STUDIES IN LABOUR AND SOCIAL LAW

GENERAL EDITORS

BOB HEPPLE

Professor of English Law in the University of London, at University College

PAUL O'HIGGINS

Professor of Law in the University of London, at King's College;
Fellow of Christ's College, Cambridge; and
Member of the Royal Irish Academy

D1555792

Discrimination: The Limits of Law

Edited by

**BOB HEPPLE AND
ERIKA M. SZYSZCZAK**

MANSELL

First published by Mansell Publishing Limited
A Cassell imprint
Villiers House, 41/47 Strand, London WC2N 5JE, England
387 Park Avenue South, New York, NY 10016-8810, USA

© Centre for the Study of Race Relations Law, University College
London, 1992

Reprinted in paperback 1995.

All rights reserved. No part of this publication may be reproduced or
transmitted in any form or by any means, electronic or mechanical
including photocopying, recording or any information storage or retrieval
system, without permission in writing from the publishers or their
appointed agents.

British Library Cataloguing-in-Publication Data

Discrimination: the limits of law.—(Studies in
  labour and social law)
  I. Hepple, B.A. (Bob Alexander), *1934-*
  II. Szyszczak, Erika M.   III. Series
  340.87

  ISBN 0-7201-2126-4 (hardback)
       0-7201-2122-1 (paperback)

Library of Congress Cataloging-in-Publication Data

Discrimination: the limits of law/edited by Bob Hepple and
  Erika M. Szyszczak.
      p.   cm.—(Studies in labour and social law)
    Revised papers from the W.G. Hart Workshop held at the Institute
  of Advanced Legal Studies of the University of London, July 1990.
    Includes bibliographical references and index.
    ISBN 0-7201-2126-4 (hb)—ISBN 0-7201-2122-1 (pb)
    1. Race discrimination—Law and legislation.   2. Civil rights.
  3. Equality before the law.   I. Hepple, B.A.   II. Szyszczak, Erika M.
  III. W.G. Hart Workshop (1990: University of London)
  IV. Series.
  K.3242.Z9D57   1992
  342'.0873—dc20
  [342.2873]   91-31336
                                                               CIP

Typeset by Colset Pte Ltd, Singapore

Printed and bound in Great Britain
by Ipswich Book Company

CONTENTS

III. POSITIVE DISCRIMINATION AND AFFIRMATIVE ACTION

IV. LOOKING AHEAD

The Contributors

Susan Atkins Visiting Fellow at the University of Southampton.

Derrick Bell Professor of Law at Harvard University.

Geoffrey Bindman Solicitor, Bindman and Partners, Visiting Professor of Law, University College London.

Trevor Buck Lecturer in Law at the University of Leicester.

Mary Coussey Director of the Employment Division at the Commission for Racial Equality.

Barry Fitzpatrick Jean Monnet Chair of European Law and Policy at the University of Newcastle upon Tyne.

Sandra Fredman Fellow and Lecturer in Law at Exeter College, Oxford.

John Gardner Fellow and Tutor in Law at Brasenose College, Oxford.

Bob Hepple Professor of English Law in the University of London at University College.

Jim Knox Management Consultant.

Nicola Lacey Fellow and Tutor in Law at New College, Oxford.

Laurence Lustgarten Reader in the School of Law, University of Warwick.

Werner F. Menski Senior Lecturer in Hindu and Modern South Asian Laws at the School of Oriental and African Studies.

Tariq Modood Commission for Racial Equality and Nuffield College, Oxford.

Jonathan Montgomery Lecturer in Law at the University of Southampton.

Paseko Ncholo Researcher at University College, London.

Joe O'Hara National Legal Officer, GMB Trade Union.

Bhikhu Parekh Professor of Political Theory at the University of Hull.

Edward Phillips Senior Lecturer in Law at the University of Greenwich.

Gwyneth Pitt Senior Lecturer in Law at the University of Leeds.

Sebastian Poulter Reader in Law at the University of Southampton.

Vera Sacks Senior Lecturer in Law at Kingston University.

Josephine Shaw Senior Lecturer in Law at the University of Keele.

Erika Szyszczak Senior Lecturer in Law at the London School of Economics and Political Science.

Preface

In convening the W.G. Hart Legal Workshop at the Institute of
Advanced Legal Studies of the University of London in July 1990, we
sought to provide an opportunity for a wide diversity of opinions to be
expressed around the common theme of the limits of law in the field of
discrimination. The papers presented at the workshop have now been
revised to form the Chapters in this book. The common theme is that
anti-discrimination laws have failed to fulfil the promise of equality
which they hold out to disadvantaged groups. How is one to explain the
limits of law in this respect? Can legal strategies and techniques be
improved and, if so, would this make any real difference to the position
of those who are disadvantaged?

The Chapters fall into three main sub-themes. The first of these is a
critique of existing civil rights models of anti-discrimination law. Since
it is the United States which, for more than four decades, has provided
the inspiration for these models, it is fitting that the first essay should
be a powerful allegorical critique by Derrick Bell. This is followed by
Bob Hepple's discussion of whether the British Race Relations Acts
have been a failure. This is a question which is also explored by Mary
Coussey in relation to strategic enforcement and by Geoffrey Bindman
in connection with proof and evidence of discrimination. New vistas for
remedying discrimination are being opened in EEC law, the subject of
Barry Fitzpatrick's essay. Developments in Northern Ireland are
regarded by some as a harbinger of change in the rest of the United
Kingdom, and these developments are explained by Jim Knox and Joe
O'Hara. No apology is made for the emphasis in Part I on legislation
concerning racial and sectarian discrimination. This is a topic which has
been relatively ignored in academic studies and even in practitioners'
works in Europe, although there is now an extensive literature on sex
discrimination law.

The Chapters in Part II explore far wider dimensions. A number of
new ideas concerning the underlying rationale of anti-discrimination
law and the interactions among discrete grounds of discrimination are
canvassed. Nicola Lacey demonstrates the significance of feminist legal

theory in providing a more throughgoing analysis of laws designed to combat racism and advocates a move from the emphasis on individual enforcement towards the rights, interests and claims of groups. Erika Szyszczak examines, from the perspective of the developing EEC law, the potential for challenging and remedying the consequences of the single market for black ethnic minorities. John Gardner argues that so long as anti-discrimination law is confined to the sphere of state action and free reign is allowed to economic choices through informal modes of community life, long-standing patterns of domination will remain. In separate essays, Sebastian Poulter and Jonathan Montgomery are concerned with the ways in which cultural and religious diversity can be protected in a pluralist society, while safeguarding basic human rights and values. Sandra Fredman and Erika Szyszczak address the complexities of the interaction of race and gender, in particular from the standpoint of black women, and they conclude that discrimination cannot be effectively tackled by the general concepts currently used by the law. Tariq Modood, too, sees 'race' as a complex concept, consisting of colour, class and culture as three relatively independent dimensions. Finally, in this part, Trevor Buck examines the similarities among ageism, sexism and racism and argues for legislation which concentrates on the collective nature of rights against discrimination. All these essayists stress the importance of 'groups' while acknowledging the difficulties of identifying these groups.

The limitations of the concept of equal opportunities as a means of changing the social and economic position of the world's disadvantaged majority—women, the poor, the 'backward clases and tribes' and other oppressed groups—have led to much debate concerning the issues of 'positive' or 'reverse' discrimination and 'affirmative' or 'positive' action. There is no agreement in this area, even concerning the appropriate terminology, as demonstrated by the variety of usages by the essayists in Part III. This part contains a number of important contributions to the debate. Bhikhu Parekh argues that there is a moral duty to help disadvantaged groups. He discusses the experiences of societies that have practised what he calls 'positive discrimination' and concludes that, on balance and within limits, this is a valuable tool of public policy. This is a theme which Gwyneth Pitt also explores in the specific context of a less-qualified candidate being preferred to a better qualified one on grounds of race or sex (what she calls 'reverse discrimination'). She argues that this can be supported on utilitarian grounds as an effective way of achieving a more egalitarian society. These general discussions are followed by a detailed examination of the Indian experience by Werner F. Menski, who draws some lessons for Britain. Edward Phillips also has a cautionary tale for Britain from the experience of positive discrimination in Malaysia. Vera Sacks reports on the extent to which provisions for positive discrimination in the British Sex Discrimination Act have been utilized, and calls for new and more effective measures. Josephine Shaw examines the use of legally binding quota systems in the Federal Republic of Germany in the context of constitutional guarantees of equal treatment. The place of rights to equality and affirmative action in constitution-making forms the theme of Paseko Ncholo's essay on the rapidly changing southern African scene.

It would be impossible to draw any specific conclusions from such a rich and diverse collection of essays. Instead, Susan Atkins looks ahead in the field of teaching and research, and Laurence Lustgarten provides a perspective as to where we are going in the field of public policy and law relating to racial discrimination.

The essays represent the individual views of the authors. We believe that individually and as a collection they make a valuable contribution to the international debate on discrimination and disadvantage.

We wish to express our thanks to all those who contributed to the discussion at the W. G. Hart Workshop, especially to those whose essays appear in this volume. Thanks also to Belinda Crothers, Seonaid Cooke, Elizabeth Durant, Vivien Fairley, Ruth Kirby and Paseko Ncholo for their assistance.

Bob Hepple and Erika Szyszczak
London, 1992

I

CIVIL RIGHTS MODELS

1

An Allegorical Critique of the United States Civil Rights Model

Derrick Bell

THE ALLEGORY: THE RACIAL PREFERENCE LICENSING ACT OF 1996

The final years of the twentieth century found much of the United States as racially segregated as it had been a century earlier when the Supreme Court's 'separate but equal' decision in *Plessy* v *Ferguson*[1] — gave constitutional status to a wave of Jim Crow statutes. That Court had distorted the necessary meaning of the Fourteenth Amendment's guarantee of equal protection of the laws in response to a society weary of racial remedies and ready to sacrifice black rights to political expediency. By 1990, the nation had again concluded that it had done enough for its racial minorities. The enforcement of civil rights laws, never vigorous, slowed to an ineffective pace which encouraged open violations and discouraged the filing of complaints which victims knew would only add futility to their misery.

In 1994, three decades after enactment of the Civil Rights Act of 1964, landmark legislation that imposed penalties for proved instances of racial discrimination, the Court held that the Act was so irrelevant to contemporary racial problems that it no longer contained that essence of rationality necessary for constitutional validity. In 1964, the Supreme Court had had little difficulty finding the various provisions of the new law constitutional.[2] But with the law's protective function seriously undermined by successive federal administrations which offered little more than lip service to enforcing its provisions, and given recent Supreme Court decisions which construed these provisions narrowly, there was much consternation but little surprise in civil rights circles when the 1964 Act was declared unconstitutional in 1994. In reversing its earlier approval of the Act, the Court found that the measure created categories based on race which failed to meet the strict scrutiny standard the Court held in 1989 applied to remedial as well as invidious racial classifications.[3] Rather surprisingly, the Court found the 1964 Act inconsistent with what it viewed as the essential principle of the landmark decision in *Brown* v *Board of Education*[4] which found state-sponsored segregation in the public schools a violation of the Fourteenth Amendment. Unlike the 1964 Act, the Court said, the *Brown* decision did not seek to identify and punish wrongdoers. The implementation order in *Brown II*, moreover, did not require immediate enforcement.[5] Rather, it recognized that delay was required, not only to permit time for the major changes required in Southern school policies, but also to accommodate the views and strong emotions of most Southern whites, which ran counter to school integration.

The 1994 Court referred with approval to the views of the late Yale law professor Alexander Bickel, who contended that any effort to enforce *Brown* as a criminal law is normally enforced, 'forthwith and without recourse', would have failed as have prohibition, anti-gambling measures, sex laws and indeed most laws policing morals. Bickel said, 'It follows that in achieving integration, the task of the law . . . was not to punish law breakers but to diminish their number'.[6] Professor Bickel's argument, the Court found, was instructive. It revealed that *Brown* was basically a call for a higher morality rather than a judicial authorization for Congress to seek to coerce behaviour allegedly unjust because it recognized generally acknowledged differences in racial groups and based public policies on those differences. This characterization, the Court felt, explained why *Brown* was as ineffective as an enforcement tool as have been other 'morals-policing' laws, all of which are hard to enforce precisely because they seek to protect the citizen's health and welfare against what a legislature deems self-abuse.

Based on this reasoning, the Court concluded that 'laws aimed at requiring cessation of white conduct deemed harmful to blacks are hard to enforce because they seek to police morality'. The Court conceded that both the states and the federal government had broad powers to protect health, safety and welfare of their citizens. But it could find nothing in the Constitution authorizing regulation of what government at any particular time would deem appropriate 'moral' behaviour. Such recognition, the Court reasoned, would seek to control the perceptions of what some whites believe about the humanity of some blacks. 'Whatever the good intentions of such an undertaking, it clearly mandated a morality that might be urged by a religion but was beyond the reach of government coercion.'

In closing, the Court urged support for educational efforts designed to gain voluntary adherence to the worthy goals of the *Brown* decision. It urged black leaders 'to emulate the life and adhere to the teachings of Booker T. Washington, your greatest leader'. Blacks, the Court admonished, must 'work harder' to the end that more of 'your people will prove themselves worthy of the many opportunities available to those prepared to enter the competitive race without special subsidies or unfair advantages. Racial remedies sponsored by government must adhere to the free enterprise principles which are the heart of our system.'

The Court's unanimous decision was widely hailed across the nation and motivated Congress to pass and the president to sign a new civil rights law incorporating what many whites but few blacks welcomed as the Court's new philosophy of 'moral materialism' in racial matters. At the signing ceremony, held in the Rose Garden and witnessed by representatives of the many right-wing organizations that had worked for its passage, the president assured the nation that the new Racial Preference Licensing Act represented a realistic advance in race relations. 'It is', he insisted, 'certainly not a return to the segregation policies granted constitutional protection under the "separate but equal" standard of *Plessy* v *Ferguson*. . . . It is no more than an inopportune coincidence that the Act was passed exactly a century after the Court announced that decision. Rather, the new law is a bold, new approach to the nation's oldest problem, one that is in harmony with our commitment to allowing the market-place rather than governmental regulation to determine public policy.'

In fact, the new Act ratified discriminatory practices that in the early 1990s had become the *de facto* norm. Under the new Act, all employers, proprietors of public facilities and owners and managers of homes and apartments, on application to the federal government, could obtain a license authorizing the holders and their agents to exclude or separate persons on the basis of race and colour. The license required payment to a government commission of a tax of 12 per cent of the income derived from whites employed, served or sold to during each quarter in which a policy of 'racial preference' was in effect. License fees were placed in an 'equality fund' used to underwrite black businesses, offer no-interest mortgage loans for black home buyers and provide educational scholarships for black students.

Opponents of the Act charged that black people, as under *Plessy*, would be segregated and would never gain any significant benefit from the equality fund. Within a year, however, the Supreme Court had heard and dismissed all such challenges to the new Act. Rejecting charges that the Act encouraged racial discrimination, the Court held the law a reasonable balance between equal protection and freedom of association rights. 'Moreover', the Court said, quoting its decision in *Plessy* v *Ferguson*:

> A statute which implies merely a legal distinction between the white and colored races — a distinction which is founded in the

color of the two races, and which must always exist so long as white men are distinguished from the other race by color — has no tendency to destroy the legal equality of the two races, or reestablish a state of involuntary servitude. . . .[7]

'Blacks as well as whites', the Court pointed out, 'are entitled to obtain racial preference licenses. If anything,' the Court noted, 'the law benefits blacks by making available an equality fund which has already issued millions of dollars to aid blacks in businesses, home mortgages and scholarships. This fund recognizes and serves as reparation for past and continuing anti-black practices which traditional civil rights laws have proven unable to eliminate.'

In conclusion, the Court found that Congress could reasonably adopt the views of those law and economics experts who contend that practitioners of bias will voluntarily cease to discriminate when the economic cost exceeds the psychological benefits they now receive from excluding people of colour. Both studies and general experience indicate that efficient black businesses, black home buyers with advantageous financing and blacks generally who are well-educated and highly skilled get ahead despite barriers based on race. 'As the numbers of truly qualified blacks increase, the perceived need to discriminate against them will decrease, a decline that the racial preference licensing tax will help to bring about.'

DISCUSSION: THE DEFICITS OF TRADITIONAL ANTI-DISCRIMINATION STATUTES

Serious contemplation of a licence to discriminate seems bizarre until we review the origins and inherent infirmities of more traditional civil rights laws. Dr Kenneth Clark, the eminent sociologist whose findings on the adverse effects of racism on black children were cited in the US Supreme Court's school segregation decisions,[8] observed that the usual response to racial unrest in America is the creation of a commission to study the situation and, in due course, to issue a report which, after an initial flurry, is filed away, its recommendations unimplemented and forgotten.[9]

Experience enables us to supplement Dr Clark's observation. When the racial unrest is serious and sustained, it may prompt passage of civil rights laws intended to recognize and protect rights of discrimination victims.[10] When these measures are enacted, their effectiveness varies, but it is clear that in majoritarian societies, the scope of laws intended to protect minority rights is limited. Yale Law School Professor Owen Fiss explained this limitation almost two decades ago in a manner amply supported by subsequent events.[11] Fiss views anti-discrimination prohibitions as applied to employment decisions as a limited strategy intended to confer benefits on a racial class — blacks. He explains:

> The limited nature of this legal strategy is not just a function of the circumstances of politics but rather reflects a deep commitment to the values of economic efficiency and individual fairness. The most troublesome question is whether the historical legacy of the class, will or should, moderate that commitment so as to yield, through enactment or construction, a more robust strategy for the law. The legacy supplies an ethical basis for the desire to improve the relative economic position of blacks, and yet it also explains why a law that does no more than prohibit discrimination on the basis of race will leave that desire, in large part, unfulfilled.[12]

Fiss provides us with a perspective, based on theory but steeped in pragmatism, covering much of the resistance to meaningful implementation of anti-discrimination laws which, even before they become law, are usually compromised during the legislative process. Currently, for example, there are bills in the US Congress designed to counteract the limiting interpretations of a series of 1989 Supreme Court decisions.[13] Proponents of these civil rights measures are making an enormous expenditure of energy and resources.[14] Even if their efforts are successful, both history and common sense tells us the new law will do no more than return civil rights law to the status of modest viability it held before the Court's series of damaging decisions.

Were this a period of social calm, we might now move to a familiar and unthreatening consideration of the relative merits of current civil rights legislation as compared to that enacted a few decades ago. The American experience might provide useful analogies for critiquing the civil rights legislation enacted in Britain, Northern Ireland, Canada and elsewhere, but for my country — and likely others — I think it is time for reflections that go beyond a comparative discussion of mainly ineffectual prohibitions.

The very visible social and economic progress made by some African Americans and other people of colour in the United States cannot obscure the increasingly dismal demographics reflecting the status of most of those whose forebears were slaves. The basic measures of poverty,[15] unemployment[16] and income[17] suggest that the slow racial

advances of the 1960s and 1970s have ended and retrogression is well
under way. Statistics, however, cannot begin to detail the havoc caused
by joblessness and poverty: broken homes, anarchy in communities,
futility in the public schools. All are the unhappy harvest of race-related
joblessness in a society where work provides sustenance, status and
the all-important sense of self-worth.

For the most part, American whites are sanguine about the massive
unemployment levels among blacks and the concomitant poverty,
broken homes and devastated lives that come with joblessness in a
society where work is equated with worth. But white America is not
at all passive about the high levels of violent street crime committed
by the young, black, male products of these communities where
discrimination-bred discouragement has given way to alcohol- and
drug-related despair. Despite the best efforts of some schools and as
a result of the *de facto* surrender of many others, whole hosts of young
black people are convinced that rejection is their lot in life. The
response — not in all cases, but in enough — is personal rebellion in
any of several anti-social forms. Employers, government agencies and
the police react to the rebellious with retaliatory measures which do not
reassure us about our safety and make the rebellious worse. Because
the repressive measures do not distinguish between rebellious and non-
rebellious blacks, some of those trying to play by the established rules
join those already convinced that there is no hope. The result is an
accelerating cycle of crime and poverty which climbs despite the deploy-
ment of more police and the imposition of heavier prison sentences.
The effects of this rebellion cycle are not limited to the black community.

The election of blacks to public office, many to positions never
before held by black persons, while worthwhile, will not have much
effect on the problems of unemployment and poverty. Incidents of
random and organized racial violence are on the rise. Moreover,
hostility to black progress, when translated into political and judicial
enmity, constitutes a clear and present threat to gains made over the
last four decades. These multiple manifestations of the end of an era
of civil rights progress provide notice that it is time to discuss seriously
whether African Americans — and since civil rights affect all racial
minorities, *all* people of colour — will ever gain real racial equality
through the workings of traditional civil rights laws and judicial
decisions.

This last decade of the twentieth century is an appropriate time to
make an assessment and to fashion plans for the future by reviewing
experiences of the past. At the end of the eighteenth century, Thomas
Jefferson's view that blacks should be free but that 'the two races,
equally free, cannot live in the same government',[18] was widely shared

by those who drafted our Constitution. Staughton Lynd, summarizing how the Framers came to include recognition and sanction of human slavery in a document committed to the protection of individual liberties, wrote: 'Even the most liberal of the Founding Fathers were unable to imagine a society in which whites and negroes would live together as fellow-citizens. Honor and intellectual consistency drove them to favor abolition; personal distaste, to fear it.'[19]

That ambivalence, founded in white supremacy and matured in the belief that the two races should not coexist in this new land, subverted the enthusiasm of even those who championed abolition and the post-Civil War amendments which granted citizenship rights to the former slaves. By the end of the nineteenth century, it was abundantly clear that the citizenship promises contained in law had been broken in fact by the terms of the 1877 Hayes-Tilden Compromise.[20] The Supreme Court's *Plessy* v *Ferguson* decision in 1896 gave legal substance to segregation policies that had been in effect for years. The Court's finding that the equal protection guarantee was met by the provision of 'separate but equal' accommodations represented a denial of social reality, self-deceit given credence because it conformed both to the nation's needs and its beliefs.

In our era, the premier civil rights precedent, *Brown* v *Board of Education*, promised to be the twentieth century's Emancipation Proclamation. Both the *Brown* decision and the Emancipation Proclamation, however, served to advance the nation's foreign policy interests more than they provided actual aid to blacks.[21] Black people ignored the self-interest motivations and, inspired by the rhetoric of freedom, initiated self-help efforts to gain long-denied rights.

Freedom efforts have fallen short in the twentieth century as they did in the nineteenth. It appears that as much as civil rights proponents criticized him at the time, the late Yale law Professor Alexander Bickel has proven correct in his dire prediction. He warned that the *Brown* decision would not be reversed but would become, dread word, 'irrelevant'.[22] Irrelevant is the seeming fate of this once-proud decision as we survey the Supreme Court's civil rights decisions of the last term. Third-year law student Radhika Rao assessed the Court's anti-civil rights thrust in a decision finding a Richmond, Virginia, set-aside ordinance unconstitutional.[23] Ms Rao writes:

> In *City of Richmond* v *Croson*, a majority of the Supreme Court chose for the first time to subject an affirmative action plan enacted by the former capital of the Confederacy to the stringent review it applies to the most repugnant forms of racism. The Court's decision to treat all racial classifications identically possesses the

same superficial symmetry of the 'separate but equal' analysis in
Plessy v *Ferguson*, and it suffers from the same flaw. The Court
denies the reality of racism when it isolates race-conscious actions
from their context and concludes that benign racial classifications
warrant the same standard of review as invidious acts.[24]

It is difficult to imagine a more apt comparison of the Court's
approach in a decision made at the end of the nineteenth century, *Plessy*,
and one made at the end of the twentieth, *Croson*. In both, modest
anti-discrimination efforts were countered with hypocritical responses
which contorted racial reality beyond recognition. These distortions,
when repeated over time, take on a disturbingly predictable pattern
which makes it difficult to maintain long-held views about the causes
of racial discrimination and the chances for its eradication.

Long before he published his findings, American blacks and their
liberal white supporters held the philosophy incorporated in Gunnar
Myrdal's study, *The American Dilemma*.[25] Racism was simply an
anomaly in a society committed to equality, the repairable failure of
liberal democratic practices (regarding black rights) to coincide with
liberal democratic theory. Our optimism relied on two assumptions
which ignored a contrary history: that the standard practices of
American policy-making were adequate to the task of abolishing racism;
and that white America did, in fact, want to abolish racism.

In *The New American Dilemma*,[26] Professor Jennifer Hochschild
examines what she calls Myrdal's 'anomaly thesis'.[27] Reviewing the
modest progress in school desegregation over almost four decades,
Hochschild concludes that the anomaly thesis simply cannot explain
the persistence of racial discrimination.[28] Rather, she finds, the continued viability of racism supports arguments 'that racism in not simply
an excrescence on a fundamentally healthy liberal democratic body but
is part of what shapes and energizes the body'.[29] Under this view,
'liberal democracy and racism in the United States are historically,
even inherently, reinforcing; American society as we know it exists
only because of its foundation in racially-based slavery, and it thrives
only because racial discrimination continues. The apparent anomaly
is an actual symbiosis.'[30]

Hochschild looks at writings supporting the symbiosis thesis,
including the historian Edmond Morgan's statement of the relationship
between slavery and the development of a republican ideology of
freedom and contemporary Marxist accounts of the functional utility
of racism within a capitalist economy. History, she points out, reveals
several occasions in which blacks have served as bargaining chips in
facilitating the settlement of differences between segments of white

society. Even traditional liberal views regarding the need for symmetry in legal principles serve to protect and perpetuate racist policies and practices.

If Jennifer Hochschild is correct, then her second dilemma explains the intractable nature of the one Myrdal (and most of us) saw as the barrier to full equality for blacks. She suggests that rather than being understood as the tension between liberal democratic theory and liberal democratic practice, the American dilemma must be understood as the more fundamental problem of reconciling liberalism with democracy. If most white citizens choose not to grant the citizens of colour their full rights, then perhaps democracy must give way to liberalism. But how do you invoke the equality policy choice in a democratic state where racial equality is the oft-heralded ideal but power-based majoritarianism is the ongoing societal stabilizing fact? More crucially, how do you convince white Americans that the nation's most pressing social problems will never be addressed meaningfully as long as opponents of the needed reforms can stigmatize them as aid for unworthy black folks?

The economist Robert Heilbroner confirms that 'there is no parallel to the corrosive and pervasive role played by race in the problem of social neglect in the United States'.[31] He observes that the

> merging of the racial issue with that of neglect serves as a rationalization for the policies of inaction that have characterized so much of the American response to need. Programs to improve slums are seen by many as programs to 'subsidize' Negroes; proposals to improve conditions of prisons are seen as measures to coddle black criminals; and so on. In such cases, the fear and resentment of the Negro takes precedence over the social problem itself. The result, unfortunately, is that the entire society suffers from the results of a failure to correct the social evils whose ill effects refuse to obey the rules of segregation.[32]

How can we explain the willingness of so many white Americans to sacrifice their interests in social reform to ensure that blacks deemed 'undeserving' by reform opponents do not gain from government benefits needed by both? What precisely are they trying to protect in this land where equality is a concept while ownership of property is a basic measure of worth.

Over time, beliefs in white dominance, reinforced by policies that subordinate black interests to those of whites, have led to an explicitly unrecognized but nonetheless powerful concept of property right in whiteness. In challenging the legality of racial segregation in the late

nineteenth century, the plaintiff in *Plessy* v *Ferguson*, recognized and
the Court acknowledged — at least for the purposes of the case — that
there was a property right in being white, an entitlement to those
advantages gained over blacks by virtue of a white identity.[33] Although
there is no such overt recognition in contemporary racial decisions,
the application to affirmative action policies of strict scrutiny standards
of review once reserved for the most invidious forms of racism reflects
a concern for 'innocent whites' and recognizes in fact what the current
Court's predecessors were not willing to acknowledge openly.[34]

On close analysis, it becomes clear that past gains in the courts and
in Congress came during periods when policy-makers deemed that
the interests of whites would be advanced or at least would not be
harmed by recognizing the claims of African Americans for racial
justice. I have been suggesting for years that civil rights progress in
general, and the historic decision in *Brown* v *Board of Education* in
particular, did not happen solely because of either the earnest efforts
of blacks or the sudden realization by white policy-makers that the
racial injustices about which blacks had complained for so long were
intolerable. Rather, progress requires a concidence with some fairly
pressing issue or situation that is aided by granting — or, as with *Brown*,
seeming to grant — a remedy for long-suffered racial wrongs. In the
case of *Brown*, there was a convergence of self-interest factors which,
consciously or not, helped convince the Court and then slowly the
society that racial segregation was an accommodation to the general
belief in white superiority that the country could no longer afford.
There is impressive evidence that the anti-Communist atmosphere
during the post-World War II era contributed substantially to the
end of official segregation.[35]

This is a concept rather hard to grasp for those who remember all
too clearly the rabid resistance to *Brown* and to the desegregation that
followed. Those memories are not flawed. The rage with which so
many whites screamed 'never!' grew out of what was to them a
threatened loss of status as white people. Segregationists were neither
impressed nor amused by contentions that it was in America's interest
to drop the 'separate but equal' charade. We must keep in mind,
however, that from the beginning of slavery, the masses of whites
have supported programmes that were contrary to their economic
interest as long as those policies provided them with a status superior
to that of blacks.

Why don't whites wake up? Professor Kimberle Crenshaw suggests:

> To bring a fundamental challenge to the way things are, whites
> would have to question not just their own subordinate status, but

also both the economic and the racial myths that justify the status quo. Racism, combined with equal opportunity mythology, provides a rationalization for racial oppression, making it difficult for whites to see the Black situation as illegitimate or unnecessary. If whites believe that Blacks, because they are unambitious or inferior, get what they deserve, it becomes that much harder to convince whites that something is wrong with the entire system. Similarly, a challenge to the legitimacy of continued racial inequality would force whites to confront myths about equality of opportunity that justify for them whatever measure of economic success they may have attained. . . .

Race consciousness makes it difficult — at least for whites — to imagine the world differently. It also creates the desire for identification with privileged elites. By focusing on a distinct, subordinate 'other', whites include themselves in the dominant circle — an arena in which most hold no real power, but only their privileged racial identity. Consider the case of a dirt-poor, southern white, shown participating in a Ku Klux Klan rally in the movie *Resurgence*, who declared: 'Every morning, I wake up and thank God I'm white.' For this person, and for others like him, race consciousness — manifested by his refusal even to associate with Blacks — provides a powerful explanation of why he fails to challenge the current social order.[36]

Novelist Toni Morrison provides a more earthy but no less accurate assessment of how the presence of blacks enables a bonding by whites that occurs across vast socio-economic divides. Thus, when in a recent *Time Magazine* interview Ms Morrison was asked why blacks and whites can't bridge the abyss in race relations, she replied:

I feel personally sorrowful about black-white relations a lot of the time because black people have always been used as a buffer in this country between powers to prevent class war, to prevent other kinds of real conflagrations.

If there were no black people here in this country, it would have been Balkanized. The immigrants would have torn each other's throats out, as they have done everywhere else. But in becoming an American, from Europe, what one has in common with that other immigrant is contempt for *me* — it's nothing else but color. Wherever they were from, they would stand together. They could all say, 'I am not *that*'. So in that sense, becoming an American is based on an attitude: an exclusion of me.

It wasn't negative to them — it was unifying. When they got

off the boat, the second word they learned was 'nigger'. Ask them — I grew up with them. I remember in the fifth grade a smart little boy who had just arrived and didn't speak any English. He sat next to me. I read well, and I taught him to read just by doing it. I remember the moment he found out that I was black — a nigger. It took him six months; he was told. And that's the moment when he belonged, that was his entrance. Every immigrant knew he would not come at the very bottom. He had to come above at least one group — and that was us.[37]

The significance of the Toni Morrison anecdote is its universality. Indeed, it is difficult to think of another characteristic of societal functioning that has retained its viability and its value to social stability from the very beginning of the American experience down to the present day. Both the nation's history and current events give reason to wonder, with Professor Tilden W. LeMelle, 'whether a society such as the United States is really capable of legislating and enforcing effective public policy to combat racial discrimination in the political process and elsewhere'.[38] So, while slavery and segregation are gone, most whites continue to expect the society to recognize an unspoken but nonetheless vested property right in their 'whiteness'. This right is recognized and upheld by the courts and society like all property rights under a government created and sustained primarily for that purpose.

There is no easy solution to this dilemma. Identifying whiteness as a property right simply calls the problem by its rightful name. One would think that it would not be difficult to identify broad areas of social reform in which the interest of most whites would be much greater than the illusory entitlement to a superior status based on whiteness. The gap between the incomes of the rich and the poor is greater than ever. Whites as well as blacks need more comprehensive health care, better schools and more affordable housing. But achieving unity on these common interests is so difficult precisely because so many whites, though they share with blacks a whole range of social needs, are willing to sacrifice their real interests to satisfy their psychic need to maintain a status superior to that of black people.

CONCLUSION

One wonders. Given the limited effectiveness of traditional civil rights laws, what kind of miracle or — more likely — how enormous a catastrophe will be required before whites realize that their property right in being white has been purchased too dearly and has netted them only the opportunity, as historian C. Vann Woodward put it, to hoard sufficient racism in their bosoms to feel superior to blacks while working at a black's wages.

Those of us who still hope for equality through unity face two enormous challenges. First, we must broaden the Constitution's protection to encompass the sacrosanct area of economic rights, not simply as was the case at the beginning to secure vested property interests, but to recognize entitlement to basic needs — jobs, housing, health care, education, security in old age — as an essential property right of all. We must mount this campaign in the face of the likely resistance from many whites who will be the principal beneficiaries of its success.

Second, to reduce this resistance, we must mount an educational campaign based on the notion that 'until whites get smart, blacks can't get free'. In his campaign for the Democratic nomination for president, the Reverend Jesse Jackson made an exciting start in this tough educational process. He did not gain the nomination, but he proved that there are substantial numbers of working-class whites willing to learn what blacks have long known: that the rhetoric of freedom so freely voiced in this country is no substitute for the economic justice that has been so long denied to whites as well as blacks.

Most black people and a respectable number of whites recognize both the need for social reform and the danger inherent in maintaining the current status quo. It is not right and hardly possible that those long held at the very bottom of this society can both sense the deadly dangers in the nation's present course and continue to give life to the fading belief in racial equality so long espoused and so infrequently practiced. Working from the bottom to gain their rights, African Americans have given substance to the Constitution's guarantees and a vibrant humanity to a nation that has oscillated between a patronizing posture when its interest dictated a feigned friendship, and cold contempt when it did not.

History shows that when the issue is justice for African Americans versus racism, racism wins every time. But when the issue is racism versus perceived self-interest for whites, the choice (it is said) is justice for blacks. Over the years, we have thus come to know what whites *really* mean when they express an interest in racial justice. Given this knowledge, civil rights advocates must consider carefully what strategies will achieve what whites will view as in their self-interest. This analysis must consider both the limitations of penalty-oriented civil rights laws and the continuing value of discrimination practices which are not only as old as the country, but which continue to provide a key basis for societal stability and order.

NOTES

1. 163 US 567 [1896].

2. *Heart of Atlanta Motel, Inc.* v *United States* [1964] 379 US 241, and *Katzenbach* v *McClung* [1964] 379 US 294 (upholding the public facilities provisions of Title II).

3. *Croson* v *City of Richmond* [1989] 109 SCt 706.

4. 347 US 483 [1954].

5. 349 US 294 [1955] (mandating an end to discrimination in public schools with 'all deliberate speed').

6. Bickel, A. *The Least Dangerous Branch: The Supreme Court at the Bar of Politics* (Indianapolis, Bobbs-Merrill, 1962) pp. 247–54.

7. 163 US 537, 545 [1896].

8. *Brown* v *Board of Education* [1954] 347 US 483, 494 note 11.

9. Platt, A. *The Politics of Riot Commissions* (n.p.,1971) pp. 376–77 (Dr Clark's statement is contained in his testimony before the Kerner Commission, established in 1967, in the wake of a series of urban racial disorders.)

10. Of course, racial unrest not deemed either threatening to the majority or politically appropriate for legislative action need not lead to new civil rights laws. For example, between 1937 and 1946, civil rights advocates introduced more than 150 bills in the US Congress intended to address lynching, the poll tax and fair-hiring practices. No civil rights acts were enacted during this time and the president during most of that period, Franklin D. Roosevelt, despite his considerable power, never pushed for or encouraged the passage of a civil rights bill. Carmines, E. and Stinson, J. *Issues Evolution: Race and Transformation of American Politics* (Princeton, Princeton University Press, 1989).

11. Fiss, O. 'A theory of fair employment laws' (1971) 38 *University of Chicago Law Review* 235.

12. Ibid. at 313–14.

13. Following are the 1989 Supreme Court rulings on civil rights that Congress may modify or reverse:

    1. *Richmond, Va.* v *J.A.Croson Co.* [1989] 109 SCt 706 (by a 6–3 vote, struck down an affirmative action plan that set aside 30 per cent of city construction contracts for minority-owned businesses).

    2. *Patterson* v *McLean Credit Union* [1989] 109 SCt 2363 (ruled 5–4 that an 1866 law forbidding discrimination in contracts applies only to hiring agreements, not on-the-job bias).

    3. *Dallas Independent School Dist.* v *Jett* [1989] 109 SCt 363 (ruled 5–4 that state and local officials cannot be held liable for discrimination unless the alleged violation was part of an official policy).

    4. *Wards Cove Packing Co.* v *Atonio* [1989] 109 SCt 2115 (held 5–4 that in cases brought under Title VII of the 1964 Civil Rights Act, burden is on the plaintiff to prove an employer had no business necessity for a practice with discriminatory effects).

    5. *Martin* v *Wilks* [1989] 109 SCt 2180 (ruled 5–4 that non-parties to a court-approved consent degree incorporating an affirmative action plan can challenge the plan as reverse discrimination, even years after it was adopted).

    6. *Lorance* v *A.T.& T. Technologies, Inc.* [1989] 109 SCt 2261 (held 5–3 that seniority plans cannot be challenged as discriminatory unless complaints are filed soon after the plans are adopted).

14. S 2104, Congressional Record, S 1019–21 (7 February 1990). In section 2(b), the Bill lists its purpose: to respond to the Supreme Court's recent decisions by restoring the civil rights protections which were dramatically limited by those decisions; and to strengthen existing protections and remedies available under federal civil rights laws to provide more effective deterrence and adequate compensation for victims of discrimination.

15. By 1987, the poverty rate for black Americans was 33.1 per cent, an increase of 700,000 people in one year. By contrast, during that year, the white poverty rate fell from 11 per cent to 10.5 per cent. Center on Budget and Policy Priorities *Still Far from the Dream: Recent Developments in Black Income, Employment and Poverty* (October 1988). The report is available from the Center, 236 Mass. Ave., N.E., Suite 305, Washington, DC 20002.

16. The black unemployment rate averaged 13 per cent in 1987, lower than in any other year in the 1980s, although higher than in most years of the 1970s. The proportion of the total black adult population which is employed is at the highest level recorded since the data were first collected in 1972. But black unemployment has declined less than white unemployment, and the gap between black and white unemployment has widened to 2.57 times the white rate in 1988 — the highest black-to-white unemployment differential ever recorded. Ibid. at ix–x.

17. The 1987 income of the typical black family ($18,098) equalled just 56.1 per cent of the typical white family ($31,935), a lower percentage than in any year since 1967 when the data first began to be collected. A factor contributing to the growing income disparity between blacks and whites is the growing income gap between upper-and-lower income families in the nation as a whole. In 1987, this gap reached its widest point in 40 years. Ibid. at vii–viii.

18. Lynd, S. *Black History* (n.p.,1968) p. 117. 'Slavery and the founding fathers' in Drimmer, M. (ed.).

19. Ibid. at 129.

20. In the hotly contested presidential election of 1876, the Democrat, Samuel J.Tilden, won a plurality of 250,000 votes in the nation, and appeared to have won the electoral count by one vote. The returns of three states were challenged and when re-counts did not resolve the dispute, it was submitted to a special electoral commission which awarded the vote to the Republican, Rutherford B. Hayes. Democrats accepted this outcome in return for several concessions, including a Republican promise to withdraw the remaining federal troops from the South, an action that removed the last barrier to the already-in-progress subjugation of the black freedmen. See Foner, E. *Reconstruction: America's Unfinished Revolution, 1863–1877* (New York, Harper and Row, 1988) pp. 575–87.

21. The benefits to the nation, including disruption of the South's economy, raising insuperable political barriers to European nations entering the Civil War on the side of the South and opening the way to the enlistment of thousands of blacks in the Union Army, are discussed in Bell, D. *Race, Racism and American Law* 2nd edn (1980) pp. 3–7. For the advantages the nation gained as a result of the *Brown* decision, see Dudziak, 'Desegregation as a cold war imperative' (1988) 42 *Stanford Law Review* 61.

22. Bickel, A. *The Supreme Court and the Idea of Progress* — (1970).

23. *City of Richmond* v *Croson* [1989] 109 SCt 706.

24. Harvard Law School, JD (1990).

25. Myrdal, G. *An American Dilemma* (New York and London, Harper and Brothers Publishers, 1944). 'The Negro problem in America represents a moral lag in the development of the nation and a study of it must record nearly everything which is bad and wrong in America. . . . However, . . . not since Reconstruction has there been more reason to anticipate fundamental changes in American race relations, changes which will involve a development toward the American ideals.' Ibid. at xix.

26. Hochschild, J. *The New American Dilemma* (New Haven, Yale University Press, 1984).

27. Racial discrimination 'is a terrible and inexplicable anomaly stuck in the middle of our liberal democratic ethos'. Ibid. at 3.

28. Ibid. at 203.

29. Ibid. at 5.

30. Ibid. at 5.

31. Heilbroner, R. 'The roots of social neglect in the United States' in Rostow, E. (ed.) *Is Law Dead?* (New York, Simon and Schuster, 1971) p. 296.

32. Ibid.

33. Justice Brown wrote:

> It is claimed by the plaintiff in error that, in any mixed community, the reputation of belonging to the dominant race, in this instance the white race, is property, in the same sense that a right of action, or of inheritance, is property. Conceding this to be so, for the purposes of this case, we are unable to see how this statute deprives him of, or in any way affects his right to, such property. If he be a white man and assigned to a colored coach, he may have his action for damages against the company for being deprived of his so called property. Upon the other hand, if he be a colored man and be so assigned, he has been deprived of no property, since he is not lawfully entitled to the reputation of being a white man (163 US 548).

34. *Martin* v *Wilks* [1989] 109 SCt 2180 (the failure of white firefighters to intervene in earlier employment discrimination proceedings did not preclude their challenging employment decisions taken pursuant to a consent decree).

35. Dudziak op. cit (note 21) p. 61.

36. Crenshaw, K. 'Race, reform, and retrenchment: Transformation and legitimation in antidiscrimination law' (1988) 101 *Harvard Law Review* 1331, 1380–81.

37. Morrison, T. 'The pain of being black' (22 May 1989) *Time* 120.

38. See, Bell, D. op. cit. (note 21) sec. 1.12.

2

Have Twenty-five Years of the Race Relations Acts in Britain Been a Failure?[1]

Bob Hepple

INTRODUCTION

Why have the Race Relations Acts of 1965, 1968 and 1976 failed to change the patterns of racial disadvantage in Britain? The question is often posed but it is based on a false assumption that law is simply an independent instrument of state power, a technical device that is capable of doing as much for ethnic relations as the microchip has done for communications. This kind of 'magic belief' is, as Otto Kahn-Freund said in the context of industrial relations, 'a superstition of political importance, but a superstition none the less'.[2] The separation of law from social life as a whole leads to the expectation that law can, in some way, 'act upon' society, and this has been followed by inevitable disillusionment as successive statutes, each more elaborate than its predecessor, have failed to achieve the stated aims of the reformers. We have been slow in Britain to absorb Derrick Bell's insight that 'the common thread in all civil rights strategies is eventual failure'.[3]

Judged in terms of the aims expressed in the White Paper on *Racial Discrimination*[4] — to reduce discrimination and by so doing to help break the 'familiar cycle of cumulative disadvantage' — the ineffectiveness of the Race Relations Act 1976 is irrefutable. The Policy Studies Institute's (PSI) third survey (1982–85) showed a continued gap in the unemployment rates, job levels, earnings, household income and quality of housing between black and white people.[5] This has been confirmed by successive Labour Force Surveys.[6] Seventeen years after the Act of 1968, the PSI found that 'even at a conservative estimate' there were still 'tens of thousands of acts of racial discrimination in job recruitment every year'.[7] The most recent report by Colin Brown[8] shows that differential unemployment rates between whites and ethnic minorities cannot be explained by differences in levels of qualifications.

They reflect instead employer discrimination against ethnic minorities and the concentration of workers from minority groups in jobs that are most vulnerable to redundancy. While there has been some narrowing of the gap between white and ethnic minority unemployment rates in recent years, this mainly reflects the tendency for unemployment among minorities to rise faster than white unemployment during economic downturns and to fall faster during periods of growth. Brown points out that ethnic minorities might benefit from changes in labour supply conditions in the next few years but one cannot expect lasting improvement without a serious assault on racial discrimination.

Even the severest critics of the Acts would concede that they have broken down some barriers for individuals in their quest for jobs, housing and services and that they have driven underground those overt expressions of discrimination which were current twenty years ago.[9] Yet most of the reformers expected more than this from the legislation. They usually acknowledge the obvious difficulties in ascribing to an Act of Parliament specific responsibility for any degree of social change, especially where the long-term aim of the Act is to alter entrenched attitudes and behaviour. But they tend to focus their critique, and strategies for future changes, on the perceived weaknesses of the legislation and its enforcement. If only the Act had 'more teeth', imposing cost-deterrent sanctions on discriminators, there would be more significant impacts upon discrimination and disadvantage, according to this line of argument.

This approach shows little familiarity with the insights provided by sociologists into law as an instrument of social change. If these scholars teach us anything, it is that law is more likely to be effective in facilitating action which people want to take than in creating new rights to protect weaker parties.[10] The lack of social change following the Race Relations Acts is not unique. It is characteristic of most legislation which seeks to protect those who lack economic and social power, through the mechanism of individual rights enforced by private litigation. Fifteen years' experience of the operation of the Race Relations Act 1976 highlights several of the reasons for this.

LIMITS OF RIGHTS-BASED LAW

The first reason is that the 'cycle of disadvantage' in which second and later generations of ethnic minorities are trapped cannot itself be brought within the scope of the law. Law, as Ehrlich[11] and others have pointed out, demands specificity. Legal concepts have to be relatively clear and they can be enforced only against identified persons. Put another way, the legal process can operate only by individualizing conflict between specific parties. We may say that government policies are a 'cause' of high unemployment among black and brown minorities, or that the police are to 'blame' for not curbing racial harassment. This kind of attribution of responsibility, which involves tracing consequences, effects or results, may lead us to pass moral judgements, but it is not sufficiently precise for the attribution of legally relevant causation. Ironically, it is those who take the first faltering steps towards living up to their moral obligation to promote equality of opportunity who are most likely to fall foul of the Act, while those who avoid moral responsibility are less likely to find a case of unlawful discrimination proved against them. For example, an employer who monitors the ethnic composition of the workforce may find the statistics used against him to prove an allegation of unlawful discrimination,[12] while an employer who simply claims to be 'colour blind' may be at less risk of having the case proved against him, since the Employment Appeal Tribunal has held that there is no power to require an employer to provide details of the ethnic composition of his workforce where such information is not readily available.[13] It is no accident that the employers most vulnerable to claims of racial discrimination have been those (like the NHS and local authorities) who are raising expectations by beginning to move in the direction of equal opportunities.

Secondly, the law is directed at only one element in the many causes of disadvantage, namely 'discrimination'. The demand for specificity has led to a narrow and technical definition of this concept. The Aristotelian notion that likes must be treated alike, unless there is a morally relevant difference between them, becomes in law 'direct discrimination'. This is defined by section 1(1)(a) of the 1976 Act as 'on racial grounds treating a person less favourably' than the respondent 'treats or would treat other persons'. The apparent precision of this concept has proved to be illusory. The courts at first allowed benign motives to exempt the respondent from liability[14] but this was later disapproved.[15] It was not until the majority decision of the House of Lords in *James* v *Eastleigh Borough Council*[16] that the long-standing controversy about the relevance of 'motive', 'intention', 'grounds' and 'reasons' appears to have been resolved — but only to raise a number of other issues relating to causation and proof. This is a sex discrimination case, but the same principles would apply to racial discrimination because of the similar wording of the two Acts.

In *James* the council provided free access to its swimming pools for those 'who have reached the stage pension age'. This meant that men (whose pension age is 65) were differently treated from women (whose pension age is 60). The Court of Appeal held that this was not discrimination 'on the ground of' sex since neither the overt nor the covert reason was the desire to treat women less favourably than men. Sir Nicolas Browne-Wilkinson V-C said that section 1(1)(a) of the Act is 'looking to the case where, subjectively, the defendant has treated the plaintiff less favourably because of his or her sex. What is relevant is the defendant's reason for doing the act, not the causative effect of the act done by the defendant'. According to the Vice-Chancellor the condition relating to state-pension age raised an issue of indirect discrimination (which could, presumably, have been justified) but not of direct discrimination (which can never be justified). In overruling this decision the majority of the House of Lords (clarifying their earlier reasoning in *R.* v *Birmingham City Council, ex parte EOC*[17]) held that the correct test is objective, namely, 'would the complainant have received the same treatment from the defendant but for his or her sex?'[18]

One implication of the majority decision is that Sir Harry Woolf in *R.* v *Westminster City Council, ex parte CRE*[19] fell into a linguistic trap in treating 'intention' and 'motive' as interchangeable. As Lord Goff pointed out in *James*,[20] the analogy with the use of these concepts in criminal law must be handled with care, and if it were necessary to identify the requisite intention, that is simply the intention to perform the relevant act of less favourable treatment. The less favourable treatment 'may derive either from the application of a gender- [or race-] based criterion to the complainant, or from selection by the defendant of the complainant because of his or her sex [or race]; but, in either event, it is not saved from constituting unlawful discrimination by the fact that the defendant acted from a benign motive'.[21] It is, however, doubtful whether the drafter of the Acts had this sensible distinction in mind when framing the provision which requires an 'intention' to treat the complainant less favourably on grounds of sex or race before there can be an award of compensation for indirect discrimination.[22] In this context, 'intention' seems to have the subjective meaning which Lord Lowry advocated in his dissenting speech in *James*.[23] This involves considering the reason why the discriminator treated the complainant less favourably, in the context of remedies for indirect discrimination, while in relation to proof of direct discrimination the defendant will be liable if it is shown that 'but for' the complainant's race or sex he or she would not have been treated less favourably. The majority decision in *James* serves as a warning that complex hurdles of causation may yet be used to deny liability, just as has happened in the 'mixed motives' cases in the USA.[24] If the burden of proof remains throughout on the complainant, this 'but for' test will be a difficult one to meet. In *Owen & Briggs* v *James*[25] the Court of Appeal had said it was enough if race was 'an important factor' in the performance of the act which formed the basis of the complaint. We are likely to hear much more in the future about whether race or gender must be a factor, or a substantial factor, or the determinative factor or the sole factor in order to make direct discrimination unlawful. Even in Northern Ireland, the new Fair Employment Act 1989 fails to heed the Standing Advisory Commission on Human Rights' (SACHR) recommendation[26] that motives should be declared to be irrelevant, and that the evidential burden of proof should shift to the respondent once less favourable treatment is shown.

Another implication of the *James* decision is that if gender-based or race-based criteria are applied to the complainant then this can qualify only as direct and not as indirect discrimination.[27] This has the important consequence that race-based criteria can never be justified. However, if a race-neutral condition or requirement is imposed, then the Race Relations Act's concept of 'indirect' or 'effects' discrimination, which may be justified, comes into play. Section 1(1)(b) of the Act is based on a similar definition in the Sex Discrimination Act 1975. This in turn was derived from the interpretation by the Supreme Court of Title VII, section 703(a) of the United States Civil Rights Act 1964 in *Griggs* v *Duke Power Company*.[28] This made it unlawful for an employer to use a practice or procedure that disproportionately affects black persons, unless this is a matter of 'business necessity'. The ambiguous language of the United States Supreme Court was translated into the specific and complex language of the British definition. The underlying theory is that in a society in which inequalities in the distribution of benefits are regarded as justifiable, the opportunities for attaining those benefits ought to be determined on a proportional basis of group entitlements. It is based on a principle of procedural justice 'which makes no assumption that a particular pattern of distribution should result'.[29] It is therefore not a simple redistributive principle; it is concerned with barriers to an equal start, with the way in which the distribution was determined rather than simply the actual outcome.

In the wording of section 1(1)(b), however, this principle is far narrower than the ambiguous notion of 'institutionalized discrimination'. The complainant has, first of all, to prove that the respondent has applied some 'requirement or condition' which on its face is racially neutral. This has to be, according to a much-criticized Court of Appeal decision, an 'absolute bar' and not simply a 'preferred profile' for a job.[30] Accordingly, it is often difficult to formulate practices which may have an adverse impact into a potentially unlawful requirement or condition, such as word of mouth recruitment, shop floor understandings, or vague and unadvertised subjective promotion procedures.

The Northern Irish Fair Employment Act 1989, s. 49(1), has simply copied the defective British definition instead of covering any practice, policy or situation which has a significant adverse impact (as the SACHR report had proposed). A particular weakness of the British definition is the rigid line drawn between direct and indirect discrimination. Instead of using the employer's practices which have a potentially adverse impact on minority groups to prove an allegation of direct discrimination, the Act obliges the complainant to formulate indirect discrimination clearly and specifically as a separate basis of claim.

The complainant next has to show that he or she 'cannot comply' with the 'requirement or condition'. The House of Lords has said that this does not mean that it must be physically or inherently impossible for the complainant to comply. The test is whether he or she can do so consistently with the customs and cultural conditions of his or her ethnic group.[31] But the courts and tribunals are dependent on evidence of those customs and cultural conditions or else must rely on their own, not always reliable, view of 'general social facts'.[32] The complainant must also show that the proportion of his or her group which 'can comply' is 'considerably smaller' than the proportion of those who are not members of that ethnic group which can comply. Although the Court of Appeal has recently attempted to provide some guidelines on proving disparate impact,[33] the tribunals have been given a free hand, by the appellate courts, to decide on the relevant pool[34] and on such crucial questions as whether it should be limited to the particular workplace or geographical area or to the country as a whole. Elaborate statistical evidence is not required, but there is no guidance (such as the 'four-fifths' rule used in the US) as to what constitutes a 'considerably smaller' proportion. Perhaps the most significant feature of the definition in the context of the present discussion is that the complainant has to show the 'requirement or condition' is to his or her 'detriment'. In effect this means that there always has to be an identifiable complainant who has suffered some disadvantage.

Only when the complainant has mounted these hurdles does the respondent have to 'justify' the 'requirement or condition'. In the United States, as already mentioned, the test is 'business necessity'. The British Act does not define what is 'justifiable irrespective of the colour, race, nationality or ethnic or national origins of the person to whom it is applied'. Necessity is a relative concept (necessary for what?). Justifiability is even more elastic. The *Ojutiku* decision[35] took refuge in the intuitive common sense of that darling of English law, the 'reasonable man', and said that the respondent must advance 'good grounds' 'acceptable to right thinking people'. Under the influence of decisions of the ECJ and the House of Lords under Article 119 of the

EEC Treaty, the Court of Appeal in *Hampson* v *Department of Education and Science*[36] reinterpreted *Ojutiku* and reasserted the notion of 'an objective balance between the discriminating effect of the condition and the reasonable needs of the party who applies the condition'. What has to be recognized is that even this more liberal definition requires a process of fact evaluation in an area in which no consensus exists among tribunal members, even less a social consensus, as to what is 'acceptable'. In practice they have been willing to go along with the views of 'englightened management', occasionally being guided by the Race Relations Code of Practice. But it is in the nature of tribunals and courts to be norm-reflecting and not to encourage more progressive norms which might change the consensus.[37] Even if the Fair Employment Act 1989 had replaced the word 'justifiable' with 'necessary' (as proposed by SACHR), this problem of evaluation by a conservative judiciary would have remained.

The legal definitions of both direct and indirect discrimination depend for their effectiveness upon the recognition of collective racial disadvantage. Inferences of adverse treatment of individuals can be drawn from proof of the treatment of others by the same respondent in similar circumstances. Because indirect discrimination turns upon the adverse impact of practices upon groups, this requires courts and tribunals to determine and evaluate social facts. However, the traditional form of civil adjudication in Britain for the resolution of private disputes is unsuitable for this task. Lawyers are familiar with the reconstruction of occurrences between individual parties. They are unaccustomed to the processes for acquiring knowledge about the recurrent patterns of behaviour which go to make up social facts. Not surprisingly, findings as to 'social facts' have been left to the 'common sense' of the courts and tribunals. Significantly, only about 31 of the 2,000 lay members of industrial tribunals (which hear complaints of discrimination in employment) come from black or Asian ethnic minorities. Consequently, very few of those judging these cases are likely to have had experience of the situations in which direct and indirect discrimination occur.

It has been argued that a more positive statutory concept, such as 'equality of opportunity' or 'fair opportunity' would transform the legal approach, making it easier to address the problems of collective racial disadvantage. But would such a concept guarantee the desired redistribution of unemployment and disadvantage any more than the negative concept of discrimination does? It has often been remarked that 'equality of opportunity' is, in Rawlsian terms, a form of 'imperfect procedural justice' in which procedures are enforced with a view to achieving a desired outcome but with no *a priori* guarantee that following the procedures will promote the outcome in every case. One assumption that both negative and positive concepts have in common is that employment, goods and services are a limited 'good' which must be allocated on grounds that do not exclude any section of those who desire them, other than on grounds of 'suitability' for the employment or 'potential' for the ability to pay for the goods or services in question. At this point, liberals are prone to endorse the 'merit' principle. For example, employers 'should be free to select the person whom the employer considers to meet the requirements of the job and is most appropriate for the employer's enterprise'.[38]

The merit principle implies that it is always possible to distinguish candidates on strictly objective job-related criteria. This would mean, for example, that if one candidate has more employment experience than the other the former should be preferred. But it is likely that the person with less experience will come from the disadvantaged group, so to apply the strictly objective criteria will perpetuate inequality. This difficulty was recognized in the SACHR Report[39] which suggested the vague compromise that the objective of appointment and promotion according to the merit principle has to be pursued in combination with the objective of equality of opportunity.

Is not the very idea of a 'merit principle' an unnecessary diversion in the context of either a negative freedom from direct or indirect discrimination or a positive right to equality of opportunity? One may say negatively that race, gender, religion etc. should not enter into an employment or other decision. But it is not a 'direct corollary' of this (as suggested in the White Paper, *Fair Employment in Northern Ireland*,[40]) that the only appropriate criterion is merit. As Bernard Williams has said: 'The grounds considered appropriate for the good should themselves be such that people from all sections of society have an equal chance of satisfying them.'[41] We know that there is a connection between lack of educational and skill qualifications and poor housing and belonging to black and Asian ethnic minorities. The appeal to merit must appear disingenuous to members of these disadvantaged communities who are rejected as 'unsuitable'. One is not supplying 'equality of opportunity' if one applies this criterion to people who are unequal because they have been deprived of the opportunity to acquire 'merit'.

The conclusion I draw is that whether we rely on negative concepts like direct or indirect discrimination or a broader positive notion of 'equal opportunity', even 'fair opportunity', it would be illusory to believe that these can be translated into legal terms of art which will lead, without more, to the promised land of substantive equality. I come back to the point with which I started this section. Law is both too *specific* and too *selective* in its choice of causes in the 'cycle of disadvantage' to be capable, in itself, of delivering real substantive equal rights.

IS THE LAW SYMBOLIC OR EDUCATIVE?

The discussion so far has focused on the rather naive instrumentalism which sees the Race Relations Acts as having a specific purpose or purposes against which their effectiveness can be measured. The measure cannot be racial disadvantage because this is outside the scope of the law, nor can it be discrimination as it is commonly understood (in terms both of adverse treatment and institutionalized adverse impact) because no legal definition or legal process is capable of embracing the social patterns of discrimination against groups, as distinct from treatment of or impact upon individual members of those groups.

Can the purposes be differently stated? The Race Relations Board, just before the Act of 1968, gave a classic liberal definition of the aims of anti-discrimination legislation:

1. A law is an unequivocal declaration of public policy.
2. A law gives support to those who do not wish to discriminate, but who feel compelled to do so by social pressure.
3. A law gives protection and redress to minority groups.
4. A law thus provides for the peaceful and orderly adjustment of grievances and the release of tensions.
5. A law reduces prejudice by discouraging the behaviour in which prejudice finds expression.[42]

This suggests that the purpose was not simply to produce symbolic legislation which would placate the victims of discrimination, but rather to give support to those who wish to resist the pressures to discriminate and to educate those who are prejudiced. It was the educational perspective which led to the inclusion in the 1976 Act of a 'persuasive' definition[43] of discrimination so as to bring within its ambit for the first time situations of indirect discrimination. The emotional repugnance felt towards adverse treatment was redirected to unintentional practices which have an adverse impact on members of an ethnic minority. The concession was made that these practices cannot lead to an award of damages, unless the discrimination is intentional,[44] but even without an effective sanction many large organizations have been led to examine and redefine those practices which might offend against this wider concept of discrimination. In time, these unintentional practices may come to be regarded as sufficiently reprehensible to justify a change in the law to enable courts and tribunals to impose awards of substantial damages.

A problem with this educational perspective is that it rests ultimately on the idea that there is a social consensus about the need to promote equality of opportunity, an idea which, as already noted, has been discredited in the context of 'justification' for indirect discrimination. In reality, the moral crusade for race relations legislation occurred at the very moment when the consensus on which Empire rested, that Britain was a society in which all British subjects were equal, had broken down. The price for the Race Relations Act 1968 was the Commonwealth Immigration Acts of 1962 and 1968 and the price for the Race Relations Act 1976 was the Immigration Act of 1971 and the British Nationality Act 1981. Once it is accepted that the Race Relations Acts were part of a process of conflict between different values and beliefs struggling for dominance, rather than an almost mechanical instrument to fulfil certain purposes, one can begin to examine the Acts in the context of social integration.

LAW AND SOCIAL INTEGRATION

The sociologist distinguishes between 'purpose' and 'function'. Functions exist independently of the stated aims of the legislators, administrators and judges, and they may change over time. The Race Relations Acts have significant functions as mechanisms for social integration. One can approach these functions in different ways. Some scholars have done so through Parsonian theory, which sees social change as the continual negotiation of conflicting pressures (control and conditioning) for stability and change. For example, Mayhew's classic empirical study of the Massachusetts Commission against Discrimination[45] examined the nature of the processes of negotiation between conditioning forces, such as the job and housing markets, and controlling forces embodied in the values of race relations legislation as interpreted by the élite of administrators and judges. Mayhew found that the Massachusetts Commission had an integrative function, establishing compromises between the opposing pressures, enforcing the law only so far as it could do so without endangering the 'precarious foundation' of the equal rights standard. Ultimately, civil rights groups felt frustrated by its methods and came to view the law as a façade behind which the black minority were misled into believing that the majority cared about them. A fertile field lies in wait for British researchers, who have only recently begun to examine the interpretation and enforcement of the Race Relations Acts from this kind of perspective. They are likely to find, as Mayhew did, that law is more autonomous and less influential than Parsons believed. Coussey's Chapter in this book[46] indicates the constraints and possibilities, from the viewpoint of a leading British practitioner.

In the case of the CRE, any such research would have to note how the controlling forces of high rates of black unemployment, increased poverty and depressed housing, have had to be accommodated within the conditioning forces of inadequate government funding, hostile judicial review (ruling out general investigations of specific bodies) and a culture (within and outside the commmission) that attaches greater value to individual rights than to social action and collective remedies. The resulting compromises include less reliance on formal investigations, and a greater emphasis on helping individuals even where this does not form the basis for wider promotional or advisory work in organizations. The increasing 'individualization' of discrimination law has been one of the features of the 1980s.

Another approach emphasizes the symbolic functions of race relations legislation. Critics of the Race Relations Acts frequently contrast the promise of equal opportunity, embodied in vague and flexible legal concepts, with the intricacies of restrictive case law and ineffective enforcement. It is precisely the combination of a legislative standard of equal rights (particularly important in Britain because of the absence of any entrenched bill of rights) with innumerable exceptions and weak enforcement which allows the law to be all things to all people. Even if the law appears to have little impact it has symbolic importance as a rallying point around which particular struggles can be organized. From this perspective it is not the Acts as such which should be the main focus of criticism, but rather those who have failed to make the most of the Acts' symbols in order to promote change. This can be done only by identifying the radical symbolic elements in the Race Relations Acts, such as indirect discrimination and positive action, and linking these elements with the structure of power in Britain.

LAW, POWER AND PROCESS

Whether one agrees with the pluralists, who believe that the Race Relations Acts were a compromise between conflicting social groups, or with the adherents of theories of power élites,[47] who hold that the Acts are used by the white establishment in order to maintain social control without eradicating discrimination, there is general agreement that the law is an expression of power relations. Social legislation is the outcome of processes of conflict between different social groups and competing ideologies. As Philip Abrams said, 'what any particular group of people get is not just a matter of what they choose to want but what they can force or persuade other groups to let them have'.[48] The powerfulness of the opponents of change has been the decisive element in the making of race relations law. In order to understand the Acts a purely functional approach is less instructive than one which emphasizes power, and views the law as simply one element in the process of change.

Such an analysis might start with the pressures and counter-pressures which led to the passing of the Acts of 1965 and 1968,[49] and it would then have to turn to the curious linkages between sexual and ethnic politics. As is well known, the Race Relations Act 1976, with its more extensive definition of discrimination and enhanced enforcement provisions, would not have reached the statute book had it not been for the Sex Discrimination Act 1975. That Act was itself based on an assessment of the weaknesses of the Race Relations Act 1968.[50] In the subsequent judicial interpretations, it is significant that the judiciary have been far more liberal and sympathetic to women's claims than to those of ethnic minorities despite the almost identical wording of the two Acts. This is partly because EEC law (as interpreted by the European Court of Justice) has a wider concept of equal opportunity than the British Sex Discrimination Act, and EEC law is not directly relevant to the interpretation of the Race Relations Act.[51] It may also be due to the more powerful social position of women than ethnic minorities. The interpretations of the Sex Discrimination Act have, in turn, been used to influence the interpretations of the Race Relations Acts on the basis of the argument that these Acts should be harmoniously interpreted as part of a single body of anti-discrimination legislation. On the other hand, it is noticeable that the CRE and EOC have taken very different views of their enforcement functions, and that the CRE has proposed far more extensive reforms in the legislation than the EOC.[52] This seems to reflect the different constituencies of the respective commissions and their expectations. Some have argued for a single human rights agency, but it is precisely these different constituencies (demanding differently composed commissions, each with its own earmarked resources) which have prevented such unification.[53]

A single code of anti-discrimination law has had tactical advantages for ethnic minorities, but has it distorted the strategic objectives of the movement for racial equality? In order to answer this one needs to analyse the use that has been made of litigation, by individuals and the commissions, to achieve strategic objectives. This is a task beyond the scope of this Chapter.[54] What seems to be clear is that while the EOC used test cases in the European Court of Justice to put pressure on the British government to extend the law on equal pay for work of equal value and on equal retirement ages and benefits, no similar avenue was open to the CRE. Only recently has the CRE moved from an emphasis upon establishing how discrimination occurs and proposing ways to prevent this to a renewed emphasis on putting things right in specific situations within defined time scales.[55] The rise of ethnic political movements (as well as the election of black MPs and councillors) could enable the CRE to move from an all-purpose agency appearing to represent ethnic minorities into a body whose primary task is seen as law enforcement, training, and acting as a watchdog over the effectiveness of remedial action taken by government, employers, unions and others. The CRE's recent decision to help fund ethnic minority complainant aid organizations is a reflection of this new trend.

The coming struggles over racial equality are likely, therefore, to focus on two symbols of great importance. The first is the improvement of the individual complaints process in ways proposed by the CRE.[56] This can be done by building on pressures within the legal system, for example, for the introduction of some form of class action.[57] A higher success rate for complainants, greater understanding and sympathy for those alleging discrimination and more effective procedures and remedies will enhance the credibility of the law in the eyes of ethnic minorities, and so serve an integrative function. The second, and more important, focus should be on a new regulatory framework which moves away from the adversarial process based on individual cases. Action by the regulatory agency should be triggered by under-representation and have the aim of achieving equitable or fair representation of different groups of the local population. At the same time, we need to move away from the culture of dependence on such an agency to 'give' fair representation. The emphasis needs to shift to self-regulation by empowering groups to defend their own interests. Employers and others with control over scarce resources must be placed under a duty to take remedial action to ensure fair representation, in ways which are discussed by Mary Coussey in the next Chapter. There must be incentives, such as contract compliance, and deterrents, such as effective monetary sanctions, to ensure that potential discriminators are placed in a significantly better position by complying than by non-compliance.

In none of this can the law be expected to remove the power that is exercised over ethnic minorities, but it can help to direct that power into legitimate procedures which recognize their interests.

NOTES

1. This essay draws on, and updates, the author's articles, 'The Race Relations Acts and the process of change' (1987) 14 *New Community* 32, 'Discrimination and equal opportunity in Northern Ireland' (1990) 10 *Oxford Journal of Legal Studies* 408 and 'Judging equal rights' (1983) 36 *Current Legal Problems* 71.

2. Kahn-Freund, O. 'Industrial relations and the law: retrospect and prospect' (1969) 7 *British Journal of Industrial Relations* 301.

3. Bell, D. *And We Are Not Saved: The Elusive Quest for Racial Justice* (New York, Basic Books, 1987) p. 248; and see his Chapter in this book.

4. Cmnd 6234 (London, HMSO, 1975) paras 11,12.

5. Brown, C. *Black and White Britain: The Third PSI Survey* (London, Policy Studies Institute, 1984); compare Smith, D. J. *The Facts of Racial Disadvantage: A National Survey* (London, PEP Broadsheet 560, 1976), and *Racial Disadvantage in Employment* (London, PEP Broadsheet 544, 1974) and Daniel, W. W. *Racial Discrimination in England* (Harmondsworth, Penguin, 1968).

6. 'Ethnic origin and the labour market' (1991) *Employment Gazette* 59-72; compare 'Ethnic origin and economic status' (1987) *Employment Gazette* 18-29.

7. Policy Studies Institute *Racial Discrimination: Seventeen Years after the Act* (London, Policy Studies Institute, 1985) p. 31.

8. Brown, C. *Racial Discrimination in the British Labour Market* (London, Employment Institute Economic Report, vol. 5, no. 4, June 1990).

9. See the selected examples of allegations of racial incidents in employment in Britain from 1 January 1961 to 31 December 1965 in the first edition of Hepple, B. *Race, Jobs and the Law in Britain* (London, Allen Lane, 1968) pp. 201-16.

10. This distinction is made and developed in the context of the Race Relations Acts by Lustgarten, L. 'Racial discrimination and the limits of law' (1986) 49 *Modern Law Review* 68 at p. 71; see generally the useful discussion of the major writers by Cotterrell, R. *The Sociology of Law: An Introduction* (London, Butterworths, 1984) ch. 2.

11. Ehrlich, E. *Fundamental Principles of the Sociology of Law* trans. by Moll, W. L. (New York, Arno Press, 1975).

12. As in the leading case of *West Midlands Passenger Transport Executive* v *Singh* [1988] IRLR 136 (CA).

13. *Carrington* v *Helix Lighting Ltd* [1990] IRLR 6 (EAT).

14. *Peake* v *Automotive Products Ltd* [1977] IRLR 365 (CA). This was a sex discrimination case in which Lord Denning MR said (at p. 973) that it 'is not discrimination for mankind to treat womankind with the courtesy and chivalry which we have been taught to believe is right conduct in our society'. The logical consequence of this reasoning would have been to permit racial discrimination where the respondent believed he or she was protecting a member of an ethnic minority from embarrassment.

15. *Ministry of Defence* v *Jeremiah* [1979] IRLR 436 (CA).

16. [1990] IRLR 288 (HL), overruling [1989] IRLR 318 (CA).

17. [1989] IRLR 173 (HL).

18. Per Lord Goff at p. 295, Lord Bridge at p. 292, Lord Ackner at p. 294.

19. [1984] IRLR 230, mentioned with approval by Lord Griffths in his dissenting speech in *James* at p. 293.

20. At p. 295.

21. Ibid.

22. Race Relations Act 1976 s. 57(3); Sex Discrimination Act 1975 s. 66(3).

23. At p. 297. This is also the approach which Lord Lowry took in *Armagh District Council* v *Fair Employment Agency* [1984] IRLR 234 (NICA), and must now be regarded as dubious in view of the majority's reasoning in *James*.

24. See e.g. *Price Waterhouse* v *Hopkins* noted in [1989] 26 EOR 35. The US Civil Rights Act 1991 has now made it clear that there is unlawful discrimination when a prohibited ground was a 'motivating factor' for an employment practice, even though other factors were also responsible for the decision.

25. [1982] IRLR 502 (CA).

26. Standing Advisory Commission on Human Rights. *Religious and Politicial Discrimination and Equality of Opportunity in Northern Ireland, Report on Fair Employment* Cm. 237 (London, HMSO, 1987) paras 6.5, 6.15.

27. Per Lord Goff at p. 294, Lord Bridge at p. 292, cf. Lord Lowry dissenting at p. 298; comment by G. Mead (1990) 19 *Industrial Law Journal* 250. This accords with later decisions of the European Court of Justice in *Dekker* [1991] IRLR 27, and *Hertz* [1991] IRLR 31 that direct discrimination cannot be justified on grounds of cost etc.

28. 401 US 424 [1971]. The Civil Rights Act 1991 has reversed later decisions and reaffirmed that the burden is on the employer to prove that a practice is 'job related for the position in question and consistent with business necessity'.

29. McCrudden, C. 'Changing notions of discrimination' in Guest, S. and Milne, A. (eds) *Equality and Discrimination: Essays in Freedom and Justice* (Stuttgart, Franz Steiner Verlag, 1985) p. 83 at p. 88; see also the same author's 'Institutional discrimination' (1982) 2 *Oxford Journal of Legal Studies* 303.

30. *Perera v Civil Service Commission* [1983] IRLR 166 (CA); and see *Jones v Chief Adjudication Officer* [1990] IRLR 533 (CA), where it is suggested that where more than one requirement is laid down the impact of all must be assessed together.

31. *Mandla v Lee* [1983] IRLR 209 (HL).

32. See e.g. *Raval v DHSS* [1985] IRLR 370 (EAT), in which it was held that an industrial tribunal was wrong to decide that a Kenyan Asian could comply with a requirement that she must have a GCE O level in English because it was possible for her to sit the examination. However, although it was found that Mrs Raval had sufficient command of English to fulfil the job requirements, the EAT upheld the tribunal's decision that the O-level requirement was 'justifiable'.

33. *Jones v Chief Adjudication Officer* [1990] IRLR 533 (CA), per Mustill LJ.

34. *Kidd v DRG* (UK) Ltd [1985] IRLR 190 (EAT).

35. *Ojutiku v Manpower Services Commission* [1982] IRLR 418 (CA).

36. [1989] IRLR 69 (CA) at p. 77. There was no appeal against this finding in the subsequent hearing in the House of Lords [1990] IRLR 302 (HL), in which the appeal was allowed on the ground that the discrimination was not protected by the statutory instrument relating to teachers' qualifications.

37. See Hepple, B. 'Judging equal rights' (1983) 36 *Current Legal Problems* 71 at p. 83.

38. SACHR Report op. cit. (note 26) para. 7.19.

39. Op. cit. para. 7.20.

40. Cm. 380 (London, HMSO, 1988) para. 1.14.

41. Williams, B. 'The idea of equality' in Laslett, P. and Runciman, W. G. (eds) *Philosophy, Politics and Society* (London, 1962) p. 110 at p. 126.

42. Report of the Race Relations Board for 1966–67 (London, HMSO, 1968) para. 65.

43. This is explained and discussed by McCrudden, C. in Guest and Milne (eds) op. cit. (note 29).

44. Race Relations Act 1976 s. 57(3), and see above

45. Mayhew, L. H. *Law and Equal Opportunity: A Study of the Massachusetts Commission against Discrimination* (Cambridge, Mass., Harvard University Press, 1968); and 'Stability and change in legal systems' in Barber, B. and Inkeles, A. (eds) *Stability and Social Change* (Boston, Little, Brown, 1968) pp. 187–210.

46. See also, McCrudden, C. et al., *Racial Justice at Work: The Enforcement of the Race Relations Act in Employment* (London, Policy Studies Institute, 1991), which was not available at the time this essay was written.

47. See e.g. Bell op. cit. (note 3) pp. 60, 61.

48. Abrams, P. *Historical Sociology* (Shepton Mallet, Open Books, 1982) p. 15.

49. See *Race, Jobs and the Law in Britain* 2nd edn (Harmondsworth, Penguin, 1970) pp. 156–74; Lester, A. and Bindman, G. *Race and Law* (Harmondsworth, Penguin, 1972) pp. 107–49.

50. See Meehan, E. M. *Women's Rights at Work* (London, Macmillan, 1985) p. 85.

51. For example, the application of an objective test of justification in *Steel v Union of Post Office Workers* [1977] IRLR 288 (EAT) (a sex discrimination case), but a subjective test in *Ojutiku v Manpower Services Commission* op. cit. (note 35). Despite the departure from *Ojutiku* in *Hampson*

op. cit. (note 36), considerable doubt still exists about the relevance of decisions under Art. 119 EEC Treaty and the Equal Treatment Directive 76/207/EEC to the interpretation of British race relations legislation in view of the absence of a basis in the EEC Treaty to deal with racial discrimination. See further the essay by Szyszczak in this book.

52. Compare CRE *Review of the Race Relations Act 1976: Proposals for Change* (1985) with EOC *Equal Treatment for Men and Women* (1988).

53. Other aspects of the interaction of race and gender are discussed by Fredman and Szyszczak in this book.

54. See McCrudden, C. et al . op. cit. (note 46) and the earlier limited study by Kumar, V. C. *Industrial Tribunal Applicants under the Race Relations Act 1976* (London, CRE, 1986). There has been more extensive research on the use of the Sex Discrimination Act, e.g. by Leonard, A. *Judging Inequality* (London, Cobden Trust, 1987) and *Pyrrhic Victories* (London, HMSO, 1987).

55. CRE *Annual Report 1986* (London, CRE, 1987) p. 7.

56. See CRE *Review of the Race Relations Act 1976: Proposals for Change* (1985), which the CRE is currently revising in the light of subsequent developments in law and practice.

57. On the merits of which in this context, see the essay by Lacey, in this volume; and Pannick, D., 'Class actions and discrimination law' (1982) 10 *New Community* 16.

3

The Effectiveness of Strategic Enforcement of the Race Relations Act 1976

Mary Coussey

INTRODUCTION

The strategic powers in the Race Relations Act 1976 are mainly those under Section 49 which enable the Commission for Racial Equality (CRE) to carry out formal investigations. The courts have defined two types of investigation. First, general enquiries which can be carried out after giving notice, without the Commission holding any specific belief that there may have been breaches of the Act. Such investigations cannot be confined to the activities of specifically named organizations and can result only in a report and recommendations. In general investigations, subpoena notices can only be issued on the authority of the Secretary of State. The second type of investigation is the 'belief', or 'accusatory' investigation into suspected unlawful acts by a named person. In these the Commission is required to specify grounds for accusation and give an opportunity for representations before embarking on enquiries. In belief investigations the Commission has a power to issue subpeona notices and non-discrimination notices, the latter preceded by another obligatory opportunity for representations.

The basis for the strategic role of the Commission was set out in the White Paper preceding the 1976 Act. In this it was envisaged that the proposed Commission would be able to carry out formal investigations on its own initiative into a specific organization. This was seen as the basis for an inspectorate and was interpreted by the Commission as a power to investigate in named organizations the effects of practices on particular racial groups, either because there was general evidence of inequality in the industrial sector or job level or because it was a leading company in an industry or sector. But the decision in the *Prestige*[1] case in 1984 precluded investigations into named organizations where no unlawful acts were suspected. In practice this has meant that the strategic or inspectorial role of the Commission has had to be carried out through general surveys across an area or sector. These surveys are far less likely to focus on specific evidence and on specific solutions.

Some conclusions about the effectiveness of the strategic enforcement powers of the Commission can be drawn from an analysis of published employment reports. This allows an identification of some of the factors which have led to action by employers.

WHAT IS THE EXTENT OF RACIAL INEQUALITY IN EMPLOYMENT?

Any discussion of the effectiveness of the strategic provisions of the 1976 Act has to be set in context. There are three main indicators of racial inequality in the labour market: unemployment rates; occupational distribution, including job levels; and levels of racial discrimination.

Throughout the 1980s, the unemployment rate for ethnic minority people was double that for white people.[2] For example, between 1984 and 1986 the ethnic minority unemployment rate was 20 per cent compared with 10 per cent for whites, with slightly higher rates for people of West Indian and Bangladeshi/Pakistani origin. Unemployment was higher among young people: 17 per cent overall for 16 to 24-year-olds, but 32 per cent for ethnic minorities. Young people of Pakistani and Bangladeshi origin had the highest ethnic minority unemployment rates. Although the gap narrowed a little by 1989, it then increased again. In 1991 there was an ethnic minority unemployment rate of 15 per cent compared with 8 per cent for whites.

People from ethnic minorities were also out of work for longer periods than white people.[3] However, the disparity in unemployment rates cannot be fully explained by differences in levels of qualifications. On the contrary, Labour Force Surveys show that the gap is greatest amongst those with higher-level qualifications; furthermore the proportion of ethnic minority people with higher-level qualifications is above the overall average.

Labour Force Surveys also show that ethnic minority people are concentrated in certain industries, in lower-level occupations and in certain metropolitan localities. For example, 27 per cent of ethnic minority males were employed in hotels, catering and repairs compared with only 16 per cent of whites. Ethnic minorities are also strongly represented in transport and communications, health services and some manufacturing. Only 5 per cent of male Afro-Caribbeans and 13 per cent of Asians were in professional and managerial occupations, compared with 19 per cent of white males.[4]

The factors of industry type and job level have been significant in explaining differences between white and ethnic minority unemployment rates, because in consequence ethnic minority people have been more vulnerable to unemployment, especially by the loss of lower-level jobs in manufacturing.

The other significant factor in explaining labour market differences is racial discrimination. The extent of racial discrimination has been demonstrated in several studies. For example, a survey in 1984–85 based on hundreds of applications for a range of jobs showed that about one-third of employers discriminated against the ethnic minority applicant in favour of an equally qualified white person, a level of discrimination found in a similar survey conducted in the mid-1970s.[6] Investigations and research by the Commission for Racial Equality have found similar disparities in graduate recruitment and in recruitment to particular sectors.[7]

In reply to the Commission's proposal[8] for a review of the Race Relations Act 1976, the government argued in 1989 that there was no need for a stronger race relations act because there was evidence of an improvement in the position of minorities; presumably this evidence relied on the recent narrowing of the gap in unemployment rates. However, an analysis[9] of the ethnic differences in unemployment rates suggests that the improvement is neither a new development nor a meaningful one. Ethnic minority unemployment rate increases and decreases have been faster than the white rate, and the recent fall simply reflected a fall in general unemployment rates. Levels of racial discrimination have not mirrored the rise and fall in employment and unemployment.

The levels were the same in the 1970s and the mid 1980s, and there are indications that they continued at the same rate in the late 1980s, after the unemployment rate disparity fell. What this suggests is that neither economic factors nor the legislation have yet had a significant effect on the extent of racial discrimination.

WHAT IS THE EFFECT OF STRATEGIC ENFORCEMENT?

It is clear from the analysis of changes in the labour market position of ethnic minorities that the law has not been able to reduce the overall

level of racial discrimination. Does this mean that the strategic enforcement powers have not contributed towards improving opportunities
for ethnic minority people, and if so why not? Has strategic enforcement
had any significant effect on the organizations concerned?

The strategic investigations carried out by the CRE before the *Prestige*
decision in 1984 were chosen with reference to the broad labour market
position. It was decided to carry out a rolling programme of general
enquiries into the extent of inequality in a number of representative
industries located in areas of significant ethnic minority population.
In this way, it would be possible to build up a range of models,
demonstrating in practical terms how discrimination operates. Over a
dozen such enquiries were started. By selecting large companies in
industrial sectors in which ethnic minorities were concentrated, it was
anticipated that the findings of the investigations would be relevant to
other employers in the same industry.

These enquiries combined a strategic and inspectorial approach.
However, their aims were not fulfilled because many of the early
strategic investigations had to be abandoned after the *Prestige* decision.
But the experience gained was the basis for many of the recommendations in the Code of Practice, as these enquiries identified most of
the potentially discriminatory practices and other barriers caused by
disadvantage in the labour market.

For example, there were five reports[10] published of general investigations, started before the *Prestige* decision, into named organizations.
The enquiries covered a wide range of personnel decision-making and
practices at different job levels. Many potentially discriminatory practices were identified. These included informal word-of-mouth recruitment, which effectively excluded ethnic minority applicants from access
to jobs, and the application of geographical preferences, which in some
circumstances disproportionately excluded ethnic minorities (e.g.
applicants should not live in Liverpool 8). Discriminatory selection
criteria were also found, such as informal oral or written English tests
which had little relation to the standards needed for the work, and
which screened out a large majority of Asian candidates. Subjective
criteria, acceptability criteria and stereotypical judgments were widespread. The use of sponsorship as a qualification for a hackney cab
licence was found to be a discriminatory practice. One enquiry was
restarted as a 'belief' investigation, and focused more narrowly on
promotion procedures, identifying the interview as a discriminatory
practice because it rejected ethnic minority candidates for lack of
communication skills. This was found to be unjustifiable because the
interview did not test the more direct work-related communication
required for the job.

Other early investigations published before 1984 (and therefore unaffected by *Prestige*) uncovered a similar array of discriminatory practices. These included direct discrimination and pressure to discriminate by shop stewards,[11] and indirect discrimination by Massey Ferguson in the use of unsolicited letters for recruitment.[12] The latter practice favoured applicants with links with the workforce. As the workforce was overwhelmingly white, the letters of application also came mainly from white people. Inside knowledge also meant that applicants wrote to apply for a specific vacancy as it arose. Ethnic minority applicants had no such networks at the plant, and tended to call at the factory gates. When this occurred, they may have been advised to 'write in', but few did so. Many had no confidence that their letters would be successful. The company argued that this recruitment practice was not a 'requirement' (which is one of the criteria in the statutory definition of indirect discrimination) because applicants who applied in other ways were sometimes considered. Had this early case come to the courts, it would have been an interesting test of the meaning of 'requirement or condition' in Section 1(1) (b) of the Race Relations Act, demonstrating as it does the ease with which employers can point to one or two exceptions to challenge the existence of a practice or 'requirement'.

This investigation also showed the powerful effect of a poor company image: the chill factor. It was known among the ethnic minority communities in Coventry, the site of the plant, that it was a 'waste of time' applying to Massey Ferguson for a job if you were black or Asian, because 'no one like me' was employed there. The 'chill factor' is still an important deterrent to ethnic minority candidates, as several recent surveys by employers have shown. See, for example, the recent survey 'Ethnic Minority Recruitment to the Armed Services', published by the Ministry of Defence in January 1990. According to this research, one-third of Asians and half of Afro-Caribbeans in the survey expected to find racial discrimination when applying to the armed services.

None of the companies involved in these pre-1984 investigations had taken steps to implement equal opportunities policies. The discriminatory practices could flourish unchecked, as there were no records of the ethnic origin of applicants or employees. Ironically; in the absence of such data, it was difficult for the commission to find sufficient evidence of discriminatory practices. The alternative was to rely on employers' records of reasons for rejection or their accounts of selection practices. Not surprisingly, the evidence gleaned from this was often too weak to justify the use of the enforcement powers. This was particularly true after 1982, when the Court of Appeal ruled in the *Amari Plastics* case[13] that in an appeal against a non-discrimination notice, the respondent could challenge the commission's findings of fact as well as the requirements in the notice to stop operating discriminatory practices. In effect, the results of a lengthy and wide-ranging investigation could be reassessed and the witnesses re-examined. There were few instances which would stand up in the face of two detailed tests, one inquisitional and the other adversarial.

Set against such judicial standards, the commission's enforcement powers seemed slight. As a result, the commission began to look for more effective ways of securing the necessary changes in practice and began using formal investigations as a basis for negotiating with companies as informed insiders. This required a different approach, which is reflected in later reports of investigations.

The *Prestige* and *Amari Plastics* cases meant that after 1984, the Commission was unable to use its formal investigations powers as envisaged by those who drafted the Race Relations Act. Investigations into named organizations were now dependent on evidence of suspected unlawful acts, and it was thus more difficult to aim these at employers who are particularly influential or otherwise significant. The requirements for representations at both ends of the investigation have led to extensive delays, and much of the litigation has concentrated on procedural requirements rather than on the substantive issues. After the Commission had made findings of fact, an appeal against any proposed notice was held to carry with it the right to challenge the facts on which the notice was based, thus reopening in a different forum an already lengthy inquisitorial process.

THE CODE OF PRACTICE

The Code of Practice in force since 1984 has had a significant effect on the Commission's law enforcement strategy. The power to issue an employment code arises under section 47 of the Race Relations Act 1976, which lays down four formal requirements. The Commission must publish a draft code and consider any representations made about the draft. Second, there must be consultation with employers' organizations, trade unions and other appropriate organizations in the course of preparing the draft. Third, the draft must be put to the Secretary of State for approval. Fourth, if the Secretary of State approves the draft, it must be laid before Parliament for 40 days.

Section 47 also defines the status of the code. Its recommendations are not enforceable, but an industrial tribunal must take them into account if they appear to be relevant to any question arising in proceedings.

The formal draft code was first issued in 1979, and consultations took place with organizations including the Confederation of British Industry, the Trades Union Congress, the Advisory Conciliation and Arbitration Service, the Institute of Personnel Management, the Department of Employment, ethnic minority and community relations groups, a cross-section of industrial organizations and a range of private and public employers, including local authorities. During the subsequent discussions with the Employment Department, concern focused particularly on the recommendations that ethnic origin data should be used to monitor equal opportunities. These recommendations were seen as controversial. However, by 1982, following the report of a House of Commons Home Affairs Committee featuring ethnic monitoring, and the 1981 Scarman report of the Brixton riots, the government gradually accepted the principle. In anticipation of the code in 1984, the Civil Service announced that it would carry out a programme of ethnic origin surveys of its staff. Other large public-sector employers, mainly in local government, also started monitoring their workforce. The code was laid before Parliament and came into effect on 1 April 1984.

The statutory basis of the code, the consultation process and the subsequent government and parliamentary approval gave it a legitimacy and authority which considerably strengthened it and gave it a much wider application than the earlier formal investigations. Moreover, the Commission's strategy changed in several ways. First, for about two years resources were concentrated on raising awareness of the code, particularly among large employers, and in gaining their acceptance of it as good practice, especially in relation to ethnic monitoring. Large leading private-sector employers were approached systematically, asked what they were doing to implement the Code of Practice and given advice on practical matters such as setting up monitoring systems. The need for practical advice on implementing equal opportunities policies has grown, as awareness and acceptance of such policies has increased, and this work has continued to make heavy demands on the Commission's resources. For example, in their evidence to the House of Commons Employment Committee in February 1989,[14] the Commission estimated that in the previous year detailed advice was given to over 300 large employers, and since 1987, seventeen national conferences and seminars had been held. In the same period, five new formal investigations were started.

The Commission also carried out research on 1985–86[15] into the extent to which employers were complying with the Code of Practice, and into the effectiveness of the recommendations in producing improved opportunities for ethnic minority people in employment. The research found that only a minority of employers was fully implementing the recommendations in the Employment Code. The proportion was significantly higher among large employers, public-sector employers and those employers with a substantial ethnic minority workforce. However, the survey showed a high level of basic awareness of the Code among employers nationally: two-thirds of the employers surveyed had heard of it, rising to 95 per cent among large employers, although the proportions were reduced for those who had actually read through it. Only 229 (25 per cent) employers had read the Code, and these formed the interviewed sample.

Of the 229 employers interviewed, two-thirds had formal, written equal opportunity policies, but fewer than 4 per cent of employers interviewed had comprehensive policies with adequate systems for monitoring their effectiveness. Over half of the employers interviewed said that they had checked their recruitment practices, and 10 per cent — mostly large employers — found evidence of racial discrimination. Many of the employers interviewed had little or no understanding of the concept of indirect discrimination. Up to one-third of employers were still using recruitment methods such as word-of-mouth recommendations for existing employees or unsolicited applications, which can exclude ethnic minority applicants. Over half were using selection criteria such as aptitude tests and minimum educational qualifications, which may not measure what is needed for the job in question, and may be indirectly discriminatory.

Other selection methods that give scope for discrimination were still in use; for example, over half the employers interviewed were shortlisting manual vacancies without use of job descriptions and employee specifications. Selection decisions that were unchecked at senior level were fairly common, such as the use of one person for both screening and for shortlisting for interview.

Over one-third of employers interviewed said that it was as a direct result of the Code of Practice that they had drawn up or revised their written equal opportunity policy, had reviewed their recruitment methods and selection criteria and had taken some form of action to encourage ethnic minority applicants. In addition 12 per cent of employers interviewed said that they had recruited more ethnic minority employees as a result of action taken to implement equal opportunity programmes.

There were also detailed case studies of employers with comprehensive policies. These showed that where employers take action specifically aimed at dealing with barriers to equality of opportunity, this is likely to increase the numbers of ethnic minority people recruited or promoted. Most case-study employers referred to the link between equal opportunity policies and good business practice. In implementing their policy they found that this improved the quality of personnel selection and led to better communications and industrial relations. These research findings suggest that the Code can be effective in reducing racial discrimination, but there is little incentive for employers to implement its recommendations voluntarily.

The Commission assists about 200 complainants each year. In most cases this will include drafting the questionnaire to employers which asks about equal opportunity policies. Between 60 and 90 of these cases reach a tribunal hearing, and tribunals increasingly refer to the Code of Practice in their decision as a yardstick for evaluating the credibility of employers claims to be practising equal opportunity policies.

The Code of Practice concentrates on employment processes. It recommends that data be used to monitor the effectiveness of an equal opportunity policy, but does not attempt to define a measurable standard by which progress should be assessed, nor does it define the 'disproportionate effect', to use as a basis for checking the extent of indirect discrimination. There have been few judicial attempts to define these standards. Industrial tribunals have relied heavily on a pragmatic approach to a particular case. Indirect discrimination cases have been few, and there are none in which the statistical standards have been directly at issue.

STRATEGIC ENFORCEMENT SINCE THE CODE OF PRACTICE

The inspectorial basis of formal investigations was curtailed both by judicial decisions and by competing demands on the Commission's resources. It also appeared that named-person investigations had not always produced the desired changes, because the accusatory process is contentious, with respondents devoting their resources to defending themselves rather than accepting the findings as a reason for introducing comprehensive changes. Moreover, there was no longer a need to use investigations to identify indirectly discriminating systems.

These were already encodified and had been well publicized in this process. The second shift in strategy after 1989 was to make more use of formal investigations as a means of negotiating changes based on an analysis of the barriers in an organization or a sector. The strategy has had a mixed success.

Formal Investigations since 1984

Case	Issue	Date published
Beaumont Shopping Centre	Recruitment	1985
Chartered accountancy training contracts	Recruitment	1987
South Manchester District Health Authority	Promotion; access to training	1988
Working in hotels	Recruitment	1991
Cardiff employers	Recruitment; promotion; & access to training	1991
JHP Training Ltd	Access to work placements	1992
Hestair Management Services Ltd	Referral services	1991

Investigations in progress in 1990

Case	Issue
Bradford school leavers	Recruitment
Leicestershire County Council	Recruitment promotion
T & T	Referral services

Experience in the Beaumont Leys[16] investigation the result of which were published in 1985 suggested that employers were more willing to accept advice and introduce widespread change when confronted privately with evidence of inequality, than they were after a more public and accusatory investigation. Tesco, the largest employer in the Beaumont Leys complex, improved their selection training, introduced monitoring and issued guidelines to their managers aimed at reducing disparities in selection rates. The investigation has been duplicated with other large retail employers, and working groups have been set up in the North-West and the Midlands, for example, to develop ways of increasing ethnic minority recruitment.

The investigation into recruitment of trainee chartered accountants, the results of which were published in 1987, was used in a similar way, to negotiate widespread changes in practices with leading firms in the profession. The Institute of Chartered Accountants was persuaded by the findings of widespread disparities in selection rates between white and ethnic minority graduates to monitor entry to the profession and to issue a code of practice. The first published results show that in 1989 over 10 per cent of new entrants were from ethnic minorities. The findings were also used to press the Association of Graduate Recruiters, which includes some of Britain's biggest companies, to look at their recruitment practices. Follow-up reports published by the Commission in 1989 show that some of the large firms of accountants have shown improvements in the number of ethnic minority graduates recruited since the formal investigation. For example, nine of the large chartered accountancy firms had taken such steps as widening recruitment sources to target ethnic minority applicants. In 1988, the three largest firms showed a sustained improvement in ethnic minority success rates.

The Beaumont Leys and chartered accountancy reports also include an attempt by the Commission to define objective standards for a statistical test of discrimination. In both investigations, tests were applied to the data for black and ethnic minority and white application and success rates: all showed high levels of significance.

For the first time the Commission also recommended that firms use application rate data as an estimate of the expected number of each group to be selected at each stage. Put simply, the Commission was recommending numerical targets for the selection process. The use of numerical targets was developed still further in the enquiry, published by the Commission in 1990, into promotion at London Underground Ltd.[17] The use of numerical targets for recruitment and promotion has become the chief means by which the Commission will monitor the effectiveness of the changes put into effect by London Underground. This report is also a good example of the way in which the Commission has recently used the threat of a formal investigation to negotiate change. The Commission decided that it was unnecessary to embark on the formal enforcement process because changes had been carried out. The London Underground findings are being used to follow up with major test producers and users, as they provide a model of what to do to avoid indirect discrimination in selection testing.

The Beaumont Leys and chartered accountancy investigations illustrate how post-*Prestige* strategic enforcement can be effective in an organization. The investigation must be narrowly defined, either by the industry or organized structure or by function or geographical location. It must include in its scope employers regarded as a model or leader by others, and it must focus on an issue or practice about which the industry itself has a concern, to maximize self-interest and the potential for negotiating change.

Weaknesses in the enforcement process — the procedural requirements and the resource investment needed to bring about change through the use of non-disrimination notices — have meant that the

Commission's strongest power has been the threat of an investigation and bad publicity. This has been the incentive for employers to change. But the effects have been limited where there has been no 'market leader' to set the pace. The investigations into the hotel industry, Cardiff employers and Bradford school leavers are examples of enquiries with much less potential for follow up, because the role-model employer and tightly focused basis of a single function or issue are missing. These are in effect pre-*Prestige*-type 'inspectorial' investigations, with the disadvantage that they have identified no new barriers or indirectly discriminatory practices. The other post-*Prestige* investigations are accusatory.

The recently published London Underground enquiry also illustrates another shift in focus, and a third phase of strategic enforcement. If all the barriers have been identified and encodified, and if the employment code is now widely enough established to be accepted good practice, the need for a historical examination of processes is reduced. The 1980s saw a significant shift in public sector management away from centralized policies and monitoring. Decisions have been devolved, with accountability exercised through the use of agreed performance outcomes. Strategic enforcement will need to develop within this framework and use outcomes expressed as targets or goals, or specific objectives to be achieved, as the basis for monitoring by the Commission.

For this to be effective, the commission will have to develop guidance and data for establishing objectively measurable outcomes.

There has as yet been no full-scale evaluation of the effectiveness of strategic enforcement in the Race Relations Act 1976. We do not know whether progress has been faster in those industries which have had sustained experience of strategic Commission activity. Changes in levels of ethnic minority unemployment seem to be due to economic factors and owe little to the law. We have seen an increase in the numbers of employers with equal opportunity policies, but few of these can show a change in ethnic minority participation rates, especially at higher levels.

Experience in the United States suggests that employers begin to take voluntary action when they see it as to their advantage to do so. In order to create this perception six conditions are necessary.[18] First, the standard must be established by law. Where standards are not so established, employers will change or waive them for economic or professional reasons. If the standards are set by employers, self-interest will influence their development and use. Although employers should participate in the development of standards, these need to be given authority by government promulgation. Arguably the employment code has such an authority and sets standards for carrying out certain employment practices, but these are not legally enforceable and so fail as regulatory standards.

The second condition for self-regulation is that there must be a vigorous enforcement programme, one in which there is significant risk of serious consequences to employers who flout the standards; for example, settlements improving the rights of workers, and extensive use of regulatory agency rule-making to support the enforcement programme. In Great Britain, there are some 285,000 private-sector employers (or 23,000 parent companies) alone. For the Commission's inspectorial role to have a sufficient impact, staffing would have to be at least at the level of the factory inspectorate (500 to 600 staff compared with the Commission's 30 staff in the Employment Division) or, alternatively, industrial tribunal complaints would have to be multiplied twenty- or thirty-fold, with a twenty-fold increase in awards or settlements and provision for class actions.

The third condition is that the results achieved must be objectively measurable. In the United States, disparate impact was defined by the Supreme Court in 1971.[19] No such definition has been attempted in British courts, and the Commission has not defined 'under-representation' in its reports or in the Code of Practice. Nor has Parliament defined 'fair participation' in the Fair Employment Act 1989 in Northern Ireland.

The fourth condition is that the law should provide for liability to individuals, so that even where an organization is carrying out equal opportunity programmes which may protect them from state regulatory action, an individual is free to litigate. This condition does apply in this country; insured individual complainants are free to bring action without the support of the Commission.

The fifth condition is that employers should be better off after voluntary compliance. There must be a regulatory inspection, or other periodic reporting requirement, of voluntary affirmative action plans. No such system exists in this country, although there is the basis for it in Northern Ireland, in that the Fair Employment Commission can call for an employer's affirmative action plan if fair participation is not being provided, and require remedial measures.

The final condition is that there must be sufficient and organized public concern. Given that there has never been an effective independent civil rights movement in Great Britain, arguably no such condition exists here.

Enforcement in Britain meets only one of these tests, that of private access to litigation. Courts and tribunals have not set standards, in the sense of defining the specific steps needed to produce equality, nor have they yet objectively defined disproportionate effect or participation levels, although the Commission has begun to do so in recent reports and recommendations.

Enforcement cannot be defined as vigorous and there is little economic pressure. Set against the estimated tens of thousands of acts of direct discrimination in employment, the few hundred cases each year cannot be seen as extensive. There is no satisfactory system for inspection or reporting, and the resources of the Commission do not allow it to attempt any such functions.

A NEW REGULATORY FRAMEWORK?

The 1991 census will provide benchmark data which could allow the introduction of a new approach to equal opportunities. Local information on the availability of different groups in the labour market would allow a more accurate and objective test of under-representation. A new regulatory framework could be developed wherein action is triggered by failure to deal effectively with under-representation within a specified timetable. This new approach would move away from the adversarial/defensive process of the present legislation, and would focus on outcomes and solutions. It would be more innovative and creative than examining historic evidence accounting for particular workplace patterns. It is more compatible with the current policy of devolved delegated decision-making, with regulation accountability exercised by the achievement of agreed outcomes.

Employers would be required to practise equality of opportunity and a new definition of discrimination would give the individual right of redress for a failure to offer equality of opportunity, if he or she can show that disproportionately few persons of his or her racial group have progressed in comparison with others, and that the employer has not taken remedial or positive action steps set out in the Code to improve access to specified work. The Commission would have the power to investigate failure to practise equality of opportunity based either on a reporting requirement, as in the Fair Employment Act in Northern Ireland, or a strategic power to examine named organizations. The Commission would issue directions to an employer requiring him or her to carry out action, tied to achieving specific objectives or goals within a specified timetable.

Incentives are also important in bringing about equal opportunities. Linkage of compliance with effective affirmative or positive action and the award of public contracts, including government contracts, could provide a commercial incentive. The Local Government Act 1988 has limited the scope for local authorities to make this link, because they cannot have access to data which would show whether contractors are monitoring employment practices. It is too soon to evaluate the effectiveness of these limited provisions. However, linking contracts with evidence of positive action and of progress towards full participation of ethnic minorities is a more direct commercial incentive because it would reward employers who can show that they are practising equal opportunities.

NOTES

1. *CRE v Prestige Group plc* [1984] ICR 473 (HL).
2. These figures are derived from the Labour Force Surveys published in the *Employment Gazette* between 1986 and March 1990.
3. Brown, C. *Black and White Britain* (London PSI, 1982).
4. Ibid.
5. Brown, C. and Gay, P. *Racial Discrimination: Seventeen Years after the Act* (London, PSI, 1985).
6. McIntosh, N. and Smith, D.J. *The Extent of Racial Discrimination* (London, PEP, 1973).
7. *Report of a Formal Investigation into Recruitment for Chartered Accountancy Training* (London, CRE, 1987); *Report of a Formal Investigation of the Beaumont Leys Shopping Centre, Leicester* (London, CRE, 1985).
8. *Review of the Race Relations Act 1976: Proposals for Change* (London, CRE, 1985).
9. Brown, C. *Racial Inequality in the British Labour Market* (London, Employment Institute Economic Report, Vol. 5, no. 4; 1990).
10. *Reports of a Formal Investigation into Bradford District of West Yorkshire PTE; Chubb and Sons; Dunlop; National Bus Co; Unigate Dairies; and Hackney Carriage Licences* (London, CRE, 1983–85).
11. *Report of Formal Investigations of BL Cars Ltd* (London, CRE, 1981).
12. *Reports of a Formal Investigation of Massey Ferguson Partnership Ltd* (London, CRE, 1982).
13. *CRE v Amari Plastics* [1982] QB 1194.
14. House of Commons. *The Work of the Commission for Racial Equality* 8 February 1989 (London, HMSO).
15. *Are Employers Complying?* (London, CRE, 1989).
16. Op. cit. Note 7.
17. *Lines of Progress* (London, CRE, 1990).
18. Blumrosen, A. 'Six conditions for meaningful self-regulation' (1983) 69 *American Bar Association Journal* 1264–69.
19. *Griggs v Duke Power Co* [1971] 401 US 424.

4

Proof and Evidence of Discrimination

Geoffrey Bindman

PROVING DISCRIMINATION

One of the commonest instant reactions to the claim that law may help to restrain racial discrimination is: how can you prove it? The assumption is that a discriminatory intention must be an essential element of the wrong, and that intention, a mental state, is not susceptible to investigation. Of course, lawyers are used to the idea that courts identify intentions as facts. The old cliché — 'the Devil himself knoweth not the thought of man'[1] — has been replaced by another: 'the state of a man's mind is as much a fact as the state of his digestion'.[2] Proof of discrimination has three elements: first, we must know what, in the legal context, discrimination is. For this we must rely on whatever statutory definitions there may be, supplemented by judicial interpretation. Second, we must identify what must be proved in order to establish that discrimination, as so defined, has or has not occurred. Here the question of intention arises. The burden of proof also comes under this heading. Third, there is the question of obtaining the necessary evidence. In discrimination cases this has caused particular difficulty.

The United States Background

Anti-discrimination law in Britain owes its origin to the United States. The Race Relations Act 1965 imported its structure from the model of the typical state human rights statute, in which discrimination, the key concept, was not defined. The Civil Rights Act 1964, which introduced the statutory prohibition of discrimination into several aspects of federal law, again failed to spell out any definition. Thus, for example, Title VII of the act outlaws a series of specific practices against individuals (including failure or refusal to employ) where they occur 'because of such individual's race, colour, . . . or national origin.' The result was to leave a wide discretion to the judges to define the scope of the law, both as to the definition of discrimination, and as to the burden and standard of proof. In general the approach of the United States judiciary was positive and purposive: regarding the broad objective of the law as the rectification and redress of an overriding social evil, they did not view the words of the statute as restrictive but as an invitation to fashion a practical and effective legal strategy.

Thus, in *Griggs* v *Duke Power Co.*[3] the Supreme Court held the words of the 1964 Act apt to cover a situation not previously thought to be within the scope of the law, namely, where black job applicants were required to possess the same qualifications as white applicants, notwithstanding that past discrimination had deprived all or most of them of the opportunity of obtaining those qualifications. The Court allowed an exception, however, where the qualifications were essential for performance of the job. In such situations (known as *adverse impact* or, when the concept was imported into United Kingdom law, *indirect* discrimination), there was no suggestion that any intention to discriminate need be proved. The mere fact of unjustified (that is, not job-related) adverse impact of a rule or practice on members of a particular ethnic group was sufficient to establish liability. In cases of differential (called in the United States 'disparate') treatment under Title VII, the question of intent had also not loomed large. Where minority members were treated less favourably than others, proof of a discriminatory purpose was not required. The need for a causal link seems always to have been assumed. A distinction appears to have been drawn, however, where allegations of racial discrimination were made under the Equal Protection clause of the US Constitution. In *Washington* v *Davis*,[4] the Supreme Court held that intent to discriminate must be established in such cases.

DEFINING DISCRIMINATION

The definitions of discrimination in the Race Relations Act 1976 are similar in form to those in the Sex Discrimination Act 1975. In the following discussion cases under both Acts will be relied upon where identical problems of interpretation arise.

Judicial tradition in Britain favours literal construction, though sometimes with an eye to legislative purpose.[5] This contrasts with the more purposive tradition in the United States. Thus, the extension of the definition of discrimination achieved by the Supreme Court in the *Griggs* case was assumed by the government when contemplating the introduction of the Sex Discrimination Act in 1975 to be beyond the scope of the United Kingdom judiciary. Hence the incorporation in the Sex Discrimination Act and subsequent Race Relations Act 1976 of a separate definition of indirect discrimination. So in both the Sex Discrimination Act and the Race Relations Act we have to consider proof and evidence separately for direct and indirect discrimination. This consequence of the legislative approach in the United Kingdom can inhibit our understanding of discrimination, which may not easily fit under either heading. This is especially apparent when one reflects that from the perspective of the victim of discrimination the distinction between direct and indirect discrimination is likely to be immaterial. Certainly, deprivation of employment or other benefit is not affected.[6]

DIRECT DISCRIMINATION

In direct discrimination, two things must be proved: that the victim has been treated 'less favourably' than another person has been or would be treated; and that such treatment was 'on racial grounds' (i.e. colour, race, nationality or ethnic or national origins).

Less favourable treatment means that different treatment must be proved between the complainant and others; it must be shown to be less favourable (i.e. detrimental) to the former. The word detriment is itself used in section 1(1)(b) and the test is similar for both direct and indirect discrimination. In *Peake* v *Automotive Products*[7] it had been maintained by Lord Denning MR that differences introduced for administrative convenience or chivalry were not to be deemed 'less favourable'. Later, in *Ministry of Defence* v *Jeremiah*,[8] he acknowledged that his former view was incorrect, but he said that the maxim 'de minimis non curat lex' could apply in discrimination cases. The notion that discrimination can ever be so trivial as to qualify under that exception has been put in doubt by a subsequent Court of Appeal decision.[9] It is thus now clear that 'being put under any disadvantage' is sufficient to amount to 'less favourable' treatment or to detriment.

The second criterion for direct discrimination involves unfavourable treatment on the ground of colour, race, nationality or ethnic or national origins. There have been a number of cases in which the identity of the protected groups has been an issue. 'Nationality' was added as a qualifying category by the 1976 Act as a result of the House of Lords decision in *Race Relations Board* v *London Borough of Ealing*,[10] which held that discrimination by the borough in the allocation of housing in favour of those of British nationality was not discrimination on the ground of ethnic or national *origins*. In *Mandla* v *Dowell-Lee*[11] the House of Lords held that Sikhs were, for the purpose of the Race Relations Act, a group defined by ethnic or national origins. Valuable guidance was given as to the characteristics by which such a group could be identified. Lord Fraser said that the essential conditions were:

1. a long shared history, of which the group is conscious as distinguishing it from other groups, and the memory of which it keeps alive;
2. a cultural tradition of its own, including family and social customs and manners, often but not necessarily associated with religious observance.

Other conditions, while apparently not essential, would, he thought, be relevant:

3. either a common geographical origin, or descent from a number of common ancestors;
4. a common language, not necessarily peculiar to the group;
5. a common literature peculiar to the group;
6. a common religion different from that of neighbouring groups or from the general community surrounding it;
7. being a minority or being an oppressed or a dominant group within a larger community. . . .

He made the further important point that such a group would be capable of including 'converts'. 'Provided a person who joins the group feels himself or herself to be member of it, and is accepted by other members, then he is, for the purposes of the Act, a member.'

The phrase 'on the ground of' identifies the link between the act of discrimination and whatever feature makes it an act of *racial* discrimination. Its meaning has caused much uncertainty, arising from the need to give it *some* meaning. In *Peake* v *Automotive Products*, there was a prior question, before the effect on the claimant came to be considered, namely, whether there had been any intention on the part of the respondent to discriminate. Mr Peake had claimed sex discrimination because his employers allowed women employees to leave work five minutes earlier than men. It was accepted that they did this for the benevolent motive of avoiding the congestion which would occur if all employees finished work at the same time. It was incontestable that men and women were differently treated, and that men were treated less favourably by having to wait or work for an extra five minutes, but was the treatment 'on the ground of' sex?

Phillips J in the Employment Appeal Tribunal held that motive was immaterial. He drew a distinction between the over-riding purpose of the employer in carrying out a discriminatory policy and the policy itself:

> [The Act] requires one to look to see what in fact is done amounting to less favourable treatment, and whether it is done to the man or woman because he is a man or woman. If so, it is of no relevance that it is done with no discriminatory motive.[12]

Lord Denning took a different view: that the employer's worthy motive justified his action. Another way to put the argument advanced by Lord Denning would be to say that it is permissible to treat a person of one sex or race less favourably than one of another sex or race, provided one does so with an overriding benevolent purpose. This would be to permit acts disadvantaging minorities in the interest of what an individual judge might decide was a counterbalancing advantage to society as a whole or to another section of it.

The tide of case law has moved against such a subjective approach. In *R v Birmingham City Council ex parte Equal Opportunities Commission*,[13] the House of Lords upheld the decision of the Court of Appeal, which itself upheld the decision of McCullough J, that the test of Phillips J in *Peake* was the correct one: motive was immaterial — what was relevant was whether the different treatment was 'because' the object was a man or woman (or member of a particular racial group).

But the problem does not end there. 'Because of' and 'on the ground of' denote a link between the sex or race of those differentially treated and the differential treatment. What is the nature of that link? It could be identified as causality, but that leaves open a number of options. First, is an unconscious act covered? Suppose an employer who rejects a black applicant in favour of an equally well qualified white applicant is ignorant of the colour of either *and has no reason from the surrounding circumstances to be aware of or suspect* that either candidate is black? A possible answer is that no unlawful direct discrimination occurs in this situation because there is no evidence of any *conscious* act of discrimination by the employer. The employer was unaware of the discriminatory effect of his or her action. Another answer would simply be to say that there is no causal link in such a case. But the employer is the instrument of the rejection of the black candidate. If he is not the cause of it that can only be because he is unaware of and connot foresee the consequences of his act.

A second situation is one in which the employer or other alleged discriminator consciously treats a person of one racial group less favourably than he would treat a person from a different group, but does so under coercion or to avert damaging consequences to his employer. These are the facts of *R. v CRE ex parte Westminster City Council*,[14] in which Woolf J, upheld by a majority of the Court of Appeal, found that the conscious refusal by an official of the council to employ a black man, in order to avoid a threatened strike by white men who objected to working with him, was 'on the ground of' race or colour.

This is a sensible and practical conclusion which Woolf J (now Woolf LJ) explained misleadingly by declaring that there could be discrimination on racial grounds without an 'intention' to discriminate. The implication was that the council officer had not intended to discriminate. What the judge meant, as he made clear elsewhere in his judgement, was that discrimination was not his overriding motive. The council officer plainly intended to reject the black applicant. He knew that by doing so he was treating him less favourably than he would have treated a white applicant (whom he would have hired). His defence could amount to no more than that he would have preferred not to discriminate if he had not felt under pressure to do so.[15]

In the Birmingham case, the Equal Opportunities Commission claimed that the city council were unlawfully discriminating by operating an educational system in which there were fewer grammar school places for girls than for boys. The consequence was that girls had to achieve better examination results to get into grammar school than boys. The city council defended itself by pointing out that it was under no obligation to provide places in selective schools and it had no control over the available number of places. Nevertheless it was abundantly clear that officers of the council were responsible for submitting pupils for the places which were available and that in doing so they consciously participated in the selection of a smaller number (and proportion) of girls than of boys. Inevitably, they were party to the rejection of some girls who had higher marks than boys who were selected. Discrimination was an undesired but not an unintended consequence of what they did.

The House of Lords has recently had to consider the same problem yet again in *James v Eastleigh Borough Council*.[16] The council allowed free admission to its swimming pool to 'persons who have reached pensionable age'. Of course, that means 65 for men and 60 for women (itself a form of discrimination which has led to challenge under European Community Law). Mr and Mrs James were both 61, so Mrs James got in free but Mr James had to pay the 75-pence admission charge. Was this discrimination 'on the ground of' sex?

The Court of Appeal said it was not. Vice-Chancellor Browne-Wilkinson drew a distinction between discrimination explicitly on the ground of sex and a rule which referred merely to pensionable age. The latter, he said, might be indirect discrimination where pensionable age is different for men and women, but in that event the additional defence would be open that an indirectly discriminatory requirement or condition may be justifiable.

The House of Lords reversed this decision, but by a majority of only 3 to 2. At first sight it is hard to see how the facts can be distinguished from the Birmingham case. Eastleigh had a benevolent motive: to assist pensioners by making a concession to them. But — assuming that they were aware of the fact that pensionable ages for men and women were different (and the contrary was never claimed) — they consciously differentiated between men and women, to the detriment of the former.

Lord Bridge and the other law lords who formed the majority in the House of Lords had no doubt of this. Lord Bridge pointed out that indirect discrimination only arises where a requirement or condition is applied *equally* to persons of different sex (or race). 'Pensionable age', he said, 'cannot be regarded as a requirement or condition which is applied equally to persons of either sex precisely because it is itself discriminatory between the sexes.' Lord Bridge regarded 'on the ground of' as denoting an objective test. '. . . the question becomes: "Would the plaintiff, a man of 61, have received the same treatment as his wife but for his sex?" An affirmative answer is inescapable.'

Lord Ackner and Lord Goff, who agreed with him on the result both accepted that motive was immaterial. Lord Ackner said:

> The reason why this policy was adopted can in no way affect or alter the fact that the Council had decided to implement and had implemented a policy by virtue of which men were to be treated less favourably than women, and were to be so treated on the ground of, i.e. because of, their sex.

Lord Goff was reluctant to accept the need to grapple with concepts such as motive or intention, but, he said:

> I incline to the opinion that, if it were necessary to identify the requisite intention of the defendant, that intention is simply an intention to perform the relevant act of less favourable treatment.

This again could be read as begging a vital question, namely: what is the act which must be intended?.

In *James* v *Eastleigh*, however, the relevance of intention does at last seem to have been clarified in determining when there has been direct discrimination. It is simply to establish a causal link between the sex or race of the victim and the act done by the discriminator. That causal link can be expressed by using the 'but for' test. It avoids over-philosophizing the problem but requires the court to determine causality as a matter of common sense.

The Burden of Proof

The burden of proof rests on the claimant, as is usual in civil proceedings, but it has been recognized that in a discrimination case the evidence is likely to be in the control of the respondent.[17]

It is now well established that once the claimant has produced evidence of having received less favourable treatment (in one of the circumstances covered by the Act), the onus shifts to the respondent to produce evidence either that there was not less favourable treatment, or evidence that such treatment was not on racial grounds. In the cases in which the issue first arose, the purpose of the ruling was to discourage the dismissal of discrimination complaints by industrial tribunals without hearing evidence from the respondent at all.[18] In subsequent cases, however, Vice-Chancellor Sir Nicolas Browne-Wilkinson and other judges have suggested that it is unhelpful to see the matter in terms of a shifting burden of proof and that it is preferable to see the burden as always remaining on the claimant.[19]

Practitioners will disagree. Burden of proof is a useful concept which identifies clearly what must be proved by each party. The current position has been authoritatively laid down by the Court of Appeal in *Noone* v *North West Thames Regional Health Authority*.[20] Lord Justice May said:

> In these cases of alleged racial discrimination it is always for the complainant to make out his or her case. It is not often that there is direct evidence of racial discrimination, and these complaints more often than not have to be dealt with on the basis of what are the proper inferences to be drawn from the primary facts. For myself I would have thought that it was almost common sense that, if there is a finding of discrimination and of a difference in race and then an inadequate or unsatisfactory explanation by the employer for the discrimination, usually the legitimate inference will be that the discrimination was on racial grounds.

This, however, is far from satisfactory. It still means that a respondent will be able to avoid a finding of racial discrimination by producing a *plausible* alternative explanation other than race for an act of discrimination (i.e. less favourable treatment of a person of one racial group than of a person from another group) without being under a positive obligation to prove that the alternative explanation was the *true* one.

To require such a positive obligation is in effect to reverse the burden of proof once a *prima facie* case of racial discrimination has been made out. This is what the CRE has recommended.[21] The EOC has made a similar recommendation but the words in which it is expressed leave some doubt as to whether the respondent should, in their view, be required to prove the *actual* grounds or that grounds (other than sex) existed which *could have* justified discrimination.[22]

The burden on the respondent needs to be more than an evidential burden if there is to be a real inducement to avoid discrimination. For it is too easy to find a plausible subjective ground, especially in recruitment or promotion cases, for choosing one candidate rather than another.

INDIRECT DISCRIMINATION

In indirect discrimination, the following must be proved by the claimant: that he or she has been subjected to a *requirement or condition*; that the requirement or condition has been applied *equally* to persons not of the same racial group; that the proportion of persons of the same racial group who *can comply* with the requirement or condition is *considerably smaller* than the proportion not of that racial group; that the claimant has suffered a *detriment*. The above having been proved, the respondent may escape liability by showing the requirement or condition to be *justifiable* irrespective of racial grounds.

For those matters which have to be proved by the claimant, the standard of proof is on the balance of probabilities, and generally the courts have interpreted the law broadly in favour of claimants.[23] The existence of a requirement or condition must be established; a mere preference is not enough, which is a defect pointed out by the CRE. From the victim's point of view, it may be immaterial — the impact is the same.[24] The nature of the evidence necessary and admissible to prove adverse impact will be considered below.

As regards the requirement or condition being applied equally, it is of the essence of indirect discrimination that the treatment given or offered to the victim should be *ostensibly* not less favourable than that given or offered to members of other racial groups. But the distinction between indirect and direct discrimination, where the opposite must be the case, may not be as sharp as previously supposed. In *James* v *Eastleigh*,[25] there were differences of opinion among the judges as to whether the discrimination alleged was direct or indirect. The council's policy was to allow free swimming to 'persons who have reached the state pension age' — on the face of it an equal rule for men and women. Vice-Chancellor Sir Nicholas Browne-Wilkinson took the view that any discrimination was the result of an unintended adverse impact.

Only by going behind the terms of the policy to determine its effect was it possible to conclude that it was discriminatory. The House of Lords judges were prepared to do this. Lord Bridge considered the vice-chancellor's reasoning fallacious:

> the fallacy, with all respect, which underlies and vitiates this reasoning is a failure to recognise that the statutory pensionable age, being fixed at 60 for women and 65 for men, is itself a criterion which directly discriminates between men and women.

However, once one is prepared to go behind the terms in which a policy, or requirement or condition, is formulated, the distinction between direct and indirect discrimination can become blurred.

The courts have been prepared to give a liberal interpretation to the 'can comply' phrase. They do not demand the ability literally to comply. If they did so they would exclude and validate many practices which cause practical disadvantages to minorities and women. In *Mandla* v *Dowell-Lee*, the case of the Sikh schoolboy,[26] the issue was whether a requirement of uniformity in the wearing of school caps indirectly discriminated against a Sikh whose religious and cultural observance required the wearing of a turban. Obviously he 'could comply' with the requirement in a literal sense. He could have physically removed his turban and put on a school cap. The issue was: could he reasonably be expected to do so? As Lord Fraser said in the House of Lords:

> . . . it must, in my opinion, have been intended by Parliament to be read not as meaning 'can physically', so as to indicate a theoretical possibility, but as meaning 'can in practice' or 'can consistently with the customs and cultural conditions of the racial group'.

The courts have accepted that statistical proof need not be produced in the ordinary case where common experience makes it evident that a substantial proportion of members of a particular group are adversely

affected by a particular practice. But in some cases proof may be
required and in such cases it is necessary to determine the appropriate
'pool' for purposes of comparison. Generally, the object is to compare
like with like, leaving out elements which themselves have a racial basis.
Thus, in the case of recruitment, where, for example, it is claimed
that an educational requirement has an adverse impact on a particular
ethnic minority because a considerably smaller proportion can comply
with the requirement, the appropriate pool might be those eligible
for recruitment apart from that requirement.

The criterion of detriment no longer causes difficulty, for the reasons
indicated earlier in relation to 'less favourable treatment'.

The test of 'justifiability' was for a long period interpreted broadly
in favour of respondents, who were allowed to escape liability by
showing that a requirement or condition was subjectively reasonable
from the respondent's own perspective.[27] Under pressure from the
European Court of Justice, the obligation on the respondent to justify
requirements or conditions which have a racially discriminatory impact
has become more onerous. A decision of the European Court of Justice
held that such requirements or conditions could only be justified by
measures which 'correspond to a real need on the part of the undertaking, are appropriate with a view to achieving the objectives pursued,
and are necessary to that end'.[28] This is closer to the US test laid down
originally in *Griggs* v *Duke Power Co.*[29]

The House of Lords adopted and applied the test laid down by the
European Court the following year in a Scottish case,[30] but since then
there have been indications of a desire to hark back to the rejected
subjective *Ojutiku* test. In *Hampson* v *DES*[31] Balcombe LJ in the Court
of Appeal said that to determine whether or not a requirement or
condition was justifiable needed a balance to be struck between its
discriminatory effect and the reasonable needs of the person applying
it. This was to follow the minority view of Stephenson LJ in *Ojutiku*,
which introduces an objective element into the equation ignored by
the majority (Eveleigh LJ and Kerr LJ).

Another subsequent decision of the European Court of Justice[32]
has re-emphasized the point that, under European Community law,
a requirement or condition with discriminatory impact on pay as
between men and women can be justified only by objective factors
unrelated to any discrimination on grounds of sex. Although racial
discrimination is not directly prohibited by European Community law,
it would be irrational to apply different tests of justifiability to racial
and sex discrimination.

EVIDENCE OF DISCRIMINATION

The recognition that in most cases the information required to prove discrimination is in the hands of the employer or other alleged discriminator led Parliament and the courts to fashion means of making the information available. The Race Relations Act 1976[33] provides for a questionnaire to be submitted by one who suspects discrimination, inviting the suspected discriminator to supply relevant information. There is no obligation to supply the information but failure to do so entitles a court or tribunal in subsequent proceedings to 'draw any inference from that [failure] that it considers just and equitable'. Thus the respondent who fails to answer reasonable questions risks an adverse finding of discrimination, though in practice there have been few cases where this has occurred.[34]

Most significantly, the courts have endorsed the need for claimants to obtain documents and information in the possession of the opposing party whenever disclosure is necessary for fairly disposing of the proceedings.[35] This includes confidential reports and documents, which may even identify other job applicants and their qualifications. Disclosure will also be ordered of statistical evidence (or evidence from which statistics can be prepared) which might establish a pattern of disparate treatment which could give rise to an inference of discrimination.[36] The recognition that discrimination against an individual claimant can be inferred from statistical evidence and that the claimant must be given access to such evidence is a development of major importance. It may form the basis for proceedings to restrain systemic direct as well as indirect discrimination.[37] 'If a practice is being operated against a group then, in the absence of a satisfactory explanation in a particular case, it is reasonable to infer that the complainant, as a member of the group, has himself been treated less favourably on grounds of race.'[38]

However, a recent decision holds that a respondent cannot be required to obtain information which he does not in fact possess.[39] This has the paradoxical and harmful consequence that employers may seek to protect themselves against liability by *not* carrying out equal opportunity policies (and, indeed, by not complying with the CRE's Code of Practice).[40]

CONCLUSION

Two factors emerge from this discussion which seem to confuse the distinction between direct and indirect discrimination. First, the elimination of the subjective element from direct discrimination equates it in that respect to indirect discrimination. Second, the willingness of the House of Lords in *James* v *Eastleigh*[41] to find direct discrimination where a requirement was on its face applied equally, suggests another way in which the scope of direct discrimination may be extended to occupy areas in which liability has hitherto existed only where indirect discrimination could be established.

The need for a sharp distinction between direct and indirect discrimination is now called in question. The only practical consequences of the current distinction are that in cases of indirect discrimination the defence of 'justifiability' is available, and, where the respondent proves that the requirement or condition in question was not applied with the intention of treating the claimant unfavourably on racial grounds, no award of damages may be made.[42] The shift away from 'intention' in cases of direct discrimination undermines the rationale of both these differences. The CRE has in any case recommended the abolition of the second.[43]

No doubt there has to be provision for cases in which an over-riding need (which may include the basic skill required for a particular job) outweighs a discriminatory impact, but in practice such an exception also exists for direct discrimination: where a person is rejected for employment because he or she cannot do the job, that is held not to be discrimination on racial grounds, but on the ground of that incapacity.

Furthermore, the assumption is often made that direct discrimination relates to individual discrimination whereas indirect discrimination has a collective quality: it is seen (often rightly) as the outcome of patterns and practices brought about for reasons unconnected with race. But this assumption obscures the frequent existence of patterns and practices of systemic direct discrimination.[44] Should a respondent be able to justify a practice from which systemic direct discrimination is inferred? The present law allows no general exemption based on overriding social value in such a case, nor, probably, should it — but the issue has never been fully examined.

Most importantly, we must guard against the assumption that because the difficulties of proving discrimination have been considerably lessened by advances in statutory interpretation, the position of the victim of discrimination seeking redress has therefore been equally improved. The success rate in tribunals and courts is still extremely low,[45] and the impact of the law as a whole seems slight. The reasons for this continuing problem need to be addressed. The following tale, which concludes this chapter, is a cautionary illustration of the gap which sometimes exists between theory and reality.

APPENDIX: THE SAD TALE OF MR JASWANT SINGH

The case of Mr Jaswant Singh and the West Midlands Passenger Transport Executive[46] is illuminating. It is the leading case on the right of a claimant who alleges discrimination in recruitment or promotion to discovery of information about other applicants for similar posts. It extended the law on discovery. But what happened to Mr Singh? Did he succeed in proving discrimination in his own case? Unfortunately, he did not.

Mr Singh had been employed by the company for 27 years when, in 1985, he applied for the post of senior inspector. He had moved up in the company through the positions of bus conductor and driver to the grade of inspector in 1977. After that he worked hard to qualify himself for further promotion. He attended a part-time course run by the National Examination Board for Supervisory Studies (NEBSS), passing examinations in management, law and communications. Then he became a part-time student at Birmingham Polytechnic, where over a period of four years he obtained the qualifications first of associate and then of member of the chartered Institute of Transport (MCIT).

In 1979 he had applied for promotion to district inspector. He was unsuccessful. The 24 holders of that post were all white but he did not suspect discrimination.

In 1985, he applied for a post as service supervisor or traffic supervisor. There were 31 vacancies for such posts and Mr Singh was the only non-white candidate interviewed (by an all white panel). At the end of the interview he was told that he had done extremely well, but after about two weeks he heard that he could not be appointed because priority had to be given to other applicants whose existing jobs were disappearing in the re-structuring of the organization. Again he accepted this as a valid explanation.

Three months later applications were invited (in a notice headed 'the Executive is an equal opportunity employer') for thirteen senior inspector posts. Mr Singh applied and was interviewed, apparently successfully, but again, after a few days, he was told that the promotion was not to be offered to him, because 'the other candidates were a little better than you at interview'. This time he could no longer accept the result. He asked for a meeting at the head office, but no meeting took place. He applied to the CRE for assistance and a s. 65 questionnaire was submitted to the employers.

Mr Singh stated in his questionnaire that he believed for two reasons that he had been the victim of racial discrimination: he had

been told that his previous application had been unsuccessful only
because others were given priority as a result of company re-structuring;
and he was better qualified and had more years of service than successful candidates.

He invited the employers to supply a detailed explanation of the
selection criteria, particulars of the ethnic origin and qualifications
and experience of all candidates and the ethnic composition of the
relevant sections of the workforce. The employer's response was careful
and detailed. It relied on its adoption of an equal opportunity policy
and a document which it had compiled in line with the CRE Code
of Practice, entitled 'Guidelines on Discrimination in Interviewing
and Selection for Interviewers'. The document claimed that short-listed
candidates were assessed at interview for leadership qualities, ability
to take control of situations, act decisively, be calm, effectively com-
municate and manage when confronted with crises, and perform with
presence of mind and quickness on the uptake. The employer disclosed
to Mr Singh in tabulated form the ethnic origin, age, professional
qualifications and experience of the 55 candidates, identified by number, and indicating which had been short-listed and which selected.
In fact only nine were appointed.

The employer declined to provide similar particulars for recruitment
to *other* traffic supervisory posts, apart from those for which Mr Singh
had applied on the occasion which gave rise to his present complaint.
It was that refusal which Mr Singh successfully challenged in the
industrial tribunal, the EAT and the Court of Appeal.

In fact, the additional information obtained as a result of the successful appeal to the Court of Appeal did nothing to help Mr Singh
to prove his case. The employer had supplied without objection the
information sought about the 55 applicants for the posts directly in
question. The information about applications and appointments
relating to other posts added little to the picture already apparent.
When Mr Singh's substantive case came before the industrial tribunal
it referred to all the appropriate precedents on burden and standard
of proof.

The tribunal concluded — it could hardly do otherwise — that there
was discrimination in that Mr Singh did not get promotion and others
did, and that there was a difference of race between him and the
successful candidates. The tribunal then concluded as follows:

> The actions of the respondents were such a shambles that had this
> been an unfair selection for redundancy for instance, we should
> have considered that they had been totally unfair to the applicant
> and to many others white and black. And in this particular

exercise, they have been totally unfair to many of the unsuccessful applicants, whether they be white or black, and that really is the crunch of this whole exercise.

What was the evidence about the qualifications and experience of the 55? First, out of the 55, 11 were of Asian and two of Caribbean origin. The rest were white. Twenty of the candidates were short-listed, of whom four were Asian (including Mr Singh) and the rest white. Nine were appointed, all of them white. Of those appointed one was older than Mr Singh, five had the same NEBSS qualification but none had his MCIT qualification. One of those appointed had longer service as inspector than Mr Singh. None had longer service with the employer.

So Mr Singh was plainly better qualified than all the successful applicants on the objective criteria. But the employer's witnesses who were concerned in the selection process denied discrimination and maintained in evidence that they had fairly assessed Mr Singh on the basis of the qualities considered relevant for the post. The company's efficency may have been questionable but the good faith and honesty of its witnesses could not be challenged.

NOTES

1. Brian CJ in *Year Book Pasch. Edw.* 4, fol. 2, pl. 2.
2. Bowen LJ in *Edgington* v *Fitzmaurice* [1883] 29 ChD at p. 483.
3. 401 US 424 [1971].
4. 426 US 229 [1976].
5. Note the way in which the House of Lords justified their narrow construction of the exemption in s. 41 of the act for acts done 'in pursuance of any instrument or enactment by a Minister of the Crown' in *Hampson* v *Department of Education & Science* [1990] IRLR 302.
6. See Lawrence, C. 'The id, the ego and racial discrimination' (1987) 39 *Stanford Law Review* 317. Other interesting discussions of a 'victim perspective' in anti-discrimination law are to be found in Freeman, A. D. 'Anti-Discrimination law: a critical review' in Kairys, D. (ed.) *The Politics of Law* (New York, Pantheon Books, 1982), and Matsuda, M. J. 'Public response to racist speech: considering the victim's story' (1989) 87 *Michigan Law Review* 2320.
7. [1977] IRLR 365.
8. [1980] QB 87.
9. *Gill & Coote* v *El Vino Ltd* [1983] 1 All ER 398.
10. [1972] AC 342.
11. [1983] 2 AC 548.
12. [1977] IRLR 105.
13. [1989] IRLR 173.
14. [1984] ICR 770, and [1985] ICR 827 (CA).
15. See the debate between Professor Michael Banton and Professor Bob Hepple in (1988) 15(1) *New Community* 125.
16. [1990] IRLR 288.
17. See the speeches of Lord Salmon and Lord Wilberforce in the House of Lords decisions in *Science Research Council* v *Nasse* and *Leyland Cars* v *Vyas*, reported together at [1979] ICR 921.

18. E.g. *Oxford v Department of Health and Social Security* [1977] IRLR 225.

19. In *Khanna v Ministry of Defence* [1981] IRLR 653. However, he made it clear that 'if the primary facts indicate that there has been discrimination of some kind the employer is called upon to give an explanation [in the absence of which] an inference of unlawful discrimination from the primary facts will mean that the complaint succeeds'. Mr Justice Wood has repeated the view that the burden of proof remains on the complainant in such a case in *British Gas v Sharma* (Winter 1990) 6 *EOR Discrimination Case Law Digest* 2.

20. [1988] IRLR 195.

21. *Review of the Race Relations Act 1976: Proposals for Change* (London, CRE, July 1985) p. 14.

22. *Equal Treatment for Men and Women — Strengthening the Acts* (Manchester, EOC, March 1988) p. 22. The words of the EOC's recommendation are: 'The Commission proposes that once the applicant proves less favourable treatment in circumstances consistent with grounds of sex or victimisation, a presumption of discrimination should arise which would require the respondent to prove that there were grounds for that treatment other than sex or victimisation.'

23. E.g. *Price v Civil Service Commission* [1977] 1 WLR 1417.

24. *Perera v Civil Service Commission (No. 2)* [1983] ICR 428; *Meer v London Borough of Tower Hamlets* [1988] IRLR 399.

25. Op. cit. (note 15).

26. Op. cit. (note 11).

27. *Ojutiku and Oburoni v Manpower Services Commission* [1982] ICR 661. See particularly the judgment of Eveleigh LJ, who said: 'If a person produces reasons for doing something which would be acceptable to right thinking people as sound and tolerable reasons for so doing, then he has justified his conduct.'

28. Case 170/84, *Bilka-Kaufhaus GmbH v Weber Von Harz* [1986] IRLR 317 ECJ.

29. Op. cit. (note 3).

30. *Rainey v Greater Glasgow Health Board* [1987] ICR 129.

31. [1989] IRLR 69.

32. Case C. 177/88, *Rinner-Kuhn v FWW Spezial-Gebaudereinigung GmbH & Co Kg* [1989] IRLR 493.

33. S. 65.

34. See *Virdee v EEC Quarries Ltd* [1978] IRLR 295 and *King v Great Britain China Centre*, reported in (1988) 22 *Equal Opportunities Review* 43.

35. *Science Research Council v Nasse and Leyland Cars v Vyas* [1979] ICR 921.

36. *West Midlands Passenger Transport Executive v Singh* [1988] 2 All ER 873.

37. Willborn S. L. 'Proof of discrimination in the United Kingdom and the United States (1986) *Civil Justice Quarterly* 321.

38. Balcombe LJ. *West Midlands Passenger Transport Executive v Singh* (see note 35).

39. *Carrington v Helix Lighting Limited* [1990] IRLR 6.

40. S. 47 of the Race Relations Act 1976 gave the CRE power to issue a Code of Practice for employment (a power recently extended to housing and education). Failure to comply with the code may be taken into account by an industrial tribunal or a county court in determining whether unlawful discrimination has taken place. This has rarely happened but a Manchester industrial tribunal recently inferred discrimination from the failure of the Manchester City Council to follow its own internal code of practice for selection for promotion: *Harris v Manchester City Council* (5 March 1990), reported in (Winter 1990) 6 *Equal Opportunities Review Discrimination Case Law Digest* 8.

41. Op. cit. (note 15).

42. Race Relations Act 1976 s. 57(3).

43. See *Review of the Race Relations Act: Proposals for Change* p. 28 (note 20).

44. See Willborn, S. L. 'Proof of discrimination in the United Kingdom and the United States (note 36).

45. In 1989, the number of cases disposed of as a result of industrial tribunal and county court proceedings declined slightly to 164, (the 1988 figure having been 172). Of these, 33 were successful at trial, 49 were unsuccessful, and 82 were settled. £67,628 in total was awarded in compensation or damages and £108,036 recovered in settlements. (*Annual Report of the CRE for 1989* [London, HMSO] p. 110).

46. See note 35.

5

The Effectiveness of Equality Law Remedies: A European Community Law Perspective

Barry Fitzpatrick

INTRODUCTION

Until recently, fifteen years of sex-equality legislation had produced little enthusiasm for the litigation process as a vehicle for greater sex equality.[1] Given both substantive and procedural restrictions within the United Kingdom system,[2] it is hardly surprising that attention has been shifting from the 'negative' model of employment protection to more 'active' models[3] of affirmative action and reverse discrimination.[4] Ironically, it is just at this moment that the dynamic interpretation of the uncluttered provisions of European Community law by the European Court has added new life to the traditional model of equality-law protection,[5] at least in conjunction with more active approaches.

This new enthusiasm for a litigation strategy will be short-lived unless the judicial process can produce effective remedies which will encourage its use for the purpose of eliminating some elements of inequality. Given the impetus already initiated by the European Court, it is appropriate that the focus of this chapter is a scrutiny of the potential within Community law for an effective system of national remedies for infringements of equality law. Although many wider issues of enforcement of equality rights might be discussed, the emphasis here is upon remedies in individual litigation, the arena within which most equality litigation occurs. First, a number of significant general principles of Community law will be considered. Second, these principles will be applied to the question of establishing effective remedies. Third, the enforcement of perceived Community law obligations on remedies will be considered. Finally, a brief survey of some particular controversies concerning United Kingdom remedies will be undertaken in the light of the analysis of Community law. Two examples might assist in this analysis: the controversy surrounding the statutory maximum on awards of compensation which might be made by an industrial tribunal under the Sex Discrimination Act 1975;[6] and the lack of power of an industrial tribunal to issue injunctive relief in sex-equality cases.[7]

Although the legislative instruments in Community law have their limitations, they are nevertheless imbued with the same dynamism which has recently characterized other aspects of the European Court's case law. As a result, many of the procedural limitations in United Kingdom law may be called into question. Some would, of course, be wary of such Community-led developments to the extent that they would bring little comfort to marginal workers other than women. However, we can already see signs of 'read across' implications[8] from sex-equality to race-equality law.[9] Indeed, a significant aspect of the analysis given here is based upon a Community law obligation to 'read across' from the most favourable national provisions into national implementation of Community sex-equality law. The pressure to harmonize such developments within all areas of national equality law would then be powerful.

RELEVANT PRINCIPLES OF EUROPEAN COMMUNITY LAW

European Community law has its own infrastructure of principles. Without knowledge of these principles, the potential of Community equality law cannot be appreciated. In the field of remedies, the European Court has not, until relatively recently, been prepared to intrude upon national sovereignty over the procedures whereby Community law is enforced through the national legal systems.[10] This caution is not surprising. Kahn-Freund warned that procedural rules, born out of the power relationships in each country, are not easily amenable to transplantation.[11] However, this reticence has now evaporated. In *Commission of the European Communities* v *Greece*,[12] a case whose significance was noted by the Legal Service of the European Commission,[13] three principles were identified which must be applied to national systems of remedies where Community law is being enforced. First, the national remedy must be effective, that is, it must provide a real deterrent against the unlawful act. Second, the remedy must be comparable to the remedy available in national law for infringements of comparable national rights.[14] Third, the remedy must be proportionate to the seriousness of the infringement of Community law. The first and third principles are essentially of Community-wide application. Hence, in the case of sex-equality rights, their fundamental nature[15] requires a high level of protection in every Member State. Even given this high base, the second principle, of comparability, may even raise it, depending upon the level of rights protection already available in a particular national legal system.

These principles are easily ascertainable from the European Court's case law both within and without sex-equality law. The principle of effectiveness has been applied to the question of judicial review of legislative action in *Regina* v *Secretary of State for Transport, ex parte Factortame*.[16] Indeed, in *Johnston* v *The Chief Constable of the Royal Ulster Constabulary*,[17] the European Court elevated the principle of 'effective judicial protection' into a fundamental principle of Community law, by invoking Articles 6 and 13 of the European Convention on Human Rights. The principles of 'comparability' and 'proportionality' are also well established in Community case law. For example, in *Watson and Belmann*,[18] in relation to free movement of persons, the Court required that a penalty for breach of Community immigration law had to be comparable with a penalty for a breach of equivalent national laws and had to be proportionate to the seriousness of the offence. The crucial question which requires close examination below is the basis upon which such comparisons can be made. At this point, it is sufficient to suggest that, given the fundamental nature of the principles of equality irrespective of sex, any comparison must take account of the proportionately serious nature of the infringement which is to be rectified. The concept of proportionality itself has played a dominant part in the development of Community law since its first recognition as a fundamental principle in *Internationale Handelsgesellschaft*.[19] In sex-equality law, it has been of significance in numerous cases, for example, *Johnston*.

It might be argued that these last two principles are only appropriate as *limitations* upon national remedies which would otherwise obstruct the proper operation of Community law, for example, by curtailing free movement of persons as in *Watson and Belmann*. However, given the approach of the European Court in *Commission of the European Communities* v *Greece*, it is now clear that these principles can be used either to maximize the remedies already available in national law, or in appropriate circumstances, to minimize them.

The three principles were brought together within sex-equality law by Advocate General Rozès in *Von Colson and Kamann* v *Land Nordrhein-Westfalen*.[20] Although the court adopted only the principle of effectiveness in that case, itself a significant event, it was established after *Greece* that all three principles are of universal application.

EFFECTIVE REMEDIES IN INDIVIDUAL SEX-EQUALITY LITIGATION[21]

There are a number of legal bases upon which Community obligations in relation to individual remedies can be constructed. At first sight, the most obvious possibility is Article 6 of Directive 75/117 on equal pay,[22] which states:

> Member States shall, in accordance with their national circumstances and legal systems, take the measures necessary to ensure that the principle of equal pay is applied. They shall see that effective means are available to take care that this principle is observed.

Already, in *Handels-og Kontorfunktionaerernes Forbund i Danmark* v *Dansk Arbeijdsgiverforening, acting on behalf of Danfoss*,[23] the European Court has extracted from this provision an obligation upon the member states to amend their national law so as to alter the burden of proof in favour of claimants in cases of 'opaque' payment systems. It might therefore be anticipated that a similar obligation can be constructed in relation to ineffective national remedies. However, Article 6 of the 1975 Directive on equal pay has its limitations. First, it would appear to leave significant national discretion to the Member States. For the purposes of ensuring effective remedies in the litigation process, there is no immediately obvious obligation to ensure that the 'effective means' involve the judicial process at all. However, given the interaction of the principles of comparability and proportionality with the principle of effectiveness, this is not an overwhelming obstacle to a Community regime of effective national remedies. More significantly, however, this 'effective means' provision has not been repeated in the later directives, in particular, for our purposes, Directive 76/207 on equal treatment in working conditions.[24]

Attention must therefore turn to Article 2 of the Equal Pay Directive, which states:

> Member States shall introduce into their national legal systems such measures as are necessary to enable all employees who consider themselves wronged by the failure to apply the principle of equal pay to pursue their claims by judicial process after possible recourse to other competent authorities.

Here, there is greater scope for a wide-ranging obligation to institute effective litigation remedies. First, the provision contains a formula repeated in each equality directive, in particular Article 6 of the Equal Treatment Directive. Second, it relates directly to the judicial process. Third, although it is concerned explicitly with the question of access to the judicial process, the European Court has interpreted it to include an obligation to instigate a system of effective remedies also. In *Von Colson*, the Court, relying upon the principle of effectiveness, concluded (at paragraph 23 of the judgment) that:

> . . . full implementation of the directive . . . does entail that that sanction be such as to guarantee real and effective judicial protection. Moreover it must also have a real deterrent effect on the employer.

An immediately apparent limitation of this provision is that it is concerned solely with litigation conducted by an aggrieved claimant, in contrast with other provisions of the equality directives which concentrate upon the correction of legislative acts and employment instruments, such as collective agreements.[25] Hence, provisions such as Article 2 of the Equal Pay Directive will be referred to as the 'aggrieved claimant' provisions. Within the scope of individual litigation, the aggrieved claimant provisions, as interpreted in *Von Colson*, offer the opportunity to set a relatively high threshold below which national systems of sex-equality law enforcement cannot be permitted to fall. In particular, the emphasis is upon both the *protective* and the *deterrent* effect of the required remedies, the latter being a function which neither United Kingdom employment law,[26] nor even tort law,[27] is today expected to perform. Once it is accepted that principles of comparability and proportionality are also to be brought into the equation, it is possible to pursue a highly interventionist approach towards the question of the adequacy of remedies in national law for breaches of Community law obligations. The principle of proportionality will require remedies of significant force to counter the infringement of fundamental Community principles. Hence, the universal 'minimum guarantee' of the aggrieved claimant provisions is relatively high.[28] Building upon this foundation, the application of the principle of comparability ensures that higher standards of enforcement in national law must be made available, particularly in relation to national principles of equal fundamental importance to that of Community sex equality.

Two points deserve further consideration. First, the discussion has so far been concerned with obligations to be extracted from the equality directives. However, this gravitation towards the directives runs counter to the trend in the European Court's case law, which is largely concerned with the maximization of the ambit of Article 119 EEC,[29] which states: 'Each Member State shall during the first stage ensure and subsequently maintain the application of the principle that men and women should receive equal pay for equal work.'

Until now, little attention has been paid to the *procedural* implications of Article 119 EEC. The emphasis in the case law has been upon the identification of directly effective[30] substantive rights. However, it is arguable that 'the application of the [equal pay] principle' includes obligations to provide effective, comparable and proportionate remedies to support the substantive rights which Article 119 EEC encompasses. If this is the case, the obligations outlined in relation to the equal pay, but not the equal treatment, directive would be subsumed within the scope of Article 119 EEC itself, an outcome of obvious significance for the ambit, if any, of directly effective *procedural* rights. Certainly, although *Danfoss* itself was argued, at the behest of the Danish arbitration tribunal, on the basis of the Equal Pay Directive, it would appear that the obligation upon the Member States to alter the burden of proof in equal-pay cases could as easily have been based upon Article 119 EEC as upon the 'effective means' provision of the directive.

Second, a constant theme of the European Court's case law on remedies has been that Community law does not require *new* remedies to be created but rather that existing remedies are to be effectively utilized.[31] Even in *Factortame*, the emphasis was upon the removal of restrictions upon the operation of existing remedies rather than the creation of new ones. However, it must be argued that, where the system of remedies in a Member State falls below the minimum guarantee of Community law, an obligation to introduce effective remedies must be invoked. Returning therefore to *Danfoss*, it can be seen that the procedural obligation in relation to burden of proof was identified without any consideration as to whether national legal systems permitted such a reversal of proof. A similar approach can be taken to remedies. Whether a directly effective right to such a new remedy can be established is, of course, a different question and one which will be addressed below.

THE ENFORCEMENT OF EUROPEAN COMMUNITY LAW OBLIGATIONS IN NATIONAL LAW

How significant are these principles in United Kingdom equality law? First, the national system of remedies must be considered against these yardsticks in order to decide whether United Kingdom law is in conformity with Community law or whether the European Commission ought to consider infringement proceedings against the UK under Article 169 EEC in view of the perceived failure of the UK to perform its treaty obligations. Second, it must be considered whether the relevant articles of the equality directives are capable of creating direct effect. Third, it must be borne in mind that Community rights in directives, if properly transposed, ought to reach Community citizens *indirectly* through national implementing legislation (the concept of 'indirect' effect)[32] and hence that such legislation must be interpreted in the light of the provisions of the directive.[33] In reality, the Court is generally anxious to point out that it is the first obligation of the national court to reconcile national law with Community law and that it is only if that exercise fails that the question of direct effect arises.[34]

But we are still confronted with a complication. Is the combined application of these three principles sufficient to establish an identifiable Community standard which national procedural rules must satisfy and, if so, is that standard sufficiently clear to be applied either by the European Court in Article 169 EEC proceedings or by national judges applying either the indirect or direct effect principles? It is suggested that, at least in equality law, the answer to these propositions is in the affirmative. Nevertheless, the starting point for this analysis, the crucial judgment in *Von Colson*, is discouraging. In paragraph 18, the Court, considering Article 6 of the Equal Treatment Directive, stated: 'However the directive does not prescribe a specific sanction: it leaves Member States free to choose between the different solutions suitable for achieving its objective.'

Nevertheless, it must be remembered that the first question from the German Labour Court which was being answered here was whether the directive required the creation of a *new* sanction in German law in relation to the awarding of a contract of employment to an unsuccessful applicant.[35] In answering the fifth question of the German Labour Court on the requirement of effective application of *existing* remedies, the Court responded with paragraph 23, quoted above, and concluded in that paragraph:

> It follows that that where a Member State chooses to penalize the breach of the prohibition of discrimination by the award of compensation, that compensation must *in any event* be adequate in relation to the damage sustained. (emphasis added)

Given this minimum guarantee of adequate compensation, to be interpreted in the context of effective deterrence against discrimination

and given the addition of the principles of comparability and proportionality to the analysis, it ought to be possible for the European Court,
in an Article 169 EEC action brought by the European Commission,
to ascertain whether UK remedies reach such a standard. In particular,
Advocate General Rozès in *Von Colson* identified aspects of German
law in relation to both racial and religious discrimination as appropriate
points of comparison.[36] Obviously, there is a danger of this comparability exercise degenerating into the assembly of a 'cocktail' of
rights from a great variety of sources, the 'best bits' being accepted
as points of comparison and the worst being carefully ignored. Nevertheless, given the *fundamental* nature of the Community rights involved,
it is only right and proper that the very best protection available in
national law ought to be available in relation to the transposition of
the principles of equality into national law also. Hence, it would be
appropriate, in a UK context, to examine, for example, unfair dismissal
law, religious equality law and the general principles of the tort system
as points of comparison. Indeed, our two examples of the statutory
maximum and the lack of injunctive relief can already be seen as being
open to challenge upon this basis.

Of greater immediate import is the possibility of enforcing enhanced
procedural standards through the national courts. Given that the *first*
obligation upon the national judge is to reconcile national legislation
with Community principles, it is arguable that the national judge is
capable of ascertaining, perhaps with the assistance of a reference to the
European Court, upon what basis national remedies can be tested.
Despite the inappropriate approach of the UK courts to the interpretation of *pre-existing* legislation in conformity with Community law obligations,[37] it is now clear that national courts are bound to do everything
possible to reconcile *all* legislation with the provisions of Community
law.[38] From a UK perspective, it remains to be seen how the House
of Lords will extricate itself from the impasse which it has constructed.
Nevertheless, in Community law, it is beyond doubt that both the Equal
pay Act 1970 and the Sex Discrimination Act 1975 are subject to the
operation of the indirect effect principle[39] and hence must be scrutinized carefully in order to see if their terms are reconcilable with the
obligation to have effective, comparable and proportionate remedies.

Finally, the question of direct effect must be tackled, although
conscientious application of the principle of indirect effect may lessen
the need for direct effect to be invoked at all. From *Von Colson*, we
have gathered that there is no perceived obligation under the directives
to *create* new remedies.[40] However, the court went on, in paragraph 35,
to *deny* that the obligation in relation to effective remedies could be
given direct effect:

[T]he directive does not include any unconditional and sufficiently precise obligation as regards sanctions for discrimination which, in the absence of implementing measures adopted in good time, may be relied on by individuals in order to obtain specific compensation under the directive, where that is not provided for or permitted under national law.[41]

Two European Court rulings suggest that this restrictive conclusion is open to challenge. First, it seems clear that where directly effective substantive rights are at issue, a national judge must disregard any national rule which prevents an applicant from obtaining an adequate remedy. This is self-evident from *Factortame*.[42] Second, it seems to follow from *Johnston* that a directly effective right to an effective remedy is required from the aggrieved claimant provisions themselves. In paragraph 19 of *Johnston*, the Court echoed *Von Colson* in declaring: '[A]ll persons have the right to obtain an effective remedy in a competent Court against measures which they consider to be contrary to the principle of equal treatment.'

However, when asked whether this 'right' was directly effective, the Court answered in the affirmative and in the process, it is suggested, made a significant departure from *Von Colson*. It is worth quoting paragraph 58 of the judgment in full:

As regards Article 6 of the [1976] directive . . ., the Court has already held in [*Von Colson*] . . . that that article does not contain, as far as sanctions for any discrimination are concerned, any unconditional and sufficiently precise obligation which may be relied upon by an individual. On the other hand, in so far as it follows from that article, construed in the light of a general principle which it expresses [that is, the fundamental principle of effective judicidal protection], that all persons who consider themselves wronged by sex discrimination must have an effective judicial *remedy*, that provision is sufficiently precise and unconditional to be capable of being relied upon as against a Member State which has not ensured that it is fully implemented in its internal legal order. (emphasis added)

The simplest way to reconcile *Von Colson* and *Johnston* is to take a common law approach and 'distinguish' *Johnston* on the basis that it was a case about *access* to the judicial process, an objective explicitly referred to in the aggrieved claimant provisions, while *Von Colson* was a case about adequate remedies. Hence, a directly effective right to enter the judicial process is available but a directly effective right to an adequate remedy is not.[43] It is suggested that this outcome is not one to which the European Court would wish to subscribe. If, despite having a directly effective right to enter the judicial process, the aggrieved claimant is then entitled only to some wholly inadequate remedy, such an outcome would provide a significant disincentive to the exercise of the directly effective right of access.[44] This is hardly a tenable position. Happily, the European Court is not a common law court. It is expressing a principle of law and that principle, as the emphasis in the quotation makes clear, is that aggrieved claimants have a directly effective right to an effective *remedy*. This is a sensible outcome for two reasons. The court in *Johnston* was distinguishing between a directly effective right to *any* effective remedy, even if one has to be created, and a directly effective right to a *pre-existing* remedy which is only ineffective because of some limitation which must be ignored. To the extent that *Von Colson* denied direct effect in *both* circumstances, the Court in *Johnston* has reinforced the first conclusion but has moved away from the second.

Moreover, there is no intrinsic difference between the process of direct effect in each case. Although the Member State has a discretion over remedies and over what form of judicial process to make available, once that choice is made, the Member State cannot rely upon the original discretion to defend itself in cases where a particular obstacle lies in the way of *either* effective access to the judicial system or effective remedies from it. This is particularly so given that, in each case, the Member State is seeking to obstruct either effective access or remedies on the basis of an impediment of its own creation.[45] Despite the various 'rules' on direct effect which surround the concept, the central issue is one of justiciability.[46] Can the judge see a single solution within the Community provision which can be applied to the controversy before the court? If the answer is in the affirmative, the provision has direct effect. If the provision is too imprecise, or if it leaves sufficient discretion to the Member States that no single solution can be ascertained, then the provision lacks direct effect. If, as discussed below, the only obstacle to adequate compensation is a statutory limitation upon damages, as in *Marshall (No. 2)*, there is no reason why such an impediment cannot be ignored as easily as the Secretary of State's certificate was ignored in *Johnston*, whether through the operation of indirect or direct effect.[47]

Indeed, this approach towards justiciability can be carried further than the analysis of *Johnston* provided here. To what extent could national judges pick and choose between remedies available within the national legal system so as to maximize the enforcement mechanisms available to successful applicants? On the one hand, the combined application of the principles of effectiveness, comparability and proportionality may well point towards only one remedy which satisfies all three principles: invariably, given the fundamental nature of the principles of equality, the most powerful sanctions which are available. Hence, it is strongly arguable that, once a directly effective right to an effective remedy is acknowledged, the process of identifying the appropriate remedy can go beyond the mere avoidance of statutory limitations upon the remedy which the court might otherwise invoke and could also include the introduction of more powerful remedies outside the scope of the court's immediate powers, for example, a power of injunctive relief on the part of an industrial tribunal in a sex-equality case.

However, here we encounter a potential limitation within the concept of direct effect, namely that directly effective rights are restricted to circumstances within the jurisdiction of the national court.[48] Of course, if this limitation was taken too literally, it would deny the operation of direct effect altogether because, if the national court did have complete jurisdiction sufficient to apply Community law effectively, there would be, at most, a need to apply the principle of indirect effect constructively and hence the application of direct effect would never arise. Nevertheless, there must be some limitations upon the ability of a national court to enforce directly effective rights in a manner outside its immediate powers. For example, in *Factortame*, the court, in paragraph 20, stated:

> The Court has also held that any provision of a national legal system and any legislative, administrative or judicial practice which might impair the effectiveness of Community law by withholding from the national court having jurisdiction to apply such a law the power to do *everything necessary* at the moment of its application to set aside national legislative provisions which might prevent, even temporarily, Community rules from having full force and effect are incompatible with those requirements, which are the very essence of Community law. (emphasis added)

Applied to the question of effective remedies, it can be contended that, so long as the national court has 'subject matter' jurisdiction over the controversy before it, it must take upon itself the obligation to do everything necessary to uphold Community law, including, arguably, enforcing a directly effective right to a remedy outside its existing powers. As if to cast doubt upon such an adventurous approach, the court proceeded, in the following paragraph in *Factortame*, to conclude: 'It follows that a court *which in those circumstances would grant interim relief*, if it were not for a rule of national law, is obliged to set aside that rule.' (emphasis added)

Hence, although the possibility of a directly effective right to what might be called 'read across' remedies is a live one, it would be necessary to assume that the European Court was determined that 'effective judicial protection' had to be pursued to its greatest possible extent before such an outcome could be sensibly predicted. Of course, there is little possibility of 'read across' remedies if only indirect effect is applied, for example in relation to injunctive relief, as the legislation in question may well not include any provisions capable of reinterpretation so as to achieve the desired result. In these circumstances, where both indirect and direct effect fail to produce the required remedy in the national legal system, recourse to Article 169 EEC becomes inevitable.

By way of conclusion on this point, we must return again to the ambit of Article 119 EEC. Even if directly effective rights to effective remedies can be constructed, to the extent that they have a provision of a directive as their basis in Community law, those rights can only be invoked in vertical relationships by a claimant against the state and emanations thereof.[49] If, however, a directly effective right to an effective remedy could be constructed out of Article 119 EEC, such rights could be applied horizontally in cases against private-sector employers as well as against public-sector employers. Of course, such an outcome could only affect equal-pay cases under Article 119 EEC and not equal-treatment cases under the Equal Treatment Directive. Nevertheless, bringing procedural questions within the scope of Article 119 EEC adds to their stature and hastens the day when national systems are obliged to develop a coherent and incisive array of remedies for the enforcement of individual sex-equality rights.

CHALLENGING THE LIMITATIONS UPON REMEDIES IN UNITED KINGDOM LAW

It is not proposed here to undertake an exhaustive survey of remedies in individual equality litigation.[50] Suffice it to say that various restrictions have been built into the system. Taking examples from the Sex Discrimination Act 1975, a finding of unintentional indirect discrimination precludes any award of compensation[51] and, as already mentioned, awards of compensation are subject to a statutory maximum.[52] Although compensation for injury to feelings is available,[53] it is assessed with the statutory maximum in mind.[54] Exemplary damages are available for breaches of equality law if the employer is a public authority but are more difficult to claim if the respondent is in the private sector.[55] The tribunals have a power to make recommendations[56] but this is heavily circumscribed.[57] Powers to order reinstatement[58] or grant interim relief[59] are not provided under the Sex Discrimination Act.[60]

The application of the analysis above to these limitations leaves many of them in doubt. For example, there is nothing in Community law to suggest that unintentional indirect discrimination is any less 'a failure to apply . . . the principle of equal treatment' than an intentional act of 'indirect' discrimination. An applicant has as much a right under the aggrieved claimant provisions to an effective remedy as has the victim of more blatant discrimination.[61] Not only ought an Article 169 EEC action to succeed, it ought also to be possible to invoke both indirect effect and, if necessary, direct effect to ensure that the minimum guarantee of an effective remedy is protected.[62] So also, despite persistent judicial resistance, it is suggested that the statutory maximum upon awards of compensation cannot survive the application of Community law principles. If an aggrieved person has suffered £20,000 worth of loss, it cannot be adequate — let alone constitute a real and effective deterrent — to award such a person just under £9,000.[63] Similarly, reliance upon the statutory maximum for assessing compensation for injury to feelings is equally flawed.

What is still open to question is whether there ought to be some higher maximum or any maximum at all. The limit of £30,000 set in the Fair Employment (Northern Ireland) Act 1989[64] is an obviously attractive point of comparison and it would also provide a basis for a significantly higher 'upper limit' for compensation for injury to feelings. However, there are three reasons why the total removal of any limit upon compensation is more appropriate. First, it is clear that compensation in sex-equality cases is to be assessed on the same basis as the assessment of damages in tort.[65] Applying comparability on the basis of national 'best practice', there ought not to be any limitation upon compensation for sex inequality either. Second, bringing comparability closer to home, there is no statutory limitation upon judgments in the county court in sex-equality cases.[66] Hence, the UK provides inadequate compensation levels in areas where Community law does apply, while providing adequate compensation where it does not,[67] an outcome hardly in keeping with the principles of effectiveness, comparability and proportionality. Finally, the setting aside of the statutory maximum is arguably possible applying indirect effect to section 65(1)(b) of the Sex Discrimination Act 1975 and can also be achieved by invoking the direct effect of the aggrieved claimant provisions. The introduction of an alternative maximum, *e.g.* from the Fair Employment (Northern Ireland) Act, would not be possible under indirect effect and would raise jurisdictional problems under direct effect.

On the question of exemplary damages, they are, despite their anomalous nature, available in a tort action[68] and therefore, applying the principle of comparability, or even merely the principle of effectiveness, they must be available in a sex-equality case also. Far from being unsuitable in equality cases,[69] it is apparent that an effective remedy must provide a deterrent effect and hence that, despite the natural reticence of the common lawyer to apply 'penal' sanctions to non-criminal liability, exemplary damages ought to be available, in appropriate cases, not merely for public-sector, but also for private-sector, applicants. If 'everything necessary'[70] to protect successful applicants includes redefining the categories for which exemplary damages are available, it would appear to be possible under indirect effect. In any event, any difficulties could be bypassed in order to satisfy a directly effective right to an effective remedy.

It is also strongly arguable that industrial tribunals must have the power to order reinstatement for discriminatory dismissals as they have in relation to any unfair dismissal application. Indeed, unless it is contended that rights to trade-union membership are of such significance that comparison with sex-equality rights is inappropriate,[71] tribunals ought to have the power to maintain a contract of employment after an allegedly discriminatory dismissal through interim relief and ought to be entitled to make awards of compensation for non-compliance with a reinstatement order in conformity with the figures available in cases of union membership and union non-membership. Here again, an Article 169 EEC action would be appropriate but it is arguable that, although the application of indirect effect to the relevant sections of the Employment Protection (Consolidation) Act 1978 would be difficult to countenance in a sex-equality case, it is nevertheless true that all these remedies are within the jurisdiction of an industrial tribunal and therefore could be the subject of the application of directly effective procedural rights.[72] Carrying the comparison with tort law to its logical conclusion, there is no reason why in appropriate cases a tribunal ought not to be in a position to issue an injunction to prevent a discriminatory act occurring. Here, however, as suggested above, the construction of directly effective rights would be difficult. Nevertheless, the pursuit of such remedies in an Article 169 EEC action ought to be encouraged.[73]

CONCLUSION

This essay, in contrast with many others in this book, has adopted an extremely narrow brief. The emphasis has been almost entirely upon a close examination of Community law to identify a powerful set of principles upon which incisive remedies in individual litigation can be constructed. Within the scope of this Chapter, the focus has been upon individual remedies, although an analysis of impediments to access to the process or obstacles to effective protection within the system could also have produced far-reaching results.

Similarly, there is still plenty of analysis to be made of other possibilities within Community law to strengthen the litigation process. For example, provisions in the equality directives require correction of both legislative instruments, at present being attempted through judicial review,[74] and the correction of employment instruments, such as collective agreements.[75] Numerous possibilities exist to exploit these provisions as vehicles for utilizing the litigation process without incurring the enormous personal sacrifices to which individual litigants, often in marginal employment positions, are subjected. Of even greater potential significance are the procedural aspects of Article 119 EEC. Despite its limitations in questions of equal pay, there is no reason why the more 'active' regime of the Fair Employment (Northern Ireland) Act 1989[76] ought not, by way of comparison, be applied to inequality on grounds of sex also. And, of course, if Community law itself encourages such 'read across' implications through the principle of comparability, it is all the easier to invoke such implications within the national equality law system.

These are heady times for Community sex-equality lawyers. Wise heads are entitled to counsel restraint. To what extent can use of litigation produce durable and workable solutions to the problems of inequality? No doubt a well-developed equal opportunities policy is worth a dozen court judgments. No doubt some entrenched areas of discrimination will not succumb easily to traditional litigation tactics. Nevertheless, so long as the European Court continues to advance towards a comprehensive code of substantive and procedural equality rights, the impact of Community law upon United Kingdom equality law and its enforcement is likely to be profound.

NOTES

1. See Gregory, J. *Trial by Ordeal* (London, HMSO, 1989) and Leonard, A. *Pyrrhic Victories* (London, HMSO, 1987).

2. For example, on the substantive level, numerous exclusions from the operation of the legislation such as the 'retirement provisions' exclusions in section 6(1A) of the Equal Pay Act 1970, as amended by the Sex Discrimination Act 1986 section 2(4) and in section 6(4) of the Sex Discrimination Act 1975, as amended by section 2(1) of the Sex Discrimination Act 1986 and, on the procedural level, the cumbersome arrangements governing 'equal value' cases in the Equal Pay Act 1970, as amended by the Equal Pay (Amendment) Regulations 1983, SI 1983 No. 1974.

3. Nielsen, R. 'Transferability of equal opportunities legislation' in Hvidtfeldt, K., Jørgensen, K. and Nielsen, R. (eds) *Strategies for Integrating Women into the Labour Market* (Copenhagen, Women's Research Centre in Social Science, 1982) pp. 265, 270.

4. A recurring theme throughout this book is a quest for alternatives to the negative model of individual litigation. See also Hepple, B. 'Discrimination and equality of opportunity — Northern Irish lessons' (1990) 10 *Oxford Journal of Legal Studies* 408.

5. For example, recent cases on sex-equality concerning references from United Kingdom courts, such as Case C-188/89 *Foster v British Gas Plc* [1990] 2 CMLR 833 (on 'emanation of the State') and Case C-262/88 *Barber v Guardian Royal Exchange Assurance Group* [1990] ICR 616 (on equality in occupational pensions) and from other jurisdiction cases such as Case 177/88 *Dekker v Stichting Vormingscentrum Voor Jong Volwassen (VJV-Centrum) Plus* [1991] IRLR 27 (on employment decisions based on pregnancy as direct sex discrimination) and even from cases outside sex-equality law such as Case C-106/89 *Marleasing SA v La Comercial Internacional de Alimentacion SA*, [1990] ECR I-4135 (cf. with *Duke v GEC Reliance* [1988] AC 618 (HL(E)) in relation to the interpretation of national law in conformity with Community law).

6. Section 65(2) of the Sex Discrimination Act 1975 as interpreted in *Marshall v Southampton and South West Hampshire Area Health Authority (Teaching) (No. 2)* [1990] IRLR 481 (CA). In *Marshall (No. 2)*, the primary dispute was over whether the tribunal could include interest within an award of compensation. However, the focus of the case was upon the legitimacy of the statutory maximum set, at the time of writing, at £8,925. This paper is written particularly with the latter controversy in mind.

7. Indeed, there is not even a power to order reinstatement under the Sex Discrimination Act 1975 as is provided in section 69 of the Employment Protection (Consolidation) Act 1978 for unfair dismissal cases, let alone interim relief, as in section 77 of the 1978 act, in relation to dismissals on grounds of trade-union membership or activities.

8. Hepple op. cit. (note 4) at 411.

9. *Hampson v Department of Education* [1989] ICR 179 (CA), on objective justification in relation to indirect discrimination.

10. For example, Case 158/80 *Rewe v Hauptzollant Kiel* [1981] ECR 1839.

11. Kahn-Freund, O. 'On uses and misuses of comparative law' (1974) 37 *Modern Law Review* 1, 17-20.

12. Case 68/88, [1989] ECR 2964. See (1990) 31 *Law Society Gazette* 31. The case concerned appropriate penalties for fraud upon EC agricultural funds.

13. 'Commission notice concerning the judgment of the Court of Justice of 21 September 1989 in Case 68/88' OJ 1990 C 147/3.

14. Also described as 'the principle of non-discrimination' (see Hepple, B. and Byre, A. 'EEC labour law in the United Kingdom — a new approach (1989) 18 *Industrial Law Journal* 129, 140).

15. Case 152/84 *Marshall v Southampton and South West Hampshire Area Health Authority (Teaching)* [1986] ECR 723 para. 36.

16. Case C-213/89 [1990] 2 WLR 818, even though the application of the principle of comparability would not have produced the same result (para. 60).

17. Case 222/84 [1984] ECR 1651.

18. Case 118/75 [1976] ECR 1185 para. 21.

19. Case 11/70 [1970] ECR 1125.

20. Case 14/83 [1984] ECR 1891, 1919. Advocate General Mancini described *Von Colson* as 'unquestionably the most important' equal treatment case (Mancini, G. F. 'Labour law and community law' (1985) XX *Irish Jurist* 1, 15). See also Curtin, D. 'Effective sanctions and the equal treatment directive: the *Von Colson* and *Harz* cases' (1985) 22 *Common Market Law Review* 505 and Shaw, J. 'European Community judicial method: its application to sex discrimination law' (1990) 19 *Industrial Law Journal* 228.

21. The following is based upon Fitzpatrick, B. *The impact of EC Sex Discrimination Law on Collective Agreements: A Comparative Study* (report for D.G. X of the European Commission, 1989, unpublished).

22. OJ 1975 L 45/19.

23. Case 109/88 [1989] IRLR 532 para. 14, noted by Szyszczak, E. (1990) 19 *Industrial Law Journal* 114.

24. OJ 1976 L 39/40.

25. Article 4 of the Equal Pay Directive and Articles 3, 4 and 5 of the Equal Treatment Directive.

26. For example, *Talke Fashions Ltd* v *Amalgamated Society of Textile Workers and Kindred Trades* [1977] ICR 833 (EAT).

27. See discussion on exemplary damages at notes 69–70.

28. See Pescatore, P. 'The doctrine of "direct effect": an infant disease of Community law' (1983) 8 *European Law Review* 155.

29. As, for example, in Case C-262/88 *Barber* op. cit. (note 5). See Fitzpatrick, B. 'Equality in occupational pension schemes: the new frontier after *Barber*' (1991) 54 *Modern Law Review* 291.

30. Directly effective rights are directly enforceable in national law without recourse to appropriate national legislation. See Usher, J. 'Legal instruments and judicial remedies' in McCrudden, C. (ed) *Women Employment and European Equality Law* (London, Eclipse, 1988) pp. 169–74 and Wyatt, D. 'Enforcing EEC social rights in the United Kingdom' (1989) 18 *Industrial Law Journal* 197.

31. Case 158/80 *Rewe* op. cit. (note 10).

32. See Fitzpatrick, B. 'The significance of EEC directives on UK sex discrimination law' (1989) 9 *Oxford Journal of Legal Studies* 336, 337, relying upon Case 222/84 *Johnston* para. 51. See also Usher op. cit. (note 30), pp. 173–74.

33. Case 14/83 *Von Colson* op. cit. (note 20) paras. 26 and 28.

34. Case 222/84, *Johnston* op. cit. (note 17) paras. 51 and 52.

35. Case 14/83, *Von Colson* para. 6.

36. At 1920.

37. *Duke* v *GEC Reliance* op. cit. (note 5) and *Finnegan* v *Clowney Youth Training Programme Ltd* [1989] ICR 462 (HL(NI)).

38. Case C-106/89, *Marleasing* op. cit. (note 5). Compare the approach of Butler-Sloss LJ in *Marshall (No. 2)* op. cit. (note 6) 486.

39. So also the Employment Protection (Consolidation) Act 1978 or, indeed, legislation concerned with procedural questions, such as the County Courts Act 1984 and the Supreme Court Act 1981 (see Shaw op. cit. (note 20) 242).

40. At para. 18.

41. Relied upon by both Butler-Sloss and Staughton LJJ in *Marshall (No. 2)* 486, 487.

42. Case C-213/89 *Factortame* op. cit. (note 16) paras. 19–21.

43. This is explicitly the basis of the analysis of Butler-Sloss LJ in *Marshall (No. 2)* (486) and implicitly that of Staughton LJ (487).

44. Rubenstein, M. ('The equal treatment directive and UK Law' in McCrudden op. cit. (note 30) 101) concludes that the low level of awards 'acts as a disincentive both to potential applicants to bring complaints and to employers to change their practices'.

45. See Lloyd LJ in *Marshall (No. 2)* 484–85. An 'estoppel' argument against a Member State can only be utilized in order to establish '*vertical*' direct effect against an 'emanation of the State' (see note 49) *after* it has been established whether the provision is capable of creating *any* direct effect at all.

46. Pescatore op. cit. (note 28) 174–77.

47. If this analysis is correct, the *Marshall (No. 2)* litigation has yet, at the time of writing, to produce the appropriate result. The industrial tribunal ([1988] IRLR 325), employing some formidable analysis of the issues, reached the right outcome, that the statutory maximum should be

disregarded, but for the wrong reasons, seeking to construct a directly effective right out of *Von Colson* when none was there (see Shaw, note 20, 241). The majority in the Court of Appeal reached the right conclusion on the European Court's stance in *Von Colson* but sought, in typical common law fashion, to 'distinguish' away the self-evident implications of *Johnston*. At the very least, it cannot be contended that the question of a directly effective right to an effective remedy is so clear that no reference to the European Court under Article 177 EEC is required.

48. Wyatt op. cit. (note 30) 208–9.

49. Case 152/84 *Marshall* op. cit. (note 15) and Case C–188/89 *Foster* op. cit. (note 5).

50. See O'Donovan, K. and Szyszczak, E. 'Enforcement' in *Equality and Sex Discrimination Law* (Oxford, Blackwell, 1988) Ch. 8; McCrudden, C. 'Legal remedies for discrimination in employment' (1981) *Current Legal Problems* 211; Hepple, B. 'Judging equal rights' (1983) *Current Legal Problems* 71; and Rubenstein op. cit. (note 44) 98–102.

51. The route to this limitation is somewhat tortuous. Under section 65(1)(b) of the Sex Discrimination Act 1975, which sets out remedies in employment cases under Part II of the Act, the tribunal has a power to issue an order requiring the respondent to pay compensation to the claimant on the basis of the powers of a county court to award compensation in a sex-equality case under Part III of the Act (concerning provision of services). Hence, in section 66(3) (which appears to apply only to Part III cases), the prohibition of compensation for unintentional indirect discrimination applies to employment cases under Part II of the Act also. See also sections 56 and 57 of the Race Relations Act 1976.

The Equal Opportunities Commission recommends that this limitation should be removed (*Equal Treatment for Men and Women Strengthening the Acts* (Manchester, EOC, 1988) para. 4.27.

52. See note 6. The statutory maximum is contained in section 65(2) of the Sex Discrimination Act 1975 (and also section 56(2) of the Race Relations Act 1976) and therefore is restricted to employment cases under Part II of the Act. Elaborate provisions in section 56(3) of the 1976 Act and section 76(2) of the Employment Protection (Consolidation) Act 1978 ensure that a claimant cannot obtain more than the statutory maximum for a compensatory award even if findings of sex discrimination, race discrimination, unfair dismissal or any combination thereof are made. The only way to breach this limit is if a reinstatement order, made under section 69 of the Employment Protection (Consolidation) Act 1978, is unsatisfied. A claimant is then entitled, by virtue of section 71(2)(b)(i), to an 'additional award' of between 26 and 52 weeks' pay, so long as the dismissal was unlawful under the 1975 or, as the case may be, the 1976 Act.

53. Section 66(4) of the 1975 act and section 57(4) of the 1976 act.

54. *North West Thames Regional Health Authority* v *Noone* [1988] ICR 813 (CA), setting a notional maximum on compensation for injury to feelings, under section 57(4) of the 1976 Act, at 40 per cent of the statutory maximum for a compensatory award.

55. *Arora* v *Bradford City Council* [1990] IRLR 165, another race-equality case.

56. Section 65(1)(c) of the 1975 Act (and section 56(1) of the 1976 act) provide for 'a recommendation that the respondent take within a specified period action appearing to the tribunal to be practicable for the purpose of obviating or reducing the adverse effect on the complainant of any act of discrimination to which the complaint relates'. It is open to the tribunal, under section 65(3), to award compensation, or further compensation, if a recommendation is not satisfied, but only within the statutory maximum set in section 65(2).

57. For example, in *Noone* op. cit. (note 54), the Court of Appeal rejected a tribunal recommendation that a claimant be employed in the next available post, although a significant factor was that recruitment was governed by a statutory procedure which could not be overriden by a recommendation under section 56(1)(c).

58. Under section 69 of the 1978 Act (for an 'ordinary' unfair dismissal).

59. Under section 77 of the 1978 Act, as amended (where the reason for dismissal is trade-union membership or activities or non-membership of a trade union). Sections 4 and 5 of the Employment Act 1982 also provide substantial 'special awards' in relation to dismissals on grounds of union membership and activities or non-membership of a union.

60. *Noone* is not an encouraging precedent in the context of a recommendation to appoint a successful claimant (see note 57). In any event, a claimant relying upon the power of the tribunal under section 65(1)(c) would not have access to compensation equivalent to an 'additional award' under section 71(2)(b) of the 1978 Act if a recommendation for reinstatement was not followed, let alone a 'special award' (note 59).

61. The European Court's case law on indirect discrimination in the field of employment has, until now, been concerned with pay cases. Indeed, after Case C–33/89 *Kowalska* v *Freie und Hansestadt Hamburg* [1990] IRLR 447 (noted by Reiland, C. (1991) 20 *Industrial Law Journal* 79), it would follow that the Equal Pay Act 1970 ought to be interpreted to require proportionate pay for part-time workers in relation to their hours of work compared with full-time work, irrespective of the employer's intention. On this basis, an exclusion of compensation for indirect discrimination under the Sex Discrimination Act 1975 would be indefensible.

62. Under indirect effect, section 66(3) would be ignored in appropriate cases. A majority in the Court of Appeal in *Marshall (No. 2)* was prepared to contemplate that 'damages' in section 65(1)(b) could include interest, the awarding of which was the precise issue under appeal in the case. However, they all agreed that the statutory maximum itself was not open to 'benevolent construction'. Following Case C–106/89, *Marleasing* (note 5), in which the European Court concluded (para. 8) that Community and national law must be reconciled *as far as possible*, it is certainly open to argument, and therefore appropriate for reference to the European Court, that benevolent construction of national law includes the disregarding of limitations such as this statutory maximum.

Under direct effect, either Article 119 EEC or the relevant provisions of the Equal Treatment Directive (Article 2, in conjunction with Article 3, 4 or 5, as appropriate) could be given direct effect, in the former case either vertically or horizontally but, in the latter case, only vertically.

63. As intimated earlier, the reasoning of the industrial tribunal in *Marshall (No. 2)* (see note 47) is impeccable, save for the reliance upon *Von Colson* rather than *Johnston*. In particular, it drew upon the experience of its lay members to conclude that compensation at the statutory maximum was 'hopelessly inadequate' (329). Indeed, Butler-Sloss LJ, in *Marshall (No. 2)* (485), accepted the inadequacy of such a compensation level.

64. Section 26(4) of the Fair Employment (Northern Ireland) Act 1976 as introduced by section 50 of the Fair Employment (Northern Ireland) Act 1989.

65. Section 66(1) of the 1975 Act (see also section 57(1) of the 1976 act).

66. As pointed out by the industial tribunal in its decision in *Marshall (No. 2)* (note 47) 329, equality cases in the county court under Part III of the 1975 Act are not even subject to the normal county court limit upon damages but are to be assessed on the basis of high court jurisdiction (section 66(2)).

67. Therefore, in *Alexander* v *Home Office* [1988] ICR 685 (CA), in which the applicant was working, but not 'employed', in a prison workshop, the case was pursued under Part III of the 1976 Act, on the basis of which the county court could award damages without statutory limitation. However, if the applicant had had the misfortune to be free of incarceration, identical circumstances would have left a tribunal bound by the maximum.

68. See *Broome* v *Cassell and Co. Ltd* [1972] AC 1027 (HL(E)) and *Rookes* v *Barnard* [1964] AC 129 (HL(E)).

69. *Bradford City Metropolitan Council* v *Arora* [1989] ICR 719, 727 (EAT).

70. Case C–213/89 *Factortame* op. cit. (note 16) para. 20.

71. See Advocate General Rozès in *Von Colson*.

72. See discussion at note 48.

73. Indeed, it is arguable that much of Pannick's list of reforms in relation to individual remedies is attainable through the application of Community law principles (see Pannick, D. *Sex Discrimination Law* (Oxford, Oxford University Press, 1985) pp. 307–9).

74. The Equal Opportunities Commission and the Equal Opportunities Commission for Northern Ireland (see press release, 27 November 1990) are both pursuing applications for judicial review in relation to discriminatory provisions in employment and welfare legislation, relying, for example, upon Article 5.2.a of the Equal Treatment Directive and the European Court's rulings in *Factortame* and in Case 171/88 *Rinner-Kühn* v *F. W. W. Spezial Gebäudereinigung* [1989] IRLR 493, noted by Szyszczak, E. (1990) 19 *Industrial Law Journal* 114.

75. Considered in Fitzpatrick op. cit. (note 21) and referred to in Fitzpatrick op. cit. (note 29).

76. Hepple, B. op. cit (note 4) 421 and Ellis, E. 'The Fair Employment (Northern Ireland) legislation of 1989' (1990) *Public Law* 161. At the very least, the principle of comparability could be used, in conjunction with the principle of proportionality to justify an Article 169 EEC action requiring comparable mechanisms in sex-equality law.

6

Fair Employment Legislation in Northern Ireland[1]

Jim Knox and Joe O'Hara

INTRODUCTION

The Fair Employment (Northern Ireland) Act 1989 was enacted after a five-year campaign involving, among other factors, economic pressure from the United States. The campaign drew attention to the persistence of large differences between the rate of Catholic and Protestant unemployment in Northern Ireland, despite the enactment of the Fair Employment (Northern Ireland) Act 1976. The government's attempt to strengthen the 1976 Act has been criticized in various quarters, not least for its failure to incorporate many of the recommendations of the Northern Ireland Standing Advisory Commission on Human Rights (SACHR). This chapter briefly summarizes the provisions of the 1976 Act before contrasting the government's 1989 reforms against the proposals made by SACHR.

THE FAIR EMPLOYMENT (NORTHERN IRELAND) ACT 1976

In 1972 the British government suspended the Northern Ireland Parliament and instituted 'direct rule' from Westminster. In the same year a working party was established 'to consider what steps should be taken to counter religious discrimination where it may exist in the private sector of employment'. The report of the van Straubenzee Committee was published in 1973,[2] and led to the first Fair Employment Act. Although the Committee's terms of reference had been limited to employment in the private sector, the 1976 Act extended to both private and public sectors. The legislation was restricted to the sphere of employment — there was no equivalent of Part III of the Race Relations Act 1976 dealing with discrimination in other fields.

Prohibition on Discrimination

The 1976 Act made unlawful discrimination on religious of political grounds, or victimization. Religious or political discrimination occurs when a person treats another less favourably than he treats or would treat another individual of different religious or political belief in the same circumstances. There was no prohibition of indirect discrimination, although there was an implicit duty on employers to refrain from indirect discrimination, insofar as such action could be found to comprise a failure to provide equality of opportunity. However, indirect discrimination/inequality of opportunity, unlike direct discrimination, was not actionable by private individuals.

Equality of Opportunity

Unlike sex and race discrimination legislation, the 1976 Act gave centre stage to promoting equality of opportunity. Whilst the van Straubenzee report recommended that religious discrimination in employment should be made unlawful, it emphasized that the fundamental aim of the legislation should be the promotion of full equality in all aspects of employment opportunity. The 1976 Act defined equality of opportunity as occurring when a person has the same opportunity as another person 'with due allowance being made for their material suitability'. There was no explicit duty on employers to provide equality of opportunity, although such a duty could be inferred from the powers of the regulatory agency established by the Act to promote equality of opportunity.

The Fair Employment Agency (headed by a part-time executive board with no specific legal training) was appointed by the Secretary of State. The Agency was authorized to investigate the existence, nature and extent of equality of opportunity and to consider what action should be taken for its promotion. In contrast to the UK anti-discrimination Commissions, the agency was granted considerable discretion by the 1976 Act over the scope and conduct of investigations. Where, following an investigation, the agency formed the opinion that there had been a failure to afford equality of opportunity, reasonable and appropriate remedial action was required. However, there was no explicit guidance in the 1976 Act as to what that action might be. The agency could require a written undertaking, which, if refused, or given but not complied with, could be superseded by directions enforceable through the courts. Appeals against agency findings, or the reasonableness of agency remedies, lay to a specially constituted Fair Employment Appeals Board.

The 1976 Act provided for the agency to promulgate a Declaration of Principle pledging subscribing organizations to abide by the Act and to strive to promote equality of opportunity. Whilst the agency was not legally able to refuse an organization wishing to register as a subscriber, it could suspend or remove from the register an employer shown by an investigation under the Act to have acted in a manner inconsistent with the declaration. In 1981 it became government policy not normally to award contracts to employers who were not registered as subscribers to the declaration.

Exemptions

Both the anti-discrimination provisions and the equality of opportunity provisions were excluded from various sectors of employment, most significantly the employment of teachers in schools. Religious and political discrimination was permitted when done for the purposes of national security or protecting public safety or public order. A certificate signed by the Secretary of State would serve as conclusive evidence that an action was done for these purposes.

Individual Complaints

Individuals who believed themselves to have suffered religious or political discrimination were able to take their complaint to the agency. Each complaint was investigated by a staff member of the agency, who would attempt conciliation. Failing this, a sub-committee of the board would reach a finding on the complaint. If the agency found discrimination it had powerful remedies at its disposal. Most notably, there was no prescribed limit on the compensation it could award, and the agency could issue directions enforceable through the county court. Appeals against agency findings were made to the county court.

THE OPERATION OF THE 1976 ACT

Despite its theoretical promise, the 1976 Act was a failure in practice. This failure of the legislation was due to a number of reasons, not least the lack of support from ministers. Although the explanatory memorandum to the bill had envisaged an annual budget of £280,000, that level was not reached until 1986–87; and the staff, originally projected at 40, numbered only 20 in 1987–88.

The agency's strategic investigations into equality of opportunity proved erratic. There was a marked reluctance to order affirmative action. No employer was ever required to adopt goals or timetables for appointments or promotions. The contract compliance scheme foundered because the enforcement process required an agency finding of failure to afford equality of opportunity — in practice no employer was ever removed from the register.

The paternalistic control by the agency over individual complaints was not a great success. Of the 605 individual complaints investigations completed by the agency up to 1988, only 52 (8.6) were upheld. Compensation in 39 cases averaged £2,266. The county courts proved hostile to applicants; although they upheld the agency's finding in ten cases and allowed one complainant's appeal, they allowed nine respondents' appeals.

Impetus for Change

The impetus for further reform came from America, where the well-organized Irish-American lobby began campaigning in the early 1980s, initially targeting the awarding of American military contracts to Northern Ireland engineering companies, where inequality was widespread. The reliance of the Northern Ireland economy on American investment, particularly in the manufacturing industry, was further used when in 1984 the 'MacBride Principles' called on American corporations with subsidiaries in Northern Ireland to avoid discrimination and to promote affirmative action. The British government's argument that the principles required unlawful reverse discrimination was rejected by an American federal court in May 1986: *New York City Employees Retirement System* v *American Brands Inc.*[3] This gave further impetus to the campaign and by 1987 state legislators were considering giving the principles statutory force.[4]

Statistics became available showing that the 1976 Act had not closed the religious gap. Catholic males were around two and a half times more likely to be unemployed than their Protestant counterparts. The religious differential for women was a factor of just under two.[5]

In December 1984 SACHR, a statutory body established by the Northern Ireland Constitution Act 1973 for the express purpose of keeping the legislation under review, declared that it would undertake a study of the adequacy and effectiveness of the legislation and its institutions.

THE SACHR REPORT AND THE 1989 ACT

The SACHR Report[6] of October 1987 is the most influential critique of the 1976 Act. The main conclusions of SACHR and the extent to which its recommendations were incorporated in the 1989 Act[7] are summarized below:

- SACHR recommended that the burden of proof in direct discrimination cases should be eased. This would be done by requiring an aggrieved individual to show only that there had been less favourable treatment, that the treatment involved individuals of different religions or political persuasions and that he or she met the requirements of the job (rather than was better qualified). Thereafter it would be incumbent on the employer to show that there was not less favourable treatment.

The 1989 Act failed to incorporate this recommendation and left the 1976 Act unamended.

- SACHR recommended that the prohibition of discrimination should be extended to include indirect discrimination. This would be defined along the lines currently proposed by the Commission for Racial Equality, rather than in the restrictive terms contained in present race and sex discrimination law. Indirect discrimination should be made actionable.
  The 1989 Act prohibited indirect discrimination but defined this in terms similar to those employed in race and sex discrimination law.
- SACHR recommended that equality of opportunity should be redefined and new legislation should place an explicit duty on employers to provide it. This duty would be fulfilled when employers refrained from direct and indirect discrimination, monitored their practices and, if inequality of opportunity was indicated, adopted appropriate lawful remedial action.
  The new legislation creates no active duty on employers to pursue equality of opportunity. There is, however, a duty on employers with over 25 employees (with over 10 employees from 1991) to register with the successor to the agency, the Fair Employment Commission. All public-sector employers and all private-sector employers with more than 250 staff must monitor and submit annual returns to the Commission. All registered concerns must review their practices at least once every three years to see if 'fair participation' is provided.

The Commission can require affirmative action if it comes to its notice that 'fair participation' is absent.

At the time of writing, the government is considering whether to amend the 1989 Act in the light of a tribunal ruling that it is a criminal offence under the Act to divulge information drawn from monitoring returns to establish the religion of a successful candidate, even for the purpose of tribunal proceedings.[8]

- SACHR considered the best way to resolve the potential conflict between those provisions in the 1976 Act prohibiting discrimination and those provisions involving remedial action directed at a religious group. SACHR recommended that the new Act should spell out what affirmative action should be permitted to employers and that this action should be explicitly exempted from the Act's discrimination prohibition. They recommended similar provisions to those contained in sex and race discrimination law for outreach advertising (i.e. targeting advertisements on an under-represented group) and single-religion training. In addition SACHR advocated measures which were not religion-specific, but which had the effect of disproportionately including one group. An example of this is adopting a practice of recruitment from the unemployed, which will indirectly benefit Catholics because they are more likely to be unemployed. A more central role was envisaged for targets and timetables.

  The 1989 Act explicitly exempts outreach advertising from the direct and indirect discrimination provisions contained in the Act. The government, however, rejected training confined to a particular religious group. Instead the 1989 Act refers to affirmative action training conducted in a certain place or confined to a particular class of person, but that class is *not* to be 'framed by reference to religious belief'. The implication is that such training might disproportionately benefit one religious group without totally excluding the other. However, if this is the purpose of the training then it must ultimately be 'framed by reference to religious belief'. Despite the attempt to limit access to training by some factor other than religion, religion is the *raison d'être* of that training (or else it is not affirmative action). The 1989 Act therefore appears to obstruct affirmative action training.

- SACHR recommended that jurisdiction of individual complaints should be transferred from the agency to the industrial tribunals. Instead, the agency's successor, the Fair Employment Commission, would play a role akin to the EOC and CRE by assisting selected complaints. This recommendation was based on a number of judgments. Among the most important were: that the obligation of the agency to hear all complaints had depleted its resources and detracted from

its work on equality of opportunity; that industrial tribunal procedures permitting full cross-examination would restore to parties a
greater measure of control over their case (under the agency's procedures, neither side had an opportunity to question or even to hear
the evidence of the other side); and that hearing religious discrimination cases in this forum would help integrate the Fair Employment
Act into the mainstream of employment law, thereby reducing
emotive political connotations. SACHR also recommended that the
tribunals be granted new remedial powers so that the remedies
available under the 1976 Act would not be diluted.

The 1989 Act transferred jurisdiction over individual complaints
to a specialist tier of the industrial tribunals (the Fair Employment
Tribunal). The Fair Employment Tribunal has power to award
victims of religious discrimination compensation up to £30,000,
although otherwise its remedial powers for individual complainants
are similar to conventional tribunals.

- SACHR proposed that any new enforcement body should retain
existing autonomy to conduct investigations but should have its
bargaining power *vis-à-vis* employers strengthened. On past occasions, the agency had declined to make public findings of a failure to
provide equality of opportunity because it thought it needed to retain
employer goodwill to ensure appropriate remedial action. The
agency claimed that experience showed that affirmative action programmes needed periodical revision. The agency preferred not to rely
on directions because they could not be easily amended. Instead it
hoped that by shielding employers from embarrassing findings it
could ensure their co-operation. Yet by failing to make a clear finding
the agency sacrificed the ultimate enforceability of remedial programmes. SACHR's solution was to bolster the position of the
enforcement body by, among other things, granting it the power to
amend directions. However, it proposed that employers should be
allowed to avoid findings of inequality of opportunity if they voluntarily entered enforceable affirmative-action agreements.

Whilst the 1989 Act provides considerable autonomy to the Fair
Employment Commission in the conduct of investigation, it fails to
take on board SACHR's other recommendations.

- SACHR concluded that the existing Declaration of Principle was
ineffectual in promoting equality of opportunity because its terms
were vague. Organizations could not be refused registration as equal
opportunity employers (no matter what their practices) and could not
be struck off the register without a full-blown investigation. SACHR
recommended that the Declaration of Principle be replaced by one

of practice which spelt out the steps employers committed to equal opportunity should take. Employers subscribing to the declaration would register with the Commission and would submit regular monitoring returns. The Commission could refuse registration and would be able to remove employers from the register if monitoring information was not supplied or if an investigation revealed inequality. A wide range of public contracts and grants would not normally be given to organizations who were not registered as subscribers.

Unlike SACHR's recommendation, the 1989 Act compels employers to register with the Commission. The denial of contracts and grants is not used as an incentive to register but as a supplementary penalty to employers who have failed to register or who have registered but failed to supply proper monitoring returns. The 1989 Act does, however, widen the range of public contracts and monies which will be withheld from unregistered employers.

● SACHR recommended that the key exemptions to the legislation should remain, but the issue of certificates by the Secretary of State stating that a discriminatory act was done for reasons of national security would be reviewable by the courts.

This recommendation was not included in the 1989 Act.

CONCLUSION

In key aspects, particularly the requirement to monitor, the introduction of a form of contract compliance and the latitude afforded to the investigatory body, the 1989 Act is stronger than the 1976 Act or for that matter both the Sex Discrimination Act and the Race Relations Act. However, in the crucial area of affirmative action, the 1989 Act is comparatively weaker than what had previously been possible (if, in fact, little used by the Fair Employment Agency). Therefore, while the mechanisms for tackling individual discrimination and detecting inequality of opportunity are improved, the scope for remedial affirmative action is limited.

It is noteworthy that the consensus which ensured a unanimous report by the van Straubenzee Committee in 1973 had broken down by the time of SACHR's report in 1987, notably over the issue of affirmative action. The reasons for the breakdown in this consensus are not clear, but they may reflect a common theme (notwithstanding opposition to discrimination) of concern about the effect of positive measures to ensure minority participation.

It is also noteworthy that both Acts were passed by Westminster, an exterior legislature. It is certain that, whatever the social consensus may have been, in neither 1973 nor the late 1980s was there a political consensus within Northern Ireland for legislation.

A further, crucial, distinction can be drawn between the 1976 Act, which was passed at the behest of a Westminster consensus that legislation was necessary, and the 1989 Act, which was due almost entirely to outside economic pressure from the United States.

In terms of the evolution of United Kingdom anti-discrimination law, the Fair Employment (Northern Ireland) Act 1989 establishes certain precedents that will be of interest to those concerned to strengthen legislation in the spheres of race and sex discrimination. However, in Northern Ireland, the fact that race and sex discrimination have some 'catching up' to do will not alter the political impetus for further action to provide equal opportunities. Rightly or wrongly, the benchmark for judging the success of the 1989 Act will be the extent to which any impact is made on the differential between rates of Catholic and Protestant unemployment. The landmark SACHR report demonstrates how much further the legislation can be strengthened. Unless the 1989 Act impacts upon the religious *differential* in unemployment, it is likely that the influential US lobby will demand such action.

NOTES

1. The foremost writer on the fair employment legislation has been Christopher McCrudden. See in particular: 'Law enforcement by regulatory agency: the case of employment discrimination in Northern Ireland' (1982) 45 *Modern Law Review* 617; 'Equal employment opportunity in Northern Ireland' (1986) 10 *Equal Opportunities Review* 17; 'Discrimination in Northern Ireland: new legal measures' (Winter 1987) *Manpower Policy and Practice* 41; 'The Northern Ireland Fair Employment White Paper: a critical assessment' (1988) 17 *Industrial Law Journal* 162; 'A fatally flawed bill' (1989) 24 *Equal Opportunities Review* 1; 'Northern Ireland and the British constitution' in Jowell, J. and Oliver, D. (eds) *The Changing Constitution* 2nd edn (OUP, 1989); *Fair Employment Handbook* (ed.) (London, Eclipse, 1990); 'The Fair Employment Bill in Parliament' in Hayes, J. and O'Higgins, P. (eds) *Lessons from Northern Ireland* (SLS, forthcoming).

2. *Report and Recommendations of the Working Party on Discrimination in the Private Sector of Employment* (the van Straubenzee Report) (London, HMSO 1973).

3. [1986] IRLR 239 (US District Court, Southern District of New York).

4. For a fuller account of the campaigns leading to the 1989 act, see McCormack, V. and O'Hara, J. *Enduring Inequality — Religious Discrimination in Employment in Northern Ireland* (London, Liberty/National Council for Civil Liberties, 1990).

5. For a full analysis of these statistics, and of the extent to which religion is a factor in the

labour market, see the research commissioned by SACHR: Smith, D. and Chambers, G. *Equality and Inequality in Northern Ireland: Part 1 — Employment and Unemployment* (London, Policy Studies Institute, 1987).

6. Standing Advisory Commission on Human Rights. *Religious and Political Discrimination and Equality of Opportunity in Northern Ireland: Report on Fair Employment.* Cmnd. 237 (London, HMSO, 1987).

7. The 1989 Act followed a number of government consultative documents, notably the Government White Paper, *Fair Employment in Northern Ireland* Cmnd. 380 (London, HMSO, 1988).

8. See 'Enforcement of Fair Employment Act collapses' (1990) 34 *Equal Opportunities Review* 2.

II

THEORIES AND INTERACTIONS

7

From Individual to Group?[1]

Nicola Lacey

Over the last few years a plentiful and challenging literature has developed in which feminist writers have constructed an illuminating critique of legal approaches to dismantling sexism and sex discrimination.[2] Much of this literature makes passing or more substantial reference to questions of racism, generally in the context of an acknowledgement of the specificity of the oppression of black women. However, most of the work[3] does not address directly the question of what the critical tools and insights of feminist social theory might contribute to a more thoroughgoing analysis of laws designed to combat racism. This silence is born partly of a recognition and respect for the specificity and complexity of racism and its relationship to law; a (proper) inhibition from too easily regarding racism and sexism as simply analogous social institutions; and an understandable concentration on the question of women's oppression and its legal constitution, stretching beyond anti-discrimination legislation, which is the central focus of feminism.

However, I think it is true to say that many of us who are concerned with this general field of enquiry are uncomfortable with the fact that, with some notable exceptions,[4] there has been a relative lack in United Kingdom law journals of critical analysis specifically focused on race discrimination law. This is not to say, of course, that the question of racism is not canvassed in legal literature. Particularly in the criminal justice area, the racist practices and attitudes of public institutions such as the prison system and the police are debated regularly in both the specialist and general press.[5] However, it would be fair to say that in terms of analysis and critique of the potential positive role of law in combating racism, there has been less published debate than in the area of gender. Given the scandalous under-representation of Afro-Caribbean, Asian and indeed people from practically all ethnic minority groups[6] on the staff of law schools (and indeed in the higher education system generally), this is perhaps (depressingly) predictable. While the contributions of members of non-oppressed groups to the struggle to understand and oppose racism in the legal sphere is to be welcomed,[7] both the prominence of ideas about the relevance of direct experience and particularity of perspective in much modern social theory and straightforward arguments of social justice identify this under-representation as a major cause for concern and activity. While working for significant improvements on this front, it is obviously important for us to familiarize ourselves with the developements in other countries, such as the United States, where black people have found a significant voice in the legal academy and have begun to subject legal practices to the scrutiny of what has come to be known as 'critical race theory'.[8]

It also seems worthwhile to ask what contribution feminist ideas, which are beginning to have some impact on the law school agenda in this country, could make to a critical understanding of race discrimination law. This is the underlying project which informs this essay. I should like to note at this point my sense of discomfort both at the possibility of being seen to pre-empt or deny the distinctive perspectives of people from ethnic minority groups by generalizing a white feminist perspective to their position and, conversely, of being marginalized as one 'loony left' approach talking to another. Certainly, there will be aspects of the issues which I am discussing to which my position as a middle-class white woman will have made me insensitive. My conviction that racism, like sexism, cannot and must not be regarded as *exclusively* the problem of its victims, and that the challenges posed by feminist and anti-racist analyses of law are challenges which must be met by all lawyers, prompts me to continue with the project nonetheless.

My argument will fall into two main sections. In the first place, I shall return to the questions I raised in an earlier article on sex discrimination law, so as to explore the relevance of feminist questions I raised there for race discrimination law. This will involve some discussion of the relationship between feminist and anti-racist approaches to law, and a more general account of the questions of social theory raised by feminism. Secondly, I shall move on from the feminist critique of anti-discrimination law to ask one specific question about possible reform: how far could we improve the symbolic and instrumental value of anti-discrimination law by employing the notion of collective or group-based rights? What legal and political questions are raised by this kind of approach? Finally, I shall try to draw some general conclusions about the usefulness of and dangers inherent in anti-discrimination legislation and make some tentative suggestions about where we might go from here. I shall in particular address the question of how reformist lawyers ought to respond to feminist and anti-racist scepticism about the gains to be had from law and legal processes.

FEMINIST PERSPECTIVES ON ANTI-DISCRIMINATION LAW

In an earlier article[9] I noted that there is now a wide consensus, among lawyers with very different political points of view, about certain intractable problems thrown up by the sex discrimination legislation. Problems of proof; the hopeless inadequacy of the available remedies; the unsatisfactory nature of the resource basis and structure of the enforcement agencies; the inexpert nature of the tribunals hearing discrimination cases; the lack of legal aid for tribunal cases — all these are widely acknowledged to hamper the potential effectiveness of the legislation.[10] All of these technical problems, and more, apply equally to the operation of the Race Relations Act 1976,[11] and have been analysed and criticized by the Commission for Racial Equality in its proposals for reform.[12] The general message delivered by these and similar proposals is that, with some fairly substantial modification, but without any major change of direction or underlying principle, the anti-discrimination law could be made to work tolerably well. Several rather different kinds of problem are, however, suggested by a feminist critique, and these seem to call into question the very structure and basis of anti-discrimination law. I shall now sketch out some of these feminist questions, and consider their relevance for race discrimination law.

The Underlying Notion of Equality of Opportunity

It is widely recognized that a legal commitment to formal equality is insufficient to guarantee the fair treatment of groups which have suffered a history of prejudice and discrimination. This is reflected in the Sex Discrimination and Race Relations Acts' commitment to 'equality of opportunity', and their instantiation of the concept of indirect discrimination. However, this fundamentally liberal notion, the precise delineation of which is in any case by no means clear, poses problems for, and puts limitations on, the achievements to be made by anti-discrimination law. For example, indirect discrimination effectively uses an unequal outcome as a *prima facie* test for inequality of opportunity. The ultimate willingness of the tribunal to interpret this as an instance of unjust, illegal inequality is modified by the underlying ideology of equality of opportunity, which invites the tribunal to be receptive to the idea that unequal results may be explained in terms of the free, autonomous choices of individuals. For example, if the sexual segregation of the labour force, the concentration of women in low paid and part-time work, and the under-representation of women in highly paid and high-prestige jobs are seen as flowing from autonomous individual choices which flow in turn from women's and men's legitimately different lives, the tribunal will be more sympathetic to arguments of justification and less persuaded by the plaintiff's argument that the result represents a legally recognized injustice. In other words, the tribunal's response to the evidence may be affected by the very stereotypes which many of us hoped that the legislation would serve to attack. Exactly comparable problems arise here in respect of race: although the hold of 'naturalistic' or 'biologistic' ideas about the appropriate place, role and characteristics of people from ethnic minority groups is perhaps now less tenacious than is the case with gender, the influence of stereotypes about what, for example, Afro-Caribbean or Asian people are like can be directly relevant in race discrimination cases. This is because they affect both the plausibility of certain kinds of arguments about justification and the tribunal's reading of whether or not the unequal outcome is something which should be regarded with suspicion, or rather as just the 'natural' outcome of people's choices. The powerful hold of racist stereotypes in areas such as police practice and the treatment of prisoners[13] can hardly be doubted to exist in most areas covered by the current Race Relations Act, and many more which are not.

The Implication of the Individual Complaint

Following on from these difficulties with the liberal ideology of equality of opportunity, there are further limitations, inherent in the nature of the liberal legal form, in the capacity of indirect discrimination to bite against structural sexism or racism. Indirect discrimination seeks to address practices which have discriminatory effects, but it works by means of individual lawsuits which, it is hoped, will have wider knock-on effects. This has indeed happened in some instances, but the relative infrequency of successful cases is, as we have already noted, often deplored.

One problem with the current legal approach is that a basic structural implication of any lawsuit is the idea that what is complained against is *abnormal*. This implication, once again, affects the tribunal's reading of both law and fact, and it constitutes a psychological and hence material barrier to success in indirect discrimination cases for a very simple reason. This is that in many areas of social life, institutional sexism and racism *are the norm*: they cannot be regarded as abnormal. Descriptive and prescriptive conceptions of 'the norm' shade into one another, generating a reluctance to conceive the statistically normal as legally proscribed: descriptive normality confers legitimacy. Doubtless this speaks volumes on the general problem of laws which seek to legislate in advance of social practice and consensus. But it can hardly be doubted to pose a special problem for Afro-Caribbean, Asian and female defendants who are addressing their complaints about heavily entrenched and rarely questioned social practices to a white, male-dominated legal forum. The statutory construction of (certain very limited kinds of) racism and sexism as abnormal has proved to be relatively impotent in the face of the broader social construction of them as normal.

This seems likely to mark a significant difference in the experience of male plaintiffs under the Sex Discrimination Acts and white plaintiffs under the Race Relations Act, whose complaints will often call into question practices (such as affirmative action) which are not so universally and unquestioningly endorsed. An interesting example of a 'majority' plaintiff who *did* meet with little sympathy from the courts arose in the *Peake* case,[14] in which the practice complained of (allowing women to leave work five minutes earlier than men) was assimilated with chivalry. This is precisely the kind of widely accepted sexist institution to criticisms of which the courts are likely to be resistant. Of course, this aspect of the *Peake* decision was later overruled, but its history is of continuing interest.

Problems of Comparison with the White Male Norm

A further problem in the operation of the Sex Discrimination Act is a function of the definition of discrimination in comparative terms: both direct and indirect discrimination depend on a comparison of the plaintiff's treatment or position with what would have been the treatment of, or what is the impact of the practice upon, a person of the opposite sex. The major problem here is that the standard or treatment or the outcome which represents the point of comparison and hence the Act's conception of what is normal or legitimate is necessarily a norm set for (and generally by) men. This poses particular problems in areas such as pregnancy, where particular treatment is legitimate yet where a discrimination claim is either ruled out in an excercise of blinkered logic[15] or allowed on the basis of an inappropriate comparison between a pregnant woman and a disabled man.[16] It also illustrates rather clearly the blunt critical edges of the legislation, which cannot provide any platform for litigants to criticize the formulation of the 'normal' standard: they must content themselves with arguing for assimilation to it. Complaint about formal difference rather than substantive critique is the name of the game.

Are similar problems posed for Afro-Caribbean and Asian people by the comparative aspect of anti-discrimination law? Certainly assimilation to a white-defined standard is seen as an eminently unsatisfactory goal by most anti-racist writers, and the desire to raise more radical questions about social justice has infused not only critical social theory but also popular culture, as for example in the songs of Tracy Chapman. As in the case of gender, appeals to specific needs, interests, ways of life or sensibilities are inherently dangerous and double-edged in the context of a legal system informed by the formally egalitarian ideology of the rule of law, just as basic challenges to the conventional construction of standards and value are quite literally ruled out of court.[17]

Problems of Symmetry

As Cotterrell has noted,[18] at a formal level, anti-discrimination legislation operates by means of decategorization rather than categorization. In other words, it picks out certain features or categories only in order to prohibit their operating as reasons for certain kinds of decisions. This reflects the liberal notion that all have *the same right* not to be discriminated against. It opens up the possibility of white male legal actions which exploit the vulnerability of any legal recognition of race or gender difference,[19] however important these may be in addressing the disadvantage of women or certain ethnic groups. It can do so precisely because the legislation is framed in terms of difference rather than disadvantage: it constructs the problem to be tackled as race and sex discrimination, rather than as discrimination against and disadvantage of women and certain ethnic groups. Quite apart from the fact that this seriously misrepresents the social problems to which the legislation purports to respond, it means that any kind of protective or remedial measure addressing disadvantage is suspect. In particular, it rules out affirmative action, even of a moderate kind, as objectionable in principle. It thus represents a serious limitation on the legal and political possibilities for tackling women's and ethnic minority people's oppression and social disadvantage.

The Implicit Validation of Sexism and Racism in the 'Private' Sphere

Related to the comments I have made about the need for individual litigants to convince the tribunal that what happened to them was 'abnormal', the converse, and equally damaging, implication of the legislation must be that less favourable treatment on grounds of sex or race or unjustified differential impact are legitimate where they fall outside the limited ambit of the Acts. As Fitzpatrick has suggested,[20] in the context of a society where racism is endemic, it is in principle impossible to have 'innocent' law: any legislation which attempts a partial attack on race discrimination implies, at the very least, that only that racism covered by the legislation is of sufficient importance to merit political intervention and to raise serious questions of social justice. This implication becomes less damaging the more thorough-going the legislation is, and as arguments about the relative ineffectiveness of legal intervention become correspondingly stronger. Yet in a racist and sexist society, it is impossible completely to escape the implication of limited anti-discrimination legislation that discrimination not addressed by it fails to raise questions of injustice calling for political redress.

Empowering Disadvantaged Groups?

I hope that these brief comments will have been sufficient to demonstrate that the problems from a feminist perspective with respect to the operation of the Sex Discrimination Act raise comparable and similarly intractable problems for race discrimination law. At every turn the critical hold offered by the legislation is severely limited, and becomes more so when applied by judges and others whose political perspective encourages them to a restrictive view of its role. At the point of deciding what constitutes less favourable treatment, sexist and racist stereotypes can creep in; in deciding what is justified, the view of anti-discrimination law as essentially concerned with dismantling restrictive practices and opening up a genuine market of equal opportunity predisposes tribunals to be sympathetic to economic arguments and discourages any clear appeal to the intrinsic value of a more egalitarian world. If we want to get at the real structures of racism and sexism, individual lawsuits on this kind of model are unlikely to be an effective vehicle.

FEMINIST SOCIAL THEORY AND CRITIQUES OF RACISM

We now need to explore how these specific criticisms of the anti-discrimination legislation relate to more general themes in critical social theory, and to consider how far these alternative critical analyses suggest ways of overcoming the problems inherent in the political framework of the present legislation. The points I have made are directly informed by the insights of feminist and critical legal theory. Several of the points turn on what has become known as the critique of liberal legalism — a cluster of ideas among which the ideal of the rule of law and the separation of the world into public and private spheres are two of the most important. The liberal legal world is one in which legal rules are applied and enforced in a politically neutral and formally equal way; the legal sphere is seen as relatively autonomous from the political sphere; all are equally subject to law and formally equal before it. There are stringent limits on the proper ambit of state intervention by means of law, which is seen positively as protecting individual rights and interests against political encroachment, and negatively as respecting a sphere of private life in which public regulation is inappropriate and indeed oppressive.[21] The place in which the line between public and private is seen as falling has shifted over time, as has the content of the rights perceived of as the object of legal protection, but this basic framework has exercised an enduring hold over legal practice, imagination and ideology.

Several features of this framework have been the object of critique. Feminists have criticized the ahistorical, pre-social view of human nature which underlies liberal rights theory and legal individualism, and have pointed out the ways in which the need to frame legal arguments in terms of individual claims systematically obstructs the project of revealing and dismantling structures and institutions which disadvantage women. These arguments have developed into a more general critique of the discourse of rights, which are seen as not only inherently individualistic, but also essentially competitive and hence anti-socialistic. They are also seen as being tied in with the notion of formal equality — hence the need to ascribe equal rights to all and the inevitable obscuring of real social problems and disadvantages. In a world in which white, male and middle-class people both have more effective access to legal forums and meet a more sympathetic response when they get there, the ascription of formally equal rights will in effect entrench the competitively asserted rights of these privileged people. Far from dismantling the disadvantage of women, people from ethnic minorities and socio-economically underprivileged groups, it may even have the opposite effect. In pursuing this potentially radical critique of liberal law, feminists have also been understandably preoccupied with questions of strategy: to what extent should and must we try to exploit legal forms despite our doubts about principle and practice, given that they are undeniably one of the socially salient forms of public argument and power? I shall return to these questions of strategy below.

Second, and related to this first point, feminists and other critics of legal theory aspire to deconstruct the asserted neutrality and objectivity of liberal legal forms, and to expose their substantive preconceptions and the ways in which they in fact systematicallly favour certain kinds of interest. An integral part of this deconstruction is the denial of the possibility of making a separation between questions of form and those of substance, and between substantive law and its enforcement. Feminism is therefore necessarily committed to a socio-legal and political analysis. One specific object of deconstruction, of particular interest in the anti-discrimination area, is that of the legal subject. Feminists claim that far from being a neutral, genderless, classless and raceless abstract individual, the legal subject (as unwittingly revealed in legal language) is in fact a white middle-class man. Hence the views and assumptions built into legal forms, rules and principles, as well as the values and goods recognized by legal arrangements, express the experiences and viewpoints not of the abstract individual (itself an incoherent idea) but of the privileged white male.

Furthermore, it has been argued that the nature of law as a closed system of reasoning, administered by a high-status profession and cast in exclusive and often obfuscating language, necessarily disadvantages the less powerful in their attempts to use the legal system for reformist purposes. Those whose interests are already reflected in legal rules and arrangements have no difficulty in participating in the closed system of reasoning. In contrast, those whose interests and perspectives are marginalized or ignored will often find that arguments which they wish to introduce and see as relevant to a legal issue are regarded as irrelevant and inadmissible. A notorious example is that of the frequent experience of female witnesses in rape trials of being silenced and of having their account excluded from the legal process.[22] This can also be a function of the individualization of legal disputes, and here anti-discrimination law is once again an important example. The individual litigant in a race or sex discrimination case may well find that evidence about her employer's practices and attitudes in different spheres or towards different people and on different occasions which have formed an important part of her recognition of her own treatment as discriminatory are not admissible in proving her individual complaint.

One possible strategy, of course, is for feminists and anti-racists to attempt to intervene in the legal forum, reworking legal concepts and definitions so as to reflect Afro-Caribbean, Asian, female and other perspectives. A notable example of such a strategy is law defining and making actionable sexual harassment — a concept which reconstructs, from a feminist perspective, behaviour conventionally regarded as acceptable and even favourable to women as unacceptable, oppressive and illegal. This kind of social and legal reconstruction is one of the most important potential contributions of critical social theory, and in the anti-discrimination area it raises a number of possibilities for reform. One example might be the recognition of groups' rather than individuals' claims, combating the notion of the legal subject as an abstract individual and putting the position and experience of an oppressed group explicitly on the legal agenda — a possibility which will be canvassed later in this paper.

Third, feminists have demonstrated the ideological power yet the disingenuousness and indeed analytic incoherence of the public/private distinction. On the one hand, the liberal argument is that there are certain areas of life (paradigmatically, the family, but also, and of relevance to anti-discrimination law, certain kinds of market relations) in which legal intervention and regulation is inappropriate or should be severely restricted. This argument is used by liberals as a justification for the non-intervention of law: the assertion of 'privacy' is then hived off from the preceding argument, presented as a matter of description, and the legal policy of non-intervention constructed as an absence or omission. Yet this stance of omission as politically innocent is disingenuous, for law in fact keeps out only where it is satisfied to leave in place the social arrangements and power relations which characterize the unregulated situation. Where law has the capacity to intervene, the decision not to do so is itself a political decision: omission, feminism argues, calls for justification as much as does intervention, for it effectively legitimizes the status quo.

On the other hand, the alleged distinction between public and private, although ideologically powerful, in fact collapses under just the kind of analytic scrutiny which liberal legalism prizes so highly. In the late twentieth century at least, even discounting the argument that omission is the political equivalent of intervention, it is quite simply impossible to find areas of social life which are legally constructed as entirely private. Even the family, to take a central example, is hedged around with legal regulation at practically every turn. This combination of the ideological power yet analytic weakness of the public/private distinction militates to its use in a way which is both intellectually vacuous, in that it is question-begging, and at the same time politically powerful. A good example of this apparent contradiction is represented by arguments purporting to justify the limited scope of anti-discrimination law by simply asserting the existence of private spheres not suitable for legal regulation without articulating just why such regulation is inappropriate. The feminist analysis sketched in this paragraph underpins the argument noted above that non-regulated areas can come to be seen as areas in which the legal system implicitly legitimizes sexism and racism, given the social facts of their existence.

Fourth, many feminists have called for a move away from analysis in terms of inequality understood in the sense of *difference* from the position of or treatment normally accorded to men.[23] This is not to say that the powerful notion of equality is abandoned: rather, it is recast in terms of the dismantling of oppressive and exploitative power relations and of a thoroughgoing challenge to the very construction of norms and values which have conventional status and which are argued to reflect the partial judgements of men or other dominant groups. This is clearly of direct relevance to anti-discrimination law, for it addresses the problem already canvassed about the limitations inherent in the notion of comparison with and equalization to a white male-defined norm in its introduction of a more radical egalitarianism. However, it also introduces one of the major problems for feminism or indeed any other critical social theory whose analysis depends heavily on the specificity of the oppression of a particular group. I want to dwell on this problem because it is of direct relevance to my further question about the potential gains to be had in terms of a move to legal recognition of group-based claims.

I shall try to illustrate the problem using feminism as my example. Feminism, put very crudely, attempts to understand women's subordination and to struggle against women's oppression. As such, it is implicit in the feminist project that some features of that subordination are common to all women in a particular society, at least at some level — although the forms and nature of women's oppression are recognized to be historically and culturally specific. As we have already seen, feminist critique draws heavily on notions such as 'women's' and indeed 'men's' point of view or experience; this specificity of viewpoint is generally held to flow from the common experience of gender oppression or domination.[24] What makes this kind of feminist claim highly complex is, of course, the fact — increasingly recognized and pondered upon in feminist thought — that not all women's oppression, even in one society, is just the same. Since the subordination experienced by Afro-Caribbean women, Asian women, working-class women, lesbian women, women who are single mothers and so on is qualitatively different, the feminist claim must be that gender is always *one factor*, and a fundamentally important one, in constituting the social position and experience of all women and men; but it is overlaid with many other factors, most notably in our society, by race and by class. Exactly the same points can be made, of course, about the experience of racial or religious oppression: the experience of Afro-Caribbean and Asian women and men is not the same, nor indeed is that of different ethnic groups, as is clearly illustrated by recent work on the prison system which shows stark contrasts in the stereotypical views held about different ethnic groups in prison.[25]

This recognition of the differentiated nature of social oppression[26] is leading critical social theorists steadily away from attractively simple, monolithic theories such as Marxism, in which everything is reduced to one explanatory concept, towards a more complex and pluralistic approach. This is certainly to be welcomed, but it has to be acknowledged that so far it has raised more questions than it has answered. For it takes us into crucially important and intractable issues such as the status of assertions about oppression generated by different individuals and groups and the role, if any, to be accorded to claims to 'truth' and 'knowledge';[27] the relationship between the different points of view generated by particular people according to their experience of different forms and combinations of prejudice and subordination; the extent to which oppression has to be understood in cultural as well as (or as opposed to) material (economic) terms; and political questions about how to move towards a society in which these different perspectives and experiences can be heard and recognized in the attempt to begin to dismantle oppressive power relations and to reconstruct human relations along non-oppressive lines. These are fundamentally important questions of social and political theory which cannot be addressed in this essay. However, the fragmentation and diversity of the experience of oppression in society is of great significance for any group-based approach to reform of anti-discrimination law.

RACE, GENDER AND CRITICAL SOCIAL THEORY

I hope that enough has been said in the last section to show both that the methodological tools of a critical feminism are powerful in analyzing a variety of social issues including those of race and ethnicity, and that this approach may be suggestive not only of critical points but also of positive future directions for anti-discrimination law. However, it must be re-emphasized that the argument is at the level of critical method, and does not imply any simplistic assumption about analogies between racial or gender oppression in this or any other society. The project so far has been to extend a certain kind of critical analysis which in the United Kingdom has hitherto been applied to sex discrimination law to anti-discrimination law more generally. However, the analogies and points of contact between sexism and racism must occupy our attention, because they raise intensely difficult and crucially important problems of principles and practice.[28] For example, Asian women who have organized against domestic violence have often found particularly strong resistance from the police when asking them to intervene.[29] The police argue that this resistance is justified on the basis of the value of the extended Asian family and the need to allow that institution to settle its own disputes (hence avoiding awkward cultural conflicts). These women point out that this denial of support is not only sexist but also racist, in that it is based on stereotypes about the way in which Asian people live. There could hardly be a starker example of the denial of respect implicit in the marginalization of an experience which these women had struggled and sacrificed an enormous amount to express. It also represents a kind of doubly oppressive situation: these women were ignored by the white state power to which they appealed at the same time as being subject to censure in the community from which they came; in putting the issue in the public domain, they also inevitably risked the propagation of stereotypes of the authoritarian role of men in Asian families by media and police.

As social institutions, racism and sexism clearly exhibit certain important differences. The centrality of naturalistic and biologistic arguments in constituting and maintaining racism and sexism, at least in the United Kingdom, is arguably different; membership of particular racial groups is significantly correlated with social class and with poverty, as conventionally understood, in a way which is not so obviously true of gender; the experience of racial oppression is arguably more diverse than that of sexism given the variety of stereotypes about different racial groups. Furthermore, the need to understand oppression in cultural terms is more contested, and the meaning of 'cultural discrimination' less clear-cut, in the case of women than in the case of ethnic minority groups. As Modood's essay in this book illustrates, even in the case of racial discrimination there has been a reductive tendency towards a focus on discrimination as colour prejudice as opposed to the devaluation of a particular set of values and ways of life.

There are also similarities between racism and sexism. Both are strongly associated with a variety of forms of political and social disadvantage — educational, economic, in the arena of criminal justice — and both rely to a significant extent on stereotyped views about what is normal to, appropriate for or to be expected of members of that group simply by virtue of that membership. Perhaps most importantly, both have been recognized as social institutions — parts of the structure and patterning of social relations — rather than as merely cumulations of individual prejudices, actions and decisions. This move from the recognition of discrimination to the naming of and struggle against sexism and racism is a crucial one, and opens up the possibility of and need for the common critical methodology outlined above. Finally, Afro-Caribbean and Asian people and feminists who have come to this kind of consciousness of racism and sexism tend to share a deep scepticism about how far their situation is likely to be improved by resort to a white male-dominated legal process which relies on individual assertions of right. Can the legal process respond positively to this scepticism? Can legal forms be de-individualized and politicized so as to reflect and tackle racism and sexism understood in this way?

FROM INDIVIDUAL TO GROUP?

There are many ways in which the legal process might try to respond to the scepticism of Afro-Caribbean and Asian people and women. In this essay, I shall canvass only one — the move from an exclusive reliance on individual enforcement in the discrimination area to include a focus on the rights, interests and claims of groups.[30] This kind of reconstruction seems to be well worth considering given the powerful criticisms of the limitations inherent in individual enforcement and the accompanying representation of the paradigm legal subject as an abstract individual who , it has been argued, is implicitly white and male. Could a move to the recognition of group rights and/or collective remedies help to overcome the problems of legal individualism or to deconstruct the notion of the abstract legal subject in acknowledging as subjects entities recognized precisely because of their substantive political position? I shall discuss this question on the assumption that such a reform would not replace but be combined with either the existing legislation, or a reformed statutory framework of individual enforcement which might move away from the liberal symmetry of the current legislation.

Group rights may be understood in a variety of different ways, several of which might be worth considering in reforming anti-discrimination law. For the purposes of this discussion, I shall distinguish between just two senses of group rights. The first I shall call 'cultural' or 'protective' rights. These may be adopted to protect and express respect for the particular and distinctive ways of life of peoples from specific ethnic, racial or religious groups.[31] An example would be the rights of a Sikh to wear the dress appropriate to his or her religious beliefs, or the right of a Muslim worker to observe traditional religious holidays or hours of prayer. This kind of right — the 'right to be different', as Sachs[32] has called it — is already recognized to some extent in UK law, both indirectly via the Race Relations Act 1976[33] and directly in legislation such as the Road Traffic Act 1988 s. 16(2) (which exempts Sikh motor cyclists from the requirement to wear a crash helmet provided that they are wearing a turban). Such cultural rights are not so much group rights as rights pertaining to a person by reason of his or her membership of a particular group, although one can certainly imagine occasions on which it would be useful to allow the group itself to take legal steps through a representative or authoritative body to ensure that such rights were met. The development of these kinds of legal rights as one means of ensuring tolerance of and promoting respect for cultural diversity is an important political issue which calls for serious and continued consideration.

In this essay, however, I want to assess the potential of a second conception of group rights, which I shall call 'remedial' rights. These 'remedial' rights focus on socio-economic disadvantage and the distribution of basic goods rather than on cultural discrimination and the value of cultural pluralism. These rights would apply to groups which were suffering disadvantage as a result either of present oppression or the present effects of past oppression.[34] The essence of the right would be that positive and effective steps be taken to combat and overcome that disadvantage within a reasonable period of time. This would mean that the holders of such rights would typically be members of minority ethnic and religious groups and women, rather than white

men, and that the very instantiation of the rights would therefore express
the perceived social problem to which they purport to respond.

The enforcement of these group rights would need to be supported
by adequately resourced public agencies which would offer counselling,
legal advice and representation, and which would monitor the effectiveness of remedies over a substantial period of time. The assertion of
group rights would be met with remedies not only of the traditional
legal kind — for example, damages distributed among or with an
impact upon assignable individuals who are members of the group —
but also a wide range of radically different remedies which would not
necessarily be susceptible of such distribution. This feature would be
crucial in breaking the conceptual link between loss and remedy which
characterizes the individual legal form.[35] Hence contract compliance,
quota systems and affirmative action programmes, urban development
programmes, educational reforms and money to set up community
projects of various kinds would be possible responses to the legal
assertion of the violation of a group right.

Should such rights be instantiated as legal rights, or must they
rather be conceptualized as political rights? Would courts and tribunals
as currently constituted be capable, politically or professionally, of
administering legal actions asserting such claims? I would argue that
it would be possible to legislate for such group rights in certain areas.
For example, this might be done by allowing a group defined in terms
of the Race Relations Act and Sex Discrimination Act categories (which
it is to be hoped might be extended to include religion and sexual
orientation) whose representation in an area of employment fell below
its numbers in the general pool by a certain margin, or a group whose
share of valuable educational resources was disproportionately low,
to bring a claim for appropriate remedial action. As such, the action
would have much in common with the procedural notion of a class
action, but would have the additional feature of de-individualizing
the legal subject and opening the way for more wide-ranging remedies
which are not tied to specific legally recognized harms. The essence
of the action would be seen not so much as an assertion of the existence
of widespread individual acts of discrimination against members of
the group, but of an unjust disadvantage suffered by the group, the
ultimate source of which would not be the subject of technical legal
proof. This would overcome some of the main problems of legal proof
and enforcement, and would be informed by an ideal of a substantive
equality of outcome which goes well beyond the commitment of the
present legislation. And although the structure of such actions would
inevitably be complex, many of the technical problems which would
arise have already been encountered and at least partially resolved

in indirect discrimination cases under the existing Sex and Race Discrimination Acts.

What would be the main advantages of such an approach? First of all, such a notion of group rights would entail a form of class action which, as has been widely argued[36] and as is reflected in American experience, has a number of procedural advantages as compared with individual litigation. The encouragement, solidarity and consciousness produced by a class action; the wider relevance of individual pieces of evidence which can add enormously to the persuasiveness of the case; the possibility of touching on discrimination as a patterned structure rather than as individual pathology; progress in terms of widening access to legal redress and moving away from a situation in which rights are in practice the preserve of the relatively privileged few among the underprivileged group; the possibility of spreading the costs of litigation — all these constitute major advantages of the class action approach. Obviously, the possibility of class actions exists without resort to the notion of group rights, but it is a natural concomitant of that notion and as such can fairly be regarded as one of its advantages.

Second, the recognition of collective rights would mean the direct and overt legal recognition of the specificity of the objects of racial and sexual discrimination. In other words, group rights would empower groups of people who experience a common socio-economic or educational disadvantage which is structured along racial, ethnic, gender or religious lines to assert themselves and the patterned nature of their disadvantage. Rather than stopping at giving all citizens *the same right* not to be discriminated against, which, as an exclusive stategy, as we have seen, obscures the nature of the real political problem, the collective approach would make those problems visible in the legal and political arena. It would represent a move beyond the obfuscating exclusive reliance on a symmetrical approach, criticized earlier in this essay, and could mean that the legal sphere might become a more symbolically, as well as a more instrumentally, powerful forum in which to assert and voice the disadvantages and injustices suffered by certain oppressed groups in our society. This would help to overcome the problem raised by the symmetrical individual enforcement model's implication that discrimination is something unusual, pathological, abnormal, and would put institutional discrimination centre stage. It would represent a significant step away from the notion of the abstract, gender- and race-neutral individual legal subject who is equal with all other subjects before the law, and towards a legal recognition that sexism and racism mean that all subjects are *not* equal before the law, and that compensatory legal recognition and remedy is called for to combat the unfair disadvantage suffered by some legal subjects. It introduces into the courtroom the historical realities of racism and sexism, which could no longer be marginalized on the legal agenda by being divided up into individual pathological acts of discrimination of no general political significance. Litigation might become a forum in which an oppressed group actually advanced its cause and further developed its sense of solidarity and resistance to its race- or gender-related disadvantage. Arguably, in other words, the notion of collective rights might help to politicize the legal process in a positive way.

Conversely, certain disadvantages and potential dangers are also inherent in the notion of collective rights. First of all, if we were to add a system of group rights to an otherwise unmodified structure of individual enforcement (and indeed to an essentially individualist liberal legal system), might the very starkness of the contrast itself serve further to marginalize racism and sexism as legal issues? Could the legal institutionalization of a specific group paradoxically undermine the struggle against racism and sexism either by calling forth political hostility or by becoming a 'specialist' or marginal area of legal practice? The first problem is met by the fact that such a change would not occur without some measure of political will and hence a change in the political climate, but the inhospitableness of the legal system even to the limited models of agency enforcement introduced by current anti-discrimination legislation suggests that we should not merely dismiss the marginalization point as a non-problem.

Important questions can be raised about whether the move from individual to group rights really overcomes feminist and other objections to the notion of legal rights, particularly if the structure of individual rights is left in place. In liberal political theory, the notion of collective rights has had the dubious honour of being both marginal and controversial, with purists tending to argue for the essentially individual nature of rights. Those liberals who are willing to countenance the notion of group rights tend to do so by analogy with individual rights, thus playing down their specificity.[37] This means that liberal notions of group rights tend to share many of the features of individual rights to which feminists, socialists and others object: their reliance on coercive enforcement and hence their oppositional and potentially divisive nature. If the liberal world of competitive assertions of conflicting rights by atomistic individuals is simply to be replaced or supplemented by a similar competition between self-interested groups, is this genuinely a political gain? Socialists like Campbell[38] have argued persuasively for a conception of rights in terms of values and goods individuals or groups may legitimately have an interest in (which could include the non-oppressive political treatment of both themselves and others). He asserts that this model escapes the disadvantages of the liberal model of competitive and coercive individual rights. As we have already seen, this kind of argument has not laid to rest feminist scepticism about the usefulness of rights discourse. But some of the most important of the relevant feminist and socialist arguments are addressed to a symmetrical liberal notion of rights, which the approach to disadvantage-based, remedial group rights would move beyond.

Another possible objection to the notion of group rights also flows from a scepticism about rights and their legal entrenchment. This is manifested in the arguments of Unger,[39] among others, who asserts that the liberal legal project of fixing categories and boundaries in the concrete form of legal rules, and in particular in the form of entrenched constitutional rights, is dangerous and oppressive. In his view, the radical liberationist political project consists of precisely the opposite strategy — that of pulling down boundaries, questioning assumptions about how things have been organized traditionally and making possible a wide variety of different kinds of social, personal and political arrangements. Unger's vision has itself been dubbed a kind of 'super-liberalism', but in the version described it suffers from a naively utopian character which arguably disqualifies it as a serious argument against practical reforms which seek to intervene in the actual legal world experienced by relatively powerless, disadvantaged groups. His argument is connected, I think, with a certain kind of scepticism about the legal process which supposes that people always have a choice about whether to use legal forms or not, whereas in the present world, such a choice often does not exist. I shall return to this point in the concluding section of this essay. Meanwhile it also seems apposite to note that Unger's objection to the objectification and concretization of particular categories and arrangements may not in any case bite against the kind of group rights which I am envisaging, which are contingent on the present existence of disadvantage and which would disappear with its dismantling.

A more serious problem for the notion of group rights seems to be the fact of fragmentation and diversity of individual and group identity. People in any social world are members of a number of different communities and groups, and suffer or enjoy a number of overlapping and interacting identities, advantages and disadvantages as a result. Those who are oppressed or disadvantaged for one purpose or in one sphere are not necessarily so in others. Hence we certainly cannot assume any kind of identity of interest among members of a group just because of one shared oppression, nor can we assume that, for example, racial oppression will have had the same kind of impact on the experiences, consciousness and life chances of all members of that group. A recognition of this kind of diversity, and a commitment to recognition of a plurality of oppression, experiences and interests, seems to bring with it a nightmarish vision of the potential explosion of overlapping groups defined along different lines all competing with each other (and implicity with parts of themselves) for the resources or changes necessary to dismantle their specific disadvantages. This is to return to the liberal, competitive notion of rights from which we are trying to move away; but the practical and conceptual difficulties raised by the diversity of social oppression and the consequent fragmentation of group identity cannot be underestimated.

Conversely, we have to ask ourselves whether the legal constitution of *certain* groups identified in terms of specific forms of disadvantage as the bearers of special claims has its own dangers, given that they would be likely to be limited in number, if only for practical reasons. For example, it could be said to reasonate with the reductionist mistakes of monolithic social theory which were criticized above, by apparently reducing the complexities of social oppression to two or three discrete, irreducible and separate axes. Furthermore, it can be argued (as indeed it frequently has been in critical discussion of reverse discrimination programmes) that the identification of women or a racial group as the object of a specific policy of this kind serves to consolidate the very suspect categories which it is necessary to dismantle, and to reinforce the notion that race and sex can be legitimate reasons for action.

This argument, which evokes Unger's critique, however, is open to challenge. For it identifies the basis for reverse discrimination (or group rights) as the shared fact of race or gender rather than as the shared fact of race- or gender-related disadvantage. The concentration on the latter rather than the former is crucially important, not least because it escapes the inference of reliance upon a more full-blooded identity of interest or indeed on any notion of the shared culture or values which may or may not characterize particular disadvantaged groups. Shared culture, values and ways of life can and often do form the basis for and can arise out of discrimination and oppression, but this is not necessarily the case. Whilst, as we have already seen, there is a strong case for having protective cultural rights to underpin respect for pluralism, not all attempts to dismantle oppression need to cast in legislation the specificities of any particular self-identified group or culture. To this extent I am in sympathy with the direction of Unger's argument outlined above. I also take very seriously the lessons of both Menski's and Phillips' essays in this book, which deal with compensatory group rights in India and Malaysia. Certainly any attempt in this country to move in the group-based direction would have to take account of the negative aspects of the Indian and Malaysian experience. However, very significant differences exist between each of those schemes and the more fluid approach which I have been considering, in which the legal structure would attempt to facilitate the self-identification of local disadvantaged groups within the broad categories of proscribed grounds of discrimination enacted in the Race Relations and Sex Discrimination Acts. Nonetheless, if any further argument is needed to support the idea that these kinds of objections to a group-based approach should be considered seriously, one has only to look at the way in which the notion of a group and indeed of group rights has been used in political debate in apartheid countries such as South Africa to see that a reliance on the notion of culturally identified groups can carry with it serious political dangers.

Arguments are likely to be raised about the impact of the kinds of remedies which I have suggested. These are arguments rehearsed in critiques of reverse discrimination (including those by Parekh and Pitt in this book). The arguments suggest that such strategies both tend unjustly to disadvantage relatively underprivileged members of advantaged groups and miss their real targets by benefiting only relatively privileged members of disadvantaged groups.[40] This criticism is not wholly misplaced in its assertion that the effects of such programmes can fall in an unfortunately patterned way, but the *basis* for the criticism is misplaced, for it depends on the move from a group-based remedy to an individual-based objection. If we regard reverse discrimination as a genuinely group-based remedy, we are not called upon to look in every case at questions of distribution between individuals, although distributive patterns over time will certainly be important. This argumentative move from group to individual is understandable because such objections are usually placed in the context of liberal discussions of reverse discrimination which attempt to defend it on the basis of individualistic theories of equal opportunity. Very sophisticated liberal arguments for reverse discrimination have been put forward,[41] but they are ultimately vulnerable. This is because they have little to say about just why an egalitarian end-state as between particular groups is seen as desirable, or why an unequal outcome is seen as problematic in the absence of clear proof that a particular individual has suffered from the unjust inequality of opportunity endured by at least some members of her group. Hence the liberal reply to the conservative objection that only the relatively privileged benefit from reverse discrimination programmes is not entirely satisfactory. Once again, I would argue that a satisfactory account can only be given on the basis of a more radical and thoroughgoing commitment to equality of outcome and the elimination of social disadvantage.

GROUPS, LAWS AND POLITICS

I hope that I have now said enough to justify the tentative conclusion that it is worth the while of those of us committed to further political and legal action to combat racism and sexism to consider the symbolic and instrumental benefits to be gained by the constitution of collective remedial rights based on present social disadvantage. I have tried to show what kinds of questions critical social theory would raise about such group rights, and how these questions might be addressed. These questions are extremely complex and require much more detailed analysis and thought than I have been able to give them in this chapter. However, I should like to draw out one or two underlying questions for further comment.

The kind of approach to group rights which I have gestured at sits right on the traditionally constructed boundary between law and politics. This boundary is in my view quite artificial, but given the conventional understanding of the specificity of legal and political processes, it is important to acknowledge that the kinds of remedies I have envisaged for breaches of group rights might well be seen as calling for political action and decision-making rather than for legal (judicial) determination. A more overtly politically significant constitutional court might well, in my view, be able to tackle such decision-making, but I would only hold to this view on the assumption that there would be radical changes in the training, selection, tenure and accountability of judges — changes which seem far from the political agenda in this country at the moment. On the present construction of the boundary between law and politics, remedial decisions with the kinds of significant resource implications likely to be effective in tackling racial and sexual disadvantage could only come from governmental institutions. As things stand at the moment, therefore, I suspect that effective recognition of group-based remedial rights would have to be at a political rather than a legal level. One compromise would be that courts should make a finding that a group right had been violated — probably on the same kind of basis as findings of *prima facie* indirect discrimination — and then refer the issue to a governmental or quasi-governmental agency with effective enforcement powers for remedial action, perhaps with a system of reference back to the court within a certain period of time.

A further implication of my arguments about group rights is that they apply in principle more widely than to the social institutions of racism and sexism alone. The implications of a commitment to disadvantage-based group rights are entirely socially contingent, but in a society such as ours such a commitment would certainly bite in principle against class oppression and socio-economic disadvantage in a variety of spheres including, significantly, education. In pointing out this kind of implication I am revealing just how radically egalitarian such an approach might be, were it to be pursued beyond the confines of the Sex Discrimination and Race Relations Acts' categories. Doubtless not everyone will accept the political attractions of egalitarian pluralism, and in this essay I have not been concerned to defend it in a thorough way. I have been concerned rather to point out how a commitment to it can overcome some of the limitations widely recognized to characterize the current equality of opportunity approach. Hence I would suggest that its attractions are implicitly recognized by many who would baulk at its radical implications, in that it underlies the move towards recognition of racism and sexism as structural and as expressive of institutionalized power relations rather than as entirely explicable as products of individual decision and action.

Finally, I should like to draw together some threads left loose earlier regarding the issue of left-wing scepticism about using the legal process to advance radical change on behalf of Afro-Caribbean and Asian people, women and others. Feminist discussions of this issue (on which there is a wide range of opinion) are sometimes reminiscent of Marxist arguments about the irreducibly oppressive nature of law, which become translated into something like a claim about its irreducible maleness. The Marxist claim has always seemed to me to mark an unusual failure of imagination in Marxist thought, and I feel the same about the feminist analogue. The claim that law under capitalism and law under patriarchy exhibit most of the oppressive features of those social systems seems to me both true and unsurprising. But we should beware both of reductionism and of a despairing and unrealistic surrender to the idea that the nature of law, unlike that of other social institutions, cannot be gradually transformed through political struggle and action. This is not to say that much progress has yet been made in this direction — although even the fiercest Left critics of the Race Relations and Sex Discrimination Acts would be loath to see them repealed.

Given its social power, we simply cannot afford to abandon the legal process as a site for political action. And we must not do so for a further reason, already touched upon. This is because in the real world disadvantaged people do not always have a choice about whether or not to defend or advance their needs and interests by legal means. Sometimes they simply have to do so because legal action is initiated by other parties, and on other occasions they have to because no other avenue of redress is available or remains to be explored. We must try to alter law so as to make it more receptive to the arguments of the powerless, so as to stop it silencing their voices: we should not completely discount law as an arena for consciousness-raising as well as for material political advance.[42]

Group-based rights, then, just might be a step in the right direction, particularly if their recognition of disadvantage spills over into wider legal recognition at the level of defence to civil and even criminal actions, for example. This would be radical change indeed, but if we are not prepared to think in this imaginative and speculative way about law, we abandon it to its current oppressive status and our sceptical stance simply becomes a self-fulfilling prophecy. I hope to have said enough in this essay to justify the conclusion that although the gains to be had from law are at the moment quite limited, we must not abandon the reformist project, just as we must not confine ourselves to a focus in anti-discrimination law. Changing law must remain one modest but important part of the radical political enterprise.

NOTES

1. I should like to thank the participants in a lively discussion of this essay at the Hart Workshop. Their comments have been influential in revising and, I hope, improving the argument. I am also grateful to Ann Dummett, Sandra Fredman, John Gardner, Bob Hepple, Laurence Lustgarten and Carl Wellman for reading and giving me helpful comments on an earlier draft.

2. See, for example, O'Donovan, K. and Szyszczak, E. *Equality and Sex Discrimination Law* (Oxford, Blackwell, 1988); MacKinnon, C. *Toward a Feminist Theory of the State* (Cambridge, Harvard University Press, 1989) ch. 12; Smart, C. *Feminism and the Power of Law* (London, Routledge, 1989).

3. Including my own contribution; see 'Legislation against sex discrimination: questions from a feminist perspective' (1987) 14 *Journal of Law and Society* 411.

4. See Fitzpatrick, P. 'Racism and the innocence of law' (1987) 14 *Journal of Law and Society* 119; Lustgarten, L. *Legal Control of Racial Discrimination* (London, Macmillan, 1980) and 'Racial inequality and the limits of law' (1986) *Modern Law Review* 68.

5. See, for example, Institute of Race Relations. *Police against Black People* (London, 1979); Gordon, P. 'Black people and the criminal law: rhetoric and reality' (1988) *International Journal of the Sociology of Law* 295.

6. The question of the proper language to be used in referring to ethnic minority groups is a difficult one, and most of the possibilities have some drawbacks. In response to the powerful arguments of Tariq Modood in his 'Black and Asian identity' ((1988) XIV *New Community* 397), I shall refer in the British context to 'Afro-Caribbean and Asian people' in preference to the more usual 'black people'. This has the benefit of marking the fact that racial prejudice is not merely colour prejudice, but is also based on culture (see Modood's essay in this book). The drawback with this usage is that it excludes other groups which are protected by the Race Relations Act 1976. I shall therefore also occasionally refer to 'ethnic minority groups'. Of course, members of majority groups are also protected by the Act, but I hope that the view of the social functions of anti-discrimination legislation which emerges from this essay justifies the focus on 'minorities'.

7. For an interesting discussion of this point, see Kennedy, R. L. 'Racial critiques of legal academia' (1989) 102 *Harvard Law Review* 1745.

8. See, for example, Bell, D. *Race, Racism and American Law* 2nd ed. (1980); Lawrence, C.R., III 'The id, the ego and equal protection: reckoning with unconscious racism' (1987) 39 *Stanford Law Review* 317; Williams, P. 'Spirit-murdering the messenger: the discourse of finger-pointing as the law's response to racism' (1987) 42 *University of Miami Law Review* 127.

9. Lacey, op. cit. (note 3).

10. See, for example, the essays by Bindman and Fitzpatrick in this book.

11. See in this book the essays by Coussey and Hepple.

12. Commission for Racial Equality. *Time for a Change?* (1983), *Review of the Race Relations Act 1976: Proposals for Change* (1985).

13. See, for example, Genders, E. and Player, E. *Race Relations in Prisons* (Oxford, Clarendon Press, 1989), Ch. 3–5; Gordon, P. op. cit. (note 5).

14. *Peake* v *Automotive Products* [1978] QB 233.

15. *Turley* v *Allders Department Stores Ltd* [1980] ICR 66.

16. *Hayes* v *Malleable Working Men's Club* [1985] ICR 703; *Webb* v *EMO Air Cargo UK* [1990] IRLR 124.

17. One potential exception here in the gender area being the law on equal pay for work of equal value; see O'Donovan and Szyszczak, op. cit. (note 2) Ch. 5.

18. Cotterrell, R. 'The impact of sex discrimination legislation' (1981) *Public Law* 469.

19. Fudge, J. 'The effect of entrenching a bill of rights upon political discourse: feminist demands and sexual violence in Canada' (1989) 17 *International Journal of the Sociology of Law* 445; Smart op. cit. (note 2) ch. 7.

20. See Fitzpatrick op. cit. (note 4).

21. For a different view of the significance of the public/private distinction, see Gardner's essay in this volume.

22. See, for example, Chambers, G. and Millar, A. 'Proving sexual assault: prosecuting the offender or persecuting the victim?' in Carlen, P. and Worrall, A. (eds) *Gender, Crime and Justice* (Milton Keynes, Open University Press, 1987) p. 58; Smart op. cit. (note 2) ch. 2; Temkin, J. *Rape and the Legal Process* (London, Sweet and Maxwell, 1987) pp. 1–8.

23. Littleton, C.A. 'Reconstructing sexual equality' (1987) 75 *California Law Review* 1279; MacKinnon, C. op. cit. (note 2); O'Donovan and Szyszczak op. cit. (note 2) ch. 1; Smart op. cit. (note 2) chs. 4, 7.

24. However, some strands of feminist thought are sympathetic (at least partially) to naturalistic explanations, and even firmly socially constructionist accounts are often vulnerable to misinterpretation as biologistic by writers hostile to the feminist project.

25. See Genders and Player op. cit. (note 3).

26. See Connell, R.W. *Gender and Power* (Polity Press, 1987) parts I, II.

27. For contrasting positions in this debate, see Kennedy *op. cit.* (note 7), and Williams op. cit. (note 8).

28. See Fredman and Szyszczak's essay in this volume.

29. An eloquent and incisive account of just such a situation was given by members of the Southall Black Women's Centre at a seminar held by the Oxford University Women's Studies Committee in its series on Race, Class and Gender held in Autumn 1985.

30. This is not a novel suggestion. In his early work on the Race Relations legislation, *Legal Control of Racial Discrimination* (note 4), Lustgarten canvassed the idea of a 'collective remedial concept of discrimination' (pp. 31–37). The disadvantage-based, remedial rights which I suggest should be considered have much in common with Lustgarten's ideas, and his discussion is illuminating in defending the practicality of the notion and illustrating its continuity with current approaches to anti-discrimination law in the US. Interestingly, his original suggestion attracted little comment or response. This may have been because of its relatively brief treatment in the context of a longer work, but it is probably also attributable to most commentators' unquestioning acceptance of the individual model at the time at which Lustgarten was writing.

31. I should like to acknowledge a particular debt to Tariq Modood, whose comments at the Hart Workshop made me aware of the inadequacy of my original formulation. My continued focus on what I have called 'remedial' rights as opposed to 'cultural' rights flows from a recognition of the complexity of the issues raised by the latter, rather than from any sense that they are of less importance. Many of the most important issues concerning 'cultural' rights are dealt with by Poulter in this volume.

32. Sachs, A. *The Future Constitutional Position of White South Africans* (London, Institute of Commonwealth Studies, 1990) p. 28.

33. *Mandla v Dowell-Lee* [1983] 2 AC 548.

34. A link between the two senses of group-based rights is suggested by Charles Lawrence's argument (op. cit. note 8) that in interpreting anti-discrimination law (and hence in ascribing any 'remedial' rights), the decision-making tribunal might be directed to consider whether the 'cultural meaning' of the existing disadvantage was a racial or religious one. While I find Lawrence's arguments about the importance of unconscious racism totally persuasive, my feeling is that, even if it would work in the US, in the British context a 'cultural meaning' test would turn out to be highly restrictive. The lack of a recent history of overt and blanket legislative exclusion of ethnic minority groups from certain goods, along with the persistence of racist attitudes, would mean that tribunals and juries would be reluctant to ascribe a 'racial meaning' to *de facto* disparities. This judgement is reinforced by what we know of tribunals' interpretation of the 'justification' test in indirect discrimination cases such as *Ojutiku v Manpower Services Commission* [1982] IRLR 418.

35. On this point, see Freeman, A. 'Legitimising racial discrimination through anti-discrimination law: a critical review of Supreme Court doctrine' (1978) 62 *Minnesota Law Review* 1049.

36. See Gregory, J. *Sex, Race and the Law*, (London, Sage, 1987) pp.34–36, 156–58; Chayes, A. ' The role of the judge in public law litigation' (1976) 89 *Harvard Law Review* 1281; Pannick, D. *Sex Discrimination Law* (Oxford, Clarendon Press, 1986) pp. 282–302.

37. See, for example, Raz, J. *The Morality of Freedom* (Oxford, Clarendon Press, 1986) pp. 198–203.

38. Campbell, T. *The Left and Rights* (London, Routledge & Kegan Paul, 1983).

39. Unger, R. M. *The Critical Legal Studies Movement* (Harvard University Press, 1986); *Social Theory: Its Situation and Its Tasks* (Cambridge University Press, 1987) chs. 2–5.

40. Again, see the essays by Menski and Phillips in this book.

41. See Dworkin, R. *Taking Rights Seriously* (London, Duckworth, 1977) ch. 9; see also the essay by Pitt in this volume.

42. See Crenshaw, K. W. 'Race, reform and retrenchment; transformation and legitimation in anti-discrimination law' (1988) 101 *Harvard Law Review* 1331, for a subtle and ambivalent assessment of the role of rights. Crenshaw recognizes the potential of legal rights in combating the 'otherness' of black people in America yet also, conversely, in risking legitimation and co-optation. In the legal arena, winning and losing are, as she puts it, 'part of the same experience'. I agree with her view that rights discourse is, however, sometimes the only available point of entry for struggle or reform, and that we need to use liberal legal ideology pragmatically, with our eyes open to its dangers.

8

Race Discrimination: The Limits of Market Equality?

Erika Szyszczak

The European Community has provided a dynamic which has brought about changes in legislation,[1] procedures,[2] remedies[3] and political lobbying in sex discrimination law in the 1980s. In addition the European Court has established a significant case law at the Community level in the key areas of migrant worker and equal treatment policies. This is remarkable when we realize that a legal discourse on non-discrimination and equal treatment at work has been fostered in a political climate hostile to individual employment rights and state regulation of the labour market.[4]

Recent rulings of the European Court[5] confirm the potential for challenging and obtaining remedies from the state when government policies run counter to Community law. While it is important that the effects of Community law are integrated into national law in order to produce change, it is necessary also to maintain a clear vision of the Community's understanding of the concept of discrimination since the limitations of using Community standards may sometimes be lost in the excitement surrounding the gains. It is timely to take this opportunity to critically assess the development of discrimination law at the Community level since the Community is poised to develop a set of social rights which will complement the completion and operation of the Internal Market in the 1990s.[6] While some of the Community's proposals may be useful in establishing a new level, or 'floor', of social rights, it is clear that the coverage of these rights is not exhaustive and, as with the employment protection coverage at the national level, some disadvantaged groups may fall through the safety net of legislative protection.[7] Also, a question emerges as to what *are* the consequences of the Internal Market for discrimination issues? Supporters of the Community Charter of the Fundamental Social Rights of Workers (the 'Social Charter') point to the success of the Community equal-treatment programme in the 1980s as a model for the gains to be made by developing a Community 'floor' of rights in other areas.[8]

Significantly, 'women's' issues figure prominently in many of the proposals put forward by the EC Commission in its Action Programme[9] designed to implement the Social Charter. The success of the equal treatment programme, the relative lack of controversy over the need for women's rights in the workplace and the fact that women command a good percentage of the European electorate make the inclusion of their rights — albeit in a regulatory form — a safe bet in order to sell the Social Charter. Clearly the early proposals on the regulation of 'atypical work'[10] pregnancy and maternity[11] will be of value to women working in the United Kingdom. Hopefully, our meagre rights in this area will be dragged up to European standards. But fears are expressed about the economic consequences of the Internal Market for women's work. For example, the Cecchini Report 1988[12] estimated that initially there will be job losses as a result of economic and industrial restructuring. These job losses are likely to fall disproportionately in the service sector of the economy — a sector that employs a high proportion of female labour. Another fear expressed by women — and this is a fear expressed by black and ethnic minority groups too — is that the fundamental premises of the Internal Market, of freedom of movement[13] tied in with the transportability of Euroskills, will not be available to women because of their lack of mobility.

THE CONSEQUENCES OF THE INTERNAL MARKET FOR BLACK AND ETHNIC MINORITIES

In contrast to the high profile given to women's issues, race issues do not figure prominently in either the Social Charter or the EC Commission's Action Programme. It is felt that many black and ethnic minorities, particularly when they are only 'guest workers' in the European economy, will be adversely affected by the consequences of the Internal Market. Wong vividly describes the future Europe as a '. . . landscape for increasing problems of social polarisation and exacerbation of racial tensions and uprisings'.[14] The fears of black and ethnic minority communities may be separated into three recognized issues for the purposes of analysis, although obviously the three areas overlap and interrelate to form a web of what could be classified as institutionalized discrimination.

Invisibility

The first fear is the invisibility of black and ethnic minority rights in the Social Charter and in Community law generally. Two reasons have been advanced by the Community for the lack of attention given to race discrimination. The first is the lack of a legal basis in the Treaty of Rome 1957 in order to legislate in the area of race discrimination. The second reason is that, unlike the equal treatment programme, there has been no *demand* for such action. Both justifications are open to scrutiny and form the focus of this essay.

Indirect Discrimination

A second fear is that indirect discrimination may occur as a result of the operation of the Internal Market. Freedom of movement is an illusory right to a non-Community national. Equally, discrimination at the national level may lead to black and ethnic minorities having difficulty in obtaining the transportable Euro-skills.

Examples of the kind of indirect discrimination which may occur are given by the Commission for Racial Equality.[15] In analyzing the implications of Council Directive 89/48/EEC on a 'general system for recognition of higher education diplomas awarded on completion of professional education and training of at least three years' duration',[16] several issues of indirect discrimination emerge. The Directive requires member states to recognize Community professional qualifications subject to the completion of one of the adaption procedures provided where the qualifications are lower than those of the host state. Article 1 of the Directive states that a diploma must show:

> . . . that the education and training attested . . . were received mainly in the Community, or the holder thereof has three years' professional experience certified by the Member State which recognises a third country diploma . . .

There is nothing in the Directive to allow a challenge by an individual alleging that a decision by a competent authority is racially discriminatory. In this respect, after the decision of the House of Lords in *Hampson* v *Department of Education and Science*,[17] it would seem that the Race Discrimination Act 1976 offers more protection against this type of discrimination than is found elsewhere in Europe. It should also be remembered that the European Court has been prepared to provide remedies in the area of freedom of movement in instances where no specific right is granted in Community legislation.[18] Resort has been made to the European Convention on Fundamental Rights and Freedoms and to the general principles of law developed by the European Court to provide further remedies.[19] The question remains as to whether the European Court is prepared to extend such rights to non-Community nationals.

It is also feared that employers may unfairly exclude applicants on the ground of non-possession of relevant European qualifications. The defence to indirect discrimination, enunciated in *Bilka-Kaufhaus GmbH v Weber von Hartz*[20] and applied by the Court of Appeal in *Hampson*[21] to race discrimination claims, may provide a measure of protection against such action but it remains to be seen how far the courts will scrutinize economic objectives and how far Council Directive 89/48/EEC will be utilized to justify discrimination against holders of non-European qualifications.

Another example of the indirect discrimination consequences of the Internal Market is in the area of public procurement. Community law has already been used by the Conservative government as an excuse not to introduce local labour contracts as a way of alleviating local unemployment after the Broadwater Farm and Handsworth disturbances.[22] Anxieties are now expressed about the decision in *Gebroeders Beentjes BV v State (Netherlands)*,[23] where a challenge was made to a Dutch land consolidation scheme which had rejected the applicants on the ground *inter alia* of their inability to employ the long-term unemployed, one of the criteria for tender selection. The European Court drew a distinction between contractual conditions on the one hand and the criteria for selection on the other. In the case of the latter it was held that the criteria used could be incompatible with the public procurement Directive if they produced discriminatory effects contrary to Article 7 EEC, which forbids discrimination on the grounds of nationality. It may be that by imposing conditions to implement equal opportunities policies in public procurement, member states infringe Article 7 EEC, particularly where firms from other Community states have difficulty in complying when they have not had any experience of such policies.

It may be that some of the rights contained in the Social Charter may benefit black and ethnic minority workers. However, issues relating to minimum qualifying periods, which have resulted in indirect discrimination in the operation of national employment protection legislation for women workers, may equally apply to black and ethnic minority workers.

Overt Racism

A third fear of the consequences of the Internal Market is that by promoting a common European identity, even further alienation of black and ethnic minority groups will occur, fuelled by the lack of legal protection in national and Community law, the indirect discrimination consequences of the Internal Market and the growth of right-wing fascist groups in Europe.[24] Even Mrs Thatcher, not the greatest supporter of the Internal Market, alluded to this in her famous speech at Bruges in 1988:

> From our perspective today, surely what strikes us most is our common experience. For instance the story of how Europeans colonised and (yes, without apology) civilised much of the world, is an extraordinary tale of talent, skill and courage.

The fostering of a common European identity may prevent the acceptance of different 'non-European' forms of religion, languages, cultural ideas and education. Sivanandan[25] has warned: 'We are moving from an ethnocentric racism to a Eurocentric racism, from the different racisms of the different member states to a common, market racism.'

Issues have already arisen in Europe over multi-racial schooling and the wearing of traditional clothes at school and at work. These are indicative of some of the features of alienation already experienced. With cutbacks in public expenditure it is felt that even fewer resources will be available to finance projects relating to the education of black and ethnic minorities and that more attention will be paid to the teaching of European languages, history, politics and culture.

THE LEGAL BASIS OF THE EQUAL TREATMENT PROGRAMME

Unlike the 'core' freedoms of the Treaty of Rome 1957, social policy law does not have a firm legal base from which an anti-discrimination programme may emerge. Article 119 EEC is the only firm legal commitment to developing a substantive aspect of social policy law, but the equal pay clause was included for economic rather than social reasons. Article 119 EEC did not provide the means whereby further anti-discrimination measures could be enacted and the subsequent equal treatment directives have been introduced using Article 100 EEC and Article 235 EEC. Both articles require a unanimous vote in the Council of Ministers and are circumscribed by the fact that any new measures introduced must be shown to further the economic aims of the Community. The European Court has utilized the preamble and Article 117 EEC of the Treaty of Rome 1957 as interpretative tools to ensure an upwards harmonization of social policy law.[26] But few concrete measures have emerged to fulfil the commitment to improving the living standards of Europeans. In legal terms the new Social Charter adds no new implementation measures to social policy law.[27]

The European Court has played an important role in developing the equal treatment programme, as a result of infringement actions and preliminary rulings. A particularly important development is the elevation of the principle of equal treatment to one of the fundamental principles of Community law.[28] Although sometimes ambiguous[29] and tentative in its approach, the court has recently delivered some bold rulings which have opened up government policy for scrutiny in the national courts and developed areas of Community law previously blocked in the Council of Ministers.[30]

The Limitations of the Equal Treatment Programme

Several criticisms may be mounted against the Community's approach to discrimination. The economic measures enacted bear little relationship to the demands of the women's movement across Europe. The European Court itself seems unprepared to move Community competence into the private sphere by refusing to regulate the public mediation of *choice* in the allocation of domestic work.[31]

Since Community law is symbiotic in nature it relies heavily on national implementation and enforcement. Thus the combination of Community and national primary and secondary legislation and case law has resulted in a plethora of sources of discrimination law rights. Despite exhortations from the Equal Opportunities Commission, no attempt has been made to codify discrimination law. As a result individuals, out of necessity, must seek specialized legal advice in order to pursue Community-based rights. It is questionable how far such advice is available, in terms of expertise to give it and financial resources to obtain it. While Article 177 EEC references from national courts have created an attractive web of substantive rights, there are limitations in this reliance on national courts to apply Community law and the haphazard nature of Article 177 EEC results in a slow, piecemeal system of Community case law. A case study of the development of indirect discrimination[32] for the purposes of Article 119 EEC shows how employees, employers and the state can be left in an ambiguous situation as to the nature of their rights and obligations under Community law. Furthermore the *concepts* of discrimination deployed in Community law are conservative, resting firmly on the basis of formal equal treatment. Little attention has been paid to the role of positive action and there is no legislative definition of indirect discrimination. While the European Court has filled this legislative gap, the test now propounded is firmly grounded in economic justifications for employers' and the state's conduct.[33]

A further limitation is the remoteness, not only of the legislative process, but also the judicial process for securing Community rights. Individuals may not compel a national court to make an Article 177 EEC reference and they have no legal standing to compel the EC Commission to mount an infringement action. It has been argued that in order to be effective, social rights in the Community must be accompanied by positive political and economic resources.[34]

A LEGAL BASIS FOR A COMMUNITY RACE DISCRIMINATION POLICY?

The fears raised by black and ethnic minority groups suggest that they may need even greater protection than other vulnerable groups from discrimination and racism as a consequence of the functioning of the Internal Market. This raises the question as to whether a legal basis for race discrimination may be found in Community law.

The Social Charter

Race discrimination is not ignored completely in the Social Charter. The preamble contains the following recitals:

> Whereas in order to ensure equal treatment, it is important to combat every form of discrimination, including discrimination on grounds of sex, colour, race, opinions and beliefs and whereas, in a spirit of solidarity, it is important to combat social exclusion.

and

> Whereas it is for the Member States to guarantee that workers

from non-Member countries and members of their families who
are equally resident in a Member State of the European Community are able to enjoy, as regards their living and working
conditions, treatment comparable to that enjoyed by workers
who are nationals of the member state concerned.

But no measures are to be found in the EC Commission's Action
Programme[35] to implement these sentiments. Paragraph 5 of the
Action Programme states: 'While the Commission is not making a
proposal in respect of discrimination on the grounds of race, colour
or religion it nonetheless stresses the need for such practices to be
eradicated.' The only measure in the Action Programme which touches
upon the area of race discrimination is a new initiative on the social
integration of migrants from non-Community states which 'will lay
stress on the quality of administrative and social services afforded to
migrants, especially in such fields as education and housing'.

Article 7 EEC

The Treaty of Rome 1957 (as amended) forbids discrimination on the
grounds of nationality in a number of provisions, the most general
being Article 7 EEC. At first sight Article 7 EEC would seem to provide
a broad legal base on which to build a non-discrimination principle:

> Within the scope of application of this Treaty, and without
> prejudice to any special provisions contained therein, any discri-
> mination on grounds of nationality shall be prohibited.
>   The Council may, on a proposal from the Commission and in
> co-operation with the European Parliament, adopt, by a qualified
> majority, rules designed to prohibit such discrimination.

It is worth noting at this stage that Article 7 EEC does not confine itself
to nationality relating to one of the member states of the Community.
It is confined to the *application* of the Treaty of Rome 1957, now
amended to embrace the concept of the Internal Market.

Article 7 EEC has been utilized to ensure the smooth functioning
of the free movement of persons provisions in the Treaty of Rome 1957.
These provisions secure a positive set of rights for Community workers
wishing to work in another member state and they have been described
as 'an incipient form of European citizenship'.[36] As with the equal
treatment programme, the European Court has categorized the rights
pertaining to the freedom of movement as fundamental rights.

A controversial issue in the application of the freedom of movement rights is that they are only available to the nationals of one of the member states. The member states retain the competence to determine their own nationality laws. An early debate focused upon the relationship between Article 7 EEC and Article 48 EEC. Böhning argued that the right to the freedom of movement was available to *all* workers, irrespective of their nationality within the Community.[37] Eden and Patijn,[38] on the other hand, pre-empted the European Court in arguing that the right to free movement was only available to Community nationals.

Article 48 EEC thus circumscribes the general protection afforded by Article 7 EEC in the area of freedom of movement. The only concession to non-Community nationals is to be found in Article 10 of Council Regulation 1612/68 whereby a migrant worker may bring her non-Community spouse and dependants to the host state irrespective of their nationality.[39] Article 11 of Regulation 1612/68 grants the spouse and children of the migrant worker the right to take up employment in the host state and Article 12 allows access to the education system for the migrant worker's children.

Attempts have been made to extend the application of the non-discrimination principle contained in Article 7 EEC, Article 48(2) EEC and the subsequent secondary legislation to cover non-Community migrants and people who are suffering from discrimination in a member state where they have nationality or residence but have not moved to another member state (the concept known as 'reverse discrimination'). The European Court has not entertained either form of claim enthusiastically.

In *Demirel* v *Stadt Schwabisch Gmund*[40] the European Court dismissed an attempt to rely upon free movement provisions contained in an association agreement with Turkey as a means to prevent the deportation of a Turkish citizen from Germany. The European Court held that the association agreement did not produce direct effects and that the resort to the respect for the right to family life contained in Article 8 of the European Convention on Human Rights and Fundamental Freedoms did not fall within the ambit of Community law in this instance. This approach might be compared to the numerous instances when Community migrant workers have successfully invoked the Convention to provide a source of human rights guarantees in Community law.[41] It may also be compared to the ruling of the European Court of Human Rights in *Berrehab* v *The Netherlands*,[42] where a Moroccan migrant in the Netherlands successfully argued that deportation after the breakdown of his marriage infringed the Convention.

Similarly, in relation to reverse discrimination the European Court has adopted a restrictive approach. A Community national must move

to *another member state* in order to trigger the advantages attached to
Article 48 EEC. However, in an Article 169 EEC action, the European
Court seemed to suggest that the absolute prohibition against discri-
mination contained in Article 7 EEC may have a wider application

> . . . guaranteeing to the State's own nationals that they shall
> not suffer the unfavourable consequences which could result from
> the offer or acceptance by nationals of other Member States of
> conditions of employment or remuneration less advantageous
> than those obtaining under national law.[43]

In *R* v *Saunders*,[44] Advocate General Warner was willing to accept
that Article 7 EEC was capable of prohibiting reverse discrimination
since the Treaty of Rome 1957 was capable of giving individuals rights
enforceable against their own state. The obvious difficulty of leaving
reverse discrimination outside Community competence is that it leaves
black and ethnic minorities outside the protection of the sophisticated
legal rights available at the Community level. Where a member state
has no effective race discrimination law such groups may be outside
of the protection of law altogether.

It could be argued that the treatment of indigenous and non-
Community migrants *within* member states has a bearing upon the
effective operation of Article 48 EEC. For example, a Community
migrant worker may only ask for and receive the same treatment as
nationals of the host state. Where there is a low level of social and
employment law protection against discrimination this may prove a
disincentive to migration. Of course, this is the purpose of the Social
Charter, to prevent 'social dumping'. The disincentive may be because
the Community national does not want to move to a lower level of
social protection or it may be that all the available jobs have been taken
because of heavy reliance on exploited migrant labour.

It is difficult to see why sex discrimination can be singled out as contributing to imbalances between national labour markets — a situation
viewed as 'wholly internal to a Member State' in the Article 48 EEC
context — whereas race discrimination is not perceived of in the same
way. While work has been carried out to assess the impact of non-
Community migrant labour and the distortion of competition, Europe
lags behind the United States in studies of the effects of *race* discrimination and labour markets.

Sundberg-Weitman[45] has argued that the general ban on discrimination contained in Article 7 EEC may be used as a general rule for the
interpretation of the Treaty of Rome 1957. It may also have an *independent function* in as much as it can be applied to cases of discrimination

not affected by any special provisions relating to discrimination in the Treaty of Rome 1957. The European Court has recently taken some bold initiatives and applied Article 7 EEC in cases relating to tourism.[46] The difficulty with these cases for my argument is that in each case the Community national had moved (or wanted to move) to another member state in order to take advantage of the services of tourism. This raises the question of whether Article 7 EEC may only apply in the context of freedom of movement. The requirements of the Internal Market may demand the integration of *all* people living and working within the geographical area of the Community as well as those possessing a nationality of one of the member states.

There are limitations to using Article 7 EEC to combat race discrimination. Its use will be of greater value in member states which employ 'guest worker' labour and do not allow such workers to take out nationality and citizenship rights. It will be of less use in the United Kingdom where many black and ethnic minorities possess British nationality.[47] It should also be realized that Article 7 EEC cannot give the same extensive 'floor of rights' protection afforded by Article 48 EEC. Like all discrimination law, it tends to operate *ex post facto* and on an *ad hoc* basis, although successful actions may produce normative change. But it is a starting point, a legal base from which to build a set of *positive* anti-discrimination rights.

A Soft Law Approach?

The question of whether Article 7 EEC could be used to combat racial discrimination which interferes with the functioning of the Internal Market may be interwoven with the arguments as to whether there is Community competence to deal with race issues under other provisions relating to social policy in the Community, in particular the attempts to create a migration policy *vis-à-vis* non-Community states.

The attempt to bring the regulation of non-Community nationals within the ambit of Community rather than national competence can be traced back to the Communiqué issued after the Heads of State or Government Meeting in Paris in October 1972. Here the Community was called upon to relaunch Community activity in the social field by providing the necessary measures or resources. In 1975 the Council adopted a resolution[48] in which 'full and better employment at Community, national and regional levels' was stated to be an 'essential condition for an effective social policy' and an undertaking was given that measures necessary to achieve that objective would be adopted by 1976. Included in this undertaking was the promise of an Action

Programme with the aims of achieving equality of treatment for Community and non-Community workers 'in respect of living and working conditions, wages and economic rights' and of promoting consultation on immigration policies *vis-à-vis* third countries.

The theme of non-Community migrants' rights was also taken up at the Heads of State or Government Meeting in Paris on 9 and 10 December 1974. Point 10 of the final Communiqué recognized the need for a stage-by-stage harmonization of legislation affecting non-Community nationals. In fact little emerged on this point. A Council resolution[49] recognized the aims of the Communiqué by committing 'political resolve' to implement the promised measures while taking account of the responsibility of the Community institutions.

The interest in non-Community migrant workers' issues stemmed from the fact that the 1960s and early 1970s saw a huge increase, in terms of numbers and geographical scope, of migration for economic reasons to and within Western Europe. But the onset of the recession resulted in an exacerbation of racial tension. A reading of articles published in *Race and Class* in the 1970s shows the 'social time bomb' created by the exploitation of migrant labour and the qualms of leaving the remedies to national competence.

The EC Commission responded by establishing the Action Programme for Migrant Workers.[50] The aim of this Action Programme was to develop a Community policy in relation to employment, social security and integration of migrant workers into European society. The measures proposed aimed to combine social justice with economic efficiency, in other words to prevent racial and ethnic tension from disrupting the smooth operation of the Community. Despite this economic underpinning, little was achieved and the role of the EC Commission became largely to enumerate the problems faced by the migrant workers rather than to produce any precise remedies.

Education was one area which figured prominently in the Action Programme but the only concrete form of legislation to emerge was a Council directive on the education of migrant workers' children.[51] The directive was based upon Article 235 EEC and in the original proposal the children of non-Community migrants were included. This provision was omitted from the final draft passed by the Council. Instead, annexed to the directive is a declaration relating to the member states' obligations towards third country migrants. This includes a recognition of the importance of creating special reception classes and tuition in the mother tongue, history and culture. The legal status of the declaration is uncertain. It would not seem to be capable of creating directly effective rights against the state in the same way as a directive may. It remains to be seen whether it can create indirect effects.[52] The recession of the 1970s, resulting in cutbacks in public expenditure, meant that little progress was made in providing positive action for migrant workers and their families.

In addition to attempting to regulate the position of non-Community nationals, it was felt that the overall position of migrants within the Community would benefit from the regulation of illegal immigration. As a first step towards the co-ordination of migrant policies within the Community, a draft directive on illegal immigration was proposed based upon Article 100 EEC.[53] The preamble to the draft directive stated that it was based upon the social aims of the Treaty of Rome 1957, in particular Article 117 EEC.

This would have been the first step to the eventual co-ordination of the member states' immigration policies. Instead the proposal was scuttled in arguments over the legal competence to issue such a proposal. Some member states argued that Article 235 EEC would be a more appropriate legal basis for the proposal; others felt the proposal was outside of Community competence altogether.

Also of symbolic significance is the recognition of non-Community migrants' basic rights in the declaration on the principles governing the living and working conditions of migrant workers which emerged from the General Committee for Euro–Arab Dialogue in Damascus in December 1978. This declaration guaranteed the equal treatment of economic rights and basic human rights to Arab workers within the Community. Once again, questions arise as to the legal status of the declaration. Is it an act *sui generis* of the Community? And after *Grimaldi*,[54] is it capable producing indirect effects?

The Single European Act 1986

Prior to the agreement on the Single European Act 1986 it was recognized that migrant labour from outside the Community could affect the functioning of the Internal Market. There are no concrete measures relating to this issue in the Single European Act 1986 but annexed to it are a series of declarations, two of which concern the regulation of non-Community migrants. There is a general declaration on Articles 13–19 of the Single European Act 1986 which states:

> Nothing in these provisions shall affect the right of Member States to take such measures as they consider necessary for the purposes of controlling immigration from third countries and to combat terrorism, crime, the traffic in drugs and illicit trading in works of art and antiques.

There is also a political declaration by the governments of the member states on the free movement of persons:

> In order to promote the free movement of persons, the Member States shall co-operate without prejudice to the powers of the Community, in particular as regards the entry, movement and residence of nationals of third countries. They shall also co-operate in the combating of terrorism, crime, the traffic in drugs and illicit trading in works of art and antiques.

The legal status of these declarations is uncertain. Toth argues that they cannot be regarded as 'reservations to the treaty' as understood in international law:

> They are more in the nature of statements containing opinions, expectations, clarifications and interpretations; in other words, expressing their authors' understanding of, or position in relation to, certain provisions of the Act.[55]

While the declarations cannot restrict, exclude or modify the legal effects of the Single European Act 1986, a question arises as to whether they impose any kind of obligation (positive or negative) upon the member states in the co-ordination of policies towards third country nationals. After reviewing the politics and litigation surrounding *Germany and others* v *Commission*,[56] it would seem that the member states do not regard themselves bound by the declarations.

On 8 July 1985 the EC Commission adopted Decision 85/381/EEC[57] initiating a procedure for prior notification of and consultation on migration policies in respect of non-Community states. The Decision was based upon Article 118 EEC, but the preamble to the Decision refers to the Council Resolutions of 1974[58] and 1976[59] and the fact that the harmonization of legislation concerning foreigners had been advocated by the European Council in 1974 and 1984 and by a European Parliament Resolution[60] in 1983. Five member states lodged an application with the European Court under Article 173 EEC to have Decision 85/381 declared void on two grounds: that the EC Commission lacked competence to adopt the Decision; and, in the alternative, that there was a breach of essential procedural requirements because insufficient reasons were given for the Decision and there was a failure to consult the Economic and Social Committee.

Looking first at the competence issue, all the applicant member states argued that Articles 117 EEC and 118 EEC were essentially in the nature of a programme, using the *Third Defrenne*[61] ruling as authority.

France and the United Kingdom argued further, stating that Decision 85/381/EEC exceeded both Article 118 EEC and Title III of the Treaty of Rome 1957 since that Title did not embrace migration policy. All five applicants argued that the Treaty of Rome 1957 made no provision for a common policy in the social field and that Article 118 EEC allowed the EC Commission to adopt only non-binding instruments. Due to procedural problems the case was not heard by the European Court until after the signing of the Single European Act 1986, wherein the member states pledged to collaborate closely on migration policies.

Advocate General Mancini was sympathetic to the EC Commission's predicament. The issue turned upon the interpretation of Article 118 EEC and he pointed out: 'As from the early 'sixties it became apparent that the Member States, or a large proportion of them, intended to restrict the Commission's use of its powers under Article 118 EEC within the narrowest possible limits.' In vivid terms he describes the 'suspicious and uncompromising attitude' of certain member states resulting in 'dissension, but above all coldness, distrust and vigorous defence of national sovereignty, even in the face of exhortatory or fact-finding instruments'.[62] The Advocate General found that the Council, through various resolutions, had indicated that Community action in the field of consultation was necessary and this is what the EC Commission was purporting to do. The aim of consultation was to enable the EC Commission to make proposals, not to adopt measures.

A legal basis for such action could be use of the Treaty of Rome 1957 *simpliciter* or the resolutions passed by the Council. While precedents could be found for this legal basis, it is clear that the Advocate General did not approve of such a move.

The European Court adopted two perspectives to the question. Asking first, did migration policies *vis-à-vis* third states fall within the scope of collaboration envisaged in Article 118 EEC? The court roundly rejected the view that such policies fell entirely *outside* this scope. The second question was the issue of whether the EC Commission had the competence to adopt binding measures under Article 118(2) EEC. Here the European Court stipulated that where an article of the treaty conferred a specific task on the EC Commission 'it must be accepted, if that provision is not to be rendered wholly ineffective, that it confers on the Commission necessarily and *per se* the powers which are indispensable in order to carry out that task'.[63]

The power given to the EC Commission was regarded as a procedural power to establish the notification and consultation machinery leading towards the adoption of a common position on the part of the member states. However, in this instance the European Court accepted the member states' contention that the EC Commission had exceeded its powers: the EC Commission had no power to determine the result to be achieved in the consultation process and it could not prevent the member states from implementing measures which the EC Commission might consider to be contrary to Community policies and action. Furthermore, Article 1, in extending consultation to cover issues relating to the *cultural integration of non-EC workers and their families* exceeded the EC Commission's competence. This singling out of cultural integration to take the decision outside the Community competence is a tenuous excuse employed by the European Court since it does not seem to be incompatible with the policies envisaged by the Council of Ministers from 1974 onwards. The reasoning employed by the European Court is criticized by Simmonds in that it 'denied perhaps the most important element of successful integration — the achievement of an inter-relationship between the two cultures in which the immigrant lives'.[64]

Thus the European Court has accepted that migration policy may fall within the parameters of Article 118 EEC and that the EC Commission may enact *binding* decisions in order to implement Community policy. This in turn may provide the basis on which to develop a policy to combat race discrimination and build a system of fundamental human rights for non-Community migrants within the Community, provided the EC Commission can show that such measures are necessary for the functioning on the Community labour market as a whole. In order to do this the EC Commission may resort to the Preamble to the Treaty of Rome 1957, Article 117 EEC and the Preamble to the Social Charter discussed above.

EUROPEAN POLITICAL CO-OPERATION

While the legal arguments continue as to how far there is Community competence to regulate non-Community migrants, there is political recognition of the need for the Member States to co-operate on the issue. The attitude of the member states in the case of *Germany and others* v *EC Commission* might be compared with the rapid progress towards concerted immigration policies within the framework of European Political Co-operation (EPC) — a *political* process beyond democratic and judicial control. Terrorism has headed the European Political Co-operation agenda for a number of years and in 1986 the foreign ministers of the Community issued a statement on combating international terrorism. This statement declared that the member states intended to intensify their efforts and promote common action against terrorism. This included co-operation on security at airports, ports and railway stations, common visa policies,[65] control of abuse of diplomatic activity and the control of persons entering and circulating within the Community. Refugee issues are also discussed in the context of EPC. At the Dublin Summit in June 1990 eleven of the twelve member states signed a convention laying down the criteria determining the state responsible for examining applications for asylum lodged in one of the member states.[66] By 1990 the Schengen Treaty had been signed and fears were expressed that it could act as a trial run for a Community-wide abolition of frontier controls for Community nationals. This in turn could lead to a greater awareness of the presence of non-Community nationals within the member states and stricter post-frontier immigration control — including the right of cross-frontier pursuit.

THE ROLE OF THE EUROPEAN PARLIAMENT

The European Parliament has played an important role in developing human rights and a concept of 'citizens' rights'. For example, in 1977 it initiated an inter-institutional declaration on human rights whereby the Parliament, Council and Commission agreed to be bound by the principle of respect for human rights in their work.[67] The Parliament has also been instrumental in keeping race issues alive on the Community agenda. In the early 1980s, at the instigation of socialist groups, a Committee of Inquiry was established to examine the rise of fascism and racism in Europe. Le Pen, the chairman of the Group of the European Right, attempted to challenge the establishment of this Committee before the European Court. The court declared the complaint inadmissible, which was unfortunate in one respect because one of the grounds of complaint was that the subject matter of the inquiry was outside of the Community's competence.[68] It would have been useful if the European Court had discussed this issue to end the speculation over legal competence in this area.

The Committee reported its findings and listed a number of recommendations.[69] These included the ratification by the member states of international conventions covering race discrimination and racism, and to allow the right of individual petition under Article 25 of the European Convention on Human Rights, Article 14 of the International Convention on the Elimination of All Forms of Racial Discrimination

and the Optional Protocol to the International Covenant on Civil
and Political Rights. Other recommendations relate to effective legal
redress at the national level for victims of race discrimination and the
introduction of national legislation to combat political extremism,
racism and racial discrimination. Paragraph 376 is important for the
purposes of our discussion.

> An effort must be made to define more broadly Community
> powers and responsibilities in the area of race relations by applying
> a teleological interpretation of the Treaties, on the basis, *inter alia*
> of seeking the useful effect of the relevant provisions and of the
> European Community's implicit powers; by recourse to the proce-
> dure under Article 235 of the EEC Treaty, and, if necessary, by
> revision of the Treaties. Action must be taken on the communica-
> tion from the Commission to the Council for a Community policy
> on migration, on which Parliament has delivered its opinion, and
> on the resolutions adopted by Parliament on the same subject.

In this respect, paragraph 376 goes on to recommend that a Declaration against racism, racial discrimination and xenophobia be adopted
jointly by the Community political institutions. Further recommendations relate to the monitoring of national legislation and the promotion
of non-discrimination in legislation.

The parliament adopted a Resolution of 16 January 1986 on the rise
of fascism and racism in Europe. On 11 June 1986 the Council and the
EC Commission joined the Parliament in adopting the Declaration
against Racism and Xenophobia;[70] it is merely a declaration of intent,
recognizing the issue of racism within the Community. Subsequent
years saw attempts to persuade the Council to adopt a Resolution on
racism and xenophobia and to give the EC Commission a mandate to
implement an Action Programme in this area. The legal basis of the
proposed Resolution was Articles 220 and 235 EEC and Article 1 of the
Single European Act 1986. Resort is also made to the 1977 Inter-
Institutional Declaration on Human Rights and the general acceptance
of human rights standards at the national level and in the jurisprudence
of the European Court. Particular attention is paid to the 'public order'
issues of racism and also the role of mediation, especially in the fields
of employment and housing. It is recognized that these two areas are
of major importance from the point of view of foreign communities,
having direct effects in terms of health, income and education. The
role of education and training are also singled out for special attention,
both for the integration of 'foreign' workers and for the education of
the indigenous population, in particular 'public servants' coming into
contact with immigrants.

On 29 May 1990 the Council found the consensus to adopt a Resolution on the fight against racism and xenophobia.[71] In the preamble reference is made to the 1977 Declaration on Human Rights, the 1985 Resolution on a Community policy on migration and the 1986 Resolution of a European Parliament on Racism. There seems to be widespread disappointment in the Resolution and it has resulted in an acrimonious exchange between the Council of Ministers and Employment and Social Affairs Commissioner Mrs Papandreou, who withdrew the EC Commission's support for the Resolution on the grounds that it had become so watered down as to be meaningless. The Resolution reiterates the Parliament's calls upon the member states to ratify the international conventions on racism and to recognize the right of individual petition. It also asks the member states to introduce and strengthen existing laws on racism. In particular anti-racist organizations should be given the right or the support to take actions in the courts against alleged racist offences.

The EC Commission is given the power (in compliance with Article 4 EEC) to undertake a comparative assessment of anti-racist laws in the member states. Reference is also made to the role of education and the media in the fight against racism. The limitation of the Resolution is that any Community action must be limited to Community citizens. The EC Commission, in its proposal, had sought to extend the protection against racism to non-Community nationals working within the Community. At the insistence of the United Kingdom government this was removed, since it was argued to be outside the Community's competence.

Once again we see the resort to Community soft law and this raises the question of how much weight can be attached to the Resolution. It may give rise to indirect effects and a Community national may be able to rely on the human rights concepts implicit within the Resolution as a means of interpreting national law so as to conform with Community law. It may also be a tenuous building block from which further measures to combat race discrimination may be enacted.

THE RESPONSES TO RACE DISCRIMINATION AND THE INTERNAL MARKET

We have seen that one response to the problem of tackling race discrimination in the 1990s has been to find a legal basis for legislation which could be modelled upon the relatively successful sex discrimination measures adopted in Community law. As the above discussion reveals, the search may not prove impossible but at best it is only a limited form of race discrimination which can be tackled under the present Community competence. Even in relation to the Resolution on Racism and Xenophobia the issues of institutional discrimination are not confronted squarely. In many respects the Community is at the level of understanding of race discrimination where the UK was in the 1960s. Subsequently we came to understand that individual enforcement of systematic discrimination was necessary in areas extending beyond the labour market. An equal treatment directive in the field of race discrimination is seen as one possible Community response to race discrimination post-1992. It is apparent from the EC Commission's own investigations and from the observations of several of the essays in this book that much more than this is needed. Rather than starting from an equal treatment basis, emphasis must be shifted to positive action in social benefits, housing and education as well as the labour market. There must be an acceptance of the multi-culturalism of European society, which embraces a notion of the protection of fundamental human rights in the sense of basic economic, political, social and civic rights enforceable by collective action.

Another response has been consciousness-raising by the Commission for Racial Equality and local authorities of the direct and indirect consequences of the Internal Market for black and ethnic minorities.[72] This has prompted action for an 'alternative agenda' for the Internal Market. Central to this strategy is the use of networking across Europe and political lobbying within the Community. Attention has been focused upon immigration issues and the need for a refugees' charter. The question arises as to whether such networking will be effective. It works for women, to some extent, because of a certain amount of homogeneity and consensus of the position of white women in the Community. Further, in the case of women the Community has facilitated networking and women's issues have received attention from the EC Commission and the European Parliament.

It is often pointed out that one of the contributory factors as to why race issues have not assumed as much political weight in the UK as they have in the US is because of the diversity of ethnic groups in the United Kingdom. That diversity is magnified across Europe. This leaves us with the question of whether there is — or whether it is necessary to have — an underlying, unified political identity among ethnic groups so as to form a basis for tackling the racism and discrimination felt by people already living and working in the Community as well as by those from outside 'Fortress Europe' who may wish to migrate in the future.

NOTES

1. Amendments to the Equal Pay Act 1970 SI 1983 No. 1974 and SI 1983 No. 1807 and to the Sex Discrimination Act 1975 by the Sex Discrimination Act 1986 were the response to infringement actions under A169 EEC and preliminary rulings under Article 177 EEC. See *inter alia*: Case 61/81 *EC Commission* v *United Kingdom* [1982] ECR 2601; Case 165/82 *EC Commission* v *United Kingdom* [1983] ECR 3431; Case 152/84 *Marshall* v *South West Hampshire Area Health Authority (Teaching)* [1986] ECR 723.

2. See the equal value amendments to Equal Pay Act 1970 ibid.

3. See Fitzpatrick's essay in this volume.

4. The Conservative governments since 1979 have claimed not to be openly hostile towards individual employment rights but incrementally they have weakened the substantive content of many rights and increased the qualifying thresholds for several of the statutory employment protection rights. See Hendy, J. *The Conservative Employment Laws* (London, Institute of Employment Rights, 1989); Wedderburn, Lord, 'Freedom of association and philosophies of labour law' (1989) 18 *Industrial Law Journal* 1.

5. Case C–171/88 *Rinner-Kuhn* v *FWW Spezial-Gebaudereinigung GmbH and Co. Kg* [1989] IRLR 493; Case C–213/89 *R* v *Secretary of State for Transport ex parte Factortame* [1990] 2 WLR 818.

6. Commission of the European Communities *Charter of the Fundamental Social Rights of Workers* (Luxembourg: Office of the Official Publications of the European Communities, 1990); Communication from the Commission concerning its Action Programme relating to the Implementation of the Community Charter of Basic Social Rights of Workers COM (89) 568 final (Brussels).

7. See Szyszczak, E. 'Employment law and social security' in Lewis, R. (ed.) *Labour Law in Britain* (Oxford, Basil Blackwell, 1986).

8. On the equality programme see McCrudden, C. (ed.) *Women, Employment and European Equality Law* (London, Eclipse, 1987).

9. See note 6.

10. COM (90) 228 Final (Brussels).

11. COM (90) 406 final (Brussels).

12. Cecchini, P. *The European Challenge 1992: The Benefits of a Single Market* (Aldershot, Wildwood House, 1988).

13. The concept of the Internal Market is described in Article 8A of the amended Treaty of Rome 1957 as 'an area without internal frontiers in which the free movement of goods, persons, services and capital is ensured in accordance with the provisions of this Treaty'.

14. Wong, A. '1992 Opportunity for oppression' (1989) I *Black Parliamentarian* 1.

15. See the research carried out by Bandopadhay, N. 'Race Equality, Europe 1992' (London, CRE, 1989) mimeo.

16. OJ 1989 L 19/16.

17. [1990] IRLR 302.

18. Case 222/86 *Union Nationale des Entraineurs et Cadres Techniques Professionnels du Football* v *Heylens* [1989] 1 CMLR 901.

19. See Arnull, A. *The General Principles of EEC Law and the Individual* (London and Leicester, Pinter and Leicester University Press, 1989). See also the essay by Fitzpatrick in this book.

20. Case 170/84 [1986] ECR 1607.

21. [1988] IRLR 69.

22. Standing Committee A House of Commons (24 November 1987).

23. Case 31/87 [1990] 1 CMLR 287.

24. See von Beyme, K. *Right Wing Extremism in Western Europe* (London, Frank Cassell, 1988).

25. A. Sivanandan. 'The new racism' (4 November 1988) *The New Statesman and Society*.

26. Case 43/75 *Defrenne* v *Sabena (No. 2)* [1976] ECR 455; Case 126/86 *Zaera* v *Instituto Nacional de la Seguridad Social* [1989] 1 CMLR 827.

27. Vogel-Polsky, E. 'What future is there for a Social Europe following the Strasbourg Summit?' (1990) 19 *Industrial Law Journal* 65.

28. See Arnull, A. op. cit. (note 19).

29. See, for example, Case 96/80 *Jenkins* v *Kingsgate (Clothing Productions) Ltd* [1981] ECR 911.

30. See Case 171/87 *Rinner-Kuhn* op. cit. (note 5); Case 109/88 *Handels- og Kontorfunktion aerernes Forbund i Danmark* v *Dansk Arbejdsgiverforening (acting for Danfoss)* [1989] IRLR 532; Case C-33/89 *Kowalska* v *Freie und Hansestadt Hamburg* [1990] IRLR 447.

31. In Case 184/83 *Hofmann* v *Barmer Ersatzkasse* [1984] ECR 3047, the court denied that parental leave fell within the Equal Treatment Directive 76/207/EEC and held that Community law did not deal with matters of family organization or alter the division of responsibility between parents. The EC Commission had hoped that the court would indirectly lend its support to a proposal for parental leave blocked by the United Kingdom government, OJ 1984 C 316/7.

32. See the discussion in Szyszczak, E. 'L'espace sociale européenne: reality, dreams or nightmares?' (1990) 33 *German Yearbook of International Law* 28.

33. Op. cit. (note 20).

34. Hoskyns, C. 'Women, European law and transnational politics' (1986) 14 *International Journal of the Sociology of Law* 299.

35. Op. cit. (note 6).

36. Plender, R. 'An incipient form of European citizenship' in Jacobs, F. (ed.) *European Community Law and the Individual* (Amsterdam, North Holland, 1976).

37. Böhning, W. 'The scope of the EEC system of free movement of workers' (1972) 9 *Common Market Law Review* 81.

38. Eden, D. and Patijn, S. 'The scope of the EEC system of free movement of workers: a rejoinder' (1973) 10 *Common Market Law Review* 81.

39. OJ Sp.ed. 1968 L 257/2. This is subject to the proviso that she must have housing available equivalent to normal standards for national workers in the region where she is employed.

40. Case 12/86 [1989] 1 CMLR 421. Cf. Case C-192/89 *SZ Sevince* v *Staatssecretaris van Justitie* [1990] ECR 3461.

41. For example, Case 36/75 *Rutili* v *Ministre de l'Intérieur* [1975] ECR 1219.

42. A/138 [1989] 11 ECRR 322. Cf. Storey, H. 'The right to family life and immigration case-law at Strasbourg' (1990) 39 *International and Comparative Law Quarterly* 328.

43. Case 167/73 *Commission* v *France* [1974] ECR 359 para. 45. Cf. Case 147/87 *Zaoui* v *Caisse Régionale d'Assurance Maladie de l'Ile de France* [1989] 2 CMLR 646.

44. Case 175/78 [1979] ECR 1129, 1142.

45. Sundberg-Weitman, B. 'Addresses of the ban on discrimination enshrined in Article 7 of the EEC treaty' (1973) 10 *Common Market Law Review* 71.

46. Joined Cases 286/82 and 26/83 *Luisi and Carbone* v *Ministero del Tesoro* [1984] ECR 377; Case 186/87 *Cowan* v *Le Tresor Public* [1990] 2 CMLR 613.

47. Unless one can argue that the varying forms of nationality status now available after the British Nationality Act 1981 are a form of discrimination on the grounds of nationality.

48. OJ 1974 C 13/1.

49. OJ 1976 C 34/2.

50. *Bulletin of the EC*, Supplement 3/76.

51. Council Directive 77/486/EEC OJ 1977 L 199/32.

52. See Case 322/88 *Grimaldi* v *Fonds des Maladies Professionnelles* [1990] IRLR 400; Wellens, K. and Borchardt, G. 'Soft law in European Community law' (1989) 14 *European Law Review* 267.

53. OJ 1976 C 277/2.

54. Op. cit. (note 52).

55. Toth, A. 'The legal status of the declarations annexed to the Single European Act 1986' (1986) 23 *Common Market Law Review* 803, 806.

56. Joined Cases 281/85, 283–85/85 and 287/85 [1988] 1 CMLR 11.

57. OJ 1985 L 217/25.

58. OJ 1974 C 13/1.

59. OJ 1976 C 34/2.

60. OJ 1983 C 184/12.

61. Case 149/77 *Defrenne* v *Sabena (No. 3)* [1978] ECR 1365.

62. Op. cit. (note 56) at p. 19.

63. Op. cit. (note 56) at para. 28.

64. Simmonds, K. 'The concertation of Community migration policy' (1988) 25 *Common Market Law Review* 177.

65. By the end of 1990 there was still no common Community visa policy and in an official

statement released by the EC ministers concerned with immigration on 13 December 1990, it was noted that nationals of 55 countries required visas to enter the EC member states. For an update, see EC Commission Background Report, *Immigration and Asylum*, ISEC/B6/92.

66. Denmark was unable to sign the convention due to imminent political elections. Non-EC migrants issues are dealt with by working sub-groups working in secret, in particular the Trevi and Immigration groups, which meet approximately every six months to assist in the development of EPC decision-making.

67. OJ 1977 C 103/1.

68. Case 78/85 *Group of the European Right* v *European Parliament* [1986] ECR 1753.

69. European Parliament *Committee of Inquiry into the Rise of Fascism and Racism in Europe* (December 1985). A further inquiry was carried out and published in 1990 with Mr G. Ford MEP as rapporteur: *Report Drawn Up on Behalf of the Committee of Inquiry into Racism and Xenophobia* (European Parliament documents A3–195/90 series A PE 141 205/final). Although controversy surrounded the parliamentary debate on the report it was accepted by the European Parliament on 16 October 1990. See 'Britain blamed by EC for "export of skinhead racism" ' *The Independent* (9 October 1990).

70. OJ 1986 C 69/40.

71. OJ 1990 C 157/1.

72. Johal, J. (ed.) *1992 and the Black Community: A Campaigning Report* (Leeds, Kaamyabi, 1989). Reports on local authority activities can be obtained from LARRIE, 35 Great Smith Street, London SW1P 3RJ.

9

Private Activities and Personal Autonomy: At the Margins of Anti-discrimination Law

John Gardner

I

It is often said that social life in the post-industrial nations of the West is fragmented into three discrete spheres. In Roberto Unger's words, we live by

> a particular ideal of democracy for the state and citizenship, . . .
> a picture of private community in the domain of family and friend-
> ship, and . . . an amalgam of contract and impersonal technical
> hierarchy in the everyday realm of work and exchange.[1]

This frequently noted separation of 'the state', 'the family' and 'the market' is invariably ascribed to the triumph of liberalism in Western political culture. The liberal tradition, it is said, held out the promise that people would be emancipated from pervasive hierarchical structures. Political influence, wealth, and standing in the community would no longer automatically go hand in hand, because each would be kept in a sphere of its own. Moreover, the norms of each sphere would be, in their own special way, sensitive to people's choices. We would all be able to express political choices through the ballot box, economic choices through the invisible hand of market forces and personal choices through a spontaneous and informal mode of community life. All in all, citizens would be to a greater extent the authors of their own lives.

But the liberal tradition, many critics now argue, has turned out to be incapable of honouring this liberating promise, and the three-way fragmentation of social life is precisely what gets in the way. We have only to look, the critics say, at legal doctrine in Britain or the United States. Legislatures and judges often speak of the need to respect 'private' activities, and seem to treat this as a reason for refusing to intervene in various economic transactions and personal relationships. So long as a particular economic transaction has a 'market' cast, it seems to be consigned unquestioningly to a sphere in which government has no proactive role to play. Here, government merely *reacts* to what it sees as the parties' own market choices, offering them a handy law of contract by means of which to back up those choices if need be. Meanwhile, if a particular relationship seems to fit into the 'family' mould, then there is a marked allergy to government intervention of any kind, proactive or reactive. People's choices here are thought not to be the law's business at all. Law is really a weapon of the 'state' sphere only. Economic and personal activities are generally assumed to be organized so that they can look after themselves. This has the practical result, however, that there are no institutional channels through which liberal citizens can call into question the long-established patterns of domination which are internal to such activities. Liberal political principles disable themselves from reaching into two-thirds of the liberal social world. And most of the domination which stops people from being authors of their own lives is situated, in today's world, in the unregulated two-thirds. This is why liberalism cannot honour its own liberating promise. Liberal law erects what we might call 'privacy barriers' in its own path.[2]

Unger relies on the United States constitutional doctrine of 'equal protection' to substantiate his version of this critique. He sets a lot of store by the fact that a complaint of race or gender discrimination under the equal protection doctrine is available only where the discriminatory conduct in question amounted to 'state action'. The point, he says,

> is to limit the constitutional constraint upon legislative freedom to the instances of disadvantage that governmental rather than private power helps to uphold. This provides a . . . chance to ward off the danger that equal protection review might be used to turn society upside down and to disrupt the institutional logic of the constitution.[3]

At first sight Unger could scarcely have chosen a worse example to bear out his argument than the example of equal protection doctrine. It is true that the United States Constitution regulates state action only. But the Constitution is not the only American legal mechanism for dealing with race and gender discrimination. The Civil Rights Act 1964 explicitly extends analogous protections to many of those who suffer race and gender discrimination at the hands of non-governmental institutions and individuals. If the state-action requirement under the Constitution can tell in favour of Unger's critique, then the absence of a state-action requirement under the Civil Rights Act can presumably tell against it. Nor is the Civil Rights Act an unusual piece of legislation by the standards of Western post-industrial nations. Britain, Canada, Australia and many continental European jurisdictions have more or less equivalent legislative packages, penetrating well beyond state action. Perhaps there are areas of the law in which the privacy barriers stand firm. But it looks as if the area of law dealing with race and gender discrimination cannot possibly be one of them. Or is this appearance deceptive?

II

The British legislation is fairly typical in its scope. Roughly speaking, race or gender discrimination is unlawful if it is perpetrated by an employer or trade union, by someone who is letting premises, by someone who is providing education or by someone who is supplying goods, facilities or services. At first sight, most of these regulated relationships and activities seem to belong firmly in the economic or market sphere if they belong in any sphere at all. There is little obvious sign, meanwhile, of legislative intrusion into the relationships and activities which we tend to describe as *personal*. What we have here, perhaps, is legislation which breaches one privacy barrier, transforming the market into a public sphere fit for proactive legal reorganization, but nevertheless comes to a halt at the second privacy barrier, accepting as unimpeachable whatever has the hallmarks of a genuine personal relationship.

Such a picture of the legislative scheme was painted by the House of Lords in the 1973 case of *Charter* v *Race Relations Board*.[4] The case concerned section 2 of the Race Relations Act 1968, retained in the 1976 Act as section 20, and applied to gender discrimination by section 29 of the Sex Discrimination Act 1975. The section makes it unlawful for those who are concerned with providing goods, facilities or services 'to the public or a section of the public' to discriminate in the course of doing so. In *Charter*, the House of Lords held that the phrase 'to the public or a section of the public' had a limiting function, namely to exclude from the scope of the Act any provision of goods, facilities or services which was 'of a purely private character'.[5] On this basis, the House took the view that a Conservative Club, admission to which was by 'personal selection' and which met in 'private premises', was not providing any of its facilities or services to 'the public or a section of the public', so that its refusal to admit black people was not unlawful discrimination.

In an important passage in *Charter*, Lord Simon outlined what he took to be the philosophical rationale for the presence of these limiting words in the legislation:

> We all have, we hope, a spark of unique personality. But every one of us plays a number of roles in life. We are children, husbands or wives, mothers or fathers, members of some association, passengers in a bus, cinema-goers, workers with varying status in industry or commerce or profession, adherents of a religious denomination, Parliamentary or local government electors, nationals of a state, together with countless other personae in the course of a lifetime—many in the course of a day—some, indeed, simultaneously. Certain of these roles lie in the public domain; others in the private or domestic. When the draftsman used the words 'provision to the public or a section of the public', he was contemplating, I think, provision to persons aggregated in one or other of their public roles.[6]

Being a member of a club counts as a role which lies in Lord Simon's 'private or domestic' realm so long as there is 'personal selection of members with a view to their common acceptability'.[7] There are echoes of this division in all of the judgments, including the dissenting judgment of Lord Morris. For these purposes, apparently, relationships and activities which have a commercial flavour are to be treated as public rather than private. Admitting new members automatically on payment of a fee, for example, would not be enough to turn member-ships of a club into a private role in Lord Simon's sense. This would not be personal selection.[8]

The personal selection test from *Charter* was applied, to interesting effect, in *Applin* v *Race Relations Board* a year later.[9] A couple had a long-standing arrangement with a local authority, whereby children were placed in their home as foster children for short periods. At any one time, they would be looking after four or five such children. They never discriminated against black children, but National Front activists tried to incite them to do so. The question before the House of Lords, in an action against the activists, was whether discrimination by the foster parents would have been unlawful had the incitement proved successful. The House answered in the affirmative, on the ground that there was no personal selection of the children by the foster parents. They took all the children who were sent to them, and thus the children constituted 'a section of the public' for the purposes of the 1968 Act. Lord Reid said that, in his view, 'an ordinary family' would not have fallen within the scope of section 2, but this was no ordinary family. Indeed this was not even a 'private household'—it was an institution which had been well and truly extended into the public domain by virtue of its non-selectivity.[10] So race discrimination would have been unlawful had it ever been practised by the foster parents.

These cases actually bear out many of the concerns voiced by Unger and his fellow critics. In the first place, once an activity or relationship is classified as 'private', then it is evidently conceived to be self-sufficient and self-justifying from beginning to end. Its norms cannot properly be subjected to scrutiny according to the norms of the public sphere, to which the norms embodied in legislation against discrimination belong. In the second place, the question of whether a particular activity or relationship is to count as 'private', so as to benefit from this abstention, is settled by looking at the procedures by which it is initiated, and asking whether these are procedures which are typical of 'private' activities and relationships. There is more than a hint of circularity here. The truth is, as Lord Reid's remarks make clear, that 'ordinary families' and 'private households' are taken to embody the paradigm 'private' activities and relationships. By persistently admitting people to and excluding people from one's facilities and services according to one's personal tastes and prejudices— by acting as a traditional *paterfamilias* would—one makes it less likely, rather than more likely, that one's practice of excluding black people according to one's discriminatory tastes and prejudices will prove to be unlawful. By traditionally selecting according to preference, one grants oneself liberty to select according to preference. By conforming to the established family way of doing things, one benefits from the privacy barrier, and exempts oneself from anti-discrimination norms altogether.

It seems unlikely that such considerations, worrying though they may be, were at the front of many parliamentary minds during the passage of the 1976 Act. Nevertheless, specific provisions were added to the Act in order to ensure that neither *Charter* nor *Applin* could have been decided the same way after 1976. This was not done by eliminating the 'public or a section of the public' requirement in the goods, facilities and services provision. Section 20 of the 1976 Act virtually reproduces section 2 of the 1968 Act. Nor was the 'personal selection' test excised as a way of interpreting the 'public or a section of the public' requirement. Instead, new sections were inserted to deal specifically with members' clubs and fostering arrangements. Those members' clubs which *Charter* excluded as not being open to 'the public or a section of the public' have been brought within the scope of the legislation by section 25 of the 1976 Act, so long as they have a membership of 25 or more. Section 23(2), meanwhile, provides that the section 20 prohibition on discrimination will not extend to

> anything done by a person as a participant in arrangements under which he (for reward or not) takes into his home, and treats as if they were members of his family, children, elderly persons, or persons requiring a special degree of care and attention.

In the result, the personal selection test no longer has significant practical consequences. The relationships and activities in which it made sense to apply it are now, for the most part, treated separately.

There happens to be a perfectly good reason why the 1976 reforms concerning the scope of the race discrimination legislation should have paid attention to particular relationships, rather than attempting to come up with a general ruling to supplant the *Charter* personal selection test. Some relationships and activities are more likely than others to be distorted or damaged by the fact that they have been directed from outside, engineered by some non-participant with influence over the participants. We could call these 'direction-sensitive' relationships and activities, using 'sensitive' in the strong sense in which medics use it when a patient is said to be 'sensitive to penicillin'. The most direction-sensitive relationships and activities in any society are the ones which have come to be identified most closely with spontaneity and self-expression. Making these subject to any significant degree of directive intervention will tend to upset their balance. The upset may occur at two levels. First, particular instances of such relationships and activities may well be tainted. A woman who has had a child only under pressure from her partner, for example, may well find that her relationship with her child is strained or ambivalent for this reason. Second, if such relationships and activities come to be associated with directive interventions, their character may be radically and comprehensively altered. They may no longer stand for the spontaneity and self-expression which they previously stood for. If the practice of arranging marriages were to enjoy a general renaissance in British culture, for instance, then marriage would become a very different institution from the one which we have come to know over the last hundred years. It would not be the same relationship with a different mode of instigation, because the mode of instigation is partly constitutive of the relationship. The widespread introduction of a directive element into the selection of marriage partners would destroy marriage as we now understand it, and replace it with a new social form sharing the same name.[11]

Of course, it might be a good thing if certain relationships, and the social forms which support them, were to be undermined. If they happen to be valueless, for example, we have reason to work towards replacing them, and if they are valuable but with attendant disadvantages, we have reason to try to improve upon them. But one has to have an eye to the place which any replacement social form will occupy in society as a whole. It may be that we could indeed improve the institution of marriage, taken on its own, by introducing a new directive element in its instigation, and perhaps then particular marriages would also be better relationships, being very different relationships. This is not, however, the only problem of value we have to contend with. We might improve marriage, but fail to improve social life as a whole. This is because we live in a society in which it is impossible to lead a fulfilling life without personal autonomy, and people do not enjoy personal autonomy unless, among other things, they can choose the path of their lives from among a reasonably wide range of valuable options. Many of those options, of course, may be supported by social forms which are not particularly direction-sensitive. A priest's move to a particular parish or a soldier's embarkation upon a particular tour of duty can be brought about by orders from superiors without in any way distorting the relationships which ensue, or breaking away from the social forms of priesthood or soldiering. But it seems certain that at least *some* activities and relationships which proceed from spontaneity and self-expression must be among the valuable options which are available in a society if the members of that society are to lead autonomous lives. A society in which every path one can choose is hedged about with rules and regulations is not a society which is particularly conducive to personal autonomy. There is insufficient variety among the admittedly numerous options.

Moreover, relationships which proceed from spontaneity and self-expression are in practice more likely than others to be adaptable at the margins, yielding new subsidiary social forms, and thus nourishing personal autonomy indirectly over time. The social form supporting the cohabitation relationship, for example, has developed from the social form supporting the marriage relationship just because of the shift from an externally directed relationship called marriage to a spontaneous and self-expressive relationship by the same name. So while we might turn marriage into a better institution, considered on its own, by adding a directive element to its instigation, we might nevertheless be diminishing the quality of social life as a whole, both by compressing the variety of options and by stunting their subsequent development. In a liberal society, where personal autonomy is of such great importance, the availability of admittedly imperfect spontaneous and self-expressive relationships is undoubtedly better than the availability of no spontaneous and self-expressive relationships at all. And this, let's face it, is the immediate choice. Alternative social forms which will support spontaneous and self-expressive relationships really cannot be brought into being by decree. That runs counter to their nature. They have to develop gradually from the ones we already have.

Now, I have argued elsewhere that our legislation against race and gender discrimination is justified by the role which it plays in enhancing the personal autonomy of people in our society.[12] It opens up valuable options to people who have previously had few, and helps people to take pride in their identities, both of which are essential if they are to lead autonomous lives. The coercive intervention involved in such legislation is justified by the harm principle, understood as the principle that the state may only prohibit activities which destroy personal autonomy and may only enjoin activities which enhance personal autonomy. The prohibition in section 20 of the Race Relations Act is no exception. Access to a reasonable range of goods, facilities and services, like access to a reasonable range of employment opportunities, is essential for those who are to lead autonomous lives in our society. Moreover, exclusion from a swimming pool or beach or bus, as black South Africans will surely testify, is liable to threaten one's pride in identity just as exclusion from a particular job does. Both as a refusal to open up options and as an attack on self-respect, race discrimination in section 20 situations may generally be prohibited by virtue of the liberal harm principle. And yet, there may obviously be situations in which the enforcement of such autonomy-based duties will be counterproductive from the perspective of personal autonomy itself. Legal regulation of race or gender discrimination, in the context of certain activities and relationships, may do serious institutional harm, depleting or skewing the society's general stock of autonomy-enhancing social forms, leaving too little space for truly spontaneous and self-expressive activities and relationships, destroying more personal autonomy than it creates.[13]

Activities and relationships which are peculiarly direction-sensitive in the sense that we have been discussing do not really have much in common with one another apart from their general association with spontaneity and self-expression. They are not exclusively, or even typically, the kinds of activities and relationships which Lord Simon had in mind when he spoke of the roles which lie in the 'private or domestic' domain. Marrying, cohabiting, and bringing up children are doubtless among the relevant activities and relationships, but voting in a central or local government election is another, and writing a novel is yet another. The fact that someone is dictating what the subject matter or length or readership of a novel will be makes for a bad novel, and the general introduction of such constraints presages the replacement of the novel as a literary form with some new, less spontaneous and less self-expressive, genre. Likewise, direction in one's choice of candidate in elections taints the relationship between voters and governments, and, were it to become current here, would amount to the overthrow of an important political form, the purely self-expressive secret ballot, which has become the centrepiece of our system of government.

Conversely, there are plenty of activities and relationships which tend to be described as 'private' or 'personal' in ordinary conversation, but which are not threatened in any way by the fact that their inception or development is in some respects subject to external direction. Club committee-rooms, for example, are the natural habitat of countless rules and regulations, often imposed by long-dead officers, and there is no reason of principle why the addition of one or two more should make any difference, just as such, to the nature of 'the club' as a social form. Employment in a 'private household' is another example. Lord Simon in *Charter* and Lord Reid in *Applin* both buttressed their view that the Race Relations Act presupposed a social life divided into a 'public' sphere and a 'private or domestic' sphere by pointing out that the employment provisions of the 1968 act did not extend to employment in a 'private household'. It is hardly surprising that the European Court ultimately disapproved section 6(3) of the Sex Discrimination Act 1975, which contained an identical exemption for household employment, on the grounds that it was inconsistent with the philosophical foundations of the anti-discrimination principle.[14] For there is nothing peculiarly direction-sensitive about the relationship of employer and employee, wherever the employee happens to be doing the job. For the purposes of gender discrimination, the exemption has been pared down by section 1 of the Sex Discrimination Act 1986, so that it extends only to certain unusual employment relationships which are more like friendships, such as the relationship between a 'lady' and her 'companion'. Unfortunately, section 4(3) of the Race Relations Act 1976 has not been similarly pared down. But to be true to the liberal principles underlying the legislation, it really should be. The exemption should focus, like section 23(2), on a particular activity or relationship which happens to be highly direction-sensitive, rather than on some general 'sphere of social life'.

So it is perfectly understandable that the legislative response to *Charter* and *Applin* in 1976 should have been a piecemeal reversal, rather than a general canon of exemption to replace the House of Lords' personal selection test. The activities and relationships which ought to benefit from exemptions because subjecting them to external direction would threaten the culture of personal autonomy are a motley collection, and it would be difficult to bring them together under a general legal definition. There is no discrete 'social sphere' to which they all belong.

The case for exemption of highly direction-sensitive relationships and activities has limits, of course. They may go badly wrong, and harm their participants in various ways as a result. The considerations which I have mentioned militate in favour of certain exemptions in anti-discrimination legislation in order to give some such relationships and activities a general place in our social forms, and a chance to succeed in particular instances. This all presupposes that the relationships and activities are not themselves more harmful than beneficial. But of course, every activity and relationship has the potential to descend to that level. The reasons for exempting, say, foster parents from the legal duty not to discriminate on grounds of race when selecting a child for fostering do not necessarily extend to, say, allowing foster parents to racially abuse their foster child without any sanction. For this reason the fostering exemption in section 23(2) of the Race Relations Act 1976 ought perhaps to have been narrower, leaving room for race discrimination proceedings in some cases where black children are abused or maltreated by their foster parents on grounds of race. But astute local authorities will supply the sanction here by taking offending foster parents off their list. The main point is that one does not necessarily help the cause of personal autonomy by failing to deal with autonomy-damaging corruptions of those relationships which, in the name of personal autonomy, one declined to dictate or constrain when they had a chance of working. Lord Simon goes wrong in this respect when he supposes that 'private or domestic' roles remain 'private or domestic' from beginning to end. Some judges and politicians likewise go wrong in this respect when they decry legal involvement in domestic violence as an invasion of privacy. This privacy fetish evinces disrespect for the personal autonomy of those who suffer in horribly deformed versions of marriage or child-care. It does not by any stretch of the imagination serve liberal values.

III

This is not, of course, a complete answer to those who think that liberal political principles create spheres of impotence for themselves. These critics may accept my view that liberal political principles only exclude themselves from 'private or domestic' activities and relationships on a piecemeal basis, and even then not on the ground that they are 'private or domestic'. Out goes the main element of Lord Simon's picture of social life. They may also accept my claim that this piecemeal abstentionism, properly understood, has limits, in that the spontaneous and self-expressive relationships which have been given a chance to succeed may nevertheless fail miserably and fall to be wound up or reorganized by external direction. Out goes another aspect of Lord Simon's picture.

But the problem for liberal values, as many critics see it, is not specifically with failed marriages or failed cohabitations or failed anythings. The problem is with prevailing man-woman and parent-child relationships which, by the standards internal to the relevant social forms, are going along quite nicely. Having *some* such social forms to choose from, and being able to embark upon the corresponding relationships, may do wonders for personal autonomy. But women who are actually in the prevailing versions of these relationships, when they are going full steam, regularly find that their personal autonomy is compromised. Certainly, women may take pride in their identities as partners in such a relationship. The relationship may also open up many valuable options for women, as it does for men. But the patriarchal family also tends to close off whole classes of valuable options for women, which it generally does not do for men. And the ones that are closed off are mainly the ones which offer income, political power and recognition. The ones that remain, while certainly valuable, often go unrecognized and unpaid, and do not make for much political power. Overall, the prevailing man–woman and parent–child relationships may indeed create more personal autonomy than they destroy, and eliminating them might destroy more personal autonomy than it would create. But as things stand, women typically get the raw end of the deal. Does liberal anti-discrimination law offer any of its liberation here?

The answer is that it does. The less a person is autonomous, the stronger the reason to secure further autonomy for her. Anti-discrimination law reflects this fact, here as elsewhere, but in this case it does not do so by directly regulating the relationship in which the domination is primarily situated. Instead, the immediate strategy is to adjust other relationships and activities, both in particular instances and at the level of their supporting social forms, so as to open up a more adequate range of options to women living in patriarchal families. In other words, the strategy has not been to alter the *scope* of the Sex Discrimination Act to take it into women's relationships with their partners and their children, but to adjust the *responsiveness* of the Act within its existing scope. This strategy reflects the fact that relationships within married and unmarried couples, and their relationships with their children, are peculiarly direction-sensitive, while many of the valuable options, access to which would enhance women's personal autonomy, involve activities and relationships which are not particularly direction-sensitive, and can often be constructively realigned, albeit gradually, by well-aimed shots of external direction.

The responsiveness of the Sex Discrimination Act is dictated, of course, by the definition of 'discrimination' on the basis of which it proceeds. In Britain, as in many of the other jurisdictions with similar legislation, the definition is bifurcated. Some unlawful discrimination is direct discrimination, under section 1(1)(a), which involves treating someone less favourably on grounds of their sex; and some is indirect discrimination, under section 1(1)(b), which involves applying a requirement or condition to somebody to his or her detriment, a requirement or condition with which he or she cannot comply, and with which fewer members of his or her sex than of the other sex can comply. The definitions are both phrased so that they apply equally to men and women. But it does not follow that the legislation must be unresponsive to the gender imbalance of patriarchal power.

In fact, judicial constructions of the indirect discrimination limb have often been quite sensitive to the very real constraints placed upon women's access to options by their so-called 'family responsibilities'. In the first place, the words 'can comply' and 'cannot comply' in section 1(1)(b) have been read so as to recognize that people who are not being literally coerced or manipulated may nevertheless be unable to comply with certain requirements or conditions because of their circumstances, including obstacles placed in their way by prevailing social forms. In *Price* v *Civil Service Commission*,[15] decided soon after the legislation was brought into force, the Employment Appeal Tribunal held that an upper age limit for executive officer recruits in the Civil Service was unlawfully discriminatory, on the grounds that women are often delayed in their career moves by time taken to rear children, a factor which affects men's careers far less often. The question, Phillips J recognized, was not whether women could have chosen not to have or bring up their children, and so could have complied in theory. The question was whether they could comply in practice with the requirement or condition that they be younger than 28 when applying for the job. The approach has been approved without reservation by the House of Lords,[16] is closely mirrored in European Community law,[17] and the same considerations have been effective to transform some kinds of discrimination against part-time workers in both recruitment and redundancy procedures into unlawful indirect discrimination against women.[18]

Again, the 'pool' of men and women within which the comparison of respective ability to comply is made has typically been adjusted by judges to make sure that the adverse impact of a particular requirement or condition is not hidden from view. For example, where a government department set a requirement that single parents with dependent children must once have been married in order to qualify for a hardship study grant, J. Schiemann refused to do the calculation by asking what proportion of 'male studying single parents with dependent children' had once been married, then asking what proportion of 'female studying single parents with dependent children' had once been married, and comparing the results. This way of doing the calculation would have failed to take into account the fact that, as a rule, mothers rather than fathers have the job of looking after children in our society. Instead he compared the proportion of 'male studying parents with dependent children' who were single and had once been married with the proportion of 'female studying parents with dependent children' who were single and had once been married. This, he observed, showed that women were much more likely than men to be single parents with dependent children, and were thus much more likely in practice to be adversely affected by the requirement.[19]

These are, of course, selected highlights. There are a number of issues, notably pregnancy discrimination, on which the law has proved totally unsatisfactory.[20] And we should not forget that the cumbersome tribunal procedures and meagre compensation awards associated with the Sex Discrimination Act and Race Relations Act are not exactly conducive to speedy progress in the adjustment of any social forms. Still, the selected highlights do show how readily liberal principles can take the fact of women's disempowerment on board. The frequently expressed view that liberalism cannot take account of patriarchal power is based on a serious misreading of the ideal of personal autonomy. It is true that the ideal of personal autonomy is hostile to coercion and manipulation in ways in which it is not hostile to other kinds of power. Coercion and manipulation have a special symbolic status in liberal societies. This is why the fact that we cannot lead valuable lives without personal autonomy generates the harm principle, which is meant to limit the availability of coercion and manipulation in our society to situations where personal autonomy itself is at stake. But the hostility to coercion and manipulation is not all that there is to personal autonomy. What personal autonomy requires, as we already know, is that one have access to a wide range of valuable options and pride in one's identity. Having access to a wide range of valuable options is not the same as being free of coercion or manipulation.[21] One may have access to a wide range of valuable options, but be coerced or manipulated not to pursue a particular one of them. One may be free of coercion and manipulation, but nevertheless lack access to a wide range of valuable options. This is because whether one lacks access to a wide range of valuable options depends on the structure of one's environment in many diverse ways. It depends on whether one is properly educated, whether one is supplied with enough information, whether one has adequate material resources, whether there are enough compatibilities and enough incompatibilities between the social forms by reference to which one formulates one's goals and develops one's identity, and so on. So the requirement of access to options is sensitive to countless power structures which fall short of being structures of coercion and manipulation. It is a myth that liberal political principles can only get to grips with really crude kinds of power.

But surely this kind of 'getting to grips' is merely tinkering with a few of the more obvious symptoms of patriarchy, rather than tackling the disease itself? Those who would raise this objection are bewitched by their own picture of social life as fragmented into discrete social spheres. Changes in working practices and education arrangements are precisely the kind of changes which will, over time, have an impact on the structure of man–woman and parent–child relationships. Social forms are interdependent to a considerable degree. By changing some of them directly, we are more than likely to alter many others indirectly. Arranging work and education in novel ways will change the expectations which men and women have of their own lives and of each other's lives, and thus ultimately the structure of all of their relationships.

Of course, these changes are difficult to predict exactly, and even more difficult to control. However, even when its coercive force is directed elsewhere, the law may be helping to guide the general direction of such changes. While accepting the facts about women's disempowerment, for example, the courts may nevertheless work against the patriarchy-reinforcing idea that those facts are necessary or natural. In *Horsey* v *Dyfed County Council*, for example, a woman applied to her employer to be sent on a training course in another part of the country, nearer to her husband's place of work. The application was turned down because the employer took the view that, once she had moved nearer to her husband for a while, the woman would not move back to her normal place of work again.[22] The Employment Appeal Tribunal held that the decision was based on an assumption that women generally follow their husband's career moves, but not *vice versa*. Treating a woman less favourably because one has a stereotyped view of how women will behave in certain situations, the tribunal went on, is simply treating that woman less favourably on ground of her sex, and thus amounts to direct discrimination within the meaning of section 1(1)(a) of the 1975 Act.

The same result would follow if an employer refused a woman some employment benefit on the ground that he assumed she would in the end only be available to work part-time. This yields the interesting result that an employer must often take into account, in designing his

employment practices, the fact that many women are unable in practice
to work full-time (the indirect discrimination provisions so require), but
he must not take into account the fact that many women are unable in
practice to work full-time as a reason for rejecting or disadvantaging a
particular woman relative to a man (for this offends against the direct
discrimination provisions). Odd as it sounds, this makes perfectly good
sense. Recognizing the *general* fact is a necessary step in reorganizing
working practices to assist in the strengthening of women's personal
autonomy. But the assumption that a *particular* woman is affected by the
relevant impediments to personal autonomy elevates those impediments
to the status of antecedently given, inevitable aspects of womanhood.
This elevation tends to legitimate the impediments themselves, reinforcing partriarchy and retarding rather than enhancing women's personal
autonomy. This is why the law steps in.

There is no abstentionism here. On the other hand, there is no
attempt to force prevailing man–woman or parent–child relationships
directly into a new mould. That would almost certainly be destructive.
There is direct coercion of an employment relationship — direct coercion, part of the justification for which is that, by means of the coercion,
we may be able to have an indirect promotional effect upon the structure
of the patriarchal family.

IV

Are there analogous dynamics in the law of race discrimination? For at
least one purpose, the courts have treated the power of ethnic customs
and traditions as analogous to patriarchal power. Just as many women
cannot comply in practice with requirements or conditions as to age
or full-time working, so the House of Lords has held that a male Sikh
cannot comply in practice with a requirement that he remove his turban
at school.[23] This is meant to allow Sikhs access to an adequate range of
options without having to compromise their pride in their identities as
Sikhs. It seems clear, however, that the courts would face some difficulties if they were required to push the analogy between ethnic customs
and traditions and patriarchal impediments to its logical conclusion.
The courts have, after all, been at pains to promote the message that
powerlessness is not a natural or necessary aspect of womanhood. They
are far less confident when it comes to promoting a message about the
naturalness or necessity of ethnic traditions and customs. One has only
to compare the courts' treatment of benign 'courtesy' measures taken

towards women in the workplace with their discussions of whether employers should implement measures which pay benign 'respect' to ethnic sensibilities. The former measures are directly discriminatory, but it is rarely mooted that the latter might fall into the same category.[24] The message in the gender cases is the valuable one that women's traditional role as an object of male protection is not natural or necessary; but the message in the race cases is kept away from any such denial of naturalness or necessity.

We should not be surprised to find that ethnic customs and traditions raise special problems of their own here. The courts are, of course, perfectly aware that such customs and traditions may sometimes pose a threat to the personal autonomy of those who are subject to them. The nature of the threat would be more obvious if the garment in question were a yashmak rather than a turban. Then it would itself stand for strong patriarchal power entrenched in an ethnic tradition, tied to a significant risk that access to an adequate range of options will be denied. But the courts and tribunals have to be alive to the possibility that there might remain sub-cultures, even within a liberal society, in which personal autonomy is not an essential component of the good life. The Rushdie affair has drawn popular attention to just such a sub-culture. It is not clear that sub-cultures of this kind are sustainable in the long run, because personal autonomy is such a pervasive concern in society at large, and it has proved itself to be an infectious ideal. But in the meantime, courts are understandably reluctant to go about invalidating the internal power structures of such sub-cultures. Here it seems safer to adjust the legal strategy to accommodate such power structures. The law can take a stronger line on the disempowerment of women within the dominant liberal culture because it is now much too late for the argument that women who belong to that culture can enjoy the good life without personal autonomy. They clearly cannot. The evolution of indigenous social forms in the last two hundred years or so has ruled out any viable alternatives.

V

The distinctively liberal strategies for dealing with the autonomy-damaging aspects of patriarchal power can only work, of course, if the relevant coercive interventions in employment practices and the like are more than merely cosmetic. We assumed at the outset that the British legislation against discrimination has no real problems at the first of the supposed privacy barriers, namely the barrier between the state and the market. We made this assumption because market relationships and activities, such as employment and trade, seem to take up most of the scope of the legislation. Our discussion of the responsiveness of the legislation — particularly as regards the concept of indirect discrimination — seems to lend weight to the view that this is liberal legislation which sanctions a comprehensive re-examination of orthodox market behaviour. But there is a catch here, and it has the potential to blunt the responsiveness of the anti-discrimination legislation considerably.

The catch has been brought to the surface by *Rainey* v *Greater Glasgow Health Board*.[25] In 1979 the respondent health board was required by the government to change its arrangements so that prosthetics fittings were provided in-house rather than being contracted out. The only way to get the service going at that time was to recruit *en bloc* the prosthetists who had hitherto been working in the contracted-out service, all of whom were men. But those prosthetists had hitherto been paid at private-sector rates, rather than at the lower public-sector rates. The only way to be sure of attracting them was to offer to continue paying them at private-sector rates. Subsequently, other prosthetists, who had not worked in the private sector, were recruited at the normal public-sector rates of pay. One of these recruits, a woman, brought an action under the Equal Pay Act 1971 claiming to be entitled to equal pay with a man of similar experience who had been recruited from the private sector at a higher rate of pay. The House of Lords held that there was a 'material difference' between the woman's case and the man's, which would justify the inequality of pay under subsection 1(3) of the 1971 Act. Lord Keith, with whom the other lords concurred, said that 'a difference which is connected with economic factors affecting the efficient carrying on of the employer's business' can be a 'material difference'.[26] It can also, and this ties back in with our discussion, yield a 'justifiability' defence under section 1(1)(b) of the Sex Discrimination Act 1975 or section 1(1)(b) of the Race Relations Act 1976, which define indirect discrimination.

This decision can be presented as having elevated 'economic factors' to a discrete sphere of activity, governed by its own internal norms, and unassailable by any other standards. If the market indicates that one should pay a certain price or implement a certain practice, then one may pay that price or implement that practice regardless of any other considerations. Of course, if one may justify discriminatory practices in these terms, then the anti-discrimination legislation gives with one hand and takes away with the other. It grants women new options by altering working arrangements, but only if these are economically attractive to employers. One way to make an arrangement economically attractive is to hire women to do it, since women typically have fewer viable options than men, and therefore cannot afford to turn work down when it is offered to suit their 'family responsibilities'. Homeworking in the clothing trade is an example. A special class of 'women's work' is preserved, which fails to supply the personal autonomy which the availability of alternative working patterns is supposed to precipitate. As it stands, part-time work very often belongs to the same category. It is often so exploitative that ensuring its availability to women almost seems to add insult to injury. The range of options remains too narrow, the possibility of enhanced pride in identity is undercut by the low status of the work and the whole patriarchal matrix is indirectly reinforced by the perpetuation of the myth that womanhood must occupy certain natural and necessary subordinate roles. So much for the great liberal legislative programme. It turns out to be largely abstentionist in relation to the very institution which it primarily claims to regulate.

But the accusation of 'abstentionism' involves a gross exaggeration of what *Rainey* stands for. The House of Lords was trying to implement the jurisprudence of the European Court, which sets explicit limits to the use of market forces as justifications. The factors pleaded in justification must themselves be 'unrelated to any sex discrimination', and the measures adopted must 'correspond to a real need' on the part of the employer's undertaking.[27] The second consideration evidently tips the balance away from mere convenience, or preference, and in the case of a solvent enterprise, from marginal profitability. The first consideration, meanwhile, rules out arguments in which the cheapness of women *qua* women is used as the basis for justification, for this is a directly discriminatory justification. It may also rule out justifications which are indirectly discriminatory under certain conditions. Even if European law does not go this far, there is strong House of Lords authority to the effect that indirectly discriminatory justifications are unavailable under section 1(1)(b) of the Race Relations Act if there is a 'close relation' between the criteria of selection on the one hand and race or nationality on the other.[28] In any case, the extent of the indirectly discriminatory effect of the requirement or condition itself is one factor which bears on the burden of justification.[29] The decision in *Rainey* is perfectly consistent with all of this. There is no sense in which the norms of the market are viewed as being exempt from scrutiny just as such.[30]

So anti-discrimination law need not stop at the provision of more flexible working arrangements at the margins of the labour market. Anti-discrimination law can also do its bit, even in the light of *Rainey*, to bring such working arrangements in from the exploitative margins, to ease them into the perceived mainstream of work options. Of course, it cannot bring about a headlong rush towards the demarginalization of part-time work, homework and so on. It cannot ignore countervailing considerations which are specific to particular cases, such as the fact that a heavy economic burden placed upon a given enterprise may lose many people their livelihoods, or may bring essential services to a standstill. But because the right not to suffer discrimination on grounds of gender *is* a right, not every countervailing consideration counts here. The effort to bring part-time work into the mainstream of work options prevails over marginal profitability considerations, inflation considerations and so on, which affect all enterprises. We have already borne all of these general factors in mind when arriving at the conclusion that there should be a right not to suffer discrimination in the first place. This is why the justifiability defence is restricted to non-discriminatory justifications involving a real need on the part of the enterprise.

Unfortunately, the market is a sufficiently organic construct that it is sometimes difficult to distinguish marginal profitability considerations from really urgent threats to the survival of an enterprise or the carrying on of its work. This is why the justifiability defence is not consistently applied from case to case, even when it is correctly interpreted.[31] However, the indirect discrimination provisions certainly do have it in them to work towards changes in the status and social role of 'marginal' modes of work hitherto dominated by women.[32] One hope is that, by de-marginalizing these modes of work, men will increasingly come to see the option of combining a working life with child-care responsibilities as a viable option for their own lives. And this is the real key to securing a social environment which is conducive to women's personal autonomy.

Of course, a great deal more could be said about the relationship between anti-discrimination law and the market. But the important point has been made. Anti-discrimination law, as it applies to 'private' employers, is not a reactive form of legislative intervention. It does not merely back up the internal norms of the market. Sometimes it is presented as if it does. Instances of race discrimination and gender discrimination are sometimes presented as instances of irrationality by market standards, failures of self-interest on the part of employers, traders and so on. But they are not cases of irrationality by market standards.[33] On the contrary, they are dictated by market standards. By market standards, women and black people are often cheaper to hire or to do business with than white men because they have fewer valuable options to choose from, and often, owing to their low pride in their own identities, lower expectations. This makes it rational, by market standards, to hire them or do business with them cheaply, which further reinforces their shortage of valuable options and further inhibits their pride in themselves. This shows why the market can only operate within certain limits in a society whose members must enjoy personal autonomy if they are to have fulfilling lives. We have stronger reason, in such a society, to secure more personal autonomy for those who have less, but markets tend to push in the opposite direction. A liberal society has to make proactive interventions to keep the market in check, and anti-discrimination law is one such intervention. It does not come up against a liberal privacy barrier around our economic transactions, any more than it comes up against such a privacy barrier around our homes and clubs. It makes carefully targeted strikes in both areas.

VI

In an important essay, Hugh Collins has documented the various ways in which modern private law makes proactive interventions in family and market transactions and relationships.[34] His argument shows how the privacy barriers erected in a previous phase of the common law's evolution have gradually been dismantled. The scope and responsiveness of anti-discrimination law fit well with this modern trend in contract law and tort law.

For Collins, however, the dismantling of these privacy barriers is associated with a rejection of traditional liberal values. He detects the emergence of a general 'communitarian' duty to respect the interests of others, a duty which

> substitutes closer bonds of social solidarity than those recognised by the ideal of private autonomy. . . . This transition in legal thought implicitly contains a rejection of the traditional liberal view that privacy is essential for human flourishing.[35]

By contrast, I have associated the absence of general privacy barriers in anti-discrimination law with the *ascendancy* of the liberal ideal, the ideal of personal autonomy. Can we both be right here?

Collins helpfully cites Isaiah Berlin's view of traditional liberal concerns. Berlin writes of the liberal commitment to

> a certain minimum areas of personal freedom which must on no account be violated; for if it is overstepped, the individual will find himself in an area too narrow for even that minimum development of his natural faculties which alone makes it possible to pursue, and

even to conceive, the various ends which men hold good or right or sacred. It follows that a frontier must be drawn between the area of private life and that of public authority.[36]

This passage mentions a liberal ideal and a strategy for furthering it. The ideal is of somebody who can conceive and pursue a variety of ends. The strategy is that of leaving parts of people's lives free from state intervention. The ideal is precisely the one which has been advocated in this essay. It is the ideal of personal autonomy, the ideal of a person who is, to a substantial degree, the author of his or her own life. On one reading of the strategy, I have endorsed that too. If it merely means that the state has authority to command some things and lacks authority to command others, then the strategy is supported whenever the harm principle is supported, as it is here. On another reading of the strategy, however, I have rejected it. I have rejected it if it means that there are private activities which can be identified in advance, and which are immune from legal intervention irrespective of their impact on particular people in particular cases. *Pace* Collins, I have suggested that this strategy has little to offer in furthering the ideal of personal autonomy, and should not be understood as a distinctively liberal strategy.[37] In reality, Collins' general 'communitarian' duty, which he contrasts with liberal concerns, is no more than a liberal autonomy-based duty. It is not surprising that Collins should call it 'communitarian', however. The liberal ideal has certain important and obvious communitarian dimensions. It requires a certain kind of common life, yielding a diversity of valuable and accessible social forms.

In the grand scheme of things, it may not be worth quibbling about who is a liberal and who is not. It matters here only because we began with an allegation against the liberal political tradition, namely that it cannot honour its own liberating promise because liberal law erects privacy barriers. We have now seen that this allegation is spurious, at least in relation to liberal anti-discrimination law. This is not to say that liberalism has already honoured its liberating promise — its promise of self-authorship — in relation to women and black people. On the contrary, many years after the implementation of anti-discrimination legislation in Britain, the United States and other post-industrial societies, women and black people are still very much less likely than white men to lead ideally autonomous lives in any of the societies in question. But this is not because of any pervasive deficiency in the liberal approach to law-making, or even in the anti-discrimination legislation in particular. It is a result of the impotence of law *tout court*.

Law is a blunt tool, which destroys more readily than it creates. The social forms which are the source of the value in our lives are delicately shaped over time, whatever their defects. There is no quick way to get them into perfect shape, although the less direction-sensitive among them can be nudged by legal means in order to get some sort of gradual adjustment underway. It is easy to understand the frustrations of those critics who see the whole business as excessively protracted. But they waste their energy in criticizing law just for being the way law necessarily is. They would be better employed arguing for improved government expenditure to increase the momentum of change. Even then, of course, they should not expect any rapid transformations.[38]

NOTES

1. Unger, R. *The Critical Legal Studies Movement* (Cambridge, Mass., Harvard University Press, 1986) p. 17.

2. For arguments along these lines, see Unger op. cit. (note 1) pp. 17–42; Walzer, M. 'Liberalism and the art of separation' (1984) 12 *Political Theory* 315; Bowles, S. and Gintis, H. *Democracy and Capitalism* (New York, Basic Books, 1986) pp. 92–120; Pateman, C. 'Feminist critiques of the public/private dichotomy' in Phillips, A. (ed.) *Feminism and Equality* (Oxford, Basil Blackwell, 1987) p. 103.

3. Unger op. cit. (note 1) p. 45.

4. [1973] 1 All ER 512 (HL).

5. Ibid., per Lord Reid at 516.

6. Ibid. at 527.

7. Ibid. at 529.

8. See Lord Reid's remarks in *Docker's Labour Club* v *Race Relations Board* [1974] 3 ALL ER 592 (HL) at 595.

9. [1974] 2 All ER 73 (HL).

10. Ibid. at 77–78.

11. See Raz, J. *The Morality of Freedom* (Oxford, Oxford University Press, 1986) p. 392.

12. Gardner, J. 'Liberals and unlawful discrimination' (1989) 9 *Oxford Journal of Legal Studies* 1. I tried to build on the analysis of liberal social life offered by Raz in The Morality of Freedom op. cit. (note 11).

13. Although the liberal state may only use coercion if doing so will serve personal autonomy, it does not follow that the liberal state must *always* use coercion whenever doing so will serve personal autonomy. Sometimes, perfectionist considerations which are not autonomy-based will dictate that coercion ought not to be used to prevent a particular harm. Sometimes, for example, using coercion would destroy social forms which are valuable apart from their autonomy-enhancing nature, or even in spite of their autonomy-retarding nature. Generally, it is open to liberal governments to bear such considerations in mind when deciding what harms to respond to and what harms to ignore. Andrew Ashworth overlooks this point when he argues for a general symmetry between the criminal law relating to actions and the criminal law relating to omissions: Ashworth, A. 'The scope of criminal liability for omissions' (1989) 105 *Law Quarterly Review* 424. However, it seems to me that one of the effects of raising a certain principle to the status of a *fundamental right* in liberal societies is that non-autonomy-based countervailing considerations (*inter alia*) are excluded from the balance of considerations when the corresponding legal duties are fixed. Because the principle of freedom from discrimination on the grounds of race and gender has been elevated to status of a fundamental right — a fact to which numerous supra-national treaties testify — the exceptions which legislation against discrimination may legitimately contain are only those exceptions which reflect autonomy-based countervailing considerations.

Raz has recently suggested that the fact that governments in post-industrial societies are ill-adapted to dealing with matters of feeling and emotion provides a reason for keeping them out of family relations as a rule. See Raz, J. 'Liberalism, skepticism, and democracy' (1989) 74 *Iowa Law Review* 761 at 766–67. As a general perfectionist consideration, this is indeed important. Governments are sufficiently clumsy that they can destroy all sorts of value in the course of protecting personal autonomy. Nevertheless, *where a fundamental right is at stake*, this general perfectionist consideration must be left aside. There is no need to be particularly responsive to feeling and emotion in order to balance up only the autonomy-enhancing and the autonomy-threatening aspects of a family relationship. Post-industrial governments are no more ill-adapted to recognize the terrors of domestic violence than those of 'football' violence, nor are they more ill-adapted to deal with domestic sexual harassment than with workplace sexual harassment. Or rather, if they are ill-adapted, this is a result of their inertia rather than an essential feature of them.

14. Case 165/82 *Commission of the European Communities* v *United Kingdom* [1983] ECR 3431 (ECJ).

15. [1978] 1 All ER 1228 (EAT).

16. *Mandla* v *Dowell-Lee* [1983] 1 All ER 1062 (HL).

17. Case 170/84 *Bilka Kaufhaus GmbH* v *Weber von Hartz* [1986] ECR 1607 (ECJ).

18. *Clarke* v *Eley (IMI) Kynoch* [1982] IRLR 482 (EAT); *Home Office* v *Holmes* [1984] 3 All ER 549 (EAT). Of course, opening up part-time work options will be worthless if part-time workers are exploited, or have low social status as a matter of course. The role of anti-discrimination legislation in de-marginalizing part-time work is discussed in section 5 below.

19. *R* v *Secretary of State for Education ex parte Schaffter* [1987] IRLR 53 (HC). See also *Kidd* v *DRG (UK) Ltd* [1985] IRLR 190 (EAT), in which the specification of a revealing 'pool' was unfortunately teamed up with the fatuous ruling that *evidence* must be adduced for the proposition that unmarried mothers find it more difficult than other parents to take on full-time work.

20. See Lacey, N. 'Dismissal by reason of pregnancy' (1986) 15 *Industrial Law Journal* 43.

21. See Raz, J. op. cit. (note 11) pp. 377–78.

22. [1982] IRLR 395 (EAT).

23. *Mandla* v *Dowell-Lee* op. cit. (note 16).

24. Compare *Gill and Coote* v *El Vino* [1983] 1 All ER 398, with *Mandla* (note 16). Notice that the ban on 'courtesy' measures in the gender cases remains — quite correctly, in my view — even if all the women affected think that courtesy is essential to their womanhood.

25. [1987] 1 All ER 65 (HL).

26. Ibid. at 70.

27. *Bilka Kaufhaus GmbH* v *Weber von Hartz* op. cit. (note 17).

28. *Orphanos* v *Queen Mary College* [1985] 2 All ER 233 (HL).

29. Case 224/84 *Johnston* v *Chief Constable of the Royal Ulster Constabulary* [1986] 3 ECR 1651 (ECJ); *Singh* v *British Rail Engineering Ltd* [1986] ICR 22 (EAT).

30. In the United States, a 'business necessity' test of justification has been imposed: *Griggs* v *Duke Power* [1971] 401 US 424 SCt; *Albemarle Paper* v *Moody* [1975] 422 US 405 SCt. However, some courts have denied that market-based wage rates can be scrutinized under the *Griggs* test at all. In *AFSCME* v *Washington* 770 F. 2d 1401 (USCA 1985), at 1407, Judge Kennedy held that *Griggs* was irrelevant because 'neither law nor logic deems the free market system a suspect enterprise. Economic reality is that the value of a particular job to an employer is but one factor influencing the rate of compensation for that job'. If the point were taken to its conclusion, of course, there would be no space for any anti-discrimination law at all.

31. Consider, for example, Balcombe LJ's slippery approach to 'real need' in *Hampson* v *Department of Education and Science* [1990] 2 All ER 25 (CA). Consider, for example, *Enderby* v *Frenchay Health Authority* [1991] IRLR 44 (EAT). This *reductio ad absurdam* of *Rainey* has now been referred to the European Court of Justice by the Court of Appeal [1992] IRLR 15.

32. See, for instance, the recent European ruling in Case C–171/81 *Rinner-Kuhn* v *FWW Spezial-Gebäudereinigung GmbH and Co. KG* [1989] IRLR 493 (ECJ), on part-time workers, and the earlier British case of *Steel* v *Union of Post Office Workers* [1987] 2 All ER 504 (EAT), on temporary workers.

33. See Posner, R. *The Economics of Justice* (Cambridge, Mass., Harvard University Press, 1981) pp. 351–63.

34. Collins, H. 'The decline of privacy in private law' (1987) 14 *Journal of Law and Society* 91.

35. Ibid. at 102.

36. Berlin, I. 'Two concepts of liberty' in his *Four Essays on Liberty* (Oxford, Oxford University Press, 1969) p. 124.

37. The second strategy is sometimes associated with J. S. Mill. But Ten has shown that Mill did not regard any actions or classes of actions, still less any 'sphere of life', as automatically insulated against state intervention. He did not subscribe to an antecedently demarcated public/private distinction. He merely regarded certain reasons for action as improper reasons for state intervention (i.e. reasons not grounded in personal autonomy). See Ten, C. H. *Mill on Liberty* (Oxford, Oxford University Press, 1980) p. 62.

38. Excerpts from earlier drafts of this essay were read at a seminar in the University of Southampton and at the 1990 W. G. Hart Workshop at the Institute of Advanced Legal Studies, London. I am grateful to participants in both sessions for their illuminating comments. Derek Parfit, Stephen Shute and Jeremy Horder gave invaluable help at the final draft stage.

10

The Limits of Legal, Cultural and Religious Pluralism

Sebastian Poulter

INTRODUCTION

Recent years have witnessed an upsurge in the identification of many peoples with their particular ethnic groups or religious communities. An appreciation of their cultural heritage, a concern for the preservation of their distinctive customs and traditions and a commitment to maintain their deeply held values and beliefs has led them to stake out claims upon the wider polity for greater recognition of their ethnicity. This ethnic (and religious) revival appears to be a worldwide phenomenon, with numerous illustrations to be found in all five continents, of which the following is merely a small sample.

In Africa, the long wars recently fought by the Eritreans and Tigrayans in Ethiopia have received much publicity, but elsewhere ethnic rivalries often simmer just below the surface. In the Americas, the plight of the Indians in Brazil (and elsewhere) has led to concern about their very survival in the face of rapid economic development, while in the United States, Hispanics, blacks and others increasingly reject the old notion of a 'melting pot'. In Australasia, the celebration both of the bicentenary of white settlement in Australia in 1988 and of the 150th anniversary of the Treaty of Waitangi in New Zealand in 1990 have provided opportunities for aborigines and Maoris respectively to protest at the ways in which their cultures have been ignored or obliterated by the Crown. In Asia, there have been recent assertions of ethnicity by the Sikhs in India, by the Tamils in Sri Lanka, by the Kurds in the Middle East and by Muslim and Christian communities in Lebanon. In Europe the 1990s have witnessed the dramatic creation of several 'new' ethnic states as first Lithuania, Latvia and Estonia broke free from the USSR (shortly before its own collapse) and then Slovenia and Croatia seceded from Yugoslavia, precipitating that country's final disintegration. The conflict between Protestants and Catholics in Northern Ireland, of course, continues and there is no prospect of an early settlement of the divisions between Greek and Turkish Cypriots.

It is vital to come to terms with ethnic and cultural diversity in the modern world since there are now estimated to be at least four times as many ethnic groups as states,[1] and a majority of the latter are by no means ethnically homogeneous in character, possessing deep religious, linguistic and cultural divisions.[2] Probably only a very small proportion of ethnic groups actually wish to become politically independent; typically, such groups have a well-defined territorial base and have enjoyed the status of nationhood at some time in the past. Most ethnic groups strive instead for more limited objectives such as fair representation in decision-making bodies, an equitable share in natural resources, legal recognition of cultural traditions, religious freedom and language rights.

Britain's various ethnic minority communities now account for an estimated 2.75 to 3 million people (representing around 4.5 per cent of the population as a whole) and they are currently increasing at the rate of around 90,000 per annum, two-thirds of which is attributable to natural growth and one-third to net migration.[3] There are thought to be over a million Muslims living here and Judaism, Hinduism and Sikhism can probably each claim more than 300,000 adherents.[4] Recently, each of these four minorities has had cause to assert itself vigorously in protecting its fundamental values — Muslims over Salman Rushdie's book *The Satanic Verses*, Jews in relation to a threat to remove their special rights to religious slaughter of animals,[5] Hindus in respect of the denial by the planning authorities of general public worship at Bhaktivedanta Manor temple in Hertfordshire[6] and Sikhs over a new legal requirement that all workers on building sites must wear safety helmets.[7] Hence, while discrimination on the basis of colour remains widespread in this country, in many respects the most important characteristics of Britain's minority communities today are not so much the (predominantly) brown or black skins of their members but their adherence to certain customs, traditions, religious beliefs and value systems which are greatly at variance with those of the majority white community.

THE CONCEPT OF A MULTICULTURAL
BRITAIN

Modern Britain is often referred to in popular parlance as 'a multicultural society'. However, if this phrase is to be more than merely platitudinous, its underlying objectives in terms of social policy must be defined with some degree of clarity. It can be constructively employed to denote a general policy of respect for ethnic minority cultures (within certain very broad limits), coupled with a determination to promote equal opportunity for everyone and to eradicate all forms of discrimination based on race, religion or ethnic or national origin.[8] Such goals are not, of course, new. In 1966 when he was home secretary in the Labour Government, Roy (now Lord) Jenkins outlined precisely this target in a speech about integration, in which he commented:

> Integration is perhaps a rather loose word. I do not regard it as meaning the loss, by immigrants, of their own national characteristics and culture. I do not think we need in this country a melting pot, which will turn everybody out in a common mould, as one of a series of carbon copies of someone's misplaced vision of the stereotyped Englishman. . . . I define integration, therefore, not as a flattening process of assimilation but as equal opportunity, coupled with cultural diversity, in an atmosphere of mutual tolerance.[9]

In his view, if Britain were to be able to claim any sort of world reputation for civilized living and social cohesion it needed to come closer to the fulfilment of this goal than it was when he spoke. Now, more than twenty years on, many people would surely echo his remarks.

It seems probable that the three objectives of 'equal opportunity', 'cultural diversity' and 'mutual tolerance' will constitute part of official government policy towards ethnic minorities for the foreseeable future, regardless of which party holds the reins of power. Naturally, significant differences of emphasis can be expected as well as varying degrees of commitment to the implementation of such policies. However, a reversion to the notion of wholesale 'assimilation'[10] (fashionable during the period 1950 to 1965), as a process that might be achieved through government pressure, is now generally recognized as totally unrealistic, though some senior Conservative politicians still occasionally refer to the need for members of the ethnic minority communities to accept 'the social and cultural standards' of the 'host country'.[11] The speech by Douglas Hurd (then Home Secretary) at the Birmingham Central Mosque on 24 February 1989 (ten days after Ayatollah Khomeini's intervention in the Rushdie affair) can be seen as particularly significant, for it clearly represented a continuation of the approach adopted by Roy Jenkins in the same office 23 years earlier.[12] Mr Hurd emphasized the 'equal opportunity' aspect by referring to the need for ethnic minority children to acquire a fluent command of the English language as well as a proper understanding of British history, institutions and democratic processes if they were to achieve success here. He reasserted the government's determination to stamp out racial discrimination and pointed to the increasing numbers of Asians and Afro-Caribbeans who were playing a full part in British public life as magistrates, local councillors, police officers and parliamentary candidates. So far as 'cultural diversity' was concerned, he expected the minorities to retain their religious faiths, traditions and mother-tongues and pass these on to their children. A portion of the Home Secretary's speech was also devoted to 'mutual tolerance' in stressing the necessity for everyone involved in protesting about Salman Rushdie's book to respect the rule of law and not to resort to violent demonstrations in the streets or to making death threats against the author or his publishers.

So far as the English legal system is concerned, its task in the promotion of equal opportunities lies largely in the successful enforcement of the Race Relations Act 1976 and the strengthening of some of its provisions[13] to try to ensure the eventual elimination of discrimination in such fields as employment, housing, education and the provision of goods and services. In terms of the maintenance of cultural diversity, the law's role is to allow and, where appropriate, facilitate the continued practice of ethnic minority customs and traditions. In a liberal democracy, such legal endorsement of pluralism can be supported by reference to fundamental beliefs about the need for individual freedom, religious toleration and social justice based upon equality of respect. Since the challenge presented by a policy of cultural pluralism may, on occasion, be a pretty stiff one, the law can assist in the creation of 'an atmosphere of mutual tolerance' by being properly enforced, in an evenhanded way, so that public order is preserved.

The overall objective which Britain should be striving to attain was well summarized in the Swann Committee Report on the education of children from ethnic minority groups in 1985:

> We would . . . regard a democratic pluralist society as seeking to achieve a balance between, on the one hand, the maintenance and active support of the essential elements of the cultures and lifestyles of all the ethnic groups within it, and, on the other, the acceptance by all groups of a set of shared values distinctive of the society as a whole. This then is our view of a genuinely pluralist society, as both socially cohesive and culturally diverse.[14]

However, the Swann Committee also made it perfectly plain that in its view the ethnic minority communities could not be allowed to preserve unchanged all the elements of their cultures and lifestyles because this would prevent them from taking on the shared values of the wider society.[15] There are, therefore, limits to the acceptance of cultural diversity which need to be imposed in support of the overriding public interest in promoting social cohesion. Cultural tolerance cannot become a 'cloak for oppression and injustice within the immigrant communities themselves',[16] nor must it endanger the integrity of the 'social and cultural core' of English values as a whole.[17] It is quite impracticable to subscribe to a policy that holds that all cultural values have equal validity in modern Britain and that no cultural practices should ever be condemned or outlawed. Indeed, in a number of legal cases in which the question of respect for foreign cultural practices has been specifically addressed, English judges have emphasized that tolerance is bounded by notions of reasonableness and public policy and that foreign customs and laws will not be recognized or applied here if they are considered repugnant or otherwise offend the conscience of the court.[18]

CULTURAL PLURALISM IN ENGLISH LAW TODAY

Unlike many other Commonwealth countries, England possesses an essentially unified legal regime. Even so, within this monistic framework it is possible to identify several examples of separate and distinctive treatment and regulation being afforded to members of ethnic or religious groups, designed to give proper respect to their own cultures and traditions.[19] Many of these are summarized below in relation to the various branches of law concerned, together with some of the most striking instances of situations where English law draws the line and refuses to give recognition to cultural diversity.

Family Law

MARRIAGE

The basic law governing the solemnization of marriages in England is set out in the Marriage Acts 1949–86. These Acts lay down detailed rules concerning where a marriage may take place, who should conduct the ceremony, at what time of day it may occur and the nature of the celebration. However, two religious denominations are exempt from all these regulations concerning the formalities of marriage, namely Quakers and 'persons professing the Jewish religion'.[20] Their special privileges go back at least as far as Lord Hardwicke's Marriage Act 1753. As a result their ceremonies may occur at any hour of the day or night; they need not take place in any particular building; they do not require the presence of any official appointed by or notified to the state authorities; and the form of the wedding merely has to follow the usages of the Society of Friends or the usages of the Jews, as the case may be.[21]

English domestic law makes no concessions, however, to other laws or customs in relation to the question of capacity to marry. A marriage in which either party is under sixteen years of age, or is within the prohibited degrees of relationship as defined in the Marriage Acts 1949–86, or is already married to someone else will automatically be void.[23] Although there has been no decided case on the subject, it is certain too that English law would disregard any prohibition falling outside its own rules, e.g. the Islamic ban on marriages between Muslim women and non-Muslim men and the Jewish prohibition forbidding Jews from marrying Gentiles.

Arranged marriages are treated as perfectly valid in themselves, although the immigration rules make it unnecessarily hard in practice for parties to such marriages to gain entry to the UK for purposes of settlement.[23] However, if an arranged marriage taking place in England is pushed to the point of compulsion so that it amounts to a forced marriage entered into under duress, the marriage is voidable.[24] The unwilling party may thus escape from it by instituting nullity proceedings within three years of the marriage, provided it can be proved that his or her will had been overborne by the pressure or threats applied.[25]

DIVORCE

The only way of obtaining a divorce in England is through a decree granted by a court of civil jurisdiction[26] on the basis of a finding that the marriage in question has irretrievably broken down.[27] Hence a Muslim divorce by *talaq*, a Jewish divorce obtained by a *get* from the Beth-Din or a purely consensual divorce arranged in accordance with Hindu, Chinese or African custom will not be accepted as valid if it occurs within the British Isles.

The English courts possess a wide discretion, within certain statutory guidelines, to decide whether to make orders for financial provision upon separation and divorce and, if so, how large an amount should be specified.[28] In *Brett* v *Brett*[29] the wife, an orthodox Jewess, had obtained a decree of divorce from the English court on the ground of cruelty under the old law. However, she also wanted her ex-husband to deliver a *get*, without which she would not be free to remarry under Jewish law. Upon her application for financial provision the court took account of this wish (and her ex-husband's adamant refusal to agree to it) by allowing him to pay a smaller lump sum than would otherwise be ordered, provided he delivered a *get* to her within a period of three months. In two other cases the English courts have been prepared to enforce contracts for the payment of deferred dower (*mahr*) by Muslim husbands upon divorce.[30]

Education

CHOICE OF SCHOOL

Parents have a right to express a preference to a local education authority as to which school they would like their child to attend, but the authority is only bound to comply with the preference in so far as this would be compatible with the provision of efficient education and the efficient use of resources.[31] Co-educational schools now predominate and there is no guarantee that there will be places at all-girls schools for all those ethnic minority parents who might seek them.

Voluntary-aided status is available, together with substantial financial benefits, for denominational schools within the state sector,[32] but while there are a few Jewish schools in this category no other non-Christian faiths have had such status accorded to their schools.

RELIGIOUS EDUCATION

The Education Reform Act 1988 attempts to accommodate the needs of non-Christian pupils and their parents in a variety of ways.[33] Although all schools in the state sector must provide for daily acts of collective worship and for classes in religious education, any parent who is apprehensive about Christian indoctrination may request that his or her child be withdrawn from either or both of these activities.[34] In local education authority schools the collective worship has to be 'wholly or mainly of a broadly Christian character' when judged over a school term,[35] but schools may obtain exemption from this provision if the local Standing Advisory Council on Religious Education (SACRE) decides that it would be inappropriate,[36] e.g. where there is a sizeable number of pupils of non-Christian faiths. The principal religious traditions of the local area have to be reflected in one of the four groups which is entitled to be represented on each SACRE.[37]

In local education authority schools classes in religious education have to follow an 'agreed syllabus' and must not be given in the form of doctrines that are distinctive of any particular denomination.[38] Many of the existing syllabuses are multi-faith and any new syllabus adopted after 29 September 1988 must 'reflect the fact that the religious traditions in Great Britain are in the main Christian, while taking account of the teaching and practices of the other principal religions represented in Great Britain'.[39] Parents who are not satisfied with their local agreed syllabus can request separate religious education for their children in accordance with their faith and the local education authority must normally arrange this so long as the cost of such tuition does not fall upon the authority.[40]

DRESS FOR SCHOOL

Pupils cannot lawfully be refused admission to a school or be sent home for a breach of the school rules about uniform simply because they are complying with ethnic rules about dress.[41] Hence Sikh boys may wear turbans at school,[42] Asian girls may wear *shalwar* (trousers) and Muslim girls may wear *dupattaas* (headscarves).

Religious Observances

Members of religious minorities are legally entitled to freedom of worship;[43] to construct, own and manage their religious buildings;[44] to register such buildings[45] and claim exemption from liability for the payment of local rates;[46] to celebrate their religious festivals and to swear their own distinctive oaths in judicial proceedings[47] (whether as plaintiff or defendant, witness or juror). They are not, however, protected by the blasphemy laws against having their faiths reviled and ridiculed in a scurrilous or contemptuous fashion. Prior to the Salman Rushdie affair the precedents strongly suggested that the law only extended this safeguard to Christianity and the particular rituals and doctrines of the Church of England. In 1979 in *Whitehouse* v *Lemon*[48] (the '*Gay News*' trial), Lord Scarman declared:

> The offence belongs to a group of criminal offences designed to safeguard the internal tranquillity of the Kingdom. In an increasingly plural society such as that of modern Britain, it is necessary not only to respect the differing religious beliefs, feelings and practices of all but to protect them from scurrility, vilification, ridicule and contempt.[49]

However, he then proceeded to indicate that the current law did not cover non-Christian religions:

I will not lend my voice to a view of the law relating to blasphemous libel which would render it a dead letter, or diminish its efficacy to protect religious feelings from outrage and insult. My criticism of the common law offence of blasphemy is not that it exists but that it is not sufficiently comprehensive. It is shackled by the chains of history.[50]

Lord Scarman's comments on this aspect of the case were merely *obiter dicta* and it was not until the decision of the Divisional Court in *R* v *Chief Metropolitan Stipendiary Magistrate, ex parte Choudhury*[51] that a decisive modern ruling was given on the subject. In that case application had been made for judicial review of the refusal by the chief metropolitan magistrate to grant summonses accusing Salman Rushdie and his publishers of blasphemy against Islam. The Divisional Court unanimously upheld the magistrate's ruling that the offence of blasphemy only related to Christianity and could not be judicially extended to other faiths.

After the decision in *Whitehouse* v *Lemon* the question of possible reform of the law was referred to the English Law Commission, where the detailed arguments and options were considered in a working paper (No. 79) published in 1981 and a final report (No. 145) published in 1985. Ultimately, the two members of the Commission who broadly agreed with Lord Scarman's views were out-voted by three commissioners who recommended that the blasphemy law should be abolished altogether. However, in the four years that elapsed between the final report and the publication of *The Satanic Verses* no action was taken by Parliament, either to abolish the offence or to extend its ambit to other faiths.

Employment

The Race Relations Act 1976 attempts to combat discrimination in the employment field by making both 'direct' and 'indirect' discrimination unlawful. Indirect discrimination involves practices and procedures which appear at first glance to be perfectly acceptable because they apply the same standard requirements to everyone (regardless of race, colour or origins etc.) but which on closer inspection have a disproportionately adverse impact upon members of 'racial groups'.[52] A 'racial group' is denoted by the Act as meaning 'a group of persons defined by reference to colour, race, nationality or ethnic or national origins'.[53] In outlawing indirect discrimination the Act is able to give protection to certain cultural practices and religious norms followed by members of such groups in circumstances where a similar protection would not be available to members of the majority community. Hence, in appropriate circumstances, Asian women are guaranteed the right to wear trousers at work when white women would not be[54] and Sikh men cannot be denied jobs simply because they insist on wearing turbans rather than the company's prescribed headwear, when white job applicants would certainly have no option but to comply with the company's rules and regulations.[55] However, a Rastafarian can be refused employment merely because he is unwilling to cut off his dreadlocks.[56] It is important to bear in mind that very few members of the ethnic minority communities actually win cases of alleged discrimination in practice and most of the indirect discrimination cases have been lost because the employers have been able to establish to the satisfaction of tribunals and appellate courts that their rules and regulations concerning dress or appearance are 'justifiable' within the Act — often on grounds of hygiene or safety.[57]

Recently it has been made compulsory for virtually all persons working on construction sites to wear suitable head protection in the form of a safety helmet.[58] However, a specific statutory exemption from this requirement has been created for turbanned Sikhs[59] in the light of the knowledge that around 40,000 Sikhs are currently employed in the construction industry. Furthermore, any employer who refuses to employ a Sikh on a construction site simply because he is unwilling to wear a safety helmet in place of his turban will be barred from being able to argue that such a policy is justifiable on grounds of safety under the indirect discrimination provisions of the Race Relations Act.[60]

Criminal Law

THE QUESTION OF GUILT

In criminal proceedings it has long been the general approach of the courts to apply a uniform and consistent standard to all those who are accused of offences, regardless of whether or not they have foreign origins.[61] Since the main purpose of the criminal law is to impose certain minimum standards of behaviour for the benefit of the community as a whole, it has seemed logical to apply, in the vast majority of circumstances, a universal set of principles to determine who is guilty and who is innocent.

This pattern of uniformity has been followed in a number of cases where the conduct of the accused was at least partly explicable and sometimes even justifiable in terms of his or her cultural background. There have been convictions of several Asians of kidnapping and false imprisonment for snatching relatives pursuant to family feuds,[62] of an African mother of assault for scarifying the cheeks of her young sons,[63] of a West Indian father of assault arising out of his overzealous punishment of his son,[64] of Rastafarians of the misuse of drugs for possessing marijuana,[65] and of an Indian Muslim under the Education Act 1944 for failing to send his teenage daughter to a co-educational school.[66]

In addition, certain alien customs and traditions have been specifically outlawed by statute. For example, all forms of female circumcision are banned by the Prohibition of Female Circumcision Act 1985 and polygamy constitutes the crime of bigamy under section 57 of the Offences against the Person Act 1861.

SPECIAL STATUTORY EXEMPTIONS

There are, however, fields in which Parliament has legislated specifically to exempt adherents to particular minority faiths from certain statutory provisions. First, under the Shops Act 1950 a 'person of the Jewish religion' may open his shop on Sundays without being in breach of the Sunday trading laws, provided he registers with the local authority and keeps the shop closed on Saturdays.[67] Secondly, under the Slaughter of Poultry Act 1967 and the Slaughterhouses Act 1974, Jews and Muslims may slaughter animals and poultry in accordance with their traditional methods without having to stun them first, provided the meat is for consumption by Jews or Muslims, as the case may be.[68] Thirdly, under the Road Traffic Act 1988, Sikh motor cyclists are excused from the requirement to wear a crash helmet, provided they are wearing turbans.[69]

Apart from these three instances, the legislature has recently made indirect provision for Sikhs to continue to be able to wear their *kirpans* (religious daggers) in public places without being guilty of an offence. New legislation designed to penalize those carrying knives and other sharply pointed articles specifically provides that it is a defence for the accused to prove that he had the article with him in a public place 'for religious reasons'.[70]

DISCRETION IN SENTENCING

When considering the appropriate sentence to impose upon a convicted person, the English courts are prepared to take account of a variety of factors of a cultural nature which may result in mitigation of the punishment imposed. The defendant's foreign origin, adherence to ethnic or religious customs or traditional values, ignorance of English law and English mores and difficulty in adjusting to life in a novel environment are all matters which a court may properly take into account at this stage in the process.[71]

RIGHTS OF PRISONERS

Although prisoners have few 'rights' enforceable through the courts, they are accorded certain privileges and can expect certain standards to be followed in the light of various sets of circular instructions issued to prison establishments by the Home Office. The current guidelines allow, *inter alia*, orthodox baptized Sikhs to wear the five symbols of their religion, together with a turban; Muslim women to wear clothes which fully cover their bodies; Hindu women to wear saris; and Rastafarians to keep their dreadlocks.[72] Religious dietary taboos are also generally respected, as are religious festivals in the sense that they are recognized as days upon which no work is required to be done by prisoners of the faith concerned.[73]

Local Authorities

The right of travellers (gypsies) to maintain their nomadic lifestyle has been endorsed through legislation which imposes a duty upon local authorities to provide adequate sites for gypsy encampments.[74] Unfortunately no time limit was set for the completion of this task and opposition from local residents, coupled with weak enforcement mechanisms, has meant that today far fewer sites have been established to meet the needs of travellers than was intended when the legislation was enacted in 1968.[75] One estimate suggests that there is still a national shortfall of at least a third, with many thousands of gypsy families having no lawful place to camp.[76]

AN APPRAISAL

It will be evident from these illustrations that English law has been adapting its provisions on an *ad hoc* basis, responding to the social needs and pressures of the time. No coherent official strategy has yet been formulated, whether in the form of a white paper or a law commission report. However, the British government has not reacted positively to all requests for the law to be made to conform with the values of minorities. In particular, ministers have not been willing to put before Parliament two particular pieces of legislation suggested to them by Muslims. The first, initially proposed during the 1970s, would have introduced a separate system of Islamic personal law to govern the affairs of all British Muslims.[77] The second, promoted passionately in the aftermath of the publication of Rushdie's *Satanic Verses*, would have extended the current blasphemy laws to cover faiths other than Christianity.

If the general philosophy behind, for example, statutory protection for turbanned Sikhs is that Britain is now a multicultural society, in which recognition of cultural and religious diversity is required as part of the tolerance expected in a liberal democracy, it is incumbent upon those who support this position to explain why the line between what is legally acceptable and what is objectionable is drawn at one place rather than another. This is especially important at a time when Britain is being brought into ever closer union with continental Europe (as with the creation of the single EC market in 1992). Arguments are currently being raised about the possible loss of national identity in the 'supra-sovereignty' of the European Community. It is therefore an opportune moment to ask precisely what it means to be 'British'. What are the fundamental values of English society today which are worthy of preservation and which define both the relationships between the various ethnic groups comprising our national community as a whole and our role in a wider European context?

The Human Rights Dimension

In seeking to frame suitable guidelines for Parliament and the courts in defining more precisely what British core values entail in regulating a multicultural society and where exactly the limits are to be set on public policy grounds with respect to the toleration of diversity, the human rights dimension must be borne in mind.[78] In most democracies the answers to profound questions involving core values, individual liberty, religious freedom, the balancing of competing interests, the protection of minorities and major public policy considerations are to be located in written constitutions containing a bill of rights. In the absence of such a constitution in Britain, it seems reasonable to suggest that reference should be made instead to those international human rights treaties to which the UK is a contracting party, such as the European Convention on Human Rights and the International Covenant on Civil and Political Rights. Although they are not directly binding in the English courts, judges pay careful attention to them,[79] both because they constitute international obligations and because they furnish important indications of public policy.[80] It is significant that powerful support for the domestic application of international human rights law was given at a colloquium of senior Commonwealth judges in 1988 in the form of the 'Bangalore Principles'.[81]

If a 'human rights approach' were to be adopted in framing suitable provision in English law for cultural pluralism, specific answers would need to be given to two questions of principle. The first would be whether a particular ethnic practice demanded legal recognition because to refuse it would be tantamount to a denial of human rights. The second would be whether an ethnic tradition required automatic non-recognition because the practice itself constituted a violation of human rights. On the basis of the second principle it is clearly appropriate to outlaw such practices as slavery, female circumcision and barbarous punishments (such as the severing of limbs),[82] while the first principle requires the provision of general guarantees of freedom of worship and freedom from discrimination, as well as, for example, the more mundane commitment to supply an interpreter for a defendant in a criminal trial who does not understand the English language.[83]

It is arguable that, on human rights grounds, Muslims should not be allowed to operate a system of Islamic personal law in England because of the risk that the rights of women will be violated in a discriminatory fashion[84] through such practices as polygamy, *talaq* divorces and forced marriages. On the other hand, it is not easy to justify the archaic English law of blasphemy in human rights terms. Even if it is regarded as operating as a legitimate limitation upon the right to freedom of expression in protecting the 'rights of others',[85] it functions in a discriminatory fashion of confining its protection to Christianity.[86] The offence of blasphemy should either be abolished altogether, as recommended by the majority of the Law Commission in 1985,[87] or extended to other faiths as advocated by the minority, as well as by Lord Scarman in *Whitehouse* v *Lemon*.[88]

The Question of Differential Treatment

Whenever ethnic minorities are accorded favourable treatment by the law which is not identical to the treatment accorded to members of the majority community, some of the latter are liable to argue that this represents unwarranted 'privilege'. These 'assimilationists' are likely to draw attention to the well-known adage, 'When in Rome, do as the Romans do', which seems to be elevated by some on the political right to a central article of faith in modern Britain. If ethnic minorities do not conform and if English law allows them to 'get away with it' then, it is often suggested, this amounts to discrimination against the majority.

Non-discrimination is, of course, a cardinal principle of international human rights law and it is therefore vital to clarify the position in this regard.

Legal departures from the general pattern of uniformity of treatment do not offend against fundamental principles of equality if they guarantee minorities genuine equality in the form of equal respect for their religious and cultural values. This is often preferable to mere formal equality which can have a tendency to undermine these values by simply affording identical treatment to all, regardless of religious and cultural differences. Special differential treatment is a well-established concept in international human rights law, dating back at least as far as the League of Nations[89] and reflected in the International Covenant on Civil and Political Rights[90] and decisions of the European Court of Human Rights.[91] Legal distinctions may properly be made between different groups in society, provided a legitimate aim is being pursued and the distinction possesses an objective and reasonable justification. It is these requirements which demonstrate the contrast between special differential treatment and apartheid, with which it is, sadly, all too often confused in the popular mind. The latter doctrine, apart from being coercive, is discriminatory because the distinctions if makes are based on colour and hence are arbitrary and irrational. On the other hand, the desire of communities with distinctive cultural and religious traditions to ensure that these are preserved affords an entirely rational justification for making some distinctions in the legal field. Hence, while the hallowed principle of 'equality before the law' (which has been cherished as part of 'the rule of law' since Dicey[92] first wrote about it in 1885) generally requires English law to be colour-blind, it certainly does not require it to ignore important religious and cultural differences.

The Future Direction of English Law

To date, the only pressure for English law to move in the direction of a full-bodied legal pluralism has come from Muslim groups seeking a separate system of personal law. Partly in view of the practical problems which this would entail (e.g. which system of Islamic law should be applied and by whom?) and partly because of the risk of human rights violations, it is suggested that this path should not be followed.[93] There are dangers of creating serious social divisions not only between Muslims and non-Muslims but also between the different Muslim communities in Britain themselves. However, this should not be taken as implying that much valuable and constructive work in the settlement of family disputes cannot be achieved through the application of Islamic principles by means of mediation and conciliation involving Muslim community welfare organizations. A *sharia* 'court' already functions informally in London (as indeed does a Jewish rabbinical 'court'), though without the power to enforce its decisions.

The wisest course would be to retain the present policy of adapting an essentially monistic structure on an *ad hoc* basis so that the reasonable religious and cultural needs of the ethnic minority communities are satisfied. Reference should be made to international human rights standards as part of this process, for three reasons. First, this will inject some consistency into the uncertain domain of 'public policy'. Second, it would furnish useful guidelines for the resolution of any conflicts between the three central objectives of equal opportunity, respect for cultural diversity and mutual tolerance. Third, it may assist in the rebuttal of any charges of ethnocentricity which may be levelled when English law repudiates certain unacceptable cultural practices, by appealing to notions of universal (or near-universal) values reflected in widely ratified international conventions.[94]

In very broad terms, the process of having regard to the human rights dimension in working out the details of a legal policy on ethnic minority customs and traditions should lead to a system of justice which is tolerant of and sympathetic towards cultural pluralism. Only comparatively rarely would such customs and traditions have to be denied legal recognition, such as some of those in the field of Muslim family law outlined earlier. The International Covenant on Civil and Political Rights not only has a provision on religious freedom along the same lines as that in the European Convention[95] but also proclaims boldly in article 27:

> In those States in which ethnic, religious or linguistic minorities exist, persons belonging to such minorities shall not be denied the right, in community with the other members of their group, to enjoy their own culture, to profess and practise their own religion, or to use their own language.

So far as action on the part of the ethnic minority communities themselves is concerned, they should ensure that they not only campaign for legal changes on specific matters relating exclusively to their own needs but also make their voices heard when more general issues of law reform arise, so that their cultural values influence the broader content of English law for the better.[96]

CONCLUSIONS

To espouse a legal policy of 'cultural pluralism within limits', as advocated in this chapter, may leave its author exposed to attack from
both assimilationists and cultural relativists, for such a stance seeks
unashamedly to capture a part of the 'middle ground'. Although it takes
up a position quite close to the endorsement of full legal support for the
maintenance of cultural diversity, it falls well short of it in practice.
Moreover, it lacks the comforting capacity to respond with certitude on
various controversial issues because the exact limits to toleration cannot
always be precisely defined in advance. It thus appears vulnerable to
assaults from those who feel able to adopt more absolutist positions.

At one end of the spectrum can be found the assimilationist who
simply insists upon the conformity of the minorities with majority values
and standards because they have chosen to live here. Yet the assimilationist cannot seriously want the English legal system to be employed
to force such compliance even in such personal matters as religious belief
and worship or in the regulation of every aspect of family and social life.
Yet, once the assimilationist concedes that a 'private domain' can be
carved out and excluded from such policies of conformity, it becomes
plain that there are huge difficulties in drawing the line between public
and private spheres.[97] Where does the education and upbringing of
children belong, for example, and to which category should the role
of women in society be allocated? Feminists and others have recently
expressed considerable disquiet at the manner in which the law is prone
to marginalize women's concerns by confining them to a private or
domestic sphere.[98]

The cultural relativist, by contrast, spurns the temptation to be judgemental about any of the values and practices of those from other societies
and is quick to brand as cultural 'imperialists' those who would outlaw
even a handful of alien traditions in England. Literally, 'anything goes',
no minimum standards are recognized and any criticism or rejection of
other cultures is regarded as taboo because it carries connotations of
'superiority' and must perforce emanate from a 'colonialist' mentality.
However, if consistency is to be maintained, the cultural relativist has
to eschew any vision of social progress and ignore blatant examples
of oppression and inequality which would be wholly unacceptable if
perpetrated by members of the white majority community. Nor can the
beliefs and practices of a minority community be safely confined to its
members, for their repercussions may directly affect the population at
large — as the furore over *The Satanic Verses* amply demonstrated.

It is surely idle to believe that future relations between the white majority community and the various ethnic minority communities will be free from cultural conflict, though it seems probable that the Salman Rushdie affair represents the high-water mark of inter-community confrontation over a legal issue and that in general terms ethnic tensions are lower here than they are, for example, on the other side of the Channel. The task for legal policy-makers is to achieve a proper balance between two competing considerations. On the one hand, there is the need to appreciate clearly the immense benefits (cultural, social and economic) which accrue to the members of the ethnic minority communities themselves through the maintenance of their values and traditions. These benefits contribute, directly and indirectly, to the well-being and prosperity of society at large. The law must therefore buttress and support the cultures of these communities so that they flourish and thrive. They constitute a substantial national asset.[99] On the other hand, very occasionally, it will be necessary for English law to interfere with alien practices, usually in the interests of protecting vulnerable members of those communities (especially women and children) and hence in support of the welfare of the public as a whole. Of course, all cultures are dynamic and many unacceptable customs are probably in terminal decline in any event.

There is certainly no reason why members of the ethnic minority communities should feel that they must always be on the defensive so far as the English legal system is concerned. English law is flexible and adaptable and several campaigns on behalf of the minority communities have already brought about significant reforms. No doubt, the long-standing rivalry between the West and Islam will continue to be prominent for some time and perhaps even intensify now that both the era of colonialism and the period of the Cold War are virtually at an end. However, in future no one should be too surprised at the clash between such profoundly different ideologies.[100]

In the final analysis it needs to be acknowledged on all sides that 'unity through diversity' is a perfectly viable option in a liberal democracy where the cardinal values of freedom, justice and tolerance provide the necessary protection for the maintenance by separate ethnic groups of many other values which are *not* shared by all members of society. Pluralism should not be seen as representing a divisive threat but rather as a positive asset. If it is viewed in the same fashion as a mosaic, blending together diverse parts in an elaborate design to form a harmony, it can surely be treasured for its own intrinsic worth and as the emblem of a truly civilized community.

NOTES

1. See 'Ethnicity in World Politics' (1989) 11 *Third World Quarterly* ix.

2. Smith, A. *The Ethnic Revival* (Cambridge, Cambridge University Press, 1986) p. 40.

3. See Shaw, C. 'Components of growth in the ethnic minority population' (1988) 52 *Population Trends* 26; Haskey, J. 'The ethnic minority populations of Great Britain: their size and characteristics' (1988) 54 *Population Trends* 29.

4. There are no official figures for religious affiliation, merely rough estimates, because no questions on the subject are asked on census forms. For the basis of the estimates given here, see Poulter, S. *English Law and Ethnic Minority Customs* (London, Butterworths, 1986) p. 206. Claims by Muslims to have 1.5 to 2 million adherents in Britain are wildly out of line with recent Labour Force Survey figures.

5. See Farm Animal Welfare Council *Report on the Welfare of Livestock when Slaughtered by Religious Methods* (London, HMSO, 1985).

6. For the announcement of the final decision by the Secretary of State for the Environment see *Hansard* (Commons) vol. 169 (written answers, 20 March 1990) cols. 600–601. See further note 44 below.

7. Construction (Head Protection) Regulations 1989; Employment Act 1989 s. 11 (see further note 58 below and accompanying text).

8. See e.g. *Education for All* (Swann Report) (London: HMSO) pp. 5–6.

9. Jenkins, R. *Essays and Speeches* (London, Collins, 1967) p. 267.

10. For illuminating analyses of the contrasts between 'assimilation' and cultural pluralism, see Parekh, B. *Colour, Culture and Consciousness* (London, Allen and Unwin, 1974) ch. 15; Parekh, B. 'Britain and the social logic of pluralism' in *Britain: A Plural Society* (London, CRE, 1990) pp. 58–76.

11. John Biffen MP in *The Independent* (5 October 1987). See also the comment of Sir John Stokes MP, reported in *The Independent* (30 May 1989): 'Those who settle here must obey our laws *and customs.*' Norman Tebbit MP has also complained that 'in recent years our sense of insularity and nationality has been bruised by large waves of immigrants resistant to absorption' (May 1990) *The Field* 78. No doubt, these sorts of sentiments are shared by a significant, if unquantifiable, proportion of the white population (see *Swann Committee Report* op. cit. (note 8) p. 6.

12. The speech was reprinted in full in *New Life* (3 March 1989). Similar views were expressed by John Patten, minister of state at the Home Office, in a letter to leading British Muslims dated 4 July 1989 (see *The Times* (5 July 1989), where the letter is reprinted).

13. See e.g. CRE *Review of the Race Relations Act 1976 — Proposals for Change* (London, CRE, 1985). There is also a need for government and all public-sector bodies to adopt stringent 'contract compliance' requirements for those providing goods and services — see e.g. Bhat, A., Carr-Hill, R. and Ohri, S. (eds), *Britain's Black Population* 2nd edn (Aldershot, Gower, 1988) ch. 4.

14. Op. cit. (note 8) p. 6.

15. Ibid. at p. 5.

16. Lester, A. and Bindman, G. *Race and Law* (Harmondsworth, Penguin, 1972) p. 18.

17. Patterson, S. 'Immigrants and minority groups in British society' in Abbott, S. (ed.) *The Prevention of Racial Discrimination in Great Britain* (Oxford, Oxford University Press, 1971) p. 30.

18. See e.g. *Baindail* v *Baindail* [1946] P 122 at 129; *Cheni* v *Cheni* [1965] P 85 at 99; *Varanand* v *Varanand* [1964] 108 SJ 693; *In the Estate of Fuld (deceased) No. 3* [1968] P 675 at 698.

19. See, generally, Poulter, S. *English Law and Ethnic Minority Customs* (London, Butterworths, 1986); Poulter, S. *Asian Traditions and English Law* (Stoke-on-Trent, Trentham, 1990).

20. Marriage Act 1949 s. 26(1)(c), (d).

21. Ibid. ss 26(1), 35(4), 43(3), 75(1)(a).

22. Matrimonial Causes Act 1973, s. 11. Concern about *foreign* marriages where the bride is under sixteen or where the marriage is actually polygamous has also led to changes in the immigration rules designed to prevent such couples settling in the UK — see HC 306 of 1986; Immigration Act 1988 s. 2; HC 251 1989–90, paras 2–5.

23. For the notorious 'primary purpose' rule, see HC 251 1989–90, paras 47, 50.

24. Matrimonial Cases Act 1973 s. 12.

25. *Hirani* v *Hirani* [1983] 4 FLR 232; cf. *Singh* v *Singh* [1971] P 226.

26. Family Law Act 1986 s. 44(1).

27. Matrimonial Causes Act 1973 s. 1.

28. Matrimonial Causes Act 1973 Part II, as amended by the Matrimonial and Family Proceedings Act 1984; Domestic Proceedings and Magistrates' Courts Act 1978.

29. [1969] 1 All ER 1007.

30. *Shahnaz v Rizwan* [1965] 1 QB 390; *Qureshi v Qureshi* [1972] Fam 173.

31. Education Act 1944 s. 76; Education Act 1980 s. 6(5).

32. Education Act 1944 ss. 18–19.

33. For a detailed analysis, see Poulter, S. 'The religious education provisions of the Education Reform Act 1988' (1990) 2 *Education and the Law* 1.

34. Education Reform Act 1988 s. 9(3).

35. Ibid. ss 6,7.

36. Ibid. s. 12.

37. In terms of s. 11(4) of the 1988 Act the four groups comprise the LEA, the teachers' associations, the Church of England and 'such Christian and other religious denominations as . . . will appropriately reflect the principal religious traditions in the area'.

38. Education Act 1944 s. 26 (as amended).

39. Education Reform Act 1988 s. 8(3).

40. Education Act 1944 s. 26 (as amended); Education Reform Act 1988 s. 9(4).

41. Race Relations Act 1976 ss 1,3,17.

42. *Mandla v Dowell-Lee* [1983] AC 548.

43. Liberty of Religious Worship Act 1855.

44. Subject, of course, to the planning laws. On 20 March 1990 the Secretary of State for the Environment announced that he would uphold the inspector's decision, following two public inquiries, to ban large-scale public worship at Bhaktivedanta Manor, the Hindu Temple at Letchmore Heath in Hertfordshire. A two-year period of grace would be allowed for an alternative site to be found. Local residents had objected that planning permission for such worship had never been obtained and too much intrusion and disruption to their lives had been caused by worshippers. The pre-existing permission for the temple to be used as a residential college for the International Society for Krishna Consciousness remains in force. A subsequent appeal to the High Court by ISKCON was unsuccessful, see *ISKCON v Secretary of State for the Environment* [1991] (unreported).

45. Places of Worship Registration Act 1855.

46. Local Government Finance Act 1988 s. 51 and sched. 5, para. 11.

47. Oaths Act 1978.

48. [1979] AC 617.

49. [1979] AC 617 at 658.

50. Ibid.

51. [1991] 1 All ER 306.

52. Race Relations Act 1976 s. 1(1)(b).

53. Ibid. s. 3(1).

54. *Malik v British Home Stores* [1980] (unreported).

55. *Kamaljeet Singh Bhakerd v Famous Names Ltd* [1988] (unreported).

56. *Crown Suppliers (PSA) v Dawkins* [1991] ICR 583.

57. See e.g. *Singh v Rowntree Mackintosh Ltd* [1979] IRLR 199 and *Panesar v Nestle Co. Ltd* [1980] ICR 144 (no beards allowed in confectionery factories); *Kuldip Singh v British Rail Engineering Ltd* [1986] IGR 22 (hard hat, not turban, to be worn in engineering workshop). The decision of the Court of Appeal in *Hampson v Department of Education* [1990] 2 All ER 25 has, however, recently stiffened the test of justifiability.

58. Construction (Head Protection) Regulations 1989.

59. Employment Act 1989 s. 11.

60. Ibid. s. 12.

61. See e.g. *R v Esop* [1836] 7 C & P 456; *R v Barronet and Allain* [1852] Dears CC 51.

62. *R v Dad and Shafi* [1968] Crim LR 46; *R v Moied* [1986] 8 Crim AR (S)44.

63. *R v Adesanya* [1974] (unreported).

64. *R v Derriviere* [1969] 53 Crim AR 637.

65. *R v Williams* [1979] 1 Crim AR (S) 5; *R v Daudi and Daniels* [1982] 4 Crim AR (S) 306; *R v Aramah* [1983] Crim LR 271.

66. *Bradford Corporation v Patel* [1974] (unreported).

67. Shops Act 1950 s. 53.

68. Slaughter of Poultry Act 1967 s. 1(2); Slaughterhouses Act 1974 s. 36(2).

69. Section 16(2), replacing the original exemption which was contained in the Motor-Cycle Crash Helmets (Religious Exemption) Act 1976.

70. Criminal Justice Act 1988 s. 139(5)(b).

71. See e.g. *R* v *Rapier* [1963] Crim LR 212; *R* v *Bailey* [1964] Crim LR 671; *R* v *Byfield* [1967] Crim LR 378; *R* v *Derriviere* [1969] 53 Crim AR 637; *R* v *Bibi* [1980] 1 WLR 1193.

72. Home Office Circular Instruction No. 2 of 1983. See generally, *Directory and Guide on Religious Practices in HM Prison Service* (London, Prison Service Chaplaincy, 1988).

73. Ibid.

74. Caravan Sites Act 1968 Part II.

75. See generally Forrester, B. *The Travellers' Handbook* (London, Interchange, 1985).

76. Hyman, M. *Sites for Travellers* (London, Runnymede, 1989) pp. 8–9.

77. See *Why Muslim Family Law for British Muslims* (London, Union of Muslim Organisations, 1983).

78. See Poulter, S. 'Ethnic minority customs, English law and human rights' (1987) 36 *International and Comparative Law Quarterly* 589 at 594–95.

79. See e.g. *Ahmad* v *ILEA* [1978] QB 36; *Home Office* v *Harman* [1983] AC 280; *R* v *Maze Visitors ex parte Hone* [1988] AC 379 at 392–94; *Re KD* [1988] AC 806 at 823–25; *Attorney General* v *Guardian Newspapers Ltd (No. 2)* [1988] 3 All ER 545 at 640, 652, 660.

80. See e.g. *Blathwayt* v *Lord Crawley* [1976] AC 397 at 426; *Oppenheimer* v *Cattermole* [1976] AC 249 at 282–83; *Attorney General* v *BBC* [1982] AC 303 at 354; *Schering Chemicals* v *Falkman Ltd* [1981] 2 All ER 321 at 331; *Attorney General* v *Guardian, Observer and Times Newspapers* [1987] 1 WLR 1248 at 1296–97, 1307.

81. *Developing Human Rights Jurisprudence* (London, Commonwealth Secretariat, 1988).

82. See e.g. ECHR arts. 3 (inhuman or degrading treatment), 4 (slavery).

83. See e.g. ECHR arts. 6(3) (interpreter), 9 (religion), 14 (discrimination).

84. See e.g. ECHR arts 12, 14; International Covenant art. 23(4); International Convention on the Elimination of All Forms of Discrimination against Women art. 16.

85. ECHR art. 10(2); *Gay News* v *UK* [1983] 5 EHRR 123.

86. Even so, in *Choudhury* v *UK* (1991) 12 *Human Rights Law Journal* 172, the European Commission of Human Rights declared inadmissible a claim that the English blasphemy law contravened the ban on religious discrimination contained in Article 14 of the European Convention. For criticism of this conclusion, see Poulter, S. 'Towards legislative reform of the blasphemy and racial hatred laws' (1991) *Public Law* 371 at 374–75.

87. Law Commission Report No. 145 'Offences against religion and public worship' (1985).

88. Op. cit. (note 49) p. 658.

89. See e.g. *Minority Schools in Albania Case* PCIJ (1935) series A/B no. 64.

90. Art. 27.

91. See e.g. *Belgian Linguistic Case (No. 2)* [1979–80] 1 EHRR 252; *Marckz* v *Belgium* [1980] 2 EHRR 330; *Abdulaziz, Cabales and Balkandali* v *UK* [1985] EHRR 471.

92. See Dicey, A. *An Introduction to the Study of the Law of the Constitution* 10th edn (London, 1959).

93. See further, Poulter, S. 'The claim to a separate Islamic system of personal law for British Muslims' in Mallat, C. and Connors, J. (eds) *Islamic Family Law* (London, Graham and Trotman, 1990) pp. 140–66.

94. For consideration of the degree to which human rights norms have attained universality in international law, see Meron, T. *Human Rights and Humanitarian Norms as Customary Law* (Oxford, Oxford University Press, 1989) ch. II.

95. ICCPR art. 18; ECHR art. 9.

96. See further Poulter, S. 'Divorce reform in a multicultural society' (1989) 19 *Fam Law* 99.

97. For an attempt to construct a 'public/private' dichotomy for this purpose, as well as an appreciation of its limitations, see Rex, J. 'The concept of a multi-cultural society' (1987) *New Community* 218.

98. See generally, O'Donovan, K. *Sexual Divisions in Law* (London, Weidenfeld and Nicholson, 1985).

99. See further Parekh, B. 'Britain and the social logic of pluralism' op. cit. (note 10) pp. 68–70.

100. See e.g. Kabbani, R. *Letter to Christendom* (London, Virago, 1989) ch. 1.

11

Legislating for a Multi-faith Society: Some Problems of Special Treatment

Jonathan Montgomery

INTRODUCTION

In the most recent edition of *Freedom, the Individual and the Law* Geoffrey Robertson has departed from the structure established by the late Harry Street and distributed the material previously collected together under the heading of freedom of religion into chapters on discrimination and freedom of expression.[1] Robertson thus denies any independent content to religious freedom. This is in some ways surprising at a period when there have been calls for the extension of blasphemy laws to other faiths, for separate schooling on confessional divisions and when there has been further entrenchment of the established religion in the latest Education Reform Act. All these issues place religious freedom closer to the centre of the political stage than it has been for some years. Rather than subsume claims about religious freedom into other categories we should be scrutinizing it more carefully than ever.

This chapter is not concerned, however, to provide a general review of the nature of religious freedom. It focuses on one particular aspect of the problem: the question of special treatment. In a country such as England, where many areas of law have been shaped by the existence of an established church, a strong argument can be presented that the general law of the land favours Christianity over other faiths. If this is the case then it follows that equal treatment will sometimes require dispensation from those general principles. Provisions providing for formal equality may result in greater restrictions of the freedom of minority groups than is experienced by the majority. Differential treatment may therefore be legitimate in order to offer equal concern and respect to all. The question of special treatment is therefore important as a redress for the impact of our legal history. In addition it can be argued that restrictions are not merely discriminatory but breach fundamental substantive rights of religious freedom.

A second reason for examining this aspect of religious freedom is that it raises a difficult set of conceptual issues concerning the nature of group rights. A number of commentators have observed that the individualistic cast of much human rights rhetoric may need to be supplemented by group rights if the needs of all minorities are to be respected.[2] It may be necessary to accept or devise special rules governing a particular group. If so this raises both technical problems of definition and theoretical difficulties in relation to the justification of special treatment. Further, the conceptual problems posed by the notion of a 'group' right are considerable. Recognizing a group right might mean allowing all members of the group to exercise the right in question. However, it may well be sufficient that only a few specific individuals are exempted, in recognition of the needs of a whole group. The concept of a 'group right' therefore needs elucidation before a satisfactory analysis of special treatment can be offered.

This chapter is concerned with these problems of offering special treatment. The specific context is that of religious minorities. Since religious traditions tend already to have a group identity independent of legal intervention, this makes some of the issues clearer. In addition, a number of special exemptions from the criminal law already exist for religious minorities, for example, in the issues of the wearing of protective helmets by motor cycle riders and construction site workers, Sunday trading and the slaughtering of animals. These provide the focus of the study.

Yet more is at stake than the technical problems of legal drafting. In addition to consideration of how things might be done, there is a need to examine the policy implications of special treatment. This chapter does not seek to establish a normative framework for special treatment, but it does try to address a set of difficulties which have been underplayed in contemporary discussions. It tries to show how the use of group rights needs to be considered in the light of the possibility of conflict between the collective freedom of religious groups and individual independence. It also contends that the arguments offered for special treatment often ignore the political context in which exemptions from the general law operate. The argument ends with a plea for a more sophisticated understanding of the variety of ways in which special treatment may be understood from different perspectives. The insights of cultural semiotics need to be absorbed if our understanding of the functions of law is to be enriched.

Although the specific context of the study is that of religious groups, the implications of the discussion range more widely. The general theoretical problems concerning special treatment and the use of group rights are of concern in respect of the search for equality in the areas of sexual and racial discrimination. So too the semiotic approach can be used as a tool to increase our understanding of sex- and race-based distinctions. It is hoped therefore, that the matters canvassed here will be of interest to all concerned with the pursuit of equality.

TYPES OF GROUP RIGHTS

At least four quite different senses of 'group right' can be identified. The first covers cases where individuals are to be treated differently *because* of their membership of the group. Once membership of the relevant class or group is established, this itself gives rise to the changed legal status. Group rights in this sense are essentially the same as any general civil right or liberty. Rights follow from having the status of group member in the same way in which certain rights follow from being a citizen (e.g. the right to vote) or from being married (e.g. the right to occupy a home belonging to your spouse under the Matrimonial Homes Act 1983).

A number of examples of group rights of this sort in respect of religious groups can be identified in English law. Quakers and 'persons professing the Jewish religion' may marry according to their own usages and are excused from the usual rules of formality.[3] All members of the communities in question are free to exercise this privilege, although there may be a discipline internal to those communities which regulates its use. If this is the case the effect of the special treatment on individual members of the group cannot be assessed without an examination of the internal norms which govern access to the privileges in practice.

A second sense of 'group right' covers not individual privilege, but the creation of a 'private' space in which a self-contained parallel system of rules would operate. An example would be provided by the claim from sections of the British Muslim community to a separate regime of family law which would enable Islamic law to be applied in the 'private' sphere of family relations.[4] This sense of group right can be usefully compared to the claims of J.S. Mill for an area of human life immune from legal intervention on the basis that it is self-regarding.[5] If this claim were accepted, a different system of personal laws would govern the Muslim citizens from that which governs the general population. There is nothing impossible about this type of legal pluralism, which was, after all, maintained by English judges in colonial India. However, such proposals raise difficult problems concerning their effect on individual members of the community.[6] How, for example, should the law respond to young Asian women who do not wish to conform to the traditional marriage customs of their communities? The creation of a completely different regime would be a form of group right which would reduce the power of the law to mediate between individuals who wish to assert a degree of independence from, but not wholly to repudiate, their cultures.

This second sense of group right is based on the recognition of a common identity for the cultural and religious minority. Support for such a right rests on a number of assumptions. First, the group must have some discrete identity which enables its members to be distinguished from outsiders. Second, the group must be essentially homogeneous in respect of its desire for the special treatment. If it is not, then special treatment will be repressive for some members of the group, however much it frees others. Third, not only must the group generally want the special treatment, but the treatment must be of a nature which creates liberties which can be exercised by all.

It is immediately clear that the first two assumptions are problematic. The boundaries of cultural groups are rarely clearly established. Values are not created in the abstract, they are shaped by their contrast and conflict with other values. Individual people are likely to feel part of one group in some contexts and of another in relation to different issues.[7] There is a significant danger that group rights of this second type will be based upon stereotypical judgements.[8] Both the nature and membership of cultural groups will fluctuate and group rights of this second type are unlikely to be able to maintain the flexibility needed to deal with this.

The third sense in which the term group right might be used covers cases where the group is allowed, acting as a collective body, to act in a way would which otherwise be unlawful. An example of this type of group right can be found in the Sex Discrimination Act 1975. Section 19 allows qualifications and authorizations to be withheld from one sex 'for purposes of organised religion' in order 'to comply with the doctrines of that religion or avoid offending the religious susceptibilities of a significant number of its followers'.[9] This does not permit an *individual* to discriminate on the basis of his religious beliefs; it only allows the religious *group* exemption when it acts collectively. It is only qualifications and authorizations, not particular appointments, which are covered and it is organized religion, not merely religion, which is protected. This, of course, would exclude religions which deny the validity of the authoritarian structure which it implies.

The fourth sense of group right recognizes the collective needs of the group, but rather than conferring special legal status on all its members or to the group acting collectively, this right permits some individual members to have special privileges on behalf of the whole. Here one might cite the law governing ritual slaughtering. In the case of the exemption covering the Jews, specific licensed individuals are not bound by the general legal provisions. Were an unlicensed person to use ritual methods of slaughtering he would have no legal excuse, despite his membership in the Jewish community. The need which the special exemption recognizes is the need of the whole community, but in order to balance the claims of the religious group against those of animal welfare, the exemption is given only to a few members of the group acting as the agents of the whole.

Both the third and fourth senses of group right can be seen as techniques used to deal with the problem of conflicting rights. Where there are competing principles the creation of a group right has to provide some sort of compromise. In the sex discrimination example this is achieved by specifying the purposes for which discrimination is permitted and requiring the religious body to have reached a high degree of agreement on its position before the exemption can come into play. In the case of ritual slaughter the limiting of the special exemption to a small number of individuals reduces the overall number of animal deaths by religious methods and the licensing system allows for monitoring.

The first and second senses of group rights seem more appropriate where the problem is less one of conflicting rights than of the infringement of religious freedom without any competing rights-based justification. The second sense is most appropriate when the problems can be said to be concerned with a separate social sphere.[10] The law can create a private space which can operate on independent principles. In this way, for example, the terms on which religious ministers serve have been consistently held to be outside the usual employment protection provisions because they are outside the normal market sphere.[11] Where the infringement of individual rights of religious freedom occurs in the public sphere, then the first category of group right will usually be required.

It must be pointed out, however, that the very idea of a group right raises a serious problem about the congruence between the rights of the group as a whole and that of its members. It may be that groups have an inherent life of their own, in which case the argument for their recognition is independent of the position of individuals. This is a different type of pluralism from that which is based on variation among individuals. It would be a pluralism which regarded group rights as flowing from the existence of the groups as independent legal persons.[12]

This is a view of religious (and civil) freedom which was espoused by J. N. Figgis in *Churches in the Modern State*.[13] Figgis saw the denial of the independent authority of groups as real and not merely fictitious persons as permitting despotic state power. He argued that where groups were recognized only as fictions in law they were seen as drawing their existence from the state. This permitted the state to disregard their claims, removing an important balancing power to the absolute power of the sovereign. Figgis also recognized that the implication of his position was a denial of absolute authority in the leadership of the church.[14] He referred to Rousseau's notion of the general will and commented:

> we must insist that every individual has and must have by the nature of things his share in forming that General Will, even though at any moment it may go entirely against his own judgment, except the one desire to continue a member of the society .[15]

On this view, he argues, the very nature of belonging to a group denies the validity of pure individualism. The actual social existence of groups contradicts absolute despotic power, but group values also preclude absolute freedom of individuals to act entirely as they please. The life of groups within society is thus more than the life of its members.

Figgis raises the paradox of group rights. On the one hand they can be used to enhance freedom: 'true liberty will be found by allowing full play to the uncounted forms of the associative instinct'.[16] Group rights, more influential and more robust than individual rights, act as a restriction on state power. They also reflect the gregarious nature of human existence, a feature underplayed, if not totally ignored, by individualistic concepts of human rights. At the same time, however, membership of a group entails the restriction of freedom, as collective decisions and values cannot be guaranteed to coincide with the individual concerns of group members.

The view that groups have an inherent life of their own can be contrasted with a second view of the basis of group rights. This view holds that group rights are instrumental, no more than a mechanism by which individual projects can be furthered more efficiently. An obvious example of group rights of this sort is the class action, whereby the individual rights of members of the class are vindicated. Similarly, where the individual members of a group can be said to have identical interests, instrumental group rights are appropriate.[17] Freedom of association can be accepted under a libertarian system on the basis that it is the only efficient way in which the rights of individuals can be protected in a state organized into a number of collective bodies. On this view, the right to join a trade union can be championed but the obligation to strike when called upon, or the closed shop, can be portrayed as contradicting the individualistic right in issue.[18]

On this second view of group rights, no special justification for their existence is necessary beyond the empirical observation that efficiency requires them. The moral and political justifications are of the same nature as for other individual rights. Group rights in the organic sense require a more complex legitimation. It has to be shown that even where there is conflict within the group, the collective position should be reinforced by the law at the expense of dissident views.

DEFINING A RELIGIOUS MINORITY

If the concept of group rights, of whichever sort, is accepted, the problem is raised of how the groups which are to be given them can be defined. A number of exemptions from the general law exist in the United Kingdom and a range of techniques for controlling access to them can be found: for example, individual self-selection; licensing powers for existing religious bodies; the creation of new commissions made up of the members of the religious group; control by those external to the tradition in question. A consideration of these existing techniques can provide a basis for discussion of the problems of definition.

The first example shows self-selection without objective scrutiny. The right of a witness, not a Jew or Christian, to take a non-biblical oath is recognized on the basis of his objection to doing so, without further limitation.[19] It is not possible to challenge the validity of an oath by showing that the way in which an oath was taken was not regarded as binding under the tenets of the religion to which a person belongs. The test is entirely subjective, it

> does not depend upon what may be the considerable intricacies of the particular religion which is adhered to by the witness. It concerns two matters and two matters only in our judgment. First of all, is the oath an oath which appears to the court to be binding on the conscience of the witness? And, if so, secondly, and most importantly, is it an oath which the witness himself considers to be binding upon his conscience? [20]

Consequently, expert evidence that a Muslim would be bound only by an oath sworn on the Koran does not invalidate testimony sworn on a Christian testament.[21] There is of course control of abuse of this provision through the law of perjury, but qualification for the special exemption is not defined by the law. It appears that it is necessary only for the witness to claim it. This would also seem to be true of the provision in the Criminal Justice Act 1988 that 'religious reasons' provide a lawful excuse for carrying a knife in a public place.[22]

Self-selection can also be combined with some degree of group definition. Persons are exempt from wearing motor cycle helmets on the basis
that they are wearing a turban as a follower of the Sikh religion.[23] As
there is no further definition of the word 'follower', this test is essentially
subjective rather than objective in that a claim that someone is a follower
of the Sikh religion will be virtually incontrovertible for practical
purposes. The same approach has been used to exempt construction
workers from regulations concerning the wearing of protective headgear, under section 11 of the Employment Act 1989.

The use of self-selection allows religious objections to be directly and
personally related to the issue in question, without distortion by filtering
access through the perspectives of a possibly unsympathetic judiciary.
Under self-selection both the right to the exemption, and its exercise,
are wholly dependent on the person claiming it. Were the meaning of
'Sikh' to be subjected to judicial scrutiny, it is likely that some who
believe themselves to be Sikhs would be denied that status in the same
way that the definition of religion in the charity law appears to exclude
even some mainstream religious positions.[24]

Self-selection can also be combined with elements of group selection.
Exemption from the prohibition on Sunday trading is available to Jews
who have registered an objection to opening on Saturdays with the relevant local authority. The application for registration must be accompanied by a declaration from the shopkeeper that the objection is held
on religious grounds and a certificate from a panel appointed by the
Board of Deputies affirming that the objection is genuine.[25] Obtaining
this certificate requires submission to the Board of Deputies and the
exemption therefore confers a new power on this body to determine
orthodoxy and to police the faith of the Jews.

The nature of this internal intervention into the politics of the Jewish
community requires a brief consideration. The Board of Deputies is a
representative body of British Jewry with a long history. It was founded
in 1760. Every recognized (itself implying the power to exclude some
claimants) synagogue is entitled to elect delegates.[26] The Board has
been criticized by some for representing communities rather than
individuals.[27] The requirement of a certificate from the Board was
introduced only in 1979 amid much controversy that its power was
abused to protect the community as a whole at the expense of individual
Jews.[28] Previously, individual Jewish shopkeepers were entitled to
exemption unless the local authority could convince a special tribunal
that the exemption was unwarranted. The Sunday trading exemption
thus combines the first and third categories of group right.

Exemption for religious slaughter works differently for Jews and

Muslims.[29] Muslims are exempted from the usual standards where the killing is 'by the Mohammedan method for the food of Mohammedans and by a Mohammedan'. Jews can only come within the exemption when they are licensed by the Rabbinical Commission specially set up under the Slaughterhouses Act 1974 for the purpose. These two methods of exemption are quite different. The former is an example of the first kind of group right, although as will be discussed shortly, access is overseen by secular licensing authorities. The latter comes into the fourth category outlined above. In the Sunday trading case the right of exemption exists to protect the economic livelihood of shopkeepers who would otherwise be forced to close two days instead of one. The exemption for ritual slaughter allows a few Jews to be exempt from the usual restriction in order to secure a supply of *kosher* meat for the whole community.

The Jewish exemption also raises a further point of interest in connection with the process by which the qualification for the exemption is defined. The licensing authority is a Rabbinical Commission set up specifically for the purpose. On the face of it this might appear to involve a greater distortion of Jewish politics than the use of the pre-existing Board of Deputies in the Sunday trading example. However, it should be noted that the new commission was set up as a compromise between that Board, which wished the licensing power to be exercised by the Chief Rabbi, and the Union of Orthodox Congregations, which feared the creation of an unrepresentative oligarchy.[30] The compromise was accepted by the Board of Deputies because it was feared that the exemption would otherwise be lost completely. Homa commented:

> The settlement thus reached was eminently satisfactory to both sides in that whilst it provided for the centralised administration of *Schechita* it also allowed freedom from the exercise of ecclesiastical monopoly against a dissident group. [31]

Thus while the setting up of the special commission altered the balance of power within the Jewish community, it is not necessary to see it as an infringement of religious freedom. To have used an existing body would also have upset the balance of power. Such an effect cannot be avoided, but if adverted to the political effect can be consciously exploited.

Having considered individual self-selection and internal group selection, it remains to consider the possibility of an outside body defining access to special treatment. In addition to the processes just described for identifying those who are permitted to carry out ritual slaughter, there is also a requirement for local authority licensing of the premises where it occurs.[32] This has the effect of submitting the religious slaughterers to secular scrutiny. Such an approach to special treatment runs risks. First, the outside, secular understanding of religious affiliation and requirements may be at variance with that of the members of the faith community in question. Second, the needs of the community may be underestimated. In 1987 the *Observer* reported that only five places in Birmingham had been officially licensed for *halal* slaughter, and that this fell seriously short of the demand. A further 45 premises were used illegally to make up the shortfall.[33]

The foregoing discussion not only raises a number of technical difficulties, but also indicates theoretical problems. First, how far are exemptions designed to further individual religious freedom and how far are they designed only to facilitate the life-style of a minority group? Ritual slaughter is not a group right in the first sense and an individual who seeks to claim it as such will be liable to prosecution.[34] Where group rights of the second type exist there will be potential for conflict between the collective interests of the group and the individual interests of its members. Careful definition of the criteria for access to special treatment can reduce, but not exclude, these difficulties.

Second, it is necessary to consider how the way in which the qualifications for exemptions from the general legal provisions are defined distorts the nature of the groups concerned. This is not a problem which can be avoided. Any exemption will inevitably do so in some way, but the relative merits of different approaches need to be considered in the course of legislating for special treatment. Even if it is appropriate to create a private libertarian space in which faiths can be lived out under religious precepts, the way in which the law defines that space may have a wide-reaching impact on the way in which life within in it operates.

THE RHETORIC OF EXEMPTION

The third section of this chapter is concerned with identifying concepts used to legitimate dispensing with the usual legal rules. This is not primarily intended to be an exercise in assessing the validity of these normative principles on their own terms, but to highlight the importance of consistently maintaining such arguments in context, considering the way in which they operate and are understood in practice. The previous section showed how the process of definition distorts the communities which are being acted upon by the law. The next section will examine the ways in which special treatment is perceived by the exempted groups. This part of the investigation bridges the gap between the two by asking what it is claimed is being achieved.

The most common principle appealed to is the need to permit 'official' or 'required' religious practices.[35] It is argued that members of religious minorities should not be required to go against their consciences where this would be contrary to 'a fundamental question of religious principle'.[36] This approach raises a series of problems of definition: what practices are 'required' and by whom or what? Where the religious groups concerned have some sort of hierarchical organization, this may not be difficult. The Church of England and the Roman Catholic Church both have internal legal systems and it would be possible to appeal to them to determine whether something was required. But this is not always the case. In the context of Rastafarianism, for example, the lack of organization would make this approach very difficult.[37]

The difficulties can be illustrated by reference to the debates in the House of Lords on the exemption of Sikhs from the obligation to wear motor cycle helmets. Because the religious status of the turban was in issue, the argument included the suggestion that the turban was not in fact obligatory. It is not one of the 'five symbols'. Correspondence in the *Sikh Courier* was cited to support the claim.[38] In the end the House sought to avoid the problem by arguing that 'so far as concerns the Sikh religion we should accept what the Sikhs themselves say'.[39] The difficulty with this is that the answer is likely to depend on who is asked. If senior members of the religious community say that a practice is not required, this will remove protection from individuals who take a more restrictive view of their religious responsibilities. Once more the potential for conflict between the collective and individual nature of religious freedom is seen.

A second problem relates to the ethnocentricity of the concept of required religious practices. While it is true that the division of approved acts into those merely encouraged and those required by the faith is not restricted to Christianity (Islam has a similar tradition of classification), there is something characteristically Anglican about the concept. The attempt to define Anglican beliefs in order to sustain the unity of the Church of England has relied on the idea that some aspects of Christian practice are 'adiaphora' or 'things indifferent'. It is therefore not necessary that there is agreement on them. This position enabled English ecclesiastical law to resist nineteenth-century attempts to use the law to enforce orthodoxy by holding that there was a significant distinction between doctrine *in* the Church of England and the doctrine *of* the Church of England.[40] The latter, the agreed and required doctrines, covered only a small proportion of the ground.

A second common justification is the need to protect members of religious minorities from injustices produced by the Christian assumptions on which English law is in part still based. Thus it is argued that it would be unjust to force a Jewish shop to be closed two days a week when a Christian could open six days. The exemption from prohibitions on Sunday trading for those whose holy day is Saturday is thus based on the 'simple ideas of holding the scales of statutory prohibition equally between Christian and Jew'.[41] The idea at stake is not, however, as simple as it might seem. It does not explain why only those religions whose holy day is Saturday should benefit from such an exemption. Section 53 (12) of the Shops Act allows 'persons who are members of any religious body regularly observing the Jewish Sabbath' to claim the exemption. If the basis were purely equality, the exemption should apply to all regular holy day observances, not merely those falling on a Saturday. The apparently objective argument would not lead to the exemption as in fact defined.

The process of definition can distort the arguments supporting special treatment in various ways. It has already been shown how the unresolved ambiguities between individual and group rights upset neat analyses. The provisions relating to religious slaughtering illustrate another feature of the problem, caused this time by the tensions between the claims to religious freedom as a substantive right on the one hand and a non-discrimination principle on the other.

The exemption granted to Muslims is for killing 'by the Mohammedan method for the food of Mohammedans and by a Mohammedan'. Where meat produced by *halal* slaughter is offered for general sale rather than just to fellow Muslims, this falls outside the protection. Thus a Muslim butcher who sold such meat to an RSPCA inspector who was wearing a crucifix committed an offence.[42] The implication of this decision is that Muslim butchers are confined to a ghetto — they must either produce meat which is suitable only for the alien non-Islamic community or restrict their activity to their own faith companions. This would prevent them competing in the open market and would thus conflict with the equality principle.

A final normative framework which is offered relies on an appeal to human rights principles. One approach is to try to work out whether an exemption is required by religious freedom. Another is to ask whether it would conflict with other recognized human rights.[43] Both these methods raise difficult questions. On the one hand the attempt to determine what the right requires could be said to beg the question. It also raises many of the difficulties already discussed under the heading of the 'required practices approach'. The major move forward from those issues concerns the availability of international agreements defining some areas more closely. However, even here accusations of ethnocentrism have been made which undermine the credibility of this approach it resolve disputes.[44]

The principle that special treatment is not justified when it conflicts with human rights carries with it a different pitfall. If special treatment is required by religious freedom then to disallow it because it conflicts with other human rights principles is to give religious freedom a very low priority. Reconciling conflict between rights is always difficult within the human rights discourse. Where derogation is permitted for some rights but not others this can give an indication of priority. Here, however, the answer would seem to be that religious freedom is supreme, as the scope for derogation from that right is highly restricted.[45] The problem of priority between conflicting rights can be resolved only by a full explanation of the justifications behind the rights in question. International documents record consensus but not its justification.

The suggestions that religiously required practices should be permitted by law or that structural discrimination should be compensated also raise questions of consistency. Why, for example, do we not exempt Rastafarians from prohibitions on the use of drugs?[46] Why do we not recognize the public holidays of non-Christian faiths?[47] Of course the claims of religious freedom must be balanced against other factors. Nevertheless, it is arguable that the normative principles provide less satisfactory explanations for the creation of exemptions than historical and political features.

The House of Lords debates on the motor cycle helmets issue refer to the contribution of Sikh troops to the Allied forces in World War II as often as they do to religious requirements. One might be forgiven for thinking that it was a sense of obligation to the community which tipped the balance in favour of the exemption. There is repeated mention of this debt in the speeches.[48] A cynical view can be (and was) expressed that such an accommodating position is related to the need to placate the Sikh community in times of racial tension.[49] On this basis special treatment is opportunistic, not rationally based.

These considerations must be related back to the issues identified in the first sections. The process of translating the desire to provide an exemption into legislation may frustrate the expressed intentions behind it. Arguments that required practices may be permitted will probably be distorted by the process of allowing one section of the minority community to determine what is required. Thus some individuals may not be allowed to act in a way in which they personally feel required to act by their religion but which the authorized body feels is not mandatory. A process of definition which relies on group selection will then fail to recognize the right to live as required by one's religious beliefs.

The problems exposed in *Saggers* v *British Railways Board*[50] provide an instructive illustration of these difficulties. Saggers was a Jehovah's

Witness who sought to avail himself of the right to opt out of closed-shop union membership, to which he objected 'on grounds of religious belief'.[51] His claim was vulnerable on two points. First, he had previously been a union member and had left after a dispute over arrears of union dues rather than on the issue of principle. Saggers argued that his beliefs had changed as his faith grew. This met the first objection, but laid him open to the second. As Saggers accepted, the Jehovah's Witness religion did not itself proscribe trade-union membership and many of its adherents do belong to trade unions.

There was therefore a conflict. If access to the right of conscientious objection were to be defined in terms of the beliefs of the religious group to which a person belongs, Saggers' objection did not qualify. If the test were subjective, he clearly qualified as the tribunal found that he was sincere and genuine. A majority verdict of the Employment Appeal Tribunal supported Saggers, but the dissenter crystallized the difficulty he found in the following terms: '[I find] it difficult to accept that people can shelter within a recognised religion or sect which enables them to claim genuine religious beliefs and then tack on personal riders such as a refusal to join a trade union'.[52] The exemption in issue was rephrased in 1980 to reinforce the tribunal's emphasis on the subjective nature of the test and to broaden it to ground of conscience and deeply held personal conviction.[53]

This section has considered some of the justifications proffered to support special treatment and noted some of the difficulties which they raise. It is not enough, however, to look at the adequacy or otherwise of the reasons offered on their own terms and in relation to the technical processes by which they can be enshrined in law. The principles expressed to be the reasons for exemption by the lawmakers must also be related to the concerns of the exempted groups. The reasons given for justifying special treatment may be quite different from the reasons for its importance to the group itself. This is the concern of the final section of the paper.

READING AN EXEMPTION

In order to understand the difference between the way in which the legislators and those given special treatment understand the significance of statutory exemptions, how cultural signs are interpreted must be considered. This chapter makes use of the distinction drawn by the French post-structuralist thinker Roland Barthes between *denoted* meaning and *connoted* meaning.[54] Denoted meaning is used by Barthes to refer to what is actually perceived when an image is considered; connoted meanings are created when those perceptions are interpreted by reference to the prior knowledge and experience of the 'reader'. Two readers may thus share the same experience at the denotative level but understand it quite differently because the connotative systems into which they place it are quite different. Thus, while denoted meaning is usually relatively uncontroversial, the scope for variation in the connoted meanings of any particular image is enormous, as these derive from widely varying experience.

In 'Myth Today' Barthes cites as an example of a complex cultural sign the photograph on the cover of *Paris-Match* of a young uniformed Negro saluting the French tricolour.

> Whether naively or not, I see very well what it signifies to me: that France is a great Empire, that all her sons, without colour discrimination, faithfully serve under her flag, and that there is no better answer to the detractors of an alleged colonialism than the zeal shown by this Negro in serving his so-called oppressors. [55]

The denoted meaning of the picture is that somewhere a young black has saluted the French flag. The connotations produced by Barthes are much fuller. Another observer might see things quite differently, such as viewing the picture as indicative of the degree of oppression achieved by French colonialism. Why does the young man need to be black — is there something unusual about it? Is it evidence of the insidious efficiency of state propaganda, misleading the black community into believing itself to be free? Barthes points out that the decoding of the connoted, second order, meanings destroys the power of the myth, preventing it from being read naively. Yet undertaking the analysis shows how important it is to excavate readings which could be accepted as natural, but which may differ significantly depending on the cultural frame into which the material is placed.

In the context of special treatment, debates about what actually may be done under an exemption are analogous to the concept of denoted meanings. Issues of statutory interpretation can therefore be debated within the standard legal discourse without overwhelming confusion. However, it is impossible to understand the significance of special treatment without also considering its connotations. Enshrining the law in statutory form privileges the interpretations given by the legislators and the application by courts privileges the decodings made by lawyers. The interpretations of the groups given special treatment are thus systematically excluded.[56]

For the legislators the connotations will be conditioned by assumptions of benevolence; the feeling that they are giving groups better treatment than they would otherwise receive. For minorities, it may be just another example of paternalism based on a misunderstanding of their values. Careful consideration of the significance of special treatment will take such problems into account. Examining these issues further undermines the claim that existing special treatment is based on objective normative principles. When case studies are considered, it becomes apparent that the immediate political context may colour the minorities' views of what sort of special treatment is appropriate or necessary.

The campaign for the right to wear a turban is an interesting example. The turban has caused more controversy than the 'five symbols' of Sikhism, which are more fundamental to the religion's way of life. This is probably best explained by its visibility, which enables it to function as a symbol of independence and solidarity. One study of young Sikhs observed a pattern of early rebellion against the practice of growing hair and wearing a turban followed by the adoption of those traditions in response to experiences of prejudice as 'a symbolic act of pride in being different'.[57] Similarly, a public dispute about the right of transport workers to wear turbans in Wolverhampton was accompanied by a revived enthusiasm for the garment, in solidarity, among the Sikh community.[58] As Taiffel has put it:

> The awareness of being a member of a separate minority group and the identification with it following upon this awareness depend upon the *perceived* clarity of the boundaries separating in common the members of the from others.[59]

The significance of the exemptions from wearing protective headgear for the Sikh community itself would therefore seem to be more that they claim the right to display a symbol of resistance to the dominant culture than that there is a religious obligation at stake. These connotations are underplayed by an analysis based on the latter assumption.

The rhetoric by which special treatment is justified in the official sphere thus excludes consideration of the importance of the issue for the Sikh community. In terms of Barthes' distinction, the existence of the motor cycle helmet exemption carries a denoted meaning perceived by all, that a Sikh wearing his turban will be free to ride without a helmet. But at a connotative level the legislators understand it as the recognition of religious obligation while the Sikh community are more concerned with vindication of their right to be different and a visible expression of otherness.

Noting this variation in interpretation is vital to the formulation of social policy on the issue. Raising the visibility of Sikh separatism would be counter-productive if a policy of assimilation were being pursued. If the motive behind the Sikh claims for exemption were in breach of such an overall policy then couching the debate in terms of religious obligation would divert attention from the main issue. In the context of a pluralist policy, enhancing the public profile of the Sikh community might be seen to have an important educative effect, bringing home the multi-cultural nature of our society. In this case the Sikh claims would be in tune with the dominant social policy.[60]

The variation of connotations in the Sikh example arises from the relationship between minority and dominant cultural communities. The control by the Jewish authorities over the licensing of Sunday trading illustrates a different aspect of the politics of special treatment. Here it is the internal politics of the Jewish community which need to be taken into account. The introduction of the need for a certificate to support a shopkeeper's declaration of religious conviction resulted from pressure from Jewish leaders motivated by fears that the reputation of their community was being tarnished because of abuses of the less strictly regulated exemption. This move has been criticized as promoting the well-being of the religious establishment at the expense of individual religious freedom. No procedural safeguards exist to protect individual interests. Proceedings are secret, the Board of Deputies is not accountable to outside scrutiny and applicants have no right to be represented or even to be accompanied by an adviser. Between December 1979 and April 1981 one third of the applications were rejected without reasons being given publicly.[61]

The courts have refused to intervene to protect individual Jews against alleged abuses. An attempt to challenge the introduction of the 1979 regulations was thrown out.[62] In a case on the licensing of ritual slaughter the Court of Appeal declined to intervene on the basis that there was 'a clear intention that such matters should be left to . . . those in the Jewish community best qualified to decide thereon'.[63] While it may seem legitimate when the relationship between the Jewish community as a whole and the dominant culture is considered, this deference to the Jewish authorities is far more problematic in the light of internal religious politics. Complete neutrality is, of course, impossible, but that does not excuse legislators from ignoring such political factors. The way in which an individual Jew in conflict with the Jewish establishment would understand the exemptions is likely to be in terms of the law failing to provide the usual protections against abuse of power, not as a recognition of religious freedom.

If contemporary political factors are vital to understanding the interpretation of special treatment, it is also important that the traces of

history are properly considered. Past grievances may play a highly significant part in shaping the understanding of issues. This point can be
made by reference both to the general debate about the extension of
blasphemy laws to protect other faiths and to the specific response of the
Islamic community to Salman Rushdie's *Satanic Verses*. It can be argued
that blasphemy has long been used systematically by the Christian tradition to ridicule rival faiths, in particular Judaism and Islam.[64] On this
view, the refusal to extend the protection of blasphemy laws to Islam is
more than an isolated piece of contemporary discrimination, it is part
of a wider historical conspiracy.

The impact of history is particularly acute in the Rushdie case because
of the author's deliberate use of the abusive name 'Mahound' in an
attempt to 'reoccupy negative images, to repossess pejorative language,
and . . . to turn insults into strengths'.[65] For many Muslims awareness
of the historical use of this name as a means of vilification must bring
pain: 'What Muslims see in Rushdie's fictional adaptations of ancient
stereotypes is not simply hatred, but the long, terrible, triumphalist
hatred which the West has had for Islam almost since its beginnings'.[66]
These historical scars go some way to explaining the surprising extent
to which the whole Islamic community, and not just its fundamentalist
elements, has been scandalized by Rushdie's book.[67]

For current purposes the important factor is not the fairness or otherwise of these Muslim perceptions of Rushdie's offence, but the significance of the fact that they exist in formulating public policy. To ignore
them is to neutralize any possibility of effective reform because the
nature of the problem will not be properly addressed. Unless the way
in which the group receiving special treatment understands what is
at stake is taken into account in formulating legislative responses,
then legal intervention risks being culturally imperialist and counter
productive.

CONCLUSION

This chapter has attempted to unravel some of the complexities of providing special treatment for religious minorities. Rather than suggesting
solutions it has tried to uncover the inadequacies of the existing criteria
which are used publicly to justify exemptions from the criminal law. It
has argued that difficulties arise from a number of sources. The ambiguities of the notion of group rights cloud discussion. Lack of attention
to the technical difficulties of drafting exemptions leads to the risk that

unintended effects of the way in which access to special treatment is defined may undermine policy objectives. The political and historical contexts out of which the calls for exemptions arise and which surround their interpretation need also to be taken into account. Consideration of these factors must supplement rather than replace existing theories of special treatment, but this chapter contends that without it those theories cannot be maintained.

NOTES

1. Robertson, G. *Freedom, the Individual and the Law* 6th edn (Harmondsworth, Penguin, 1989). Compare, e.g. the 5th edition (Harmondsworth, Penguin, 1982).
2. See Lacey's chapter in this book.
3. Marriage Act 1949 s. 26(1).
4. Union of Muslim Organisations *Why Muslim Family Law for British Muslims* (London, UMO, 1983).
5. For a discussion of the history of this approach and an assessment of its implications in the modern context, see Lustgarten, L. 'Liberty in a culturally plural society' in Phillips Griffiths, A. (ed) *Of Liberty* (Cambridge, Cambridge University Press, 1983).
6. For a general discussion, see Poulter, S. 'The claim to a separate Islamic system of personal law for British Muslims' in Mallat, C. and Connors, J. (eds) *Islamic Family Law* (London, Graham & Trotman, 1990).
7. Verma, G. K. 'Pluralism: some theoretical and practical considerations' in Commission for Racial Equality *Britain: A Plural Society* (London, CRE, 1990).
8. See, e.g. Modood, T. 'Colour, class and culture' (1990) 30 *Equal Opportunities Review*. 31–33 and his essay in this volume.
9. Sex Discrimination Act 1975 s. 19(2).
10. For discussion of the idea of separate social spheres in the discrimination context, see Gardner's essay in this volume.
11. See, e.g. *re National Insurance Act 1911; re Employment of Church of England Curates* [1912] 2 Ch 563; *re Employment of Ministers of the United Methodist Church* [1912] 107 LT 143; *Methodist Conference (President) v Parfitt* [1984] QB 368; 'Rabbi loses appeal against dismissal' *The Times* (11 January 1985); *Davies v Presbyterian Church of Wales* [1986] 1 WLR 323 (see [1986] CLJ 404); *Santokh Singh v Guru Nanak Gurdwarah The Times* [1990] ICR 309.
12. This would be a corporate form of structural pluralism; see Lynch, J. 'Cultural pluralism, structural pluralism and the United Kingdom' in Commission for Racial Equality *Britain: A Plural Society* (London, CRE, 1990) discussing Gordon, M. *Assimilation in American Life: The Role of Race, Religion and National Origins* (New York, Oxford University Press, 1964).
13. Figgis, J. N. *Churches in the Modern State* 2nd edn (London, Longmans, Green & Co, 1914); see also Lustgarten op. cit. (note 5) for discussion in the modern context.
14. Ibid. lecture IV 'Ultramontanism'.
15. Ibid. at 159–60.
16. Ibid. at 171.
17. See Atkins, S. 'Women's rights' in Cooper, J. and Dhavan, R. (eds) *Public Interest Law* (Oxford, Blackwell, 1986).
18. See the discussion by Summers, C. 'Trade unions and their members' in Gostin, L. (ed.) *Civil Liberties in Conflict* (London, Routledge, 1988). See also Marfarlane, L. J. *The Right to Strike* (Harmondsworth, Penguin, 1981).
19. Oaths Act 1978 s. 1, 4.

20. *R v Kemble* [1990] 1 WLR 1111, 1114.

21. Ibid.; contrast the position under the Oaths Act 1888, *R v Moore* [1892] 66 LT 125.

22. Criminal Justice Act 1988 s. 139(5).

23. Motor-Cycle Crash Helmets (Religious Exemption) Act 1976 s. 1.

24. See, for example, the problems in including Buddhism within definitions based on the worship of a supernatural god discussed in *Barralet v A-G* [1980] 3 ALL ER 918 and *R v Registrar General ex p. Segerdal* [1970] 3 All ER 886.

25. Shops Act 1950 s. 53, SI 1979/1294.

26. *Halsbury's Laws of England* 4th edn (London, Butterworths, 1975) vol. 14 paras 1426, 1432.

27. Kimmel, H. 'The structure and regime of the Board of Deputies of British Jews' (1968) 4 *Jewish Public Affairs*.

28. Alderman, G. 'Jews and Sunday trading: the use and abuse of delegated legislation' (1982) 60 *Public Administration* 99–104.

29. Slaughterhouses Act 1974 s. 36(3).

30. Homa, B. *Orthodoxy in Anglo-Jewry* (London, Jewish Historical Society of England, 1969) pp. 28–30.

31. Ibid. at 30.

32. Slaughterhouses Act 1974 part I.

33. Smart, V. 'Muslim anger as slaughter shops face crackdown' *Observer* (19 April 1987) 5.

34. *R v Efstathiou* [1984], unreported but discussed in Poulter, S. *English Law and Ethnic Minority Customs* (London, Butterworths, 1986) para. 10.14.

35. E.g. Poulter, S. *English Law and Ethnic Minority Customs* (Butterworths, London, 1986) para. 10.17.

36. Lord Avebury Hansard HL vol. 374 col. 1058 discussing exempting Sikhs from the wearing of motor cycle helmets.

37. Ethnic Minorities Unit *Rastafarianism in London* (London, Greater London Council, 1984).

38. HL vol. 374 col. 1064; HL vol. 376 col. 1163–66. See also the debate in *New Community*: Thompson, M. 2 *New Community* 429; Gurinda, S. 3 *New Community* 427.

39. HL vol. 374 col. 1059.

40. Montgomery, J. 'The ordination of women' (1984) 87 *Theology* 447. See especially *Gorham v Bishop of Exeter* [1850] 2 Robb Ecc 1; Moore's Special Report.

41. *Thanet DC v Ninedrive Ltd* [1978] 1 A11 ER 703, 705. The exemption is to be found in the Shops Act 1950 s. 53.

42. *Malins v Cole* [1986] CLY 89.

43. Poulter, S. 'Ethnic minority customs, English law and human rights' (1987) 36 *International and Comparative Law Quarterly* 589; Australian Law Reform Commission *Report on the Recognition of Aboriginal Customary Laws* Rep. 31 (Canberra, Australian Government Publishing Service, 1986). See Poulter, S. 'Cultural pluralism in Australia' (1988) 2 *International Journal of Law and the Family* 127 for comment.

44. 'Summary of discussion' in Commission for Racial Equality *Britain: A Plural Society* (London, CRE, 1990)

45. Poulter, S. 'Cultural pluralism and its limits: a legal perspective' in Commission for Racial Equality *Britain: A Plural Society* (London, CRE, 1990) pp. 17–20.

46. See Poulter, S. *English Law and Ethnic Minority Customs* (London, Butterworths, 1986) para. 10.17.

47. Ibid. at para. 9.26.

48. HL vol. 374 col. 1060; HL vol. 374 col. 1062; HL vol. 376 col. 1169.

49. HL vol. 374 col. 1064.

50. *Saggers v British Railways Board* [1977] ICR 809; *Saggers v British Railways Board (No. 2)* [1978] ICR 1111.

51. Trade Union and Labour Relations Act 1974 schedule 1 para. 6(5).

52. *Saggers v British Railways Board (No. 2)* [1978] ICR 1111, 1115.

53. Employment Protection (Consolidation) Act 1970 s. 58(4), as amended: 'genuinely objects on grounds of conscience or other deeply-held personal conviction to being a member of any trade union whatsoever or of a particular trade union'.

54. See Barthes, R. 'Rhetoric of the image' in *Image-Music-Text* (London, Fontana, 1977).

55. Barthes, R. 'Myth Today' in *Mythologies* (London, Paladin, 1973) p. 125. This edition was

selected, and translated, from the original French edition of 1957 by Annette Lavers.

56. 'Law . . . can be described linguistically or, more importantly, discursively, in terms of its systematic appropriation and privileging of legally recognised meanings, accents and connotations (modes of inclusion) and its simultaneous rejection of alternative and competing meanings or accents, forms of utterance and discourse generally as extrinsic, unauthorised and threatening (modes of exclusion)' Goodrich, P. *Legal Discourse* (London, Macmillan, 1987) p. 3; see also pp. 183–204.

57. James, A. *Sikh Children in Britain* (Oxford, Oxford University Press, 1974) p. 50.

58. Beetham, D. *Transport and Turbans* (Oxford, Oxford University Press, 1971).

59. Taiffel, H. 'The social psychology of minorities' in Husband, C. (ed.) *Race in Britain* (London, Hutchinson, 1982) p. 222.

60. See Poulter's essay in this volume and Parekh, B. 'The social logic of pluralism' in Commission for Racial Equality *Britain: A Plural Society* (London, CRE, 1990) for brief discussions of the nature of policies of assimilation and pluralism.

61. Alderman, G. 'Jews and Sunday trading: the use and abuse of delegated legislation' (1982) 60 *Public Administration* 99–104.

62. *R v London Committee of Deputies of British Jews ex p. Helmcourt The Times* (16 July 1981).

63. *R v Rabbinical Commission for the Licensing of Shochetim, ex p. Cohen The Times* (22 December 1987).

64. Webster, R. *A Brief History of Blasphemy* (Southwold, Orwell Press, 1990) esp. ch. 1.

65. Rushdie, S. 'Choice between light and dark' *Observer* (22 January 1989) 11.

66. Webster op. cit. (note 64) 40.

67. Modood, T. 'British Asian Muslims and the Rushdie affair' (1990) 61(2) *Political Quarterly* 143–60.

12

The Interaction of Race and Gender[1]

Sandra Fredman and Erika Szyszczak

We . . . often find it difficult to separate race from class from sex oppression because in our lives they are most often experienced simultaneously.[2]

Of course I am afraid, because the transformation of silence into language and action is an act of self-revelation, and that always seems fraught with danger.[3]

Issues concerned with race and gender discrimination are frequently dealt with along the same or parallel lines. In the United States, a single enforcement agency has jurisdiction in respect of both types of discrimination. In Britain, although race and sex discrimination are handled under two separate statutes and the law is monitored and enforced by two separate Commissions, the structure and conceptual framework of the legislation have close parallels. Moreover, reforms generated in one affect the other. For example, the Sex Discrimination Act 1975 was originally modelled upon the United States' race discrimination law, developed in *Griggs* v *Duke Power Co.*,[4] and European Community law regulating sex discrimination continues to make an impact on the Race Relations Act 1976.[5] This prompts the central question addressed in this paper. Is it appropriate to deal with race and gender as sub-categories of the same overall problem of discrimination or are there fundamental differences? This question is of more than just theoretical importance. It also has two important practical implications. First, should the law deal with both types of discrimination in the same way, or are the differences between them so great as to warrant a strategy which deals more specifically with issues raised in each area? Second, how should the law deal with situations in which both sex and race discrimination are targeted at the same individuals, namely black women?

This latter question is particularly pressing in the context of recent feminist legal writing and research, which has concentrated on women's relationship with and experience of the law.[6] Gradually the gaps and silences of masculinist legal theory have been filled, only to reveal even further frontiers of enquiry. In both Britain and the US, black female academics have mounted a critique of the narrow focus of white feminist legal scholarship on the grounds of its tendency to overlook racial identity, and thus to define issues in a manner which addresses more significantly the experiences of white women.[7] This has led to a colour-blindness in feminist research and to an over-simplification of the sites of women's oppression. In particular the argument is made that white feminists fail, or are unable, to recognize that women from black and ethnic minorities experience various forms of oppression simultaneously. For black women, the status of being both a woman and a black is not regarded as additive, but synergistic. It creates 'a condition for black women which is more terrible than the sum of their two constituent parts'.[8] While black women cannot forget or ignore the complexity of the interaction of race and gender in their lives, equally they cannot separate experiences attributable to their gender or their race, or indeed other characteristics which may lead to disadvantage.

The purpose of this essay is to address the complexity of these issues as they have arisen in academic debate and practical reality. We cannot pretend to offer any clear answers, or even coherent strategies for the future. What we hope to achieve is a first step in a dialogue which will confront some of the issues raised. We begin by considering the weaknesses in the existing conceptual apparatus for dealing with race and sex discrimination, our argument being that there is an urgent need for reform in both arenas, and that simple amalgamation on the basis of existing concepts will continue to be inadequate. In the second part, we take the argument further by considering in abstract terms the specific differences between race and sex discrimination, as a foundation for the proposition that the law should recognize and address each issue more specifically. In the final sections, we turn to the position of black women and argue for a more holistic approach towards them as a particular group with special economic and social needs, and for a recognition of the specific disadvantage felt by women who are black.

CRITIQUE OF EXISTING CONCEPTS OF DISCRIMINATION

Other chapters in this book deal in detail with the current criticisms of the existing legal framework in Britain; here we merely outline two major reasons for the ineffectiveness of the law. First, both the Sex Discrimination Act and the Race Relations Act place too much reliance upon the individual, both in terms of conceptualizing a group wrong in individualistic terms and by leaving the burden of enforcement to the individual complainant. The role of the two enforcement agencies, the Equal Opportunities Commission (EOC) and the Commission for Racial Equality (CRE), in incorporating a collective dimension to the issue of discrimination is too restricted. This is compounded by the problems of proof facing an individual: in both Acts the hurdles relating to the burden of proof and the provision of acceptable evidence to show discrimination are difficult to surmount.[9]

Second, the law is based on a flawed concept of equality. Instead of concentrating on correcting disadvantage resulting from systematic discrimination against a particular group, the existing legal framework of both race and sex discrimination assumes a false symmetry, prohibiting discrimination in favour of a disadvantaged group to the same extent as discrimination against that group. In addition, the notion of equality requires a standard against which the position of different groups can be measured. The answer to the question 'Equal to what?' becomes 'Equal to white males'; ultimately the white male is the underlying norm which must be mirrored and adhered to. The effect is that women are expected to conform to a world based on male values and black people to white values.

The concept of equality is also open to a wide range of interpretations. Only some forms of inequality are considered worthy of legal redress; in particular, economic inequality is not sufficient *per se*. The Acts are ostensibly based on the less radical concept of equality of opportunity. However, equal opportunity is predicated on equalizing the starting point of different groups. Yet the legislation makes no commitment to supplying sufficient resources to ensure such equality. This is compounded by the provision that commercial justifiability may excuse discriminatory practices. Thus in jobs where educational standards or a level of skills are required, previous disadvantage will disqualify certain groups even though that disadvantage is itself due to discrimination. This remains true despite the fact that the objective test to justify alleged discriminatory practices, derived from *Bilka-Kaufhaus GmbH* v *Weber*,[10] has improved upon the test based on merely 'sound and tolerable' reasons emanating from *Ojutiku* v *Manpower Services Commission.*[11]

Could the above weaknesses be surmounted by an amalgamation of the sex and race discrimination legislation and enforcement mechanisms? The chief attraction of such a move would be to overcome the limited resources of each agency and the *ad hoc* manner in which the EOC and CRE co-ordinate their strategies. When a case arises involving sex and race discrimination it seems that in considering funding the EOC and CRE decide which form of action has the best chance of succeeding. This decision is made not on the basis of a quantifiable factor (that is, has *more* sex discrimination than race discrimination occurred?) but by posing a legal question: is the sex or the race discrimination claim more likely to succeed? Thus black women are forced into involuntary choices. As Wilson argues, black women 'are more likely to perceive racism and racial discrimination as the main issue confronting them in terms of employment, housing, education . . . and not sex discrimination'.[12]

It may be that from a personal and a political perspective a claimant may prefer to categorize the discrimination as either race or sex discrimination. The CRE does provide assistance for cases with an element of sex as well as race discrimination, illustrated in the case of *North West Thames Regional Health Authority* v *Noone,*[13] and now the issue of women is part of CRE annual work plans.[14] Coussey[15] has made powerful arguments for a joint strategy, arguing that there is enough common ground, in terms of cause, effect and results to mount a common equal opportunities strategy in Britain. Fortunately we can turn to the US model of a single agency tackling equal opportunities to assess the implications of a closer interaction of sex and race discrimination issues. The experience of the US, however, indicates that a simple amalgamation is not sufficient to surmount the fundamental weaknesses in the conceptual structure; indeed, the composite is even weaker than each of the two parts.[16] We thus turn to the second section of this essay, considering the differences between race and sex discrimination, and point to the need to maintain separate and more specific strategies.

THE DIFFERENCES BETWEEN RACE AND SEX DISCRIMINATION

The major difference between race and sex discrimination lies in the causes of each. Only by addressing the basic causes can the law effectively deal with the problems that result. Thus it is essential to consider the causes of each type of discrimination in detail.

For women there are two central causative features of sex discrimination: issues relating to child-care and domestic responsibilities, and issues relating to violence. Child-care and domestic responsibilities (including both domestic work and unpaid caring for other family members) play a crucial role in defining women's place in society. Women with such domestic responsibilities are limited in their hours of paid work, mobility, access to training and education and trade-union activities. Prospects of promotion are restricted by a career structure which assumes a continuous paid working life. Clearly these limitations will vary between white women and women from different ethnic groups, as well as between women with actual domestic responsibilities and those without. But *all* women, regardless of their real responsibilities are limited by assumptions that women are primarily child-bearers and rearers. Thus women are stereotyped as lacking seriousness about work, as dependent upon a male breadwinner in a family unit, as inevitably about to leave or limit their paid work for children. This in turn affects expectations about girls' education, the education and training received and ultimately the nature of the paid and unpaid work carried out by women in society. Moreover, many of these stereotypes are translated into other areas of law which affect women in a discriminatory way, the best example being social security regulations. Outside of the world of paid work there are other issues relating to reproductive capacity and women's health.

Violence is the second central issue of women's specific experience of the public and the private world. But here the nature of violence is specifically gender-related. The primary manifestations are in the form of pornography, sexual harassment at work and rape.

What are the implications of this analysis for the legal framework in respect of sex discrimination? We would argue that the law should address each of these causative factors in a specific and focused manner. Thus for a woman to achieve equality in the world of work, the law must facilitate the provision of flexible working hours, career-breaks, child-care facilities, maternity and paternity leave. As Findlay[17] has argued, for true equality to emerge between the sexes law must transform and transgress the public/private divide which it itself has helped to create. Such a strategy should also include consideration of reproductive issues. Such questions are not specifically dealt with by the Sex Discrimination Act 1975 (as amended), although they have appeared as issues in litigation under that Act.[18] As Kenney[19] points out, reproductive capacity affects both men and women and yet only the European Community has recognized this fact in its legislation concerning health and safety at work. The women's movement, in its campaigns around 'body politics', has brought home the centrality of reproductive issues to all aspects of women's lives. However, in Britain these issues are seen as scientific questions of access to technology or resources (such as fertility techniques, contraception or cervical cancer screening); or as 'moral' issues based on conscience (such as abortion, sterilization and embryology research). In respect of gender-related violence, the law has made significant strides as regards sexual harassment.[20] But pornography is still characterized as a freedom of speech issue, and the law concerning rape remains heavily weighted against the victim. Most striking is the law's reluctance to intervene in cases of domestic violence.

In contrast to sex discrimination, we would argue that the concept of race discrimination is more diverse. As a starting point race discrimination is targeted at a wider range of characteristics than gender discrimination and includes nationality, ethnicity, colour, racial group or a combination of these characteristics. Each target demands a different response from the law. We can only outline a few examples here. Thus, if discrimination occurs on the grounds of nationality, immigration laws may need to be scrutinized (a role hitherto limited *by* law), specific recognition given to external qualifications and indirect discrimination removed in requirements relating to work experience within the host state.[21] If ethnicity is the dominant form of discrimination, then the law must be prepared to recognize different cultural norms as well as deal with the possibility of conflict between those norms and non-discrimination ideals. For example, Muslim women's needs may conflict with central aspects of a non-discrimination programme, such as multi-cultural schooling and the abandonment of single-sex schools. This is a complex problem which is addressed in several other essays in this book. At the heart of the issue is where to strike a balance between the recognition of ethnic minority groups' needs for different treatment in order to preserve ethnic traditions on the one hand, and observance of other fundamental anti-discrimination principles, such as equality in marriage, on the other. In the accommodation of difference, however, we would agree with Poulter's essay in this book that law must be able to distinguish between acceptable differences and those differences which must be subordinate to other values, such as the elimination — or at least control of — sex discrimination.

Similarly, where race is the dominant issue, the main causes of discrimination differ yet again. One important factor relating to race discrimination is the effect of residential segregation, a feature which does not generally fall into the main causative factors of gender discrimination. It is arguable that women who live within patriarchal family structures are subjected to very different forms of control (often

involving private forms of power) from those affecting blacks who live
in ghettos, where power is often exercised in a very public form, particularly through policing and state control of family life. In addition,
residential segregation on racial grounds is closely associated with
economic disadvantage. Although there is a strong overlap with class,
as Modood's essay in this book shows, race is often the *cause* and not just
the description of disadvantage. Ghettoes usually mean poorer housing
and low quality education across *all* subjects. This contrasts with the
educational disadvantage of girls, which occurs largely in the lack of
availability of 'masculine' subjects for girls. In the context of violence,
which exists in both sex and race discrimination, racial violence is often
more public and overt and exemplified in abuse and assault.

This analysis shows that, as in the case of sex discrimination, the law
needs to concentrate upon the specific causes of racial disadvantage,
particularly the material causes such as inferior housing and education.
It is not sufficient to identify and outlaw prejudice at the point of selection for employment. In other words, legislation related to sex and race
discrimination must provide a clear programme of resource allocation
to meet different needs.

This analysis also reveals that similar concepts are manifested quite
differently within the different arenas of sex and race. Equality is the
clearest example. For women, 'equality' means conforming to a world
of work based on the assumption that the child-care responsibilities
of workers are handled outside the labour market. Traditionally, the
worker was a man whose wife worked unpaid at home. For a woman
encumbered with child-care or other caring responsibilities, 'equal
treatment' means no more than conforming with this stereotype. This
in turn leaves few alternatives: either she must find other low-paid
women to look after her children, or she must work in subordinate conditions such as those associated with part-time work and home-working.
For black and ethnic minority groups, 'equality' means the need to conform to white cultural and social values, such as those relating to family
structure, dress and religion.

The ideology of racism differs from that of sexism, with the former
having a stronger element of coercion, and the latter relying more on
consent.[22] The ideology of racism pervades the use of state power to
coerce, seen in the heavy policing of black residential areas, policing of
welfare claimants, violence in prisons and public places. Equally, everyday racism and race discrimination coerce blacks into occupying only
a small space in society, evidenced by their under-representation in the
media, public office, politics, skilled jobs and managerial positions. The
ideology of sexism also produces coercion — in the form of rape and
sexual harassment. But sexism is primarily based upon consensual

ideas concerning the 'natural' role of women and ideas of 'femininity'. This type of coercion, which women have argued has a public and general dimension, is nonetheless treated by law as a private, individual issue.

BLACK WOMEN AS A DISCRETE LEGAL GROUP

While it is clear that sex and race discrimination merit different handling by the law, we are left with questions concerning one group which falls under both heads of disadvantage: black women. The cumulative effect of race and sex discrimination is not simply additive. Black women experience problems not shared by either white women or black men. Scales-Trent[23] argues:

> By creating two separate categories for its major social problems — 'the race problem' and 'the women's issue' — society has ignored the group which stands at the interstices of these two groups, black women.

In the United States a third way forward has been explored in recognizing the dilemma posed by the interaction of race and gender. This is the holistic approach of recognizing black women as a distinct group, worthy of legal protection, with its own legal identity. It is to this question that we now turn.

Black women may be seen as a discrete group in relation to both white women and black men. Differences in family organization, education, culture and employment patterns make it difficult for black women to share the same legal and political concerns as white women. One example concerns abortion. Black women often experience abortion as a coercive mechanism, whereas for white women abortion is seen as a question of autonomy.[24] The power structures within black families often differ from those of white families and across different ethnic groups. For example, high rates of unemployment among black men result in black women playing a pivotal role in maintaining family income. Often black women provide the main source of income. Child-care for black women takes a variety of forms depending upon family structure, geographical location and income. These factors have led some black women to avoid or delay marriage.[25]

Another difference between black and white women which has both economic and legal consequences is that while paid employment participation rates vary among black women, such women have always been portrayed as workers occupying a subordinate role to white women, for whom the myth of passive and delicate femininity has been a preserve. This has resulted in different images of black women in society as well as the distortion of those images in pornography.[26]

In the US, black activists and scholars have addressed the issue of how a new legal status for black women could be derived by using the disadvantages of their multiple status. Initially the US courts were not sympathetic to multiple status claims. As in Britain, black women were forced to separate their sex and race discrimination claims. In *Degraffenreid* v *General Motors Assembly Division*,[27] the court foresaw the potential for moving discrimination law beyond the standard of comparability with the white male norm and rejected a joint sex and race discrimination challenge to a 'last-in-first-out' lay-off policy. The justifications for the rejection of a *combination* of sex and race claims were well rehearsed. First, it was argued that by allowing the interaction of race and sex claims the courts would create a 'super remedy' for black women that 'would give them relief beyond what the drafters of the relevant statutes intended'.[28] Black women should come to the courts on an equal footing with white women and black men. They should not, and could not, obtain better *locus standi* and remedies by creating an unauthorized class of plaintiff. (At this juncture it is interesting to note that the US courts have not encountered any difficulty in recognizing white men as a distinct class deserving special treatment in reverse discrimination claims.) A second justification was that by allowing the growth of 'special group' interests, Title VII would become unmanageable. It would open the door to allow other interest groups to make special pleadings. Finally, the creation of a new group interest would open a 'Pandora's box' or lead to the creation of a 'many-headed Hydra'.[29] It is easy to understand the reasoning of *Degraffenreid*. As Crenshaw points out, black women have difficulty making any gains under the present law because they are two steps removed from the legal norm which 'is not neutral but is white male.'[30] Sex discrimination and race discrimination are relatively easy to tackle because they are politically acceptable targets for legal intervention and reform. Asking law to listen to a plurality of voices upsets the hegemony of law and forces it to 'lose a sense of ready solutions and steady certainties'.[31]

Some progress was made in the USA in 1980 in *Jeffries* v *Harris County Community Action Association*[32] when a court rejected the *Degraffenreid* approach and substituted the analogy of the 'sex-plus' concept, the situation utilized in sexual harassment claims whereby it is alleged that a person discriminates against another person on the basis of sex, *plus* an additional characteristic or factor related to sex. In *Jeffries* the court addressed the race and sex discrimination claims separately and then categorized the claim as one of sex discrimination with a secondary category of race discrimination. Although this decision recognizes the possibility of a claim based on both sex and race discrimination, it required the race claim to be subordinated to the sex discrimination issue. The decision has been heavily criticized since it merely repeats the choice that black women must make in bringing legal claims, 'thereby perpetuating a fundamental misunderstanding of the nature of the discrimination experienced by black women, most of whom do not consider their race to be secondary to their sex.'[33]

Despite criticism, the sex-plus analogy has been allowed by other courts in the United States. However, in order not to splinter Title VII 'beyond use and recognition' the subsequent decision of *Judge* v *Marsh*[34] has limited the use of the sex-plus concept to the combination of only one 'plus' with the dominant protected immutable trait (or fundamental right). Thus black women are limited to arguing only that their sex *plus* their race have been the cause of their discriminatory treatment. This prevents the courts from addressing other factors which may be contributory causes, for example, their colour, religion, national origin, marital status. The limitations and the irony of this approach are summarized by Scarborough:

> The more someone deviates from the norm, the more likely s/he is to be the target of discrimination. Ironically, those who need Title VII's protection the most get it the least under *Judge's* limitation.[35]

In addition to these limitations of the 'sex-plus' approach, the doctrine has come under attack from black scholars since it refuses to recognize the reality of black women's lives. By combining sex and race discrimination the law is seeing and conceptualizing black women as the *sum* of two parts, sex + race, rather than as whole persons. Attempts have been made to argue beyond the sex-plus approach to establish that black women, because of their unique historical, social and economic experiences, form a separate and special class worthy of particular attention in law.[36] Such a holistic approach is capable of being achieved in the US because the Constitution already recognizes the complexity of the *forms* discrimination can take. Although technical, it also provides a process whereby groups may establish their distinct identities. In Britain this process is limited to the establishment of groups defined by the Race Relations Act 1976.

There are critiques of using a holistic approach in the United States;

for example, it stands as a challenge to the Critical Legal Studies' scholars, since ultimately it is a rights-based approach to improving the situation of minorities in society. However, the claims brought by black women in the United States show the importance of engaging in a rights-based discourse. It is the first step in engagement with the law, speaking a language it understands. As a result, the invisibility and silence of a whole host of issues not tackled by discrimination law have been uncovered.

Another criticism of the holistic approach is one that was levelled against us when we presented this essay at the W.G. Hart Workshop in 1990. A black woman was offened by the ideas put forward by black applicants and black scholars since she felt it stereotyped black people in general as suffering from disadvantage. We are well aware of this dilemma but feel that there are advantages to be gained in adopting an approach which is not based upon competition but has its basis in difference. It may be that there are losses in the approach. By re-emphasizing disadvantage in law it may reinforce stigma by strengthening the very stereotypes that produced the differences.[37] But there are gains to be made. First of all, it moves away from comparisons with one norm. Second, it turns an individual claim into a group claim. Third, group identity may provide an empowering notion for both individuals and groups, developing a sense of pride. The group inhabits a legal forum wherein an individual may identify with, and become part of, an entity recognized as distinct in law. In turn the group may link itself to, and become part of, the broader society. This is the challenge already raised in — and to some extent recognized by — law in relation to the acceptance of multi-culturalism. Black women have taken that challenge one step further.

A HOLISTIC APPROACH TO DISCRIMINATION LAW?

The result of this tentative exploration of the interaction of race and gender leads us to conclude that discrimination cannot be tackled by general concepts, such as equality of opportunity, currently employed by law. Law must be more specific about the factors which make up particular types of discrimination and recognize that a multiplicity of forms of discrimination exist. Sometimes these forms of discrimination may be cumulative, in terms of, say, a race *and* a gender — the two politically acceptable forms of anti-discrimination law. At other times it may be difficult for a person suffering disadvantage to pinpoint in law — and in reality — the precise *cause* of their disadvantage. The causes may be recognizable, but as of yet unprotected, in law: for example, disability, learning difficulties, sexual orientation, sexual transformation, age, HIV positive, height, class. The list is endless.

At a pragmatic level the way forward may be to consolidate resources and push for concerted strategic action on the sex and race front. Equally, there are good pragmatic reasons to tackle the specificity of sex and race discrimination separately. A holistic approach provides the legal methodology whereby the complexity and interaction of different and several forms of disadvantage may be addressed in, and by, law. At present the attempts to enforce legal rights by black women, who are making a claim based on a position two steps removed from the white male norm, seem to pose problems the courts cannot understand or refuse to hear. Minow argues that when those in the mainstream of legal power are asked to listen to people 'many steps away from the norm' the task 'seems both overwhelming and incapacitating'.[38] This is the challenge the interaction of race and gender poses to the whole conceptual basis of discrimination law.[39]

We are aware of the critique of a rights-based approach to tackling disadvantage through the legal system. But the losses suffered, and the few gains made, by black women in the United States and in Britain begin to uncover the invisibility and silence of one particular group in society. Their claims add another dimension to the issues being debated in Britain as to whether we should amalgamate equal opportunities policies or move in the direction of addressing the specificity of different forms of discrimination.

NOTES

1. We are grateful to Deirdre Stanley for providing research assistance on this paper.

2. The Combahee River Collective 'A black feminist statement' in Hull, G., Scott, P. and Smith, B. (eds) *All the Women Are White, All the Blacks Are Men, but Some of Us Are Brave* (New York, The Feminist Press, 1981).

3. Lorde, A. *Sister Outsider: Essays and Speeches* (New York, Crossing Press, 1984) pp. 41–42.

4. 401 US 424 [1971].

5. *Hampson v Department of Education and Science* [1989] IRLR 69.

6. See *inter alia* O'Donovan, K. *Sexual Divisions in Law* (London, Weidenfeld and Nicolson, 1985); Smart, C. *Feminism and the Power of Law* (London, Routledge, 1989).

7. See *inter alia* Kline, M. 'Race, racism and feminist legal theory' (1989) 12 *Harvard Women's Law Journal* 115; Monture, P. 'Ka-Nin-Geh-Heh-Gah-E-Sa-Nonh-Yan-Gah' (1986) 2 *Canadian Journal of Women and Law* 159; Bhavnani, K. and Coulson, M. 'Transforming socialist feminism: the challenge of racism' (1986) 23 *Feminist Review* 83; Scales-Trent, J., 'Black women and the

Constitution: finding our place, asserting our rights' (1989) 24 *Harvard Civil Rights–Civil Liberties Law Review* 9; Scarborough, C. 'Conceptualizing black women's employment experiences' (1989) 98 *Yale Law Journal* 1457; Austin, R. 'Sapphire bound!' (1989) *Wisconsin Law Review* 539.

8. Scales-Trent *op. cit.* at p. 9.
9. See Bindman's essay in this book.
10. Case 170/84 [1986] ECR 1607.
11. [1982] ICR 661.
12. Wilson, M. 'Racism is the main issue' (1989) 2 *Between Equals* 9.
13. [1988] IRLR 195; [1988] IRLR 530.
14. Op. cit (note 12).
15. Coussey, M. 'Why we need a joint strategy' (1990) 3 *Between Equals* 26.
16. See Scales-Trent op. cit. (note 7); Crenshaw, K. 'Race, reform, and retrenchment: transformation and legitimation in antidiscrimination law' (1988) 101 *Harvard Law Review* 1331.
17. Findlay, L. 'Transcending equality theory: a way out of the maternity and the workplace debate' (1986) 86 *Columbia Law Review* 1118.
18. *Page* v *Freight Hire (Tank Haulage) Ltd* [1981] IRLR 13.
19. Kenney, S. 'Reproductive hazards in the workplace: the law and sexual difference' (1986) 14 *International Journal of the Sociology of Law* 393.
20. See *Porcelli* v *Strathclyde Regional Council* [1986] ICR 177.
21. See Szyszczak's essay in this book for the implications of the Internal Market for race issues in the European Community.
22. See Scarborough op. cit. (note 7).
23. Op. cit. (note 7) p. 10.
24. Bryan, B., Dadzie, S., and Scafe, S. *The Heart of the Race* (London, Virago, 1985) p. 105.
25. Baca Zinn, M. 'Family, feminism and race in America' (1990) 4 *Gender and Society* 69.
26. Bryan, Dadzie and Scafe op. cit (note 24) pp. 191–94.
27. 413 F. Supp. 142 (ED Miss. 1976).
28. Ibid. at p. 143.
29. *Judge* v *Marsh* 649 F. Supp 770, 780 (DDC 1986).
30. Crenshaw, K. 'Women and the law: a feminist jurisprudence' (1986) p. 30 mimeo.
31. Minow, M. 'The Supreme Court 1986 term — foreword: justice engendered' (1987) 101 *Harvard Law Review* 1, 82.
32. 615 F. 2d 1025 (5th Circuit 1980).
33. Scarborough op. cit. (note 7) p. 1471.
34. 649 F 2d 1025 (5th Circuit 1980).
35. Op. cit. (note 7) p. 1472.
36. See the discussion in Scarborough and Scales-Trent, op. cit (note 7).
37. See the discussion by Minow, M. 'When difference has its home: group homes for the mentally retarded, equal protection and legal treatment of difference' (1987) *Harvard Civil Rights–Civil Liberties Law Review* 111; Scales-Trent op. cit (note 7).
38. Ibid.
39. See the comments in 'Note, invisible man: black and male under Title VII' (1991) 104 *Harvard Law Review* 749.

13

Cultural Diversity and Racial Discrimination in Employment Selection

Tariq Modood

INTRODUCTION

Progress in equal opportunities, as elsewhere, requires us to continually review our understanding not only of what we are trying to achieve but of the phenomena we are dealing with. The relationship between race and culture is a case in point. The need to review our understanding is particularly acute, as some recent forms of minority assertiveness, most notably in the Salman Rushdie affair, have caused confusion among egalitarians about the obligations of racial equality and, indeed, about the very question of what is race.[1]

When it comes to defining what we mean by race some people reach for a dictionary, others for elaborate biological or sociological theories. I prefer to start with the Race Relations Act 1976. It defines a 'racial group' by reference to: 'colour, race, nationality or ethnic or national origins'. What is interesting here and is rarely remarked upon is how the definition not only includes the very term it is defining but includes it as only one of a number of alternative possibilities.[2] A 'racial group', it seems, can be constituted by one of a number of things, one of which is 'race'. The incoherence of this can only be removed if we appreciate that the terms 'race/racial' are being used in two different ways: the law is using a *narrow* concept of race to elucidate one of the dimensions of the *broad* concept of race. And while it is on this broader concept that the law rests and which it attempts to define, it acknowledges that an aspect of the broader concept is the more specific understanding of race needed to complete the list of colour, nationality, ethnic or national origins. Presumably, this narrow conception is of race as physical appearance or phenotype — what to some people, but not the law, *is* race.

To understand the broader, legally comprehensive conception of race, we have to turn to the House of Lords judgement in *Mandla* v *Dowell-Lee*[3] which took great care to lay down the test for 'ethnic group'. In their opinion there were two essential characteristics of an ethnic group: a long shared history; and a cultural tradition of its own. Arguing, however, that other characteristics were also relevant, they included: a common geographical origin, or descent from a small number of common ancestors; a common language; a common literature; a common religion; being either a minority or a majority within a larger community.

This reasoning was used to establish that Sikhs are an ethnic group within the meaning of the act, and has been referred to in other cases to establish that, among others, Jews, gypsies and Rastafarians are 'racial groups'.[4] Indeed, it more or less matches the ambiguities of ordinary usage. Thus nobody is confused when a vicar who describes Islam as an 'alien *culture* thriving in our midst' is admonished by the Bishop of Wakefield as having 'set back *race* relations 20 years' and the story is reported in a popular newspaper under the headline: 'Vicar's alien *race* jibe makes a Bishop see red' (my italics throughout).[5] Indeed, the law would have a better grip on the social reality of racial discrimination if it were broadened to make direct discrimination against Muslims unlawful in the same way that it currently protects the employment and other rights of religious minorities such as Sikhs and Jews.[6]

The legal concept of racial discrimination (and hence of race) is incomplete without the concept of indirect discrimination. Indirect racial discrimination arises where practices which cannot be shown to be justifiable (e.g. in selecting the most able candidates for particular kinds of posts) have disproportionate impact upon some racial groups compared to others.[7]

This has the effect of deepening the concept of ethnic discrimination so that, for example, rules which affect members of certain minority religions can be captured within the notion of indirect discrimination: so under certain conditions it is unlawful to insist that Muslim women employees wear skirts, for even though Muslims are not a racial group, the unjustified prohibition will have a disproportionate impact upon those ethnic groups in which Muslims are a significant number. The concept of indirect discrimination also links race with class, for the concept captures certain practices (e.g. requiring excessive academic qualifications for certain jobs) which may rest on social inequalities (the distribution of educational opportunities) which the lay person would not at first glance think of as relevant to the concepts of race and racism.

I propose therefore to offer an understanding of race as a complex concept consisting of colour, class and culture as three relatively independent dimensions in order to better identify the social reality behind the law. I do this so as to focus attention on the dimension of culture, which

I think has been least explored in race equality employment thinking and practice. My analysis is of social processes and outcomes at the level of observable experience, for I remain unconvinced by Marxist and other forms of structuralism which explain race and racism by reference to some deeper level of sociological abstraction.

THE THREE Cs OF RACE

Colour

It is obviously the case that being anything but European in physical appearance is enough in white societies to make one a possible object of racist treatment. For some, therefore, this is the crucial feature of racism. Van den Berghe defines racism as 'an ideology of superiority based on phenotypic differences'.[8] But it is difficult to see how differences in physical appearances can indefinitely sustain assumptions of superiority. Arab oil wealth or Pacific Asian achievement are examples of changes in circumstances which erode the basis of a historical discrimination (Arab and Japanese visitors to South Africa did not once but later did enjoy official white status). Colour prejudice or colour hierarchy cannot therefore, I think, be equated with racism. It is best seen as the ground floor of racism rather than the whole building.

Class

Inferior treatment on the basis of colour can create a subordinate class which by virtue of its socio-economic position can continue to suffer competitive disadvantage even were colour prejudice to wane. Even in a colour-blind society historically oppressed racial groups often suffer class discrimination. Jobs which prefer a public school, Oxbridge background will disadvantage the majority of society but will have a disproportionately greater impact on racial minorities. Most writers on race and most egalitarians readily understand the sociological connection between systematic historical discrimination and current socio-economic disadvantage. It is, therefore, worth emphasizing that there is no *necessary* link between colour and class. It has, for instance, been the case for some time in the USA, Canada and Australia that some non-white groups exceed standard levels of socio-economic achievement and I believe that this may now be the case with Indians in Britain.[9] Not only is there no absolute correlation between the colour discrimination a group suffers and its socio-economic under-performance, but it is quite likely that a group's perceived success will lead to a heightening of resentment and discrimination against it.

Culture

Culture in the broad sense — which includes community, ethnicity and
religion — is, like class, the ground of one of the more universal forms
of discrimination. Again, like class, it has no necessary relationship with
colour, yet when they are linked it constitutes the third dimension of
race. Ethnic hierarchies and religious discrimination can and do exist
in an all-white or all-black society. Nevertheless, racial groups which
have distinctive or 'alien' cultural identities or community life will suffer
an additional dimension of discrimination and prejudice. Moreover,
just as class can disadvantage by denying access to leisure activities
or the acquisition of skills and understanding, so can membership of a
minority cultural group deprive one of, say, excellence in the dominant
language and modes of thought, or access to certain forms of social networks. Again, just as colour-blind class discrimination can be a form of
indirect racial discrimination, so membership of a minority community
can render one less employable on the grounds of one's dress, dietary
habits, or desire to take leave from work on one's holy days rather than
those prescribed by the custom and practice of the majority community.

Each of the three dimensions, then, can be the focus of prejudice and
stereotyping, and the last two are clearly related to institutional discrimination. Each dimension can vary in degree (e.g. the darker in colour
the less acceptable) and can be the basis of discrimination and a disadvantaged social position, though no one dimension necessarily implies
another (it is possible to be black, middle-class and to be in, say, the
mainstream youth culture). The worst position is where all of the dimensions are in play. The more distant an individual or group is from the
'norm' of white middle/upper-class British Christian/agnostic, the
greater their marginality and exclusion. The hostility of the majority is
likely to be particularly forceful if the individual in question is a member
of a community (and not just a free-floating or assimilated individual)
which is sufficiently numerous to reproduce itself as a community and
has a distinctive and cohesive value system which can be perceived as
an alternative to and a possible challenge to the norm. The Rastafarians
are one example of where these three dimensions are active; Bradford's
orthodox Muslims are another.

It is particularly important to recognize that racism constitutes opposition and less favourable treatment not just to individuals but, above
all, to communities or groups. For it then becomes clear that while
colour discrimination is a necessary condition of racism (as opposed to
the ethnic discrimination and ethnic stratification experienced by, say,
the Irish in Britain),[10] it cannot be equated with racism. The presence
of colour or phenotypical differences may be the distinction between

what in ordinary (though perhaps not in legal) discourse we might call racial rather than ethnic discrimination. Nevertheless, objecting to an individual who is like oneself in all other respects except skin colour, while common enough, is not typical of the more intractable forms of racism. Racism is normally not just unequal treatment on the basis of a difference in physical appearance, though such treatment can take place as a residual prejudice derived from fuller-scale forms of racism. Racism normally makes a linkage between a difference in physical appearance and a difference in group attitudes and behaviour. In contemporary settings the linkage is unlikely to be crudely genetic or biological, but is likely to rest on history, social structure, group norms, values and culture. The causal linkage is unlikely to be perceived as scientific or law-like but as probabilistic. Thus, we all know of white individuals who have good personal relations with certain non-white persons and yet have stereotypes about the groups those persons are from and believe that the groups in question have major problems (chips on their shoulders, lazy, frightened of responsibility, religious fanaticism, etc). The white individuals in question are likely to deny that they are racists ('my best friend is black'). Indeed, this denial can be genuine, for it is possible to not be a racist in individual relationships or in the context of cultural homogeneity, and yet be a racist about groups. For behind the immediate issue of colour or physical appearance are a number of other issues — the historical relationship, size of respective populations, scale and speed of shift in the distribution of status and power and many others.

I would just like to focus on an issue which develops the link between group differences and racism against groups. It is the idea of behavioural acceptability. Whole groups of people can be stereotyped in terms of pathological social behaviour, such as trouble with the law, street crime, use of violence, etc. It is easy to see how this form of 'demonizing', which received considerable analytical attention at one time,[11] can be highly suggestive and, feeding off existing or latent prejudices, can create racist treatment, including policy and institutional response, of the group in question. It is also possible to see that where *this* is the main form of racism it can, on the one hand, be transcended in respect of inter-racial friendships when a black person can demonstrate that he or she is the exception to the behavioural stereotype; yet on the other hand, it is also clear that despite such one-to-one relationships, the stereotype may still be thought, by the white person in question, to apply to the group as a whole.

Other kinds of group stereotypes that can be associated with colour or differences in physical appearance are to do with a community's structure, norms and values. Whole communities can be objects of suspicion and hate because they are deemed to be backward or illiberal, unduly religious, oppressive of women or unwilling to mix socially with other groups. Individuals, even when they are white, are likely to experience prejudice where they are preceived to be culturally or religiously different; if the community in question which is perceived as 'alien' should be non-white, yet greater is the likelihood of stereotyping and less likely the forming of inter-racial, inter-communal individual relationships. The price of 'acceptability' may be for minority individuals to exhibit signs of rejecting their origins and disassociating themselves from their communities. France provides an example of how this cultural-racism can be stronger than colour-racism, where the hostility, for instance, against light-skinned Arabs is far more intense and ruthless than that against Francophone West Africans and Afro-Caribbeans.

Cultural-racism is likely to be particularly acute if the minority community actually, and not just defensively, wants to maintain some of the essential elements of its culture or religion; if, far from denying their difference (beyond the colour of their skin or exacerbated social deprivation), they want to assert it and demand respect just as they are. On the basis of this analysis it comes as no surprise that a recent European Commission survey showed that of all minorities in Britain, Asians are the most disliked.[12] This was also the finding of Dervla Murphy in her sojourns in Bradford and Birmingham, and of a Scottish-Nigerian writer on race in his travels around Britain.[13] Part of the explanation must lie in Michael Banton's observation in 1979 that

> the English seemed to display more hostility towards the West Indians because they sought a greater degree of acceptance than the English wished to accord; in more recent times there seemed to have been more hostility towards Asians because they are insufficiently inclined to adopt English ways.[14]

While this probably marks a long-term shift, such attitudes are of course formed by current controversies — the kinds of controversies that are currently threatening to make 'Muslim', like 'Jew' before it, into a racial category.

Racial discrimination can, then, be understood to operate at the three different levels of colour, class and culture. Most research shows that at a first encounter or face-to-face level, colour is the decisive consideration: responses to enquiries about rooms to let or job vacancies, in usually about a third of the cases, will be negative to people who are not white even though the rooms or jobs in question are in fact available.[15] It would be too simplistic to say that in these cases the white respondents see only the colour of the non-white person, but the evidence now over a number of years shows that in these cases colour is the material factor. Secondly, there is the indirect racial discrimination associated with non-racial forms of socio-economic inequalities and forms of class exclusivity. Third is the unfavourable treatment of non-white people (though also white people like the Irish, Jews, Poles, Greek Cypriots and so on) on the basis of their perceived ethnicity. A particularly fertile area of this third form of discrimination is job selection, especially where the jobs in question are not of the simple manual sort but where the individual's personal and social skills and qualities are part of the basis of assessment. It is here that subtle and unsubtle forms of stereotyping are most at play.[16] What is interesting is that the most thorough emprical study of white manager's stereotypes about non-white people found that the stereotypes are not about, to use the most favoured term, 'coloured' people *as such* but are about particular groups. The groups are perceived as being mainly two: Jamaicans/West Indians/blacks/Afro-Caribbeans on the one hand, and, Asians/Indians/Pakistanis on the other. No significant stereotype was found to apply to both groups.[17]

CULTURE AND THE INDIVIDUAL

Over the last decade or so British race equality thinking and action has been geared towards eliminating colour discrimination and the socio-economic educational disadvantages associated with some racial groups. The time is long overdue, I think, to take the dimension of culture or ethnicity seriously. Let me illustrate by an example of how current thinking is inadequate. Equality policies and trainers often state that equality and fairness require treating everyone the same: but how can one do that if people have different norms, sensibilities and needs? There is often a plea to treat everyone as an individual, but is it possible to treat someone as an individual if you are ignorant about his or her cultural background and the things that matter to him or her? Everyone is agreed that much discrimination is the result of (often unconscious) negative racial stereotyping, but what are we to put in its place?

Stereotyping is an intellectually crude, patronizing and unfair method of providing a context in which to judge individuals who are deemed to be of a collective type; in the extreme case individuals are seen completely in terms of a collective type. The greater the ignorance about a group of people by an outsider or observer, the greater the reliance on a stereotype (which may not be completely unfavourable to the group). It follows that to decrease the use of unfavourable stereotypes one has to increase the level of knowledge about the groups and to make sure that the knowledge used is not only of the outsider's generalizing type but includes some understanding of how the group understands itself, of what it believes to be some of its distinctive qualities or virtues. We need to allow favourable as well as unfavourable generalizations to come into play. The more one knows about a group the more one is able to penetrate beyond the group to the individual; it is when the context is easily understood and taken for granted that the individual stands out and so can be noticed in his or her own right. The less familiar one is with the group, the less one is able to perceive the individual for 'they all look alike' (not just in terms of physical appearance but also in terms of behaviour). See for instance how easily all assertive Muslims have been branded as 'fundamentalists' by the media, and indeed how there *was* no media interest in Muslim concerns until they were seen as a threat.[18] The choice, then, is not between identifying someone as an individual and identifying him or her as a group member; without understanding the group, one lacks the context for identifying the variables out of which individuality is composed. Until one can penetrate into the forest one cannot see one tree as being different from another.

These generalities are relevant to the employment selection process. Consider the cultural variables of an interview for example. What I have in mind are the following types of features: desired length of interview, desired ratio of talk between interviewer and interviewee, length of introductions, eye-contact, posture, body language, deference, willingness to talk about oneself and various areas of one's life, tendency to answer directly or in circumlocutions and elaborate context-setting ways, standards of politeness and informality, willingness to 'sell oneself' and inhibitions about boasting, sexual modesty, anxieties built up from previous rejections and fear of discrimination, etc. How we treat and evaluate other people in an interview is dependent on how we relate to them, how comfortable we are with them. The very same qualities that in one individual may be perceived as pushy and aggressive may in another be commended as the raw materials to be developed into leadership skills. The difference in perception may be nothing more than racial — or for that matter, sexual — prejudice. Such prejudice may be unconscious and unexamined because it is shared and reinforced by our own peer group and, when combined with a lack of familiarity with the nuances of a different cultural manner, is bound to produce mutually unsatisfactory interviews and fail in bringing out or identifying the capabilities of ethnic minority candidates. Where we as selectors do not make an effort to guard against unconscious discrimination, we invariably select those individuals who are most like ourselves — for after all not only are they the people it is easiest to get close enough to for their strengths to be spotted, but they are the ones whom we are likely to feel we had a good interview with because they are the individuals that we are likely to enjoy the experience of being with. Conversely, with those that we don't easily hit it off with, we do not make the same effort to seek their positive qualities and therefore undervalue them.

THE NEED FOR RESEARCH AND NEW TRAINING MATERIALS

BBC TV's *Crosstalk* (1976) and *Multi-Cultured Talk Swap* (1977) are virtually the only training materials among those currently available which even touch on these things, but even they are far from comprehensive and are somewhat dated. Yet the monitoring evidence is that ethnic minority groups have a particularly bad interview success rate. Some of this is, I believe, due to imperfect understanding and lack of cross-cultural sensitivity, which even with well-intentioned interviewers can lead to the devaluing of candidates' abilities and stereotyping of groups. And yet it is my impression that very little equal opportunities recruitment and selection training attempts to deal with this and most trainers are unwilling or unable to handle it. The typical course warns against racist stereotyping without giving any guidance as to how to be culturally sensitive, leaving the impression that such skills are not necessary.

This rather bleak training situation fortunately looks set to change. A BBC sequel to *Crosstalk*, as well as a CRE video on interviewing, are in production (1990–91) and the American Bureau of National Affairs' set of videos and training pack, entitled *Bridges: Skills for Managing a Diverse Workforce*, is soon to be available in Britain. Some of the most promising developments consist in applying ideas in other areas of expertise — history, anthropology and the preparation of staff to work abroad — to equality training. Satie Sethi of Pathway (Southall), for instance, put on a 13-week course for the top management of London Borough of Hounslow in 1990 which involved studying 'the history of the Indian sub-continent, the main religions of South Asia and the cultural traditions of its people'.[19] There is a danger, however, that training courses which concentrate only on minority cultures or which introduce such material at too early a stage will unproductively emphasize the 'otherness' of those cultures and possibly even reinforce stereotypes. More promising is the approach devised by Ashok Ohri for Voluntary Service Overseas which, by beginning with getting individuals to think about their own 'cultural baggage' aims to break the cast of mind in which 'we are normal, they are ethnic' and so make one receptive not just to information but to the thoroughgoing acceptance of diversity.[20] Also helpful is the approach which begins with an analysis of the internal culture of the organization.[21]

While these innovative ways of going beyond the simplicities of anti-colour-racism are most worthwhile, what we really need, I think ,is a serious programme of research to examine the inter-relationships between challenging negative stereotypes; recognizing cultural differences; setting objective selection procedures; and treating each individual equally. While the backdrop of this research will be the question of to what extent cultural diversity is a long-term feature of race equality, it should ideally include an examination of some existing equal opportunities training courses and materials with a view to producing model courses and material.

I appreciate that some may wonder whether this is not to open a can of worms. The issue of cultural differences, it may be said, has not been ignored due to an oversight but to a genuine worry that heightening cultural or group differences will erode the principle and legal requirement that each person, each job applicant for example, should be treated as an individual and not judged in terms of group qualities. After all, some industrial tribunal cases, for example, *Bradford City Council* v *Arora* have actually been won on the basis that interview questions were designed to highlight that a candidate was from a distinct ethnic and cultural background. I acknowledge there is a real problem here and that is why I emphasize that research is needed on the *inter-relationship* between recognizing differences *and* treating each individual as an individual; and, moreover, I think the research needs to be carried through into the production of sound training materials. It is also worth bearing in mind that contemporary sex-equality is increasingly being structured around the facts of gender difference. While on one level this means differential provision (maternity and child-care), on a more interesting level the issues are about organizational culture and the difference between men's and women's value profiles and management styles. Indeed, the Industrial Society actually offers a course on the benefits of gender difference.[22]

The idea of group difference is the key distinction between narrow and broad concepts of racial and sexual equality. While the narrow concept of equality is about allowing individuals, whose only differences are hormonal or of pigmentation, to compete for positions within existing social structures and systems of rewards, the broad concept involves changing norms, procedures and entitlements to take account of groups whose needs, values and forms of fulfilment are different from those accomodated by existing arrangements. Oddly, current race-equality wisdom interprets the demands of the broad concept as a soft option. Hence, a *Labour Research* survey of the UK's top employers has been interpreted as showing

> that the only areas [in which] they were doing anything tangible were those which could be called 'multi-cultural': the granting of time for religious observance and extended leave arrangements to visit families abroad, making allowances for special dietary requirements traditions. However, anything to do with tackling racism, racial discrimination and racial harassment was rare.[23]

This is a most surprising conclusion. For not only is there the false contrast in the passage between the cultural and the racial (the denial of the right to be culturally different, such as the wearing of *shalwar-kameez*, has been found to be unlawful racial discrimination by industrial tribunals), my own experience is quite the opposite. The standard response of private- and public-sector managers to equal opportunity initiatives is along the following lines:

> I don't care whether they are yellow, green, purple or what have you, as long as they can do the job and are willing to muck in like everyone else, and not harp on about their differences, or make special pleading or demand privileges but try to become just like the rest of us.

Of all egalitarian ideas, this assimilationist, individualistic interpretation of racial equality is the most prevalent among all social classes and supporters of all major political parties, certainly among white, and perhaps also black, people. To deny group differences, however, is to embrace a concept of racial (and sexual) equality which is narrower than that available in current law and social and employment policy provisions. It is to deny the fact of one of the principal dimensions of self-fulfilment and of racial discrimination.

Two other worries are likely to be present in most people's minds: First, immigrant groups, especially after the first generation, are subject to considerable cultural adaptation and flux and it would be wrong to form group generalizations which are in the process of becoming out of date and which clearly have little relevance to significant numbers of assimilated individuals. Second, the real issue is not about correct group generalizations but the systemic inequality which allows dominant groups to continue without penalty to stereotype subordinate groups: cross-cultural understanding and respect is not possible unless it goes hand-in-hand with altering the power relationships.

Both these points have some substance. They, however, qualify the issue of ethnicity without destroying it. They bring in important wider considerations which have to be properly taken into account; they do not show that ethnic difference is a non-issue. This issue will increase in prominence rather than, as was once assumed, go away. If so, the race-equality agendas of the 1980s will not be adequate for the 1990s.

NOTES

1. For an attempt to construct a basic ethnography of British Asian Muslims in respect of the Rushdie affair, see Modood, T. 'British Asian Muslims and the Rushdie affair' (1990) 1(2) *Political Quarterly* 143–60; for a discussion of how the Rushdie affair challenges certain sociological conceptions of British race relations, see Modood, T. 'Catching up with Jesse Jackson: being oppressed and being somebody' (1990) 17(1) *New Community* 85–96; and for how it connects with the existing legal concept of incitement to hatred, see Modood, T. 'Muslims, incitement to hatred and the law' in Horton, J. (ed.) *Liberalism, Multiculturalism and Toleration* (London, Macmillan, 1992).

2. Banton, M. 'Science, law and politics in the study of racial relations'. Presidential address to the Royal Anthropological Institute, 1989.

3. [1983] IRLR 209. This may be regarded as the foundational decision of moderate legal pluralism. For discussion of what this means, see Poulter, S. 'Cultural pluralism and its limits: a legal perspective' and Parekh, B. 'Britain and the social logic of pluralism both in Commission for Racial Equality', *Britain: A Plural Society*. (London, CRE, 1990).

4. The decision recognizing Rastafarians as an ethnic group was overturned by a majority of 2–1 at the EAT, *Crown Suppliers (PSA)* v *Dawkins* 24 April 1991.

5. *Daily Express* (9 March 1990). For the Commission for Racial Equality's understanding of the term 'race', see its evidence to the House of Commons Employment Committee, *Recruitment Practices*, (1989–90) p. 94.

6. In *Nyazi* v *Rymans Ltd.* (10 May 1988 EAT 6/88) the EAT upheld an industrial tribunal's ruling that Muslims are not a 'racial group' for the purposes of a complaint under the Race Relations Act 1976. The recent IT decision in *CRE* v *Precision* (26 July 1991) confirms that a refusal to employ someone because he or she is a Muslim is not unlawful direct discrimination, though in many circumstances it would be unlawful indirect discrimination. Cases such as these have led the CRE to consider whether legislation is now needed to cover religious discrimination and incitement to religious hatred (Commission for Racial Equality, *Second Review of the Race Relations Act 1976*, London, June 1991).

7. For practical examples, see Commission for Racial Equality *Indirect Discrimination in Employment: A Practical Guide* (London, CRE, 1989), and *Code of Discrimination for the Elimination of Racial Discrimination in Education* (London, CRE, 1989).

8. Van den Berghe, P. L. 'Class, race and ethnicity in Africa' (1983) 6(2) *Ethnic and Racial Studies*.

9. See Modood, T. 'The Indian economic success: a challenge to some race relations assumptions' (1991) 19(3) *Policy and Politics* 177–89.

10. In two recent industrial tribunal cases both applicants were found to have suffered unlawful racial discrimination because the interviewers had stereotyped views of the Irish: *Killian* v *Boots The Chemist* unreported (London North 1107989/1A) and *O Driscoll* v *The Post Office* unreported (Leeds 25671/89).

11. E.g. Hall, S. et al. *Policing the Crisis* (London, Macmillan, 1979).

12. *Today* (14 March 1990).

13. Murphy, D. *Tales from Two Cities* (London, John Murray, 1987), and Maja-Pearce, A. *How Many Miles to Babylon?* (London, Heinemann, 1990) p. 72.

14. Banton, M. 'It's our country' in Miles, R. and Phizacklea, A. (eds) *Racism and Political Action in Britain* (London, Routledge and Kegan Paul, 1979) p. 242.

15. See Brown, C. And Gay, P. *Seventeen Years after the Act* (London, Policy Studies Institute, 1985); Commission for Racial Equality *'Sorry It's Gone': Testing for Racial Discrimination in the Private Sector* (London, CRE, 1990); and Foyster, R. et al. 'I landed twice as many jobs as my two friends — but then *they* are black', *Today* (11 September 1990).

16. Commission for Racial Equality *Chartered Accountancy Training Contracts: Report of a Formal Investigation into Ethnic Minority Recruitment* (London, CRE, 1987) pp. 19–21.

17. Jenkins, R. *Racism and Recruitment* (Cambridge, Cambridge University Press, 1986) ch. 4. Laziness perhaps is a feature of the stereotypes of both West Indians and Asians but as it is a salient feature in the former and a minor one in the latter, the contrast, again, is more striking than the similarity.

18. With particular reference to the Rushdie affair, see Modood, T. 'Religious anger and minority rights' (1989) 60(3) *Political Quarterly* 280–84, and Parekh, B. 'The Rushdie affair and the British press: some salutary lessons' in Commission for Racial Equality *Free Speech* (London, CRE, 1990) pp. 59–78.

19. *The Times* (16 July 1990) 3.

20. Legum, M. 'Whose culture needs attention?' (1990) 2(1) *Cross-culture* 16–17, and 'Traveller, know thyself' (1990) 2(6) *Eurobusiness* 24–27.

21. Guptara, P. 'How to approach 1992: step 1 — understand yourself' (July 1989) *Training and Development*.

22. For some conceptual and policy debates, see Rhode, D.L. (ed.) *Theoretical Perspectives on Sexual Difference* (New Haven, Yale University Press, 1990); for a British feminist perspective with explicit reference to race and gender, see Brah, A. 'Difference, diversity and differentiation' in Donald, J. and Rattansi, A. (eds) *'Race', Culture and Difference* (London, Sage, 1992).

23. Wrench, J. 'Employment and the labour market' (1990) 16(4) *New Community* 578.

14

Ageism and Legal Control

Trevor Buck

INTRODUCTION

It is essential to have a reasonable idea of the social phenomenon of 'ageism' before making any assertions about the relevant forms of legal or other controls that might be thought appropriate to regulate it. The first section of this Chapter selects several important factors for brief exploration in order to clarify the concept. The second section is directed at comparing and contrasting the concept of ageism with those of sexism and racism. The third section reviews relevant case law developments in the UK and in the European Community. The final section, based on the implications of the previous discussion, makes some tentative propositions for devising a legal model to accommodate ageism.

THE SOCIAL PHENOMENON OF AGEISM

The study of ageing and ageism is contained within the relatively new discipline of gerontology.[1] This comprises three fairly distinct aspects: biological, psychological and social. Social gerontology can in turn be subdivided into three dimensions: the individual experience of ageing, the social context defining ageing and the societal consequences of ageing.[2] The social phenomenon of ageism would appear to be associated with the last of these two elements, though an individual's experience of ageing must include a measure of internalization of the values and expectations that society has placed on age-related questions.

Theoretical approaches utilized within social gerontology have been somewhat deficient in the past and it is arguable that at least some of the earlier theoretical approaches have actually contributed to negative attitudes and stereotypes of older/elderly persons. For example, two approaches, termed 'disengagement' and 'activity' theory respectively, have been seen to contain serious flaws. Disengagement theory asserts that ageing involves a process of withdrawal from participation in society.[3] Criticized almost from the outset principally for its deterministic character, activity theory asserts almost the opposite: people reaching the stage of life when they are divested of accustomed roles require restitution of their situations through compensatory activities.[4] Both theories have been criticized for their oversimplification and lack of empirical support.

Social gerontology has not been immune to the general theoretical developments in the social sciences and there have been various attempts at applying labelling, exchange, sub-cultural and age-stratification theories.[5] Some commentators have preferred certain theoretical formulations as particularly appropriate in the age context. For example, Victor argues that symbolic interactionism might be a particularly appropriate approach.[6] It is always going to be the case that the multi-disciplinary nature of gerontology will pose difficulties in the search for an adequate theoretical foundation. However, this essay is confined to delineating several key factors which it is thought influence the social context of ageing and ageism.

Demography

The proportion of the population in the UK and other advanced industrial societies defined as 'elderly'[7] has increased over the last century. This is because of a decline in mortality (especially infant) rates and a decrease in fertility rates. The table below illustrates the increases for men and women this century.

Table 1
Percent of Elderly in the English Population Aged 60 +

Year	Male	Female
1901	7	8
1911	7	9
1921	9	10
1931	11	12
1951	14	18
1861	14	20
1971	16	22
1981	17	22

Source: Laslett P. 'The comparative history of ageing and the aged: with particular reference to the household position of aged persons in Gilmore, A.J., Svanborg, A., Marois, M., Bettie, W., Piotrowski, P. (eds) *Aging: Challenge to Science and Society* vol. 2 (Oxford University Press, 1981)

Towards the year 2000, it is predicted that the total proportion of elderly will decrease but this disguises the large proportionate increase in the very elderly (i.e. 75 +).However, the increase in this group, although large proportionately, is not so dramatic an increase in absolute numbers.

As Table 1 illustrates, there is a growing imbalance between the numbers of men and women surviving into old age. Studying old age will involve more attention to older women. In explaining some of the defects of early theorizing about old age it is significant to note that elderly women were frequently left out of such accounts. Feminist discourse has increasingly recognized that the experience of old age by men and women is different in many respects.

One of the important factors distinguishing the life expectancies of men and women has been the greater frequency of smoking among men and the resultant health effects. It remains to be seen how far the adoption of smoking by women in the post-war era will affect the balance between the sexes as these cohorts of women enter old age. One may also speculate, in terms of life expectancy and other social dimensions, what the impact will be of the more widespread experience of divorce since 1971. In 1986, life expectancy at birth was 71.9 (males) and 77.6 (females) in the UK.[8]

From a policy point of view, the 'dependency ratio'[9] is much more important than proportionate increases in the elderly population. The dependency or 'support' ratio is the ratio of the economically active population to elderly persons who are economically dependent. Table 2 provides an indication of this 'support ratio'.

Table 2

The Numbers of Adults of Working Age in the Population per Person over Pension Age

Year	Children under 16	Adults of working age	Persons of pension	Ratio
1984–85	11,405	33,372	9,977	3.3
1995–96	12,096	33,647	10,174	3.3
2005–06	12,387	34,113	10,139	3.4
2015–16	11,706	34,347	11,153	3.1
2025–25	12,274	33,636	12,344	2.7
Ultimate	12,123	33,947	12,540	2.7

Source: Reform of Social Security Background Papers (June 1985) Cmnd. 9519 vol. 3 p. 45, Annex B, Table 1.

No profile of the ageing population can be complete without some account of the changes in types of household inhabited by the elderly. Most older persons now prefer to live in their own independent households (either on their own or with a spouse). Others live in some form of 'extended' family group. It is interesting to note that, despite popular belief, the fraction of elderly people living in institutional homes has probably remained at about 5 per cent throughout the twentieth century.

The so-called 'demographic time bomb' is used to refer to several different aspects of demographic prediction. In the present context, the term relates to fears surrounding the economic consequences of the increase of elderly persons in our society. Given the fact that it is the proportionate (not absolute) increase in the very elderly that is significant, the question must be asked whether some of the public responses to these predictions are justified by the evidence. Similarly, panic responses to the movement in the support ratio do not take account of numerous factors, such as the balance of public and private social security provision, which would ameliorate such developments.

Historical and Cultural Context

It is tempting to come to certain conclusions about ageing and old age by looking at the status of old/elderly persons across time and across different cultures. One well-known theory is the 'modernization thesis' developed by Cowgill and Holmes.[10] Basing their analysis on fourteen different societies ranging from pre-literate to modern industrialized societies, they argued that modern developments have resulted in significant changes in the status of the elderly. Improvements in health care and the resulting ageing of the working population caused a consequent decrease in job opportunities for the young. The social institution of retirement, therefore, was based on the need to create jobs for the young. However, the importance of economic activity in modern societies meant that retirement was devalued; in addition, technological change reinforced the process of devaluation of older workers as their skills became redundant. Furthermore, the process of urbanization contributed to the dissolution of the extended family structure. All such factors have combined to marginalize, devalue and isolate today's elderly in comparison with those in pre-literate societies.

However, there are serious problems with the thesis. First, it is assumed that pre-industrial societies are fairly uniform and the status of the elderly within such societies is high. Second, it is assumed that the pre-literate primitive cultures studied were equivalent to pre-industrial societies. Studies conducted with greater historical rigour have not confirmed any 'Golden Age' for the status of the elderly in pre-industrial society.[11] Even a cursory knowledge of such studies will disabuse the reader of any romanticized notion of the position of older persons in pre-industrial society as one of high status. Clearly the evidence varies enormously across different cultures, but too often the facts are that old age is generally a time of humiliating poverty and loss of status.[12]

Labour Market Economics

'Modernization' theory may have been seriously flawed in many respects, but it seems clear that there is an important relationship between the process of industrialization and ageing. The relationship, however, is very complex, as the demands of the labour market have changed over time and across different types of employment. Phillipson argues, for example, that in the period after World War II and up to the mid 1960s, the demand for labour was such that the government wished to encourage the employment of older workers for the longest possible time and much research done during this period seems to reflect this policy objective.[13] Indeed, the National Advisory Committee on the Employment of Older Men and Women[14] was formed largely in response to the disruption in 'normal' work patterns after World War II. They issued two reports indicating the need for making use of the elderly in the workforce.[15] However, relative economic expansion in the 1960s and early 1970s shifted concern to *reducing* the size of the labour market, encouraging early retirement and lower retiring ages. Given the crucial importance of employment in determining income, social class and status in modern industrial societies, it is not surprising that the issues of retirement and the position of older (and younger) workers have been seen to be important elements influencing the experience of ageing and the position of the elderly generally. The strength of the work ethic is sufficiently persistent for many retired persons to describe themselves as 'a retired civil servant' or 'a retired school teacher' many years after they actually undertook those occupations.

However, despite the complexities in the relationship between employment and ageing, public policy initiatives in the UK, (certainly since at least World War II), seem to be based on an assumption that the older/elderly worker is a marginal labour resource only called upon when needed. For example, a recent (1990) government White Paper[16] called upon employers to utilize marginal groups (older workers, the disabled, long-term unemployed) given the present shortages of young recruits. It can be argued that the particular demands of the labour market are reinforced by convenient ideologies concerning the required qualities of workers who happen to be in short supply. Similar findings have been made in relation to the need for more women in employment during war-time and the development of certain types of child-care theory to reinforce women's withdrawal from the labour market when their participation is no longer required. According to this reasoning ageism might be viewed as a necessary ideological corollary to the needs of the labour market.

Politics and Ageing

In the United States the Depression in the 1930s generated the beginnings of lobby groups acting on behalf of the elderly, but many of these dissolved with increased social security provision. Nevertheless, there are now numerous organizations dedicated to the needs of the elderly. Hendricks and Hendricks[17] identify ten such major organizations; three are associations with general membership, four are trade associations and the rest are composed of members from a professional society, of social welfare workers and of specialists concerned with the black elderly. The National Council of Senior Citizens is one of the largest.[18] There is no doubt that now the elderly have a significant stake in national politics sufficient for there to be a distinct 'Gray Lobby'.[19] However, achievements so far have been confined to improving benefits within the existing social security, Medicare and Older Americans Act[20] legislation. There is still much speculation as to how far age-consciousness in the US will result in a coherent political bloc. Certainly, the militancy of the Gray Panthers, founded by Maggie Kuhn, remains on the fringe. The objectives of this latter group are to challenge the negative attitudes towards and by the old by encouraging 'solidarity' between generations, a position taken against the view that ageism is a product of some inherent conflict between age cohorts.[21]

By contrast, such activism in the UK has been sporadic until very recently. There have been indications, however, throughout the post-war era, of some concern especially in relation to the employment of older workers and also the movement for 'sheltered' housing. Age discrimination in employment has frequently been the subject of Private Member's Bills[22] and another such bill intended to make age discriminatory advertising unlawful was initiated in the House of Lords in Autumn 1990. The first Campaign against Age Discrimination in Employment in the United Kingdom was launched in 1990.[23] Pensioners' associations generally have exhibited increasing activism over the past five years.[24]

Perhaps of more long-term political significance than the current developments of pressure group politics in the UK is the proposal for a European Community Council resolution on a Community action

programme for the elderly and the recent recognition of the rights of
elderly people in the Charter of Fundamental Social Rights of Workers.
The Community programme is to be carried out from January 1991 to
December 1993, the latter year being designated as 'European Year of
the Elderly and Solidarity between Generations'. The objectives of the
programme are:

1. To contribute to the development of preventive strategies
   to meet the economic and social challenges of an ageing
   population;
2. To identify innovative approaches to strengthening solidarity
   between the generations and integration of the elderly population, involving all economic and social agents, in rural as well
   as in urban contexts;
3. To develop and highlight the positive potential of elderly
   citizens in contributing to the Community. (Article 2)[25]

It seems quite likely that such European influences (as distinct from
the European Community case law developments discussed briefly
below), will combine with increased activism in the UK to provide the
context for enhanced legal protection of older workers and the elderly
generally across many different areas. It is possible too that these sorts
of initiatives will provide the empirical data upon which to base reform
proposals which, in the United Kingdom, have been lagging behind
efforts in, for example, the United States.[26]

AGEISM, SEXISM AND RACISM

The term 'ageism' is usually attributed to the American psychologist
R. N. Butler,[27] and there are some immediately apparent similarities
between this concept and sexism and racism. All three identify negative
attitudes and stereotypes ascribed to a person by virtue of nothing more
than belonging to one of these categories. It can be established through
empirical evidence that these pejorative attitudes have been, to a greater
or lesser extent, institutionalized, although one has to say that the
empirical evidence in relation to ageism in the UK is still at a formative
stage. The problem in relation to ageism, certainly in the UK, is that
it has not fully emerged in the public consciousness. Thus, although
racism and sexism have not disappeared from our society, there has been
an increased consciousness of what these phenomena signify. Age consciousness, by contrast, has not yet made much impact.

There are perhaps four qualifications to be made however, to the latter proposition. First, 'youth culture' has on occasion been a significant social and political entity in Europe and elsewhere. Second, on the personal and psychological plane, individuals persist in being acutely aware of their age, whether they have become 'middle-aged', whether they are older or younger than they look, etc.; indeed many individuals could be described as obsessed with their chronological age. Third, in public affairs, sporadic outbursts from politicians and the press may be occasioned by firms refusing to employ anyone over 35 or 40.[28] Finally, there would appear to be an increasing interest among feminists in the particular position of older women. It is tempting to speculate as to whether the politically active cohorts of feminists from the 1960s and 1970s and the 'New Men' of the next decade will have any impact on 'age consciousness' when they enter old age in the next twenty years or so.

Apart from the relative absence of public consciousness, another difference between ageism and sexism and racism is that the available evidence would appear to demonstrate that ageism occurs in a much more subtle or covert form. Some of the evidence relating to the use of age as a criterion in employment decision-making is equivocal.[29] The balance of evidence relating to the use of age limits in job advertising (the subject of a Private Members' Bill introduced in 1989),[30] would suggest that age is frequently a marginal factor in the decision. Furthermore, employers frequently breach their own age limits in recruitment.[31] Of course, the difficult question here is whether ageism is more covert precisely because age consciousness is generally low or whether it is in the nature of the phenomenon that it operates in a less potent fashion than either sexism or racism?

Even if this latter question were to be satisfactorily resolved (in favour of the view that ageism has slightly less significant power than sexism or racism), one would still have to determine whether and how legal processes could be used to tackle it. The fundamental difficulty of defining the concept of ageism is that lack of good empirical evidence, and ignorance as to the extent to which age consciousness might develop in terms of a social-political movement, make it almost impossible to predict its impact. However, there are some remaining comparisons with sexism and racism to be usefully made.

In relation to sexism, the impact of ageism would appear to be additive. There is an increasing literature on the subject of the 'double jeopardy' of being female and old. Sontag,[32] for example, argues that men are 'allowed' to age without the same penalties as women. Men's ageing crisis is often linked to pressures on them to be 'successful', while women's ageing crisis relates to their sexual attractiveness and loss of reproductive function. Women, much earlier than men, undergo a 'humiliating process of gradual sexual disqualification'. Lines in a man's face might symbolize 'character'; the social meaning for a woman of such outward signs of ageing are very different. Although awareness of ageist images is more recent than sexist ones, Itzin[33] argues that ageism is integral to sex-stereotyping from childhood to old age. She draws attention to the media images of older women; frequently they display older women selling mood-changing medicines. A content analysis of the magazine *Woman* from January to June 1983, she argues, shows that every issue had a major feature concerned with women and age in some particular way.

Of course the relationship between age and sex translates in British sex discrimination law as 'indirect discrimination', as in, for example, *Price* v *Civil Service Commission & another*.[34] However, the extension of existing discrimination law to accommodate age discrimination is fraught with difficulties as will be discussed below.

The relationship between racism and ageism is also problematic. Each ethnic group imposes its own distinctive social meaning on the individual's experience of ageing. Some commentators have argued that black Americans do not suffer the same discontinuities in their lives as their white peers. Others argue that the 'triple jeopardy' of being old, poor and belonging to a racial minority has an additive discriminatory effect.[35] Life expectancy tends to be shorter among black Americans and this has certain consequences for the age distribution of the various ethnic groups.[36]

The concept of ageism can also be approached from the perspective that the elderly constitute some kind of 'minority group',[37] or even sub-culture.[38] Such views suffer from similar conceptual difficulties as occur in seeing women as a 'minority' or 'sub-cultural' group. It is difficult to find homogeneous categories when describing old/elderly persons; one aspect of unravelling the myths surrounding the elderly is to address their heterogeneity. Although some sections of the elderly population can be described as living in poverty or otherwise deprived, for example, this is clearly not always the case. Similarly, as the elderly do not normally live in age-segregated communities,[39] nor confine patterns of social interaction to their own age peers, it is difficult to see the usefulness of this type of theory.

A similar conceptual difficulty arose in the context of the Age Discrimination in Employment Act 1967 in the United States concerning whether the aged had an adequate 'history of oppression'. In *Murgia* v *Commonwealth of Massachusetts Board of Retirement*[40] the state statute provided that the board retire uniformed police officers at the age of 50 years. It was alleged that this violated the Fourteenth Amendment. The

Supreme Court held that this had to be determined under the 'rationality' standard. The Court found that, applying this standard, the age limit was rationally related to the objective of protecting the public by ensuring the physical preparedness of its uniformed officers, although it was conceded that use of an age limit to achieve this objective was not ideal. The court rejected the use of the 'strict judicial scrutiny' test on the grounds that age was not a sufficiently 'suspect' classification. A 'suspect' class was defined as one 'saddled with such disabilities or subjected to such a history of purposeful unequal treatment, or regulated to such a position of political powerlessness as to command extraordinary protection from the majoritarian political process'.[41]

Whether older workers ought to come within this definition is a moot point. It can be argued that there was already sufficient evidence available in the US of a 'history of oppression' at the time of the passing of the Age Discrimination in Employment Act 1967.[42] It has also been said that the increase in the number of mandatory retirement laws suggests that we are now living through the 'history' which the courts could not find.[43] Other commentators seem more confident that ageism is a phenomenon of a simply different order.[44]

There have been a few attempts to apply a more scientific method to the problem of the relationship between ageism, sexism and racism. Palmore and Manton[45] devised an 'equality index' in 1973 to compare these three concepts. They argued that the operational measure of equality should be comparable between any two groups in terms of any kind of characteristic (they used income, occupation and education). Once this was determined one would have to interpret how much of this inequality was due to various forms of prejudice. Their main findings were that age inequality is greater in education and weeks worked but least in occupation (of those working). Age also produced more income inequality than race. The joint effects of any two of the factors were generally additive, with the age-sex combination producing the lowest equality in terms of income. Combining all three factors produced the lowest equality in both income and occupation. Age inequality was found to be greater among men and non-whites than among women and whites. Finally, changes since 1950 showed that non-whites were making small gains in all three areas, women were barely maintaining their inferior status, but the aged were actually losing ground in income and education. However, such approaches frequently beg more questions than they answer.

The obvious difference about being old compared with being female or a member of a racial minority is that it is an attribute achieved over a long process of time and (subject to living out the normal life span) it is achieved by most members of society. The experience of ageing can,

therefore, claim to have a more universal application. If equality legislation can be made wide enough to accommodate some rational model
of equality between age cohorts, it is arguable that *all* members of
such a society will have a direct interest in supporting the equality
principle.

THE LIMITS OF LEGAL CONTROL UNDER ENGLISH AND EUROPEAN COMMUNITY LAW

The case law development in both English sex discrimination and
European Community equal pay/equal treatment legislation demonstrates various age-related issues reflecting some of the increasingly
vociferous economic claims being made by particular age cohorts. For
example, in *Price* v *Civil Service Commission*[46] it was held that the Civil
Service upper age limit of 28 for direct entry to the executive officer
grade constituted indirect sex discrimination; women would have more
difficulty than men in complying with the age bar as more women in
their twenties are caring for young children and often only return to the
job market in their mid-thirties.

It is easy to overlook the fact that such age limits also constitute
'direct' age discrimination for all persons over the prescribed limit. But
such cases are often revealing in so far as the employer will be pressed
to argue that while such a 'condition or requirement' cannot be complied with by women in proportion to men who can comply (Sex Discrimination Act 1975, s. 1(1)(b)(i)), nevertheless, it is 'justifiable'
(s. 1(1)(b)(ii)). In *Price* the Civil Service Commission contended that the
age limit was necessary to control the direct entry to the executive officer
group because this was one of the main sources of recruitment for more
senior grades; appointment below the prescribed age of 28 was necessary
to ensure that there was sufficient time ahead to obtain the skills and
experience required for the more senior jobs. However, such claims for
a 'balanced' age/career structure are never fully articulated in the cases,
and indeed, where there is some attempt to do so, as in *Price*, such
arguments are frequently revealed as insubstantial. Counsel for Mrs
Price actually showed that there were positive arguments against the age
bar; it limited 50 per cent of female executive officer direct entrants to
an age where they were most likely to leave the jobs they had obtained
by direct entry and it eliminated from consideration 'mature people of
both sexes'.

In the *Price* litigation the Civil Service Commission revealed something of its past practice in relation to the age bar for direct entry executive officers: from 1946 to 1958 entrance was limited to 17½–19-year-olds; from 1959 to 1965, 17½–23-year-olds; and from 1966, 17½–27-year-olds. It was clear from the evidence that the age limit was simply extended in 1966 to attract more applicants for executive officer posts in the context of an expanding workforce capacity in the Civil Service. Despite the attempted justifications for the age bar in terms of creating a 'balanced' age structure in the workforce, whatever that might mean, it was clear that in fact the age limit was being used as a convenient administrative device to regulate the numbers of job applicants.

The *Huppert* case[47] follows *Price* as regards the finding of indirect sex discrimination. This case concerned a woman academic, aged 39 at the relevant time, who had gone through a successful interview for a 'new blood' post at Cambridge University, but was later refused the job on the ground that she was over the 35-year age limit prescribed in the scheme. The scheme, operated by the University Grants Committee since 1983, was therefore inherently age discriminatory. It was based on a view that academics over 35 years old are 'burnt out' to a greater extent than their younger colleagues. The industrial tribunal took the view that there had been indirect discrimination. The 'pool' of qualified persons tended to include women who had children in their early thirties (after completing doctoral and post-doctoral work). The tribunal accepted that this resulted in a considerably smaller proportion of women who could comply with the age limit and the limit was held not to be 'justifiable'.[48]

The dangers of the fundamentally ageist assumptions behind the setting up of the 'new blood' scheme are that such assumptions, in a different context, may well provide the foundation to resist a claim of indirect sex discrimination. Cases such as *Price* and *Huppert* establish firmly that using such an age limit may well constitute a 'condition or requirement' which women cannot comply with in proportion to men, but the various arguments produced claiming the necessity for a balanced age structure in the workforce have potential for making such discrimination 'justifiable'. This potential appears to have been realized in some cases. For example, in *Leavers v Civil Service Commission*[49] applicants for appointment to the Diplomatic Service were required to be 'under 32'. This practice was held to be justifiable as it was argued that it took 25 to 30 years to reach a senior grade such as ambassador and given a mandatory retirement age of 60 an entrant over 32 could not expect a reasonable period in a senior post before retirement. In this case the element of age discrimination involved in the mandatory retirement policy appears to have stimulated age discrimination at the recruitment stage as well.

Issues of age have also arisen tangentially to litigation under the European Community principles of equal pay and equal treatment for men and women. One of the principal uses of the equal treatment Directive 76/207/EEC[50] in the United Kingdom has been to challenge the differential retirement ages between men and women. However, the economic factors which underpin much of this litigation reveal a number of age-related issues which the European Community legislation, like English discrimination law, as yet fails to respond to directly. For example, in *Burton* v *British Railways Board*[51] the litigant wished to take early retirement at the age of 58, but on the basis of parity with his female colleagues, who had access to a voluntary redundancy scheme at 55, while males could only benefit from the scheme at 60. It was held that the equal treatment directive applied in principle, but since the age limits were calculated by reference to statutory retirement ages of 60 and 65, then Article 7 of Directive 79/7/EEC[52] (equal treatment in social security) applied, permitting the exclusion of the equal treatment principle in the 'determination of pensionable age'. Thus his claim failed, but *Burton* was distinguished in *Marshall* v *Southampton & South West Hampshire Area Health Authority*.[53] Ms Marshall's claim was held not to be within the derogation of Article 7 of Directive 79/7/EEC. It should be remembered that her claim was made in response to the health authority's policy of mandatory retirement (at 60/65).[54] *Marshall* and other authorities have severely limited the scope of the derogation in Article 7 by holding that the determination of pensionable age had not been '*for the purposes of* granting old-age or retirement pensions' (my emphasis).

The impact of the European Community developments on UK law has been that the awkward exclusions of the Equal Pay Act 1970 and Sex Discrimination Act 1975 concerning 'provisions relating to death or retirement' have been amended by the Sex Discrimination Act 1986 which makes discriminatory retirement ages illegal and the Employment Act 1989 which fixes a single retirement age of 65 for men and women for the purposes of redundancy benefit. In addition, as regards occupational pensions, Directive 86/378/EEC[55] now specifically prohibits the fixing of differential retirement ages for men and women (Article 6(f)).[56] Although the equality principle in European Community law has had some significant implications for UK discrimination law, feminist discourse contends that the predominantly economic objectives of the European Community directives will limit the development of the equality principle.[57] *A fortiori* the litigation under the EC legislation is unlikely to widen the equality principle to accommodate a recognition of ageism even in the limited arena of employment. A more positive source of protection for older workers and the elderly is likely to emanate from the recent initiatives alluded to briefly at the end of the first section of this essay.

AGE DISCRIMINATION LAWS

The Age Discrimination in Employment Act 1967 (ADEA) in the United States has produced a well-developed body of case law, and has been amended several times, most notably to make adjustments on the issue of mandatory retirement.[58] The availability of remedies under this law, in terms of dollar awards, can only be described as impressive in comparison with the operation of British discrimination law. It has to be said, however, that the ADEA has suffered numerous procedural difficulties in its development. Some commentators have noted that age discrimination laws were very much pushed along the conveyor belt of civil rights legislation in the 1960s without perhaps too much thought to the particular needs of legislation in the age context. The lesson seems to be clear. Although there are some real distinctive features of the social phenomenon of ageism which correspond to those of sexism and racism, it would be foolhardy to frame laws on any glib comparisons.[59] Notwithstanding the shortcomings of the ADEA, legal reform in the United Kingdom can be strengthened and proceed on a more well-informed basis because of the experience gained from the operation of the Act in the United States.

The first issue for policy makers in the UK to decide will be whether there is a need for a specifically *legal* response. Government ministers responding to questions regarding the plight of older workers routinely reply that employers should be 'encouraged' to accommodate older workers. The Watkinson reports of the 1950s concluded that a legal response might make older persons a special class which would then be vulnerable to stigmatization. Employers themselves, of course, would be largely unwilling to be subjected to further regulation. However, there is no doubt that a developing perspective in relation to 'equal opportunities' in general will reinforce any support for the enactment of such laws. It may also be the case that one of the strongest arguments in support of age discrimination legislation in employment law in the UK is that it is (potentially) a protection for *all* workers. It is interesting to speculate, in this context, how an increased awareness of ageism, consequent upon the enactment of such a law, would impact on sex and race consciousness generally.

Assuming a legal response is appropriate, where is the starting point?
Arguably, a clear, simple measure is required, perhaps predominantly
as a public relations exercise. A law making age-discriminatory advertising unlawful has much to recommend it in this respect. There is ample
evidence to show that age limits in employment advertising are fairly
widespread, particularly in relation to certain types of occupation.[60]
Such a law would 'bite' in a clearly defined area and cause many
employers, for the first time perhaps, to pause and reconsider their equal
opportunities policy in the age context.

Greater problems arise when deciding the shape of a more substantial legal framework to regulate age discrimination in employment
generally. Would, for example, a 'quota' model of regulation be appropriate? It can be argued that there are advantages in the legislative
model provided by the Disabled Persons (Employment) Act 1944.[61]
However, recent suggestions that this measure should be repealed
because of its ineffectiveness in supporting disabled persons might cast
doubts on whether this legal formulation is apposite. Could the existing
model of sex and race discrimination law be adapted to accomodate age
discrimination? There would be advantages in such an approach. As
already mentioned, the concept of indirect sex discrimination has on
occasion involved an element of (direct) age discrimination; for example, *Price* and *Huppert*. What would be the content of indirect age
discrimination? It could apply to work situations where older workers
were being unjustifiably laid off.[62] For example, in *Franci* v *Avco Corp.,
Avco Lycoming Div. D. C. Conn.*[63] the plaintiffs were within the protected
age range, each was performing his or her job satisfactorily, none were
laid off for 'cause', but the employer continued to employ young people
to perform duties which the plaintiffs were qualified to do. There was
also statistical evidence that the 'facially neutral' action of reducing
the work force because of economic necessity had a disparate impact
on employees within the protected age group. It was held that the
evidence showed a *prima facie* case of age discrimination. Indirect age
discrimination has also been used to control an employer's use of
discriminatory retirement plans. In *Betts* v *Hamilton County Board of
Mental Retardation*[64] a disability retirement plan offered by the county
board had a disparate impact upon those in the protected age group who
had not accumulated sufficient retirement benefits to compensate for
denial of disability benefits based solely upon their age. The plan denied
benefits to employees 60 years or older and over 60-year-olds were
precluded from the option of returning to work after a period of
disability.

The concept of indirect discrimination as originally developed in the
United States and imported into the UK legislation, resonates with the

rights of people as a *collective* group, rather than as individuals. Any effective use of the concept of indirect discrimination in the age context would have to involve a better use of statistics in the courts than has been shown hitherto. It is evident that the Commission for Racial Equality and the Equal Opportunities Commission both currently favour such developments in the race and sex contexts but are also aware of the dangers of meaningless computer print-outs littering the floors of such agencies. McGinley argues that the British approach of relying largely upon 'common sense and common knowledge' in deciding whether a requirement indirectly discriminates [may be] adequate in dealing with the grosser forms of discrimination. Subtler forms of discrimination, however, will probably require more precise statistical showings'.[65] Such an approach is, of course, far more evident in the US. With regard to age discrimination cases, a former solicitor of labor has said:

> the development of meaningful statistics is essential to the successful prosecution of the large pattern and practice cases and this is the kind of case that we intend to develop more of. This does not mean that we will not continue to bring cases involving a single employee. We will. At the same time we must concentrate our efforts of those cases which will have the greatest impact on the community and which will establish precedent for the important legal issues.[66]

If one accepts these lessons from the American legislation then the focus of age discrimination legislation ought to concentrate upon the *collective* nature of such rights rather than the *individual* level. This indicates, therefore, the particular suitability of the concept of indirect discrimination, in the age context, and secondly, the need for the development of a 'class action'.[67] Arguably, this is particularly the case given that it would seem to be accepted by most commentators that age discrimination is likely to take much more subtle and covert forms than other types of discrimination.

At present, in the UK, there are signs that a collective consciousness with regard to age-related issues is beginning to emerge. Any age discrimination legislation will have to reflect and reinforce such developments rather than run too far ahead of them.

NOTES

1. See Bromley, D. B. *Human Ageing: An Introduction to Gerontology* 3rd edn (London, Penguin, 1988), for a useful introduction to gerontology.

2. See Victor, C. R. *Old Age in Modern Society* (London, Croom Helm, 1987) p. 1.

3. See, for example, Cumming, E. and Henry, W. E. *Growing Old: The Process of Disengagement* (New York, Basic Books Inc., 1961).

4. See, for example, Lemon, B. W., Bengtson, V. L., and Petersen, J. A. 'An exploration of the activity theory of aging: activity types and life expectation among in-movers to a retirement community' (1972) 27 *Journal of Gerontology* 511.

5. See Hendricks, J. and Hendricks, C. *Aging in Mass Society: Myths and Realities* (Massachusetts, Winthrop, 1981) for a useful summary of the relevant theoretical approaches.

6. This approach stresses the individual's interaction with the social world. Through language the individual is a social actor as well as reactor living in a symbolic environment of meaning as well as a physical one. It is through this interaction that social reality is constructed. Despite there being few empirical studies employing this approach, Victor believes it is appropriate because it views ageing as 'a dynamic process', it does not involve prescriptions for how people 'ought' to live later life and 'it suggests that the influence of negative labelling, low expectations, and negative stereotypes of old age can be overcome by more positive attitudes from the rest of society'. See Victor op. cit. (note 2) p. 50.

7. 'Elderly' and 'old' are of course relative concepts in different societies and over different times. A fashionable distinction now is between the 'young old' (60–75), and the 'old old' (75 +).

8. (1990) *Social Trends* table 7.2.

9. This is generally defined as the ratio between the working population and dependants; this may or may not include older adult and child dependants.

10. See Cowgill, D. O. and Holmes, L. D. *Aging and Modernization* (New York, Appleton-Century-Crofts, 1972).

11. For example, Thomas, K. 'Age and authority in early modern England' (1976) 62 (205) *Proceedings of the British Academy*, for early modern England, and Steams, P. N. *Old Age in European Society* (New York, Holmes and Meir, 1976) for France.

12. For example in de Beauvoir, S. *Old Age* (London, André Deutsch/Weidenfeld & Nicolson, 1972).

13. See Phillipson, C. *The Emergence of Retirement* (University of Durham, 1978).

14. The committee held its final meeting in November 1958; *HC Debates* vol. 668 (26 November 1962) col. 6.

15. *Employment of Older Men and Women, 1st Report* 11 September 1953 (Chairman: H. Watkinson, MP), Cmd 8963; *Employment of Older Men and Women, 2nd Report*, 20 October 1955 (Chairman: H. Watkinson, MP) Cmd. 9628.

16. 'Employment for the 1990s' Cm. 540 (1988). See also 'The employment patterns of the over-50s' (House of Commons Employment Committee, 2nd report, 1988/89 session, HC 41).

17. See Hendricks and Hendricks op. cit. (note 5) ch. 12 'The aged in the political arena' for a concise account of age groups in the political sphere and also political attitudes of the aged. See also National Council on the Aging *The Myth and Reality of Aging in America* (Washington, DC, Louis Harris and Associates, 1977), s. viii 'The politics of old age'.

18. It was founded in the 1960s to support Medicare legislation and became sufficiently visible in the 1970s to be put on the White House 'enemies list'.

19. See for example, Pratt, H. J. *The Gray Lobby* (Chicago, University of Chicago Press, 1976).

20. The Older Americans Act 1965, as amended, provides federal funds to support social services for the elderly.

21. The militancy of the 'Gray Panthers' has not been matched in the UK, although miscellaneous publications in the alternative press have appeared from time to time, e.g. Search Project, *Against Ageism* (Newcastle upon Tyne, 1983).

22. E.g. 'age level of employment' bills: 1968 [Bill 98]; 1969 [Bill 124]; 1973 [Bill 141]; 'age discrimination' bills: 1983 [Bill 127]; 1989 [Bill 811]; 'employment (age limits)' bill: 1986 [Bill 88]; 1989 House of Lords [26]. See Buck, T. G. *Age Discrimination in Employment: A Comparative Study of the Law in the United States and the United Kingdom* (Unpublished LLM thesis, University of

Lancaster, 1988), ch. 3, s. 3 and app. V, 'Parliamentary attempts to find an appropriate legislative formula'. See also note 29 below.

23. In (Winter 1989) *Skills Bulletin* (Department of Employment, Training Agency), it was reported that Baroness Phillips will chair a new campaign to ban age discrimination by employers. The Campaign against Age Discrimination in Employment (CAADE) 'will try to adopt a more realistic approach towards the recruitment of the over-50s and will organise, motivate and encourage job seekers who face age discrimination' (p. 2). At its launch CAADE drew attention to the recent findings of the Commons Employment Committee that between 250,000–500,000 people, however well qualified, were unable to find jobs because of age discrimination.

24. The Association of Retired Pensioners, the Over-50s Club, Age Concern and other groups are all participating in CAADE. The Pensioners' Rights Campaign has also made recent TV broadcasts arguing for enhanced social security benefits for pensioners.

25. OJ no. C-120 (16 May 1990) p. 8.

26. See, for example, *The Older American Worker — Age Discrimination in Employment* (Report of the Secretary of Labor to the Congress under section 715 of the Civil Rights Act, 1964, June 1965). This report provided the evidence upon which the American Age Discrimination in Employment Act 1967 was based. See also National Council on the Aging op. cit (note 17).

27. See Butler, R. N. 'Ageism: another form of Bigotry' (1969) 9 *Gerontologist* 243: 'Age-ism describes the subjective experience implied in the popular notion of the generation gap. Prejudice of the middle-aged against the old . . ., and against the young . . ., is a serious national problem. Age-ism reflects a deep seated uneasiness on the part of the young and middle-aged — a personal revulsion to and distaste for growing old, disease, disability; and fear of powerlessness, 'uselessness' and death. . . . Age-ism might parallel . . . racism as the great issue of the next 20 to 30 years and age bigotry is seen within minority groups themselves.' See also Butler, R. N. 'Dispelling ageism: the cross-cutting intervention' in Riley, M., and Riley J. (eds) *The Quality of Aging: Strategies for Interventions*. The Annals of the American Academy of Political and Social Science (London, Sage Publications, 1989) for his more recent views.

28. E.g. in 1983, a Hitachi factory in Wales had invited workers over the age of 35 to take 'voluntary' redundancy. In a letter to all its employees the company said that older workers caused problems through sickness, slower reactions, poor eyesight and resistance to change. They invited their over 35-year-olds to leave the company and make way for younger (!) people, offering them a tax-free payment of £1,800 and giving them a chance to nominate a 16-year-old school leaver to take their place. The incident directly inspired the Private Members' Bill introduced by Ann Clwyd MP in 1986. See Buck, T. G. op. cit. (note 22) p. 211.

29. See, e.g. Jolly, J., Creigh, S. and Mingay, D. *Age as a Factor in Employment* Research Paper no. 11 (Department of Employment, 1980) and Makeham, P. *Economic Aspects of the Employment of Older Workers* Research Paper no. 14 (Department of Employment, 1980).

30. Employment (Age Limits) Bill 1989 House of Lords [26]. This bill, introduced by Baroness Phillips on 2 March 1989, would have prohibited the use of age limits in job appointments, training schemes, promotion, retirement and advertising of jobs. A bill 'to abolish age discrimination' was introduced in the House of Commons by Barry Fields, MP on 22 February 1989; Employment Age Discrimination Bill, 1989, House of Commons, (81).

31. See Slater, R. 'Age discrimination' (1973) *New Society* 301, and Jolly, J., Creigh, S. Mingay, D. op. cit. (note 29).

32. See Sontag, S. 'The double standard of ageing' in Institute of Gerontology *No Longer Young: The Older Woman in America*. Proceedings of the 26th Annual Conference on Aging part 1 no. 3 (The Institute of Gerontology, The University of Michigan, Wayne State University, 1975).

33. See Itzin, C. 'The double jeopardy of ageism and sexism: media images of women' in Bromley, D. B. (ed.) *Gerontology: Social and Behavioural Perspectives* (London, Croom Helm, 1984).

34. [1978] ICR 27.

35. See Bengtson, V. L. 'Ethnicity and aging: problems and issues in current social science inquiry' in Gelfand, D. E. and Kutzik A. J. (eds) *Ethnicity and Aging* (New York, Springer, 1979).

36. See Hendricks and Hendricks, op. cit (note 5) p. 405, table 3 'Age distribution of white, black, Spanish, and Indian Americans'.

37. See Breen, L. Z. 'The aging individual' in Tibbitts, C. (ed.) *Handbook of Social Gerontology* (Chicago, University of Chicago Press, 1960).

38. See Palmore, E. B. and Whittington, F. 'Trends in the relative status of the elderly' (1971) 50 *Social Forces* 84.

39. There are, however, some such communities in the United States; see Hendricks and Hendricks op. cit (note 5) pp. 318-24; and Victor, C. R. op. cit (note 2) pp. 120-125.

40. 376 F. Supp. (D. Mass. 1974) (three-judge court holding statute unconstitutional), reversed 427 US 307 [1976] *per curiam.*

41. 427 US 307, 313/4 [1976].

42. See note 26.

43. See Edelman C. D. and Siegler I. C. *Federal Age Discrimination in Employment Law: Slowing Down the Gold Watch* (Charlottesville, Virginia, Michie Company, 1977), p. 57.

44. E.g. Eglit, H. 'Of age and the Constitution' (1981) 57 *Chicago Kent Law Review* 859 concludes that 'Ageism is not as pernicious as is racism. Granted, this is a judgmental assertion. Some may disagree. But, if a history of degradation, and the elements of isolation, stigma and powerlessness have significance in identifying those most in need of judicial interventionism — and they do — most age categorisations simply miss the mark' (pp. 901-2).

45. See Palmore, E. B. and Manton, K. 'Ageism compared to racism and sexism' (1973) 28 *Journal of Gerontology* 363, and references therein.

46. See note 34.

47. Industrial tribunal decision, reported in *Times Higher Education Supplement* (25 April 1986) 12.

48. It was not 'justifiable' because 'it would have been the easiest thing in the world to have said the 35 age limit would be reconsidered in respect of a suitable candidate who had been delayed in her academic career by reason of the fact that she had children'. See *Times Higher Education Supplement* (25 April 1986) 12.

49. (1986) 8 *Equal Opportunities Review* 38.

50. OJ 1976 L 39/40.

51. Case 19/81 [1982] ECR 555 (ECJ).

52. OJ 1979 L 6/24.

53. Case 152/84 [1986] ECR 723 (ECJ).

54. Other important European Community cases, such as Case 151/84 *Roberts* v *Tate & Lyle Industries Ltd* [1986] ECR 703 (ECJ) and Case 262/84 *Beetes-Proper* v *F. Van Lanschot Bankiers NV* [1986] ECR 773 CJEC have also been founded on the litigant's desire to challenge such compulsory retirement schemes.

55. OJ 1986 L 225/40.

56. See also Case C-262/88 *Barber* v *Guardian Royal Exchange* [1990] 2 All ER 958, where the European Court of Justice held that Article 119 EEC applied to employers' contracted-out occupational pension schemes and to all redundancy schemes.

57. See O'Donovan, K. and Szyszczak, E. *Equality and Sex Discrimination Law* (Oxford, Basil Blackwell, 1988) ch. 7. A good illustration of the limits of the law here is Case 184/83 *Hoffman* v *Barmer Ersatzkasse* [1984] ECR 30, where a claim for paternity leave based on Directive 76/207/EEC failed. It was stated that the EC measures were not intended to settle questions concerned with the organization of the family or to alter the division of responsibility between parents.

58. For leading texts of the American age discrimination legislation, see Edelman and Siegler op. cit (note 43) and Northrup, J. P. *Old Age, Handicapped, and Vietnam-era Anti-discrimination legislation* Labor Relations & Public Policy Series no. 14 (Philadelphia, University of Pennsylvania, 1980).

59. See Schuck, P. H. 'The graying of civil rights law: the age discrimination act of 1975' (1979) 89 *Yale Law Journal* 27.

60. See discussion of this in Buck op. cit (note 22) ch. 3 s. 1 'Age discrimination in the U.K. — the empirical evidence'.

61. Ibid at ch. 4 s. 1, 'Reform — quota system'.

62. For a suggestion as to how a legislative provision on indirect age discrimination might be drafted, see ibid. at 163-65.

63. 538 F. Supp. 250 [1982].

64. 631 F. Supp. 1198 [1986].

65. McGinley, G. P. 'Judicial approaches to sex discrimination in the United States and the United Kingdom — a comparative study' (1986) 49 *Modern Law Review* 413.

66. Statement of Labor Solicitor Kilberg on age discrimination submitted to sub-committee on House Select Committee on Aging (1976) *Daily Lab. Rep.* (BNA) E-2 (18th February 1976).

67. See generally Buck op. cit. (note 22) ch. 4 s. 3, 'Reform — enforcing collective rights'.

III

POSITIVE DISCRIMINATION AND AFFIRMATIVE ACTION

15

A Case for Positive Discrimination

Bhikhu Parekh

In this essay I intend to examine the nature and basis of action pro-grammes designed to favour and promote the interests of disadvantaged groups. In Britain it is called either positive or reverse discrimination, and in the United States it is often referred to as preferential treatment. In the first section I shall argue that we have a variously derived moral duty to help disadvantaged groups in our society, and in the second I shall show why the duty entails a programme of positive discrimination. In the third section I shall briefly discuss the experiences of societies which have practised positive discrimination on a significant scale and conclude that, although it has its dangers, it is on balance and within limits a valuable tool of public policy.

I

Every society today, be it rich or poor, developed or developing, capital-ist or communist, includes large sections of men and women who are disadvantaged and unable to develop their human potential. They include such groups as blacks, the ethnic minorities, the indigenous population, the poor, the underclass, the long-term unemployed who have become virtually unemployable, large sections of the working classes, the untouchables and the tribal communities. With some quali-fications, women too belong to this category. Though they are inti-mately associated with and cannot be economically and socially isolated from the dominant sex, thereby making their problems at once both more and less intractable, they too suffer from cultural and psycho-logical if not always material disadvantages. Victims of a long history of exploitation, repression, discrimination and marginalization, all these groups have for generations been denied adequate opportunities for growth and treated as 'naturally' inferior, almost as if they belonged to a separate and congenitally flawed species.

Most of them are poor and suffer disproportionately from inadequate medical attention resulting in ill-health, high incidence of infant mortality and shortened life expectancy. In their crucial formative years they receive poor education, limited intellectual and emotional stimulus, and very few opportunities to develop their intelligence, character, imagination, will-power, ambition, self-discipline, self-confidence and a sense of their own worth. Haunted all their life by a deep sense of injustice and existential marginality, they are crippled by cartloads of frustrations, deep inhibitions, half-articulated fears and anxieties, and collective memories of persecution and discrimination. They feel that the world in which they live is not theirs and that they do not really belong to it. For women it is a 'man's world' in which they can only succeed by becoming like men and thus by ceasing to be themselves; for blacks it is a 'white man's world'; for the poor it is a 'middle-class world'; for the working classes it is the world of the 'bosses'; and for the Indian untouchables it is a world of higher castes. The language of inequality and injustice is too feeble to capture their feeling of superfluity and marginality, and no amount of legal and political equality is able to overcome or even significantly reduce that feeling.

A large number of writers have argued over the centuries that such 'half-men' of 'exiguous moral resources' will always be with us, that they have none but themselves to blame, and that nothing can or should be done about them except to keep them under firm control.[1] Such a view is not only callous and arrogant but also untenable. The so-called 'half-men' have not always been with us; their number has varied from one historical period to another and continues to vary from society to society; and some of them have succeeded in reclaiming their humanity when given adequate encouragement and opportunities. They are thus not naturally inferior and their condition *can* be altered. This raises the question whether it *should* be altered and whether those in a position to do something about it have a duty to do so. I suggest that they have, and that the duty has at least three sources.

Whatever else the much-debated concept of morality may involve, minimally it involves recognizing that human beings have claims on each other arising from the fact that they belong to a common species, are similarly constituted, have similar basic needs and are equal at the deepest level. Such expressions as the spirit of humanity, common humanity, human community, fellow-feeling and human fellowship used by moral writers over the centuries and regarded by them as lying at the basis of moral experience, capture this basic insight. Wherever there is suffering and a cry for help, a moral being feels addressed. He cannot remain indifferent to it and has a duty to alleviate it within the limits of his abilities and resources. If he is unable to help, he should draw it to the attention of those who can, but he cannot leave the suffering unaddressed without at least some feeling of regret and sadness. A man to whom it makes no difference whether a human being lives or dies, grows or decays, fulfils himself or wastes away, is not a moral being at all. He lacks compassion, that is, the capacity to suffer with others and to be moved by their suffering, which is one of the essential constituents of what it means to be human and the basis of moral life.

Suffering takes many forms. It may be physical and visible to the naked eye, as in the case of a person dying of hunger or lying wounded by a hooligan's gun, and we then have a duty to help him in an appropriate manner. Or it may be psychological, moral or spiritual and only accessible to a sympathetic imagination, as in the case of a person frustrated for lack of opportunities, or denied self-expression, or systematically humiliated and insulted by his fellow men and paralysed by self-pity and self-hatred. In such cases we have a duty to heal his wounded soul, to help him pull or put himself together, to enable him to secure the opportunities he needs to find a measure of joy in his unbearably empty life. We can hardly be said to respect another's dignity or to treat him as an end in himself if we treat him as dirt, or participate in practices that treat him as such, or passively watch him disintegrate under the pressure of inhuman circumstances.

Restoring broken or wounded selves and helping men and women flourish and lead meaningful lives, the central inspiring principle of moral conduct, obviously makes demands which none of us can individually meet. I may, of course, adopt or finance the education of my poor neighbour's son, contribute generously to worthwhile charities, join voluntary organizations, or rigorously examine and overcome my deep-seated prejudices and treat my female, black or untouchable students, colleagues and neighbours in a spirit of full and unpatronizing equality. All this is necessary to sustain the spirit of humanity, to deepen the feeling of compassion and to create a moral climate conducive to collective effort. And such personal actions reach areas inaccessible to collective action. However, they are by their very nature too disjointed and episodic to tackle the extensive and tenacious causes of human suffering. We have therefore no choice but to turn to the state, the sole available instrument of collective action. The state can reach areas and undertake activities our individual efforts cannot, making it the only or at least the most effective vehicle for realizing our moral aspirations. Our inescapable moral commitment to help disadvantaged groups remains an impotent rhetoric unless translated into a collective political commitment. Morality and politics are integrally related. Morally lacks power and efficacy unless it finds adequate potitical articulation. And politics lacks depth and significance unless it becomes a medium for realizing socially relevant moral values.

The second source of the duty to help disadvantaged groups has to do not with their suffering but with the moral interests of all, including the privileged.[2] At the deepest level and in the profoundest sense, the fundamental moral and spiritual interests of all men and women coincide. No group can for long degrade and brutalize another without degrading and brutalizing itself as well. To degrade others is to imply that a human being may be so treated, and thereby to lower the prevailing level of the moral minimum widely acknowledged as due to all human beings, and to dissipate the collective moral capital. Furthermore, to degrade and dehumanize others, to damage their pride, self-respect and capacity for growth, is both to deny ourselves the benefits of their possible contributions and to increase the collective moral, psychological and financial cost of repairing the damage they are likely to do to themselves and to others. Again, as human beings endowed with a moral sense and a capacity for reflection, no social group can degrade or maltreat another without hardening itself against the latter's suffering, building up an elaborate and distorted system of self-justification, and constructing a powerful coercive apparatus to put down the inevitable discontent. In so doing it dehumanizes itself as well as others and lowers the collective level of humanity. In short, humanity is indivisible. Either we all grow together or none will. It is not possible for one group fully to develop its moral, intellectual, emotional and other distinctively human capacities at the expense of another.

Such dominant groups as the whites in South Africa and the rich and the powerful in every society are naive to believe that their exploitation and degradation of their victims does not in any way damage them as well. In fact they suffer as much as their victims, and sometimes even more. The white South Africans could not deprive the blacks of their basic human dignity and treat them as an inferior species without suppressing their own doubts and tender feelings, damaging their capacities for critical self-reflection and becoming victims to moral conceit, morbid fears and irrational obsessions. The colonial rulers met the same fate. They could not dismiss the natives as 'effeminate' and 'childlike' without thinking of themselves as tough, hypermasculine and unemotional adults, a self-image to which they could not conform without distorting their growth and impoverishing their potential. In misrepresenting the natives, they misrepresented themselves as well, and fell in their own traps. They took home the attitudes, habits and styles of government acquired abroad, and corrupted their own society. This is no less true

of the economically privileged and powerful, whose lives remain superficial, pleasures crude, minds full of fear, and hearts narrow and hateful.
Deeply inequalitarian and exploitative societies exact a heavy psychological and moral toll from all involved. These permit no winners; all
alike are losers, albeit in different ways and degrees.

The third source of the duty to help disadvantaged groups is more
specific in nature and historical in its origin. It arises when their predicament is a result of the past actions and practices of the privileged group,
as is quite often the case. The current condition of the untouchables
in India is largely a result of what the caste Hindus did to them for
centuries. The latter created the category of untouchability, defined its
membership, and subjected them to the most degrading treatment.
Similarly, whites created the institution of *modern* slavery, decided that
only the blacks and not browns or yellows could be slaves, defined who
were to count as blacks, and enforced racial discrimination by the most
brutal means. In all patriarchal societies men have drawn and defined
the boundaries of public and private realms, confined women to the
latter, and monopolized the public world of culture, knowledge, power
and wealth. In these and similar other cases the dominant groups
systematically maltreated the dominated groups and caused them much
moral, material and psychological harm. They therefore bear a special
responsibility for the plight of their victims, and have a duty not only
to end the harm but also to heal their wounds and help them become
whole human beings.

The nature and basis of this duty has become the subject of much
unnecessary debate, especially in relation to American blacks, largely
because it has been cast in the misleading language of restitutive justice.
Even this would not have much mattered had justice in turn not been
defined in narrowly legal or judicial terms. Legal justice is largely a
matter between two identifiable individuals, one an identifiable victim
and the other an identifiable agent of unjust harm. It is concerned to
punish the guilty and to protect the innocent, and is perverted when the
latter gets punished. When in the late 1960s American blacks demanded
reparations or compensation from whites for past harm on grounds of
justice, they therefore exposed themselves to such obvious criticisms as
that the whites living today could not be held responsible for past acts
of harm, that the harm could not be identified, that not all whites owned
slaves, and that not all blacks alive today are descendants of slaves. Black
leaders had great difficulty answering these criticisms. They were right
to believe that they had a case but, since most of them sought to make
it in the currently dominant but largely inappropriate and judicially
articulated language of restitutive justice, they found that such case
as they made was incoherent and unconvincing. If they were to be

persuasive, they needed to do one of the following, which only a few of them did with varying degrees of success. They could have argued that historical justice between groups was very different in nature from legal justice between individuals and that it involved non-individualistic notions of causality and responsibility, and they could then have gone on to develop appropriate conceptual and moral tools. Or they could have abandoned the language of justice altogether and replaced it with one more hospitable to their aspirations. Or thirdly, they could have articulated their demands in a language which retained the notion of justice but redefined and located it in a broader and more satisfactory theoretical framework. Since it is not relevant to our discussion to pursue the inquiry further, I shall but briefly and tentatively sketch one possible way in which we could ground white Americans' duty to redress the situation of their black compatriots.

It is a historical fact that white Americans owned black slaves. Although not all whites owned slaves, many did. More importantly the America state which represented and spoke in the name of all its members endorsed and enforced slavery. Slavery was not a cluster of unrelated individual acts but a collective practice or institution legitimized by the state and embedded in American society. As for blacks, almost all of them were brought to American as slaves, and of those alive today the vast majority are descendants of slaves. Unlike the composition of the whites, that of the blacks displays greater historical continuity. Although we cannot quantify or define the exact nature of the harm caused by slavery, we know that it was severe and material, moral and psychological in nature. Such an extensive and deep damage which affected the innermost beings of the victims did not and could not disappear with the abolition of slavery. It lasted for generations and continues to haunt and cripple them today. White Americans today are confronted with the sad legacy of their past. While their ancestors might have sincerely believed that slavery was not immoral, they today take a very different view. As moral beings they cannot but regret the past and have a duty to redress its painful consequences.

First, slavery in America was a social institution sanctioned and enforced by the state. Unlike almost all other forms of political organizations, the modern state is like a corporation whose identity is unaffected by changes in its composition. It transcends both government and society and remains the same despite changes in its governments and subjects. That is why its international and national obligations derived from such things as international treaties, national commitments and public loans continue over generations. The American state, which once sanctioned and enforced slavery, remains morally accountable for its deeds for broadly the same reasons that it remains legally bound by past treaties. Individuation of states and determination of their identity do of course raise extremely complex issues, and the view I have proposed needs to be considerably tightened up. But it is difficult to see how it can be altogether rejected consistently with our current legal practices and ideas.

Secondly, an organized society is not a contingent collection of men living in perpetual present. It exists in time and is aware of so existing. It has a past and a future, both of which make claims on the present. To be a member of it is to be related to past and future generations in a specific manner. It involves recognizing that the resources of society do not belong to the present generation alone, and that future generations too have claims on them. Similarly it involves recognizing that although the present generation is not answerable for the past, it remains accountable for the claims arising from it. If the past has left behind victims who were not then full members of society but now are and who demand and need conditions necessary for such membership, we need to find ways of creating these conditions and earning their civic friendship. Now that black and white Americans are at last equal fellow citizens of a single community, they need a common past, one they are happy to own and to which they can all subscribe, just as much as they need a common future. And that cannot be done without coming to terms with its legacy. A divided past cannot permit a shared present and a shared future unless the present generation finds ways of pacifying its aggrieved and tormented victims.

Thirdly, thanks among other things to slavery, although not only to slavery, 'white' today is a symbol of power and status instinctively feared and deferred to by blacks. It triggers off in blacks extremely complex reactions, including those of fear and inhibitions and anxieties, which even they have not been able fully to articulate. In this minimal sense if no other, every white American continues to be a beneficiary of slavery. His colour is a source of material, psychological and other privileges, just as his black compatriot's colour is a source of some of his handicaps. The white American cannot give up his colour-derived benefits even if he wants to, and the only adequate moral response to such an inherited privilege is to acknowledge its origins and concomitant obligations.

Finally, every generation enters the flow of history at a particular point in time and inherits a past with its painful and pleasant memories. Although it cannot undo the past and disown the burden of painful memories, it can lighten their weight by undoing at least some of the effects of past injustices and cruelty. In so doing, it civilizes the past, reduces its moral burden, redeems the honour and good name of its forebears, and bequeaths to succeeding generations a better past and a less fractious society. Although the sentiments of inter-generational piety can be easily exaggerated, they are not wholly without a moral basis.

That all this is not too high-minded or moralistic is evident in the fact that this is how we cope with the past in our individual and collective lives. We sometimes feel guilty about our past unjust, immoral or foolish deeds and make appropriate amends to those involved or to others. We feel troubled by some of the things our parents might have done in their own interest or ours, and we seek to redeem their honour and good name in whatever ways we can. Many a colonial power, especially the Dutch, felt this way about their imperial history and did much to help their ex-colonies. Even Britain, which apparently feels morally less troubled than most about its imperial history, recognized its historical obligations to its colonial immigrants, and for several years allowed them unrestricted entry and gave them full rights of citizenship on arrival. This was also how Germans felt about the Jews after World War II. Although only a handful of them had worked in concentration camps or been involved in rounding up Jews, most Germans felt deeply ashamed of the way they and their parents had behaved. They felt they had to redeem their parents' and country's good name and to find ways of coming to terms with their unbearable past. Rightly or wrongly, their unstinting economic and political support for the state of Israel is an expression of that sentiment.

If what I have said is correct, white Americans *do* have a historically derived moral obligation to do all in their power to help blacks overcome the legacy of slavery and repair their fractured selves. This is not a simple case of restitutive justice, nor an admission of guilt for past harm, but something far more complex. It is at once a collective expression of regret, a long-overdue gesture of historical reconciliation, a form of ancestral loyalty, and an attempt to take the moral sting out of the past as well as to leave the succeeding generations a better society. What is true of the relations between white and black Americans is true also, albeit with appropriate adjustments, of those between all dominant groups and their erstwhile victims.

II

I argued in the previous section that we have a strong moral duty to help disadvantaged groups become whole men and women capable of competing with others as equals and energetically pursuing their self-chosen ends. This require a comprehensive and well-thought-out programme of action for disadvantaged groups, involving multiple strategies to tackle the diverse but interrelated causes of their disadvantages. The point of the programme is not to 'throw money' at them in the naive belief that it will solve their problems, nor to turn them into wards of the state and so perpetuate the culture of dependency, but to build up their strength, nurture their self-confidence, initiative and energy, and in general to help them regenerate themselves.

Any such programme is by definition a programme of positive discrimination.[3] It is positive because it calls for action and aims to offer substantive and well-targeted help. It is discrimination because it is biased towards and designed to favour and promote the interests of disadvantaged groups. Although ultimately all alike benefit from a rich and just society created by such a programme, in the short term one group of people receives a larger allocation of resources than another. Since resources are always scarce, allocating them to one group means taking them away from or denying them to another. In a conflictual situation we cannot favour one side without acting against the other.

Since positive discrimination is intended not just to improve the economic condition of the disadvantaged but to restore their fractured humanity and facilitate their self-renewal, it cannot be confined to education and employment, as is often suggested, but must cover all areas of social life. Obviously it involves allocation of considerable resources to the disadvantaged groups' education, training, health, material well-being, and so forth. It implies programmes designed to encourage them to enter educational, social, political and other institutions which they might find intimidating and beyond their reach and from which they may have hitherto shied away. Instead of being moulded in the image of or in a manner suited to the interests of dominant groups, the disadvantaged and marginalized groups should be able to define their identity themselves. A programme of positive discrimination therefore involves encouraging and helping them evolve their own distinct forms of cultural self-expression. It may also involve helping them build up their own autonomous communities, not as walls behind which to hide but as ways of regaining and mobilizing their strength with a view to their eventual integration into mainstream society on equal terms. As we shall see, under certain circumstances positive discrimination may also involve preferential treatment and even the system of quotas in such areas as education, employment and political representation. Above all, it requires a clear statement of the goals to be achieved in different areas of organized life, measuring progress towards these goals, and monitoring the progress.[4]

Contrary to the general impression, positive discrimination is not committed to proportionality, that is, to ensuring that disadvantaged groups are represented in all, most or even major institutions in proportion to their number in the population at large. To do so is to ignore their diversity of talents and aptitudes, to control and curtail their right of self-determination, and to mould them in the image of the dominant world. Rather the point of positive discrimination is to give them the capacity and the confidence to decide their goals for themselves, to empower them, to remove their existential marginality, and to assure them that no area of life is necessarily and inherently inaccessible to them. If they then freely choose to confine themselves to certain areas of social life, including those devoid of power and prestige, there is no reason for concern.

I have argued that our social structure has for centuries been controlled by and used to promote the interests of dominant groups, and that it has damaged the dignity, life-chances and basic human capacities of large sections of men and women. Since we ought to feel deeply troubled by this, we need to give the social structure a very different though not necessarily opposite impulse and orientation. I have analyzed the concept of positive discrimination in this context, and used it to refer to programmes designed to favour and promote the interests of *all* disadvantaged groups irrespective of whether they are based on race, colour, gender or class.[5] In so doing I have departed from the current discussion of the subject in two important respects.

First, in much of the literature, the term positive discrimination is largely confined to blacks and women, especially the former. It is not difficult to see why this is so. Unlike all other groups, blacks have for centuries been treated not just unequally but as sub-humans. Thus they have suffered the most vicious and unacceptable form of discrimination, so much so that the term discrimination became inseparable from them. This also meant that the discourse on race developed in isolation from the older and more established discourse on inequality, and became more or less self-contained. The fact that blacks had to fight for their emancipation without the coalitional support of other oppressed groups meant that they did not feel the need to expand the parameters of the racial discourse.

There is no reason why we should allow this historical accident to dictate and bias our vocabulary. Though discrimination against blacks is most acute, they are not its only targets. More importantly, their problems are inseparable from those of the other disadvantaged groups, and we need a vocabulary that allows us to recognize and articulate these common concerns and build up a broad-based coalition. Again, during its period of separate development, the racial discourse threw up important insights into the phenomenon of oppression in general. It is about time we appropriated and integrated them into the general discourse on oppression. This has the added advantage of de-marginalizing the racial discourse and incorporating it into the enriched general discourse on inequality and injustice without losing its specificity. We cannot integrate blacks into mainstream society without integrating the racial discourse into the mainstream discourse on discrimination in general.

Secondly, in much of the literature on the subject, the term positive discrimination is confined to preferential treatment, especially in the fields of education and employment.[6] By and large this narrow usage is preferred by those who approve of all or most forms of substantive help to disadvantaged groups but baulk at preferential treatment in education and employment. They do so because they draw a fairly rigid distinction between need and merit, and argue that while preferential treatment is appropriate or just at the level of need, it is wholly unjust at the level of merit. In their view it is right to give extra help to the weak to enable them to compete as equals, but once the competition is joined merit alone should matter.

I find this view unconvincing. There is no obvious reason why preferential treatment should be called positive discrimination when it is considered unjust, and something else when it is not. Such a distinction rests on no rational basis and serves no useful purpose. There is no reason either to accept the distinction between need and merit, at least in the way it is drawn here. The distinction has a deep ideological bias. Merit is almost invariably dignified as a right and given a superior moral status, whereas satisfaction of need is treated as an act of compassion or charity and subordinated to the demands of merit. What is more, it is not easy to distinguish between merit and need. If we thought that blacks or women should be given preferential treatment in certain areas in order to provide them with role models or to to tap their latent talents, then the jobs would become a communal resource, a collective need no different from and no less urgent than material and other needs. The collective *need* for a job becomes an important part of a black or female applicant's *merit*, and one of the bases of his or her right or even *entitlement* to it.

Although for these and other reasons we should not confine the term positive discrimination to preferential treatment in such areas as education and employment, the fact remains that the latter is highly contentious not only in Britain where it is rejected outright but also in the United States where it is viewed more charitably. In both countries preferential treatment is more or less accepted as a matter of course in several areas of life. No objection is raised if a political party fields black or women candidates in preference to equally or more 'meritorious' whites or males, or if the government appoints less qualified blacks or women to head important official and semi-official bodies. Even in the fields of education and employment there is a wide acceptance of such preferential measures for disadvantaged groups as special training and outreach programmes, appointments of additional teaching staff, allocation of greater resources and even setting up minority educational institutions. But any attempt to give them preferential treatment in *admissions* to educational institutions or in *appointments and promotions* is strongly resisted.

Prima facie it is puzzling why the two areas of education and employment have become a site of bitter struggle. The puzzle is deepened when it is realized that the number of people involved is extremely small and not enough to make much difference to either the dominant or the disadvantaged groups. An issue does not generally arouse such strong passions unless it touches a deep nerve and is seen, directly or indirectly, to affect important principles or interests. This is in fact the case with preferential treatment in education and employment, which is not just about who gets what percentage of a small number of admissions and jobs but about how a society should be organized and what general principles should guide its choices and policies.

The opponents of preferential treatment for disadvantaged groups in education and employment object to it on three grounds.[7] First, it disregards merit. If asked why this matters, they reply that merit alone is a proper or fair basis for selection in these areas, that it is the only antidote to a system of patronage, that it alone can ensure that the opportunity given to a person will not be wasted, and that it alone guarantees efficiency without which all alike suffer. Second, preferential treatment is unjust and violates individual rights. This is so because it introduces irrelevant and arbitrary criteria, excludes deserving candidates, and favours those with no claim to be favoured. It is unjust also because it punishes the present generation for the deeds of its predecessors, unjustly penalizes members of the dominant group, especially those superseded in specific cases, and privileges all disadvantaged groups, particularly those lucky enough to receive preferential treatment in specific cases. Third, preferential treatment represents a thin end of the wedge. If injustices and violations of rights are tolerated in one area, however worthy the cause, a bad precedent is set and there is no saying how it could be used in future. The last argument is parasitic upon the first two and loses its force if they are shown not to be open to the objections raised against them. We shall therefore concentrate on the first two arguments.

The first argument makes important points. It rightly stresses that admissions and appointments should be based on clearly specified, rationally defensible and impartially applied criteria, that merit should never be disregarded, that the better qualified should not be passed over in favour of the less qualified, that patronage in all its forms must be avoided, and that efficiency is an important value. However, the definition of merit is far more problematic than its advocates realize.

When people talk about merit, whether in educational institutions or in employment, they define and determine its content in the following three rarely articulated stages. First, an organization or an area of life is abstracted from its wider social context, and its purposes are defined without reference to its place and role in the society at large. Second, a job is abstracted from its larger organizational context and treated as a self-contained unit. An organization is broken up into and viewed as an aggregate of so many separate tasks or jobs, each requiring a specific kind of competence. As a result the overall culture, ethos, ambience of the organization in question is left out of consideration and its claims are defined out of existence. Third, the complex requirements, of a job are reduced to and defined almost exclusively in terms of relevant intellectual qualities as measured by examination results and, where appropriate, interview . Merit thus comes to be defined almost entirely in terms of the intellectual requirements deemed necessary to undertake an abstractly and insularly defined job.

When the critics of preferential treatment insist on the inviolability of merit, they have broadly this view of it in mind. There is no reason why we should accept this view, or agree that to depart from *this* view of merit is to depart from merit *itself*. We may question each of the three stages by which the dominant view of merit is arrived at. We might argue that no organization exists or flourishes in a vacuum, and that its purposes cannot be defined without reference to its obligations and responsibilities to the wider society. We might argue too that if the reified concept of job were to be deconstructed, we could find that it is not some independent entity with a unitary structure, but a fragment of a process, a cluster of tasks embedded in and deriving meaning from a larger structure. We might therefore conclude that the very concept of 'qualifications for a job' or of 'job-related qualifications' is misleading and even logically incoherent. Finally, we might argue that a job is not a task but a social relationship in the sense that it is done by an individual in association with other individuals and involves relating to a specific group of men and women whom it is designed to serve, and that it therefore calls for a complex range of skills and abilities of which the intellectual qualities are only a part. As a result of such a critique we might arrive at a very different conception of merit to the one currently dominant, or we might find the very concept of merit problematic, or we might arrive at some other concept of which merit as traditionally defined is an important but only one constituent.[8]

Take admissions to medical schools. The purpose of medical schools is to produce good doctors, and our admission requirements are necessarily determined by our conception of a good doctor. By and large we define him or her as one who is competent at his or her job, and ask for good grades at public examinations as conditions of admission. But we would easily take a different and perhaps more satisfactory view of a good doctor. We could argue that a good doctor should be not only intellectually competent but also possess specific qualities of character and temperament, compassion and a sense of social concern. We could argue too that in a culturally and racially diverse society like ours, he should be able to relate to and inspire the confidence of people of different backgrounds, and be knowledgeable about their life-styles, stresses and strains, needs and approaches to health and disease. We could also argue that he should be able to appreciate that modern medicine is not the last word in scientific knowledge and that it can benefit from a dialogue with other medical traditions.

We might conclude that a man is more likely to acquire a well-rounded education and to become a better doctor if he had in his medical school students from different cultural, racial and social backgrounds, provided of course that they were reasonably bright and capable of coping with the demands of medical education. They might not have very high grades at public examinations, but they might bring with them invaluable cultural skills, intuitions and experiences necessary for creating an environment conducive to the production of better doctors overall. Judged by the criterion of narrowly defined merit, they do not deserve admission. But judged by the standards of a broadly defined 'merit' based on differently defined purposes of medical education, they do. There is no reason why, subject to certain minimum necessary qualifications, we could not trade off one set of qualities against another. We could go a step further and argue that as a highly visible and elite institution, the medical school has an obligation to set a good example to a divided society, to tap new talents and to provide them with role models. The case for admitting competent but a little less 'meritorious' black and other candidates then becomes even stronger.

Since the terms merit and qualification carry considerable ideological baggage and create confusion, it might be helpful to replace them with the neutral and equally precise term 'prescribed requirements'. We could say that students would be admitted on the basis of their ability to meet the prescribed requirements, and define the latter to include academic merit and whatever else we consider essential and relevant. Merit here is not ignored, rather it is broadly defined.

Our remarks about admission to medical schools apply also to other areas of education and to employment. Organizations employing people do not exist in a vacuum and have wider obligations to their local areas and to society at large. Furthermore, as we saw, they are not collections of tasks and jobs but wholes with their distinct collective culture and ethos and requiring each of their interdependent parts to function in a co-operative spirit. Organizations therefore need to attract and co-ordinate different kinds of skills, sensitivities and talents. An individual unfit for *a* specific job or indeed for *any* specific job might nevertheless be indispensable to the creation of a desirable collective ethos. He or she might be needed not so much to do *a* specific job as to sensitize the *entire* organization in a particular direction, and thus as a background to *all* jobs within it. In short the allegedly irrelevant qualities of colour, gender and class may become vitally important for creating the right kind of culture in an organization.

As for the second argument that preferential treatment is inherently unjust and violates individual rights, it is open to several objections. We have already conceded that the present generation cannot be held responsible for the deeds of its predecessors. Insofar as the case for preferential treatment rests on such a view, it is obviously untenable. However, we have shown that a different kind of case can be made out for the present generation's responsibility for the consequences of past harm, and hence preferential treatment is not without a moral basis. The other points made by its critics are equally unconvincing. Preferential treatment does introduce irrelevant criteria when a person is preferred *solely* because of his or her sex or colour, but not when he or she comes out better on a broader definition of merit or when he or she makes a distinct contribution to the culture and functions of an institution. In such cases merit in the narrow conventional sense of examination results, intelligence tests and so forth is *not* disregarded but balanced against other equally legitimate considerations. And people are not selected simply because of their colour or sex, for they do satisfy the necessary requirements of competence *and* additionally possess qualities declared and shown to be desirable. A more 'meritorious' or formally better qualified candidate has then no right to complain against his or her rejection if the criteria of selection are widely known, rationally defended and impartially applied.

The argument that he has a *right* to the job and that his rejection is *unfair* rests on two fallacies. It views merit as the sole basis of desert, which it is not. As we saw, educational institutions and employing organizations might rightly take a broader view of the kinds of qualification they deem essential, and merit is but one of them. As such it is an important source of claim, but not the only one. Secondly, the argument wrongly assumes that merit's claim to reward is morally self-evident and needs no justification. Whether or not to reward merit, how much, and what constitutes merit are social *decisions* and a matter of social *policy*. We reward merit because we value what it signifies and produces. For example it generally ensures efficiency. But efficiency is never a sole value in any society, and is largely regarded as the most important value only in a society that has already attained a substantial measure of cohesion, harmony and integration and can therefore afford not to worry about these. A society deeply divided on racial, tribal, caste or religious lines and precariously hovering between survival and collapse might feel that it cannot survive unless its major institutions recruit from and develop better understanding between its contentious groups. Or a country like India in which caste Hindus will never mix or work with millions of untouchables might find that it has no choice but to require its major institutions to admit or appoint a specific percentage of the latter if it is to break down mindless taboos and survive as a cohesive and civilized society. In such cases merit is not ignored, but it is defined differently and assigned a somewhat limited value. In short, each society has to decide how to define and reward merit in the light of its problems, values and level of development. Merit does not inherently or necessarily *deserve* anything. The invidious distinction between justice and utility, and the questionable tendency to subsume merit under justice, obscure the element of social choice lying at the basis of merit and give it a false naturalistic orientation.

III

We have seen that preferential treatment of disadvantaged groups is not inherently unjust and incompatible with the principle of merit, and that it cannot be ruled out on moral grounds. The case for or against it must therefore rest on its ability to contribute to the realization of the larger objectives of positive discrimination mentioned earlier. And here the experiences of such countries as the United States and especially India, where it has been tried out on a large scale, are relevant.[9] The experiences cannot be accepted as conclusive, for preferential treatment there has been practised half-heartedly, in the face of concerted opposition, in societies suffused with intense racist and casteist prejudices and, above all, without adequately preparing the background by means of the several measures of positive discrimination listed earlier. However they can be viewed as useful pointers.

The advantages of preferential treatment are several. As both the American and Indian experiences show, it has a great symbolic significance. It reassures the disadvantaged that the dominant groups appreciate their predicament, accept the responsibility to do something about it, and have the political will to act decisively, including reconsidering such traditional bastions of their power as the principle of merit. Preferential treatment is also a powerful means of integrating disadvantaged groups into the mainstream of society and reducing their feeling of existential marginality. True, it benefits only a small number of men and women and its effects are necessarily limited. However, that is enough to persuade the rest that the dominant and otherwise frightening world is not inaccessible to them and that, if they were to exert themselves, the coveted prizes will not be denied to them.

As we saw, disadvantaged groups cannot overcome their handicaps without substantial help. But such help is often blocked by vested interests, or is of the wrong kind, or is subverted by those in charge of implementing it. It is here that preferential treatment becomes important. It ensures that those knowledgeable about the needs of, and committed to promoting the interests of the disadvantaged are involved in making and implementing decisions, offering advice and keeping a critical watch on the policies of the organisations in question. Such people also act as points of contact for their communities. There is, of course, a danger that they might become self-serving, get co-opted into the dominant group, or move away from their communities. Although real, the danger is often exaggerated. Leaders of the disadvantaged retain their value for dominant groups only so long as they remain credible within their communities, which they cannot therefore long afford to neglect. Furthermore, they remain tied to their communities by countless social, cultural, historical and emotional bonds and are subject to their constant pressure. When they prove self-serving, they risk being exposed and replaced by more determined leaders. In the early years, Untouchable leaders in India tended to ignore their community, but as the discontent mounted and the community became familiar with their manoeuvres, they were challenged and replaced by a new generation of committed leaders. Afro-Caribbean and Asian leaders in Britain and black leaders in the US have met a similar fate.

Preferential treatment also serves the valuable purpose of providing role models. This is a difficult area about which much remains unknown. We do not know how people are inspired and motivated, why and how they pluck up the courage to take their first tentative steps along a road they have never travelled before, and how over time they build up their confidence and cultural resources. But we do know that men and women whose pride and self-confidence have been shattered often draw their courage and strength from the struggles and achievements of those with whom they identify. Obviously role models only work when people are eager, willing and able to model themselves after them. If there is no churning within a disadvantaged group and if ambition, drive and talent are not beginning to emerge, role models have no or little impact. However, the churning dies down, the ambition atrophies, and the drive withers away unless those involved are encouraged, guided and reassured that the desired goals are not beyond them. If a community is unable to throw up talented men and women, a judicious helping hand in the form of preferentially appointed role models might become necessary. Such individuals become powerful catalysts — sustaining fragile ambitions, strengthening shaky resolves, and releasing that elusive and indefinable but vital impulse which often shakes a community out of its mood of despondency and despair.[10]

While preferential treatment can in these and other ways play a valuable role in uplifting[11] disadvantaged groups, it is not without its dangers. It calls for great understanding and moral commitment as well as some sacrifice on the part of the rest of society. And these are unlikely to be forthcoming unless the latter is persuaded that disadvantaged groups are making a serious effort to raise themselves and that other measures are proving ineffective. The success of preferential treatment therefore depends to a considerable extent on the initiative and resourcefulness of the disadvantaged themselves. Since the commitment to preferential treatment is difficult to sustain for a long time, it must be time-bound if we are to avoid popular resentment and backlash all too easily exploited by its opponents. Again, there is a danger that the elites on both sides might collude in making preferential treatment an end in itself, leaving unattended the acute problems of the vast majority of the disadvantaged. As the Indian experience shows, the benefits of a programme of preferential treatment can be easily cornered by small sections of disadvantaged communities. The programme must therefore be carefully monitored, and mechanisms devised to ensure that its benefits are broadly spread.

Like any other policy, positive discrimination, including preferential treatment, is a complex practice whose value depends on how it is used, and whose results and side effects cannot be accurately predicted. Preferential treatment can be misused, and then it becomes counter-productive. But it can also deliver worthwhile results if used judiciously and as part of a comprehensive and carefully thought out programme of positive discrimination. In spite of its limitations it is one of the few policy tools capable of breaking through the self-perpetuating cycle of deeply entrenched inequalities, and weakening the visible and invisible walls the disadvantaged and weak often find almost impossible to scale. The market, free competition and the much-vaunted trickle-down effects have largely failed to accelerate disadvantaged groups' upward mobility, significantly reduce inequalities, or arrest the relentless process of human decay. This is being increasingly recognized, which is why in one form or another and in varying degrees, almost every Western society has thought it to proper to follow the policy of positive discrimination.

Even in Britain where it is officially disavowed, it is being increasingly used, albeit quietly, tentatively and often in a less provocative guise. For years the Home Office has ensured that one of the ten governors of the BBC is black. There is no reason to believe that the black appointee is among the top ten 'most distinguished' men and women in the country or is 'uniquely equipped' to look after black interests. When shorn of rhetoric, it is a form of preferential treatment designed to integrate blacks into the mainstream of society and to give them public visibility and a measure of power. The same is true of the appointments of blacks and women to the Independent Broadcasting Authority, the Equal Opportunities Commission, the Commission for Racial Equality, and to countless other government bodies. Local authorities are guided by similar considerations when they appoint school governors. And all political parties, albeit in different ways and with different degrees of enthusiasm, appoint blacks and women to important committees or select them as their local and parliamentary candidates.

Several private and public organizations too have begun to stress the value of a 'multi-ethnic workforce'. They set informal quotas (or what are euphemistically called targets) and go out of their way to recruit black and female staff, sometimes to important positions and in preference to equally or more qualified whites and males. Although their motives are mixed, they include a sense of social responsibility, the need to integrate blacks and other disadvantaged groups into mainstream society, the desire to encourage and tap talent, and the concern to counter the still pervasive preferential treatment of the traditional racist and sexist kind.

Even the law is beginning to catch up with practice. Sections 47, 48 and 49 of the Sex Discrimination Act 1975 as amended by the Sex Discrimination Act 1986 authorize trade unions to reserve seats for women on their governing bodies, and permit employers to offer exclusive training to women for jobs where their number is 'comparatively small'. The Trades Union Congress has taken advantage of the law and been able to reserve twelve seats for women on its highest body. It is difficult to see what all this amounts to if not preferential treatment and informal quotas. Indeed by insisting that all public bodies should set themselves the 'target' of ensuring women equality of representation with men, the present British government has embarked on a programme of systematic positive discrimination for women.

Whatever their rhetoric, the government, industries, trade unions, business, and other organizations in Britain and elsewhere have come to appreciate that deeply disadvantaged groups cannot be integrated and uplifted without a carefully planned and limited use of positive discrimination and preferential treatment. This is a slow and grudging but significant shift of opinion. There is still considerable moral unease about this policy, which is why it is applied half-heartedly, quietly, tentatively and without public debate. I hope to have shown in this chapter that the unease is unjustified.

NOTES

1. For a recent statement, see Oakeshott, M. *On Human Conduct* (Oxford, Clarendon Press, 1975) p. 321.

2. I borrow this argument from Mahatma Gandhi and the Indian philosophical tradition, where it is developed more fully than anywhere else. For a fuller discussion see my *Gandhi's Political Philosophy* (London, Macmillan, 1989) ch. 4 and *Colonialism, Tradition and Reform* (London, Sage Publications, 1989) ch. 4.

3. For good discussions see Edwards, J. *Positive Discrimination, Social Justice and Social Policy* (London, Tavistock Publications, 1987); Blackstone, W. T. and Heslep, R. P. (eds) *Social Justice and Preferential Treatment* (Athens, University of Georgia Press, 1977); Bittker, B. *The Case for Black Reparation* (New York, Random House, 1973); and Gross, B. R. (ed.) *Reverse Discrimination* (Buffalo, Prometheus, 1977).

4. These objectives go well beyond John Rawls' primary goods. Rawls has little interest in the nature, development and psychological and cultural preconditions of human capacities. As a result, his theory of justice does not come to grips with some of the most complex and intractable problems involved in 'benefiting' and uplifting the worst-off sections of society. See his *A Theory of Justice* (Oxford, Clarendon Press, 1972) pp. 5ff.

5. For an interesting though in places unconvincing analysis of the concept of discrimination, see Somerville, J. 'Some supposedly new sorts of discrimination' (1987) 4(2) *Journal of Applied Philosophy* p. 18ff.

6. See, for example, ch. 2 in Edwards op. cit. (note 3), where the author surveys the changing meanings of the term in Britain and the United States.

7. For good discussions, see Cohen, M., Nagel, T. and Scanlon, T. (eds). *Equality and Preferential Treatment* (Princeton, Princeton University Press, 1977); Lustgarten, L. *Legal Control of Racial Discrimination* (London, Macmillan, 1980); and Edwards, op. cit. (note 3).

8. For stimulating discussions, see Dworkin, R. *Taking Rights Seriously* (London, Duckworth, 1977); Why Bakke has no case' *New York Review of Books* (10 November 1977), and his reply to criticisms in ibid. (26 January 1978); Thomas Nagel's introduction and article in Cohen, Nagel and Scanlon op. cit. (note 7); and Walzer, M. *Spheres of Justice* (New York, Basic Books, 1983) ch. 5.

9. See Shaw, J., Nordlie, P. and Shapiro, R. (eds) *Strategies for Improving Race Relations: The Anglo-American Experience* (Manchester, Manchester University Press, 1987); Gallanter, M. *Competing Equalities: Law and the Backward Classes in India* (Delhi, Oxford University Press, 1984); Mitra, S. K. (ed.) *Politics of Positive Discrimination: A Cross National Perspective* (Bombay, Popular Prakashan, 1990); and Sharma, B. A. V. and Reddy, K. M. (eds) *Reservation Policy in India* (Delhi, Light and Life Publishers, 1982).

10. A wealth of material is to be found in the autobiographies and biographies of many women, blacks and people from working-class backgrounds.

11. Here and elsewhere in the essay I talk about uplifting the disadvantaged and eschew the language of equality and equalization. Unlike the latter, 'uplift' has crucial moral and spiritual overtones, is more comprehensive, and free of the ideological and polemical baggage associated with equality. Our basic concern surely is to help the disadvantaged become strong and self-determining, rather than to equalize them with whatever other group we take as a norm.

16

Can Reverse Discrimination Be Justified?

Gwyneth Pitt

INTRODUCTION

Observers are increasingly convinced that no serious impact will be made on the problems of sex and race discrimination in the future without some measure of reverse discrimination. While the Sex Discrimination Act 1975 and Race Relations Act 1976 have been in force now for over fifteen years, there do not appear to have been the hoped-for advances in the position of women and ethnic minorities, and so more radical solutions are sought. However, the argument that *all* race-conscious or gender-conscious discrimination is bad has a powerful appeal. After all, the main argument used to justify the outlawing of discrimination against women and ethnic minorities is the requirement of formal justice that like cases should be treated alike, coupled with the denial that gender, race, colour or ethnic or national origin are relevant distinctions between human beings rendering them unlike cases. To allow reverse discrimination to help one group seems as much a violation of this principle as the former use of discrimination to limit its opportunities. This is the dominant theory in British legislation,[1] and even in the United States, where reverse discrimination has been allowed to some extent, there seems at present to be a backlash against it, based on this kind of thinking.

In a landmark decision at the beginning of 1989, *City of Richmond* v *J.A. Croson Co.*,[2] the Supreme Court considered the constitutionality of a scheme whereby the City of Richmond set aside 30 per cent of its construction contracts for businesses controlled by minority racial groups. Minority business enterprise (MBE) set-aside schemes have been commonly used by state and city governments in recent years in the US in order to improve the position of black workers and to encourage minority entrepreneurs. The Supreme Court held that the scheme violated the Fourteenth Amendment, which guarantees equal protection of the law. While there is debate as to precisely what the court meant by this decision[3] (which applies only to public, not private, employers), it seems fairly clear that the majority of the court set its face against racial preferences except in limited circumstances where there is proof of past discrimination and the scheme in question is narrowly tailored to meet the particular problem identified. This seems indicative of a general feeling by the present majority of the Supreme Court that there is no real distinction between what has been termed 'benign' or 'inclusive' discrimination and 'malign' or 'exclusive' discrimination.

Before examining the strength of the arguments for and against reverse discrimination, it is necessary to have some definition of the terms used. There are as yet no generally accepted definitions of these terms, no doubt because all are seen as value-laden and thus as attracting favourable or unfavourable connotations. Parekh (in his Chapter in this book) uses the term 'positive discrimination' in a wide sense to cover all steps taken to promote the interests of disadvantaged groups. Fullinwider[4] and McCrudden[5] use instead the term 'preferential hiring'. Greenawalt[6] points out that the negative connotations of the word 'discrimination' can itself be seen as conveying criticism of positive or reverse discrimination. In their chapters in this book, Phillips refers to 'compensatory discrimination' and Menski to 'protective discrimination', but as both phrases presuppose a particular kind of justification for the policy, I reject them, at least at this initial stage. No doubt the most neutral term is 'differential treatment', adopted by Poulter and Montgomery in this volume, but its lack of particularity perhaps indicates why it is not in general use. I will use the term 'reverse discrimination' on the basis that it is in general use.[7]

As I will use the term, reverse discrimination refers to a situation where a less-qualified applicant may be preferred to a better-qualified candidate on account of race or sex. Positive or affirmative action (which I treat as synonymous)[8] refer to programmes designed to eliminate invisible as well as visible discrimination and to encourage under-represented groups to reach a situation where they are more likely to be the best candidates for a post or place. In the employment context, examples given in the Codes of Practice issued by the Equal Opportunities Commission and the Commission for Racial Equality include advertising in publications more likely to reach minority groups and providing career counselling or training which may encourage people to have the confidence to apply for promotion. The distinction between reverse discrimination and positive action is not always clear-cut.[9] One of the strategies of a positive action programme could be the use of reverse discrimination. But the important point is that positive action is not *committed* to the preference of a less-qualified candidate. Hence positive action not involving reverse discrimination is lawful in the United Kingdom and is encouraged by the relevant commissions. Reverse discrimination, on the whole, is not lawful.

There are borderline cases where it is unclear whether an action constitutes reverse discrimination or positive action. Suppose two candidates are equally well qualified in every way and the only point of difference between them is gender or race. If the woman or black is preferred, is this reverse discrimination? On the definition given above, it is submitted that it would not be reverse discrimination, since it does not involve preference of a *less* well-qualified candidate. If the only point of difference between the two candidates was that one was unemployed whereas the other had a secure job, we would probably not think it wrong if the employer gave the job to the unemployed candidate. The decision would have a rational and acceptable basis, and is arguably better than tossing a coin. However, it is true that to choose the woman or the black in such a case does involve the use of gender or race as a criterion, so even if it is not reverse discrimination, it is only justified if we are satisfied that in some cases it is acceptable to use race-conscious or gender-conscious classifications — which is what must be justified by advocates of reverse discrimination.

Again, suppose a training programme is open only to women or to members of a minority group (permitted, of course, to a limited extent under British legislation).[10] Is this reverse discrimination or positive action? The answer, it seems, is that it is both. So far as access to a job is concerned, it is no more than positive action: for training does not guarantee that the trainee will be the best candidate for the job and therefore appointed, although it makes it more likely. So far as access to the training itself is concerned, it is reverse discrimination, for only members of the disadvantaged group will be accepted. It may be objected that this is not really reverse discrimination — it is merely using limited resources in the most effective way by concentrating them where there will be most benefit. So, for example, a course confined to women returners to the job market makes sense in regular business terms. But this is not so if it is rigidly confined to women. It could have been set up as a course for anyone returning to the labour market after a lengthy break. The requirement of absence from the labour market might then have been attacked as indirectly discriminating against men, although no doubt it would be found to be justifiable; but if it is limited at the outset to women, then it is an example of reverse discrimination.

This leads conveniently to another point. In considering reverse discrimination, it is very likely that it will not be possible to come up with a single answer for all situations. First, there are significant differences between sex and race discrimination.[11] Greenawalt notes that sex discrimination has been historically perceived as being for the benefit of women, fitted 'by nature' for a different role from men; also that practices such as limitation on hours worked by women can be seen as advantageous as well as disadvantageous.[12] Most importantly, women have not been clustered in lower social strata or geographically removed from the powerful group in the same way that racial minorities have. In the United States, the roots of race discrimination in slavery give an urgency and importance to the removal of race discrimination which is not present when sex discrimination is considered. In the United Kingdom, the enormous impact of the European Community on sex discrimination has led to a greater emphasis on that problem than on race discrimination. A problem faced in relation to gender but not race is that work or other activities performed predominantly by women are consistently undervalued; indeed an occupation may even lose status when a substantial number of women start to enter it — which partly accounts for the need for special provision for equal contract terms for women. Thus it is possible that reverse discrimination may be justified in the one case but not the other.

There may also be different arguments according to what field of activity is under consideration. Possible areas are not only appointments to jobs and promotion, but also access to further education, access to training programmes, public and private activities and set-aside programmes such as that in the *City of Richmond* case outlined above. These distinctions should be borne in mind in considering the arguments which follow.

ARGUMENTS BASED ON COMPENSATION

A popular justification for reverse discrimination is that it is intended to make up for past systemic discrimination against women or ethnic minorities. Thus it is a kind of remedy for past deprivation of opportunity. Compensation is a familiar, 'safe' notion to appeal to, based on the non-controversial and well-understood principle that the perpetrators of wrongs should compensate their victims, which no doubt is one reason why this argument is so often used. But it is prayed in aid in a wide spectrum of situations and is not always equally effective. Suppose, first of all, that X has been turned down in the past by an employer because of sex or race discrimination, and as a result it is ordered that X should be given the next available vacancy. Fullinwider[13] argues convincingly that this is *not* reverse discrimination, even if there is by that stage a stronger white or male candidate. X is clearly entitled to be compensated for the discrimination, and the best way of doing this is to give X the next job. The reason for giving X the next job is not X's race or sex, but compensation, proved by the fact that X is entitled to the next job not only if there is a better white or male candidate, but also if there is better candidate from X's own group. It is, then, an example of genuine compensation, where the particular wrongdoer compensates the particular victim for the actual wrong. Insofar as it is unfair to the better candidate for the next post, it is no more unfair than it would be unfair for a creditor of mine to discover that I am unable to pay a debt because I have used up my assets in paying compensation to someone injured by my negligence at a time before I incurred that debt. It is a chance we all take. In practice, it might not even be clear that there is a better, later candidate, because the post will not be advertised.

But the example of genuine compensation given above, where the perpetrator of a wrong compensates the victim, demonstrates the difficulties of using the compensatory approach to justify reverse discrimination generally. The major objection is that the real victims of discrimination are the earlier generations living in a society when discrimination was allowed. Compensation now will benefit the wrong people. To this it may be answered that present generations are still disadvantaged because their forebears were relegated to the lowest positions in society. This argument is obviously more convincing in relation to race discrimination than to sex discrimination, and more convincing in relation to race discrimination in the United States than in the United Kingdom. Even in the United States, its force gets weaker as time passes.

Even if present generations do continue to suffer disadvantage, the position is not really redressed by reverse discrimination, which benefits only *some* members of the group, who are likely to be those who have suffered least from the effects of past discrimination. They have at least managed to get themselves into the position of being serious candidates for the desirable opportunity.

Another variation on this point is to say that the successors of the original discriminators are still enjoying their wrongful benefits. But there is no necessary correlation between those of the majority group who are receiving wrongful benefits and those who will not get jobs if reverse discrimination is permitted. Job applicants are on the whole younger and less powerful members of society. They would bear the brunt of the burden of compensation when they are the least responsible for the original wrong, and this does not seem fair.

In essence then, the criticism of arguments based on compensation is that either the people getting compensated deserve compensation because they have suffered a wrong at the hands of the compensator — in which case the situation is not one of reverse discrimination — or they have not so suffered, in which case they have no right to compensation, and reverse discrimination cannot be justified on that basis.

A different kind of compensation argument is not backward-looking in the way that traditional notions of compensation are. It claims (accurately, in my view) that the institutional framework of society is so stacked against women and members of ethnic minorities that even though discrimination is now prohibited it still occurs and is bound to continue to occur. Reverse discrimination is a counter-balancing measure, attempting to compensate for the inherent bias in the system. It is a crude remedy, but then social rules can rarely be made to apply with precision. Even for those who accept the factual basis for this justification, it may seem that reform of the anti-discrimination law in order to make it more effective is a better option than limited and therefore arbitrary programmes of reverse discrimination.

Despite the demonstrated difficulties with a justification based on compensation, this is essentially the principle on which the United States' Supreme Court has permitted reverse discrimination to date. However, confirming the recent trend in its decisions, in *City of Richmond* v *J. A. Croson Co.*,[14] the Court refused to accept general 'societal discrimination' as sufficient justification for a reverse discrimination programme by a public body. It accepted that the policy would be justified if there were definite evidence of past discrimination, if the policy were narrowly tailored to deal with the specific discriminatory practice identified (and such identification had to be possible) and if it were used as a means of last resort. This case, being concerned with government action, was decided under the Constitution.

Private employers need not comply with the Fourteenth Amendment but only with Title VII of the Civil Rights Act 1964. In this context reverse discrimination without proof of past discrimination remains permissible, under the decision in *United Steelworkers* v *Weber*.[15] In this case the Kaiser Aluminium Company voluntarily implemented a scheme at its plant in Louisiana whereby admission to a programme to train existing employees for skilled work was based on seniority, but with the proviso that one black would be promoted for every white until the proportion of blacks in skilled jobs was comparable to their proportion in the local population. (The question of representative proportions raises other questions, discussed below). It was held that this did not violate Title VII: emphasis was laid on the fact that it was designed as a temporary measure and that whites were not altogether excluded from the scheme. American commentators who favour this approach point out that if past discrimination must be shown before such programmes are implemented then no employer will so act, because of the risk of individual suits based on the past discriminatory acts, and that it is in any case counter-productive and divisive to rake over past grievances: employment policies should be forward-looking. But as stated already, compensation is always retrospective; those who favour reverse discrimination as the way to achieve a more just society more quickly than might otherwise be possible must look for a different justification, perhaps utilitarian.

Parekh takes account of these defects in the compensatory argument by framing his main argument as essentially forward-looking, resting on the recognition of an existing situation of disadvantage, linked strongly with particular groups in society. If we are dissatisfied with that sort of society, and wish to leave a better kind of community behind us, then it behoves us to take prompt and effective action — which, presumably, may include reverse discrimination.

However, as expounded by Parekh, the driving force for doing something about the problem is not just expediency. Where it is recognized that the reason for the group's disadvantage is because of society's actions towards them in the past, actions which society now thinks were wrong, then society should accept a moral obligation to do something about the situation. It seems to me that this suggests an element of compensation, although Parekh would not characterize the obligation in those terms. His account of the source of the obligation places more emphasis on action by society now as a demonstration of its good faith in wishing to break the chain of past discrimination, and as an attempt to redeem the honour of the past. There are obvious problems with attempting to assign collective rather than individual responsibility, although Parekh's explanation would seem to offer a reasonable justification for governmental action in the public sphere at any rate. But while it may be a good argument for positive action in general (positive discrimination in Parekh's terminology), it does not seem necessarily to justify reverse discrimination in particular. Nor was it intended to do so. Parekh concedes that a preference based on race or sex *alone* would be an improper use of an irrelevant criterion. Insofar as he relies on satisfying the wish of society for a different kind of community, Parekh is appealing to essentially utilitarian considerations, which will be considered next.

ARGUMENTS BASED ON UTILITY

Proponents of social policies frequently justify them by claiming that they will result in greater social benefits than the alternative. Increased social welfare seems an entirely acceptable goal, so it is not surprising that advocates of reverse discrimination also appeal to greater social utility as a justification. It is claimed that a number of social advantages may result from reverse discrimination. In the case of race discrimination, it is felt that minority communities will benefit if there are more minority professionals, because they will tend to live in and serve those communities. Arguments of this kind were heavily relied on by the Davis medical school of the University of California to justify its quota system for minority entrants in the famous case, *Regents of the University of California* v *Bakke*,[16] where Bakke did not gain one of the 100 places in the school although his grades were higher than some minority students admitted under the school's special admissions programme, for which sixteen places were set aside each year.

In the case of women, it is often argued that there is a need for more women professionals, so that women can always consult a woman if they want to. Or it may be felt in general that women and minorities will have more empathy with the concerns of their peers. In the United States it is suggested, for example, that black police officers may get co-operation more easily than white officers in black communities. This is getting close to saying that race or sex may actually be a job qualification, which will be examined shortly. But even if sex or race is not an actual qualification, it can be argued that more women or blacks in prestigious or powerful positions will produce a more just society. In the case of ethnic minorities, this is thought to have another social benefit — it will defuse the resentment they might feel, which could otherwise find violent expression. This argument cannot be used in the case of women, who do not seem likely to accept invitations to revolt in any violent manner against their condition. On this kind of argument, as Dworkin puts it, reverse discrimination is not about aiding people who are entitled to aid, but about a strategy for coping with a national problem.[17] Of course, this is a blatant appeal to expediency rather than to any high moral principle, but many people seem to find that kind of argument actually more convincing than one based on principle.

There are other benefits which may flow from reverse discrimination. It will lead more quickly to women and blacks achieving high positions, and these examples will then provide role models to encourage the next generation and help break down stereotyped assumptions that tend to relegate women and minorities to lower positions in professions and institutions. Finally, it may be argued in the context of access to higher education (but not, I think, in relation to access to employment) that ensuring multi-racial experiences (or a mixed-sex environment) has a positive educational value in itself, and can also be justified as preparing students for the society in which they will live and work.[18]

To this it may be objected, using the same kind of argument, that reverse discrimination will have the opposite effect and will actually decrease overall welfare. The policy might reinforce feelings of inferiority in those who benefit from it, and cause others to assume that they must be second rate. Indeed, it might lead people to think that *all* women or blacks in senior positions only got there because of reverse discrimination and to assume that they were second rate. (This point is regarded as particularly forceful by women and blacks in senior positions).

There might be an increase in social tension because the dominant group would feel a strong sense of grievance if they were themselves victims of discrimination. And far from healing divisions in society, reverse discrimination would actually make people more aware of race and gender. Also, as Justice Powell pointed out in *Bakke*, what evidence is there to suggest that the goal of more doctors, lawyers and other professionals to serve minority communities is actually promoted by recruiting from those communities? There is no guarantee that they will return to the same place to live and work. They may well prefer to move away.

In a similar vein, it is suggested that not to choose the best person for the job regardless of race or gender would lead to overall inefficiency. This is an argument to be treated with caution. In the first place, it assumes that present selection procedures used in employment and education are effective in choosing the person who will perform best — which is a highly debatable proposition. Secondly, it is often overlooked[19] that reverse discrimination does not mean giving people tasks which are beyond their abilities. It is assumed that the choice will be made among candidates who all have the requisite qualifications,[20] even though some may be more qualified than others. Thus it would seem that differences in efficiency would be marginal. Some who are impressed by the efficiency objection suggest in consequence that reverse discrimination should be confined to fairly low-level jobs where the spread of skills and qualifications is not very large,[21] but this is open to the charge of hypocrisy: that writers on reverse discrimination are happy to advocate it as long as they are unlikely to meet it in their own particular job market! Lastly, Fullinwider poses the question, how sacred is efficiency?[22] In balancing aggregate welfare, the benefits to be gained from a policy of reverse discrimination may outweigh any loss of efficiency.

A different utilitarian argument on efficiency suggests that reverse discrimination may not be the most efficient way of achieving the looked-for benefits. This is a fair point. In *City of Richmond* v *J. A. Croson Co.*[23] the Supreme Court expressed the view that race-neutral measures should be used first to increase minority participation, and reverse discrimination only if they failed. At present in the United Kingdom, as Sacks' essay in this book shows, little use appears to have been made of the positive action provisions in the legislation, or of positive action provisions generally. It may be that encouragement to implement positive action is the right way forward, at least for the time being, although it would be essential to monitor its success over a confined time span to see whether stronger measures are necessary. But deferring the issue is unlikely to appeal to those who feel that they are at present denied their rightful opportunities, who may regard it as indicating a lack of good faith. This perception would also be relevant in a utilitarian calculation.

The virtue of all utilitarian arguments is that they are capable of empirical verifiability. Their drawback is that the factual data is frequently not available to carry out the verification process. The experience of reverse discrimination in the United States is too limited for much assessment to be made. There has been general ignorance in this country of the experience in India and Malaysia, which other essays in this book may help to dispel,[24] but it could be argued that the experience of any other country is of limited relevance in another, because of different social and cultural conditions. Such experience as there is has also principally been confined to reverse discrimination on racial grounds, and is not necessarily relevant to gender. It may seem reasonable to conclude, along with Dworkin and Fullinwider, that the utilitarian arguments in favour of reverse discrimination at least raise a good case for experimentation in this direction.

However, a serious drawback of the utilitarian approach is that it could have the result not only of disallowing reverse discrimination, but also of permitting old-style 'malign' sex and race discrimination, if it could be shown that aggregate welfare would increase as a result. We may be prepared to take this risk, believing it to be highly unlikely that discrimination against women or minorities could ever increase aggregate welfare. But more to the point, are we prepared to go along with a philosophy which even countenances this as a possibility?

We are here brought up against the fundamental objection to utilitarianism in all circumstances: that it allows the sacrifice of an individual's interests to the collective good. Provided that collective welfare is increased, it does not matter to the utilitarian how it is distributed, and the unhappy state of an individual or members of a permanent minority may be ignored.[25] This is unacceptable to most people, who therefore argue the need for a system of individual rights which cannot be overridden by collective welfare. Whether reverse discrimination would be incompatible with such a system of rights is the final issue to be addressed here. First, however, it is necessary to touch on two issues raised above: the situations where sex or race may actually be regarded as a qualification, and the question of representative proportions.

GENDER OR RACE AS A QUALIFICATION

It is certainly possible to envisage situations where being a man or a woman, or being a member of a particular ethnic group, is an essential requirement for the job. This is recognized in British law by the exceptions for genuine occupational qualifications provided in the Sex Discrimination Act 1975[26] and the Race Relations Act 1976.[27] One exception is in relation to authenticity — although the ambit of this is far from clear, as evidenced by the furore in 1990 over whether or not the white British actor, Jonathan Pryce, who created the role of a Eurasian pimp in the musical *Miss Saigon*, should be allowed to play the role on Broadway.[28] The most important exception is where 'the holder of the job provides individuals with personal services promoting their welfare or education, or similar personal services, and those services can most effectively be provided by' a woman, or man, or member of a particular racial group.[29] This received a restricted interpretation by the Court of Appeal in *London Borough of Lambeth* v *CRE*,[30] where the council had advertised the post of housing benefits officer, limiting applications to Afro-Caribbeans and Asians. As the post was managerial, with little or no contact with the public, the court held that there was no element of personal service being provided.

Various writers have argued that an expanded notion of what is a qualification for a job, or for admission to a course, would result in recruiting more women or blacks. If a law school believes, as Harvard reputedly does, that it is beneficial to have a mix of students from different racial and geographical backgrounds, and a mix of men and women, why may it not take those characteristics into account as well as test scores? As Parekh points out, 'merit' is assigned by humans to a characteristic: intelligence, diligence, musicality and so on have no independent moral significance. But race and gender are not job-related, it is objected. Perhaps they are: in the admissions policy of the law school they may be — because all students will benefit from an environment which better mirrors the society they will work in. This could apply in employment also, as Parekh notes: if a company wishes to promote an image of being forward-looking, committed to equal opportunity and keen to serve all sections of the community, it may well decide that this will be best achieved by having more managerial staff who are women or blacks. Thus having those characteristics would be a qualification for the job. Bad luck if you do not possess this quality — just as it is bad luck if you are not intelligent enough for the job in hand.

This is the preferred solution to the problems raised by reverse discrimination of Dworkin,[31] Singer[32] and Radcliffe Richards.[33] Since the merits necessary for the job have been redefined, then the best person for the job is being chosen, and so reverse discrimination is not in fact occurring anyway. But in a sense this sidesteps the problem rather than solving it. What if there is clear evidence that all sections of society have more confidence in white male financial advisers? Can this argument cut both ways? Only if we can draw a meaningful distinction between malign and benign discrimination. This is returned to below.

REPRESENTATIVE PROPORTIONS

In *London Borough of Lambeth* v *CRE*,[34] the council argued that since the majority of its tenants were of Afro-Caribbean or Asian origin, the racial profile of the staff serving them should be similar. Certainly it may seem just that all groups of society should have fair shares of the best jobs and opportunities. But does this mean that there should be representative proportions in local councils, universities, the professions and Parliament?

I think not. The issue of proportional representation is essentially relevant to proof. If there are inexplicable divergences between the number of blacks and women available, and their actual representation, then it strongly suggests that conscious or subconscious discrimination is occurring and it should be looked into. Setting goals or targets for recruitment related to proportions thus makes sense. It is not an invitation to engage in reverse discrimination, but rather provides a standard for measuring the success or otherwise of positive action programmes, based on reasonable expectations. Naturally, it would be expected that the goals themselves would be subject to regular review, until eventually they might be unnecessary.

Thus understood, working towards a goal does not necessarily involve reverse discrimination, and is sharply distinguished from a quota (such as was used for the admission of minority candidates in the *Bakke* case), which is related to ideas of proportional representation, and does. Dworkin argues that goals slide into quotas and lead to reverse discrimination, but it is not obvious that this is inevitable.

However, my suggestion that statistical information about representation of women and minorities should be confined to evidential purposes and the establishment of goals is not based on an objection to reverse discrimination. It is because insistence on representative proportions could result in an *upper* limit being placed on these groups. If the ethnic minority community in Britain is now just under 5 per cent, it may be argued that no more than 5 per cent should be admitted to further education, or supervisory posts on the buses or railways — which would surely be wrong. As Greenawalt points out, there are disproportionate numbers of Jewish doctors and lawyers, but this hardly indicates discrimination against non-Jews in these spheres,[35] and it would not justify an upper limit on Jewish people seeking training in these professions. Nor is this an idle example: allegations of upper limits on numbers of Asian-Americans admitted to West Coast universities are presently being made.[36] But if we are saying, no upper limits on women or blacks, but reverse discrimination for them is acceptable, are we trying to have our cake and eat it? This issue will be addressed in the next section, on rights.

ARGUMENTS BASED ON RIGHTS

People should not be used as a means to an end. The main problem identified with utilitarianism was that it would allow the interests of some people to be overridden in the interests of the majority. A system of rights is necessary to stop this happening. The term 'rights' is used here not to refer to legally enforceable rights, but to what might be argued for as moral rights. Perhaps the strongest argument against reverse discrimination is that it infringes the rights of the white or the male who is a better candidate and who would otherwise be chosen.

Precisely what 'right' is being infringed in this kind of situation? Is it the right to the job, or to the place in law school or medical school (to take the examples which have caused the most litigation in the United States)? But, as Dworkin convincingly argues, while we might regard elementary education as part of everyone's basic rights, surely we would not say that everyone, or everyone who was capable, should have a right to further education? If so, then an awful lot of people have had their rights infringed in the past, and will in the foreseeable future also. The same must go for employment. We might talk about a 'right to work' — as some do, usually in the context of the need to eradicate unemployment — but again it would be novel to suggest that anyone has the right to any particular job.

Perhaps, then, it is a right to equal treatment that is infringed: in the

United States the Fourteenth Amendment to the Constitution provides that no one shall be denied the equal protection of the laws, and it is this that has been claimed to be violated by reverse discrimination programmes. But what do we mean by 'equal treatment' or 'equal protection' here? Presumably we do not mean that everyone should be treated in exactly the same way. It is precisely because the community charge or poll tax treats each person in the same way, regardless of their means, that it is regarded as unjust by many people. Equal grants given to two hospitals where one is new and well-equipped but the other is dilapidated and in urgent need of repair would hardly be considered fair.

Perhaps it is a right to equal opportunity that is appealed to. You have the right to be considered only on criteria related to the matter in hand — which are unlikely to include gender or race. Three points can be made here. First, as mentioned above, merit is a value-laden concept. No characteristic has intrinsic merit, only what is ascribed to it by humans. Thus there is no particular moral worth in the meritocracy argued for by proponents of equal opportunities. Secondly, and more pertinently perhaps, at present selection procedures of whatever kind frequently *do* take account of irrelevant criteria: many of us are familiar with the exhaustive lists of interests and good works squashed into the five or six lines allowed on University entrance forms. It may be that demonstrated compassion or an interest in the theatre shows an individual who will make an above-average contribution to the life of an institution; and no one is excluded from the opportunity of scoring points in this way. But sporting or musical ability is quite different — yet more often taken into account. Indeed, in the United States sporting scholarships are extremely common. If it is acceptable to take account of irrelevant criteria which are beyond people's control, why not race or gender? If it is not acceptable, proponents of reverse discrimination are at least entitled to see steps taken towards the exclusion of other irrelevant criteria before reverse discrimination is ruled out. The third point is that a right to equal opportunity is often used as a justification for reverse discrimination. Taking the famous analogy used by President Johnson, there is no equal opportunity if you remove the shackles from one runner 40 yards into a 100-yard race. Thus it is argued that reverse discrimination is necessary to ensure *genuine* as opposed to *formal* equal opportunity. However, as Fullinwider points out,[37] this is essentially an argument about compensation, and thus open to similar objections as made above.

Dworkin argues that the sensible content to give to this right is the individual's right to be treated with equal respect and concern, 'that is, he has a right that his interests be treated as fully and sympathetically as the interests of any others'.[38] Much the same is Hare's principle of universalizability.[39] Thus in the *Bakke* case, his interests were equally considered, but in the end he lost out because he was not qualified on the criteria used. Failure to meet the criteria is a misfortune, but not a violation of rights. Dworkin distinguishes the use of race as a criterion here from the use of race to *exclude* black candidates (as in *Sweatt* v *Painter*,[40] for example) because in the latter case, race is included as a criterion because of prejudice and contempt — there is a failure to treat blacks with equal respect. There is no such failure to treat whites with respect in the *Bakke* case. Reverse discrimination is used to try to achieve a more just society, and only after proper concern has been given to the interests of all those applying. It is not wrong to use race as a criterion here, according to Dworkin, even though it is an arbitrary criterion, because all selection procedures use arbitrary criteria.

Against this view we could argue as above, that arbitrary criteria should not be taken into account whatever they are. But as long as it is regarded as a permissible practice, then Dworkin's analysis seems reasonable as a justification. Dworkin's discussion of reverse discrimination has been entirely in the context of access to higher education, but it is submitted that the argument is equally strong when employment is considered.

In the *Bakke* case, of 100 places available in medical school, 16 were set aside for minority candidates. Bakke did not score highly enough on the selection criteria to get one of the other 84 places, but it was conceded that had he been a minority candidate, he would have been admitted with his score.

It has been suggested that if a certain number of places are reserved for a certain class of candidates, then their unavailability to another class is irrelevant. So the 85th white has no right to complain, any more than the 101st, or the 17th minority candidate. The competition was for 84 places, not 100.

It is submitted that this sidesteps the issue: it does not answer the question whether or not it is justifiable to set aside a number of places on grounds of race or sex, nor how many ought to be set aside, if any.

Of course, it might be possible to say that in addition to the 100 places, some *extra* places would be made available for minority candidates. This involves some difficulty in establishing whether places are genuinely 'extra' or not. In admission to higher education in the United Kingdom at present, for example, numbers are so flexible that convincing demonstration of a clear baseline plus extras would not be easy. In employment, the idea of making available 'cadetships' or 'shadow' posts to blacks has been suggested.[41] These would be supernumerary; the benefit is that when a real post becomes vacant, the minority candidate is both on the spot and has had the opportunity to gain experience which will help make him or her the best candidate for the job without reverse discrimination. In this case, the status of the cadetship or shadow post as supernumerary would be clear. However, insofar as both situations involve reverse discrimination at the admissions stage (because the extra places or supernumerary places are available to one group only), then it remains necessary to put forward some convincing justification for this.

A final version of the rights argument would be to claim that wherever a post or opportunity is open to competition, then the best candidate ('best' according to the criteria used by the selection board) has the right to be offered it. This is what Fullinwider means by his 'right to equal consideration'. If this right is accepted, then it seems that reverse discrimination should be ruled out. But would we accept a right in these terms? Suppose that the best candidate for the job already has secure well-paid employment but the second-best candidate has been unemployed for some time and has dependants. Would we think the selectors had done wrong, or violated the right of the best candidate, if they gave the job to the next best? I suggest we would not. In fact, since we would never say that there is a *duty* to make a job available, it looks odd to say that once it is available, then it *must* be offered to the best candidate. If the selection board capriciously decided not to make an appointment at all, we might regard them as having acted heartlessly, in raising doomed expectations among the interviewees, but not as having violated their rights. It also seems odd to suggest a right in the best candidate when there is no obligation for selection boards to justify the criteria that they will use or make them known to the candidates. Thus I would suggest that reverse discrimination is not to be ruled out by an appeal to this right.

DISTINGUISHING DISCRIMINATION AND REVERSE DISCRIMINATION

If reverse discrimination is to be allowed, we must have clear guidance on what is 'benign' and what is 'malign' discrimination. Dworkin's answer is to look for the purpose of the discrimination: if it is because of prejudice against or contempt for blacks or women, then it is malign. If it is designed to bring about a more equal society, then it is benign. This seems reasonable, although it is not quite obviously applicable to situations such as exist in Malaysia or Fiji, where indigenous races feel that they are losing out to other groups, who are very large and powerful minorities. Their protective measures are not based on contempt or prejudice for the other groups. Perhaps a better formulation getting at the same point is the American usage of *exclusionary* or *inclusionary* purposes: measures taken to bring groups into the mainstream of society and industry are acceptable; discrimination to keep them out are not. It is submitted that the recognition of the difference is unlikely to cause problems in practice.

CONCLUSIONS

Since it does not seem to me that the policy of reverse discrimination involves violations of rights, then it seems that such programmes should be supported on utilitarian grounds, to see if it is an effective way of achieving a more equal society. At present there are very few positive action programmes, whether in employment or higher education, and it may be that reverse discrimination should be deferred until it is clear that other measures alone will not work, given that there is clearly some disutility attached to the idea of reverse discrimination. No doubt it is always better for reverse discrimination to be used as one measure in a variety of positive action strategies than to be relied on as a panacea on its own. One suspects that at present there is a certain amount of reverse discrimination occurring under the guise of formal equal opportunity. It is submitted that underhand methods increase hostility and that it would be better to be upfront about using it. Note that as things stand at the moment, this would not necessarily require a change in the law. Although in *Lambeth* the Court of Appeal refused to countenance race as job qualification outside the statutory exemptions, in *Meers* v *Tower Hamlets*[42] they upheld their earlier decision in *Perera* v *Civil Service Commission*[43] to the effect that a discriminatory condition which does not operate as an absolute bar is permissible. Thus to express a preference for those with direct experience of Afro-Caribbean or Asian communities, or speaking relevant languages, would be all right, even if they were not strictly necessary for the job.

Because of the resentment that would be caused by compulsion to engage in reverse discrimination, it seems to me that it should be voluntary only; in the present climate I do not think that the kind of programme, for example, in *United Steelworkers* v *Weber*[44] would be acceptable as a remedy to be ordered by a court, although in the true compensation situation it does seem appropriate that a court should be able to order that the next post should be offered to the victim of discrimination. However, since public bodies are in some sense an organ of government, and since they are not subject to the same market pressures as private institutions, it seems to me that it would be proper for public bodies to take a lead in implementing positive action programmes, and arguing the case for at least limited reverse discrimination programmes, with close monitoring of their effectiveness.

NOTES

1. See *London Borough of Lambeth* v *CRE* [1990] IRLR 231 (CA).
2. 109 SCt 706 [1989].
3. See the opposing views in (1989) 98 *Yale Law Journal* 1711 and (1989) 99 *Yale Law Journal* 163.
4. Fullinwider, R. K. *The Reverse Discrimination Controversy* (Totowa, NJ, Rowman and Littlefield, 1980) pp. 10–13.
5. McCrudden, C. 'Rethinking positive action' (1986) 15 *Industrial Law Journal* 219, 223.
6. Greenawalt, K. *Discrimination and Reverse Discrimination* (New York, Alfred A. Knopf Inc., 1983) pp. 16–17.
7. E.g. Dworkin, R. *Taking Rights Seriously* (London, Duckworth, 1978) ch. 9; *A Matter of Principle* (Cambridge, Harvard University Press, 1985) chs 14–16; Radcliffe Richards, J. *The Sceptical Feminist* (London, Routledge & Kegan Paul, 1980) pp. 107–8; Singer, P. *Practical Ethics* (Cambridge, CUP, 1979) p. 40.
8. The phrase 'affirmative action' is used in Title VII section 706(g) of the American Civil Rights Act 1964, and in Executive Order 11246, promulgated in 1965 by President Johnson. 'Positive action' is used in Britain by the EOC Code of Practice paras 41–43 and the Code of Practice of the CRE, paras 1.44–1.45.
9. The two are confused in the judgment of Balcombe LJ in *London Borough of Lambeth* v *CRE* op. cit. (note 1).
10. Sex Discrimination Act 1975 s. 48; Race Relations Act 1976 s. 38. See Sacks' chapter in this book.
11. See Fredman and Szyszczak, essay in this book.
12. Greenawalt, op. cit. (note 6) pp. 35–37.
13. Op. cit. (note 4) pp. 127–8. Greenawalt argues similarly: op. cit. (note 6) pp. 44–5.
14. Op. cit. (note 2). See also *Wygant* v *Jackson Board of Education* [1986] 476 US 267 (SCt).
15. 443 US 193 [1979] (SCt).
16. 438 US 265 [1978] (SCt).
17. Dworkin, R. *A Matter of Principle* op. cit. (note 7) ch. 14. Note he refers to affirmative action, but the reference clearly includes what I have called reverse discrimination.
18. These arguments were also put forward in *Bakke*. In relation to mixed-sex education, it should be noted that there is a view that while boys are better off in a mixed environment for secondary education, girls flourish in a single-sex environment, where they are not under any peer pressure to defer to males.
19. For example, by Radcliffe Richards op. cit. (note 7) pp. 107–12.
20. Using the term 'qualifications' in its widest sense, to mean not only formal qualifications, but also other skills or characteristics regarded as necessary for the job or course.
21. See Greenawalt op. cit. (note 6) pp. 66–68; Fullinwider op. cit. (note 4) pp. 88–89.
22. Fullinwider op. cit. (note 4) p. 90.
23. Op. cit. (note 2).
24. See the essays by Parekh, Phillips and Menski in this book.
25. The objections are well summarized by Hart, H. L. A. 'Between utility and rights' (1979) 79 *Columbia Law Review* 828.

26. Section 7, as amended by the 1986 act, following the determination of the European Court that the original exceptions were too wide: Case 165/82 *Commission of the European Communities* v *UK* [1983] ECR 3431 (ECJ).

27. Section 5, *not* amended in line with the Sex Discrimination Act! Note that under the American Civil Rights Act 1964, sex can be a bona fide occupational qualification, but not race.

28. Attracting the majestic attention of a *Times* leader on 4 September 1990 (saying he should).

29. Sex Discrimination Act 1975 s. 7(e); Race Relations Act 1976 s. 5(d).

30. Op. cit. (note 1). See also *Tottenham Green Under Fives' Centre* v *Marshall* [1989] IRLR 147 (EAT).

31. See *Taking Rights Seriously* op. cit (note 7) ch. 9; *Matter of Principle* op. cit. (note 7) ch. 14.

32. Singer op. cit. (note 7) ch. 2.

33. Radcliffe Richards op. cit. (note 7). See also McCrudden, C. op. cit. (note 5), p. 225.

34. Op. cit. (note 1).

35. Greenawalt op. cit. (note 6) p. 52.

36. Tsuang, Grace W. 'Assuring equal access of Asian Americans to highly selective universities' (1989) 98 *Yale Law Journal* 659.

37. Op. cit. (note 4) pp. 93–96.

38. *Taking Rights Seriously* op. cit. (note 7) p. 227.

39. Hare, R. M. *Moral Thinking* (New York, OUP, 1981).

40. 339 US 629 [1945].

41. E.g. Lustgarten, L. 'Racial inequality and the limits of law' (1986) 49 *Modern Law Review* 68, 84.

42. [1988] IRLR 399 (CA).

43. [1983] IRLR 167 (CA).

44. Op. cit. (note 15).

17

The Indian Experience and Its Lessons for Britain

Werner F. Menski

INTRODUCTION

India's post-colonial policies of protective or positive discrimination for certain groups in society indicate and pose major social and legal difficulties over the achievement of equality before the law and equality of opportunity in modern India. Modern Indian law has also been concerned with outlawing what in Britain would be called race discrimination, but more attention has been focused on the country's schemes of protective discrimination for Scheduled Castes and Scheduled Tribes (SC/ST) and, more recently, Other Backward Classes (OBC). Before looking at the complex Indian legal regulation of the reservation policies, I shall first place the issue into the wider context of legal pluralism and theories of legal uniformity/diversity and shall later seek to draw potential parallels with the current British situation.

To focus attention on this potential comparison, and to understand the magnitude and boldness of the Indian policies better, let us imagine for a moment that it became government policy in Britain at some time in the near future to compensate all groups of 'black people' (whose definition[1] is now based on the *factum* of discrimination rather than skin colour) for past injustices by a policy of positive discrimination. This, in essence, is precisely what India did in 1950, soon after Independence, and what some local equal opportunities policies in Britain appear to be seeking to achieve, too.

The consequences of this bold policy in India have stimulated a rich literature full of controversy, of which many Western lawyers and policy-makers remain woefully uninformed. What is there to learn from India? In fact, not only do we find a stream of socio-political literature on discrimination, there is also a torrent of case law and a considerable body of legal writing. Any serious study today, as Galanter's monumental work shows,[2] will have to be rather long and may be, as is Galanter's book, almost unreadable. In other words, access to the complex Indian material is not easy.

India's policies of protective discrimination are, at first sight, not of the same kind as Britain's attempts to control racial discrimination. However, as we shall see, Britain may have been moving, without being aware of this and certainly without wishing to acknowledge it, in the direction of Indian-style policies of protective discrimination. At the moment, one will be more inclined to accept that British policies may be following an American model. But as Galanter's detailed study of the Indian situation demonstrated, even America has quite a lot to learn from the Indian experience, which extends over the last 40 years.

The present contribution, constrained by limited space, attempts to be a guide through the maze of irreconcilable expectations in India today. I start with a brief look at the pre-Independence situation, in which we find an intricate system of legalized status inequality. This was explicitly challenged by the reforming spirit of post-Independence Indian leaders, who seem to have opted for the 'rule of law' model with its implied equality principles, but combined it with preferential treatment for certain groups of people. An elaborate and yet simple constitutional scheme was, thus, drawn up, supplemented by further legislation and implemented from the top down. This ongoing process has given rise to enormous labour pains that have become visible in protracted litigation struggles in the high courts and the Indian Supreme Court.

After a brief look at the constitutional policy debates, I first chart the progress of the Indian policies of protective discrimination and their implementation. I then focus on those major policy issues that have arisen in the Indian context and contain, it would appear, many useful lessons for any country contemplating such policies.

THE TRADITION OF LEGALIZED INEQUALITY IN INDIA

It is far too little known and appreciated, even by Indians, that over time (from at least *c.* 1500 BC) the Indian subcontinent developed an intricate system of hybridization of cultures, a truly complex amalgam of quite disparate and at times really irreconcilable elements at various local and national levels. Not only Hindu culture in its various aspects, but also Buddhist, Jaina, early Christian, Muslim, Jewish, Parsi and Sikh influences, not to speak of more recent Western components, combined to create what in Britain we would call a multi-cultural society. The dominant elements of Hindu and Muslim culture seem most prominent and may be seen as important 'legal postulates'[3] that have been influencing the actual operation of any particular sub-system and of the whole. But it will be impossible to locate any one element that dominates the whole, though Indian and Western authors alike often tempt us with simple, yet quite false, models of legal authority based on traditional textual evidence.[4]

In other words, central elements of Hindu culture (e.g. *dharma*) and of South Asian Muslim traditions (e.g. *shariat*) are themselves complex and diversifying entities that not only contribute to, but actually promote and demand various forms of status inequality. This does not mean that there are no uniform and uniformizing tendencies in traditional South Asian cultures and legal systems. Nor does it mean that the colonial influence on India was entirely negligible.[5] But it remains unquestionably a hallmark of all pre-Independence South Asian societies that there was an intricate system of legalized status inequality in full operation. Manifold forms of discrimination and of inequality on the basis of gender, age, caste, religion, economic power, etc. were not only not prohibited, but were in fact expected as systemic elements.

The extreme manifestation of such inequalities in India has been emphasized by many authors.[6] It is no accident that we also find a conspicuous stress on hierarchy in the Hindu legal order.[7] Only in this way, it appears, could the intricate Hindu vision of a universal system of Order/order (*ṛta*, later *dharma*) be accomplished and maintained. Indeed, it is not just current fashion to talk in 'green' terms about Hindu culture as emphasizing a complex symbiotic ecosystem of a holistic nature.[8] The adoption of the ecological motif, as Cromwell Crawford has recently explained,[9] helps to achieve a better understanding of the organic relationship among ethics, morality, religion, philosophy and law in the Indian context, as indeed in other Oriental and African socio-cultural systems. In this way, Hindu law must be seen as a closely interlinked sub-system in a complex matrix,[10] operating on the assumption of *inequality* of all parts rather than equality.

The reason for this is clearly that the central Hindu concept of *dharma* ('righteousness', 'individual duty') demands and expects that all individual beings should, within their means and limits, do what is conducive to the maintenance of the total systemic order, ultimately macrocosmic Order. Thus, the *dharma* of most animals is to serve as food for others; human *dharma* was circumscribed in terms of service to others — in the 'public interest', to use a term that is rather fashionable in India today. In essence, this element of human symbiosis is also what the much-abused caste system seeks to emphasize.

Similarly, Islam has recognized the equality of all individuals before Allah, but accepts that social reality demands manifold divisions of labour and differential treatment of individuals. Such traditional Asian concepts are quite evidently at variance with modern (and, it is claimed, even some ancient) Western theories of justice, in which equality is an integral part.[11]

It is therefore not surprising that around the time of Independence a vigorous discussion developed in India about policies of dismantling the traditional systems of status inequality, which came to be widely perceived as obstacles to modernization, secularization and uniformization, not only of law, but of the system as a whole.

THE RATIONALE OF POST-INDEPENDENCE REFORMERS

During the twentieth century, the potent mix of continuing traditional expectations, based on assumptions of inequality, and various modern concepts of equality has led to growing awareness of the need for reform.[12] While Indian society has largely persisted in a traditional mould, interacting at times quite uncomfortably with the modern legal regime, movement has been seen on the political and legal front, in the typical fashion of 'social engineering through law'.

The background to the emergent modernizing policies has been studied in detail by a number of authors.[13] The important debates of the Indian Constituent Assembly are a rich source of information.[14] In my view, it is quite apparent that an inadequate understanding of their own past appears to have seduced many modern Indian leaders into rejecting the traditional system wholesale, while an equally inadequate conceptualization of the modern models of equality has led to the uncritical adoption of 'simple' strategies for the abolition of all inequalities. That this could not work in practice has never been a surprise to South Asianists. It should not puzzle legal scholars either: it is quite naive to assume that Western legal concepts are necessarily the ideal developmental tools for countries like India.

Galanter has emphasized that the traditional Indian caste system 'was in bad odor' after Independence:

> It was widely viewed as an impediment to individualism and to broad national loyalties and thus inimical to progress and democracy. The hardships inflicted on the lowest castes inspired humanitarian revulsion. It was widely accepted that caste would have

no place in independent India and that efforts to ameliorate the effects of past inequalities were in order. As power passed into Indian hands, the exclusion of untouchables from public facilities and from Hindu temples were made statutory offences throughout most of India. Reservations for untouchables were established in the central services, and a program of educational assistance was begun.[15]

But even fundamental cultural basics, including the implications of the caste system, are not fully understood today. Leading researchers remain critical of cultural insensitivity[16] and emphasize the role of personal bias.[17] Also, while we have known for a long time that under the British the classical Hindu texts were given an inflated legal role,[18] the earlier conceptual errors are widely perpetuated today.[19] Such confusions crucially impinge on our present discussion: *varna* (caste) and *jati* (also 'caste', but really the socially more important numerous sub-castes) are often mixed up and the local variability of the latter is not realized. While bashing caste has been fashionable for a long time, *varna* has become 'a valuable fiction' in a number of ways.[20]

My argument is, then, that modern India's social engineers failed to understand a few crucial facts in their zeal for legal reform. Still today, many people believe that all Brahmins and higher-caste Hindus are rich and powerful, while all Shudras, being the lowest 'caste', are deprived of power and money. The implications that such sweeping assumptions have had for the operation of caste-based policies of protective discrimination in India will have to be discussed below. It is intriguing to find parallels here in the scholarly creation of a similarly deficient discourse on modern Britain's 'black' underclass, which rears its head frequently and in many contexts.[21]

Significant inequalities, strengthened by discriminatory practices of all kinds, continue to be perpetuated in modern India. In the present context, it is most relevant to consider the lower end of the caste spectrum and its fringes. Here we see the low-caste Shudras further sub-divided into clean and unclean castes, with different socio-economic statuses, displaying much internal discrimination. Attention is focused on a fifth 'caste', the former Untouchables or Harijans, who suffer yet more disabilities than others, and on tribals, who stand somewhat apart from the fold of Hinduism.[22] It is the position of such people that evoked the particular concern of modern India's law reformers.

The rich literature on the protagonists of reforms focuses in particular on Dr B.R. Ambedkar, who is often seen as the architect of India's Constitution of 1950 and in particular of the protective discrimination provisions.[23] He was in several respects opposed by Mahatma Gandhi, who lost to Ambedkar in the end.[24] Ambedkar's first-hand experience of discrimination and untouchability and his attitude of anger and frustration have been emphasized.[25] His was a politico-economic approach as opposed to Gandhi's religio-social stance; he argued that by acquiring political and economic power, the SC/ST members would eventually get rid of social and religious disabilities. He had an assimilationist vision of the eventual merging of all minorities into a body politic that knew no caste distinctions.

> His ardent desire that the minorities should ultimately 'vanish' is the key to understand better the spirit underlying the safeguards for minorities in the Indian Constitution. The imprint of his philosophy is too obvious to be missed by any one.[26]

My argument here is that this resourceful leader's desire for social equality and assimilation of minorities was, of course, very idealistic, a dream-like vision, akin to calling the projected Uniform Civil Code of India a 'distant mirage'.[27] While Western and Japanese jurisprudential realism is now echoed in India to some extent, an interesting book by a powerful Harijan leader still shows the confusions of modern Indian thinking on equality.[28] Jagjivan Ram argues that India's desired socio-economic re-organization will take a long time and speaks of 'a kind of grudging adjustment' while acknowledging that in a state of caste plurality communalism will not be eliminated.[29] Consequently, he calls for 'a revolution in the way of our thinking, and our living', leading to the abolition of caste,[30] which he had earlier characterized as 'a cancer',[31] unacceptable in modern India[32] and to be removed as soon as possible. Like so many others, Ram indulges in fantasies:

> Though it is still a dream, Indian society after becoming a casteless society will be utterly transformed. It may take many years, may be even centuries in the case of villages, though taking less time in urban societies. Only then will it be a working, vibrating and vigorous society. Only then will it reflect the humanistic strands of our thought and tradition. Only then will communalism be eliminated root and branch. I know, it is aiming high, very high .[33]

Such appeals for the creation of a new man, tempered by reluctant admission of social facts, are followed by sweeping assertions about the homogeneous nature of modern democracy with its minimal disparities.[34] A major aim of development in modern India, thus, has to be the promotion of homogeneity through the creation of a casteless society. Only then will all individuals become 'partners in creating a united nation'.[35]

It is conveniently overlooked here that many Indians may not see any benefit for themselves in belonging to a huge central state. Like in the parallel 'barren controversy'[36] of the Uniform Civil Code debate, I find here a deep-seated confusion about fundamental issues of equality and Indian national unity. How one creates a society of equals is never explained. In fact, Ram concedes that:

> With the best of intentions, a change in mental attitudes is bound to take some time. Till then, discrimination is inevitable and equally inevitable is the disability which flows from discriminating attitudes. It is nothing written, formal or tangible but it is bound to be ever present.[37]

This statement, in fact, concurs with Dahrendorf's earlier persuasive argument about the inherent operation of inequality in all societal and legal functions.[38] Ram recognizes the present continuation of inequality, now no longer explicitly legitimated by state law, but justified by social norms and more or less tacitly accepted by the state. Indeed, Ram explains that the abolition of untouchability, for example, already achieved by legislation, is meaningless in reality, since legislation can only show the way, but can never be effectively implemented unless the attitude of the people is changed.[39]

Ram then goes on to justify the existence and perpetuation of post-Independence positive discrimination for SC/ST groups:

> Therefore, so long as the caste feelings are there — and with all efforts it will take some time before caste feelings are completely eliminated — some kinds of reservations, some kinds of safeguards, have to be there and special concessions and facilities will have to be provided for educational, economic and cultural advancement of the downtrodden .[40]

Significantly, Ram tries to deny at once that such deliberate discrimination policies may create their own conflicts rather than improve national consensus: reservations will not, he insists, give rise to divisive and fissiparous tendencies leading to disintegration.[41]

Of course, this is just wishful thinking. Arguing that the backward communities will be fired by enthusiasm because opportunities for self-advancement are no longer denied to them, Ram envisages whole-hearted co-operation from them.[42] But recent studies on the effects of positive discrimination policies have concluded that many potential beneficiaries have not even come to *know* of the benefits, let alone enjoy any.[43] Ram's study, too, contains strong evidence of the resentment against preferential treatment for certain backward classes and shows that the implementation of such policies leaves much to be desired.[44] In line with other researchers he reports that the attitudes against reservations are hardening,[45] leading to campaigns[46] and increasingly violent atrocities against SC/ST members.[47]

The apparent backlash of upper-caste Hindus, which 'threatens to tear our social and national structure and blow up the whole fabric of the state'[48] can hardly be conducive to achieving national integration through a process of status equalization. Instead of reducing caste differences, the reservation policies have evidently contributed to an increased awareness of differential statuses and caste and class competition in India today. They have also lent themselves to open political manipulation[49] and have deteriorated into 'a vote-catching, quarrel-making and jealousy-inspiring device'.[50] All this has contributed to the noticeable reassertion of ethnicity, and thus diversity, in modern India. The Indian equivalent of 'community relations', then, often subsumed under the negative term 'communalism', may well have been damaged by the protective discrimination policies, i.e., by the 'rational' policies of the modern Indian state, whose protagonists naively planned for a reduction of the potential for such conflicts.

The social reformer's dream of an egalitarian society as the result of 'equalizing policies',[51] then, has clearly not been achieved in modern India. It is, of course, a moot point whether it was achievable in the first place. Few authors say as clearly as one could that the modern Indian social reformers, in their characteristic hubris, really had no clear understanding of the concepts involved. Mumtaz Ali Khan indicates this problem in very general terms:

> Though the move for improving the conditions of this section is indeed welcome and laudable, the various steps so far taken have been inspired more by the spirit of social reform than by a scientific consideration of the problems with the result that their aptness and adequacy are open to question. The problem is further confounded by the lack of any definite and reliable body of knowledge about the actual results of the efforts so far made in this regard.[52]

My critique of the rationale of post-Independence Indian social reformers should not, however, be read as a repudiation of the Indian policies. This would be far too simplistic, though deceptively persuasive from the perspective of the advanced sections, who would also today insist on the overriding importance of merit criteria.

Merit is a relative and often highly subjective criterion. Traditional merit criteria tend to imply that 'only the best' will be chosen in a kind of natural selection process that requires no central state intervention. Many writers have, indeed, emphasized that the merit principle on its own would certainly not be conducive to creating a more egalitarian society. One of the leading scholars of inequality in India has put it thus:

> But in a society where great inequalities exist, as in India, the unqualified adoption of merit or efficiency as a principle of distribution will, instead of diminishing inequalities, tend to increase them, as individuals belonging to the disadvantaged sections are not in a position to compete on an equal footing.[53]

Similarly, when commenting on the implications of relevant constitutional provisions, the same author argued that:

> An unqualified acceptance of the meritarian principle in a society where there are great inequalities will instead of reducing inequalities, tend to perpetuate them. If jobs are given solely on the basis of efficiency and merit, the ex-Untouchable groups who are traditionally engaged in 'unclean' occupations and who constitute a large proportion of landless agricultural labour can hardly be expected to compete with the advanced sections of the community.[54]

In the context of economic development generally, it has been argued that the vast potential of the traditionally backward communities of India justifies special remedies and special concessions. These should be generally related to development plans and need to be strong to overcome the serious ailment of inherited disabilities, which 'are so deep-seated that a separate and special treatment is justified'.[55] Conversely, the higher castes would have to endure a temporary injustice, so that the wrongs of several thousand years may be righted and a new era of justice and equality may begin.[56]

It is in this wider context that we have to read the reservation provisions in the Indian Constitution of 1950; they aimed to accelerate the process of building an egalitarian social order:

> Equality of opportunity and secularism would prove to be meaningless if a very large section of the society continued to remain poor and deprived of opportunities to secure political and administrative positions. They needed special safeguards and reservations, though there were no two opinions about the fact that protective

discrimination was not an ideal course. But under the given circumstances and the social structure, the founding fathers of the Constitution were faced with limited options.[57]

It has been argued that it is mainly because of Ambedkar's ardent support for the cause of the depressed classes that the Indian Constitution of 1950 contains such explicit provisions for protective discrimination.[58] But there is also evidence that the discussions in India's Constituent Assembly between July 1946 and November 1949, apart from minor disagreements, reflected a near unanimity and general consensus that certain classes of Indians would need special constitutional protection.[59] Significantly, the debates were held in the wider context of minorities and their position in the emerging post-Independence Indian polity.[60] Leaving aside the Muslims (however important as a minority, they were never considered as belonging to the SC/ST category), much attention was focused on the SC/ST groups; they began to emerge as separate entities from the much more general category of 'depressed' or 'backward classes'.[61]

The Scheduled Castes were specific groups of very low-caste Hindus, including a few Sikh groups in Eastern Punjab. The Constituent Assembly debates brought out the historical guilt complex of the upper-caste Hindus and led to an argument, eagerly supported by Ambedkar, that the time had come for a modicum of reverse discrimination. Thus, the redress of historical imbalances argument was applied, at least initially, only to certain low-status Hindu groups as well as the generally marginalized tribals. Protective provisions did not cover those former low-caste Hindus who had converted to other faiths, notably Christianity, Islam and Buddhism.

The various Indian minorities were at this stage led to believe that they were not in need of special treatment. Thus, the elite representatives of these groups gallantly stepped back in favour of the SC/ST. High-caste Hindu rhetoric, in an odd symbiosis with low-caste leadership, had a fairly easy task persuading all minorities that absolute preference needed to be given to the lowest of the low among the Hindu castes. This has been seen in typically Indian positive terms as:

> A golden page from our contemporary history when the religious minorities of the country voluntarily withdrew their claims to the reservations and special safeguards envisaged for them while agreeing that the Scheduled Castes and Scheduled Tribes needed these the most.[62]

On the other hand, this led to the gradual realization that non-Hindu minorities were losing out and would have to compete for special treatment in the difficult OBC category. It seems that the elite minority representatives initially did not realize the negative repercussions for the impoverished members of their respective communities; they were probably flattered by the illusion of being part of the 'mainstream' of modern Indian society.

Two elements have, thus, been combined in the Indian policies of compensatory discrimination. First was the strong desire to achieve a caste-less, classless society, a somewhat idealized state of society which inspired many leaders of post-colonial India. This preoccupation with equality has been seen as 'itself part of a historical process that grew with the movement for freedom from colonial bondage'.[63] Secondly, a policy of redress of historical imbalances was seen as the only way to compensate and uplift India's traditionally backward communities. The awkward combination of these two approaches could not but lead to much resentment and frustration, which also overcame the protagonists of these policies.[64] One may wonder which of the above two motivations has inspired the reformers and their followers more, but the real crux appears to be that neither limb of this strategic policy-making could be subjected to comprehensive planning. It was perhaps the most expedient compromise between reformist ideals and social realities that one could achieve at that time. The fate of the policies would have to be closely monitored.

THE CONSTITUTIONAL PROVISIONS

The debate on discrimination policies in India developed in the wider context of minority rights.[65] Thus, in the Constituent Assembly, Nehru could initially move a resolution to the effect that adequate safeguards should be provided for minorities, backward and tribal areas and depressed and other backward classes.[66] This assurance of protection for the interests of all minorities and backward classes was warmly received, but it soon emerged that more specific constitutional guarantees for certain classes of people would be introduced into the Indian Constitution. While the special treatment of 'backward classes' generally was justified by socio-economic criteria,[67] the historical legacy of the SC/ST groups led, as we saw, to a very special place for this category.

The resulting fundamental rights provisions are found in Articles 14–16 of the Indian Constitution of 1950. In essence, this cluster of provisions epitomizes the dilemma of modern Indian constitutional law: a desire to follow the 'rule of law' model of professed equality before the law in Article 14,[68] grafted onto a traditional society in which status inequalities continue to be the prevailing norm. This led to what Galanter, in his concluding sentence, called 'a tempered legalism — one which we find more congenial in practice than in theory'.[69] Thus, various forms of discrimination are explicitly prohibited in Article 15, while preferential treatment for certain groups is explicitly allowed. Racial or sex discrimination *per se* would clearly violate the fundamental rights guarantees of Articles 14, 15(1) and 15(2). But Articles 15(3) and 15(4), as well as Article 16(4), explicitly allow discrimination on the ground of sex or age or 'backwardness' of some kind. Articles 15(3) and 15(4) provide as follows:

(3) Nothing in this article shall prevent the State from making any special provision for women and children.

(4) Nothing in this article or in clause (2) of article 29 shall prevent the State from making any special provision for the advancement of any socially and educationally backward classes of citizens or for the Scheduled Castes and the Scheduled Tribes.

More specifically, Article 16(4) provides:

(4) Nothing in this article shall prevent the State from making any provision for the reservation of appointments or posts in favour of any backward class of citizens which, in the opinion of the State, is not adequately represented in the services under the State.

The fundamental rights provisions of Articles 14–16 are fully justiciable and thus potentially very powerful. But apart from these rather general indications of policy, the Constitution itself does not lay down how the Indian policies of protective discrimination are to be implemented. This has, of course, led to some legal insecurity and to the rapid and direct involvement of the superior courts, i.e., the Indian Supreme Court in New Delhi and the more than twenty state-based high courts. Article 32 of the Indian Constitution guarantees the right to move the Supreme Court directly and *by appropriate proceedings* for the enforcement of any of the fundamental rights. Similar provisions guaranteeing access to the high courts and their powerful writ jurisdiction are found in Article 226 of the Constitution.

I have highlighted the phrase 'by appropriate proceedings' to indicate that today, in the wake of the remarkable developments brought about by public interest litigation in India, it is in fact possible to claim one's fundamental rights by writing a postcard to a superior court. Admittedly, knowledge of this has not yet reached every Indian citizen and access to the simplest of services remains a problem for many. But the potential for public interest litigation in our particular area has been recognized and will, no doubt, sooner or later become obvious from the Indian law reports.[70]

These powerful fundamental rights provisions are supported and strengthened, in today's climate of taking the non-justiciable Directive Principles of State Policy (DPSP) of the Indian Constitution more seriously, by Article 46, which provides that:

> The State shall promote with special care the educational and economic interests of the weaker sections of the people, and, in particular, of the Scheduled Castes and the Scheduled Tribes, and shall protect them from social injustice and all forms of exploitation.

This article would seem to give specific recognition of the need for protection of the SC/ST category, but it makes clear enough reference to *all* weaker sections of the Indian people. In practice, as academic writing tends to confirm, such provisions may not have had much impact so far.[71]

Since the important Forty-second Amendment of the Constitution in 1976, there has been a further and potentially very powerful provision that is relevant here. Article 38(2), also a DPSP, provides as follows:

> The State shall, in particular, strive to minimise the inequalities in income, and endeavour to eliminate inequalities in status, facilities and opportunities, not only amongst individuals, but also amongst groups of people residing in different areas or engaged in different vocations.

This provision is aimed very much wider than specifically at the SC/ST or OBC categories. It serves to point Indian legal development in the direction of securing greater equality for all citizens, so can be seen as an important support mechanism for India's protective discrimination policies generally.

The Indian Constitution has further detailed provisions in Part XVI, 'Special Provisions relating to Certain Classes'. Articles 330–42, heavily amended over the years, provide a number of interesting details that are relevant here. Articles 330–34 focus on seat reservations and special representation for SC/ST and the Anglo-Indian community in the

House of the People (*Lok Sabha*) and the Legislative Assembly of every state. These reservations, says Article 334, were to cease after 30 years, but the Constitution (Forty-fifth Amendment) Act 1980 extended this by a further 10 years, and this extension has now been perpetuated by the Constitution (Sixty-second Amendment) Act of 1989 for a further decade. Probably because of the size of the SC/ST population, electoral considerations have become more important.

Artical 335 seems fairly reticent about SC/ST claims to services and posts. It merely says:

> The claims of the members of the Scheduled Castes and the Scheduled Tribes shall be taken into consideration, consistently with the maintenance of efficiency of administration, in the making of appointments to services and posts in connection with the affairs of the Union or of a state.

It may be assumed, I think, that the argument of damage to efficiency, which is now so often and prominently used against reservations for SC/ST (see below) has been strengthened by this particular provision.

Article 338 provides that there shall be a special officer for the SC/ST who shall be appointed by the president and shall report directly to him. Articles 339 and 340 relate to the appointment of a commission and other supervisory mechanisms designed to strengthen the position of the centre in monitoring progress with regard to the SC/ST and OBCs. Articles 341 and 342, focusing on SC/ST, provide the authority for the Indian government to specify 'the castes, races or tribes or parts of or groups within castes, races or tribes' (Article 341) which shall be deemed to be SC/ST.

Modern India's constitutional scheme for the protection of SC/ST and OBC from continued exploitation and discrimination by the upper castes and classes is, thus, very impressive. Anything similar, it seems, could not be imagined in Britain. Endowment with the authority of a central scheme has helped to ensure no let-up in modern India's attempts to be seen to implement certain policies of protective discrimination; the recent attempts of the Indian government to strengthen the reservation policies are symptomatic of the centre's claim to a leading role in this regard. The entrenchment of these provisions among the fundamental rights must, no doubt, be seen as a clear indication of full commitment to such policies. But there can be equally little doubt that these policies have not been accepted by all Indians without a measure of dismay and frustration, if not anger. At the same time, the implementation of the policies is apparently far from perfect.

We should briefly note here that the absence of explicit race relations legislation in modern India is due to the fact that Artical 15 of the Constitution appears to cover this ground. I would argue that India's fairly low-key approach to questions of discrimination in this field is due to two reasons. First, the predominance of the communal rather than racial factor makes issues turn up as 'religious', so that in India, as distinct from Malaysia or Britain, we do not and cannot really talk of 'race relations', but focus on 'communal relations'.

Second, the modern law and its makers remain quite aware of the traditional concepts of legalized inequality and their persistence in modern India. As a result, we see only rather feeble attempts to eradicate such practices as untouchability, despite Article 17 of the Constitution, which outlawed the practice, the Untouchability (Offences) Act 1955[72] and the Civil Rights Act 1970.[73] The phenomenon itself is even found in Britain today.[74]

IDENTIFYING THE BENEFICIARIES

The huge task of identifying the various beneficiaries of the Indian positive discrimination policies is a crucial aspect of the implementation of such policies, so important that its foundations were laid in the Constitution itself. Throughout, we find many indications that beneficiaries would be identified on a group basis, not as deserving individuals. In view of the fact that there are major differences in identifying the SC/ST category and the OBCs, we must look at them one by one.

The Identification of the SC/ST

The steps taken are fairly simple to report. In accordance with Articles 341–42 of the Constitution of India, the president of India rapidly consulted the governors of states. Already in 1950 we find the result, two important orders, the Constitution (Scheduled Castes) Order 1950 and the Constitution (Scheduled Tribes) Order 1950. Both, with some amendments, are still in force today, serving as an important basis for the implementation of state policy. They are tedious statutory instruments, containing little else than lists of castes, communities or tribes, or parts of castes or tribes. Details of the lists are quite immaterial here, but it should be emphasized that the selection took place on a group basis, the major criterion being traditionally low position within the Hindu caste system or tribal origin, respectively.

It may be relevant to point out here that Section 3 of the Constitution (Scheduled Castes) Order 1950 specifically provides that 'No person who professes a religion different from the Hindu or Sikh religion shall be deemed to be a member of a Scheduled Caste.' This confirms that the benefits of the protective discrimination policies (thus the term 'compensatory discrimination') are to accrue first of all to the historically disadvantaged lowest sections of the Hindu population. The reference to Sikh groups was inserted by the Scheduled Castes and Scheduled Tribes Lists (Modification) Order 1956 when it was found that certain low-status groups of Sikhs in the Punjab ought to be included to prevent communal ill-will. The category of beneficiaries continues to exclude the Muslims, Christians and Buddhists, who would inevitably, at a later stage, complain about this in the context of reservations for OBCs.

It may have been comparatively easy to ascertain group membership among the Scheduled Tribes. However, an important additional criterion apart from tribal status appears to have been place of residence, so that tribals who stayed in their traditional districts were included in the lists, while more mobile groups were in danger of being excluded.

Obviously, this original exercise of ascertaining the groups of beneficiaries would not go unchallenged. The Indian courts have, however, been very firm on this issue, refusing to add to the lists and pointing to Article 341(2) of the Constitution, which provides that the duty to amend these lists falls on Parliament, not the courts. This is probably a wise move, given that local power structures would inevitably have brought pressure on the respective high courts to amend the lists in favour of powerful groups. The parallel struggles of ascertaining who are the OBCs (see further below), clearly illustrate the frequent interference of local politics.

By 1976, pressure for the inclusion of certain groups had grown so strong that Parliament made the Scheduled Castes and Scheduled Tribes Orders (Amendment) Act 1976. In two fairly lengthy schedules, again long lists of caste names, this Act consolidates the lists provided by the 1950 orders into statewide lists, abandoning the system of district classification. This may facilitate administration of the system, but the changes also indicate a strengthening of the traditional caste criterion, in that members of certain castes, no matter where they live, qualify as beneficiaries. It must be presumed that this includes urban settlers from those communities, some of whom will be upwardly mobile and thus, as we shall see below, better able to avail themselves of the manifold benefits of the reservation policies. As far as I can see, the 1976 Act may be largely the result of pressure from certain middle-class SC/ST groups for their inclusion as beneficiaries. Also, it is very likely that expediency in terms of electoral calculations played a role yet again.

The range of tribal beneficiaries has recently been amended by the short Constitution (Scheduled Tribes) Order (Amendment) Act 1987, which provides for the addition of three further tribes in the Eastern Indian state of Meghalaya to the list of beneficiaries.

The Identification of Other Backward Classes

A neat classification, as has superficially been achieved with regard to the SC/ST category, has not been possible for the OBCs and will continue to elude us. The reasons for this are quite apparent. Clearly, the 'backward classes' will always include a large number of Indians, irrespective of the criteria applied. The numbers issue itself is proving a major stumbling block to any realistic attempts at identifying potential beneficiaries in this open category. For whatever criteria you choose to define 'backwardness', you end up with a few hundred million claimants! We have in India today a very sizeable middle class, estimated at more than 150 million people, out of a total population of now more than 850 million. This, no matter how one counts, leaves hundreds of millions as potential candidates for the 'backward' label, which is now so heavily prized.

Government statistics in 1980 estimated that 316 million Indians lived below the poverty line.[75] While economic criteria would recommend themselves and are strongly favoured by many authors,[76] there can be little doubt that they, too, would yield a far too large group of beneficiaries. An excellent recent article reports on various earlier attempts to define 'backward classes', coming to the conclusion that this term 'never had any definite meaning that could have received acceptance at the national level'.[77]

After Independence, especially after the Indian Constitution made explicit reference to 'Other Backward Classes', finding agreed criteria became an urgent task. Under Article 340 of the Constitution, a Backward Classes Commission, chaired by Kaka Kalelkar, was appointed on 29 January 1953. Its brief was to determine criteria for the identification of socially and educationally backward classes and to prepare a list of such classes. This Commission's report came to the conclusion that 70 per cent of India's population was backward and prepared a list of 2,399 castes and communities.[78]

A detailed study of the tests applied by the Commission shows that traditional caste factors had been given overwhelming importance; the Commission's report was severely criticized on that ground and for failing to evolve viable and acceptable criteria for determining backward classes.[79]One could argue that the Commission's policy of including all and sundry in its classification had the desired effect of showing the near impossibility of further action. In other words, this report must probably be seen as a stalling device.

Indeed, it took until 1979 for the central government to make a second attempt at a comprehensive definition of socially and educationally backward classes. The Second Backward Classes Commission, chaired by B. P. Mandal (the Mandal Commission), produced eleven indicators or criteria for determining backwardness. Of these, four were social criteria, three educational ones, and four were economic indicators.[80] At first sight, this seems an interesting and promising combination of criteria. But the Commission went on to give a weightage of three points each to the social criteria, but only two points to the educational ones, and one to the economic criteria. Again, thus, too much emphasis had been placed on 'caste', and the Commission's report has been severely criticized for its 'lack of vision and insincerity of purpose'.[81] In other words, the centre's second attempt to evolve viable criteria for backwardness has been boycotted, quite probably by forces inimical to any clearly defined policy in favour of backward classes. The current violent opposition to the implementation of the Mandal Commission Report, indeed, focuses on 'caste' rather than economic criteria.

The unsuccessful attempts at the centre have been matched by equally debateable measures at state level to evolve a system of identification that may be more in line with local conditions. Constitutionally, there is no obstacle to such a path, and a number of state governments have therefore taken steps to identify the backward classes in their realm. The results are clearly a mixed blessing for those who hoped to be able to develop a national policy. Local conditions in the various Indian states prompted a diversity of policies and approaches (as would probably be the case in Britain today). Thus, in Mysore (today's Karnataka), in line with traditional South Indian concepts,[82] almost all non-Brahmins were initially classed as 'backward', making that term virtually synonymous with 'non-Brahmin'.[83] This is as though in the US all non-WASP people were to be classed as 'backward'. Such an arrangement inevitably led to practical difficulties, and the whole scheme was struck down by the Indian Supreme Court in the leading case of *Balaji* on the basis that the resulting reservation quota were excessive and should in any case be limited to 50 per cent.[84] This important judgment soon led to modifications in ascertaining backwardness in Karnataka by using the tests of income and occupation, no doubt a positive development.

In Kerala, too, we see some progress. In this state with large Muslim and Christian populations, a Backward Classes Reservation Commission was appointed (the Nettur Commission). In its report of 1970, the

commission emphasized the role of educational and economic criteria
rather than social and caste factors and thus identified groups of
beneficiaries from all communities. This was found agreeable by the
government of the day and the recommendations of the report were
implemented.

In Jammu and Kashmir, much troubled by minority politics, here on
the bipolar Muslim-Hindu axis, a Backward Classes Committee under
the chairmanship of Mr Justice J. N. Wazir came up with a report, in
November 1969, that amounted to an allocation of communal quotas.
The recommendations of the committee were accepted by the government, but a reservation scheme on this basis was later struck down as
unconstitutional by the Supreme Court in *Janaki Prasad*.[85]

We see here that any definition of 'backwardness' that is too closely
dependent on any *one* factor (mainly this has been 'caste' in India; in
Britain it would probably be 'race') has not proved acceptable. The
Indian courts, as watchdogs over the implementation of the various
reservation schemes, have given a clear and fairly consistent message
that monocausal models of identifying backwardness are unacceptable.
While this seems the correct approach, certainly in view of the fundamental rights mandates of the Constitution, the discussion has not been
moved forward beyond this general point. In other words, the courts are
just as overawed as everybody else by the practical difficulties of identifying beneficiaries. It would be fruitless to construct a conflict between
judiciary and government in this area, though the *Champakam* case,[86]
leading to the insertion of Article 15(4) by the Constitution (First
Amendment) Act 1951, seemed to initiate such a long-drawn battle.

In fact, everyone is frustrated by the complexity of the issue and the
magnitude of the task, and with the best will in the world it has not been
possible to devise agreed criteria. One need only read the five separate
judgments of the Supreme Court in the important case of *Vasanth
Kumar*,[87] symptomatic of the prevailing lack of co-ordination, which is
in itself indicative of the fact that any purely rational treatment of
this complex task is bedevilled by the irrationality of Indian socio-
economic realities. No matter how well-considered a scheme one may
devise, the practical difficulties of its implementation, let alone lack of
resources, preclude any easy solution. We find here an example of the
limits of law.

It must be apparent, then, that with regard to the OBCs, India has
embarked on a well-meaning policy of seeking to achieve greater
equality, but the road to success (if there is any) is blocked by a mountain
of confusions as well as scarcity of resources. On the other hand, India
already has a huge pool of educated and well-trained people, many of
whom are unemployed or underemployed, and it would be unrealistic

in the extreme to expect that government policies should aspire to provide higher education or government jobs for all deserving individuals from the OBC category.

I have been rather dismayed at the hostile attitude of many Indian academics to the policies of protective discrimination. There is often a notable difference between detailed academic studies, published in book form, and shorter articles. The former tend to be positive and constructive, while the latter are often polemic attacks on the reservation schemes.[88] Since these policies work against the class interests of such writers, one should not be too surprised about the widespread absence of a spirit of constructive criticism. But upper-class hubris and politicking cannot be excused in view of India's constitutional mandate to create greater equality which can, as we saw earlier, only be realized through some form of positive action programme.

The only way forward, it appears, lies in seeking to develop more sophisticated criteria for identifying backwardness. There is a need to move away from the rather crude group labels based on caste, but one cannot ignore this very basic criterion altogether. Actually, the Constitution itself, by outlawing discrimination based on any *one* ground in Article 16(2) shows the way: India needs fine-tuning mechanisms for the existing policies on SC/ST and on OBCs.[89] My argument below shall be that the implementation of policies regarding the SC/ST categories over a couple of decades contains useful lessons on how to manage policies of protective discrimination for the OBC category. In essence, caste and community criteria need to be supplemented by consideration of the individual claimant's situation. In other words, on top of the low-caste criterion, means testing on an individual basis recommends itself as a standard all-India policy; it already exists in some Indian states.

Whether the important policy basis of group allocation should be abandoned altogether is a very big question. It would then presumably be replaced by individual criteria, among which caste membership will inevitably resurface as a major factor.[90] I do not accept, thus, that abandoning the group focus altogether will serve a useful purpose. Of course, applying an income ceiling on top of caste criteria means that one has already partly abandoned the group membership criterion.

If we were to consider the same issue for Britain, we would probably have to decide between protective discrimination for all poor 'blacks', or for all poor people. The latter path, no doubt, recommends itself on a number of grounds, but we may need a reminder here of India's predicament of numbers. It is doubtful whether Britain would be able or willing to bear the considerable economic implications of such policies.

I conclude this section by saying that following the regional models of Karnataka and Kerala, seeking to identify the most deserving individuals *from within* certain backward classes seems the most sensible solution in the Indian context. That the implementation of such models will be subject to many strains is certainly not peculiar to India at all.

THE IMPLEMENTATION OF INDIA'S POLICIES OF PROTECTIVE DISCRIMINATION

While it remains correct to say that the Constitution of India does not lay down criteria for determining backwardness,[91] we have seen above that the constitutional provisions have contributed significantly to the implementation of SC/ST policies and, to a lesser extent, of the policies on OBCs. I have already shown that the position of these provisions among the human rights guarantees, supplemented and strengthened by several Directive Principles of State Policy, led to an immediate involvement of the highest courts of the land. The implementation of India's policies has, thus, been negotiated at the judicial top level straight away, rather than at local tribunal level, as would seem to be the case in Britain's set-up.

A major impetus for these policies comes, then, from the Indian federal centre in two ways: first, by the promulgation of the Constitution itself and the 1950 orders made under it, which have determined the classifications of SC/ST statewide; and second, by the supervision of the Supreme Court, which may sometimes appear confused and divided, but which has had a broadly consolidating influence on the implementation of the policies.

At the same time, the 1950 orders clearly locate the various Indian SC/ST beneficiaries within a state context. This is obvious from the way in which the orders are organized. Every state could, thus, make its own rules for the implementation of the reservation policies. Not surprisingly, local political and communal power structures would then often crucially determine the genesis and implementation of such policies, especially with regard to the OBCs. Such particular local conditions led to the leading case of *Balaji*[92].

The Mysore government had made an Order in July 1962 reserving seats in technical institutions for backward classes. Under this order, the classification was based solely on caste; it was therefore declared invalid on this count. More important in this case is the question of the extent of reservations. In Mysore, the traditional Brahmin/non-Brahmin divide was used as a major determinator for 'backwardness', so that close to 90 per cent of the population of the state came to be classified as 'backward'. This nonsensical classification was then followed by a reservation in favour of backward classes to the extent of 68 per cent of seats. It could, of course, be argued that in such circumstances a 68 per cent reservation was too little for 90 per cent of the population and amounted to discrimination in favour of the non-backward class. However, the Supreme Court, having already thrown out the state's classification scheme for backwardness, decreed that the total of reservations should never be more than 50 per cent. This has become a firm precedent in Indian law. The ruling was also justified by the commonly heard appeal to efficiency: 'Reservation should and must be adopted to advance the prospects of the weaker sections of society, but care should be taken not to exclude deserving and qualified candidates of other communities.'[93]

We see here that the implementation of India's policies of protective discrimination does not take place in a vacuum. Various socio-economic restraints, in particular simply the scarcity of resources, have made this a much-contested area of the law, reflected not only in huge masses of case law, but also in the fact that communal consciousness has been aroused by these policies, leading to a spirit of aggression that has, in some states, led to periodic violent communal clashes.[94]

Apart from reservations of seats for certain communities in political bodies, a much-maligned legacy of British policy, which we are not concerned with here, the Indian reservation policies have become prominent in two areas: admission to medical and engineering colleges and employment in government departments and promotion prospects.

Soon after 1950, there was resistence to the system of communal quotas, especially in South India. Two important Supreme Court decisions in 1951 seriously challenged the whole constitutional framework for the implementation of protective discrimination. In the *Champakam* case,[95] a reservation system in educational institutions was struck down. At the same time, the judges refused to uphold a system of quotas in government posts in Madras for all groups other than the Scheduled Castes and the so-called 'Backward Hindus', giving a rather narrow interpretation of Article 16(4) of the Constitution.[96]

The resulting debates have clearly shown that SC/ST reservations were much more widely accepted than those for the OBCs.[97] It was, of course, much easier for the government to strengthen the constitutional guarantees for the OBCs than to define them more clearly; this is the path that was taken. Thus Article 15(4), already quoted above, was swiftly added to the Constitution by the Constitution (First Amendment) Act 1951.

In his discussion of the definition of OBCs, Galanter has emphasized the failure to centralize policy.[98] While I partly agree with this argument, it appears that by amending the Constitution the Indian government, clearly more progressive at that time than the Indian judiciary, reaffirmed the centre's commitment to the reservation strategies, just as V. P. Singh may be seen to have strengthened this commitment. True, backwardness remains ill-defined, but the above constitutional amendment has tied the hands of anti-reservationists by introducing a new justiciable fundamental right, elevating it from its earlier position as a directive principle of state policy. In this way, a strong centre within India's federal set-up has laid down important general parameters for the future development of the policies, while leaving most details of the implementation to individual states.

At the same time, it is also obvious that the continual involvement of the Supreme Court of India, in its watchdog function as guardian of human rights, has frequently subjected all state schemes to central control. Thus, no reservation scheme anywhere in the country has been allowed to deviate from the 50 per cent rule in *Balaji*.[99] On other issues, though, the Indian Supreme Court has spoken much less with one voice. It is easy to detect, as many writers have done, inconsistencies and contradictions in the verdicts of the Indian Supreme Court on a number of questions, prominently the issue of criteria for determining backwardness, which occupies centre stage in this enormously complicated debate and figures prominently in the next section.

MAJOR POLICY ISSUES IN THE CONTEXT OF INDIA'S PROGRAMME OF PROTECTIVE DISCRIMINATION

There are a number of major issues which can only be outlined here, since the material on any one issue is enormous. A topic of great importance is the application of criteria for determining backwardness. Extensive debate on this issue has led to a growing realization that a simple strategy of group reservation based on caste does not, in practice, yield the desired results of benefiting the really deprived masses. A consequent policy of fine-tuning of the traditional approach is now under way. Income ceilings and other criteria have been developed to avoid the 'creaming-off effect', that is, to separate out those members of backward classes that are already able to compete without the help of positive discrimination policies. Apart from this, the courts are seeking to control a number of other abuses of the system, which shows that India has already moved away, to a considerable extent, from the pure group rights approach and has begun to focus on individuals.

While this may seem a good way forward, it still does not get rid of the fundamental problem of equality, namely that no amount of discrimination policies will achieve the founding fathers' vision of absolute equality. The noticeable reluctance to debate this issue must at least be pointed out here.

We also cannot avoid the question of time-scale and are likely to see that any reservation policies, once implemented, develop their own momentum and are not likely to be abandoned altogether, though they may of course be modified. This, looking at Britain, may be a very important issue to which I shall return in the concluding section.

The Extent of Reservations

We have already seen that the Supreme Court's early definitive statement in *Balaji*[100] about a 50 per cent limit in reservations has been widely respected. Galanter has argued that since the Constitution does not explicitly lay down any maximum or limitation on the extent of preferential treatment, the Indian courts in their watchdog function had to develop a system of limitations.[101] The courts have been crucially influenced by considerations of policy and public interest, as well as efficiency and maintenance of standards. With reference to the fundamental rights provisions, the Indian Supreme Court:

> Characterised the purpose of these special provisions not merely as conferring special privileges on the backward, but as serving the interests of the whole society by promoting the advancement of its weakest elements. Thus, any scheme for preference can be weighed in terms of the interests of the whole society.[102]

In other words, modern Indian law cannot simply be concerned with the protective discrimination policies alone; they have to be seen and applied in a wider context. This, as Galanter has so impressively shown, is the underlying continuous dilemma of 'competing equalities'.

Clearly, therefore, an expansive view of reservations, which would in the extreme allow reservation of all posts, is now discredited.[103] Similarly, for this is precisely what such a system would amount to, community-based allocation of all seats has been rejected vigorously. While Galanter argues against it in view of the American experience of racial segregation, the Indian Supreme Court has rejected such communal allocations as were proposed in Kashmir, for example, by reference to the Indian Constitution's prohibition of discrimination on the basis of any single criterion, such as religion.[104]

Apart from the numerical aspect, the extent of communal allocation becomes a much more explosive issue as soon as one seeks to implement reservations for OBCs. In other words, the primary focus on the historically disadvantaged SC/ST category with its limited extent of communal quotas (for that is precisely what these reservation categories amount to) did not cause any significant problems. Comparatively little objection to reservations for the SC/ST is probably due to two factors. First, they take away only a small slice of the whole cake, normally about 10 per cent of the whole. Second, overt hostility to the SC/ST categories 'is taboo in legislative and many other public forums';[105] However resentment appears in stronger tones in the debates on the OBCs.

In conclusion, at this point, I would say that the extent of reservations required to uplift the SC/ST posed and poses no major problems in India. However, real difficulties continue to surface in the implementation of the much more ambitious action programmes for OBCs, primarily because of the sheer size of potential groups of beneficiaries and the magnitude of this task in India.

The Efficiency Argument

The question of extent of reservation policies has been immediately linked, also by Galanter,[106] with the hotly debated and much-politicized allegation that any reservation policy will inevitably lead to a lowering of standards. This may be dismissed as a bogus argument, but is a hydra that rears its head everywhere. The issue was already raised in *Balaji*[107] and there has been much debate subsequently. Notably, the Indian academic literature is full of middle-class allegations that unsuitable and unqualified individuals grab precious reserved seats, with ruinous consequences for academic and other standards.[108] Such comments are, however, often easily recognized as communalist 'sour grapes', indicating that the reservation policies bite and have been effective to an extent.

Significantly, Galanter criticizes the allegation that compensatory discrimination is a major factor in the lowering of standards in education and in the lack of effectiveness of government bureaucracy.[109] Thus, having earlier assessed the costs and benefits of India's reservation policies in interesting tables,[110] he concludes that the undeniable substantial redistributive effects of these policies have been achieved at enormous costs.[111] But these costs are not so much seen in an economic sense as in terms of their impact on the potential beneficiaries, many of whom have been unsuccessful in their endeavour to reach the required standards.[112]

Though often advanced in discussions with middle-class Indians, the efficiency argument does not, therefore, seem to be that convincing. The allegation of inefficiency was also forcefully rejected by the Supreme Court in *Vasanth Kumar*.[113] Some courts are refusing to consider reservations irrespective of merit.[114]

The almost proverbial inefficiency of Indian bureaucracy is not, then, due to lack of suitable qualification and skills, but a familiar air of officialdom's superiority *qua* office, coupled with lack of a sense of accountability. If, as I was explicitly told in India, the situation had got worse after the appearance of SC/ST clerks on public counters, we may have to take this with a pinch of salt. In fact, many Indian pen-pushers and bureaucrats are overqualified in formal terms.

The significant fact remains, however, that there is an influential *public perception* in India that the effect of reservation policies has been to bring about lower standards and to encourage inefficiency. Perhaps this is an inevitable consequence of openly abandoning the pure merit principle. As we saw above, India's conscious decision to do so involves a recognition of the fact that all criteria for merit are, to an extent, socially and culturally determined. In other words, they are not purely objective criteria and are changeable in accordance with a society's needs. This, then, is really where the shoe pinches: a classic case of the uncomfortable effects of social engineering through law.

Thus, allegations that SC/ST candidates get college places, for example, on the basis of much lower percentages than other candidates (which is, of course, factually true), are an implied attack on these new merit criteria, which offer themselves for criticism as promoting inefficiency, though this need not be the case.

Interestingly, a recent example of abandonment of traditional merit criteria in India is offered by some new policies in the area of promoting promising sportsmen, aiming to improve the country's international standing. A wide-ranging talent search yielded, for example, tribal experts in traditional shooting methods who made an almost instant impact in international archery competitions. In such cases, it would seem most obvious that the traditional high-caste dominated set-up had earlier left little space for the consideration of relevant merit criteria; birth and connections clearly mattered more than any measurable standards of efficiency.

While an open-minded talent search among a few sportspeople is not likely to cause major disagreements (I am sure one could finds parallels with Britain here), applying the same principles to all walks of life may well upset the traditional hierarchies, leading almost inevitably to negative reactions that yield intentionally garbled discourse.

Further Benefits after Entry

This issue was bound to arise, sooner or later, after certain SC/ST members had begun to gain entry to higher education and access to government jobs. Once admitted into a position as a result of protective discrimination policies, would such people have to compete on an equal footing within their new peer group? To what extent would it be permissible to continue to give them preferential treatment? Here again, the efficiency debate raises its head; it would surely be encouraging the lowering of standards if one were to continue to condone deviations from qualifications required for promotion, to take the most obvious example.

Here, like in Britain today, outright discrimination and certain forms of preferential treatment have been shown to be intimate bedfellows: one encourages the beneficiary category of applicants at the entry stage, possibly to fill the expected 'ethnic' or SC/ST quota, but then keeps such employees in lowly positions without promotion prospects, claiming that certain efficiency barriers have not been crossed. British Rail, it was recently alleged, had an astonishing test system that was able to identify and fail all non-white candidates.[115]

Inevitably, the Indian courts had to address this issue sooner or later. The leading authority here is the *Thomas* case, which has been much discussed.[116] The case arose among clerks in the services of Kerala state. It was filed by a lower division clerk who had passed the necessary tests for promotion to higher division clerk, yet found himself superseded by more senior SC/ST lower division clerks who had not passed these qualifying exams, but had been promoted nevertheless as a result of new government rules which appeared to exempt SC/ST clerks from such qualifying tests.

A full bench of the Supreme Court, in seven separate judgments, created a leading case on this issue. It seemed radical, but it has been argued by Galanter that it merely enlarged state power in a dangerous way and, above all, continued to treat SC/ST members as passive recipients of government largesse. It was, thus, perhaps a 'false victory' for the Scheduled Castes,[117] but in producing a decision that allowed and in fact required the state to implement protective discrimination measures to produce substantive equality, it also opened what seemed to some a 'Pandora's box'.[118]

A balance has to be struck, thus, between efficiency criteria and the constitutionally guaranteed preferential treatment for certain groups or even individuals. By allowing extra time for passing qualifying exams, the Supreme Court in this case attempts to find this balance, but some judges and commentators also criticized the lack of attention given to certain measures to improve efficiency. For example, why were the clerks not given special tuition to enable them to pass the required exams?

Generally speaking, though, this case created awareness that in this 'conceptual disaster area'[119] individuals who had once been able to benefit from preferential treatment could not necessarily expect such positive discrimination to continue. The earlier case of *Rajendran* had already established that promotion to higher ranks cannot simply be claimed by reservation.[120] In the *Thomas* case, the clearest indication of disquiet came from Mr Justice Beg, who agreed that special treatment should continue in this case, but argued:

> When citizens are already employed in a particular grade, as Government servants, considerations relating to the sources from which they are drawn lose much of their importance. As public servants of that grade they could, quite reasonably and logically, be said to belong to one class, at least for purposes of promotion in public service for which there ought to be a real 'equality of opportunity', if we are to avoid heart burning or a sense of injustice or frustration in this class. . . . Their entry into the same relevant class as others must be deemed to indicate that they no longer suffer from the handicaps of a backward class.[121]

In other words, when members of an economically and socially backward group have reached a certain level of achievement, they would have to compete in the open merit category again. This principle, as we shall see, links in with the 'creaming-off' syndrome and is likely to assume even greater relevance in the future.

Abuses of the System

Much could be written under this heading. There are a lot of interesting cases, some of them quite funny, about attempted abuses by individuals declaring themselves backward to become beneficiaries of the protective discrimination policies. This indicates the emergence in India of a vested interest in backwardness, both of individuals and of whole caste groups, which has been criticized by scholars[122] and the courts alike.[123] For example, it has been argued by Mr Justice Chinnappa Reddy that the stark reality of people competing for the claim of supreme backwardness may be unique to India, but this should not be promoted by the law.[124]

Abuses occur in several areas. Since the beneficiaries in the SC/ST categories are fixed by state by the 1950 orders and the acts of 1976 and 1987, some individuals are trying to assert that they are members of those beneficiary groups, though this is manifestly not the case. The easiest way to do this legally appeared to be through adoption into an SC/ST or backward class family.[125] But the courts have been alert and have even spotted the notable refinement of adoption practices in a number of South Indian states that have income ceilings. Thus, in *Srinivasa* a rich backward class family gave a son in adoption to a poor family of the same community. An alert high court here foiled the student's clever bid for the highly prized MBBS course, refusing to accept this adoption as genuine.[126]

The claim to backward status has also been advanced by young Indian Christians coming from communities that were formerly Scheduled Caste Hindus. Since backward Christian communities never fall under the SC/ST category (we have seen that they may be among the OBCs), reconversion to Hinduism became a quick device to take advantage of one's backwardness. In *Guntur Medical College*, a young man won a place to study medicine by the argument that a Scheduled Caste person need not be a Hindu by birth.[127] It was sufficient that he had reconverted to Hinduism, i.e., to the previous lowly Scheduled Caste position. The Supreme Court was clearly impressed by evidence that the young man had been accepted by his new community. In a similar case, however, another student failed to convince the court of community acceptance and lost his college place.[128]

That the offspring of upper-class Indians can now no longer rely on nepotism and 'connections' when it comes to getting prestigious college places may be deduced from the ridiculous case of a college principal's son, whose manipulation of 'the system' miserably collapsed in court.[129] Similarly, rich Indians from backward communities find it increasingly difficult to 'cook the books' to get round income ceilings. Few petitioners will be as foolish, though, as the young man who submitted two different applications, the first indicating that he was above the income ceiling, the second one giving figures below it.[130] He was easily found out for having learnt the law too slowly!

Frequently, cases of nepotism involving influential politicians come before the courts.[131] The Supreme Court has sought to control corruption at state government level.[132] The high court of Gujarat showed some courage in rejecting the argument that the sons and daughters of government servants should be treated as a separate class for reservation purposes.[133] The Supreme Court lambasted the brash North Indian approach to forcing one's way into college by hook or crook, knowing that it might take years for the courts to sort out the resultant mess — by which time the devious students would be so far advanced in their studies that concerns of efficiency would make it virtually impossible to terminate their admission.[134]

The various kinds of abuses show that the operation of the discrimination policies does indeed have the effect of restricting access in the open merit category to only the very best applicants, thus clearly increasing competition. This could justifiably be seen as a positive factor in terms of efficiency audit. On the other hand, the increased competition undoubtedly leads to more sophisticated attempts to circumvent the new rules of law. This, I would think, is not peculiar to India, though the magnitude of the problems, in view of the limited size of the cake, may well be seen as unique.

The Time Limit for Reservations

When the protective discrimination policies were debated soon after Independence, Ambedkar and others seem to have backed off from this important issue by appearing to give in to the claim that reservations should not be forever. Thus, as a kind of palliative to the superior classes, special protection for the SC/ST category was agreed for a specific period of time, which was initially fixed as ten years from the promulgation of the Constitution.[135] Apparently, Ambedkar would have preferred a longer period, but he accepted the consensus: 'He knew fully well that a centuries old malady cannot be cured within a decade. The ten year period was unrealistic, though it was realistic in providing for its extension at the end of the period.'[136]

In his concluding assessment of India's reservation policies, Galanter has attempted to argue that the policies will, over time, by themselves lead to a reduction of the beneficiary groups:

> Compensatory preference involves a delicate combination of self-liquidating and self-perpetuating features. Reservations of upper echelon positions should become redundant as preferential treatment at earlier stages enables more beneficiaries to compete successfully, thus decreasing the net effect of the reservations. A similar reduction of net effect is produced by the extension to others of benefits previously enjoyed on a preferential basis (e.g., free schooling). Judicial requirements of more refined and relevant selection of beneficiaries (and of periodic reassessment) and

growing use of income cut-offs provide opportunities to restrict the number of beneficiaries.[137]

I do not find the first argument convincing. Rather, one may conclude that reservation policies, once introduced, are there to stay. They may be modified, revised and streamlined, but it will be difficult, politically and otherwise, to abandon them altogether. Galanter says as much when he argues that 'the periodic necessity of renewal provides an occasion for assessment and curtailment'.[138]

Galantar also makes the point that preferential treatment 'has proved durable if not popular among politicians'.[139] Other writers have pointed out that the extension of the policies 'gets politicised and exploited by political parties'.[140]

The Indian example clearly shows that indefinite reservations and concessions are in danger of becoming vested interests over time.[141] Academic authors, too, make this point frequently.[142] Some have consistently argued that indefinite reservations will not lead to real integration.[143] But then, as already indicated, no amount and time of reservation policies will lead to absolute equality anyway. At the same time, though, it is a valid point that perpetual positive discrimination will tend to reinforce the beneficiary mentality on the one hand, and antagonism against beneficiary groups on the other. The vital element of self-respect must be considered in policy debates[144]. At the same time, it has been argued that not enough has been done yet:

> The scholarship to Harijans on a more liberal scale and representation in higher services must continue for an indefinite period till such time when a majority of them, with key posts, would be self-reliant and will be a source of inspiration to other members of their community. After the advent of freedom their progress in this direction has been satisfactory. It should be kept going.[145]

On the other hand, there is worrying evidence about cruel atrocities and increasing harassment of individuals belonging to the SC/ST categories, not even necessarily beneficiaries themselves, and also of members of castes that are claimants under the backward label.[146] Galanter is, no doubt, correct to conclude that 'the amount of preference afforded the Scheduled Castes and Tribes is widely overestimated'[147] but there can be no doubt that this widespread perception has disastrous implications for communal relations in India. Yet, the correct remedy is certainly not the abandonment of the SC/ST policies, since a major reason for the exaggerated perception of the benefits of protective discrimination for the SC/ST category seems to arise from the frightful politicking over who are the 'Other Backward Classes'.

The Indian Supreme Court has attempted to be constructive and has established several important propositions to the effect that the reservations should be carried well into the next century, but should be periodically assessed[148]. We have seen above that the Constitution (Sixty-second Amendment) Act of 1989 has recently extended the reservations policies into the twenty-first century. There is, thus, indeed no end in sight of the Indian policies of protective discrimination.

Appropriate Identification of Beneficiaries: The Scheduled Castes and Scheduled Tribes

The historical criteria for identifying the SC/ST beneficiary groups and the resultant policy of positive discrimination for the purpose of redressing a historical imbalance have already been explained above. This scheme has apparently become a fairly widely accepted aspect of India's complex discrimination policies. The result is that we have had clearly identified classes of SC/ST beneficiaries based on state since 1950, with few changes in the 1976 and 1987 Acts and the courts refusing to adjudicate on any change of membership.

The only major issue here is the so-called 'creaming-off' effect. It was, of course, far too simplistic to assume that all SC/ST members are uniformly poor, downtrodden individuals at the bottom of all hierarchies. Rather, internal social stratification within the SC/ST groups, which has always existed, but was probably not well enough understood by modern India's social engineers, has led to a remarkable (but, with the benefit of hindsight, entirely predictable) phenomenon: from among the wide range of SC/ST beneficiaries, only the more advanced and more upwardly mobile individuals, i.e., those who had some resources in the first place, would be able to avail themselves of the benefits offered. In principle, this problem is not limited to the reservation policies: rural credit facilities, for example, have often been snapped up not by the poorest of the poor farmers, for whom they were perhaps intended, but by the upper and middle layers of the farming communities.

While such an outcome was perhaps reasonable and could have been expected in the first instance, a perpetuation of such differential benefits has led, some decades later, to an unacceptable level of 'creaming-off'. The benefits of the SC/ST category are now snatched away and appropriated by a thin elite layer of SC/ST members and their offspring, while the vast majority remain as backward and disadvantaged as ever. Numerous fieldwork-based studies have shown this and there is no escape from this uncomfortable conclusion.[149]

As a result, a fine-tuning of the existing policies is urgently required. This has been recognized by the Supreme Court in the important case of *Vasanth Kumar*,[150] where Chief Justice Chandrachud established among his four brief propositions two that are relevant here:

1. The reservation in favour of scheduled castes and scheduled tribes must continue as at present . . . without the application of a means test, for a further period not exceeding fifteen years. Another fifteen years will make it fifty years after the advent of the Constitution, a period reasonably long for the upper crust of the oppressed classes to overcome the baneful effects of social oppression, isolation and humiliation.
2. The means test, that is to say, the test of economic backwardness ought to be made applicable even to the Scheduled Castes and Scheduled Tribes after the period mentioned in (1) above. It is essential that the privileged section of the under-privileged society should not be permitted to monopolise preferential benefits for an indefinite period of time.

Thus, notice is here given that the negative effects of the 'creaming-off' problem will be remedied soon. As we already noted, this shift to more fine-tuned economic criteria will lead automatically away from a pure group-rights approach to a more individual-centred ascertainment of beneficiaries.

Who Are the Other Backward Classes?

There can be no doubt that the controversy has, more recently, increasingly shifted to identifying socially and educationally backward classes of citizens.[151] This new focus is also reflected in a growing body of legal literature concerned with the OBCs.[152] We have already seen that vast numbers of Indians could qualify in this category, depending on the criteria used. There is no agreement on these criteria, though two themes are prominent in the discussion: that caste membership should not be the only criterion, but cannot be ignored, with low-caste status being probably a prerequisite for qualification; that economic criteria are very important indeed and should be given more importance to assess backwardness.[153] Chief Justice Chandrachud (as he then was), whose advice on the SC/ST policies I cited above, also made a number of important dicta concerning the Backward Classes:

In so far as the Other Backward classes are concerned, two tests should be conjunctively applied for identifying them for the purpose of reservations in employment and education: One, that they should be comparable to the Scheduled Castes and Scheduled Tribes in the matter of their backwardness; and two, that they should satisfy the means test such as a State Government may lay down in the context of prevailing economic conditions.[154]

This is eminently sensible advice. Following it would cut out poor high-caste claimants as well as rich low-caste pretenders. In essence, this seems the only feasible approach, but quite how to determine the beneficiary categories in every state is easier said than done, precisely because of local politics and power-play, as locally dominant backward classes and their supporters tend to allocate disproportionate reservation quotas to themselves. This is what has made reservations such a burning issue.

At this moment, clearly, India has not developed a nationally agreed strategy for identifying beneficiaries of the OBC categories, while the SC/ST policies have been in place for a long time. Therefore, the local power struggles to determine who are the OBCs are far from over. Considerable legal insecurity, but also the fact that so much is at stake, have continuously been reflected in a large volume of case law. It seems almost that all that could reasonably be said on the issue has been said already by the courts. This does not mean, however, that the policies work smoothly: a number of studies complain that the policies are marvellous, but their implementation is very seriously flawed in a number of ways.[155] It is too early now to assess whether the current attempts by the central Indian government to achieve better implementation and higher quotas of reservations can be realistically sustained.

CONCLUSION: THE RELEVANCE FOR BRITAIN

The historical experience of post-colonial India is, of course, quite different from that of Britain. At first sight, thus, one may be inclined to dismiss any suggestion that the Indian experience could possibly contain any useful lessons for Britain today. Indeed, this dismissive attitude is quite apparent in the British literature on discrimination, which may be inspired by some American material, but shows hardly any awareness of potential parallel developments in India, Malaysia or other non-European countries. Here, again, is an area of the law in which our Eurocentric hubris prevents us from learning from other legal systems that are quite simplistically perceived as inferior to ours or as dependent on our own guiding spirit. Marc Galanter, though, built this idea of learning from the Indian experience into his monumental study and showed that some useful lessons can indeed be learnt.[156]

I shall be arguing here that India's policies of protective discrimination over the last four decades, with separate provisions for different kinds of beneficiaries, offer very useful lessons for the development and monitoring of such policies anywhere in the world. In view of the fact that there is now some pressure in Britain to institutionalize ethnic monitoring and to use positive action programmes of various kinds to improve the position of certain disadvantaged groups in society, India's experience is bound to be of considerable relevance.

Of course, the resource restraints operating in modern India make the identification of beneficiaries from among more than 850 million people a major issue. But any country seeking to institute a positive discrimination policy is bound to face resource implications, especially if part of the scheme involves the educational uplifting of a substantial section of the population. In this regard, Britain with its resource-restrained and cash-starved education system looks distinctly like a Third World country and would face problems similar to India's.

In India, we have seen the need to distinguish SC/ST and OBC policies and strategies. There are clearly several similarities between the two kinds of policy and their impact, especially the detrimental 'creaming-off effect', with the resulting call for income ceilings and other economic criteria to be applied in either case. India is, in my view, painfully learning at the moment that reservations for a clearly defined, fairly limited number of potential beneficiaries are manageable with greater ease than a spray-can system of giving some form of preferential treatment to a large number of groups of people. In India's situation, it is clearly impossible to help all claimants of backward status unless one has very strict definitions of 'backwardness'. The Indian policies on the OBC categories have clearly moved into troubled water, promising too much to too many people, raising expectations in the process which, if not fulfilled, turn dreams of benefits into nightmares of communal riots. Such violent disturbances, now reported almost daily, may appear to be motivated by religious and communal fanaticism, but are more often simply over access to scarce resources in the context of reservation policies. The Indian state here, as in the similarly explosive context of the Uniform Civil Code, may be seen as responsible for these riots by pitting communities against each other in the struggles for maximum benefits from the reservation policies.

I have already indicated that I can see little chance for Britain to institute Indian-style reservation programmes from the top down. There are several reasons for this. First, we do not have a written constitution with an entrenched bill of rights, in which such provisions have been centrally enshrined in India. There is, of course, no guarantee that central state provisions of this kind would necessarily lead to an active policy of reducing inequalities. But as a result of the present set-up in Britain, the English courts are probably prevented from taking an active stance, quite unlike the Indian courts. On the other hand, the example of the Race Relations Act 1976 and the CRE's persistent involvement in attempts to curtail the various rampant forms of discrimination in Britain show that some progress can, indeed, be made.

Second, and probably this is just as important, there is no national policy, and certainly no national consensus in Britain about the extent of protective discrimination policies needed in this country. In India, at least, the need to assist the SC/ST claimants seems an agreed agenda item. In Britain, however, the myth of an egalitarian society based on the principles of equality, fairness and merit seems so pervasive that an attitude of complacency, if not indignation at the suggestion that not all may be as fair as claimed, seems quite dominant. There is no central recognition of the fact that noticeable inequalities have existed for a long time. There is clearly no national strategy for positive action programmes of the Indian kind. This is not because we don't need them — we are also told that we don't want them. As a result, differences in the approach to social welfare issues have long been portrayed as party political issues, and there is some evidence that this may indeed be the case. Thus, positive action programmes tend to be associated with a particular political party, which then claims to speak for the beneficiaries of those programmes. All this is very familiar from the Indian scene today.

Given that there is a largely negative attitude at central government level, it becomes even more significant here that Britain has a large variety of opinion in favour of positive action programmes at local government level. This has already resulted in a most remarkable fragmentation of legal policies, so that whether you are a 'black' person in Leicester or Bradford, or in Norwich or Worcester, may make a huge difference in terms of many facts of daily life.

Like in India, these local policies are, of course, open to power-play, and the party politics angle looms large. How else are we to explain that Ealing Council, for example, has recently announced plans, and has already implemented others, to shelve a considerable number of positive action programmes, arguing that these programmes were designed to buy votes for the other party. That very party, on the other hand, feels by some strange logic entitled to the benefit of the 'ethnic vote'. The real concerns that should perhaps be overriding all these vote-catching strategies appear, thus, only of secondary importance.

In Britain today, it needs to be ascertained first whether one *wants* a policy of historical reparation for all 'blacks', as a kind of compensation for centuries-long, clearly continuing inequities and injustices. If the answer to this question is an outraged negative, as it may well be, this is not the end of the positive discrimination issue, however. For is it not true that many local councils in Britain and other local bodies already operate similar policies? They will rather be phrased in terms of 'equal opportunities', but what else is this than saying that some people should now be given 'more equal' treatment to compensate for past or present discrimination?

A major problem with the various haphazard British policies of positive action seems to be that they focus on group characteristics like 'race' and, more recently, 'ethnic group'. This is going to lead to a number of difficult policy dilemmas, very similar to those faced by India in the context of 'caste'. Quite apart from the problem of how one measures 'race', or defines 'ethnic group' (the latter issue already having occupied our courts with most intriguing questions,[157] the 'creaming-off effect' will be just as much in evidence in Britain as in India the moment we have ethnic quotas in Britain. I have been criticized for implying that such quotas already exist. I think they do, though I also appreciate that this would be against the law as we think it is. Quotas exist, for example, as agenda items in monitoring exercises at local council level, and it is precisely there that the 'creaming-off' effects are already visible.

In other words, an obvious lack of central policy, and thus also lack of guidance, on this issue in Britain leads to a dilemma for policy-makers committed to working towards real equal opportunities. Perhaps one cannot always afford to be totally honest about what one is doing, which makes the development of adequate policies an even more difficult issue. It has been argued that we should talk about margins rather than quotas, but what difference does this make in reality?

As in India, moves towards various forms of positive action programme have also raised apprehensions in Britain that potential or actual claimants or beneficiaries are being given undue favours and that individuals or whole groups may feel inferior as a result of being singled out for preferential or simply different treatment. But such objections come, it appears, from the privileged majority. From a minority perspective, so I have been told on several occasions, if you know that you are being treated differently anyway because of the colour of your skin or some other reason, it could be a rather positive feeling to know that you are being given some form of compensatory treatment. In fact, we should become aware of the fact that many young 'black' people in Britain are actually demanding differential treatment, almost as of right.

Within the wider strategic considerations of anti-discrimination policies, one cannot, of course, entirely dismiss the possibility that recognition of differences and steps to decrease them may actually perpetuate and increase such divisions rather than create greater equality. You cannot have a multi-cultural society and then insist on uniform standards in all spheres of life. The attempted division into spheres of public and private life does not, in my view, get us out of this dilemma. Thus my argument is that in Britain, too, we are never going to see a truly egalitarian society, rather a different mix of diversity[158].

In the Indian context, there is much continued objection to the application of caste criteria. There must, then, be many doubts whether British policies of differential treatment purely on racial or 'ethnic' lines are appropriate and will work satisfactorily. This is so especially since 'black people' are so internally divided and many Asians, in particular, do not want to be seen as 'black'. It is, thus, rather certain that positive discrimination programmes and policies on the basis of colour alone will not be manageable, nor will they be widely acceptable. Worst of all, their benefits may go to those who do not really need special treatment.

Such problems of operation, however, do not get the issue itself off the agenda. For rather than taking racial or ethnic criteria, it may be possible to identify beneficiaries on the basis of social class and economic indicators. An approach in Britain today that stereotypes all 'blacks' as trapped in the lower classes[159] is just as manisfestly stupid and short-sighted as the Indian post-colonial idea that all SC/ST members must be uniformly poor, backward and downtrodden. The considerable internal differentiations among Asians in Britain, for example, have rightly been emphasized in recent socio-legal literature.[160] Within the wide variety of ethnic minority groups in Britain today, thus, we have millionaires as well as vagrants; to treat them all together as one potential beneficiary group for protective discrimination seems utterly absurd. We already have evidence that Asians are beginning to dominate the British retail trade, that certain groups of Asian children are doing better in schools than even white children, so policies that would identify all Asians, for example, as potential beneficiaries, are not only superfluous, they would be extremely dangerous for community relations, as the Indian example clearly shows, too.

But since discrimination at all levels and in a variety of ways continues in Britain, it could not be argued that there is no need for any action. Whether anti-discrimination laws in themselves are enough, though, may be doubted. There is no guarantee, for example, that a brilliant ethnic minority school leaver, once she or he has successfully negotiated the hurdles of a school system that traditionally allocates low expectations to 'black' children, will not find some hurdles at recruitment level for further education or the right kind of job. The apparent trend of some ethnic minority parents to push their children to academic success and through higher education, as an indicator of achievement, skills and status alike, seems also motivated by acute awareness of discrimination.

Certain anti-discrimination measures are therefore needed, rather than quota allocations on a group basis, and here India could probably learn from Britain. For the complaints about the ineffectiveness of the Indian reservation programmes are to a certain extent based on the fact that India does not have an effective anti-discrimination law, despite its apparently powerful foothold in the fundamental rights provisions. It is no accident, I think, that the current movement in Britain towards more effective ethnic monitoring, which has already uncovered scores of institutional discriminatory practices, is becoming so strong and powerful. If it could be ensured that 'creaming-off' effects do not become too strong in Britain, such positive action programmes may yet prove very effective.

In other words, what I am saying is that it is better to have action programmes that focus on deserving individuals rather than whole groups of beneficiaries. This will enable more focused action and yet, at the same time, avoid the stigma of racial quotas. For example, a grant system that helps all poor students, irrespective of ethnic status, would seem to be an appropriate mechanism to improve access to further education for all gifted and promising youngsters. Of course, current central government policies are certainly not developing in that direction.

In conclusion, while current British experience shows that certain forms of positive discrimination are already in operation locally, the present Indian models of group reservation for certain classes of people do not commend themselves for Britain. They would inevitably deteriorate into a system of communal quotas, which I see as extremely dangerous and damaging for community relations in the long run. It would inescapably create an atmospehre of 'white backlash', comparable to the upper-caste in India; to an extent we have this in Britain already, in various forms that are probably masked as racial attacks.

The efficiency argument is also of some relevance here. Any relaxations specifically for certain ethnic groups will breed resentment. Significantly, the British debate on this issue is fundamentally misguided and seems unaware of basic facts: Britain should not so much debate relaxations in terms of lower educational standards, which lead to the familiar allegation of 'them' getting away with sub-standard qualifications: 'they' have now often got better and higher qualifications, but still face discrimination, whether they are lawyers or factory workers. Thus, in Britain today, one needs to reconsider many customary, but now quite discriminatory practices and merit criteria. A case in point may be the minimum height requirements for police recruits, which have already been lowered.

One of the sorest issues must be the non-recognition of overseas qualifications, which has received less publicity and also less consideration than the question of height requirements for police officers. Britain has now started inviting overseas teachers, even from Bangladesh, while well-qualified potential applicants in Britain have for a long time been discouraged from a teaching career. Also, proficiency in English as a prerequisite for certain jobs may not always be appropriate. Conversely, proficiency in one or more Asian languages may be rather essential, as in the recent case of the white Birmingham home liaison officer whose appointment was challenged, *inter alia*, on the grounds that she would not be able to work effectively with Asian parents since she knew only English. Britain has changed in the recent past, and the nature of those changes, though not nationally recognized, is often locally quite remarkable and unmistakeable. This has many implications for equal opportunities programmes that we are yet to understand fully.

The experience of India contains a number of important warnings for responsible policy-makers in this country. It is not too late to avoid some of the pitfalls of over-ambitious social engineering, but the Indian model will also strengthen the confidence of those that have doubts whether Britain really needs any equal opportunities or positive action programmes. It has recently been argued that we have no choice but to accept today that Britain is a culturally and socially plural society.[161] In our present context, the real question in Britain today, I submit, is no longer whether to develop certain reservation policies, but rather how to make them as effective as possible. In this respect, the rich Indian experience can certainly contribute to our development today.

NOTES

1. See Commission for Racial Equality *Racial Justice in Magistrates Courts: The Case for Training* (London, CRE, 1989) p. 7.

2. Galanter. M.: *Competing Equalities: Law and the Backward Classes in India* (Berkeley, University of California Press, 1984).

3. This term was introduced in Chiba, M. (ed.) *Asian Indigenous Law in Interaction with Received Law* (London and New York, KPI 1986) pp. 6-7.

4. See, for example, Kamble, J. R. *Rise and Awakening of Depressed Classes in India* (New Delhi, National, 1979) pp. 5-6.

5. On this see in detail Galanter, M. *Law and Society in Modern India* (Oxford, OUP, 1989).

6. See, for example, Beteile, A. (ed.) *Equality and Inequality: Theory and Practice* (Delhi, OUP, 1983) pp. 17-18).

7. Ibid.; p. 18.

8. See, for example, Jhingran, S. *Aspects of Hindu Morality* (Delhi, Motilal Banarsidass, 1989) p. IX.

9. Ibid. at VII.

10. On this see generally Allott, A. N. *The Limits of Law* (London, Butterworths, 1980).

11. Beteile op. cit. (note 6) p. 32.

12. For details of this approach see ibid.; also Sharma, B. A. V. and Reddy, K. Madhusudhan (eds) *Reservation Policy in India* (New Delhi, Light & Life, 1982) especially the essay by Sharma, Development of reservation policy'.

13. See especially Kamble op. cit. (note 4); Sharma and Reddy op. cit. (note 12); Galanter op. cit. (note 2) pp. 18-40 with further references.

14. They have been analysed in detail by Saksena, H. S. *Safeguards for Scheduled Castes and Tribes: Founding Fathers' View* (New Delhi, Uppal, 1981).

15. Galanter, op. cit. (note 2) p. 37.

16. See e.g. Vatuk, V. P. in Berreman, G. D. (ed.) *Caste and Other Inequalities: Essays on Inequality* (Meerut, Folklore Institute, 1979) p. vii.

17. See ibid. at 1.

18. Galanter op. cit. (note 2) p. 19 correctly emphasizes this, as did Derrett, J. D. M. *Religion, Law and the State in India* (London, Faber, 1968) with considerable force.

19. This is done not only by experts on religion (see Jhingran op. cit. (note 8)) persistently overstating the role of the textual sources as legal authorities, but even by lawyers. The worst recent example is Funk, D. A. 'Traditional orthodox Hindu jurisprudence: justifying dharma and danda' (1988) 15 (2) *Southern University Law Review* 169. Even modern Indian socio-legal scholars (see Kamble op. cit. (note 4) pp. 4, 5, 6 and elsewhere) are unable to resist the temptation of portraying 'law-givers' like Manu, the merely mythical author of a major Indian *dharma* text, which is by no accounts a code of law! Even Scharfe, H. *The State in Indian Tradition* (Leiden, E. J. Brill, 1989) seems unsure about the place of law.

20. Ram, J. *Caste Challenge in India* (New Delhi, Vision Books, 1980) p. 35.

21. See even in 1989 Commission for Racial Equality op. cit. (note 1) p. 7.

22. See in detail Mahar, J. M. (ed.) *The Untouchables in Contemporary India* (Tucson, University of Arizona Press, 1972); Fuchs, S. *At the Bottom of Indian Society* (New Delhi, Munshiram Manoharlal, 1981); Ghurye, G. S. *The Scheduled Tribes of India* (New Brunswick and London, Transaction Books, 1980).

23. Rajasekhariah, A. M. 'Dr B. R. Ambedkar on reservation policy' in Sharma and Reddy op. cit. (note 12) pp. 23-35.

24. Ram op. cit. (note 20) p. 60.

25. Rajasekhariah op. cit. (note 23) pp. 24-25.

26. Ibid. at 31.

27. Allott op. cit. (note 10) p. 216.

28. Ram op. cit. (note 20).

29. Ibid. at 59-60.

30. Ibid. at 60.

31. Ibid. at 49.

32. Ibid. at 17.

33. Ibid. at 61.

34. Ibid. at 62.

35. Id.

36. Dhagamwar, V. *Towards the Uniform Civil Code* (Bombay, N. M. Tripathi Pvt. Ltd, 1989) p. 71.

37. Ram op. cit. (note 20) p. 63.

38. Dahrendorf, R. 'On the origin of inequality among men' in Beteille, A. (ed.) *Social Inequality* (Harmondsworth, Penguin, 1969) pp. 16–44.

39. Ram op. cit. (note 20) p. 65.

40. Ibid. at 66.

41. Id.

42. Ibid. at 66–67.

43. See, for example, Malik, S. *Social Integration of Scheduled Castes* (New Delhi, Abhinav, 1979); D'Souza, V. S. *Educational Inequalities among Scheduled Castes: a Case Study in the Punjab* (Chandigarh, Panjab University Press, 1980); Ghosh, S. K. *Protection of Minorities and Scheduled Castes* (New Delhi, Ashish, 1980).

44. Ram op. cit. (note 20) pp. 74, 80, 87, 112, 117.

45. Ibid. at 118.

46. Ibid. at 88.

47. Ibid at 96–97; Galanter op. cit. (note 2) p. 40; see in detail Kamble, N. D. *Atrocities on Scheduled Castes in Post-Independent India* (New Delhi, Ashish, 1981).

48. Verma, G. P. *Caste Reservation in India: Law and the Constitution* (Allahabad, Chugh Publications, 1980) p. 2.

49. Ram op. cit. (note 20) p. 49; Nehru, B. K. 'The politics of reservation' (15 October 1986) *India Today* p. 30.

50. See Jadhav, K. R. 'Dr. Lohia on reservation policy' in Sharma and Reddy op. cit. (note 12) pp. 36–42.

51. Galanter op. cit. (note 2) p. 40.

52. Khan, M. A. *Scheduled Castes and Their Status in India* (New Delhi, Uppal, 1980) p. 1.

53. Sivaramayya, B. 'Equality and inequality: the legal framework' in Beteille op. cit. (note 6) pp. 28–70 at 34.

54. Ibid. at 39–40.

55. Ram op. cit. (note 20) p. 68.

56. See Jadhav op. cit. (note 50) pp. 38–40.

57. Shah, G. 'Protective discrimination, equality and political will' in Shah, V. P. and Agrawal, B. C. (eds) *Reservation: Policy, Programmes and Issues* (Jaipur, Rawat, 1986) pp. 1–12 at 2.

58. Arora, K. K. 'Backwardness in India — a judicial dilemma' in Saraf, D. N. (ed.) *Social Policy, Law and Protection of Weaker Sections of Society* (Lucknow, Eastern Book Company, 1986) pp. 80–90 at 82.

59. Saksena op. cit. (note 14) p. vii.

60. Ibid at xv.

61. Arora op. cit. (note 58) pp. 82–83.

62. Saksena op. cit. (note 14) p. vii.

63. Beteille, A. *The Backward Classes and the New Social Order* (Delhi, OUP, 1981) p. 8.

64. On Ambedkar see Galanter op. cit. (note 2) pp. 39–40.

65. Saksena op. cit. (note 14) pp. xiii–xv.

66. See Arora op. cit. (note 58) p. 83.

67. Id.

68. See Galanter op. cit. (note 2) p. 563.

69. Ibid. at 567.

70. Galanter's pioneering study of 1984 op. cit. (note 2) p. 546) appears to remain unaware of the scope for public interest litigation or social action litigation in this field.

71. See, for example, Erabbi, B. 'Protective discrimination: constitutional prescription and judicial perception' in Saraf op. cit. (note 58) pp. 133–153 at 135.

72. For details see, for example, Mahar op. cit. (note 22) and Borale, P. T. 'Problem of untouchability and former untouchables' in Saraf op. cit. (note 58) pp. 154–168.

73. Ibid. at 159.

74. Kelly, J. 'Apart, and hated?' *The Times* (6 June 1990).

75. Shalla, T. N. 'Dynamics of reservation policy under Indian Constitution: a working paper' in Saraf op. cit. (note 58) pp. 99–132 at 132, n. 82.

76. See, for example, Arora op. cit. (note 58) p. 97.

77. Ibid. at 82–83.

78. Ibid. at 84.

79. Ibid. at 85.

80. For details see ibid. at 86–87.

81. Ibid. at 87.

82. Ibid. at 82.

83. Ibid. at 85.

84. *Balaji* v *State of Mysore* 84 AIR 1963 SC 469.

85. *Janaki Prasad Parimoo* v *State of Jammu and Kashmir* [1973] SC 930.

86. *State of Madras* v *Champakam Dorairajan* AIR 1951 SC 226.

87. *K. C. Vasanth Kumar* v *State of Karnataka* AIR 1985 SC 1495.

88. See, for example, Jariwala, C. M. 'State interference in medical education through compensatory discrimination: *Amalendu Kumar* v *State* AIR 1981 57–60.

89. See Verma op. cit. (note 48) pp. 12–13.

90. This would be rather like the re-emergence of the guilt factor in matrimonial litigation in England as soon as 'irretrievable breakdown' had been made the 'sole' ground for divorce.

91. Arora op. cit. (note 58) p. 88.

92. Op. cit. (note 84).

93. Ibid. at 651.

94. Prominently perhaps in Gujarat initially, on which see Shah, G. *Caste Association and Political Process in Gujarat: A Study of Gujarat Kshatriya Sabha* (Bombay, Popular Prakashan, 1975); Sheth, P. and Menon, R. *Caste and Communal Time Bomb* (Ahmedabad, Golwala, 1986).

95. Op. cit. (note 86).

96. *Venkataramana* v *State of Madras* AIR 1951 SC 229.

97. See, for example, Galanter op. cit. (note 2) pp. 165–66.

98. Ibid. at 167.

99. Op. cit. (note 84).

100. Id.

101. See in detail Galanter op. cit. (note 2) pp. 396–420.

102. Ibid. at 400–1.

103. Ibid. at 399.

104. *Triloki Nath Tiku* v *State of Jammu and Kashmir* AIR 1969 SC 1.

105. Galanter op. cit. (note 2) p. 549 clearly indicates this.

106. Ibid. at 401.

107. Op. cit. (note 84).

108. See Jariwala op. cit. (note 88); Ramchander, M. 'Elite attitudes' in Sharma and Reddy op. cit. (note 12); Singh, P. 'Reservations, reality and the Constitution: reflections on the current crises in India' in Menski, W. F. and Conrad, D. (eds) *Government Policy, Law and Society in India* (London, SOAS Centre of South Asian Studies, forthcoming).

109. Galanter op. cit. (note 2) pp. 550–51.

110. Ibid. at 81–82, 106–7.

111. Ibid. at 547.

112. Ibid. at 550–1.

113. Op. cit. (note 87) pp. 1508–9.

114. See, for example, *Dr Anand Kumar Mishra* v *State of Bihar* AIR 1981 Pat 164.

115. *The Independent* (30 June 1990).

116. *State of Kerala* v *N. M. Thomas* AIR 1976 SC 490.

117. Galanter op. cit. (note 2) p. 391.

118. Ibid. at 393.

119. So Mr Justice Krishna Iyer at p. 527 of the case.

120. *C. A. Rajendran* v *Union of India* AIR 1968 SC 507.

121. Op. cit. (note 116) pp. 521–22.

122. See, for example, Shalla op. cit. (note 75) p. 132.

123. For example in *Vasanth Kumar* op. cit. (note 87).

124. Ibid. at 1507.

125. Singh, P. 'Preventing exploitative acquisition of reservation benefits through adoption strategem' *Journal of the Indian Law Institute* (1987) 29 (1) 100–9.

126. *R. Srinivasa* v *The Chairman, Selection Committee* AIR 1981 Kant 86.

127. *Guntur Medical College* v *Mohan Rao* AIR 1976 SC 1904.

128. *J. Das* v *State of Kerala* AIR 1981 Ker 164.

129. *Atul Kumar Singh* v *State of Uttar Pradesh* AIR 1983 All 281.

130. *C. P. Sagar* v *The Chairman, Selection Committee* AIR 1983 Kant 199.

131. *Rahul Verma* v *Himachal Pradesh University* AIR 1983 HP 53; *Savita* v *State of Haryana* AIR 1983 P&H 262.

132. See, for example, *Suman Gupta* v *State of Jammu and Kashmir* AIR 1983 SC 1235.

133. *Patel Rajesh Motibhai* v *State of Gujarat* [1981] Guj 30.

134. *Punjab Engineering College, Chandigarh* v *Sanjay Gulati* [1983] SC 580.

135. Rajasekhariah op. cit. (note 23) p. 32. We already saw that this has now been extended to 50 years.

136. Id.

137. Galanter op. cit (note 2) p. 550.

138. Ibid. at 550.

139. Ibid. at 77.

140. Rajasekhariah op. cit. (note 23) p. 32; similarly Nehru op. cit. (note 49).

141. See, for example, *Vasanth Kumar* op. cit. (note 87) p. 1507.

142. See, for example, Gupta, S. S. *Preferential Treatment in Public Employment and Equality of Opportunity* (Lucknow, Eastern Book Company, 1979) pp. 83–84.

143. See Rajasekhariah op. cit. (note 23) p. 33 and especially Galanter op. cit. (note 2).

144. See Zelliot, E. 'Gandhi and Ambedkar — a study in leadership' in Mahar op. cit. (note 22) pp. 69–95 at 94.

145. Kamble op. cit. (note 4) p. 281.

146. For details see Kamble op.cit. (note 47); Ram op. cit. (note 20) pp. 96–97.

147. Galanter op. cit. (note 2) p. 560.

148. In *Vasanth Kumar* op. cit. (note 87) p. 1499, *per* Chief Justice Chandrachud.

149. For example Malik op. cit. (note 43); Parvathamma, C. and Satyanarayana *New Horizons and Scheduled Castes* (New Delhi, Ashish, 1984); Khan op. cit. (note 52).

150. Op. cit. (note 87) p. 1499.

151. See the comments of Mr Justice D. A. Desai ibid at 1503.

152. See especially Singh, P. 'Equal opportunity and compensatory discrimination: constitutional policies and judicial control' *Journal of the Indian Law Institute* (1976) 18 (2) 300–19; Singh, P. 'Some reflections on Indian experience with the policy of reservations (1983) 25 (1) *Journal of the Indian Law Institute* 46–72; Dutt, N. N. 'Need for review of the criteria for determining "Backward Classes"' AIR 1987 J 101–5.

153. See *Sagar* v *State of Andhra Pradesh* AIR 1968 AP 165.

154. *Vasanth Kumar* op. cit. (note 87) p. 1499.

155. Malik op. cit. (note 43) pp. 172–73.

156. Galanter op. cit. (note 2).

157. See especially *Mandla* v *Dowell-Lee* [1983] 1 All ER 1062.

158. See to the same effect Lynch, J. 'Cultural pluralism, structural pluralism and the United Kingdom' in *Britain: A Plural Society: Report of a Seminar* (London, CRE, 1990) pp. 29–43.

159. For an example, see above n. 21. On America see Ringer, B. B. and Lawless E. R. *Race-Ethnicity and Society* (New York and London, Routledge, 1989).

160. See, for example, Pearl, D. *Family Law and the Immigrant Communities* (Bristol, Jordan & Sons, 1986).

161. Lynch op. cit. (note 158) p. 29.

18

Positive Discrimination in Malaysia: A Cautionary Tale for the United Kingdom

Edward Phillips

HISTORICAL AND DEMOGRAPHIC BACKGROUND

Malaysia is a multi-racial, multi-cultural, multi-religious and multi-lingual society.[1] As a reflection of this diversity, three components have historically acted in partnership to create modern Malaysia: the British colonial administration, the Malay aristocratic and bureaucratic elite and the non-Malay business and labour sectors. These three components have produced the, by no means unique, tensions which exist today in modern Malaysian society. They also explain the existence of the constitutionally entrenched provisions on positive discrimination.[2] To a large extent, they also explain the reasons why these provisions have failed to achieve what they were intended to accomplish. Ironically, the attempt to create a more egalitarian society through this means has resulted in a society which, quite apart from the view of external commentators, perceives itself to be fragmented along racial lines.

The fact that Malaysia is a plural society is nothing extraordinary; modern Britain is itself a plural society.[3] What is unusual is that Malaysia, at the time of independence in 1957, was a plural society of minority communities, where no one racial group constituted an absolute majority.

Ethnic Composition of Malaya/Malaysia

Year	Malays	Chinese	Indians
1957	49.8%	37.2%	11.3%
1970	46.8%	34.3%	8.9%
1986	53.9%	33.6%	9.6%

As the figures indicate, there has been an increase in the Malay population, although this does still not represent a significant majority. In any event, the figures ignore the fact that the term 'Malay' is itself an inclusive grouping.

The traditional analysis of Malaysian society has been that the Malays control political power while the non-Malays, particularly the Chinese, wield economic power. There is some argument regarding the accuracy of this analysis but there is no doubt that at the time of independence, the Malays were substantially more economically disadvantaged than their non-Malay counterparts. The Chinese and Indians had contributed to, and were beneficiaries of, a prosperous colonial economy. They were concentrated in the urban and more developed parts of the country and had enjoyed a measure of control over trade, commerce and finance. They were, therefore, well placed to take maximum advantage of the period of sustained growth both before and after independence.

In contrast, the Malays, as much through mistaken colonial policy as by choice, were left on the land. Only a small stratum, drawn exclusively from the ranks of the feudal and aristocratic elite, were recruited into the lower grades of the civil service. More often than not, this was regarded as a token conciliatory gesture. Before and after 1957, the Civil Service was in fact the principal avenue of social and economic advancement for the Malays. This avenue was, however, open only to a few. The vast majority of the Malays continued to live in the rural areas. While the Chinese and Indians were actively participating in a capitalist economy and being subjected to the modernizing influences which flowed from abroad, the Malays were engaged in a subsistence economy and otherwise restricted to the traditional and feudalistic constraints of a rural and agricultural existence.

CONSTITUTIONAL DEVELOPMENT

When the 1957 Federation Constitution was in the process of being drafted, there was a recognition of the backward position of the Malays. The terms of reference of the Constitutional Commission included a reference that provision should be made to provide for the 'special' position of the Malays. In actual fact, the Constitutional Commission found that in at least four areas the Malays were already receiving preferential treatment as a result of colonial policy.

(1) In most of the States there are extensive Malay reservations of
    land and the system of reserving land for Malays has been in
    operation for many years. . . .
(2) There are now in operation quotas for admission to the public
    services. . . . In services in which a quota exists the rule
    generally is that not more than one quarter of new entrants
    should be non-Malays. . . .
(3) There are now also in operation quotas in respect of permits
    or licences for the operation of certain businesses. . . .
(4) In many classes of scholarships, bursaries and other forms of
    aid for educational purposes preference is given to Malays. The
    reason for this appears to be that in the past higher education
    of the Malays has tended to fall behind that of the Chinese,
    partly because the Chinese have been better able to pay for
    it and partly because it is more difficult to arrange higher
    education for Malays in the country than for Chinese in the
    towns.[4]

What is interesting about the findings of the Constitutional Commission is its account of the existence of positive discrimination. The
popular view among Malaysians of all races that positive discrimination
was introduced after independence by the ruling Malay class is therefore
false. Positive discrimination was in fact a major plank of colonial
policy. It also provides an illustration of a situation where positive
discrimination was being utilized to compensate for lack of development
rather than being used to remedy past discrimination.

As far as the attitude of non-Malays was concerned, the Commission
reported:

> We found little opposition in any quarter to the continuance of
> the present system for a time, but there was great opposition in
> some quarters to any increase of the present preferences and to
> their being continued for any prolonged period.[5]

The Commission then went on to make the following recommendations:

> We are of the opinion that in the present circumstances it is
> necessary to continue these preferences. The Malays would be at
> a serious disadvantage compared with other communities if they
> were suddenly withdrawn. But with the integration of the various
> communities into a common nationality which we trust will
> gradually come about, the need for these preferences will gradually
> disappear. Our recommendations are made on the footing that
> the Malays should be assured that the present position will con-

tinue for a substantial period, but that in due course the present preferences should be reduced and should ultimately cease so that there should be no discrimination between races and communities.[6]

CONSTITUTIONAL PROVISIONS

The results of the Constitutional Commission's recommendations, modelled on the protective discrimination provisions of the Indian Constitution,[7] are to be found in the Federal Constitution.

Article 153
(1) It shall be the responsibility of the [King] to safeguard the special position of the Malays and natives of any of the States of Sabah and Sarawak and the legitimate interests of other communities in accordance with the provisions of this Article.
(2) Notwithstanding anything in this Constitution . . . the [King] shall exercise his functions . . . in such manner as may be necessary to safeguard the special positions of the Malays and natives of any of the States of Sabah and Sarawak and to ensure the reservation for Malays and natives . . . of such proportion as he may deem reasonable of positions in the public service . . . and of scholarships, exhibitions and other similar educational or training privileges or special facilities given or accorded by the Federal Government and, when any permit or licence for the operation of any trade or business is required by federal law, then, subject to the provisions of that law and this Article, of such permits and licences. . . .
(8) Notwithstanding anything in this Constitution, where by any federal law any permit or licence is required for the operation of any trade or business, the law may provide for the reservation of a proportion of such permits or licences for Malays and natives of any of the States of Sabah and Sarawak: but no such law shall for the purpose of ensuring such a reservation —
  (a) deprive or authorise the deprivation of any person of any right, privilege, permit or licence accrued to or enjoyed or held by him; or
  (b) authorise a refusal to renew to any person any such permit or licence or a refusal to grant to the heirs, successors or assigns or any person any permit or licence when the renewal or grant might in accordance with the other provisions of the law reasonably be expected in the ordinary course of events, or prevent any person from transferring

together with his business any transferable licence to operate
that business; or

(c) where no permit or licence was previously required for the
operation of the trade or business, authorise a refusal to grant
a permit or licence to any person for the operation of any
trade or business which immediately before the coming into
force of the law he had been *bona fide* carrying on, or authorise
a refusal subsequently to renew to any such person any permit or licence, or a refusal to grant to the heirs, successors
or assigns of any such person any such permit or licence
when the renewal or grant might in accordance with the
other provisions of that law reasonably be expected in the
ordinary course of events.

(8A) Notwithstanding anything in this Constitution, where in
any University, College and other educational institution
. . . the number of places offered by the authority responsible
for the management of the University, College or other
educational institution to candidates qualified for such
places, it shall be lawful for the [King] by virtue of this Article
to give such directions to the authority as may be required to
ensure the reservation of such proportion of such places for
Malays and natives of any of the States of Sabah and Sarawak
as the [King] may deem reasonable. . . .

Two points may be noted at this stage. First, an attempt was made
to ensure that the legitimate interests of the non-Malays received some
protection, especially in the light of the right to equality provisions in
Article 8 of the Constitution.[8] Second, the original recommendation of
the Constitutional Commission was that the 'special rights' provisions
of Article 153 would remain in place for a period of fifteen years from
the date of independence. In other words, they would have been
repealed in 1972. However, this was not to be. The course of events,
in particular, the race riots of 1969, led to the removal of the fifteen-year
time limit and Article 153 is now a permanent feature of the
Constitution.

The question which must be asked is why did the non-Malays accept
the introduction of Article 153? A number of reasons have been put
forward. First, of course, was the assurance that this was not to be a
permanent feature of the Constitution. Second was the fact that the
Draft Constitution was introduced by the colonial authorities as a
'package' without any possibility of negotiation on individual points.
Third, and more important, the non-Malays were offered a *quid pro quo*.
This took the form of an informal 'bargain' among the three main

political parties. These were the United Malay National Organisation (UMNO), the Malayan Chinese Association (MCA) and the Malayan Indian Congress (MIC). As their names imply, these parties were communal in nature but their leaders realized that the British, learning from their experiences elsewhere in the Empire, were not about to turn political control over to one ethnic group.

By 1954, these three parties had united under the common banner of an umbrella organization called the Alliance (the predecessor of the present-day *Barisan Nasional* or National Front), although they retained their independent structures. The leaders of these three parties agreed that the Malays, as the indigenous race, should be recognized as *primus inter pares* and should assume major political control. In return, the non-Malays were promised that there would be no interference in their economic pursuits. In return for acceptance of Malay special rights, the non-Malays would be granted favourable revisions in citizenship regulations including the granting of *jus soli* (automatic citizenship by right of birth) in the Federation after independence. The UMNO, MCA and MIC succeeded in 'selling' the bargain to their respective communities as the best deal possible in the circumstances. In the elections to the colonial Legislative Assembly held a year before independence, the coalition made up of these parties demonstrated the extent of their success when the Alliance won 51 out of the 52 available seats.

The existence of the bargain among the main parties representing the Malays, Chinese and Indians is often conveniently forgotten by all sides in modern Malaysia. This is especially true of the non-Malays, who prefer to espouse the view that the special position of the Malays has been forced upon them since independence, ignoring the fact that this was decided through negotiation and with consent.

RESTRUCTURING OF THE ECONOMY AND THE NEW ECONOMIC POLICY

The period between 1957 and 1969 was a volatile one. As far as the constitutional structure of the Federation was concerned, the period saw the formation of the new Federation of Malaysia and the subsequent withdrawal of Singapore within two years. There was the external threat from Indonesia (the so-called Confrontation period) and the internal threat from the communist insurgency (the Emergency). It was also a time when the advocates of moderation were in retreat. The entire period was characterized by a heightened sense of ethnic militancy. This manifested itself, on the one hand, by calls from the non-Malays for the ending of positive discrimination in favour of the Malays, and on the other hand by demands from the Malays that much more needed to be done to remedy their disadvantages. There was some substance to this claim. This was a period of growth in the economy. For instance, the GNP had risen from $9,652 million in 1967 to $12,155 million by 1970.[9] Yet there was no tangible evidence of economic improvement among the Malays.

Attacked by ethnic radicals on every side, the governing moderates found compromise difficult. One example may be cited. 1967, ten years after independence, was the date set for the Malay language (Bahasa Malaysia) to become the country's sole official language. Malay radicals lobbied for there to be no compromise whatsoever on this issue while Chinese groups, who viewed the introduction of the Malay language as another manifestation of positive discrimination, pressured the government to either make Chinese an official language also, or failing that, to make major concessions. The Malay radicals countered that if the non-Malays were not going to readily and fully accept the status of the Malay language and of their own 'special' position, then there ought to be a review of the citizenship provisions granted to non-Malays. Some compromise on the language issue was made by the government; Malay was made the official language, but the continued use of English for some official purposes was allowed. Ultimately, it was a compromise that pleased no one. All these tensions came to a head in the May 1969 electoral campaign.

The campaign was fought largely on racial issues. The Alliance recorded its worst electoral performance and there were doubts as to who would form the government in two important states. The tensions were compounded by rallies which took on ugly racial overtones and which then degenerated into violence. Parliament was suspended and the country was ruled from May 1969 until February 1971 by the executive of the ruling party through the National Operations Council (NOC). The 1969 riots and the subsequent NOC administration were, in many ways, the death knell of moderation in racial issues.[10]

The NOC concluded that the major cause of the riots was widespread Malay economic discontent. There can be no doubt that this was the case. While a small group of the ruling elite had benefited from the positive discrimination schemes, the overall economic position of the Malays, the majority of whom were concentrated in the rural areas, was adverse. One study shows that 44.2 per cent of rural households in 1957 earned a monthly income below the poverty line. By 1970, after thirteen years of continued and vigorous growth of the economy, 41.7 per cent were still in this category.[11] Despite undisputed Malay domination in politics and governmental decision-making, there was little tangible evidence of benefits. In actual fact, the ruling Alliance had been concerned primarily with pooling the resources of the Malay political elite with non-Malay, particularly Chinese, business interests. It had done more to consolidate the dominant status of these elites than to fulfil the basic aspirations of the poor, rural Malays. One despised manifestation of this was the so-called *Ali Baba* (*Ali*, the Malay and *Baba*, the Chinese) business. This refers to the practice whereby a Malay who has taken up his business licence under the positive discrimination provisions transfers the right to use his licence to the Chinese in return for money, referred to as a 'pension'.

To address Malay economic grievances, a New Economic Policy (NEP) was introduced with the Second Malaysia Plan in 1971. The main objective of the NEP was to 'restructure Malaysian society to correct economic imbalance so as to reduce and eventually eliminate the identification of race with economic function'. In practical terms this meant increasing the share of the *Bumiputra* community (the term *Bumiputra* means literally 'prince of the soil' and was coined to refer to the Malays and the other tribes and natives who made up the indigenous population) in the modern corporate sector in terms of share ownership and employment. In 1970, Malays owned only 2 per cent of the share capital of limited companies in Peninsular Malaysia, while other Malaysians owned 37 per cent and foreigners 61 per cent. The NEP target was that by 1990 Malays and other indigenous people would own and manage at least 30 per cent of the total commercial and industrial activities of the economy in all categories and scales of operation. Thus the NEP's underlying strategy was to increase *Bumiputra* ownership by about 28 per cent, doing this by drastically cutting down the foreign share by 31 per cent, while allowing other Malaysians to slightly raise their share by 3 per cent.[12]

The NOC was also determined to avoid the racial politicking that had contributed to the race riots. It sought to do this through the Constitution (Amendment) Act which was passed when Parliament was restored in 1971. This amendment, in s. 3(1)(A) of the Act, permanently removed from legal public debate certain 'sensitive' issues, such as language, citizenship and the special position of the Malays by entrenching these articles in the Constitution and by amending the 1948 Sedition Act so that it now is seditious, even in Parliament, to question the principle underlying these 'sensitive' issues. In practical effect, therefore, it became an offence even to discuss Article 153 and the positive discriminatory provisions accorded to Malays. Despite constitutional challenges, these amendments have been upheld by the courts. In *Fan Yew Teng* v *Public Prosecutor* the Federal Court upheld a conviction for seditious publication of an article which criticized the Alliance government for their alleged partiality towards Malays. The court held that 'these provisions cannot be questioned and are necessary to assist the less advanced or fortunate in the light of the circumstances prevailing in the country at the time of independence'.[13]

The wide-ranging nature of this draconian provision may be seen from the fact that while s. 3(2)(b) provides a defence if the words or publication was intended to 'point out errors or defects', it was specifically provided that this defence did not apply to any comments relating to the provisions on positive discrimination. Similarly, while it would be a defence to call for a change in the law by peaceful or lawful means under s. 3(2)(c), this did not apply to the provisions on positive discrimination. Finally, the Act turned its back on one of the basic principles of a parliamentary democracy by providing that its restrictions also applied to anything said in Parliament or in any of the state legislatures.

RACE, CLASS AND POWER

The widespread belief is that in Malaysia the non-Malays control economic power and so constitute the wealthy and exploiting class while the Malays as a whole are the poor and the victims of exploitation. There is, of course, objective evidence to support this belief. First, as the urban-rural gap is divided largely between the Chinese and the Indians on the one hand and the Malays on the other, the former stand to gain and the latter stand to suffer in terms of the great difference in economic, cultural, educational and social development between the two sectors. The Chinese hold a dominant position in the business field in the cities, occupy most of the roles of middlemen and shopkeepers and, until recently, have had almost total control of the transportation system. As the upper classes of the Chinese and Indians have a greater access to the consumerist symbols of wealth and status, they are easily regarded as exploiters.

Undoubtedly, the Chinese and the Indians are generally richer and better off than the Malays, but this does not mean that the *Bumiputra*/non-*Bumiputra* cleavage corresponds exactly to the gap between poor and rich. The poor Chinese and Indians who work in the rural areas as farmers, rubber tappers or miners, and in the urban areas as menial workers, are as much exploited as their Malay counterparts.

They are all victims of inter-racial as well as intra-racial exploitation. Exploitation is a matter of class and power as well as race, a matter of economics as much as ethnicity. It is absurd to argue that the Chinese wealthy elite engages in exploitation while the Malay wealthy elite does not. It is equally absurd to argue that the Malay poor are subjected to exploitation while the Chinese and Indian poor are immune from the same treatment.

The belief that the non-Malays control the larger part of the Malaysian economy has been perpetuated as a convenient avenue of communal agitation, as part of the divide-and-rule policy first initiated by the British in colonial times. It has been used to justify the retention of the positive discrimination provisions as well as to divert attention away from the fact that the majority of the Malay community has not received any benefit from these provisions. The actual implementation of these provisions has done more to benefit the Malay and non-Malay upper classes rather than the Malay masses by giving only symbolic allocations to Malay communal sentiment and substantive allocations to Malay and non-Malay private interests.

It is true that the New Economic Policy is aimed at reducing poverty among all races. However, taken as a whole, the NEP is still conceived within the framework of a capitalist economy and is being implemented within a system of free enterprise. It looks like a programme for the advancement of a selected few of the Malay community while at the same time further benefiting the non-Malay capitalist class. It appears to be designed more as a means to strengthen elite accommodation and co-operation than to solve the basic and urgent question of poverty and social inequality in Malaysian society.

LESSONS FOR THE UNITED KINGDOM

The Malaysian experience provides important lessons for a multi-racial United Kingdom coming to grips with the most effective way of dealing with the effects of past and present discrimination. Primarily, it demonstrates that positive discrimination does not work. It is submitted that the Indian experience of protective discrimination also offers the same conclusion. It might be argued that this failure would not be repeated in the United Kingdom and it must be admitted that the situations are vastly different. Nonetheless, the Malaysian experience does illustrate some basic problems.

First, there is the problem of targeting disadvantaged groups. Just as it is absurd to treat all Malays as disadvantaged, so too would it be absurd to treat all Asians and Afro-Caribbeans as disadvantaged and deserving of preferential treatment. No one would suggest that this should be the case, which still leaves the question of how such groups should be targeted. A simplistic targeting would lead to positive discrimination being exploited by groups who have no need of such preferential treatment, as has happened in Malaysia. Any effective targeting has to be based upon a combination of class and location, for instance, inner-city areas, rather than on ethnic groupings.

Second, the New Economic Policy was formulated at a time when the economy was booming. According to World Bank data, the export: GDP ratio in 1980 was 60 per cent for Malaysia compared with 28 per cent for the United Kingdom and 37 per cent for South Korea.[14] The assumption made was that positive discrimination for Malays could be justified since it would not deprive non-Malays and, in fact, it was intended that the non-Malay share of the economy would increase from 23 per cent to 40 per cent. However, the economic recession and the collapse of the primary commodities market has wrecked the chance of this happening. Similarly, positive discrimination might have some small chance of succeeding in the United Kingdom at a time of economic prosperity but not at times, like the present, when the economy is on a down-turn and when spending budgets are being cut across the board. During such periods the effect of introducing compensatory discrimination for one group is to positively disadvantage another group. 'The irony of equality is that in trying to correct one type of outcome, policies have resulted in contradictory outcomes or complex institutional procedures that have brought about new types of inequality.'[15]

Third, the Malaysian experience has shown that compensatory discrimination is counter-productive in the effect it has upon race relations; it encourages and feeds racial xenophobia. The method adopted in Malaysia to control the problem by labelling any discussion of the issue seditious cannot seriously be considered an option in the United Kingdom. In any case, this method does not work either: it simply drives resentment underground and the resentment manifests itself in other ways.

Fourth, positive discrimination is counter-productive as it, in effect, devalues real ability. In Malaysia, a stigma attaches itself to any successful Malay, through a belief that success was only possible because of a system of preferential treatment and not through real ability. This is a stigma which would similarly apply to any successful member of a disadvantaged group in the United Kingdom should positive discrimination ever be adopted. Moreover, positive discrimination may produce a sense of hopelessness among the groups who are the beneficiaries of preferential treatment. As the Malaysian experience indicates:

> . . . the irony of the government's paternalism is that the groups being favoured often become disillusioned with and even hostile to the government for two reasons. First, special programs have raised great expectations among those groups but actual opportunities are limited by the constraints of resources [for educational expansion] and of the labour market [jobs]. Second, having once shown itself capable of providing unprecedented career opportunities in the public sector, the government is expected to continue to do more of the same in the future.[16]

Positive discrimination may be counter-productive on the national level as well, as indicated by a number of studies in the area: '[R]everse discrimination has resulted in considerable allocative inefficiency and lower rates of economic growth both of which have allowed poverty to persist.'[17]

The best thing that may be said for positive discrimination is that it has a symbolic value, proving that society regards discrimination as a serious issue. This is not reason enough when compared to its counter-productive side effects. The worst that may be said of it is that it offers the comforting illusion that something is being done to deal with discrimination. Both the Malaysian and the Indian experience demonstrate that this is an illusion which unscrupulous politicians are quick to exploit. Unfortunately, the allure of positive discrimination may be just as much of a trap for well-meaning politicians and interest-groups.

NOTES

1. Malaysia was granted independence in 1957, as the Federation of Malaya. In 1963 it was joined by the three former British colonies of Sabah, Sarawak and Singapore to form the new Federation of Malaysia. In 1965 Singapore left the Federation.

2. The term 'positive discrimination' is adopted here for the purposes of conformity. It might be argued that the term 'compensatory discrimination' would be more appropriate to describe the technique of 'compensating' a particular group for previous disadvantages.

3. See Poulter's essay in this book.

4. Report of the Federation of Malaya Constitutional Commission 1957 Colonial 330 (HMSO, 1957) para. 164.

5. Ibid. at para. 165.

6. Ibid.

7. See Menski's essay in this book.

8. Article 8 was closely modelled on the equivalent Indian provision.

9. Ministry of Finance *Economic Report* (1970).

10. There is a substantial body of literature on the causes and actual sequence of events concerning the riots. See, for instance, von Vorys, K. *Democracy without Consensus* (Princeton, Princeton University Press, 1975).

11. Snodgrass, D. R. 'Trends and patterns in Malaysian income distribution, 1957-1970' in Lim, M. (ed.) *Readings on Malaysian Economic Development* (Kuala Lumpur, Oxford University Press, 1975).

12. *Mid-Term Review of the Second Malaysian Plan, 1971-1975* (Kuala Lumpur, Government Printer, 1973) p. 81.

13. *Fan Yew Teng* v *Public Prosecutor* [1975] 2 MLJ 235, 238; see also *Melan bin Abdullah* v *Public Prosecutor* [1971] 2 MLJ 281.

14. World Bank *World Development Report 1982* table 5.

15. Mekherjee H., and Singh, J. S. 'Education and social policy: the Malaysian case' (1985) 15(2) *Prospects* 289 at 298.

16. Wang, B. L. C. 'Government intervention in ethnic stratification: Effects on the distribution of students among fields of study' (1977) 21(1) *Comparative Education Review* 110.

17. Tzannatos, Z. 'Reverse racial discrimination in higher education in Malaysia: has it reduced equality and at what cost to the poor?' (1990) *International Journal of Educational Development* 26.

19

Tackling Discrimination Positively in Britain

Vera Sacks

INTRODUCTION

While positive discrimination is seen by some as being a possible remedy for the consequences of past discrimination, there are many who are strongly opposed to this concept. Despite the arguments against such policies, legislators responsible for the Sex Discrimination Act 1975 clearly took the view that in certain circumstances practices of this kind should be permitted. Section 47 of the Act enables trainers to provide training especially for women where they have traditionally been under-represented and section 48 enables employers to do the same. The latter section, together with section 49, also enables trade unions to train female members for posts in their union, to take measures to increase the number of women trade union members and to set aside seats for women on their elected bodies (presumably nationally or otherwise).[1] As Baroness Seear commented, 'to discriminate in favour of women in the area of training is the *sine qua non* of turning the intention behind this legislation into a reality'.[2]

This paper describes a research project[3] undertaken to establish the extent to which the three sections of the Act have been utilized by trade unions, public-sector employers and trainers. The research also sought to discover whether their use had raised any particular legal problems. The work was stimulated by growing concern over two related issues. First, the persistence of job segregation and the low employment status of women; in Joanna Foster's words: 'Women are still over-represented in low-status, low-paid jobs with few opportunities available for improving status and working conditions and enhancing their skills.'[4] This was acknowledged by the Secretary of State for Employment, who was reported recently as saying that 'active efforts are necessary to redress women's lack of training specially in non-traditional areas'.[5] Secondly, there is concern over the lack of training in the United Kingdom generally. The proportion of Britain's vocationally trained workforce is 38 per cent — half that of France.[6] It seemed appropriate to explore to what extent a large reservoir of labour, said to be increasing, is being offered the opportunity to develop and capitalize on its talents and thus help to meet the national need for a well-trained workforce.

METHODOLOGY

The research was confined to surveying the activities covered by the legislation, that is, courses specially designed for women, or which set out specially to attract women, and employers' initiatives in offering women employees special training in under-represented jobs or encouraging them to take advantage of opportunities to do that work. No attempt was made to evaluate the quality of the courses nor to determine whether single-sex courses are preferable.[7] All the employers surveyed were in the public sector, as were the training providers. The public sector should provide a model of good practice and, as nearly one-third of women in employment are in the public sector, their policies and practices affect a significant proportion of the national workforce. A representative number of trade unions was also surveyed; the sampling method will be explained in the relevant section. Information was collected from the employers, trainers and trade unions by writing to them in the first instance. The information was analyzed and then followed up by telephone interviews and, in a number of instances, one or more personal interviews were also conducted. This essay describes the main findings of the research on a sector-by-sector basis.

TRADE UNIONS

Between 1979 and 1988 trade union membership dropped from 12.2 million to just under 8.7 million. Currently women represent one-third of all trade union members but around 46 per cent of all workers, a number expected to rise to 50 per cent by the mid 1990s. Two of the major themes of the TUC Women's Conference were how to ensure that women's issues are not marginalized in the bargaining process and how to promote better representation of women members at all levels within the union structures.[8] Throughout the conference it was made clear that improving women's representation in decision-making bodies is the key way of ensuring that equality issues are on the bargaining agenda.

When the Sex Discrimination Act 1975 was being discussed in Parliament, this was clearly understood and resulted in the inclusion of two sections which, although not confined to trade unions, were in fact intended for them specifically. Lord Jacques, introducing the clause which is now section 49 Sex Discrimination Act 1975, stated that 'women may need special encouragement' to take part in trade union affairs and that unions should not be prevented from making special arrangements for women by the non-discrimination principle of the Sex Discrimination Act 1975.[9] Thus section 48(2) enables unions to offer special training to women members to encourage and qualify them to hold union posts. Section 48(3) allows unions to take positive action to encourage women to become union members while section 49(1) enables unions to reserve seats for women on elected bodies where the union believes this is needed to secure a reasonable lower limit of women.

Ten unions were surveyed to establish the use which had been made of these sections. Seven of the ten unions had the largest female membership while the other three had a small but not negligible female membership (see Table 1) and were chosen as comparators. Only two of these unions (20 per cent) had reserved seats on their executive. Of those which had not reserved seats but had considered doing so, one said that they thought this measure smacked of tokenism while another, BIFU, had actually abandoned the practice. Despite the objections of some unions, it was noteworthy that the two unions which did reserve seats had the highest number of women on their executive and believed that their presence facilitated the presentation of issues affecting women in particular. While the issue of reserved seats is controversial, those who had occupied such seats felt more able and willing to stand for National Executive Committee seats and thus helped to bring women into the mainstream of union life.[10]

Women are under-represented in union posts and section 48(2) enables unions to train women to hold such posts. Of the unions surveyed, all except two had organized some training for women members which could be said to be within section 48(2). These ranged from courses on public speaking and union organization (SOGAT) to workshops on women's issues (COHSE) and courses for female shop stewards (GMB/APEX). The continuing small numbers of women union officers[11] might lead to the conclusion that such measures that are taken by unions to encourage and train women to hold posts have been ineffective and too minimal. However, other research indicates that many factors — including women's domestic responsibilities — are responsible for the small numbers and that the long and unsocial hours worked by union officers is a real disincentive.[12] Nevertheless

Table 1
Measures Adopted by Trade Unions under Sections 49(1); 48(3) and 48(2)

Trade union	Percentage of Women		Reserved Seats	Equal Opportunities organizations	Literature Targeting Women	Women-Only Training
COHSE (Confederation of Health Service Employees)	1989 1985	79 66	None; 19% of executive seats held by women	Since 1979 national Equal Opportunities Com; regional com. encouraged	✔	1. National & regional courses
NUPE (National Union of Public Employees)	1989 1985	74 66	5 since 1975, 50% of executive seats held by women, 2 on each divisional council	Since 1982 national and divisional women's com.	✔	1. National regional assertiveness courses 2. Course on women's issues, e.g. health 3. Proposed course on com. skills
IRSF (Inland Revenue Staff Federation)	1989 1985	61 62	None (a conscious decision in 1988 because tokenism was feared); 32% of executive seats held by women	Since 1988 national Equal Opportunities Com.	✔	1. Workshops on equality issues. 2. Self-assertiveness courses since 1989
USDAW (Union of Shop & Distributive & Allied Workers)	1989 1985	61 61	None; 25% of executive seats held by women	Since 1985 national and regional women's com.; Annual Women's Conference	✔	1. Courses on com. skills. 2. Confidence-building workshops. 3. Day & weekend workshops on women's issues; e.g. harassment
BIFU (Banking, Insurance & Finance Union)	1989 1985	55 52	None (abandoned in 1976); 23% of executive seats held by women	Since 1976 national Equal Opportunities Com.; since mid-1980s institutional Equal Opp. sub com.	✔	None at national level
NALGO (National & Local Government Officers Association)	1989 1985	53 52	None; 41% of executive seats held by women	Since 1977 national Equal Opportunities Com.; regional coms. encouraged (11 exist)	✔	1. Public-speaking sessions 2. Introductory workshop for new members 3. Assertiveness courses 4. Equal

Table 1 *(cont.)*

Trade union	Percentage of Women		Reserved Seats	Equal Opportunities organizations	Literature Targeting Women	Women-Only Training
						Opportu-nities weekends
GMB/APEX (Gen. Municipal Boilermakers & Allied Trades Union/Assoc. of Prof. Executive, Clerical & Computer Staff) (Amalgamated 1989)	1989 1985	32/54 n/a	10 since 1987 (re GMB, none re APEX). 30%/37% of executive seats held by women	Women's Officer since 1980s; National Equal Rights Com.; Equal Rights dept.; Annual Conferenced; since 1988 Branch Equality Officers mandatory	✔	1. Courses for female shop stewards 2. Assertive-ness and confidence-building courses
UCW (Union of Communication Workers)	1989 1985	29 25	None; 14% of executive seats held by women	None	✔	None
SOGAT (Society of Graphical & Allied Trades)	1989 1985	28 33	None; 8% of executive seats held by women	Since 1982 national women's com.	✔	1. National & regional courses on public speaking, union organiza-tion, etc. 2. 5-day residential women's course
TGWU (Transport & General Workers Union)	1989 1985	18 16.2	None; 5% of executive seats held by women	Since 1984 National Women's Advisory Com.	✔	None

growing concern in some unions with this situation could lead, *inter alia*, to more training and encouragement programmes specifically for persons interested in becoming union officers. Thus far, at any rate, section 48(2) has achieved little.

Section 48(3) permits unions to take special measures to attract women members. Declining union membership numbers have led to attention being paid to this permissive section. Literature on 'women's issues' is seen as the primary means of attracting women members and some unions have established women's sections and women's officers to raise the interest of potential members, to develop expertise and to promote women's interests. The effectiveness of these measures can be determined by drawing conclusions from the statistics on membership (Table 1) and comparing them with similar figures on male membership in the context of overall employment numbers. By that criterion more women have joined unions while their male counterparts have left, and it therefore seems that these efforts have been reasonably successful. But if women are now joining unions in greater numbers than before why are they not significantly represented on executive committees and as office holders? Their under-representation echoes the same theme as that seen in employment — numbers rise but status does not. For example, some unions, like BIFU, had issued recommendations as far back as 1980 specifying that special encouragement should be given and practical measures taken to ensure that women are more active in the union. These included crêches and other child-care arrangements so that women could attend union meetings and union training courses. The percentage of women members of that union has risen from 49 per cent (1949) to 52 per cent (1985) and 55 per cent (1989) yet only 20 per cent of women are full-time paid officers and only 23 per cent are members of the union's National Executive Committee. It is suggested that increased use of section 48(2)(a) and 49(1) might now be timely and with the adoption of the Charter for Women at Work at the 1990 TUC Conference this might happen.

TRAINING[13]

The training provisions of the Sex Discrimination Act 1975 are crucial to the reality of equal opportunities.[14] Section 47 (as amended) permits *any person* to take action to afford members of one sex only access to facilities for training which would help equip them to do work which has, in the previous twelve months, been wholly or mainly done by members of the opposite sex. These bodies can also provide special encouragement to the under-represented sex to undertake such training. A special provision extends the same possibilities to all 'returners', that is, those who the law has defined as persons who are in special need of training by reason of a period spent discharging domestic or family responsibilities to the exclusion of full-time employment. Since this provision applies to men and women equally, it was not included in this research. But as women are the primary carers in our society in reality, the many courses on offer mainly attract women, but should be available to everyone. The importance of section 47 was underlined by the removal of the designation requirement[15] in 1986, enabling 'any person' (and not only specially designated bodies) to offer single-sex training. This change meant application to the Department of

Employment is no longer required and literally any person can offer such training. This research sampled 60 training bodies which offered single-sex training (see Table 2). It did not set out to assess how many public training establishments provide single-sex training, but was looking at the range of courses, and a number of related matters pertinent to the availability of such courses.[16] It also looked at the legal context.

Of the organizations researched many had put themselves forward for an award for Positive Action Training given by the Fawcett Society[17] for exemplary single-sex training, while the rest were women's skill centres (there are now about 50 in the UK), which were set up either by women's groups or by local authorities to offer single-sex training. Thus all the bodies in the sample hold themselves up as models of good practice or as existing specifically to fulfil the objectives of legislation. The range of courses was found to be sufficiently uniform to conclude that they are reasonably representative of training offered by other bodies.

Courses offered by colleges of further education were revealed to be within a very narrow range: 50 per cent of them were on information technology and eletronics, 25 per cent on management training and the remainder were mainly engineering courses. Since colleges generally acknowledge the difficulty of attracting students to such courses, it may be inferred that their motivation was a desire to increase student intake; women are sometimes seen as a likely target group for this purpose. Such pragmatic motivation would seem to indicate only a temporary commitment to women's concerns. About a third of the courses were of the access type of one year's duration and are an example of 'encouragement' within the meaning of section 47(1), rather than training under section 47(2). An example of this type of course was one offered by Bedford College: a one-year introduction to electronics which would qualify women for a two-year course leading to the BTEC Diploma in electronics. Most of these courses are tailored to meet the needs of women with children insofar as hours of attendance and term dates were specially arranged and child-care facilities made available. Thus, for example, Blackburn College offer a BTEC Diploma in Software Engineering with similar arrangements to those at Bedford, and of the 30 hours per week required for the course, 10 can be spent at home with a computer and a telephone link to the mainframe, which are provided.

The courses on offer by women's skills centres were far more wide-ranging and generally provided training for many trades where women have largely been absent. These courses were concerned with trying to deal with the problems common to many women, that is, lack of pre-qualification or experience, domestic responsibilities, lack of confidence and lack of money. Thus the South Glamorgan Women's

Table 2
Educational Institutions Providing Women-Only Training in Non-Traditional Skills Areas

Trainer	Skills		Comment
South Glamorgan Women's Workshop	Computing	Programming theory; systems architecture	1. All courses are for women over 25 with no qualifications
	Electronics		
	Asian Women Computer Course	(Access course to the main computing course) Basic skills in computers; Maths; Business	2. All tutors are women 3. Child-care facilities 4. Arranged to accommodate domestic commitments
	Personal, Social & Vocational Skills	Supplementary course to the computing and electronic courses	5. Advertisements specifically target women.
Thameside: WOTEC	Electronics Computing Personal, Social & Vocational Skills Women into Management Home Maintenance Courses	Supplementary course to all courses offered Brickwork; plumbing; glazing and tiling; wiring; woodworking; computing	1. All courses are for women with no qualifications 2. All tutors are women 3. Child-care facilities 4. Arranged to accommodate domestic commitments
	Everyday Engineering	Machining; computing; sheet metal; electrical engineering; motor vehicle servicing	5. Advertisements specifically target women.
Edinburgh Women's Training Centre	Computing Electronics Personal, Social & Vocational Skills	Supplementary course to the computing and electronics courses	1. All courses are for women are over 25 and unemployed 2. All tutors are women 3. An allowance of £35 per week is paid to all who attend 4. Advertisements specifically target women 5. High subsequent employment rate
Nottinghamshire Women's Training Scheme	HGV Driving Building Trades Engineering	Plumbing; painting Mechanical; electronics	1. All courses are for women over 25; preference is given to disadvantaged persons 2. All tutors are women 3. Child-care facilities
	Personal, Social & Vocational Skills	Supplementary course to all courses offered	

Table 2 (*cont.*)

Trainer	Skills		Comment
			4. Arranged to accommodate domestic commitments 5. Advertisements specifically target women 6. High subsequent employment rate 7. Limited monitoring
Bedford College	Electronics	A one-year introductory course, teaching basic skills to qualify women for a two-year OND course	1. Course is for women over 21 2. Limited child-care facilities 3. Arranged to accommodate domestic commitments 4. Advertisements specifically target women
Calderdale Business & Innovation Centre	Women into Technology Women into Management		1. All courses are for women over 25 2. Child-care facilities 3. Arranged to accommodate domestic commitments 4. Advertisements specifically target women 5. Limited monitoring
Open University	Women into Technology		1. Course is for anyone 2. Courses are offered in all areas of technology; successful completion leads to a degree 3. Bursaries are offered to women who have technical qualifications, previous work experience and have been out of education for at least two years
City & East London College	Furniture-Making	Includes a specially designed mathematics course	1. Course is for women over 25 2. High subsequent employment rate 3. Monitoring

Table 2 (*cont.*)

Trainer	Skills		Comment
Cranfield Institute of Technology	Management		1. Tailor-made for each individual company
Ashridge Management Training Centre	Women into Management		1. Aimed at existing managers
Suffolk College of Further Education	Computing	Specifically trains women to use special dockside computers	
	Language	French and/ or German (supplementary course to the computing course, necessary because the women will work in customs)	
East Birmingham College	Women in Technology	Computing; electronics; electrical engineering	1. Course is a one-year access course 2. Child-care facilities 3. Arranged to accommodate domestic commitments
	Personal, Social & Vocational Skills	Supplementary course to the Women in Technology course	
Croydon College	Management Information Technology Assertiveness		1. Aimed at returners and women changing careers
Blackburn College	BTEC Diploma in Software Engineering		1. Course is for anyone 2. Child-care facilities 3. Arranged to accommodate domestic commitments 4. 30 hours per week; 10 hours are done at home with a computer and telephone link to the mainframe provided
Nelson & Colne College	Women and Management Women and Technology	Content negotiable Electronics; computer-aided design & manufacture; micro-electronics & robotics; computer applications & software; maths	1. All courses are women returners and others seeking jobs; priority given to women with no qualifications 2. Child-care facilities

Table 2 (*cont.*)

Trainer	Skills		Comment
			3. Arranged to accommodate domestic commitments
	Personal, Social & Vocational skills		
Lewisham Women's Training Centre	Plumbing Electrical Skills		1. Course is for those with few qualifications 2. All tutors are women 3. Child-care facilities 4. Arranged to accommodate domestic commitments
Camden Training Centre	Business Tech	Applying software packages	1. Priority given to unemployed applicants seeking work
	Micro-Elects	Training to become a technician Silk-screening; off-set litho printing; photographic techniques	2. All courses include work experience 3. Child-care facilities 4. Arranged to accommodate domestic commitments
	Introduction to Building	Handling, use and care of tools; carpentry & joinery; bricklaying; plastering	5. Allowance of £42 per week
	Carpentry	Making basic joints; laying floors	6. Travel money 7. 75p per day for lunch
	Plastering		8. High subsequent employment rate
	Women's Self-Employment	Basic business skills; finding premises; finding finance	
	Women Returning to work	Confidence-building; job-seeking skills; skills sampling; work experience	
Women's Motor Mechanics Workshop Limited	Car Mechanics Personal, Social & Vocational Skills	Supplementary course to the car mechanics	1. Priority given to applicants with few qualifications 2. Course includes work experience 3. Short and long courses are offered 4. All tutors are women 5. High subsequent employment rate
Bristol Women's Workshop	Woodwork Home Maintenance	Plumbing; electrics	1. Courses are offered in the day, evening and

Table 2 (*cont.*)

Trainer	Skills		Comment
			as intensive weekend and four-day courses (only the day time ones are free) 2. All tutors are women
Women's Technical Training Workshop— Sheffield	Service Engineering Electronics and Computing	Servicing videos, TVs, etc.	1. Courses are for women over 20 2. Child-care facilities 3. Arranged to accommodate domestic commitments 4. Allowance of £16 per week for books and travel
Haringey Women's Training and Education Centre	Painting and Decorating Computing and Electronics Carpentry and Joinery Plumbing Personal, Social & Vocational Skills	Supplementary course to all courses offered	1. Courses are for women over 25 with no qualifications 2. Some courses are full-time and some are part-time 3. Child-care facilities 4. Arranged to accommodate domestic commitments
WEB Builders	Plumbing Electrics Bricklaying Painting and Decorating Plastering Carpentry		1. Courses are 6 months long 2. 12-week taster courses are run 3. Supplementary courses in computers and mathematics are provided 4. Child-care facilities 5. Arranged to accommodate domestic commitments
Leicester Outwork Campaign	Machining	For women employed by the garment trade, working from home	1. Child-care facilities 2. Arranged to fit in with domestic commitments 3. Transport paid for 4. Women encouraged to work in this area
Lancashire Polytechnic	Women in Self-Employment Women into Employment	Basic business skills; confidence-building Mathematics; creative	1. Courses are open to anyone; priority given to under-privileged 2. All tutors are women

Table 2 (*cont.*)

Trainer		Skills	Comment
		writing; information technology	3. Child-care facilities 4. Arranged to fit in with domestic commitments
Sheffield City Polytechnic	Women in Communication	Assertiveness; word-processing; writing; media studies; video-making	
Hackney College	Women in Technology	Word-processing; basic computing; database; mathematics; computer architecture	1. Course is for unemployed women with no qualifications 2. Child-care facilities 3. Arranged to fit in with domestic commitments
Leicester University	Vocational Course	Career direction; confidence-building	1. Course is for unemployed women over 25
Hatfield Polytechnic	Professional Updating Polyprep NOW (New Opportunities for Women)	Confidence-building; update on relevant profession; modern business structure Training to return to study any course Training women returners to choose a career	1. Courses are for women returning to profession already qualified for 2. Child-care facilities 3. Arranged to fit in with domestic commitments 4. High subsequent employment rate
Oxford Women's Training Centre	Returning to Work Computing Applying Software Packages Painting and Decorating Brushing up on English and Maths Business Start-up Skills English as a Second Language Business English and Computing	Confidence-building	1. Child-care facilities 2. Arranged to fit in with domestic commitments

Note: Personal, Social & Vocational Skills courses involve confidence-building, job-seeking skills and CV-writing. Any programme subsidized by the European Social Fund is required to run such a course as a supplementary unit to all other skills courses offered.

Workshop, having identified the growing need for skilled personnel in computing and electronics as new industries were being attracted to South Wales, offer such courses to women over 25 without any qualifications, provide child care and arrange classes at times to fit in with school times. They also employ women tutors exclusively. This scheme, started by a group of concerned women in 1984, has been singled out as a model of good, successful training practice and has represented the United Kingdom abroad. It is now much in demand by employers in the area as a source of training and skilled labour. The City and East London College, which offer a one-year part-time furniture-making course leading to a City and Guilds qualification for women with no qualifications, discovered that many of these women had difficulty reading drawings and translating them into furniture. Consequently the maths department devised a special maths course for woodwork in which students learn by the manipulation of actual materials. This is designed for those whose maths training is insufficient (a common problem for women) and is now available nationally. Help is also given for those whose basic reading, writing and numeracy needs improvement. The course is only for mature women. This was another common feature of courses, trainers having recognized that this was the group who had missed out the first time and who needed remedial training which could not be accommodated within the normal education system.

Many examples could be given of courses designed to meet other particular difficulties experienced by many women; some seek to build on those skills which women acquire as organizers of households. Calderdale Business and Innovation Centre, for example, in their open access Women into Management course for mature women, try to do this while including something extra to give their students an employment edge. Because mature women need a lot of confidence-building and employers need to be persuaded to interview them, they give their management students an extra skill by including German and European Studies in the course.

In summary, what the best courses had on offer were:

1. Components which dealt specifically with actual difficulties typically experienced by women;
2. Child care facilities;
3. Nominal fees or even no fees so that women without incomes had a real possibility of training; and
4. Introductory access training which led women slowly back into education — a vital step for those whose early education had been inadequate or who had been away from education for a long time.

There remain, however, terrible gaps such as lack of resources, piece-meal availability and lack of monitoring of the courses or of the students' subsequent careers. What is needed is *comprehensive* coverage of the population offering access to skills courses such as those already described and a model of such courses to enable skill-providers to build on each other's knowledge.[18]

PUBLIC EMPLOYERS

Section 48 permits employers to offer women employees access to facilities for training to help fit them for particular work of the employers, subject to the criteria of there being none or a comparatively small number of persons of that sex doing that work within the previous twelve months. It also permits employers to do any act to 'encourage' women (or men) only to 'take advantage of opportunities' for doing that work. Thus under this section employers can open up areas of work for their female employees from which women are noticeably absent. This would range from middle to senior management roles to non-traditional skills. The section seeks to alleviate job segregation, which is responsible for women's continuing poor pay, status and prospects.

The Civil Service, local authorities and the NHS together employ nearly a third of all women in employment in the United Kingdom. The NHS is the largest employer of women in the European Community. Yet the profile of women employees remains stubbornly unchanged. In this research, the Civil Service and twelve local authorities were surveyed and current NHS policies on this matter were reviewed. As all district health authorities are responsible for their own personnel practices but receive general advice and guidance from the Ministry, the relevant reports were examined and analyzed.

Civil Service

There is little evidence of positive efforts to train women in the Civil Service. Each government department is responsible for its own prac-tices, and they all have an equal opportunities officer whose job it is to promote equal opportunities for women and minorities. But as far as women are concerned, efforts have been largely confined to estab-lishing part-time posts, child care and career breaks,[19] while individual women are able to go on courses if managers agree. Although this is a service employing women in every skill, trade and profession, only 13 out of 22 departments report women-only training and this is confined to management training. The statistical profile broken down by grade continues to reveal a dearth of women at senior management level[20] so that there must even be doubts about the numbers of women able to go on management courses. Government has a responsibility to lead with enlightened employment policies but our government does not offer a credible model of successful practice.

Australian experience reveals that when a voluntary Equal Employment Opportunity programme was introduced in their public service in 1975, efforts were sporadic and produced totally inadequate results. This led to legislation in 1984 which placed a duty on government departments to develop programmes designed to eliminate unjustified discrimination against, *inter alia*, women. Within the programmes plans to increase the number of women in non-traditional jobs were developed and in some cases quotas were established. Permissive voluntary measures are no longer seen as effective. Canada, like Australia, now has mandatory affirmative action programmes with the objective to secure equitable representation of women at all levels of the public service. By 1987 the number of women in the management category had increased by nearly 60 per cent (from 5.9 per cent in 1983 to 9.3 per cent in 1987) while departments were asked to increase their appointments of women in areas such as air-traffic control, civil engineering and motor vehicle repairs. Since 1986 affirmative action has been extended to Crown corporations and federally regulated industries such as transport and communications and other companies doing business with the government.[21] The brief examples drawn from common-law English-speaking countries highlight and underline the slow progress of the United Kingdom government.

Local Authorities

Local government employs about 17 per cent of all women in employment (1.6 million) and women constitute one-half of all local government employees (NHS employs 9 per cent of all women in employment — three-quarters of a million). This survey, in sampling twelve local authorities, chose six London boroughs, two metropolitan areas (Birmingham and Bristol) and four small towns in the south-east (Kingston, Slough, Woking and Oxford). These towns are in a region suffering labour shortages where the council, a big employer, could have been expected to take measures to improve its own workforce. The political complexion of the majority of the sample was, as it happened,

Labour[22] which, from previous research, could have been expected to have shown active initiatives. But, as Table 2 shows, the political complexion of the authorities did not significantly improve women's prospects; nor did the fact that all the authorities had adopted equal opportunities policies which included training.

Because local authorities are often quoted as examples of employers with good equal opportunity policies, the research also looked at other measures taken by councils outside section 48 which could be regarded as supportive of women.[23] These measures included the establishment of women's committees and council policies on job-sharing, career breaks and child care. Conclusions to be drawn from the findings (see Table 3) show that councils are more interested in schemes which will alleviate their employee shortages by keeping women in their present jobs than in developing their workforce's potential. A few councils which did provide training showed imagination but, as little monitoring is undertaken and special training is expensive, there is little evidence to convince others of its usefulness.

The training course most commonly on offer was assertiveness. Its legality is doubtful (see later) unless linked with skills training for 'particular work'. But training of the kind envisaged by the Act is offered very minimally and reflected the low priority that training is accorded generally. Given the existence of a full range of jobs within local government employment, the numbers of women employed, and the scale of job segregation, the absence of non-traditional training is striking. Two of the authorities investigated (Birmingham and Southwark) exemplified local authorities with a commitment to equal opportunities and detailed policies to support this. Birmingham's reports show that they are aware of section 48 possibilities and the city treasurer's department reported that they intended to encourage secretaries to study for other qualifications. But another report from the personnel director states that new strategies are required to attract women into higher-level jobs, raising questions about the outcome of this initiative and the management training already offered.

It would seem that local authorities need to do an audit of their workforce in order to identify the jobs in which women are under-represented, set targets and instruct managers to change the workforce profile. But what is really needed is the political will, for such positive actions are controversial. To establish programmes for women's training, promoters who are both influential and committed to eradicating inequalities are needed. The support of the party in power is also essential because resources need to be allocated and training, let alone women's training, is rarely a popular cause. Those currently charged with the task of developing personnel practices with regard to

Table 3
Measures Adopted by Local Authorities Including Those under Sections 47 and 48

	Camden (Labour)	Islington (Labour)	Hammersmith & Fulham (Labour)	Southwark (Labour)	Westminster (Conservative)	Wandsworth (Conservative)	Kingston (Conservative)	Slough (Labour)	Woking (Conservative)	Birmingham (Labour)	Bristol (Labour)	Oxford (Hung)
Women's Officer	For providing community services for women only	For providing community services for women only	✓	✓	–	–	–		–	–	✓	✓
Women's Unit Committee	For providing community services for women only	–	✓	✓	–	–	–		–	Abandoned by council in 1987	✓	✓
Monitoring	✓	✓		✓			–			✓	✓	✓
Assertiveness Training	–	–	✓	✓	✓		–	✓	✓	✓	✓	–
Management Training (s. 48)	–	–	Under discussion	✓	–	–	Distance learning programme		–	✓	✓	–
Other Training (s. 48)	Traineeships are offered to women in non-traditional areas	✓	Proposed	–	–	–	Career-planning seminars; sponsoring further education courses		–	Proposed for female manual workers	Training officer and employee choose a suitable course together	–
Advertising* (s. 48)	✓	✓		✓	–	–	–		–	✓	✓	✓
Job-sharing	✓	✓		✓	✓	–	✓		✓		✓	✓
Career-break Schemes	✓	✓		✓	–	–	✓		✓	Proposed	✓	✓
Child-care Facilities	–	–	✓	✓	–	–	–		✓	Proposed	✓	✓

* This is the only form of 'encouragement' under s. 48 which has been used—the advertisements encourage women to apply for jobs.

women in particular do not have sufficient clout to do much. Stone found that they experienced difficulties and had low levels of political support.[24] It may be that trade unions have a bigger role to play in ensuring better training opportunities for their female members employed by local authorities. But, as has been shown above, there are few full-time paid women officers of NALGO, NUPE and GMB/APEX (13, 8 and 4 per cent respectively) and 'lack of female representation has meant that trade unions often overlook the interests of women'.[25] Mandatory measures are necessary to change the unsatisfactory picture of women's employment by local authorities.

National Health Service

Many of the three-quarters of a million women who are employed by the NHS are the most highly qualified in the country and yet 'there is an absence of women in any numbers from senior positions, a segregation of jobs according to whether they are 'men's' or 'women's' and unnecessary burdens caused by the unwillingness to adapt working structures to the needs of women with families'.[26] Over the last two years the Ministry of Health has become concerned about demographic changes and unfairness in its policies towards women and is experiencing a general staffing crisis. As a result of a number of initiatives by the department, which resulted in research into the position of women in the Health Service, managers have been issued with training packs and guidance on the development of policies which are intended to change the employment profile and ensure a more even distribution of the sexes through the service as well as increased career opportunities for women. This research analyzed these manuals in order to determine whether sections 47 and 48 are at least on the agenda for action. It did not investigate individual health authorities who are responsible for implementation of personnel policies. But the guidance to managers contains little about women-only training, and enquiries made from a small number of authorities showed little knowledge of such possibilities. When interviewed, a spokesperson at the Ministry indicated that more could be done centrally by way of encouragement and promotion, and that the Minister did regard such actions as important, but that ultimately it would depend on the commitment of regional managers individually. Further research is needed to evaluate the success of these initiatives.

THE LEGAL DIMENSION

Sections 47 to 49 of the Sex Discrimination Act 1975 prescribe the conditions which enable organizations to invoke these exceptions to the equality principle. The first condition is that the number of women doing 'that work' must be nil or comparatively small, either in Great Britain as a whole or within an area of Great Britain. Of the organizations researched, none of the smaller ones had sought the statistical evidence required, and indeed a significant number of them were either totally unaware of this requirement or somewhat hazy as to the precise conditions. Most had taken an impressionistic approach and had set up courses without regard to the need for a precise statistical base. Apart from the obvious fact that this part of the Act is little known or understood, difficulties would have lain in wait even for those more legally aware. Statistics are not collected by the Department of Employment on a trade-by-trade basis; for example, the numbers of people employed in the construction industry are collected on the basis of whether they are managerial, administrative or manual, and not on the basis of skills such as welders, plumbers, bricklayers, etc. Thus for many occupations compliance with the letter of the Act is not possible. Only the professions collect statistics of the relevant kind. If any trainer is challenged on this basis, the courts and the parties would be faced with a tedious problems.

In 1986, the Sex Discrimination Act 1975 was amended[27] and the words in italics have been added so that it now reads 'where it *reasonably appears* to any person that . . . there were no persons or . . . the number of persons of that sex was comparatively small', perhaps indicating that the government were aware of the above difficulties, and the adjective 'reasonably' might be taken by the court to imply that the trainer must have made some effort to establish that an imbalance exists but need not show actual numbers. There is no indication in the parliamentary materials on this aspect but, as the intention behind these sections is clear, one might hope that the court would adopt a broad view and require only evidence of some investigation. This is unsatisfactory, however, as it makes it difficult to advise trainers.

The question as to what is meant by 'comparatively small' also remains to be answered. Supposing an organization established that 25 per cent of dentists are women — is that 'comparatively small' and would it enable a dental school to encourage women to apply for dentistry? One might be tempted to analyzed the court's approach to section 1(1)(b)(i) Sex Discrimination Act 1975, which takes a numerical approach;[28] here it is indirectly discriminatory to apply a condition or requirement with which comparatively few women can comply. Before doing so it must be remembered that sections 47 and 48 are permissive and facilitating, intended to encourage trainers to remedy past problems, whereas section 1 proscribes practices which may adversely impact on a significant number of persons of a particular sex. These different intentions may make comparisons inapt despite the superficial similarities. Even if comparisons are helpful, little light would shine, as the Employment Appeal Tribunal has said that the problems must be approached on a case-by-case basis and that proof of the 'considerably smaller numbers' must be submitted. In *Kidd* v *DRG Ltd* Mr Justice Waite said 'the court will not accept generalised assumptions or a submission that the matter was self-evident'.[29] The problem might become greater as the numbers of women in non-traditional jobs increase, and the cut-off point will become more crucial. Furthermore, the same approach is used in the Sex Discrimination Act 1975 in the provisions which deal with trade unions[30] (and other organizations of employers or bodies which govern professions or trades). Although trade unions do collect statistics by gender, the question just discussed remains to be answered. Would fewer than 50 per cent of women officers in a union constitute a comparatively small number, or would the number have to be related to the number of women who are members of that union? Thus as NUPE had 74 per cent of female members but only 11 per cent hold union posts, can they use section 48 (2) to enable them to train women specially for union posts as long as their numbers fall below 74 per cent? Or should the court adopt a 'rule of thumb' approach and lay down that, for example, 25 per cent or less is 'comparatively small', following Mr Justice Waite's remark in *Kidd* when he said 'how large a proportion is 'considerable' is very much a matter of opinion'.[31]

The same difficulty is faced in the 'encouragement' provisions of section 47(1)(b). The tax inspectorate advertised in 1988 for tax inspectors, and in the text called for more women, stating that 42 per cent of its recent recruits were women and they wanted more. While this did not indicate what percentage of the whole inspectorate were women, clearly that is crucial and illustrates the need for clear guidelines. This point is not a theoretical one, as a number of employers and trainers and trade unions do more 'encouraging' than they do actual training, and the point at which such advertisements become unlawful must be important for public bodies.

While section 48(1)(a) and (b) does not raise the same problem of establishing the gender of the workforce, since employers can (and many do) collect statistics on a departmental or job basis, the definition of comparatively small might be more acute for them than for trainers, since male employees might well object to attempts to recruit more women and/or train them. To sum up then, three problems stand out:

1. The nonexistence of a sufficiently refined statistical base for most occupations;
2. The lack of definition of 'comparatively small'; and
3. The problem of establishing the relationship between actual numbers and the relevant pool.

Only section 47(3) and section 49 avoid the difficulty by not using the numbers approach and instead permit special training for all those who have been at home discharging domestic responsibilities (in the former case) and permit seats to be reserved for women (in the latter case) where in the opinion of the organization more are needed to 'secure a reasonable lower limit'.

A further point is that the sections apply to the whole of Great Britain, or 'for an area within Great Britain'. This was intended to address the problem of local or regional imbalances, which may be realistic on the basis that women in some parts of the country are in greater need of training than in other areas, but the same problems as already described apply and may even be compounded by the greater scarcity of regional as compared to national statistics.

It may be that the legislature was unduly cautious and vague in order to avoid controversy. Or it could be argued that there is no other approach possible where affirmative action is involved. Certainly the Employment Appeal Tribunal has warned of the minefield of forcing litigants to use sophisticated statistics.[32] But the research did reveal a wayward approach, with little attention given to the legislative language, and reinforced the conclusion that the law was little known or understood. Thus a reasonable approach is needed and the following might be adopted in the absence of case law.

Either government should collect more refined statistics or, in the absence of these, the correct approach for any organization is to use the best available figures. This should constitute sufficient evidence to satisfy the criterion of reasonableness. As far as the phrase 'comparatively small' is concerned, it has already been intimated that a rule of thumb approach is preferable to a case-by-case approach, and for this purpose 25 or 30 per cent might be reasonable. Finally, the problem of the pool should be approached on the basis that the pool is always the numbers in the trade, profession or job in the whole of the country or a part thereof.

Researching the actual courses on offer brought other legal difficulties to light. The training most commonly offered by employers and by many training providers was assertiveness. Where offered in conjunction with training for non-traditional work its legality is not at issue, for the Act confers legality on any act done in relation to *'particular work* . . . in connection with encouraging women only . . . to take advantage of opportunities for doing that work.'[33] Since there is considerable evidence that women need to have their confidence improved in order to venture into unfamiliar pastures, courses which do so can certainly be said to constitute 'encouragement'. But often these courses were offered without any skills component and it can be argued that, *prima facie*, these must be unlawful unless they could be considered a facility for training, within the meaning of section 47(1)(a), which would help fit women for particular work.

Another fairly common practice, occurring in about one-quarter of the organizations studied, was the employment of only women tutors. Only one of the organizations was aware that this practice might be unlawful but thought that it was vitally important for the trainees to be with women who could serve as role models and who would be more sympathetic and understanding. The same rationale was put forward by other organizations which, however, had apparently given no thought to the lawfulness of such a practice. While it might be argued that the presence of women tutors constitutes a personal service within section 7(e) of the Sex Discrimination Act 1975, Pannick[34] doubts whether customer preference would persuade a court. He argues that the sex of the provider of the service must be vital to the job and the recent decision in the Lambeth case[35] relating to race reinforces this view.

Some courses were found to be outside the law in that they offered women only training for traditional work. Such an example was the Leicester Outwork Campaign, which provides training for women machinists in the garment trade who are working from home. Since homeworkers are predominantly women, the only way such a course would be lawful would be to offer it for women returners, for in such cases there is no requirement of under-representation. The same might be true of a number of other courses which offered mixes of traditional and non-traditional skills. The providers of these courses seemed unaware of the limitations contained in the Sex Discrimination Act 1975.

CONCLUSIONS

When enacting the Sex Discrimination Act in 1975, Parliament had thought that a sensible balance had been achieved between proscription, prescription and permission. In permitting persons to discriminate in favour of women in defined circumstances, a remedy for past discrimination and lack of opportunity had been provided while avoiding the minefield of affirmative action.[36] But, as has been shown above, this survey found that the law in this field is little known, misunderstood, and minimally used. How has this come about?

Two related factors provide important clues. One is the symmetrical approach of the Sex Discrimination Act 1975 which, as Lacey argues, 'does not match the nature of the social problem to which sex discrimination legislation should be addressed . . . The result . . . of this symmetrical principle . . . is to outlaw any form of reverse discrimination or affirmative action'.[37] Yet experience over the past fifteen years has underlined the fact that men and women are running different races and that a neutral stance tends to legitimize and confirm inequality. The second fact is the obvious one that such exceptions as are presented by sections 47 to 49 are permissive and not mandatory. Experience elsewhere reveals that little is done as long as employers are not compelled to develop affirmative action measures.[38]

In the course of this research many organizations of both employers and trainers emphasized the resource problem and the lack of commitment by those in charge. Doubtless, resources in the public sector are always subject to competing demands, and diverting resources to women's promotion and training is seen by decision-makers as controversial, expensive and unpopular, and therefore as of low priority. Commitment is essential and that is most likely to come from women, but women thus far constitute only 20 per cent of local councillors, and are in even smaller proportions in the managerial and trade union hierarchy. Thus placing a duty on employers, at least in the public sector, to provide training for women and to achieve a more balanced workforce is essential here as it has been elsewhere.[39] To quote Marano: 'All of the systematic studies done on the issue indicate that affirmative action has had a positive effect and has resulted in increased employment opportunities and training programmes for women and minority men.'[40] Marano also described how, in turn, this more highly trained part of the workforce continued on the same path but without compulsion. In Australia and Canada recent legislation places employers under a duty to submit a programme whose objective is to achieve tangible changes in the employment profile as it relates to women, and the same should be done in this country.

Little of what has been argued is new and equal opportunity specialists are unlikely to disagree with these conclusions. What some people may find disagreeable is commitment to the course of action recommended. It is undesirable to urge it as merely a matter of economic necessity in times of shortage, for its success should depend on more than the needs of the moment. Instead it should be seen as a moral imperative. The British conception of equality of opportunity is not necessarily just, 'but no popular informed debate has taken place. . . . Three successive Conservative governments have succeeded in replacing a political discourse which could accommodate social justice with one which emphasised market forces and therefore could not'.[41] Since the bottom line is political, the time has arrived for the parties to renew their commitment to equality with a new debate, followed by new and more effective measures.

APPENDIX

Trade Unions

S. 12

(1)   This section applies to an organisation of workers, an organisation of employers, or any other organisation whose members carry on a particular profession or trade for the purposes of which the organisation exists.

S. 48

(2)   Nothing in section 12 shall render unlawful any act done by an organisation to which that section applies in, or in connection with,

   (a)   affording female members of the organisation only, or male members of the organisation only, access to facilities for training which would help to fit them for holding a post of any kind in the organisation, or

   (b)   encouraging female members only, or male members only, to take advantage of opportunities for holding such posts in the organisation,

   where at any time within the twelve months immediately preceding the doing of the act there were no persons of the sex in question among persons holding such posts in the organisation or the number of persons of that sex holding such posts was comparatively small.

(3)   Nothing in Parts II to IV shall render unlawful any act done by an organisation to which section 12 applies in, or in connection with, encouraging women only, or men only, to become members of the organisation where at any time within the twelve months immediately preceding the doing of the act there were no persons

of the sex in question among those members or the number of persons of that sex among the members was comparatively small.

S. 49

(1) If an organisation to which section 12 applies comprises a body the membership of which is wholly or mainly elected, nothing in section 12 shall render unlawful provision which ensures that a minimum number of persons of one sex are members of the body

   (a) by reserving seats on the body for persons of that sex, or

   (b) by making extra seats on the body available (by election or co-option or otherwise) for persons of that sex on occasions when the number of persons of that sex in the other seats is below the minimum,

where in the opinion of the organisation the provision is in the circumstances needed to secure a reasonable lower limit to the number of members of that sex serving on the body; and nothing in Parts II to IV shall render unlawful any act done in order to give effect to such a provision.

Training

S. 47

(1) Nothing in Parts II to IV shall render unlawful any act done in relation to particular work by any person in, or in connection with

   (a) affording women only, or men only, access to facilities for training which would help to fit them for that work, or

   (b) encouraging women only, or men only, to take advantage of opportunities for doing that work,

where it reasonably appears to any person that at any time within the twelve months immediately preceding the doing of the act there were no persons of the sex in question doing that work in Great Britain, or the number of persons of that sex doing the work in Great Britain was comparatively small.

(2) Where in relation to particular work it reasonably appears to any person that although the condition for the operation of subsection (1) is not met for the whole of Great Britain it is met for an area within Great Britain, nothing in Parts II to IV shall render unlawful any act done by that person in, or in connection with

(a) affording persons who are of the sex in question, and who appear to be likely to take up that work in that area, access to facilities for training which would help to fit them for that work, or

(b) encouraging persons of that sex to take advantage of opportunities in the area for doing that work.

(3) Nothing in Parts II to IV shall render unlawful any act done by any person in, or in connection with, affording persons access to facilities for training which would help to fit them for employment, where it appears to any person that those persons are in special need of training by reason of the period for which they have been discharging domestic or family responsibilities to the exclusion of regular full time employment.

The discrimination in relation to which this subsection applies may result from confining the training to persons who have been discharging domestic or family responsibilities, or from the way persons are selected for training, or both.

(4) The preceding provisions of this section shall not apply to any discrimination which is rendered unlawful by s. 6.

S. 48

(1) Nothing in Parts II to IV shall render unlawful any act done by an employer in relation to particular work in his employment, being an act done in, or in connection with,

(a) affording his female employees only, or his male employees only, access to facilities for training which would help to fit them for that work, or

(b) encouraging women only, or men only, to take advantage of opportunities for doing that work,

where at any time within the twelve months immediately preceding the doing of the act there were not persons of the sex in question among those doing that work or the number of persons of that sex doing the work was comparatively small.

NOTES

1. See Appendix.
2. *HL Debates* vol. 362 (1 July 1975) col. 107.
3. Funded by the Economic and Social Research Council. Additional funds were provided by Kingston Polytechnic. I would like to extend grateful thanks to Alison Humphrey, my research assistant, for her invaluable work and suggestions. The research was concluded in August 1989.
4. Equal Opportunities Commission *1989 Annual Report* (London, HMSO, 1990).
5. Michael Howard, reported in *The Times* (22 January 1990). He also said that many women were trapped in jobs below their potential because of lack of training.
6. Britain has the least-qualified workforce among ten EC countries: *The Independent* (22 June 1990).
7. But a strong impression was gained that, at least during initial training, courses designed and run for women only make the participants comfortable and help their progress.
8. 'Equality for women in trade unions' (1990) 31 *Equal Opportunities Review* 18.
9. *HL Debates* vol. 362 (15 July 1975) col. 1218.
10. Op. cit. (note 8) p. 23.
11. COHSE — 27%; NUPE — 11%; BIFU — 20%; GMB/APEX — 3.6%; NALGO — 18%; USDRAW — 18.6%; TGWU — 3%.
12. Ledwith, S., Colgan, F., Joyce, P. and Hayes, M. 'The making of women trade union leaders' (1990) 21(2) *Industrial Relations Journal* 112. Research commissioned by SOGAT into this problem revealed other factors relevant to women becoming active in the union.
13. This section does not cover employer training.
14. Baroness Seear and Joanna Foster have both stressed this point.
15. Sex Discrimination Act 1975 s. 4.
16. The matters surveyed were the existence of child-care facilities, fees, age limits, timing of courses, monitoring and types of course.
17. *Women's Training Matters — Report on Award Conference on Positive Action Training 1989.* (London, Fawcett Society, 1989).
18. Recent reports indicate a decline in the number of government-supported training courses: *The Independent* (13–20 June 1990).
19. 'Equal opportunities in the Civil Service' (1989) 26 *Equal Opportunities Review* 26.
20. *Ibid.* at. 27.
21. *2nd Conference on Civil Service Change — Ottawa 1987: Report on Affirmative Action in Australia and Canada.*
22. See Table 3.
23. Coyle A. (1989) 67 *Public Administration* 10.
24. Isabella Stone *Equal Opportunities in Local Government* (London, HMSO, 1988).
25. Coyle A. op. cit. (note 23).
26. Harding, N. 'Equal opportunities for women in the NHS: prospects for success' (1989) 67 *Public Administration* 51.
27. Sex Discrimination Act 1986 s. 4.
28. The section states that:

> A person discriminates against a woman in any circumstances relevant for the purposes of this Act if — (b) he applies to her a requirement or condition which he applies or would apply equally to a man but (i) which is such that the proportion of women who can comply with it is considerably smaller than the proportion of men who can comply with it . . .

29. *Kidd* v *DRG Ltd* [1985] IRLR 190.
30. Section 48(2)(a) and section 48(3).
31. Op. cit. (note 29).
32. *Perera* v *Civil Service Commission* [1983] IRLR 166.
33. Section 47(1)(b) and section 48(1).
34. Pannick D. *Sex Discrimination Law* (Oxford, Oxford University Press, 1985) p. 260.
35. *London Borough of Lambeth* v *CRE* in (1990) 32 *Equal Opportunities Review* 38.

36. *HL Debates* vol. 362 (1 July 1975) col. 107. Baroness Seear commented: 'I would also congratulate the Government . . . on the successful balance which they struck between reverse discrimination in regard to training and resisting the pressures for a more widespread application of the policy of reverse discrimination.'

37. Lacey, N. 'Legislation against sex discrimination: questions from a feminist perspective' (1987) 14 *Journal of Law and Society* 411.

38. *Affirmative Action for Women* (Canberra, Office of the Status of Women, 1985). Also see *The Times* (25 June 1990), where it is reported that the president-elect of the law society has proposals that the lord chancellor adopt affirmative action to remedy lack of women judges: 'Sometimes you have to put aside one consideration in the interests of a higher political objective.'

39. Op. cit. (note 21).

40. Marano, C. speech to conference on 'Equal Opportunities through Contract Compliance: The British and American Experience', organized by the RIPA, CRE and GLC (London, February 1986).

41. Lovenduski, J. 'Implementing equal opportunities in the 1980s: an overview' (1989) 67 *Public Administration* 1.

20

Positive Action for Women in Germany: The Use of Legally Binding Quota Systems[1]

Josephine Shaw

INTRODUCTION

Quota systems and numerical targets represent a controversial if largely unproven means of improving the representation of disadvantaged groups in sectors of employment and training to which they have traditionally been denied access. In the Federal Republic of Germany, considerable efforts have been devoted at the administrative, party political and legal levels in the last decade to securing the introduction by law of quota systems for women in public employment. This is part of a general policy of *Frauenförderung*, literally the 'advancement of women'. So far, only the states (*Länder*) of North Rhine-Westphalia and Saarland[2] have adopted a quota law — covering, in the case of North Rhine-Westphalia, the *Land* bureaucracy, schools, universities and other public bodies as well as the local and district administrations (*Kommunen* and *Landkreise*) — but other north German states such as Hamburg, Bremen, Berlin and Schleswig-Holstein are actively considering the introduction of legally binding quota systems. Hamburg[3] and Bremen[4] already operate quota systems based on State administrative rather than legislative measures.

The object of this essay is to examine the legal context in which quota systems for employment and training[5] operate, in particular the constitutionality of such a legally binding form of positive action in the face of constitutional guarantees of equal rights and equal treatment regardless of sex. The interpretation of the relevant constitutional norms has undergone a remarkable and dynamic development which has opened up the legal space for political arguments about gender equality which would previously have been dismissed as constitutionally irrelevant. This development will be charted in some detail, as will the terms of the North Rhine-Westphalia law.[6] Thanks to the passing of this law, the Federal Republic can lay claim to be the first European Community country to adopt legislative measures to give legal substance to pious statements of intent about the inadequate representation of women in certain sectors of employment and at the higher levels in all sectors.[7] It should be noted that these developments have taken place at state and not federal level,[8] as the Christian Democrat party (CDU) which leads the governing coalition in the federal government has yet to put into concrete form its rhetorical commitment to women's rights, and indeed pursues social welfare, employment and family policies which could be described as 'anti-woman'.[9] The situation in the Federal Republic is thus deserving of attention from a wider audience, although such attention unavoidably entails detailed consideration of both technical doctrinal points concerning the attribution of powers between *Bund* (the federal government) and *Land* in the German federal system, and a precise textual and contextual (in the sense of its context in relation to other constitutional provisions) understanding of the guarantees of equality contained in the federal Constitution or Basic Law.

For reasons of space, a number of important questions concerning the history, context and possible future development of positive action programmes in the Federal Republic cannot be considered or can be considered only briefly in this chapter. First, and this is clearly the most significant omission at the present time, this essay will not attempt to consider the impact of the reunification of Germany on positive action programmes.[10] That impact is likely to take a number of forms. Clearly, reunification will lead to alterations in the structure of the labour market, operating to the detriment of women. While many women in the eastern part are undergoing a 'back to domesticity' reaction to enforced labour market participation in what was the German Democratic Republic (GDR), the collapse of industry in the east is causing a surplus of relatively cheap male labour which will squeeze the labour market opportunities of women in the west. The demographic pressure for positive action measures for women will consequently drop.

On the other hand, reunification could in the long term provide an opportunity to clarify the continuing uncertainty as regards the constitutionality of quota systems. Reunification has entailed the amendment of provisions of the Basic Law, and the Reunification Treaty explicit provides for consideration of further amendments,[11] including the possible inclusion of 'state goals' in the Constitution. If adopted, these would probably include protection of the environment and the commitment of the state to strive for the material equality of the sexes.[12]

An additional argument for incorporating an enhanced guarantee
of equality is, of course, that the GDR, for all its faults, had a comprehensive network of legal and practical structures to facilitate and
promote women's participation in the labour force.[13] Although eastern
women may prefer in the interim to use the benefits of the market
economy to allow them to stay at home with their children, many
western women would dearly love to have been able to take full advantage of the network of state-run crèches, fully paid maternity leave, and
child support payments which used to exist in the GDR.

The second major political question which cannot here be considered
is the political 'pedigree' of demands for positive action measures in
the form of quotas. It would appear that the origin of demands for quotas
falls firmly within the conventional political domain, and does not come
from the grass-roots women's movement. Cynics might suggest that
quota systems are a high-profile but relatively cheap method for a
political party courting the female vote to signify its 'women-friendly'
image. The major beneficiary of such politics is the Social Democratic
Party (SPD). The danger is, of course, that excessive concentration on
the details of implementing a quota policy diverts much-needed attention from the real problems of female employment: part-time, low-
status, poorly paid work; lack of child-care facilities and conflicting
school hours; vulnerability to unemployment; sexual harassment; the
particular problems of female immigrant or 'guest' workers.

Further legal questions which cannot be considered include the
relationship between positive action strategies of a collective nature
and the seriously inadequate individual remedies for discrimination
available under federal German law,[14] as well as the possibilities for
instituting quota systems in the private sector — for example, through
contract compliance or the granting of subsidies to companies with
commitments to training, employing and promoting women. The
latter question raises an additional complex of legal and constitutional
matters, including compatibility with European Community law,[15]
which have not yet been fully explored in the Federal Republic itself.[16]
Nor can this essay consider the voluntary introduction of quota systems
through collective agreements,[17] or the successful campaigns in the
public sector to introduce other forms of positive action, in particular
the right to work part-time.[18]

Brief consideration should, however, be given to the impact and
influence of the institutional structures for promoting equality which
have emerged at all levels of public administration since the early
1980s.[19] The Federal Republic now has a federal minister with significant designated responsibility for women's affairs. At *Land* level,
although the situation is in flux as a result of shifts in government

between Social Democratic and Conservative-led coalitions, six of the *Länder* have, or have had in the recent past, ministries of Women, or Ministries in which women feature a central designated sphere of responsibility (Lower Saxony, Saarland, Hessen, Schleswig-Holstein, North Rhine-Westphalia and Berlin). In many cases, the transformation to ministry from equality unit makes little or no difference in terms of available resources, or range of work. In the other largely SPD-governed *Länder* in the northern part of the country, the equality units tend to be independent, often responsible directly to the prime minister (or mayor in the city-states) with a cross-ministry responsibility for matters relating to women. In the conservative-governed *Länder* in the south, the units are more often attached to an 'appropriate' ministry such as social of family affairs. It remains to be seen what form of representation of the interests of women will be adopted in the five new *Länder* in the former GDR, most of which are conservative-ruled.

At local level, many district and local administrations have set up women's offices or units, although with varying powers, resources and policy remits. In all cases, these ministries and units have a responsibility and interest in relation to the employment of women in the public service, and it is the bodies in states such as North Rhine-Westphalia, Hamburg, Bremen and Berlin which have been at the forefront of developing positive action measures: urging the appointment of equal opportunities officers in departments and sections of the administration, requiring the elaboration of positive action plans by ministries, schools, universities and other public bodies and promoting the adoption of legally binding quota systems.

The political space within the administration which these bodies have carved out for the discussion of issues of gender equality has given the woman question a hitherto unknown position of priority on the political agenda. These bodies themselves are the result of tireless work in the political parties by women, often veterans of student radicalization in the 1960s and early 1970s, to force widespread recognition of the unequal position of women in German society and of the unequal share of the benefits of German prosperity which they receive. Without these bodies, without this work, it is unlikely that the quota measures would ever have been adopted. For they have created the atmosphere in which the nature of the constitutional commitment to equality in the Basic Law, in the context of the development of the *sozialer Rechtsstaat* or 'welfare state under the rule of law', has come to be significantly reconceptualized. It is an atmosphere in which support for positive action has become political orthodoxy.

One final introductory point must be made. It will become clear as the argument develops in this chapter that a number of promising avenues of theoretical debate are not being explored. These debates are of paramount importance: they include the extent to which a liberal Constitution can support and give effect to social rights; where individual and collective interests may come into conflict; the competing conceptions of formal and substantive equality which such interests may articulate; the extent to which these conceptions can be implemented through law; and the particular question of whether law can successfully operate to provide 'compensation' for historical disadvantage and detriment. Most significantly, little attempt is made in this essay to develop a feminist critique of the response which quota systems guaranteed by law offer to the social reality of gender-based oppression, or to apply feminist theories of law and the state to the development of positive action through the medium of a liberal Constitution. In this it largely mirrors the existing work in German on which it comments. German feminist writers themselves have rarely engaged in legal debates, and little work has been done on developing a feminist conception of the state. Feminist writers have tended to eschew questions relating to engagement with the state, regarding this as co-option and corruption of feminist ideas, and the 'autonomous' women's movement has focused instead on issues around 'body politics': abortion, reproductive technology, violence against women, feminist psychology.[20] Insofar as feminists have engaged with law it has generally been in the areas of criminal and family law. Work on the law[21] and politics[22] of sex equality has been more practical in nature, and has rarely been based on a feminist critique of the key notions of 'equality' and 'difference' on which the concept of discrimination is premised.[23]

The absence of such work is to be regretted. Clearly a feminist critique would add to our understanding of whether and, if so, how quotas work; a feminist critique of liberalism and liberal legalism would form a challenge to the co-option of the politics of gender into mainstream constitutional debate conducted entirely in 'legal' terms; it could reveal an irreconcilable conflict between the goals of law, conventionally understood, and the goals of feminism. This work, however, has a much more modest goal: its primary aim is simply to set out for the English-speaking readership developments in legal thinking and legal practice which have accompanied the adoption of legally binding quota systems in the Federal Republic.

EQUALITY UNDER THE FEDERAL CONSTITUTION

The key provisions of the Federal Constitution or Basic Law are Articles 3(II) and (III) and 33(II). 'Men and women shall have equal rights' (Article 3(II)); 'no-one may be prejudiced or favoured because of his sex' (Article 3(III)); civil servants shall be chosen according to 'merit' and without regard *inter alia* to sex (Article 33(II)). All laws in conflict with the constitutional guarantee in Article 3 ceased to have effect from 31 March 1953 (Article 117(I) of the Basic Law) and the legislature, judiciary and executive are bound directly by its provisions. It also applies to collective agreements between unions and employers' associations which have normative effects, thus guaranteeing, in principle at least, that women are entitled to equal pay and equal treatment under collective agreements. Article 3 is generally held not to govern private relationships between citizens. Thus it does not protect private-sector employees against discrimination. This issue, however, and the extent to which non-discrimination in employment is adequately guaranteed by the legislative provisions of the civil law or by the provisions of European Community law, like the issue of the constitutionality of contract compliance, are questions falling outside the ambit of this essay, which focuses exclusively on the public sector.

The state as an employer, on the other hand, is bound by Article 3 and Article 33(II) (the so-called 'merit' principle),[24] thus preventing, for example, the dismissal of married female civil servants. However, the merit principle would appear on first sight to preclude the adoption of quota systems which systematically favour women over men. Such systems, although pursuing material equality for women as a group, might appear to contravene the right of individual men to be treated equally. This argument is strengthened by the classical interpretation of Article 3(II) as embodying simply a prohibition on legal differentiation, operating primarily as a guarantor of individual rights *vis-à-vis* the state rather than other individuals, and not as an instrument for attacking structures of male dominance within society which perpetuate women's inequality. In the 1970s, the prevailing academic view was that Article 3(II) was concerned only with ensuring that the difference between men and women had no legal effects, not with other consequences of that difference of a social or psychological nature.[25]

The prohibition is subject to two qualifications only: a difference in treatment may be justified (or indeed mandated) by differences of a biological or functional nature between men and women.[26] Biological differences relating to women's procreative capacity justify protective legislation in the employment field, as well as special measures relating to pregnancy and maternity to encourage and protect motherhood. In addition, prior to the intervention of European Community law, the federal courts were able to use the biological exception to uphold the exclusion of men from the profession of midwife.[27] This exception does not appear to require strict scrutiny of any measure purporting to base disparate treatment on biological difference, or to require proof that the same objective (e.g. of protection) could not be achieved by some other means that does not entail discrimination between men and women. Moreover, Harvey has shown how the protective rules, such as prohibitions on night work and on certain forms of heavy work, operate inconsistently, since they protect only *Arbeiterinnen* ('blue-collar' workers) and not *Angestellte* ('white-collar' employees).[28] They are also subject to exceptions for work in restaurants and bars, hospitals and other establishments where women are employed in large numbers, often in physically strenuous work. Harvey finds the most plausible explanation of the policy to be that of 'keeping women — in particular mothers — home at night'.[29] Such a policy, even if it does not in practice protect women against strenuous work at unsocial hours, also fulfils an ideological function of creating a veneer of 'respect' for women's supposed biological weaknesses.

As regards functional differences, these are subject to much stricter scrutiny, requiring the difference to be so great that 'there are no other means by which the purpose of the law can be achieved'.[30] Moreover, the functional difference must in general be derived directly from a relevant biological difference. Although the Federal Constitutional Court has struck down laws requiring employers to give women time off each month to do housework,[31] and denying an automatic pension to widowers[32] on the grounds in each case of no relevant functional difference, it has upheld a law laying down different pensionable ages for men and women. The legislature is entitled to treat men and women differently in order to equalize, on broadly 'welfare state' grounds, the disparate burdens that fall upon them, where the disadvantages can be related back to biological differences. In other words, giving women an earlier pensionable age is an admissible 'compensation' for the double burdens carried by working (married) women.[33]

What is interesting about such an analysis is that, applied critically to real gender-based differences in the situations of men and women, it could be used to justify quota systems and other positive action measures in favour of women in employment, judged against a historical background of oppression and disadvantage. This would be a use of the concept of difference which focused not on women's supposed weakness, but their social disadvantage in a world shaped according to the needs, life-styles and desires of men.[34] However, few German scholars and feminists have chosen to pursue this argument for quotas, with its dangers of slipping into biological essentialism.[35] The particular analysis of Article 3(II) to support positive action for women in employment undertaken by scholars, practitioners and now courts has followed a rather different path.

THE CONSTITUTIONALITY OF QUOTA SYSTEMS

Forms of Quota Systems

There is, of course, no one single meaning to the term 'quota'. On the one hand, it can refer to very general goals aimed at improving the numbers of women employees or students/trainees/apprentices which employers and educational establishments can set themselves either unilaterally or in agreement with relevant interest groupings (unions, works councils, equality units in the public administration). These have no binding effect and cannot be enforced either individually by disappointed potential beneficiaries or collectively by the partners to such agreements. A number of universities, such as the FU Berlin and Bielefeld, have adopted statements similar to the 'equal opportunities statements' appended to job advertisements in the United Kingdom, indicating their receptiveness to applications from men and women[36] and their concern to increase the number of women staff. Alternatively, quotas in the sense of binding targets can be introduced by collective agreements between employers and unions (*Tarifverträge*) or by administrative or legislative action — in the latter case, in relation to employment in the public service.

Broadly, there are four variables according to which quota systems can be judged:

1. Whether they are binding or not;
2. The level of representation of women in the section, department or enterprise which they seek to achieve (women as a proportion of applicants; women as a proportion of the employees in that particular enterprise or in public employment; women as a proportion of the labour force as a whole; women as a proportion of the population);
3. The nature of the preference given to women (whether they are to be preferred where they have equal qualification for the job with any male competitors, where they have the minimum

qualifications to do the job — even as against men with better
qualifications — or regardless of qualifications);

4. Whether the quota is to be applied automatically where the
   relevant criteria are satisfied, or whether there must be an
   individual examination of each case to ensure that there are no
   overwhelming countervailing factors concerning the identity of
   the competing candidates which might preclude the application
   of the quota (e.g. the male candidate is disabled).

The efficacy of quota systems is by no means proven.[37] Nor is it clear
that quota systems framed in terms of helping the 'under-represented
sex' will necessarily help women. They may restrict the progress of
women (for example in university studies, where their better examination results have already secured them more than half of the places in
popular subjects); they raise the possibility that the concept of 'qualification' or 'merit' may be manipulated to women's disadvantage; they
presume always that women *want* to participate in equal or near-equal
numbers in a male-defined world, under male-defined conditions.[38]
Nonetheless, pressure for the introduction of quotas has grown out of
disillusionment with the effectiveness of individual complaint-based
discrimination law, which has long had minimal impact, and with the
failure of measures introduced by the law on the Promotion of Employment of 1969, which were intended to facilitate the management of
women's employment through specific measures within the framework
of the promotion of employment generally. This solution has proved to
be not only impracticable in an era when full employment has become
a dream, and recession almost endemic, but also rather too costly for
the liking of the federal government. Thus many of the special measures
to promote women's employment, including social security support
during training, have subsequently been repealed. Current measures
have generally fallen to be adopted by the *Länder* rather than *Bund*, in
a cold climate of hostility to anything which might increase the bill of
the welfare state.

Promotion of Equality by the State under Article 3(II)

The starting point[39] for the consideration of recent changes in the
interpretation of Article 3(II) of the Basic Law is the *Benda Report*,[40]
prepared for the Hamburg Equality Unit in 1986 by the eminent constitutional lawyer Ernst Benda, not previously noted for his commitment to the goals of feminism. Benda starts from the premise of the
under-representation of women in senior and responsible positions

within the public service. Within the service as a whole, where the proportion of women employed tends to equal if not exceed the proportion of women in the labour market, they are not under-represented. He attributes the under-representation in senior positions to structural and social factors, not inferior qualifications, as is sometimes alleged, and argues that experience has already shown that the time has passed when one could convincingly argue that it is sufficient to wait for enough suitably qualified women to put themselves forward for that under-representation to disappear. Accelerated progress towards equality will only be achieved if the state takes positive measures.

From this social analysis, Benda finds the authority for the state to act in favour of the equality of women in employment by reading together the constitutional provisions on equality with those in Article 20(I) and 28(I) of the Basic Law, which give the state general responsibility in relation to social conditions (the *Sozialstaatsprinzip*).[41] 'Equal rights' (*Gleichberechtigt*) in Article 3(II) means not just formal equality under the law (equal rights and duties), but an equal entitlement to a share of society's goods and resources (equality of opportunity, or even of result), for the principles of the *Sozialstaat* require the state to intervene to ensure the just distribution of scarce resources. However, Benda argues that the Constitution does not prescribe how this objective form of equality should be achieved. Although it is the task of the state to bring about equality between men and women as regards social conditions, he argues that the state has a discretion as to means. Thus it has an 'authority to act' (*Gestaltungsbefugnis*), rather than being subject to a 'constitutional mandate' (*Verfassungsauftrag*).

The Constitution read in this way does allow the institution of quota systems which do not offend against any other provisions of the Constitution such as the employer's freedom of contract, the protection of property, and the right to exercise a profession, as well as, of course, a man's individual right to equal treatment. The Article 33(II) 'merit principle' represents the most serious fetter upon the use of quotas, and Benda draws out the limitations he suggests from this provision.

Thus he rejects 'inflexible' quotas which guarantee women a certain proportion of senior positions without regard to qualifications, but finds 'flexible' quotas, which require a systematic preference for women in jobs or training places wherever male and female applicants are equally qualified, to be permissible for the purpose of ensuring that the proportion of women in those jobs or training place sequals some percentage — such as the proportion of women in the labour force as a whole — which has been fixed in advance. A specific proportion must be chosen, since it is too vague simply to introduce quotas to correct the 'under-representation' of women, or to ensure that women represent an 'appropriate' proportion of a particular group. A quota which limits, albeit within permissible parameters, the labour market opportunities of men must be specific in content. The measure of 'qualification' or merit must be gender-neutral, and cannot systematically favour one sex. In order to give effect to Articles 3(II) and 33(II) as individual rights, consideration must always be given when applying the quota to counter-vailing considerations of a 'welfare state' nature (such as disability), which may preclude the use of the quota. Benda stresses always the individual nature of the application of the quota, arguing that it is not a question of giving effect to some collective or group right on the part of women to compensatory action. Finally, the quota must be intro-duced by legislation, not by administrative measure. Benda therefore proposes that the 'directive' which currently governs positive action in the public service in Hamburg should be replaced by a statute, and that a vague reference to 'removing the over-representation of men' should be reworded in more precise terms.

Thanks no doubt in part to the eminence of its author, a former president of the Federal Constitutional Court, the Benda Report has come to represent the new orthodoxy in the Federal Republic on the interpretation of the Constitution,[42] and his findings have largely shaped subsequent legislative and judicial activity in the field.[43] However, controversy still continues to rage in the academic arena about the broad admissibility of quota systems, the precise constitu-tional legal basis which can be claimed for them, and the exact form which they may take. If one attributes the middle ground to Benda, it is possible then to identify two other positions, which could be charac-terized as radical and conservative.

The radical position can be found in the work of Pfarr and Fuchsloch,[44] Slupik[45] and Majer.[46] These writers, all active in some respect in women's organizations, are firmly in favour of quotas. Pfarr has called positive action plans incorporating enforceable preferential quotas 'the *only* effective way' of achieving women's equality in less than 400 years.[47] Like Benda, Pfarr and Fuchsloch differentiate between the subjective and objective content of Article 3(II), arguing that while the former protects the individual's personal guarantee of equal treatment, the latter focuses on the objective state of inequality faced by women as a consequence of historical male dominance. However, they reconcile potential conflicts between these two aspects not by relying on the principle of the *Sozialstaat*, but by using the concept of proportionality. Quota measures which give effect to the objective content of Article 3(II) will be lawful when judged against other com-peting provisions of the Basic Law, provided they are appropriate to pursuing the goal of equality, they are necessary to that end, and they are no more restrictive of other rights than is absolutely necessary.

Pfarr and Fuchsloch also challenge the concept of 'qualification', as articulated in Article 33(II), and as the accepted basis for quota systems in Benda's argument. They point to the ineffectiveness of the quotas using the 'same qualification' criterion as practised in Hamburg, for example, since the mid 1980s. Early results indicated that the numbers of women in senior positions had risen by 0.2%.[48] Pfarr argues that in lower-grade positions, the level of qualification demanded is often determined not by the actual requirements of the post, but by the available supply of labour. In times of high unemployment, apprenticeships previously requiring only minimal school qualifications now require a final school certificate. At higher levels, she argues, the concept of 'qualification' is inevitably coloured by the fact that men have previously occupied such posts, and those responsible for making appointments are looking for similar 'qualities' in newcomers.[49] Once the plastic nature of the concepts of qualification and merit has been demonstrated, Pfarr and Fuchsloch go on to argue in favour of quota rules based on operating a preference for women provided they have a minimum qualification, not necessarily the same qualification to their male competitors. This should lead to accelerated increases in the numbers of women occupying relevant posts and training places. They claim that such a move would not represent a violation of the individual rights of men, since it is already established that deviations from the merit principle in Article 33(II) are permitted for certain 'welfare state' reasons: in favour of disabled persons, evacuees, army veterans and others. Article 33(II) is therefore not an absolute principle.

All the writers adopting a more radical position argue firmly in favour of a duty on the state to enact quota measures to give effect to the 'equal rights' of women. Majer argues that it was the concern of the authors of the Constitution that the fundamental rights enshrined in the Basic Law should not remain mere paper declarations but should actually be put into effect. The principle of the *Sozialstaat* obliges the legislator to act to remove existing social inequalities. This implies also a duty to enact 'compensatory' law for women, since the Basic Law can require temporary preference to be given to women through quotas if this represents the most effective means of giving effect to the requirements of the Basic Law.[50]

In contrast, the conservative position, as put forward by writers such as Sachs,[51] Stober[52], Kempen[53] and Suerbaum,[54] denies the constitutionality of quota systems altogether. Broadly, they argue that it is impossible to postulate both an objective and a subjective content to Article 3 (II), the two being in irreconcilable conflict. The 'no preference on grounds of sex' clauses in Articles 3(III) and 33(II) require that the subjective, 'individual rights' content must prevail. This is in conformity with the underlying purpose of the fundamental rights provisions of the Basic Law, which is to protect the citizen against arbitrary state action, not to promote paticular social goals. Stober argues that insufficient attention has been paid to the 'merit' clause in Article 33(II) as a fetter upon systematic preferences for women; 'equal rights' is not the same as 'parity' or a particular proportion of positions. Kempen, too, insists on maintaining the contrast between giving people 'equal rights' (*Gleichberechtigung*) and putting them in 'equal positions' (*Gleichstellung*).[55] He, like Sachs, is against all quotas. To Sachs, quotas represent the return to feudalism, where an individual is judged according to status rather than ability.[56]

Stober, however, who vehemently pleads his credentials as being fundamentally in favour of the 'advancement of women',[57] has no objection to some form of 'influencing' quota, although he does not go into details as to how this would work. He also argues that the concept of 'merit' in Article 33(II) should be reworked in order to take additional account of the benefits and skills which women as 'housewives and mothers' could bring to the public service. Suerbaum, on the other hand, argues that it is inadmissible in any circumstances to prefer a woman over a man unless it can be proven that in the individual case the woman has suffered and the man has benefited from concrete discrimination.

The lack of understanding of the true nature of gender relations embedded in this conservative position is revealed perhaps most starkly by Stober's declaration that quotas are unnecessary for the advancement of women. He points to the fact that almost all the assistants he employs at the university are women, indicating that necessarily these women will eventually go on to occupy the position of 'professor'. He fails to mention the serious obstacles that these women will face in academic life if they try to combine career and motherhood, which may mean that the minority of men will come racing past the majority of women in ten years' time in the battle for promotion. He also fails to question *why* so many women are employed in such positions. The reason is doubtless in part the excellent marks achieved by women in law-qualifying examinations. It may also be that the academic life is no longer seen by men as a viable career option, with promotion blocks to reaching the level of professor caused by reductions in resources and constricted growth. This aspect of the feminization of certain sectors of academic life finds a parallel in the United Kingdom, particularly in law teaching, where pay is the single most powerful discouraging factor.

Kowal adopts an approach which contrasts with all the above writers.[58] She acknowledges openly that choices in favour of or against quotas are political and ideological choices about the nature of 'equal rights'. Broadly, there are three possible options: radical, liberal and neo-conservative. The radical position which focuses on equality of result is excluded, she argues, by reference to the underlying individualist premises of the Basic Law; the neo-conservative position which requires merely formally equal treatment would reject the use of quotas, even if it acknowledges the need to combat the inequality of women; only a liberal interpretation of the meaning of 'equal rights', focused on the notion of 'equality of opportunity', both satisfies the requirements of the Basic Law and recognizes the utility and desirability of quotas. Kowal, who regards her work as a contribution to developing a theoretical basis for substantive discussion of equal opportunities and equality for women as regards access to the public service, clearly sees the possibility of a compromise position (termed 'liberal') rooted in the *Sozialstaat* principles of the Basic Law. The question is, as the 'radical' writers would have it, whether this liberal position is one which limits the transformative potential of quotas to such an extent as to render them almost useless in practice, by allowing them to operate only where the relevant candidates have the same qualification.

Like many writers, Kowal refers to the Federal Constitutional Court decision on pensionable ages[59] as representing the highest judicial support for the argument that Article 3(II) contains elements of a compensatory rule in favour of women. Opponents of quotas, however, argue that the pensions decision does not represent a break from existing jurisprudence on biological and functional differences justifying distinct treatment of the sexes, since the Federal Constitutional Court in fact refers back to such differences.

Sokol also refers to the pensions decision as a possible example of compensatory law for women in her work on equality and discrimination, which, in contrast to the work so far discussed, is firmly rooted in feminist theory,[60] being 'woman-centred' rather than 'Constitution-centred'. To illuminate the different ways in which legal norms treat and are applied to women, Sokol returns to feminist discussions of equality in terms of 'sameness' (equal treatment) and 'difference'. In particular, she discusses the Scandinavian School of Women's Law, which rejects the simple ideal of equal treatment on the grounds that it conceals in a perverted form of its own conception the further oppression of women. It treats them simply like men. Sokol rejects the concept of 'women's law' as risking the exclusion of women from the material benefits and opportunities of society, arguing instead in favour of 'equal rights as material equality of opportunities and results'.[61] To counter the eternal trap for women of having to argue constantly in favour of 'sameness' *or* 'difference'[62] she offers the following criteria as tests according to which women can judge the nature of the demands which they place upon law: first, the demand must not be for a special women's law which can be used to exclude women; second, the demand must be capable of giving effect in legal terms to the reality of women's lives; third, the demand must be based on a gender-neutral, general standard which can be used to change the life situations of women and men, and to move them both in the direction of equal rights.[63] Sokol justifies the use of compensatory measures such as quotas on the grounds of the urgency of the need to achieve equality for women in the field of employment, but urges that progress be made in reconceptualizing the standards of 'merit' and 'qualification' which currently condition the application of quotas, so that their existing gender bias in favour of maleness can be removed.

RECENT LEGAL DEVELOPMENTS IN THE FIELD OF POSITIVE ACTION

As yet, little positive law has emerged from parliaments or courts to support or refute the arguments of scholars. What has so far emerged has been largely shaped by the Benda Report, and what Kowal would identify as the 'liberal' position.

Case Law

The case law so far has been somewhat mixed in its reaction to the legal issues posed by the adoption of quota systems. As yet, there is one first-instance decision by the Bremen administrative court on the operation and legality of the Bremen positive action directive,[64] and two decisions by the administrative courts in North Rhine-Westphalia on the validity of the appointment decisions made under *Frauenförderungskonzept*,[65] an administrative measure on positive action which was applied in that *Land* prior to the adoption of the quota law.[66]

In the Bremen case, a judge in the Bremen *Landgericht* (District Court) brought a case before the administrative court seeking, in effect, a declaration that the relevant quota provision of the positive action directive applying to senior positions in the public service would not at any future time be applied to him. The administrative court dismissed his application, arguing that it could only make such a declaration if the directive itself were invalid for violation of some superior rule of law.

Basing its reasoning largely on the *Benda Report*, the court propounded the doctrine of the subjective/objective content of Article 3(II) of the Basic Law to justify the validity of the positive action measures. It departed from Benda only in so far as it held that such measures could validly be contained in a directive, and did not require statutory authority.[67]

It is this finding in particular which was challenged in the first of the North Rhine-Westphalia cases, which involved a challenge to an appointment decision brought by a disappointed male school teacher. His application for a post of deputy director of a school was rejected in favour of that of an equally qualified woman, as required by the North Rhine-Westphalia *Frauenförderungskonzept*. In proceedings akin to inter-locutory proceedings, the administrative court of appeal of Münster left open the question of whether such a measure could ever be in conformity with Articles 3(II) and (III) of the Basic Law, but quashed the rejection in any event on the grounds that a basic right guaranteed by the Con-stitution may only be limited or affected in some way by a legislative, not an administrative measure. Again the court referred to Benda as support for its reasoning.

The Münster decision has been strongly criticized by Lange on two counts.[68] In the first place, he objected to the taking of such a substan-tive decision in the context of interim proceedings. The order made by the court went well beyond simply maintaining the status quo prior to a full hearing, which is the main objective of such proceedings.[69] The decision, which ordered the relevant official to retake his decision and to choose between the two candidates without taking into account the criterion of sex, in effect rendered the main proceedings pointless. Second, and in this respect he differs from Benda, Lange objected to the court's finding that a specific quota law is needed for the introduction of binding quotas. He points to the federal law of 25 April 1985[70] ratifying the UN Convention on the Elimination of All Forms of Discrimination against Women as sufficient legal basis for putting into operation such a constitutionally mandated deviation from the strict terms of an individual fundamental right.

Legislation

The North Rhine-Westphalia quota law should not be regarded simply as a response to the Münster court's rejection of the *Frauenförderungskonzept*. The draft law had been published more than a year[71] before the date of the judgment.[72] In so far as it was breaking new legislative ground, and, as we shall see, operating in a field where its legislative competence remains controversial, the North Rhine-Westphalia Parliament proceeded with considerable caution. After a first reading in plenary session in January 1989,[73] the Parliamentary Women's Committee held a public hearing on the proposed draft law. This hearing received written and oral contributions from invited legal experts, and from interested organizations within the *Land* such as unions and groupings of local authorities.[74] Members of the committee had the opportunity to question those submitting opinions. The law was finally adopted in October 1989[75] with the SPD in favour and the CDU and FDP (liberals) against; it came into force on 1 December 1989. Formally it amends the state Law on Civil Servants to include a quota rule for appointments and promotions as regards civil servants as well as instituting a similar rule for employees and workers in public employment who are not civil servants. The quota rule provides that where candidates have 'equal' aptitude, qualifications and professional achievements (the constituent parts of 'merit'), the female candidate is to be appointed in preference to the male candidate, so long as there are more men than women in the relevant section or department, unless there are relevant factors relating to the person of one of the candidates which displace the application of the preference.

Of course, no one expects the simple enactment of a law on quotas to solve all the problems relating to the employment of women in the public service. In particular, a law will not bring about the necessary changes in the individual consciousnesses of those who evaluate the qualities of applicants for posts and promotions, and who make the appointments decisions. However, it does stress the role of the public service in providing an ideal in terms of practice which other bodies, such as private employers, may choose to follow. By making certain practices a legal requirement, it is hoped thereby that perceptions of normality in gender relations might gradually be altered towards greater sensitivity to the particular problems of women. These, as well as concrete improvements in the representation of women, are the gains to be derived from the quota law.

The quota law was bound to be challenged. However, it was not challenged in direct proceedings for unconstitutionality by the CDU in the state parliament, as would be their right as a parliamentary *Fraktion* (group). Such a move would be judged an electoral liability, since quotas are popular, even among CDU voting women.[76] The law has, however, now been challenged indirectly in the courts by a disappointed male 'victim' of its operation, and the Münster administrative court of appeal, noted already for its opposition to the earlier *Frauenförderungskonzept*, has expressed a preliminary view that the law is unconstitutional and referred the matter to the Federal Constitutional

Court for final decision. However, pending a decision on this reference, which could take several years, the law is provisionally valid and may be applied.[77] The outlook is hopeful for the quota law, since although there was considerable disagreement among the legal experts contributing to the hearing regarding certain key questions of legislative competence and substantive content, a comparison between the text ultimately adopted and the *Benda Report* would seem to indicate that the law is cautiously worded.

Stober and Kempen challenged the competence of the *Land* parliament to legislate not only for civil servants, but also for other public employees who do not have the formal status of civil servant (*Beamte*). The federal legislature has a framework competence in relation to civil servants under Article 75 Nr. 1 of the Basic Law, which it has exercised by enacting the Federal Framework Law on Civil Servants, but the terms of this law do not exclude the possibility of the state legislatures enacting particular terms governing the employment of civil servants, as indeed all states have done. The relationship between the federal and state competence in this field has already been clarified by the Federal Constitutional Court, if not in relation to quotas.[78] Given this state of affairs, the objection to the power of the state legislature to enact a quota law for civil servants amounts to no more than a repetition at a different level of the objections to quota systems based on the merit principle rehearsed already in the context of Article 33(II) of the Basic Law. The merit principle is re-enacted in section 7 of the Federal Framework law. If it is not an absolute principle when enshrined in the Constitution, then neither can it be one when enshrined in ordinary legislation. This objection is therefore more of a substantive than a formal nature,[79] and the debates during the course of the hearing brought little more to the issue than the broader discussions in academic literature outlined above.

Serious objections can also be raised against the competence of the state to legislate for ordinary employees. Article 74 Nr. 12 of the Basic Law gives concurrent competence to legislate in respect of labour law to the federal and state legislatures. Thus the states may legislate so long as, and to extent that, the *Bund* does not exercise its right to legislate.[80] The statement of reasons attached to the draft law asserted that the state has competence to legislate for quotas in respect of employees and workers under the same terms as those governing civil servants by virtue of the Federal Framework Law, quotas being arguably specific public law aspects of employment law, thus falling under Article 75 Nr. 1 of the Basic Law. Battis however argued persuasively in his evidence to the hearing[81] that the route via Article 74 Nr. 12 of the Basic Law should be taken. Since the federal legislature has not exhaustively regulated the question of equal rights in employment in the Civil

Code, as the relevant provisions in section 611a *et seq.* contain only a meagre guarantee of equal treatment, Battis in any case concludes that the state does have competence to legislate. This conclusion is strengthened by the fact that the European Community Equal Treatment Directive which directly motivated the adoption of section 611a *et seq.* (the so-called European Community Adaptation Act)[82] specifically allows for positive action in favour of women.[83] Kempen, on the other hand, objects that section 611a *et seq.* do represent an exclusive set of rules, precluding state legislation.[84] He agrees with Battis, that Article 74 Nr. 12 rather than Article 75 Nr. 1 is relevant here. Surprisingly little attention has been devoted to the further exploration of this important question in the discussions at the hearing.

Stober raises a rather different formal objection to the quota law.[85] He objects to the application of the quota rule to appointments and promotions made by local administrations, universities and other autonomous bodies subject to public law. As the *Argumentationspapier*[86] makes clear, the bodies bound by the law include the state itself as an employer, other public administrations in the state (*Kommunen, Landkreise*), and all other bodies governed by public law. That includes the universities, the state banks, the chambers of industry and commerce and the *Westdeutscher Rundfunk*, the regional television company. Stober argues that placing such a fetter on the autonomy of separate sovereign bodies is in breach of federal and state constitutional law. Although the other legal experts do not allude to this point, or refute Stober's argument, it is clear from the contributions of the two representatives of groupings of local and regional administrations present at the hearing that there is a marked lack of enthusiasm for what could be perceived as state interference with local decision-making processes.[87] Both argued for a time limit to be placed on the application of the law, so that it would not continue in force unless it could be proven within five years to be an effective response to the acknowledged problems concerning the employment of women in the public service.

The quota law operates so long as there are fewer women in the relevant section than men; in other words, it is a fifty-fifty quota system. In his original report,[88] Benda had raised some doubts about the operation of such a quota system, preferring a system which attached to the percentage of women in the labour force — a varying figure, currently around 39–40 per cent.[89] He argued that a fifty-fifty quota gives women, who represent a smaller percentage of the overall workforce, a greater chance than men to be appointed or promoted. In oral discussion at the hearing,[90] however, Benda made it clear that he did not regard these earlier statements as containing any major constitutional objection to the quota draft as it stood, and indeed he evaluated the whole draft as being in conformity with the requirements of the Basic Law. He indicated that in circumstances where women represent such a small proportion of groups of senior civil servants or employees (in many cases less than 5 per cent, disputes about whether it should be 39 per cent, or 50 per cent, or whatever percentage female labour force participation subsequently attains, are rather irrelevant to the basic problem.

'Equal qualification' is a prerequisite for the application of the quota law. Thus, preference will only be exercised in favour of women where, on an overall evaluation of their merits, male and female candidates are found to have achieved the same standard: average, above average, below average, etc. No provisions are laid down for altering the concept of 'merit' in the light of the gender bias that the current male-defined standards undoubtedly contain. Nor does the law follow the suggestion of Pfarr and Fuchsloch that in certain circumstances at least a minimum rather than an equal qualification should be necessary.[91] Furthermore, the law attaches to 'equal' qualification, not qualification of 'equal worth' or 'weight' (*gleichwertig*), as proposed by the representatives of the union OTV.[92] On purely semantic grounds it is difficult to imagine any two persons having 'equal' (in the sense of the same) qualifications where that characteristic is made up of the three separate elements of aptitude, qualifications and professional achievements. In contrast, equal worth or weight is easier to identify, and is a reconceptualization which may enable additional account to be taken of the aptitudes which women, particularly after a career break, might typically bring to work. Clearly, the operation of the concept of qualification will make or break the quota law.

Finally, controversy also surrounds the operation of the so-called *Überwiegensklausel* or *Öffnungsklausel* (derogation clause) which requires each individual application of the quota rule to take into account any relevant countervailing considerations concerning the person of the individual candidates. This clause is phrased in the quota law in general terms, and Slupik objected to it on these grounds. She argued[93] for a definitive list of permissible deviations from the quota principle to be enshrined in the legislation, in order to avoid possible misuse by appointments and promotions bodies unsympathetic to the principle of quotas, or to the appointing of women. Her concern in particular was to exclude considerations such as the double income principle and the breadwinner concept, both factors which in general work in favour of men with dependent spouses and children and against women. Other factors which could be ruled out are the fact of having undertaken military service, and (arguably) length of service. The most important positive factor to include would be disability, although clearly race and ethnic origin, or membership of some similar disadvantaged group, might be factors which ought to be taken into account in the future. While receiving support from the representative of at least one union,[94] this suggestion was not incorporated into the final version of the law.

CONCLUSIONS

It will be seen from the discussion in this essay that the Federal Republic of Germany is beginning to develop a distinctive law and practice in relation to quota systems. The shift in the middle ground in terms of legal and constitutional ideology, matching the shift in political orthodoxy, has marked a significant tactical victory for women in their claim for equality in relation to employment. The achievements in North Rhine-Westphalia and other north German states hold out hope for women in other countries struggling to entrench in law positive measures to assist women.

These developments have yet to receive the seal of approval from the Federal Constitutional Court. However, the conservatism of those writers currently to be found propounding the 'liberal' position in relation to quotas and the caution with which the North Rhine-Westphalia legislators have approached the problem would seem to indicate that the new quota law is, as Battis put it, 'at low risk of being quashed by the Federal Constitutional Court'.[95] The approbation of the Federal Constitutional Court, if and when it comes, will lend significant weight and legitimacy to quota practice.

It is too early to tell whether the modest form of quota rule enacted by North Rhine-Westphalia in 1989 is having any significant effect on the position of women in public employment. The prognosis is unlikely to be good, since it is similar in form to that used since the mid-1980s to little effect in Hamburg in the form of an administrative provision, and a quota regulation of that nature does not attack some of the deep-seated sites of gender bias such as the notions of qualification and merit. It may be that the intangible benefits of holding up the public service and public bodies as models of good practice may be greater than the tangible ones.

Recent debates about quotas in the Federal Republic have been dominated by the legal, and in particular constitutional framework within which quotas are required to operate. In that context, it is difficult for feminists to contribute to the debate, unless they are in possession of a formidable array of arguments concerning the interpretation of the Constitution; law, because it mystifies issues of employment equity in the language of rights and powers, excludes from the debate all except those who speak the language. Moreover, as the Basic Law is widely accepted in German society as the appropriate framework for political debate, it is even more difficult to mount an argument which ultimately questions the utility of that or indeed any constitution as a vehicle for women's liberation.

Nonetheless, it is already a not inconsiderable achievement on the part of the legal and political pressure groups agitating for quotas to have demonstrated that the Basic Law is a much more supple document than might previously have been thought. Work is progressing to maximize this positive side to the constitutional debate, by achieving the legitimacy of constitutional approval for positive action measures such as quotas. Proponents of quotas intend to win the arguments in the constitutional challenge to the quota law.

NOTES

1. This essay was written on the basis of research undertaken with the assistance of a grant from Exeter University which is acknowledged with thanks.

2. *Gesetz zur Förderung von Frauen und zur Änderung sonstiger dienstrechtlicher Vorschriften* (10 May 1989) *Amtsblatt des Saarlandes* (1989) p. 977.

3. *Richtlinie zur Förderung von Frauen im öffentlichen Dienst der Freien un Hansestadt Hamburg* Mitteilung für die Verwaltung Nr. 1/84 p 2; reprinted in Pfarr, H. *Quoten und Grundgesetz* (Baden-Baden, Nomos, 1988) p. 213.

4. *Richtlinie zur Förderung von Frauen im öffentlichen Dienst der Freien Hansestadt Bremen* (9 April 1984) *Amtsblatt* p. 351; reprintd in Pfarr, H. op. cit. (note 3) p. 213.

5. It does not cover the separate question of quotas for parliamentary seats, political party offices and other public bodies such as the boards of public television companies: see Lange, K. ' "Frauen-quoten" in politischen Parteien' (1988) *Neue Juristische Wochenschrift* 1174; Blechschmidt, F. L. 'Die rechtliche Beurteilung von "Frauenquoten" und ihre Durchsetzbarkeit in der politischen Praxis' 1989 *Recht und Politik* 40; Ebsen, I. 'Quotierung politischer Entscheidungsgremien durch Gesetz', (1989) *Juristenzeitung* 553.

6. *Gesetz zur Förderung der beruflichen Chancen für Frauen im öffentlichen Dienst: Frauenförderungsgesetz* (31 October 1989) *Gesetz-und Verordnungsblatt für das Land Nordrhein-Westfalen* no. 51 (17 November 1989) p. 567.

7. Positive action is permitted by Article 2(4) of the European Community Equal Treatment Directive of 9 February 1976, OJ 1976 L 39/40. Denmark has already enacted measures ensuring the representation of women on political bodies: see Ketscher, K. 'Geschlechtsquotensystem als ein Mittel zur Verbesserung der rechtlichen Stellung von Frauen' (1989) *Streit* 83. For Danish action on developing the leadership potential of women, see Thomsen, K. 'Strategies to advance women in the public sector: example: Denmark' in Documentation of a Conference on *Frauen in Führungspositionen im öffentlichen Dienst* 1–4 July 1987 (Bonn; Friedrich-Ebert-Stiftung, 1987).

8. The existing federal directive on *Frauenförderung* is framed in very vague terms: *Richtlinie zur beruflichen Förderung von Frauen in der Bundesverwaltung* Information from Federal Minister of Internal Affairs GMBI (24 April 1986); reprinted in Pfarr, H. op. cit. (note 3) p. 239. Both the Greens (Die Grünen (eds) *Entwurf eines Antidiskriminierungsgesetzes* 3rd ed (Bonn, 1986)) and the Social Democrats

(*Entwurf eines Gleichstellungsgesetzes* BT-DR 11/3728) have put forward draft federal laws incorporating quota systems but neither is likely to achieve parliamentary approval.

9. See the political statements of the CDU reproduced in Kolinsky, E. *Women in West Germany* (London, Berg, 1987) p. 293 *et seg;* Wiegmann, B. 'Widerstand gegen Gleichberechtigung' in Gerhard, U. and Limbach, J. (eds) *Rechtsalltag von Frauen* (Frankfurt/Main, Suhrkamp, 1988).

10. See generally on the impact of reunification on women: Fischer, E. and Lux, P. *Ohne uns ist kein Staat zu machen. DDR Fraun nach der Wende* (Cologne, Kiepenheuer & Witsch, 1990).

11. Article 5.

12. For an initiative led by women arguing for a new German constitution, see Frankfurter Frauenmanifest, 'Frauen für eine neue Verfassung' (1990) *Streit* 155.

13. See generally, Bastian, K. et al. 'Zur Situation von Frauen als Arbeitskraft in der Geschichte der DDR' (1990) *Streit* 59; Scheurer, U. 'Der Preis fürs einig Vaterland — was Mütter in der DDR zu verlieren haben' (1990) *Streit* 109. A less rosy picture of the former GDR is painted by Mocker, E., Rüther, B. and Sauer, B. 'Frauen-und Familienpolitik: Wie frauenfreundlich war die DDR?' (November 1990) *Deutschland Archiv* 1700.

14. Pfarr, H. and Eitel, L. 'Equal opportunity policies for women in the Federal Republic of Germany' in Schmid, G. and Weitzel, R. (eds) *Sex Discrimination and Equal Opportunity: The Labour Market and Employment Policy* (Aldershot, Gower, 1984); Bertelsmann, K. and Rust, U. 'Equal opportunity regulations for employed women and men in the Federal Republic of Germany' in Verwilghen, M. (ed.) *Equality in Law between Men and Women in the European Community. National Reports* (Louvain, Presses Universitaires de Louvain, 1987).

15. Case 31/87 *Gebroeders Beentjes BV* v *Netherlands* [1990] 1 CMLR 287; [1988] ECR 4635; Commission Communicaton (22 September 1989) *Public Procurement: Regional and Social Aspects* Com (89) 400 final, OJ 1989 C311/7.

16. The Trade Ministry of North Rhine-Westphalia has commissioned a report on the constitutionality of contract compliance, and on introducing positive action into public procurement decisions from Prof. L. Osderloh of the University of Trier; as yet unavailable at the time of writing, it should clarify some of the basic issues. One lucrative spin-off of the centrality of the Constitution in discussions around quotas in the Federal Republic is the commissioning of reports (*Gutachten*) from academic lawyers setting out semi-authoritative interpretations of the Basic Law.

17. E.g. Fritsche, U. et al. 'Frauenförderung durch Tarifvertrag' (June 1988) *Der Personalrat* 143; 'Positive action for women: the private sector' (December 1987) no. 167 *European Industrial Relations Review* 14.

18. See generally 'Positive action for women: the public sector', (November 1987) No. 166 *European Industrial Relations Review* 12.

19. See generally Shaw, J. 'Equal opportunities for women in the Federal Republic of Germany: institutional developments' (1990) 9(6) *Equal Opportunities International* 15.

20. Hoskyns, C. ' "Give us equal pay and we'll open our own doors" — a study of the impact in the Federal Republic of Germany and the Republic of Ireland of the European Community policy on women's rights', in Buckley, M. and Anderson, M. (eds) *Women, Equality and Europe* (Basingstoke, Macmillan, 1988); Haug, F. 'The women's movement in West Germany' (1986) 155 *New Left Review* 50.

21. Pfarr, H. and Bertelsmann, K. *Diskriminierung im Erwerbsleben* (Baden-Baden, Nomos, 1989); Pfarr, H. and Bertelsmann, K. *Gleichbehandlungsgesetz* (Wiesbaden, Hessendienst der Staatskanzlei, 1985).

22. Däubler-Gmelin, H. et al. (eds). *Mehr als nur gleicher Lohn!* (Hamburg, VSA, 1985); Weg, M. and Stein, O. (eds) *MACHT macht Frauen stark* (Hamburg, VSA, 1988).

23. See the work of Sokol, B. 'Feministische Rechtspolitik — rechtliche Diskriminierung und Gleichberechtigungskozepte' (1989) *Streit* 3.

24. Also enacted for federal civil servants in s. 8 of the *Bundesbeamtengesetz* (Law on Federal Civil Servants) and for state civil servants in s. 7 of the *Beamtenrechtsrahmengesetz* (Framework Law on Civil Servants).

25. Löwisch, K. 'Welche rechtliche Maßnahmen sind vordringlich, um die tatsächliche Gleichstellung der Frauen mit den Männern im Arbeitsleben zu gewährleisten?' in *Verhandlungen des 50. Deutschen Juristentages* vol. 1. part D. (Munich, CH Beck, 1974).

26. See Dürig in Maunz-Dürig *Grundgesetz Kommentar* 6th edn (Munich, CH. Beck, 1990),

Article 3(II), RZ 9 et seg.; see also the Federal Constitutional Court cases BVerfGE 15, 343; 37, 249; 43, 225.

27. BVerwGE 40, 17.

28. Harvey, R. 'Equal treatment of men and women in the work place' (1990) 38 *American Journal of Comparative Law* 31 at p. 42.

29. Ibid, at 43.

30. Ibid.

31. BVerfGE 52, 369.

32. BVerfGE 39, 769.

33. BVerfGE 74, 163 at 179; NJW 1987, 1541 at 1542. Compare the approach of the House of Lords in *James* v *Eastleigh Borough Council* [1990] 2 All ER 607 and the European Court in Case 262/88 *Barber* v *Guardian Royal Exchange* [1990] IRLR 240 to 'discriminatory' (i.e. different) pensionable ages.

34. An example would be the Scandinavian School of Women's law. The work of Tove Stang Dahl ('Frauen zum Ausgangspunkt nehmen: der Aufbau eines Frauenrechts', (1986) *Streit* 115) and Kirsten Ketscher (op. cit. note 7) has been translated into German and published in the Federal Republic.

35. Sokol, B. op. cit. (note 23) discusses and rejects the Women's Law approach to conceptions of equality.

36. S. 611b of the Civil Code contains only a strong recommendation to employers to phrase advertisements in gender-neutral terms, and many are still gender-specific. The federal government now proposes to change this to a legal requirement: *Entwurf eines Gesetzes zur Verbesserung der Gleichbehandlung von Frauen und Männern am Arbeitsplatz* Bundestag Drucksache 11/6946 (23 April 1990).

37. See, for example, the case study on affirmative action at a North American university: Webb, J. 'The ivory tower: positive action for women in higher education' in Coyle, A. and Skinner, J. *Women and Work: Positive Action for Change* (Basingstoke, Macmillan, 1988).

38. See Ketscher, K. op. cit. (note 7) for these and other objections.

39. This work in turn draws on that of Schmitt Glaeser, W. 'Die Sorge des Staates um die Gleichberechtigung der Frau' (1982) *Die öffentliche Verwaltung* 381; Friauf, K. H. *Gleichberechtigung der Frau als Verfassungsauftrag* (Bonn, Schriftenreihe des Bundesministeriums des Innern, vol. 11, 1980).

40. Benda, E. *Notwendigkeit und Möglichkeit positiver Aktionen zugunsten von Frauen im öffentlichen Dienst* (Hamburg, Freie und Hansestadt Hamburg, 1986).

41. Article 20 (I): 'The Federal Republic of Germany is a democratic and social federal State'; Article 28 (I): 'The constitutional order in the *Länder* must conform to the principles of republican democratic and social government based on the rule of law'.

42. See, for example, Hofmann, J. 'Das Gleichberechtigungsgebot des Art. 3 II GG' (1988) *Juristische Schulung* 249; Zuck, R. 'Die quotierte Frau' (1988) *Monatsschrift für Deutsches Recht*, 459.

43. See note 64 et seq. and accompanying text.

44. Pfarr, H. and Fuchsloch, C. 'Verfassungsrechtliche Beurteilung von Frauenquoten' (1988) *Neue Juristische Wochenschrift* 2201; Pfarr, H. op. cit. (note 3).

45. Slupik, V. *Die Entscheidung des Grundgesetzes für Parität im Geschlechterverhältnis* (Berlin, Duncker & Humblot, 1988); see also her oral and written opinion in the Report of the Hearing of the Women's Committee of the North Rhine-Westphalia Parliament on the Proposed Quota Law *Ausschußprotokoll* 10/1211 (8 May 1989) p. 10 and annex 5.

46. Majer, D. Written Opinion *Protokoll 10/1211* op. cit. (note 45) annex 4. Her views are also those the *Deutsche Akademikerinnenbund* and the *Deutsche Juristinnenbund*, for both of which organizations Majer acts as a legal expert.

47. Pfarr, H. 'Gleichstellung der Frau in der Europäischen Gemeinschaft aus der Sicht Beteiligter' *Streit* (January 1986) 19 at 23.

48. Report of the Leitstelle Gleichstellung der Frau (9 December 1986) p. 2; the 1988 report of the Bremen Zentralstelle für die Verwirklichung der Gleichberechtigung der Frau (3 June 1988) Bremen Parliament Doc. 12/229 p. 9 also indicates that initial experiences with the similarly worded Bremen provisions are proving unsatisfactory.

49. Pfarr, H. op. cit. (note 3) p. 216.

50. Op. cit. (note 46) pp. 19–20.

51. Sachs, M. 'Gleichberechtigung und Frauenguoten' (1989) *Neue Juristische Wochenschrift* 553; 'Frauenquoten im öffentlichen Dienst' (1989) *Jura* 465.

52. Stober, R. 'Frauenquoten im öffentlichen Dienst' (1989) *Zeitschrift für Betriebsrecht* 289; see also his outspoken oral contribution to the hearing on the draft quota law in *Protokoll 10/1211* op. cit. (note 45) p. 6 et seq. as set out in Zimmermann-Schwartz, C. 'Neues von der Frauenförderung' (1989) *Nordrhein-westfälisches Verwaltungsblatt* 396.

53. Kempen, B. 'Die Gleichberechtigung von Mann und Frau und der nordrhein-westfälische Entwurf eines Frauenförderungsgesetzes' (1989) *Zeitschrift für Tarifrecht* 287; 'Gleichberechtigung und Gleichstellung. Zum Entwurf eines Bundesgesetzes zur Gleichstellung von Frau und Mann im Berufsleben' (1989) *Zeitschrift für Rechtspolitik* 367.

54. Suerbaum, J. 'Affirmative action: positive Diskriminierung im amerikanischen und im deutschen Recht' (1989) 28 *Der Staat* 419.

55. Kempen, B. 'Gleichberechtigung und Gleichstellung' op. cit. (note 53) p. 368.

56. Sachs, M. 'Gleichberechtigung' op. cit. (note 51) p. 558.

57. See *Protokoll 10/1211* op. cit. (note 45) pp. 8–9.

58. Kowal, M. 'Frauenquotierungen beim Zugang zum öffentlichen Dienst und Art. 3 II GG' (1989) *Zeitschrift für Rechtspolitik* 445.

59. Op. cit. (note 33).

60. Sokol, B. op. cit. (note 23).

61. Ibid. at 10.

62. See the criticisms of this approach in Smart, C. *Feminism and the Power of Law* (London, Routledge, 1989) p. 82 et seq.

63. Sokol op. cit. (note 23) p. 12.

64. VG Bremen (1988) *Neue Juristische Wochenschrift* 3224, discussed by Sachs, M. 'Frauenquoten' op. cit. (note 51). See also the decision of the Labour Court of Bonn of 16 September 1987, (1988) *Neue Zeitschrift für Arbeitsrecht* 133, rejecting the claim for discrimination brought by a man claiming to have been unfairly treated as a consequence of the equal opportunities in employment policy operated by the Greens in the Bundestag; see Pfarr, H. and Bertelsmann, K. *Diskriminierung im Erwerbsleben* op. cit. (note 21) p. 169 et seq.

65. Decision of the Minister of Employment, Health and Social Affairs of 8 May 1985 *Ministerialblatt für das Land Nordrhein Westfalen* Nr. 45 (27 June 1985) p. 858. A *Konzept* is a form of internal administrative measure which binds only the administration itself; accordingly, the local and district authorities were not bound by the *Konzept*.

66. Administrative Court of Appeal of Münster decision of 15 June 1989 (1989) *Neue Juristische Wochenschrift* 2560; (1989) *Neue Verwaltungsrechtliche Zeitschrift* 1080; (1989) *Deutscher Verwaltungsblatt* 1162, discussed by Lange, K. 'Quote ohne Gesetz? — Zur Quotenentscheidung des OVG Münster' (1990) *Neue Verwaltungsrechtliche Zeitschrift* 135. Administrative Court of Cologne decision of 12 July 1989 (1990) *Streit* 175. Both cases are discussed by Degen, B. (1990) *Streit* 177.

67. The decision was predictably criticized by Sachs, '*Frauenquoten*' op. cit. (note 51) on this point in particular.

68. Lange, K. op. cit. (note 66).

69. S. 123(I)(1) of the *Verwaltungsgerichtsordnung*.

70. Gesetz zu dem Übereinkommen vom 18.12.1979 zur Beseitigung jeder Form von Diskriminierung der Frau BGBl II (1985) 647.

71. Vorblatt zum Gesetzesentwurf der Landesregierung *Gesetz zur Förderung der beruflichen Chancen für Frauen im öffentlichen Dienst* (8 March 1988); see the early criticisms of Kempen, B. 'Die Gleichberechtigung' op. cit. (note 53).

72. OVG Münster decision of 15 June 1989.

73. See *Plenarprotokoll 10/99* of 26 January 1989.

74. *Protokoll 10/1211* op. cit. (note 45).

75. *Gesetz zur Förderung der beruflichen Chancen für Frauen im öffentlichen Dienst, Frauenförderungsgesetz* 31 October 1989 Gesetz-und Verordnungsblatt für das Land Nordrhein-Westfalen, Nr. 51 (17 November 1989) p. 567.

76. A prominent CDU supporter of quotas is Dr Rita Süßmuth, the former Federal Minister for Youth, Family, Women and Health, now President of the German Bundestag. Ambivalence towards quotas is also evident in the contributions of female CDU Members of the North

Rhine-Westphalia Parliament during the course of the hearing: see *Protokoll 10/1211* op. cit. (note 45) p. 50.

77. See a brief news report in *EMMA* (January 1991).

78. BVerfGE 4, 115; BVerfGE 38, 1.

79. This point is made also by Benda, E. *Protokoll 10/1211* op. cit. (note 45) p. 23.

80. Article 72 of the Basic Law.

81. Battis, U. *Protokoll 10/1211* op. cit. (note 45) p. 13.

82. *Arbeitsrechtliches EG-Anpassungsgesetz* BGBl I (13 August 1980) p. 1308, also sometimes known as the *Gleichbehandlungsgesetz* (Equal Treatment Law).

83. Op. cit. (note 7).

84. Kempen, B. *Protokoll 10/1211* op. cit. (note 45) p. 18.

85. Stober, R. op. cit. (note 52) p. 293.

86. A statement of the reasons for and issues raised by the law, indicating in outline how it works, and written in plain German. Unreferenced, copy on file with the author.

87. See the contributions of the representative of the *Städtetag Nordrhein-Westfalen* and the *Landkreistag Nordrhein-Westfalen* and of the representative of the *Nordrhein-Westfälische Städte- und Gemeindebund Protokoll 10/1211* op. cit. (note 45) pp. 78, 81.

88. Benda, E. op. cit. (note 40) pp. 225, 226.

89. See Commission of the European Communities *Women in Graphics* Women of Europe supplement no. 30 (December 1989) p. 36.

90. *Protokoll 10/1211* op. cit. (note 45) p. 31.

91. Pfarr, H. and Fuchsloch, C. op. cit. (note 44) p. 2206.

92. Gewerkschaft Öffentliche Dienste, Transport und Verkehr *Protokoll 10/1211* p. 69; their suggestion draws on the work of Pfarr, H. *Quoten und Grundgesetz* op. cit. (note 3) p. 203 et seq.

93. Written Opinion *Protokoll 10/1211* op. cit. Annex 5, (note 45) p. 10 et seq.

94. Deutsche Angestellten Gewerkschaft *Protokoll 10/1211* op. cit. (note 45) p. 72.

95. *Protokoll 10/1211* op. cit. (note 45) p. 14.

21

Equality and Affirmative Action in Constitution-making: The Southern African Case

Paseka Ncholo

This essay examines the provisions for equality and non-discrimination in the emerging constitutions of southern Africa and argues for a new conceptualization which recognizes the differences between the protection of minorities and the advancement of the disadvantaged majority of the population in the post-apartheid context.

THE BACKGROUND

The history of the various territories of southern Africa has been closely intertwined since colonial days when most of the area fell under direct or indirect British rule and influence, with the exception of Mozambique and Angola, which were Portuguese colonies. Moreover, Roman-Dutch law is the shared common law of South Africa, Swaziland, Lesotho, Botswana, Zimbabwe (formerly Rhodesia), and Namibia (formerly South West Africa). These legal links were further strengthened by the impact of apartheid laws in all the former colonies until the attainment of independence, save for South Africa. These countries' economies have been so interwoven with that of South Africa that their independence has been undermined. Thus any discussion of South African development has to be seen in the context of the regional experiences as a whole, particularly of the countries which most recently attained independence, Zimbabwe and Namibia.

Lesotho, Botswana and Swaziland

Lesotho, Botswana and Swaziland, known as the High Commission Territories during the colonial period evolved their laws from their close relationship with both Britain and South Africa. Upon independence in the mid-1960s, these countries adopted constitutions based on the Westminster constitutional model, but with entrenched bills of rights. The Lesotho Independence Order No. 1171 of 1966 provided for its independence with a justiciable bill of rights. This instrument protects freedom of speech, freedom of movement, liberty of the individual, the right to a fair trial and freedom from discrimination.

Cowen, who was then Lesotho's constitutional adviser, has said that Lesotho had intentions of including socio-economic rights in its independence constitution, but was advised against this. The main reason was that the realization of such rights would demand positive action on the part of the government, which would have been impossible to attain or fulfil.[1] Another reason was that in providing for non-discrimination, the constitution foreclosed all possibilities of invoking any programmes of affirmative action.

Women have been the most hard-hit by the absence of affirmative action programmes. Women constitute the majority of the population, yet their legal status within Lesotho has been almost that of perpetual minors. Although they were granted the right to vote after independence, one may argue that women's civil rights have failed so far to uplift their socio-economic status. Women are the majority of the poor and underprivileged; most are still engaged in subsistence farming and menial jobs, which makes them heavily dependent on their husbands or their male relatives' earnings from South African mines. There is a need for the government to allocate more resources for the advancement of women in the form of affirmative action. This would help to redistribute jobs and educational resources to the most disadvantaged. However, this is unlikely to occur given the current political situation in Lesotho. In 1970, there was a *coup d'état* when the government refused to step down after losing the elections. Since then, the country has been governed without a democratic constitution and a democratic government.[2]

Botswana adopted a similar constitution with a bill of rights which protected traditional civil rights. There is no evidence of deliberations in the direction of providing for substantive equality in areas of resources and opportunities.

The Swaziland Independence Order No. 1377 provided for a similar constitutional order, but that constitution was repealed in 1968. The present Proclamation of 16 April 1973 and the Establishment of

Parliament of Swaziland Order 1978 make no provision for a bill of rights.

In all three countries there have been no policies geared towards affirmative action for any group. In all these countries women continue to be treated in the same way as minors,[3] and have limited rights and consideration in matters of employment and education.

Zimbabwe

Upon independence, Zimbabwe had a much bigger settler community than the High Commission Territories, and this community was in control of the wealth and resources of the country. Due to the nature of the negotiated settlement of the conflict, matters relating to affirmative action were not included in the Zimbabwean Bill of Rights. Instead, section 16 of the Constitution provided for a comprehensive protection of property, while at the same time requiring equal treatment before the law. It also outlawed all forms of racial discrimination. The entrenchment of property rights and the absence of affirmative action provisions made it difficult for the new government to implement any sensible redistribution of resources and wealth. However, the president was given power by the Constitution to issue directives to correct previous racial imbalances in the civil service and other uniformed services. In discharging this function, he issued the Directive on Black Advancement.

Namibia

The Constituent Assembly of Namibia adopted in Windhoek on 9 February 1990 the Independence Constitution with a justiciable bill of rights for the Republic of Namibia. The country has a white minority community (mainly of German and Afrikaner origin) which has a monopoly over the resources of wealth of the country. Apartheid policies had been implemented along similar lines as in South Africa.

Article 10 of the new Constitution provides for equality and freedom from discrimination. It states that all persons shall be equal before the law and that no person shall be discriminated against on grounds of sex, race, colour, ethnic origin, religion, creed or social or economic status. Article 23(2) provides for affirmative action in favour of the victims of apartheid. Article 23(3) provides for special regard to be had for women who have traditionally suffered from special discrimination, and need to be encouraged and enabled to play a full, equal and effective role in the political, social, economic and cultural life of the nation.

Article 24(3) of the Constitution provides that there can be no derogation from Article 10 on equality and non-discrimination, but provides no similar protection in respect of Article 23. So the principles of non-discrimination and property rights take priority over affirmative action, which is seen as exceptional. How these provisions will be interpreted by the courts remains to be seen. However, it is important to note that Namibia has taken a bold and positive step to remedy the gross inequalities of past discrimination. It is understood that the government proposes to introduce an Affirmative Action in Employment Bill in order to give effect to these policies. For South Africa the lessons are relevant to the emergence of a democratic constitution.

SOUTH AFRICA

South Africa has had continuous contact with the legal thinking of the West since the Dutch settlement of 1652. By 1909, South Africa had four colonies: Cape of Good Hope, Natal, Transvaal and the Orange River Colony. Each of these colonies was self-governing but subject to the overriding authority of the United Kingdom. The legislatures of each of these colonies agreed to send delegates to a national convention to consider the possibility of a union. At that convention, the delegates agreed upon a constitution whose provisions were cast in the form of a draft bill to be ratified by the legislatures of the colonies. Delegates were selected to take the draft bill to the United Kingdom to be enacted by the British Parliament. The bill received royal assent in September 1909 under the title of the South Africa Act (9 Edw. VII, c. 9), and came into force on 31 May 1910. While in law this was an Act of the British Parliament, in actual fact it was the product of deliberations by white South Africans only. The black people of South Africa were not included.

The main issue considered by the national convention was the question of the franchise for black people. Before union, each of the colonies had its electoral system. In the Transvaal and Orange River Colony, all black people were denied the right to vote while in Natal laws were discriminatory. Only in the Cape of Good Hope were the qualifications the same for all people irrespective of colour. In theory, one could say it was possible for a black person to be elected into the Cape legislature, though this never occurred in practice. At the convention, the Cape argued for the inclusion of black people on the voters' rolls, but was strongly opposed by the Transvaal and the Orange River Colony.

This disagreement resulted in the adoption of a compromise arrangement whereby the status quo in each colony was to be maintained until
the matter could be settled later. Means were thus devised for the
Cape franchise to be protected and it was then specifically entrenched.
The entrenchment was not substantial in that the Cape had to concede
that black people (at the time mainly coloured people were qualified)
should not have a right to become members of the Union Parliament.
This effectively limited the participation of black people in the political
process to the provincial level only.

It was further agreed upon that the Constitution was to be amendable
in the same way as other laws. This meant amendment could be by
Parliament itself legislating by a simple majority in each of the two
houses. Further, after a period of ten years, Parliament was free to
legislate in the ordinary way to change its own composition and powers
as well as the composition and powers of the executive and judicial
branches of government. However, a special procedure was laid down
for amendment in relation to three issues: the electoral system in the
Cape; equality of the two official languages (English and Afrikaans);
and the amending procedure for the Constitution itself. Section 10 of
the South Africa Act 1910 provided for the prohibition of discrimination
in voting rights in the province of the Cape of Good Hope by reason
of a voter's colour or race only. Section 137 of the same Act guaranteed
the equality of English and Afrikaans as the official languages, while
section 152 set forth the agreed provision for amending the Constitution. Amendments were to be passed by both houses of Parliament
sitting together and agreed to at the third reading by not less than
two-thirds of the total members of both houses.

The Period 1910–1983

The South African Constitution operated smoothly for some time, even
without a bill of rights, other than sections 35, 137 and 152. This lack
was due to the pervasive influence of English constitutionalism, which
regarded constitutional guarantees as unnecessary. Another factor
could have been fear of the judicial testing power which had been
asserted in the resounding judgment of Kotze CJ in *Brown v Leyds*.[4]
This testing power was labelled by Paul Kruger[5] the 'principle of the
devil' which the devil had introduced into paradise to test God's word.
An entrenched bill of rights would have legitimated judicial intervention. Further, Thompson[6] argues that there was a distrust of the
American constitutional model, which was blamed for the Civil War
and seen as raising the expectations of black people. Most importantly,

a bill of rights would not easily have survived the racism displayed by white people at the convention, particularly those from the Transvaal and Orange River Colony.

It was only after World War II that a greater interest in human rights and their protection began to grow, both internationally and nationally. The misery caused by racism necessitated a guarantee of basic rights for a variety of minority groups. It further brought concern over the protection of citizens of nation states to the fore. The adoption of the Universal Declaration of Human Rights meant their internationalization. But such progressive events as the US Supreme Court decision of *Brown* v *Board of Education*, the independence of India and Pakistan and the adoption of bills of rights in former colonial countries took place, ironically, as South Africa was engaged in the erosion of the very basic human right of suffrage guaranteed under the 1910 Constitution. The erosion of this right could be traced back to the 1936 Smuts-Hertzog coalition government that ensured the passage of an act which provided for the removal of the African voters in the Cape of Good Hope from the common voters' roll and placed them on a separate voters' roll. Then they were given the right to elect three representatives to the House of Assembly — white representatives.

In *Ndlwana* v *Hofmeyr*,[7] the appellate division noted that the Union Parliament, created in the image of the British Parliament, had had at the time of the Union certain limitations upon its full sovereign power, among them the requirement of the special procedure to amend the three entrenched sections. The court further said that the Statute of Westminster 1931 had removed all limitations upon sovereignty and as a result Parliament's will could no more be challenged in South Africa than in England.

In 1951 the government passed legislation altering the franchise rights of coloured voters in the Cape Province by the procedure of the two-thirds majority specified in the Constitution. Thereafter, coloured people would be given the right to vote for four special white representatives in the House of Assembly. The legislation, called the Separate Representation of Voters Act 1951, was passed by a simple majority of each house sitting separately. Its validity was challenged and the appellate division held the legislation invalid in *Harris* v *Minister of the Interior* [1951] (2).[8] An attempt was made by an ordinary majority of members of Parliament to convert themselves to a high court which then attempted to overrule the appellate court. This was struck down by the appellate division in *Harris* v *Minister of the Interior* [1952] (4).[9] The government responded by increasing the size of the appellate division from five to eleven judges, choosing judges sympathetic to its cause. It further increased membership of the Senate with government supporters to ensure that it secured the two-thirds majority. Thus, the Coloured Voters Act was passed with the requisite majority and attempts to declare it invalid were unsuccessful. From then onwards, the government relentlessly fought to erode even the slightest constitutional or fundamental rights accorded to the black people of South Africa.

However, calls for a bill of rights in the light of the naked violation of blacks' rights were kept alive by academics like Cowen in the 1960s.[10] The need for the bill of rights was asserted by the Molteno Commission of Enquiry of the Progressive Party.[11] In 1961 attempts by the Progressive Party in the Natal Provincial Council to have a Bill of Rights included in the Republican Constitution of 1961 failed dismally. This period was followed by the banning of organizations and individuals who advocated changed in South Africa. South Africa became virtually a police state.

The new Constitution of 1961, which is described in its preamble as one 'best suited to the traditions and history of our land', brought little change to the institutional life of South Africa. All that happened was that a formal change was made in the person of the head of state — the queen was replaced by the state president. The powers of the state president were as limited as had been those of the queen before him.[12] Section 59 of the new Constitution provided that:

(1) Parliament shall be the sovereign legislative authority in and over the Republic; and shall have full power to make laws for the peace, order and good government of the Republic;

(2) No court of law shall be competent to enquire into or to pronounce upon the validity of any Act passed by Parliament, other than an Act which repeals or amends or purports to repeal or amend provisions of sections 108 and 118.

As a result of the new Constitution's firm adherence to legislative supremacy, and the restriction of the courts' testing right to matters affecting the equal language rights alone, Parliament was able to erode individual liberties without fear of judicial intervention. The role of the courts was now limited to the interpretation of Parliament's will, as the appellate division had already declared in *Sachs* v *Minister of Justice*.[13] Nevertheless, one would have expected the courts to interpret any statutory ambiguity in favour of individual freedom. Recent studies indicate that this has not been the case. The courts have frequently given executive-minded decisions.[14]

The South African regime, despite its negative attitude to a bill of rights, had its own understanding of what rights, if any, could be protected. The Nationalist government's starting point was based on separate development or apartheid, and the notion that groups as such have rights. The groups in question are the different ethnic communities, which the government treats as 'nations'. The claim is that such groups have identity and a right to preserve that identity. For example, the Tomlinson Report of 1955, on the socio-economic development of the 'Bantu' areas, spoke of 'the European people' in South Africa as having a 'right of existence as a separate national and racial entity'.[15] It is on this basis that Prime Minister Verwoerd built the whole notion of separate development as the 'right we [whites] have . . . to preserve ourselves'.[16]

> It is a fundamental right . . . of the White man to protect his own nation from disaster. Every nation has the right to continued existence. That is the most basic human right. It is a fundamental right to preserve one's nation and to protect one's identity as a nation. That is the basis of our whole policy.[17]

It is on this basis that the Nationalist government laid claim to a right to self-determination for whites and rejected any form of integration and majority rule. This, they argued, would lead to domination by Africans. The State Department of Information said:

> Majority rule is only applicable within a nation and depends upon the assumption that the nation is pre-existent and has sufficient unity to be a viable body politic. It does not apply to multi-national bodies such as the United Nations or the European Community and it does not apply to multi-national South Africa.[18]

Instead the Nationalist government called for separate development, offering to concede to the other 'nations' of the country the same right to self-determination that they claimed for themselves. This right to self-determination could be exercised by these other 'nations' in territories designed by the government for them — called homelands or *Bantustans*. It is interesting that some of the *Bantustans* created in pursuit of apartheid were granted 'independence' from South Africa. It was at this stage that they could lay claim to protect human rights if they so chose, as in the case of Bophuthatswana, which opted for a bill of rights upon 'independence'.

Apartheid meant that Africans, coloureds and Asians would not enjoy the same rights as whites in the so-called 'white' areas. The minister of Bantu Administration and Development said:

> In White areas the Bantu are not being granted equality or potential equality in respect of any single aspect of social life whatsoever;

> not as far as the say in the government of the country is concerned,
> not as far as property rights are concerned and not as far as
> social amenities are concerned. They had not potential or actual
> equality.[19]

The logic of this position was that blacks were 'mere guests' in white
areas and could not lay claim to equal treatment. The interesting aspect
is that these 'mere guests' were born in the so-called white areas just
as the whites themselves were. The coloureds and the Asians were not
scheduled to have homelands of their own. Instead, they were to have
the 'fullest opportunity' for self-determination and with constant
mutual consultation on matters of mutual and common interest.

What is interesting is that the Nationalist government hoped to divide
African people into segments based on ethnic groups like Zulus, Sothos,
Tswanas, Xhosas, etc. in its efforts to allocate them *Bantustans*. This it
bases on the grounds of different languages and culture, forgetting
that South African whites are not themselves a homogeneous group,
consisting of persons of Dutch, German, English, Scottish, Welsh,
Irish, French Huguenot and other 'ethnic' extractions.

The 1983 Constitutional Dispensation

The 1983 Constitution was preceded by lengthy political debates, which
included substantial support among whites for a bill of rights.[20] This
does not imply that there was no opposition at all. In fact in 1982 the
Constitutional Committee of the President's Council, published a
report rejecting a bill of rights primarily because it emphasized individual rights, rather than the 'volk' or white 'nation'.[21] A different
approach was taken by the Buthelezi Commission Report,[22] which
suggested the establishment of a new political order for the Natal/
Kwazulu region on the basis of a new constitutional arrangement. The
report suggested that certain checks and balances of powers be
introduced, among them a bill of rights and a totally independent
judiciary under which legislation would be testable in court.

The 1983 Constitution makes provision for two categories of entrenched provisions: a procedural obstacle of a two-thirds majority of the
total members in each house of Parliament; and a relatively easy procedure of a simple majority of the total number of members of each house
of Parliament. The first procedure ensures the equality of English and
Afrikaans as official languages. The second procedure provides for the
entrenchment of the racially defined structures.

It is interesting to note that the 1983 Constitution refers in its preamble to a commitment 'to respect, to further and to protect the self-determination of population groups and peoples', indicating that the Nationalist government's adherence to the nation's policies of separate development, its vision of the people of South Africa as forming different 'nations', continued. The 1983 Constitution was not the result of the full and free participation of all the adult citizens of South Africa. It also failed the basic test of equality for every individual within South Africa.[23]

Since the Buthelezi Report in 1982, Kwazulu (one of the self-governing *Bantustans*) has pursued the bill of rights issue. A draft bill of rights was tabled for discussion and adopted by the Kwazulu/Natal *indaba*. The *indaba* (meeting/conference) was convened at the initiative of the Natal Provincial Council and the Kwazulu government. Its purpose was to negotiate a new legislative dispensation for Kwazulu and Natal as a single geographic, economic and administrative region. This bill of rights guaranteed human dignity and equality before the law; rights to liberty and privacy; protection of the family and property; ethnic, religious, linguistic, cultural and educational rights; freedom of movement, conscience and religion; freedom of opinion and expression; freedom of association, of work and of contract. All these rights were to be binding on the legislature, the executive, the judiciary and all government institutions in the province insofar as they 'fall within the purview of and flow from the powers and functions developed on the province'. These rights and freedoms were to be enforceable through the Supreme Court.

The Current Debate in South Africa

It goes without saying that a bill of rights and apartheid are incompatible with each other. Central to any bill of rights would be provisions guaranteeing the equal allocation of basic rights without distinction based on race, colour, sex, religion or political opinion. This means any effective operation of a bill of rights entails the total abolition of all apartheid laws that interfere with civil and political rights. What is surprising is that some of today's most vocal supporters of a bill of rights are those whose interests lie with minority group protection and values which are wholly European. Some of them were at one stage or another ardent supporters of apartheid policy and the balkanization of the country into *Bantustans* and the adoption of the 1983 Constitution.[24]

An important issue is the time for introducing a bill of rights. Scholars like Dugard[25] have argued that a bill of rights should be introduced as soon as possible before apartheid policies do more damage than

presently. This view is also shared by Greenberg,[26] who argues that it
would be advantageous for the Nationalist government to introduce a
bill of rights while it is still in power. Saunders,[27] on the other hand,
strongly rejects the argument and says it is good government that
people want first. He states that a bill of rights will be a matter of free
negotiation and should take account of the broader spectrum of social
values.

It was at a time of intense debate by white academics and pro-
government institutions that the Anti Bill of Rights Committee, the
Democratic Lawyers' Association and the Inter-University Law
Students issued a statement which read:

> We take the view that the conflict in the country today stems from
> apartheid and its massive unequal distribution of rights, privileges
> and political power. Furthermore, the introduction of the 1983
> Constitution has not brought reform, but introduced neo-
> apartheid under the guise of 'own affairs' and 'general affairs'.
> The introduction of a Bill of Human Rights would have the effect
> of entrenching this constitution and above all entrench all the right
> of the white minority to 87% of South Africa's land surface and
> 95% of its productive capacity. A Bill of Rights would therefore
> not be promotive to a just solution which would ensure stability,
> progress and sound human relations in South Africa. We believe
> in a common value system and reject the concept of entrenching
> group values which would generate the differences and create
> tension in the country. We therefore call on all lawyers and
> Lawyers' Associations to join our movement.[28]

Opposition to a bill of rights has also been traditionally strong among
the Afrikaner intellectuals, due either to a misunderstanding or mere
ideological hostility. Their hostility could be due to the fact that a bill
of rights presupposes restraints on the government based on the Rule
of Law and fundamental rights. According to F. Venter, 'the Rule of
Law should be rejected on the grounds that it "presupposes" the notion
of "fundamental rights" accruing to the individual against [state or
government] authority and this reflects a humanist philosophy which is
unacceptable in South Africa'.[28] Venter bases his idea on the preamble
and section 2 of the South African Constitution of 1961, in which the
sovereignty of God is acknowledged and argues that this Christian
premise stands in radical opposition to the humanistic point of departure which makes the individual the sovereign consideration. He
therefore suggests that South African lawyers should not approve the
Rule of Law but rather embrace 'Christian government', necessarily

including the juridical ordering and administration of justice with a
Christian touch. In fact the same view has been stated by the President's
Council. Their argument is that a bill of rights is unacceptable due to
its humanist emphasis as against the maintenance of the state and its
authority.

Van der Vyver's criticism[30] of the President's Council is based on
the assertion that at no time has the Calvinist tradition supported
fascism. If the government is fascist and committed to oppression and
injustice, then it should not commit Calvin and the Afrikaners to its
cause.[31] He states that Calvin himself asserted that justice is an essential ingredient of legitimate government. Positive law which does not
reflect the norms of justice is in reality not law. It is the duty of the
repositories of state authority to care for the well-being of their
subjects.[32]

Recently however, the idea of a bill of rights has gained popular acceptance within South Africa and thus the focus of the debate has shifted.
At issue now is what rights and concerns should be protected should a
bill of rights be introduced. It is interesting that the South African
government, itself through the Minister of Justice (who had earlier
opposed a bill of rights), instructed the South African Law Commission
to investigate the issue of such a bill and devote attention to 'group
rights' in particular.[33] The commission was to report to the Minister in
two years from the date of instruction in April 1986. The resulting
proposals will be discussed below.

Since then, two divergent views concerning a bill of rights have
emerged, represented by the government on the one hand and the
African National Congress (ANC) on the other. The South African
government's approach so far overemphasizes the protection of group
rights. This approach sees in a bill of rights a mechanism whereby
political and economic interests of the privileged white minority may be
protected. The second approach is represented by the majority black
opposition groups led by the ANC and the United Democratic Front
(UDF). Their approach seeks to protect the interest of the black majority. It sees the central purpose of the bill of rights as the inclusion of
blacks into the political process with guarantees of fundamental individual rights to all citizens.[34] The desire to redress past discrimination
and injustice on the basis of race is a strong element of this approach.

ANC Proposals

In January 1988, the ANC issued a set of constitutional guidelines
intended to expand on the general wording of the Freedom Charter

424 *Paseka Ncholo*

which was adopted at Kliptown in June 1955.[35] The ANC's constitutional guidelines must be understood not as a draft constitution but simply as setting out the general principles upon which a post-apartheid constitution could be based. The ANC stated:

> The drafting of a constitution for a democratic non-racial South Africa can only be the task of elected people of our country in a constituent assembly. These guidelines are being tabled for discussion by all our people irrespective of their political inclinations, ideological leanings or party affiliations. They are meant to set in motion a process of national debate. It is hoped that finally a position would emerge out of these discussions which would reflect the broadest national consensus. It is in this spirit that these guidelines have been tabled for consideration by all South Africans.[36]

The introductory paragraphs of the guidelines reaffirm the ANC's commitment to:

1. The establishment of a non-racial democratic South Africa;
2. The termination of apartheid and the outlawing of all instances of racism;
3. The creation of instruments for the redistribution of wealth;
4. The promotion of the equality of the sexes;
5. The protection, on the basis of equality, of the rights of all, including cultural, linguistic and religious rights;
6. Embarking on a programme of affirmative action to redistribute resources;
7. The granting of a franchise based on the principle of one person — one vote;
8. The creation of a comprehensive bill of rights;
9. The implementation of a land reform programme;
10. The protection of women, the family and workers.

The guidelines present a vision of a post-apartheid South Africa which will be struggling with reconstruction after the long history of exploitation and oppression. They would impose a positive duty on all state and social institutions to eradicate racial discrimination and ethnic, racial or regional exclusiveness. The guidelines recognize that past oppression concerns not only racism but sexism too. It should be noted that black women suffer from the triple oppression of being black, women and workers. But for black and white women alike the South African laws in every sphere, i.e. the common law, statutory law and customary laws, have treated women in many respects as on a par with minors and as having limited rights.

Of particular interest is the inclusion of a bill of rights in a future constitution of South Africa. Sachs states that a bill of rights has been viewed with suspicion by many involved in the liberation struggle because of a number of interconnected factors:

(a) The push for a Bill of Rights comes not from the heart of the freedom struggle, but from the people on the fringes, many of whom have criticised apartheid but few of whom have been actively involved in the struggle against it.

(b) The objective of the Bill of Rights is seen as being primarily to protect the existing and unjustly acquired rights of the racist minority rather than to advance the legitimate claims of the oppressed majority.

(c) The attack on majoritarianism which underlies many arguments in favour of a Bill of Rights is manifestly racist since South Africa has been governed without a Bill of Rights and in accordance with the principles of majority rule (for the minority) since the Union of South Africa was created in 1910, and the need for checks and balances suddenly becomes self-evident when blacks are about to get the vote.

(d) The key role given to what are called experienced lawyers in controlling the implementation of the proposed Bill would have meant inevitably an interpretation in favour of the existing and unjustly acquired rights and against any meaningful re-allocation of rights.

(e) While protection of the individual was accepted as necessary, the failure of the proposed Bill of Rights to address the question of grossly disadvantaged communities rendered it largely irrelevant to the human rights needs of the country.[37]

Indeed one is bound to be suspicious of the need for a bill of rights when calls for it come from right-wing quarters like the University of Pretoria, the South African government, and several judges and Afrikaner academics.

The guidelines are silent so far as the mechanism of enforcement of the bill of rights is concerned. This poses a problem in that the enforcement mechanism cannot be confidently left with a predominantly white judiciary after their history of flagrant disregard of human rights and collusion with the executive in implementing apartheid policies. The guidelines take as their basic premise the notion of individual rights. In the preamble it is stated that 'there shall be equal rights for all individuals irrespective of race, colour, sex or creed'. However, one should not lose sight of the group rights which are referred to in the subsequent sentence. These relate to equal cultural, linguistic and religious rights for all. Such group rights do not necessarily refer to a specific racial group but are to be enjoyed by *all* people without reference to their race or colour.

Government Proposals

After almost two years, in 1988 the Law Commission produced its report.[38] In a fairly wide-ranging examination of the concept of a bill of rights and with reference to the international debates on the issue, the commission made substantial recommendations. The Working Paper, as it is referred to, seeks to incorporate much of what is contained in the classical liberal democratic human rights instruments, such as the Universal Declaration of Human Rights and the various European Conventions. It has rejected the idea of group rights while protecting cultural, linguistic and religious rights. It puts the principles of non-discrimination, individual integrity and judicial review firmly on the agenda. Its tentative recommendations are:

1. The adoption in principle by Parliament of a bill of rights;
2. The repeal or amendment of existing legislation that would be inconsistent with a bill of rights;
3. That the drafting of any such document be the outcome of negotiations and through consensus; and
4. That there should be a national referendum of all South Africans to determine the acceptability of the bill of rights in order that the document receive legitimacy.

In paragraph 16.6, the report emphasizes that absolute fairness and equal treatment are essential or else the whole effort should be abandoned. It further highlights the fact that a bill of rights will not be accepted as legitimate if black people are not given the vote. It recommends that every individual and every group should have the right to associate freely with other individuals and groups in order to promote common interests.

The report accepts that South African law knows only the protection of individual rights and notes that in public law South African courts have never recognized an entity known as a group. It defines the object of a bill of rights as being to protect the individual against legislation and resultant administrative acts which infringe his basic rights and freedoms. At the same time there are suggestions of another, less liberal, theme relating to group rights in the report. It notes that every individual should have the right to dissociate himself from groups and individuals (para. 23.50). It states that the protection of minorities is essential in South Africa since to ignore the rights of minority groups would be to invite endless conflict (para. 13.70). For this reason it would appear the commission recommends that political group rights in the context of the legislature's composition should be protected in the Constitution subject to the principles of equality. One is bound to be sceptical about such a provision in that it may end up classifying people according to the Nationalist Party's thinking of 'own affairs' and 'general affairs' as between and among difference races. This would imply that a form of apartheid is still intact — it is simply more sophisticated.

On the economy, the report claims that a bill of rights is not the proper place for propagating a particular economic system (para. 14.120). Nevertheless it follows the view that a bill of rights must include adequate guarantees of the right to acquire, own and dispose of property. The report suggests that ownership is one of the most basis aspirations of all South Africans and that even those who would like to see the redistribution of wealth would also like to have the right to property protected (para. 14.120). It therefore concludes that to the vast majority of South Africans a bill of rights without a property clause would be totally unacceptable (para. 14.121). Consequently, it recommends that the right to property be guaranteed and that compensation be paid from expropriation. In short, the commission's recommendations in this regard show a clear commitment to a free enterprise model of economy which, while doubtless encouraging free marketers, will run counter to the political programmes set out in the Freedom Charter and for long expressed by the mass democratic movement.

Likewise the commission's treatment of affirmative action is problematic. It only appears to favour affirmative action in cases where it will benefit a minority group which has been discriminated against in order to afford them certain advantages temporarily with the object of achieving equality (para. 14.63). This does not seem to recognize the reality of the South African situation, where it is the *majority* against whom social and economic discrimination has been aimed, and not separate ethnic minorities. Yet it seems that only specific minorities would qualify for affirmative action. This divisive approach, based on ethnicity, has been unacceptable to black people for a long time because apartheid used ethnicity and tribalism as a divisive method to enable the government to control people.

Unlike the ANC guidelines, the report makes no reference to workers' rights like the right to strike or to have a job. One wonders how this is likely to be received in South Africa with its highly politicized and unionized working class.[39]

The report leaves the enforcement mechanism of the bill of rights to the Supreme Court and the normal process of law (para. 14.90). In so doing, the commission seems to underestimate the lack of confidence by the majority of the people in the South African judicial system. In order to give credibility to any protection of human rights, a more independent body is necessary.

CONCLUSIONS

The ANC's guidelines and the South African Law Commission's recommendations indicate a great deal of consensus. Both documents envisage the end of apartheid and its laws. The need for the basic protection of civil and political rights is referred to by both sides. It should be emphasized that the Commission's recommendations are more detailed and comprehensive on this aspect. There is also general agreement on the need for the independence of the judiciary. This is, however, to be reached through different methods. For the ANC and the broad opposition groups, the present South African judiciary is not seen as independent, but as an arm of the dominant white minority. On the other hand, the Commission believes that the judiciary has been independent and respectable. The Commission goes further by proposing the Supreme Court and the ordinary process of law as the methods of enforcement of a bill of rights. The Commission rejects the idea of a special constitutional court. The most worrying aspects of this relate to the methods of appointment and the accountability of the South African judiciary. There is a need for a wider spectrum of interest groups to be instrumental in the appointment of judges and magistrates. One would expect that if the present judges and magistrates are to continue in office under a new regime, then they will have to be given the opportunity to readjust and be re-educated on sensitive issues like racism and sexism.

Parliamentary democracy is embraced by both sides for the future. (This has been crucial, considering the fears of the Nationalist government of a takeover of power by the ANC.) The actual method of representation presents a serious problem and a stumbling block. The anti-apartheid forces have expressly called for 'one person — one vote' in a unitary, non-racial democratic South Africa, while the Commission, though it accepts a 'one person — one vote' proposal, hopes to do this by at the same time emphasizing group rights in the composition of the legislature. This could lead to separate, if not racially divided, representation in Parliament, a reversion to the Nationalist Party's 'own affairs' and 'general affairs' approach in the 1983 Constitution.

There is disagreement on the exact nature of what a bill of rights should include. The ANC's guidelines refer to civil and political rights and socio-economic rights. The Commission refers basically to civil and political rights only. Of interest is that the Commission at one point mentions the right to acquire, own and dispose of property. Undoubtedly, property rights are mainly socio-economic rights. Albie Sachs[40] believes that these two sets of rights are not mutually exclusive and in conflict. This he supports by stating that the constitutional divergence has narrowed, with the liberal states moving towards accepting at least a minimum platform of welfare rights, while the former socialist states have gone in the direction of greater judicial guarantees of individual rights.

Addressing socio-economic rights is a pragmatic question when one considers the inequality in the distribution of resources and wealth in South Africa. The ANC's guidelines propose a bill of rights with affirmative action so as to redress centuries of exploitation of the majority of the people. The Commission's provision for affirmative action only relates to certain minority groups so that they may attain equality. A bill of rights, by its operation *prima facie*, implies that all executive acts must be non-discriminatory and non-racist. Such provisions would then prevent any governmental efforts in improving the situation of those previously discriminated against. Thus affirmative action, if constitutionally provided for, gives ground for such help by way of exception to the principle of equal treatment. A bill of rights limited to the equality principle could also be used to block any effective and material support for the victims of apartheid. A provision for affirmative action is essential to ensure that a well-regulated and equitable procedure of redistribution and reconstruction is embarked upon. The entrenchment of property rights may conflict with this and seems not to be appropriate in the peculiar circumstances of South Africa. Presently, approximately 87 per cent of the land belongs to the white minority, while blacks occupy only 13 per cent. This is not through the dictates of free trade, market forces or even the will of the people, but through the force of law as enunciated in the Land Act of 1913 and the Group Areas Act of 1950. Despite the repeal of these measures, any entrenchment of property rights would only serve to nullify centuries of struggle by the landless and dispossessed majority, if this is taken to override affirmative action.

As mentioned earlier, the Commission's report does not refer specifically to women and to workers' rights, unlike the ANC's guidelines. For any bill of rights to work sensibly there is a need to look into the ills of society and to try to remedy such. The guidelines, for their part, are silent on the question of implementation mechanisms. The Commission, on the other hand, has set up a five-phase implementation process. This proposal, in phase two, relates to the purging of the statute book, including the repeal of all legislation promoting separate development and the dismantling of all local government institutions that are racially structured, such as community councils and regional services councils. It also means the dismantling of the Kwazulu *indaba* created as a regional arrangement in the Province of Natal.

Much has recently been achieved in terms of thinking over the building of a new non-racial democracy in South Africa. However, this still leaves much to be desired in the approach the Commission has taken in preparing a draft bill of rights for discussion.[41] Mainly its work has been done by professionals with a limited consultative base, despite the Commission's attempts to solicit comments from a wide spectrum of people. The bill of rights is likely to be acceptable to the majority of the people only if the draft bill is referred to a national referendum of all South Africans.

Affirmative action in a bill of rights should be a permanent feature of the Constitution so as to serve as a regulating force in the allocation of burdens and resources. It should regulate the entire economy, the distribution of land, the position of women and the educational sphere. Questions may be asked as to why affirmative action is needed in a South African Constitution rather than simply a programme of post-apartheid reconstruction, particularly since the majority will be in power and could legislate anything in its favour. Affirmative action has often been perceived as a method of dealing with discrimination against an ethnic minority that is not able to effectively influence legislation. How then can it be applied to a majority?

The answer is that affirmative action in the South African context is being seen as part of a political promise and ideal. Concepts like equality and affirmative action are not cut-and-dried formulas, but are ideas that are continually built upon and redefined in the course of struggle. Such conceptions must be goal-directed and are to be realized in action rather than simply articulated in discourse. Bills of rights are living documents that grow and mature within different societies. Thus in the South African context, it is necessary for the people to create a bill of rights that provides the maximum room for advancing the interests of the disadvantaged majority. In this context, affirmative action provides a programme upon which people can lay claim to advancement. It obliges Parliament to adopt certain standards in implementing corrective action. The role of the courts should be minimized so that they are not obliged to review the substance of legislation authorizing affirmative action, but simply to ensure that appropriate procedures have been followed.

The term affirmative action may be found objectionable in some quarters due to its apparent transplantation of a concept relevant to the position of disadvantaged minorities, as in the US. A more indigenous conceptualization is needed in the South African context. Any half-measures in the formulation of equality and affirmative action in the bill of rights for post-apartheid South Africa which do not recognize the peculiarities of the situation will only serve to heighten frustration and undermine the credibility of the bill of rights itself.

NOTES

1. Cowen, D. V. *The Foundations of Freedom* (Cape Town, Oxford University Press, 1961).

2. Palmer, V. V. and Poulter, S. M. *The Legal System of Lesotho* (Morija, Lesotho, 1972).

3. Bennett, T. W. 'Application of customary law in southern Africa' in *The Conflict of Personal Laws* (Cape Town, Juta and Co. Ltd, 1985).

4. *Brown v Leyds N. O* [1897] 4 Official Reports 17 (South Africa).

5. Dugard, J. *Human Rights and the South African Legal Order* (Princeton, NJ, Princeton University Press, 1978), p. 24.

6. Thompson, L. M. *The Unification of South Africa: 1902–1910* (Oxford, Oxford University Press, 1960), p. 95.

7. *Ndlwana v Hofmeyr N. O.* [1937] AD 229 (South Africa).

8. *Harris v Minister of the Interior* [1952] (2) South African Law Reports 428.

9. *Harris v Minister of the Interior* [1952] (4) South African Law Reports 769.

10. Cowen, D. V. *The Foundations of Freedom* (Cape Town, Oxford University Press, 1961). Cowen, D. V. 'Constitution making for democracy', (1960) pamphlet.

11. Molteno, D. B. 'Commission report on franchise proposals and constitutional safeguards' (1960) *Annual Survey of South African Law* 12.

12. Dugard, J. 'Changing attitudes towards a bill of rights in South Africa' in van der Westhuizen, J. V. and Viljoen, H. P. *A Bill of Rights for South Africa* (Butterworths Publishers Ltd, 1988) p. 31.

13. *Sachs v Minister of Justice* [1934] AD (South Africa).

14. Forsyth, C. F. *In Danger for Their Talents: A Study of the Appellate Division of South Africa from 1950–1980* (Cape Town, Juta, 1985); Corder, M. *Judges at Work* (Cape Town, Juta, 1984); Matthews, A. S. *Freedom, State, Security and the Rule of Law* (London, Sweet and Maxwell, 1988).

15. Tomlinson, F. R. Summary of the report Commission for the Socio-Economic Development of the Bantu Areas, U.G. 61/1955 (Pretoria, 1955) p. 103.

16. Republic of South Africa *House of Assembly Debates (Hansard)* vol. 107 (23 March 1961) col. 3507.

17. *Ibid.* vol. 2 (23 January 1962) col. 92.

18. State Department of Information *Multinational Development in South Africa: The Reality* (Pretoria, 1974) p. 94.

19. Quoted by Mervis, J. 'A critique of separate development' in Rhoodie, N.J. (ed.) *South African Dialogue: Contrasts in South African Thinking on Basic Race Issues* (Philadelphia, Westminster Press, 1972) p. 71.

20. Corbett, M. M. 'Human rights: the road ahead' (1979) *South African Law Journal* 192; Hiemstra, V. G. 'Constitutions of liberty' (1971) 88 (1) *South African Law Journal* 47; 'Republic

of South Africa, rule of law in' (1962) 99 *Acta Juridica* 137.

21. Republic of South Africa Constitutional Committee of the President's Council 2nd report *The Adaptation of Constitutional Structures in South Africa* (Government Printer, Cape Town, P.C.4/1982) ch. 9 para. 9.10.1.

22. Buthelezi Commission Report *The Requirement for Stability and Development in Kwazulu and Natal* (1982) p. 114. It should be noted that this commission was in fact chaired by Prof. Schreiner of the University of Natal but named after Mangosuthu Buthelezi.

23. Kentridge, S. 'Civil rights in southern Africa: the prospects for the future' (1987) *Lesotho Law Journal* 97; Saunders, A.J.G.M. 'The bills of rights issue — good government first' (1985) 2 *Journal of Judicial Science* 212.

24. The University of Pretoria held a symposium entitled 'A Bill of Rights for South Africa' on 1-2 May 1986; see 'Proceedings' in van der Westhuizen and Viljoen op. cit. (note 12).

25. Dugard, J. *Human Rights and the South African Legal Order* (Princeton, Princeton University Press, 1978).

26. Greenberg, J. 'South Africa and the American Experience' 54 *New York University Law Review* 3.

27. Saunders op. cit. (note 23).

28. Quoted in Ibid. at 213-14.

29. Venter, F. 'The withering of the rule of law' (1979) 8 *Speculum Juris* 69 at 86-89.

30. Van der Vyver, J. D. 'The bill of rights issue' (1985) 10 *Journal of Juridical Science* 4.

31. Ibid.

32. Ibid.

33. The Republic of South Africa *House of Assembly Debates* (23 April 1986) col. 4014-15; General Notice 303 of 1988, GG 11288 of May 1988; The Promotion of Constitutional Development Act 86 of 1988.

34. Sachs, A. *Towards a Bill of Rights in a Democratic South Africa* 2nd edn (Maputo, Omni, 1988) pp. 11-12, 20-21; see too Sachs, A. *Protecting Human Rights in a New South Africa* (Cape Town, Oxford University Press, 1990).

35. Raymond, S. and Cronin, J. *Thirty Years of the Freedom Charter: A Blue-print for a Democratic South Africa* occasional paper No. 9 (University of Witwatersrand, Centre for Applied Legal Studies, 1985).

36. African National Congress (document undated). See van de Vyver, op. cit. (note 30).

37. Sachs, A. *Protecting Human Rights*, p. 5.

38. South African Law Commission 'Group and Human Rights' (Working Paper no. 25) (1988).

39. *New Nation Newspaper* (South Africa) (29 September-5 October 1989) 7; also (4th quarter 1989) No. 119 *The African Communist* 100.

40. Sachs, A. 'A bill of rights for South Africa: areas of agreement and disagreement, human rights in the post apartheid South African Constitution' (London, South African Constitution Studies Centre, Institute of Commonwealth Studies, 1989) p. 17.

41. See note 33 in its emphasis on group rights.

IV

LOOKING AHEAD

22

Teaching and Research:
Where Should We Be Going?

Susan Atkins*

INTRODUCTION

The development of anti-discrimination law as a coherent academic discipline resembles in many respects the development of other 'single issue' subjects, such as consumer law, welfare law, patients' law, children's law. All developed from the 1970's concerns with a new 'law and society' or 'law in context' approach, whereby legal academics, often involved with the client group as activist or adviser, aimed to challenge the positivist stance of legal scholarship and the legal curriculum. Heavily involved in practical issues, these academics sought to close the gap between knowledge and reality, to look behind the creation of law by legislators and judges and to bring a critical awareness of the effect of law in practice.[1]

In both race and sex discrimination law in this country, academics in the seventies had easy access to empirical data, sociological research and primary resources as the legislature debated the form, content and objectives of first the Sex Discrimination Act 1975 and then the third Race Relations Act in 1976. In race discrimination in particular, academics had access to a substantial body of empirical and theoretical material, legal as well as sociological,[2] which could later be updated by the energetic work of the newly established Commission for Racial Equality in its formal investigations.[3] Although feminist research and publications developed later, even in the seventies academics had access to the early sociological works of the new women's movement, legal texts and the empirical work by such bodies as the Department of Employment and Equal Opportunities Commission. Much of the legal writing of this period was concerned, as with law in context research,

* This paper reflects the personal views of the author, based on her twelve years' experience as an academic.

with the structures and efficacy of procedures in realizing policy objectives.[4] Those concerns remained a large part of the research programme throughout the next decade,[5] but were joined, as the legal jurisprudence developed through the courts, by the more traditional legal scholarship in which academics comment on and analyse statutes and cases, deriving from them legal principles and prescribing legal norms.[6]

Traditionally, legal research and legal education have been regarded as separate activities, the first superior to the second. Thomson neatly sums it up thus: 'Research and scholarship are perceived as operating at the frontiers, while education is seen as transmitting relatively well established truths and skills.'[7] That division has not been so clearly defined in the law and society courses. As in anti-discrimination law, the relationship appears to be somewhat symbiotic. The research interest of an individual academic leads to the establishment of a new course, through which she or he explores and develops its principles and internal coherence. The very process of teaching, selecting and presenting topics and materials, forms part of the research process. Although many institutions have been willing to widen their curriculum to accommodate individual interests, academic criteria, as well as more practical and logistical concerns, have resulted in selectivity. One aspect to be taken into consideration is the existence of a substantial body of publications, evidence of the importance, intellectual standing and legal integrity of the subject. Moreover, particularly in recent years, publishers have looked to the existence of academic courses as a gauge to the market for new books. The wheel turns full circle when the existence of specialist law books is taken to confirm the existence of a new legal discipline.

To draw attention to the interplay between research and education is not to make any claims of exclusivity. Responsibility for the developement of any new legal subject also rests on legal practitioners, some of whom have also made particularly important contributions to legal scholarship in anti-discrimination law in this country.[8] But for most academics in this field, at least for some of the time, the two activities are linked and in looking at where teaching and research should be going this chapter will in part look at the importance and form of that interplay for the future.

The discussion above may be read as suggesting that anti-discrimination law has been taught only in specialist courses. This is far from the case. Courses in anti-discrimination law have evolved slowly from other courses, mostly but not exclusively from labour law. Historically, labour law courses included first equal pay (after Equal Pay Act 1970) and later, with the introduction of individual complaints to industrial tribunals in Sex Discrimination Act 1975 and Race

Relations Act 1976, sex and race discrimination. Even in the early eighties, the relatively small body of case law[9] made such topics easy to contain within the broader employment law perspective. The explosion of case law over the last decade has also been largely employment related, so that even where separate courses have developed it has been natural that employment law should remain the focus of attention and the conceptual home.

There has been little challenge to this predominance of employment law and traditional legal methodology from any of the other courses in which aspects of anti-discrimination law have been taught, for instance, courses covering administrative law, civil liberties, poverty law, women and law and EEC law. In each case, these course have looked at more discrete aspects of discrimination and done so clearly within the conceptual framework of the particular course.

The law and discrimination course I taught for twelve years was different in that it evolved out of a research interest in discrimination *per se*. The course was started as a half-yearly, optional race and sex discrimination course by Albie Sachs and Judith Mayhew in 1974; I ran it for two years before changing it in 1979 to a full year's course for third-year law and joint honours undergraduates. By the mid-eighties, the course was also being offered (with additional tuition) to law postgraduates and as a core course for an innovative MSc in Equal Opportunities, intended primarily for administrators and personnel managers. Employment aspects, of course, played a large part, but in devising the course structure, topics and reading list (which changed frequently), I was able to build on the particular interests of the students, topics of current importance and developments both within the equal opportunities field and in other legal subjects. Thus the course over the years included (in alphabetical order): comparative constitutional law, crime, education, housing, immigration, motherhood, nationality, the police, religious discrimination and social security, as well as employment and EEC law. The connections and disjunctions between topics at a variety of levels were explored to build up a better understanding of the nature, dynamics and ideologies of anti-discrimination law.

My own experience reflects what has happened generally. The diversity of courses within which anti-discrimination law has been and is being taught has played a part in the development of the subject, not least because it has increased the numbers of academics concerned with it and thus the amount of legal research and numbers of publications. But the disparity of background and context has also hindered the development of anti-discrimination law as a subject in its own right. The W. G. Hart Legal Workshop in July 1990 was unique and important in that, unlike previous conferences and seminars which had looked at particular aspects, it set out to explore and pull together the diverse strands of thinking and research in and around the subject. The very holding of the workshop recognized the potential claim to be a new subject.

Anti-discrimination law is not the only subject to have been developed over the last fifteen or so years. Feminist law, or women's law as it is known in Scandinavia, is one of the other new subjects now being recognized across the Western world. Unlike anti-discrimination law, it has paid particular attention to legal theory. Moreover, it has rejected the centrality of law and the liberal concepts on which anti-discrimination law is based.[10] Within the critical legal studies movement, feminist theory has been singled out for its positive approach and potential creativity. So in answering the question where we are headed, this essay will look first at feminist theory in research and teaching and will then go on to see whether the approaches have any application to anti-discrimination law generally.

FEMINIST LEGAL RESEARCH

Feminist legal research shares the fundamental understanding of all feminist research: that 'woman' is a socially constructed concept. It shares with other parts of critical legal research an understanding that law is also a social construct and a desire to analyse and explain the ideologies of law. But the critical legal studies approach is not merely an analytical activity, it is also purposive, founded on a desire to transform legal consciousness and the ways in which legal ideologies interplay with other social constructs in the creation of social ordering. In feminist law, the purpose is gender-specific, to examine and understand how women are considered in law, how the law corresponds to women's realities and needs, and how the law acts to suppress women. Feminist research has the explicit aim of changing the position of women in society. The research is not only *about* women (which of course it is only partly, as it is the role *law* plays in women's relationships in society which is under examination) — the research is also *for* women.[11]

Being part of the women's movement of the last twenty or so years has been important for individual researchers not only socially but also academically. For feminist theory has provided feminist legal research with a critical tool of supreme importance. Feminism provides a very clear analytical world view within which to locate law and legal institutions. In critiquing the positivists' stance on law, feminist scholars can draw on a theory which points to a set of conceptual dichotomies within which Enlightenment science and epistemology are constructed: reason vs emotion and social value, mind vs body, culture vs nature, self vs others, objectivity vs subjectivity, knowing vs being. In each dichotomy, the former is to control the latter lest the latter threaten to overwhelm the former, and the threatening 'latter' in each case appears to be systematically associated with 'the feminine'.[12]

Put another way, feminist legal scholars show not only how the construction of law stems from and furthers male interests, but also how the very processes of that construction are based on values which are, in our society, assumed to be male.[13] Thus the law assigns meaning to concepts through processes which are selective, reductionist, oppositional and hierarchical, and which seek to objectify, classify, individualize and depoliticize the people and experiences under scrutiny.

Traditional academic research and legal scholarship does nothing to challenge the 'maleness' of these processes. Most legal research focuses on the written word, where even primary sources tend to be court records, most particularly appeal court records, rather than the processes leading up to and including court trials whose dynamics will include much non-verbal communication. In the positivist tradition legal scholarship is abstractive, making 'sense' of a discipline from rarefied principles which avowedly bear little relation to the facts which produced the need for them. Thus, legal scholarship, in contributing to the development of a legal discipline, supports and furthers the male value. Not only does legal scholarship play an important part in the construction of a legal discipline, it also plays a significant role in shaping the discourse of that discipline. For the most part these academic discourses result from and revolve around material which is entirely 'male' within the meanings outlined above. Legal scholarship has little direct contact with reality. Little legal research is empirically based and few academics also practise professionally. Even if this were not the case, the methodologies by which reality is translated and presented in research incorporate those Enlightenment values which produce the gender bias.

Thus feminist legal research (in common with other feminist research) has focused much attention on the search for new methodologies, recognizing the intertwining of methodology, epistemology and ideology. Although not exclusive in these concerns,[14] the Scandinavian School of Women's Law has been at the forefront of an international search for new methodologies which are principled, systematical and free from bias.[15]

RESEARCH METHODOLOGIES IN WOMEN'S LAW

Women's law takes as its starting point the experiences of women, rather than the experiences of lawyers. Thus it differs from the 'Women and law' approach, of which it is highly critical,[16] in being women-centred rather than law-centred. Research is based on empirical material drawn from women's own identification of problems, through meetings with women collectively, e.g. women's groups, or individually, e.g. women clients in legal advice clinics.[17]

This ground upward-based approach has several important aspects. First, it enables a construction of legal subjects which are interdisciplinary within legal doctrine, cutting across traditional classifications, and often exposing contradictions and inconsistences within legal policies. These exposures provide openings in which women's lawyers can press for legal reform. Thus the use of empirical data is a critical tool for an analytical process which is both deconstructive and reconstructive. Second, the approach can bring to light laws which have been obscured by the present focus of law. This is particularly so in the case of administrative law, whose effects are well known by those whose interests are determined by it.[18] Women's law on birth law, money law and housewives law has shown how some women in Scandinavia are predominantly governed by administrative law.[19] Work in this country in relation to motherhood has found similar results.[20] Administrative law is regarded by women's law as a particularly important source of law.

> As regards the relationship between the administration of justice and government administration in general, the latter is increasing in size and significance both beyond and at the cost of the former. While judicial decisions continue definitely to occupy a more important place in the legal hierarchy and methodology, general administrative agencies' application of law and regulation-making powers today are of greater significance for the procedural and substantive rights and liberties of the individual.[21]

Stang Dahl goes on to point out how the new legal disciplines, such as social security law and tax law, are changing the scope of legal sources to include lower-level court and tribunal decisions and other administrative guidance.

Empirical data plays an important part in identifying these extra sources of law and Stang Dahl has from it produced new theories of sources of law which include custom in areas of life controlled by neither legislative nor administrative unit. In order to be regarded as a legal source, historically custom had to satisfy certain criteria, e.g. to be uniformly practised, over a period of time, in the belief that it was binding. The scope for custom in developed welfare states may be limited but its rediscovery within a feminist judisprudence enables lawyers to research the operation of law in those private areas positivists declare not to be the concern of law.[22] The legally constructed public/private divide is well recognized as one which operates to women's disadvantage and one which does not a hold up under scrutiny.[23] The women's law approach allows systematic analysis of law across the public/private divide and particularly into negotiations and social orderings, individual as well as collective, which take place in the shadow of the law.

Empirical data is at the base of the women's law approach, but the skills it uses are those of legal scholarship. It is engaged no less than traditional legal scholarship with systematizing legal doctrine, but it is a system through which it is possible to explore relationships between rules, rather than a linear, hierarchical superstructure based on ever-increasing abstractions. Torstein Eckhoff, professor of jurisprudence at Oslo University, has called special attention to the potential of the new systematics and what he defines as 'operative connections' — 'the fact that the applicability of certain rules at one stage of a process of development has a determinative effect on what other rules are applied at the next stage of development'.[24] Stang Dahl has proved the transferability of the approach in the work her institute has done with women lawyers from Eastern and southern African countries, where links have been drawn between different and sometimes competing legal systems and hierarchies, including customary law.

It is this ability to cut across legal systems and legal disciplines from the starting point of a particular group interest which is of most importance to anti-discrimination law. It enables the different, often hidden, effects of law on groups, such as black women, to be identified. But as a legal method it can be used by and for interests far beyond women or other disadvantaged groups. It widens the legal base and our understanding of law while remaining a legal rather than a socio-legal or a sociological science. The women's law offers all academics, but particularly women, alternative methods of research which are not 'male' within the meanings described above with which to develop a scholarship and technical skills which are universally recognized as legal.[25]

Research and legal scholarship based on the women's law method has the capacity to challenge not only the substance of law but also discourses in law. The values of justice and freedom, which underpin the theoretical basis of women's law and which act as criteria for its structure and methodology have been criticized as vague, to the point of being meaningless and political. Yet its emphasis on equity, (a fundamental concern for fairness) dignity, self-realization and self-determination, offer a hopeful alternative to the increasingly sterile Anglo-American equality/difference debate.[26]

It is undoubtedly true that women's law assumes women's difference from men and research at Oslo University is challenging the equality politics now prevailing in Norway. But the discourses in women's law centre not around a comparison between women and men but around the experiences of women. Women's experiences of being defined as the Other, as Simone de Beauvoir identified it, of being defined in relation to men, are exactly what the women's movement in general is fighting. No less so in women's law. Thus if it is important for women to have access to the labour market on terms currently enjoyed by men, that has to be determined by women on their own terms. It is likely that these will include those values of dignity (the right to respect from colleagues and employer), physical integrity, self-realization (recognition of intellectual, technical or financial worth) and self-determination (the right not to have one's choices unfairly denied) rather than equality.

It is the potential of the women's law research methodology, to deconstruct and reconstruct law, to offer openings and programmes for law reform and to challenge existing discourses on law which seem worth exploring with regard to anti-discrimination law.

A NEW RESEARCH AGENDA?

Law academics have fulfilled a most important role over the last ten to fifteen years in analysing, systematizing and criticizing a body of anti-discrimination law in this country which continues to increase in volume and complexity. Through publications, conferences and a wider engagement in public debate, they have raised the profile of anti-discrimination law generally and within legal circles. Yet there exists simultaneously an increasing despair that, despite all this activity, in reality little has changed. This essay suggests that at present we cannot answer the question why the law has failed to deliver on its promises because until now we have not had the necessary analytical tools. Feminist theory, and in particular the women's law methodology, fills those needs.

A research agenda on this model would take as its starting point not law but the empirically determined needs, values and experiences of women and ethnic minorities. Legal research using this methodology would begin to gather and analyze information about the lives of women and ethnic minorities, starting with those experiences which at present we understand to be discriminatory. But the researchers must be very open to the variety of meanings assigned by people in these situations and be actively willing to extend the search for other experiences, other aspects which may be more hurtful or offensive than those currently perceived to be discriminatory. One of the questions that this research programme would hope to answer would be why some people find certain behaviour discriminatory, when others do not, and in particular whether there are any patterns behind these differences.[27] Moreover, there is a need for a more complex understanding of the phenomenon of discrimination. Legally some work has been done, in the development of the concepts of indirect discrimination and sexual harassment. But our present legal construction may not correspond to the meanings assigned by those for whom the law seeks to provide a service, and it is no answer to say that the example of sexual harassment proves that it does. Anti-discrimination law is a means by which the less powerful can challenge their disadvantage. That this phenomenon could be carefully constructed to fulfil the criteria of a particular legal concept may be fortuitous (and precarious, as the legal arguments in *Porcelli* v *Strathclyde Regional Council* show).[28] But it does not mean that that concept provides the 'best fit' or that it necessarily meets the objectives of those seeking to use the law.

As well as gaining a fuller understanding of discrimination, a legal research agenda needs to address the meanings given to law. Lawyers tend to perceive the notion of law as relatively unproblematic — at least for most practical, as opposed to philosophical, purposes. But, as the women's law experience has shown, we need to investigate the understanding, experiences and expectations that women and ethnic minorities have of law. Research into race and policing indicates the potential of this line of enquiry. We need to know, for instance, whether terms and conditions in the workplace are perceived to be a law superior to, possibly simply because of its immediacy, any other type of law, including anti-discrimination law. Research in this area could begin to provide an analysis of the dynamics within employment which operate to deny women and ethnic minorities access to law and shape their unwillingness to fight for what they recognize are their rights.

The research programme would also address why people are willing to use the law, what are their motives and goals. Alice Leonard's work has already shown that the objectives of some of the women taking cases bore no relationship to the goals assumed in the legislation. Leonard

asked all successful applicants of equal pay and sex discrimination cases
between 1980 and 1984 whether bringing a case had been worthwhile.

> The responses were surprising in two respects. First despite
> the problems and unpleasantness encountered by so many
> applicants — often from the time they first discussed their claim
> with an employer until well after the tribunal hearing, and even
> when looking for other jobs — and despite the fact that nearly
> three-quarters of them felt that the 'compensation' they received
> had not fully compensated for the discrimination they had suf-
> fered, 61 of the 70 (87%) started that it *had* been worthwhile.
> Second in explaining the *reason* for their opinion, there was
> remarkable consistency among applicants, who repeatedly stated
> it had been worthwhile because they had proved a matter of princi-
> ple or had helped others by winning their cases: fully 50 applicants
> (82% of those who said it had been worthwhile) gave these as
> their reasons.[29]

The research also set out very clearly the costs to women bringing cases,
which for the most part was not felt to be adequately covered. So this
sort of research could be used to inform not only law reform but judicial
awards of damages. But perhaps most interesting is the groundswell
support it appears to give for collective and/or test case action.

In questioning the fundamental objectives of the legislation, the
research might also reassess remedies and provide a desperately needed
coherent and principled set of criteria for determining appropriate outcomes of complaints. Empirical work in the criminal law field indicates
the potential of such an approach.[30] Studies of victims of crime have
provided a clear guide to the ranges of compensating and punitive action
they feel are appropriate for different types of crime. Such studies have
created a context in which more reparative sentences, such as community service, are being advocated. At a local level, probation services
are getting involved in individual meetings between criminal and victim
through which the perpetrator has to acknowledge the harm he or she
has caused and the victim expunges fears, apprehensions or other
negative emotions caused by the offence. Research on the model
advocated could establish what people wanted out of a legal case, could
build up a model for determining a range of results to be applied and
criteria for selecting from that range in individual cases. It might also
lead to new policy options in civil law, as has happened in criminal law.

Meetings between criminal and victim are part of a wider movement for alternative forms of dispute resolution. In marked contrast to
traditional dispute resolution these alternatives are characterized by

openness, flexibility, and a search for consensus and conciliation. The adjudicator/sentencer assumes a facilitative role rather than a judgemental role. The process aims towards enabling parties to a dispute to come to an agreement that is acceptable to both, although the adjudicator does not necessarily abrogate any judgemental role. The adjudicator may influence the terms of any settlement by indicating his or her reading of the merits of the case. At the end of the day, the adjudicator can and will decide the issues if no agreement has been reached. The strength of this approach is that it allows differences to be aired and compensation given while at the same time allowing the parties to continue their previous relationship. The benefits to women and ethnic minorities in the employment sphere, where for a variety of reasons, suitable alternative jobs may not be so easy to find, are obvious.

Thus I would expect the new research agenda to include the definition of discrimination, the definition of law, a deeper and more realistic appreciation of the dynamics and constraints of legal intervention, new remedies for discrimination and alternative models for legal intervention and dispute resolution. Because the research would start from and be centred on the experiences and meanings of the world as felt and determined by women and ethnic minorities, it would have a secondary purpose, that of changing the discourses about them. However, the very nature of this research method makes it impossible to know in advance the exact agenda or to predict how those discourses would be changed.

'OTHERNESS' AND THE LAW SCHOOL[31] — FEMINIST CRITIQUES OF TEACHING

At the beginning of this chapter, I noted the links between teaching and research in the development of anti-discrimination law. When there was little 'legal' material from which to teach, it was less likely that teachers would pass down an established set of truths. The increasing body of law and its increasing complexity has required more 'legal' teaching, that is to say, teaching centred around the interpretation of statute and the analysis and ranking of case law. The political realities of race and sex discrimination in our society make the subject attractive to some students and certainly inject an interesting context in which to teach it. In comparison to other subjects in the curriculum, race and sex discrimination is accessible and usually has an enviable immediacy.[32]

But feminist scholarship on teaching methodology exposes the 'hidden curriculum' of law teaching which effectively undermines the substance of this particular subject. If the research agenda is to be changed in the way I have suggested above, dramatic changes are required in teaching.

Feminist critiques of teaching generally focus on its hierarchical nature. The teacher, for example, controls the curriculum (at least *vis-à-vis* the students);[33] determines what is taught; awards and penalizes students with regard to demonstrations of correct knowledge. Even at higher levels, the terminology of student participation and greater autonomy (for example, 'reading for a degree') misdescribes a much-directed activity. Lectures are unilateral occasions, the imparting of information from the one to the many. Tutorials operate to quiz students, to check whether they have understood the material (that is to say, that their interpretation matches that of the lecturer). Even seminars, which in theory allow for student innovation and exploration of meanings, operate within boundaries and parameters set by the lecturer, through the choice of topics, the reading list, etc.

The subject matter of a law degree adds another dimension. Law academics will often claim that there are no right answers. They tell students that academic law is about creating reasoned arguments and that so long as they can present a logical argument supported with authorities (note the use of that word), what the student has to say will be as valid as the lecturer's opinion. To the extent that much law teaching, at least in the early part of the degree, is about obtaining academic skills, the statement is true, for in that context the lecturer is little interested in the subject matter taught. But when the subject is important it is palpably *not* true and the students know it right from the start. Legal analysis of case law, for instance, means taking apart two lines of argument and deciding which one is right. The student does not do this for herself. Rather she has to follow the authorative opinions of a figure(s) in the judicial hierarchy. Students are told to find the ratio of a case, that is to say find the answer, see which lawyer's arguments won. Where there are conflicting judgments the student will also have to decide who got the right answer. Sometimes the answer is mathematical, 'there are more of us than you so we are right'. Sometimes the answer can only be discovered by reference to hierarchies, for instance in the case of majority decisions where each judgment is based on a different premise. In that particular case the student may get another reminder of the power of the lecturer to determine the truth, for it will usually be she or he who assesses which judgment is right (by references of course to the 'authorities'), and determines what the case is really about.

A conflict may appear if another academic opines a different interpretation. Even here the student has good rules for determining the truth. The written word is superior to the spoken word (research superior to teaching). Journals are ranked in order of prestige and thus relatively easy to classify. Books published by the two legal publishers are more prestigious than those by non-legal publishers (particularly non-British publishers) and straight textbooks (the distillation of the law by one authoritative voice) more prestigious than a case book or worse, a mixed case and text-book which presents many voices, a choice of often conflicting messages, space for interpretation (i.e. non-authoritative). The everyday ranking within institutions of lecturers is readily transferable to assessing the written word. These rules enable students to negotiate quite happily the most complex clashes of opinion — a lecture by an eminent 'textbook' professor easily beats the written word of a junior academic; the written word of a textbook professor (or two) will be backed in preference to a majority opinion of the House of Lords.[34] No doubt students mark well the reliance of even that august body on the writers of textbooks from time to time. There is not just a right answer, there is a pyramid of deciders of truth and we teach the students skills of negotiating the pyramid in search of that right answer.

Although many women students do very well in law degrees, the mode of law teaching is not what may be described as 'female'. It is assertive, rather than questioning or hesitant; there is no room for conditional answers, negotiations of meanings. Many female students develop strategies for dealing with the masculine mode of law. For instance they do not speak in class, a gesture which may be interpreted as one of resistance and independence. Few academics appear to understand this tactic and express surprise when such a student does well, with comments such as 'one of those bright girls who take it all in but say nothing'. This tactic is interpreted as being 'not fair' (although the student has correctly assessed what in fact is required), and it may go against her in situations requiring the exercise of discretion. Yet to participate in such a system may simply be to support the status of the lecturer, to confirm his or her position in the pyramid as a determiner of the right answer.

In common with the rest of the critical legal movement, of which it is a part, the feminist critique does not reject the legal method. The basic skills of analysis, ordering, ranking, assessing hierarchies, presenting reasoned arguments and being assertive are valuable. Rather, critical legal theorists suggest that one should work through the legal method to achieve a rather different end.[35] A case will be analysed not to find the right answer but to determine the processes by which that particular conclusion is reached, looking as much (and sometimes more) at what is rejected or never selected in the first place, as at what is selected and for what reasons. In order to make those assessments students need access to a different framework. Mary Jane Mossman, summing up fifteen years' experience of teaching a gender equality course, explains the process:

> Just as sex equality cases provide a unique vehicle for criticizing the law and the legal process, the theoretical framework offered by feminism presents an opportunity for students to probe the underlying values of their own legal education. The existence of a competing framework for analyzing concepts and objectives establishes a basis for analyzing and comparing the actual results of legal education and it also produces an intellectual tension that compels students to explain contradictions and inconsistencies between different points of view.[36]

The teaching of legal method with this approach should serve to empower the student, who does not learn as if by rote (thus taking up her place at the bottom of the pyramid) but rather is enabled to gain control of the system. This process of empowering may be enhanced if it occurs in a course concerned with women or ethnic minorities challenging those structures through which their subordination is maintained.

A NEW ROLE FOR ANTI-DISCRIMINATION LAW TEACHING

The section above describes briefly how feminist critiques of law teaching have drawn attention to the hidden curriculum. Individual law teachers have tried in teaching a range of subjects to explore the hidden subjugation of women by law. In so doing they not only puncture the gender-neutrality of law but expose and challenge the discourses of law, for example about women's sexuality in criminal law, or about motherhood in tort law. This, often *ad hoc*, work greatly enhances the teaching of anti-discrimination law, for it prepares students to read cases in a new way, to focus on legal construction and ideology, and provides an epistemological background for critiquing the new subject of study. It is interesting that some institutions have formalized this experience, offering broad women and law type courses in the first years of a degree, which are then a compulsory requirement for subsequent entry to a feminist theory course.[37]

Little work appears to be taking place with regard to ethnic minorities, who remain as largely invisible outside race discrimination law classes as women did previously. The conjunction of racial disadvantage and the construction of a legal curriculum around the interests of the monied classes (and appeal court judgments) results in few examples of ethnic minority interests. Even in cases concerning people from ethnic minority communities, race is rarely deemed to be a relevant factor in the construction of legal argument. And in the very few cases where it is, few students (or indeed teachers) have access to a theoretical framework within which to make sense of the values underlying the decision.[38] Yet imperial antecedents remain — in past precedents, in legal assumptions and attitudes shaped by an English judiciary who before independence formed part of the central governing mechanism for those very countries from whom Britain's ethnic minorities have come, and through the operation of the Privy Council. Much more work needs to be done into the ethno-centrism of British law schools before the teaching of race discrimination law can be developed in the way suggested for sex discrimination.

The research agenda proposed earlier would have obvious benefits for such teaching. And, as with the early development of race and sex discrimination law as an academic discipline, the possibilities for teaching would have benefits for research. Desan Husson posited a new role for academics as receptive communicators, interposing in the process of communication between the powerless and the powerful, the ruled and the rulers.[39] In developing a jurisprudence centred on women or ethnic minorities, students may have a crucial critical role to play, particularly the stage of developing principles from empirical data. In order to do so, lecturers have to change their ideas about who is the 'expert' and relinquish the power to determine the 'truth'. It involves a greater recognition of teaching as an exchange process of skills for experience and of mutually enhancing ideas. Other aspects of teaching are similarly transformed. For example reading lists, far from enabling students to reach 'right answers', are drawn up so as to facilitate a creative exchange.[40]

To some teachers, all this will be a very familiar description of existing best teaching practice. But its underlying equal opportunities purpose may be very new. A law curriculum in which few women or ethnic minority members feature, which is based on white, male, middle-class values, which is not interested in diversity and difference, sends a clear message that the law and legal establishment is for white middle-class males. Attention is increasingly being given to discrimination within the legal profession[41] but so far little attention has been given to the part played by legal education and educational institutions.

I would suggest that the changes outlined above in the substance and methodology of teaching within those establishments are a necessary part of any equal opportunities policy.

Where then does anti-discrimination law as such fit in to this new approach? The first point to make is that this approach recognizes and is compatible with a diversity of courses within institutions. Since the approach encourages the development of gender and race throughout the curriculum, lecturers are free to use the jurisprudence in whichever contexts their academic and institutional constraints allow. This does not mean a continuation of the present situation. A prerequisite is the building up of a theoretical basis for anti-discrimination law, which would inform the development of the different facets of the subject. The elements concerning discrimination in each course would then be taught within the framework of the new subject rather than, as often now, within the framework of the 'host' course. As well as exploring the potential of the anti-discrimination law framework, lecturers can use its inclusion to raise different questions about the assumptions and underlying hypotheses of the other subject. In this way, it is possible to enrich academic debate, whether in teaching or research. Moreover, such a strategy is likely to be feasible logistically given the relatively small numbers of discrimination 'experts' in each institution. A concomitant of this wider involvement with non-discrimination lawyers at an institutional level is a closer involvement of discrimination law experts nationally. National networks, informal and intermittent or more formal, such as subgroups of SPTL (Society of Public Teachers of Law), could provide such a service across institutions.

The second point to make is that such an approach encourages the development of aspects of anti-discrimination law which are at present in danger of being overlooked in the moves to create a new legal discipline. For example, the relationship between the state and the citizen, which is central to the subject in jurisdictions with explicit constitutional provisions, can be overwhelmed by considerations of rights between citizens, the subject of the UK legislation.[42] The necessity for such wider development can be seen in the difficulty which judges and commentators have in articulating this constitutional human rights dimension, as evidenced by references to quasi-criminal standards, guilt and innocence, as the more usual discourse for state interest in actions between individual citizens.

Finally, I would suggest as a part of this diversity that there is a special role for anti-discrimination law in the introductory/legal method/ jurisprudence courses for law student entrants. Some institutions have recognized the importance of feminist perspective and have either offered a special course on Women/Gender and Law in the first year (as at Osgoode Hall) or inserted that perspective into compulsory first-year courses (as at Oslo University). Such a move in England could open up opportunities for more critical legal education, and lead to a student body willing and able to cope with such an education. Perhaps of more immediate and in this context pertinent concern, it would symbolize an institution's commitment to equal opportunities in practice.

CONCLUSION

This chapter addressed the question of where we should be going in teaching and research in anti-discrimination law. It suggests that we should take a critical approach, following the models developed by feminist legal scholars, with the purpose of creating a future legal profession and legal institutions which welcome and foster diversity; that the challenge for those teaching and researching in this area is to subject themselves, their institutions and practices to the scrutiny their discipline purports to impose on others; that this involves a radical reconceptualization not only of the practices of teaching and research but of the very notion of law itself. The essay warns that unless this happens, the creative potential of the subject will be lost and with it any possibility of answering questions concerning the law's effectiveness, reform, procedures, etc., which have been identified in this book as being so important.

NOTES

1. Thomson, A. 'Critical legal reduction in Britain' in Fitzpatrick, P. and Hunt, A. (eds) *Critical Legal Studies* (Oxford, Basil Blackwell, 1987) pp. 184–86.

2. E.g. Street, H. et al. *Anti-discrimination Legislation: The Street Report* (sponsored by the Race Relations Board and the National Committee for Commonwealth Immigrants); Hepple, B. *Race, Jobs and the Law in Britain* 2nd edn (London, Penguin, 1970); Rose, E. J. B. and Deakin, N. *Colour and Citizenship: A Report on British Race Relations* (London, Panther, 1970); Lester, A. and Bindman, B. *Race and Law in Great Britain* (Harmondsworth, Penguin, 1972); Smith, D. J. *Racial Disadvantage in Britain* (Harmondsworth, Penguin, 1977) (the first PEP report); Lustgarten, L. *Legal Control of Racial Discrimination* (London, Macmillan, 1980).

3. By 1990, the CRE had published reports of formal investigations, research papers on different aspects of discrimination and disadvantage in housing and education, and had put out the consultative draft of a Code of Practice in Employment.

4. See, for instance, Nandy, D. 'Administering anti-discrimination legislation in Great Britain' and Jowell, J. 'The enforcement of laws against sex discrimination in England: problems of institutional design' in Ratner, R. S. (ed.) *Equal Employment Policy for Women* (Philadelphia, Temple University Press, 1980).

5. Gregory, J. 'Equal pay and sex-discrimination ' (1982) No. 10 *Feminist Review*; Graham, C. and Lewis, N. *The Role of A.C.A.S. Conciliation in Equal Pay and Sex Discrimination Cases* (Manchester, EOC, 1985); Leonard, A. *The First Eight Years* (Manchester, EOC, 1986); Leonard, A. *Judging Inequality* (London, Cobden Trust, 1987); Leonard, A. *Pyrrhic Victories* (London, HMSO, 1987); Gregory, J. *Trial by Ordeal: A Study of People Who Lost Equal Pay and Sex Discrimination Cases in the Industrial Tribunals* (London, HMSO, 1989); Chambers, G. with Horton, C. *Promoting Sex Equality: The Role of Industrial Tribunals* (London, Policy Studies Institute, 1990).

6. Pannick, D. *Sex Discrimination and Law* (Oxford University Press, 1985) is an outstanding example of this approach.

7. Thomson op. cit. (note 1) p. 184.

8. Names here include Geoffrey Bindman, Bob Hepple, Alice Leonard, Anthony Lester and David Pannick, some of whose work is cited in notes 2, 5 and 6.

9. Reported in the employment law reports, industrial cases reports and industrial relations law reports.

10. See, for instance, Schneider, E. 'The dialectics of rights and politics: perspectives from the women's movement' (1986) 61 *New York University Law Review* 584.

11. See, for instance, on this point, Cain, M. 'Realism, feminism, methodology and law' (1986) 14 (314) *International Journal of the Sociology of Law* Special Issue: Feminist Perspectives on Law 255.

12. Harding, S. *The Science Question in Feminism* (Milton Keynes, Open University Press, 1986) p. 165.

13. See, for instance, Olson. F. 'Feminism, post-modernism and critical legal studies' in McLoughlin, S. (ed.) *Women and the Law* (London, UCL Working Papers no. 5, 1987). Carol Gilligan's influential book, *In a Different Voice* (Cambridge, Harvard University Press, 1982), has been read oversimplistically by some to be asserting that the gender assignations of such qualities are in fact sexual and thus immutable. The adjectival use of the terms 'male' and 'female' connotes only a recognition that, for historical and political reasons, the one has been associated with men, the other with women.

14. See, for instance, Rhode, D. L. 'Gender and jurisprudence: an agenda for research' (1987) 56 *Cincinnati Law Review* 521, 534; Cole, D. 'Getting there: reflections on trashing from feminist jurisprudence and critical theory' (1985) 8 *Harvard Women's Law Journal* 59; Lahey, K. A. 'Until women themselves have told all there is to tell' (1986) 23 (3) *Osgoode Hall Law Journal* 519.

15. See Stang Dahl, T. *Women's Law: An Introduction to Feminist Jurisprudence* (Oslo, Norwegian University Press, 1987); and also Stang Dahl, T. 'Taking women as a starting point: building women's law' and Weiss Bentzon, A. 'Comments on women's law in Scandinavia' (1986) 14 *International Journal of Sociology of Law* 239, 249.

16. For example, Frost, L. (1986) 14 *International Journal of Sociology of Law* 415.

17. Fastvold, M. and Hellum, A. give a full account of the methodology used in their research project on the distribution of money and work in marriage in *Money and Work in Marriage — Women's Perspectives on Family Law*,'Oslo, Oslo University, Institute of Public Law, Working Paper no. 6, 1988).

18. Academics who have taught extra-mural classes or been involved with legal advice centres will be familiar with the discovery of an alternative and extremely detailed legal expertise among welfare claimants.

19. Stang Dahl, T. op. cit. (note 15) and Stang Dahl, T. (ed.) *Kvinnerett* vols. 1,2 (Oslo, Norwegian University Press, 1985).

20. Kelly, P. 'Not just a woman . . . (Unpublished dissertation, Southampton University, 1986).

21. Stang Dahl, T. op. cit. (note 19) pp. 64–65.

22. Poulter's essay in this book makes a persuasive case for the use of custom for ethnic minorities within a family law system which empowers parties to decide the state of their affairs.

23. O' Donovan, K. *Sexual Divisions in Law* (London, Weidenfeld & Nicolson, 1985).

24. Eckhoff, T. 'Can we learn anything from Women's Law?' in Christensen, A., Stang Dahl, T., Eckhoff, T. and Eriksson, L. D. *Methodology of Women's Law* Institute of Public and International Publications Series no. 7 (Oslo, University of Oslo, 1988).

25. An issue also identified outside Europe: see, for instance, Cole, D. op.cit. (note 14); Thornton, M. 'Feminist jurisprudence: illusion or reality?' (1986) 3 *Australian Journal of Law and*

Society 5. The Scandinavian experience heralds, however, a note of caution. Christensen, A. 'Women's law and legal positivism' in Christensen, A. et al. op. cit. (note 24) outlines the struggle for recognition of Women's Law at Oslo University and of Professor Stang Dahl's competence for a full professorship, granted only after being honoured by the University of Copenhagen. Not all commentators agree that the search for such a feminist jurisprudence is worthwhile or sound. Carol Smart has recently denounced such attempts, alleging that, far from decentring law as they claim, they 'end with a celebration of positivistic scientific feminism which seeks to replace one hierarchy of truth with another' (*Feminism and the Power of Law* (London, Routledge & Kegan Paul, 1989) ch. 4, particularly p. 89). Yet the approach she appears to advocate, 'not to challenge legal method so much as to ignore it and focus on legal practice' (p. 25), fails to address the central issue: how to define law. Without such a definition it is impossible to decide what is and is not legal practice, unless she intends it to be confined to practices in the hands of lawyers, which appears to run counter to her demand to take the debate out of the exclusive hands of lawyers. Smart appears to have reached her position by confining, mistakenly, legal method to case-law analysis. In so doing, she not only ignores the diversity of legal methods familiar, for instance, to public lawyers, an area of law of particular importance to women, she also misrepresents the nature of Stang Dahl's work, which is to seek to build a new legal science, to create what is explicitly called a feminist jurisprudence.

26. For a concise critique of the equality/difference debate, see Smart, C. op. cit. (note 25).

27. The obvious difference is of course between the parties to a case and adjudicators who express their difference of opinion in terms of finding for or against the complainant, in their analysis of the issues involved or, more bluntly, in the amount of damages awarded. It is also suggested that the rules by which damages are determined are the result of an interpretation of the concept of discrimination not often shared by those who experience it. See Atkins, S. and Hoggett, B. *Women and the Law* (Oxford, Basil Blackwell, 1984) pp. 34–38. But differences quite clearly exist between people of the same sex or ethnic background.

28. *Porcelli v Strathclyde Regional Council* [1985] ICR 177.

29. Leonard, A. *Pyrrhic Victories* op. cit. (note 5) pp. 37–41 (Emphasis in the original).

30. Hough, M. and Mayhew, P. *Taking Account of Crime — Key Findings from the Second British Crime Survey* (London, Home Office Research Study 85, 1985); Jones, T., MacLean, B. and Young, J. *The Islington Crime Survey* (Aldershot, Gower, 1986).

31. From Mary Jane Mossman's article. '"Otherness" and the law school: a comment on teaching gender equality' (1985) 1 *Canadian Journal of Women and Law* 213.

32. In the last few years of my Law and Discrimination course I opened each session with a news and current events item, inviting student contributions. This not only shared the task of keeping up with events and created an interest and involvement in the subject, it also demystified it as a 'legal' subject.

33. There is of course another hierarchy of control over the legal curriculum in which the legal profession plays a significant part, particularly in relation to radical or critical legal education. See in this regard Chesterman, M. and Weisbrot, D. 'Legal scholarship in Australia' (1987) *Modern Law Review* 709–24.

34. As happened a few years ago when both Professors Glanville Williams and Smith, the two leading textbooks writers in British criminal law, disagreed with two consecutive opinions of the House of Lords on the meaning of recklessness.

35. Mossman works through and comments on this approach with regard to the Person's cases in 'Feminism and legal method: the difference it makes' (1986) 3 *Australian Journal of Law and Society* 30. See also Stubbs, M. 'Feminism and legal positivism' (1986) 36 *Australian Journal of Law and Society* 63.

36. Mossman op. cit. (note 31) p. 217.

37. As at Osgoode Hall; see Mossman, op. cit. (note 31) and Oslo University.

38. Sebastian Poulter has attempted to develop such a framework: see 'African customs in an English setting: legal and policy aspects of recognition' (1987) 3 *Journal of African Law* 207; and *English Law* and Ethnic Minority Customs (London, Butterworths, 1986). See also Atkins, S. 'Legal history and women's law in commonwealth countries', *Working Papers in Women's Law* no. 21 (Oslo University, Institute of Women's Law, 1989).

39. Desan Husson, C.A. 'Expanding the legal vocabulary: the challenge posed by the

deconstruction and defense of law' (1986) 95 *Yale Law Journal* 969.

40. Professor Hepple informs me that the Anti-Discrimination Programme research seminars at University College adopt this approach.

42. As, for instance, in the Courts and Legal Services Act 1990.

41. European Community law does provide a quasi-constitutional framework, but of a particular kind, in which considerations of national autonomy and women's position under capitalism compete with a constitutional analysis.

23

Racial Inequality, Public Policy and the Law: Where Are We Going?

Laurence Lustgarten

In one sense, the answer to the question this Chapter title asks can be very brief and to the point — we are going nowhere fast, round and round in ever decreasing circles. In fact in more depressing moments it seems to me that a more appropriate answer is that we are walking backwards with our faces to the future, as if determined to ignore the evidence of our eyes and to exacerbate the inequalities and divisions within our society. But there are two dimensions to the question when more analytically considered: the predictive and normative. The first — where are we going? — is based on a reading of social realities and trends. The second — where *should* we be going? — is grounded in some conception of what is morally and socially desirable. One cannot criticize actual developments without some clear normative conception, so it is there that I want to start.

WHERE SHOULD WE BE GOING?

Perhaps the best way to approach this is to ask oneself what are the goals of racial equality policy. I use the term 'equality' rather than 'non-discrimination' for the latter suggests a mere negative, while equality implies more wide-ranging aims. I would identify these goals in the following way.

First, the just treatment of individuals; that is to say no unfavourable treatment on the grounds of race, ethnicity, etc. Several essays in this volume have referred to the inadequacies of formal liberal equality.[1] I would strongly endorse this, and in fact have tried elsewhere to sketch a conception of substantive equality that might be workable in public law.[2] Nonetheless the imperative need to deepen our legal conception

of equality to take adequate account of real material power relations
does not displace the fundamental premise of the equality of human
persons.[3] On the contrary, that is the bedrock on which we must build.
This is so for several reasons, of which the most important is the ethical
one that individuals alone can claim moral status. The collective dimension of social life is obvious and undeniable; indeed no discussion of
discrimination could make any sense without it being at centre stage.
But it becomes a matter of concern for morality, and also for social
policy, only because of the effects — positive or negative, as the basis
of cultural self-definition or discriminatory exclusion by others — on
individuals.

At this point I would mention only one other reason why we must
take the fair treatment of individuals as our starting point, a reason
which is frankly political. The value of fairness in the sense of formal
equality is one that is deeply rooted in British culture, however much
honoured in the breach. It has been the driving force behind much of
the efforts to counter discrimination; and it should be remembered that
the majority of the public has consistently supported the enactment of
anti-discrimination legislation precisely on this basis, even as they
simultaneously supported restrictive immigration laws.[4] To abandon
or even to minimize this goal would be politically suicidal.

But of course we cannot stop there. We need to go further and take
as the second goal *group distributional equality*. By this I mean — to take
what is probably the most important single indicator — that the income
distribution of each racial or ethnic group of significant size should be
proportionately equivalent to whites; and, as a byproduct, that rates of
unemployment should be roughly equal.[5] It is important to emphasize
that I am not suggesting that there is some one indisputably correct
income distribution or acceptable level of unemployment. What I am
saying is that the societal distribution, whatever it is, should apply iden-
tically to all ethnic groups. Thus — to pull some figures out of the
sky — if among whites the top 10 per cent of earners are earning over
£25,000, while the median is £12,000 and the bottom 25th percentile
mark is at £8,000, the pattern among ethnic minorities should echo
this. The figures are hypothetical, but what is very real at the moment
is the concentration of ethnic minorities in the lower percentiles.[6]

Now one may believe that the present distribution of income is
excessive in its inequalities. For my part I would strongly agree, but that
is beside the point. We are talking about *racial* inequality, which means
insisting that, whatever the general social pattern, ethnic minorities are
not concentrated at the bottom of the pile. I have chosen to emphasize
income and employment because together they are the single most
important source of inequality in our society, in which, to quote from

Derek Bell's essay in this book, 'work provides sustenance, status and the all-important sense of self-worth'. But exactly the same group-equality analysis should be applied to other important areas of material life, especially housing and education. By talking in these collective terms, one makes proper allowance for variations in individuals' abilities, efforts, luck and everything else that goes into the making of success. It is not that individuals are equal — patently they are not — but that within a mix of abilities present in groups containing several hundred thousand people, the distribution of those success factors should be roughly proportionate among each group even if the economic strength of each group may lie in very different activities or areas.

Once it becomes clear that ethnic minorities are concentrated at the bottom, it becomes the responsibility of government to adopt policies to bring about group equalization in the sense I have described. What those specific policies will be would depend on one's diagnosis of the causes, which would vary significantly from sub-group to sub-group within the ethnic minority population. Examples might include targeting Afro-Caribbean (but not Asian) would-be entrepreneurs for various forms of financial and advisory assistance with their ventures; providing special English classes for Bangladeshi immigrants; or strengthening efforts to reduce discrimination in promotion, a matter particularly affecting Indians at the moment. The key point is to further group distributional equality.

The third and final goal that I would want to establish is the acceptance in principle of the equality of cultural norms and beliefs, which means adjustment and accommodation to customs and practices of significant minority groups. I would make this subject to two provisos. First is the paramountcy of human rights norms, and here it is sufficient to refer to Sebastian Poulter's essay on the subject in this book. Second, some notion of proportionality   must operate, which will balance the seriousness of the minority's interest against the degree of disruption the accommodation will cause.[7] Moreover, while insisting that equality requires respect and acceptance of different cultural norms, I would equally insist upon the principle that each individual retains the right of self-definition about group membership or identity; it is not a matter of external characterization by some outside body. Many people will not wish to be regarded as members of any ethnic group and many more will be of mixed parentage or otherwise have dual attachments that lead them to want to retain what they see as the good or desirable elements within each. They must be permitted to choose for themselves.

WHERE ARE WE GOING?

Having identified the goals, we may then consider how well we are placed to achieve them. Perhaps the best way to approach this question is to consider how developments of the past decade have affected the chances of reaching them. It must be said that the 1980s were pretty disastrous in terms of achieving racial equality, with the exception of the economic, professional and educational gains apparently made by Indian and East African Asians. But the reality of racial disadvantage and the persistence of high levels of direct discrimination,[9] let alone more subtle variations, indicate that the government has been destructive at two levels: actively, in its particular policies, and ideologically, in the realm of ideas, consciousness and expectations. The latter is perhaps even more effective for being so insidious and indeed is often a by-product of other things — a sort of ideological indirect discrimination.

WHERE WE HAVE BEEN

Take the policies first. We may start with education, for if things go wrong, the Education Reform Act 1988 could turn out to be the single worst measure of the last decade. The practical facilitation and symbolic encouragement of so-called parental choice has been coupled with a criminal indifference to the ensuing segregation. This was exemplified by the manifest self-contradiction in the statement of Baroness Hooper, the government spokeswoman in the House of Lords: 'Segregation is no part of this Bill. We underline the fact that in giving parents choice we do not wish to circumscribe that choice in any way.'[10] This policy seems almost guaranteed to produce a significant increase in ethnically separate schooling.[11] Secondly, it is possible that there will be further segregation emerging from the opt-out provisions for schools,[12] though this is very unclear as yet. Everything will turn on whether future legislation permits schools to devise selection criteria for pupils, creating a huge range of possibilities for indirect and covert direct discrimination.

Third, in the same piece of legislation there is the emphasis on a Christian character of collective worship.[13] This was not the Education Secretary's intention, but rather the Bishop of London's contribution to race relations in the 1980s which the then Prime Minister gratefully accepted. It is a slap in the face to the value of religious equality, even granted the provisions allowing for individual or collective exemption.[14] Several essays in this volume tell us about legislation sending messages, and that was about the worst possible one which could have been broadcast in this context.

Finally, there is the matter of student loans. I may have got the wrong end of this particular stick, but it does seem to me that if one were seeking to devise an examination question involving indirect discrimination, it would be very difficult to come up with a better hypothetical. As virtually everyone who has commented on the issue has noted, the prospect of incurring large debts (increasing each year of study as inflation erodes the value of the fixed grant) seems particularly likely to deter two sorts of applicants: mature and working class. Since these are the two groups from which ethnic minority students are disproportionately drawn, the mathematically inevitable conclusion is that the loans scheme will be particularly effective in blocking ethnic minority access to university (and presumably all higher) education. This can only be a prediction, since the scheme has just been introduced.[15] But unless something strikingly unexpected emerges, I fear this will be the outcome.

Moving from education to housing, there is another matter which has not received the attention it deserves. Afro-Caribbeans especially attempted to enter into the council-house sector relatively soon after they arrived. Initially they were kept out by residence requirements, but as those either were dropped or surmounted with time they joined the system. They usually ended up in inferior housing, as the consequence of various direct and indirect discriminatory practices.[16] Having gone through that process there would in the normal course of events have been at least a reasonable expectation that they would succeed to better housing stock as resident whites moved on or died. But of course that housing stock isn't there any more. It has been sold off. The full impact is very difficult to measure, but in my view the selling off of council houses (which can be defended on other policy grounds) had in London and the West Midlands the consequence of destroying the opportunity for accession by Afro-Caribbeans to good and reasonably priced accommodation.

In relation to employment, the 1980s were the decade of the great shakeout. This 'restructuring' of the economy hit black people particularly hard because of their labour market position; the deindustrialization of Britain affected above all those who had come here to do unskilled and semi-skilled labouring jobs. Remember the rate of unemployment: 21 per cent at its peak in the mid-1980s, and at least double that in many cities for young people.[17] Now this restructuring was common throughout Western economies but in Britain it was accompanied by a distinctive policy of high interest rates and deflation which benefited substantial wealth holders — who were, of course, overwhelmingly white — at the expense of the disproportionately black working class. Moreover — something else whose ethnic impact seems to have been missed — the cuts in social security benefits to the under-25s as the system was stripped of its social support elements and became wholly geared to labour market discipline, have hit black people in quite a disproportionate way because they are heavily represented among the young.[18] Recently there has been an economic upturn and, following the classic cycle that Colin Brown and others have identified, the ethnic minority unemployment rate has declined more rapidly than that for whites. Nonetheless, according to Brown's figures, the rate for Afro-Caribbeans is twice and for Pakistani/Bangladeshis is more than three times that of whites. It is only when we look at Indians that some sort of equalization appears.[19]

Furthermore, training programmes in Britain, which by European standards are narrow in access and grossly underfunded, are failing to equip young/black people with the skills needed for productive and economically rewarding careers.[20] Indeed about the only piece of good luck ethnic minority youth have enjoyed is the relative scarcity of young people generally, the so-called 'demographic downturn' of the 1990s.[21] Yet even here there has been a counter-development which is full of irony. It is good in principle that more opportunities are opening up for women. On the other hand, the problem is that many women are coming into the labour market well qualified, whereas in the absence of this pool of labour, there would have been a much greater incentive, indeed necessity, for employers and government to establish training schemes for working-class people in general and ethnic minorities in particular. Such programmes cost money, and with such limited incentive for private industry especially to invest in training, opportunities that in earlier times might have become available to ethnic minority men may well remain closed.[22]

Another issue is the so-called 'deregulation of business', particularly small firms,[23] exemplified by measures like the weakening of the Wages Councils and repeal of the Fair Wages Resolution, lengthening the qualifying periods for employment rights and erecting cost barriers for industrial tribunal litigants.[24] A more jaundiced description of the policy would be boring holes in the legislative floor of rights, leaving the poorest and most vulnerable workers at risk of exploitation while making redress more difficult. Like all the other economic policies I have mentioned, this has had a particularly harsh impact of ethnic minorities because of their position in (or involuntarily out of) the labour market. None was *designed* to penalize black people; indeed all were devised without a moment's thought given to the impact upon them. It is a classic example of institutional racism (which we lawyers have rather awkwardly simplified into the notion of indirect discrimination), but no less devastating in its effects for that.

At the level of politics and government, constitutionally one of the most significant developments in the 1980s was the growth of centralization.[25] The attack on local government has ranged right across the board, from curtailing financial independence[26] to taking over or hiving off various functions in relation to transport, housing and education[27] — and when the voters in all our major urban areas elected councils which opposed central government policy, those councils were simply legislated out of existence.[28] The hallmark of government policy has been to draw power to the centre, cut out the local authorities and replace them, either with detached and unelected bodies like development boards and housing associations and opted-out schools, or through imposed privatization. The ethnic dimension is that the only real ground of political power black people can occupy — because of their small numbers and geographic concentration — has been badly eroded. In the current debate about regionalism and centralism, it needs to be emphasized that ethnic minorities are particularly empowered by localism. It should be added too that contract compliance, one very useful and effective policy in which local government has led the way, in part because of political pressure from black groups, has largely been gutted by the Local Government Act 1988.[29]

Finally, another subject (which has received virtually no discussion at all in the essays in this volume but is extremely important) is that of criminal justice. The economic conditions I have been describing are of themselves criminogenic, but they have been coupled in the 1980s with an emphasis on punitiveness, the need for imprisonment (belatedly reversed at the decade's end) and the encouragement of longer sentences: all factors leading to a significant criminalization of black youth. Now we have not, thank God, reached the American stage. According to a study issued by a pressure group called the Sentencing Project, nearly *one in four* black American males in his twenties is in gaol, on parole or on probation.[30] In Britain the figures are not so alarming, but they are still pretty bad. Statistics are fragmentary, but two deserve attention. First, there was a NACRO report a couple of years ago which suggested that one in twenty young men under 21 would have either been in prison or received a suspended sentence. Second, Home Office prison surveys show that the proportion of black male prisoners is about double those in the comparable age groups of the general population; and the generalized category 'black' here obscures the even greater proportion of Afro-Caribbeans, whose numbers in prison are statistically offset by the relatively small numbers of Asians.[31] A reasonable estimate, deliberately erring in a conservative direction, would therefore be that about one young Afro-Caribbean man in eight has received some form of custodial sentence. We lack the precision of American statistics, but the inescapable fact is that we face a serious prospect of the emergence of a criminal underclass of black youth.

THE IDEOLOGICAL DIMENSION

Here there are three matters I want to emphasize. First, the general decline in egalitarianism as a public value and a social goal. Egalitarianism was a cornerstone of the post-war era regardless of which political party was in office, and was considered a standard with regard to which all policies, even those with wholly unrelated objectives like the pay freezes of the 1970s, were judged. What we now get instead is typified by Kenneth Baker's proclamation on education at the Conservative Party Conference in 1987: 'The pursuit of egalitarianism is over.'

Now this means that the assumption that something is wrong when there are racial inequalities, which derived from the idea that any significant inequality bore a heavy burden of justification, no longer governs in the minds of large numbers of people. What has partly replaced it is the ethos of blaming the victim, which is much stronger than a decade ago. Redistribution is out of favour. It is very interesting that now the Labour Party, rather than talking about equality, is talking in loose terms about freedom of choice and other catch-phrases which sound like the Levis jeans advert of several years ago.

Second, there has been an ethos of selfish consumerism, of egocentric individualism, coupled with the denigration of the very idea of a public interest. This has been propagated very energetically by government leaders and those opinion-moulders who follow in their wake.

Third, we are in an era of distrust of public institutions. In their place we are offered the exaltation of the market and its purported virtues. Reliance on the market sounds good — after all, everyone in Eastern Europe is now talking about markets, aren't they? — though we tend to forget the context, which is an economy in which virtually all enterprises outside agriculture have been state-owned. But we should think more rigorously about the implications of pursuing policies in this mould.

The market has certain salient characteristics. First of all, it is not merely decentralized but fragmented. Second, it does not and cannot look beyond immediate preferences, in fact it has no concern at all for the wider impact of particular transactions. Third, it is totally indifferent to non-economic factors, for example, the social and demographic characteristics of the participants in the labour market, let alone the historical factors shaping those characteristics. The market takes its participants as it finds them; it has no interest in how they got there. Finally, the market is invariably plagued by what economists are pleased to call imperfections or failures, of which the most important is the ease with which various costs can be externalized. Throughout the world — from Seveso to Chernobyl to Bhopal — we have had lethal experience of what this means in terms of the environment and health, but it is equally true that discrimination involves externalization of costs of a quite different kind. Along with the victims, it is society as a whole — but never the discriminator — which bears the costs of the multiple cycles of deprivation in which those who suffer discrimination, their families and their descendants too often become trapped.

Now in many respects the market is a fiction — a heuristic and at times ideological construct. Reliance on the market means in reality allowing institutions and individuals to undertake activities without restrictions imposed by any public authority. This leaves them free to act in ways that economic theory itself would brand as irrational, notably in refusing to make efficient use of productive workers. That, however, merely shows how impoverished the economists' conception of reality actually is. Status and power considerations or relations are equally influential in shaping actions, and are often the driving forces behind direct discrimination. And if we keep talking about market forces, we let those influences run riot.

Public institutions, on the other hand, whether regulating or directly controlling, have certain advantages of which we should remind ourselves. One is that, because they can take account of social and demographic characteristics and the cumulative result of private actions, they can consciously alter the emergent pattern. They can be redistributive. They can, and indeed if the rationale of their existence is to be satisfied they must, get an overview — monitor and evaluate the cumulative results of a stream of activities. This intelligence function should then provide the basis for determining whether redistributive policies are necessary and, after a time, what impact particular policies have had.[32]

Public institutions, though they can act by prohibition, can also act in conjunction with or supplementation of market-based activities by various forms of subsidies or investment (for example in training, job creation or construction), none of which would be provided spontaneously by the market. Thus, whatever views one may have about the extent to which regulation, public enterprise, public/private partnerships or total reliance on the private sector should dominate the economy, or what the proportionate mix of each should be, it does seem clear that unless the virtues and values of public institutions can be incorporated into the running of the economy, racial inequality will persist, and indeed in many respects will probably worsen.

AGENDA FOR THE NINETIES

Now with these policy and ideological legacies of the 1980s setting the context, how can we move forward towards the goals outlined earlier? There is first of all the more modest goal of avoiding what in the worst case could be the British nightmare of the 1990s — one in which we go down the American road of virtually equating ethnic minorities with an unemployed or poor economic underclass, stigmatized with mass criminality (that last feature particularly applying to Afro-Caribbeans), coupled with the growing isolation, partly self-imposed, of a Pakistani Muslim community that feels itself culturally estranged from the rest. If we clear this first fence, we need then to think about how to achieve the more ambitious equality goals. This is best considered at two levels. The first is that of broad constitutional and political developments and macro-economic and social policies; the second, of policies specifically devoted to countering racial inequality including — though not necessarily as the primary element — legal changes that strengthen anti-discrimination law.

Starting at the first, it will be necessary to reverse most of the policies and trends of the 1980s. We must be honest and recognize that this will require a change of government, but I am not giving a party political broadcast on behalf of the Labour Party. I merely regard it as the least bad alternative. The change of government in the present circumstances is a necessary but absolutely by no means sufficient condition. I would like to outline relatively briefly what I believe are the minimum changes necessary in this respect.

Employment

In employment, we need to initiate well-designed and adequately funded training programmes to reach the unemployed and under-employed, those whom the education system has failed and those who encounter roadblocks on the ordinary avenues of occupational recruitment.

We need also to strengthen workers' rights. This is of great importance to ethnic minorities because of their subordinate market position. It is also a matter peculiarly sensitive to party politics. The United Kingdom government has been the main opponent of the EC Commission's proposals for strong measures of employment protection within the Community Charter of Fundamental Social Rights of Workers, and has succeeded in securing considerable dilution. It would take but one change of government and agreement on a rigorous standard of protection at the workplace to put the matter beyond reversal by any further UK government; that is the necessary implication of the unanimity rule that governs these matters. The provisions of the Community Social Charter need to be accepted, implemented and in some instances strengthened.[33]

Education

In education, not only must we rediscover egalitarianism, we need to initiate sustained compensatory efforts to ensure — and here I would agree with the government about aims — a solid grounding in basics like literacy, numeracy, computer skills, and the ability to write clearly. Moreover, a big investment in second-chance education for early leavers and mature students in further and higher education will be required.

Housing

In housing, good quality homes must be built at public expense and sold at the preferential rates now in effect in order to reach poorer tenants, many of whom have not been able to take advantage of the presently existing purchase schemes. More imaginative programmes will have to be developed. Interestingly, the government is already on this trail with pilot schemes both in Scotland and Wales.[34] Although one can argue about the desirability of selling council houses, it does seem to me that once the policy has proceeded so far, to exclude one group because of their lack of funds is the wrong way to go about reversing it.

Local Government

At the political-constitutional level, the trend of centralization needs to be reversed, with localities regaining power over finance, service provision and economic policies. There is now a debate going on in both Opposition parties over what to do about local government. The Labour Party seems to be moving towards adopting a policy of regionalization, whose structures are not yet clear. If it entails bigger units than the old conurbations, and above all if it means diluting the urban areas where blacks are concentrated with the white suburban areas surrounding them, it would be a seriously retrograde step.

Criminal Justice

Finally, when it comes to criminal justice, we must attack not only the criminogenic conditions of unemployment and social resentment I have described, but it is also imperative to subject legal institutions — including where necessary the judiciary — to investigation and regulation where patterns and practices of discrimination emerge. It is important to remember that the Race Relations Act has never covered the operation of institutions of repression. This has only partly been the result of the narrow judicial construction of what constitutes 'goods, facilities or services' in relation to immigration control.[35] It was never intended that the Act apply to discriminatory practices by the police, the prison service,[36] or the judges. I think that is a very serious defect.

Now this last point, which involves enforcement of laws against discrimination to some extent, is connected with what contributors to this volume have been creatively discussing: the strengthening of laws devoted specifically to combating discrimination. But it is not merely because the others have written so well that I shall say relatively little about this, and have left it towards the end of my comments. It is also because I believe that the analysis of policy and politics that I have offered focuses on matters of greater importance — those which speak to the ultimate sources of racial inequality. They affect more people in more dimensions of their lives than do legal measures, because they are aimed at removing economic and social bases of indirect discrimination.

Nonetheless those policies will not be sufficient of themselves. In terms of a specifically anti-discrimination strategy, it seems to me there are three elements or dimensions that are worth stressing. Before detailing them, I want to emphasize one point I became convinced of some years ago, which is that the private law model — litigation by individuals under a statute designed to protect the socially or economically vulnerable — is likely to have only limited societal impact.[37] To expect much from this approach is to court disappointment and a needlessly pessimistic judgement that the law has 'failed'. Professor Bell's essay in this book discussing the United States seems to me to reinforce the view that even if one added useful technical devices like the class action to broaden the impact, the effect of private suits would still remain marginal. I should stress though that this perception does not mean that we should forget about providing effective redress for aggrieved individuals, because there are important social values in enabling and assisting people who have been done an injury to get that rectified. We don't deny victims of accidents adequate compensation because we may have different theories about the economic impact of tort law. But we should not ask more of this branch of anti-discrimination law than it can possibly provide.

There are three main lines of approach I would suggest that anti-discrimination efforts should take in the 1990s. First, and one that would not involve much law, is for government to act as a model employer, rather as it did with things like the Fair Wages Resolution a long time ago[38] — to lead by example. Second, government at all levels should use its market power to further racial equality. Contract compliance is only the most obvious example. Other important practices, such as building an ethnic impact audit into the critical formulation stage of all policy-making and executive actions — *before* the public agenda is set — would take the approach still further. There are, I am sure, numerous other ideas that others could offer in this vein.

Finally, public power and public policy must establish a framework of legal, political and psychological support and stimulation for the private sector — which after all is where most people work — to institutionalize equal opportunity efforts. If there is to be sustained progress the goals, practices and values of racial equality policies must be internalized by managers in the private sector. Here, as is seldom the case any longer, the United States does provide a useful example. A fascinating student Note describes the resistance of corporate management to efforts by the Reagan administration in the mid-1980s to dismantle affirmative action programmes.[39] After some years of initial resistance, management had built affirmative action into the ordinary conduct of business, and had discovered that the programmes were bringing other, unexpected advantages. These included diversity of outlook within the organization, access to minority markets, and an improved international image at a time when access to world markets had become increasingly important. In simple profit terms equal opportunity had become an asset; hence management resisted the ideologically motivated attempt to upset the applecart. A related point is that major companies have come to include, as part of their remuneration-incentive package for top executives, achievement of equal opportunity targets, which has become one of the prerequisites for a higher rate of pay.[40] Thus the policy is built into the corporate structure at all levels:

it is not seen as some kind of moral gloss, but actually internalized in the profit-and-loss operations of the enterprise. I have no idea what proportion of the economy is covered in this way, but it is probably substantial. In view of the importance of the initial federal guidelines in launching the efforts, I would suggest that a somewhat tougher Code of Practice embodied in the higher-profile form of delegated legislation — that is to say, issued by the government rather than merely by the Commission for Racial Equality — is needed to spark a parallel development here.

Moreover, if I may repeat something from an earlier article,[41] there need to be incentives, carrots as well as sticks. People learn better with rewards than with punishment; they are also better motivated. And carrots can take a whole lot of different forms, economic or psychic. We need Queen's Awards for equal opportunity achievement, just as they are given for exports, and to provide racial equality incentives we should be using tax breaks, grants, special deferred loan schemes and all the rest of the devices that have been used in relation to Enterprise Zones and a whole range of economic policies in the 1980s.

The third line of approach for anti-discrimination efforts in the 1990s must be the effective public enforcement of equality laws. Now this has two sides; the one we are most familiar with is the traditional punitive enforcement, devoted to uncovering and rooting out discrimination by stopping certain conduct by individuals or ending particular practices. I don't suggest that we jettison this; I think however that it needs to be supplemented by widening and reorientating the substantive laws themselves, to incorporate positive duties.[42] We are going to be feeling our way, and in this respect, the experience of Northern Ireland may be very important. We may come to take as our baseline many of the provisions of the Fair Employment Act,[43] and impose require-ments such as targets, timetables or even establishment of training programmes, backed up by periodic compliance reports and proposals for new initiatives where sufficient advances towards a representative workforce have not been achieved. The legal structure would be supportive of good faith efforts and also contain sufficient sanctions to goad, pressurize and if necessary punish the recalcitrant, but the main running would be made by those best placed to make it: the employers themselves.

Most readers will agree that this is all a very tall order. There is no chance of it even beginning to happen in the next year or two, and it will be a struggle to achieve a good part of this agenda in this decade. This pessimistic view derives from a simple political fact. Why should one expect that a group which is small in numbers and economically disadvantaged would have the power to bring about policies needed to improve their conditions? How best to build alliances that draw upon the moral force of the case against racial inequality and connect that to the disadvantages suffered by many groups within the white majority is the critical question, though best left to other forums. But it is important for us as scholars and practitioners to understand what has gone wrong with policies which have been indifferent to ethnic minorities in principle and disastrous in practice, and also with those which have sought to assist them, where there have been failures as well.[44] This will enable us to provide guidance for those who will be in positions to implement policies geared to advancing racial equality when the right political moment arrives.

NOTES

1. See, for example, the essays by Fredman and Szyszczak, and Lacey in this book.
2. Lustgarten, L. 'Socialism and the rule of law' (1988) 15 *Journal of Law & Society* 25.
3. This does not require that we give equivalent moral weight to artificial legal persons, such as companies or trusts. See ibid. at 32–33.
4. From the point of view of the black or Asian settler whose family or friends are excluded or humiliated by the immigration authorities, this looks like mere hypocrisy. From the point of view of someone of that generation of English which grew up with the globe painted red and an extraordinary insular sense of superiority to the rest of the world ('the wogs begin at Calais' is xenophobic, but certainly not racist), it seemed a reluctant but inevitable application of fair play to those who settled here. In my view it is the continued discrimination by whites of the post-imperial generation against British blacks which is most despicable.
5. One would have to disentangle sex and race. Comparisons among women are probably not reliable, in view of the extremely low levels of reported labour force activity among Muslim women, and the high levels among blacks. See Brown, C. *Black and White Britain — the Third PSI Survey* (London, Heinemann, 1984) p. 150.
6. See especially ibid. at ch. VII.
7. To take a hypothetical example, someone whose religious convictions required them to refrain from work on Friday could easily be accommodated as a university teacher, a job in which timetables are flexible and there is no requirement that a person be present every day of the working week. Any emergency arising in relation to student care could be handled by a colleague. It is unlikely that the same conclusion would apply to a stockbroker, whose clients need their services during all market hours and whose colleagues already work under conditions of high pressure.
8. To take just two examples from law and accountancy, in 1989, while 2.5 per cent of barristers were Asians, the proportion of pupil entrants was double that. In 1988, Asian candidates received 7 per cent of trainee contracts from the three largest City chartered accountancy firms. (Information kindly supplied by Tariq Modood of the Commission for Racial Equality).
9. Documented thoroughly in Brown, C. and Gay, P. *Racial Discrimination: Seventeen Years after the Act* (London, PSI, 1985).
10. Quoted in *Times Educational Supplement* (13 May 1988) A6.
11. Education Reform Act 1988, Ch. II.
12. Ibid. at Ch. IV.
13. Ibid. at ss. 6.
14. Ibid. at ss. 7(6), 9.
15. Education (Student Loans) Act 1990, which is purely an enabling measure. The substance

of the scheme is to be found in Education (Student Loans) Regs. 1990, S.I. 1990 no. 1401.

16. On tenure and quality of housing, see the third PSI survey op. cit. (note 5) ch. V. The best exploration of discriminatory practices in council-house allocation is the CRE's Formal Investigation Report, *Racial and Council Housing in Hackney* (London, CRE, 1984).

17. Brown, C. 'Racial inequality in the British labour market' (June 1990) 5 (4) *Employment Institute Economic Report*.

18. A detailed age profile appears in note 21 below. After the Social Security Act 1986 came into force, single people under 25 received nearly 25 per cent less weekly benefit than those 'non-householders' above the age limit.

19. Op. cit. (note 17), fig. 2.

20. For a discussion of training readily accessible to lawyers, see Wikely, N. 'Training for employment in the 1990s' (1990) 53 MLR 354.

21. Based upon Labour Force Survey population data for 1985–87, the Central Statistical Office produced the following table:

Age Distribution of Population by Ethnic Group (Percentage)

Age	White	Afro-Caribbean	Indian	Pakistani	Bangladeshi
0–15	20	25	31	43	50
16–29	22	33	27	25	21

Source: CSO *Social Trends* 20 (London, HMSO, 1990) p. 25.

Thus throughout the 1980s, the proportion of young people among West Indians was 50 per cent higher than among whites. It will remain higher, though less radically so, in the 1990s, but than the proportion among some of the Asian groups will be more *double* that among whites.

22. Working-class women of course share the same difficulties of gaining access to education and training, with additional disabilities related to sex. The conflict of interest is, more precisely, between ethnic minority men and middle-class women.

23. Proclaimed most forcefully in two White Papers, 'Building businesses not barriers' Cmnd. 9794 (1986) and 'Lifting the burden' Cmnd. 9571 (1985).

24. Wages Act 1986 pt. II (Wages Councils); The Fair Wages Resolution was rescinded by the House of Commons in 1982 and the government denounced the ILO Convention underpinning it. The qualifying period for protection against unfair dismissal was first raised from six months to two years for employees of small firms by the Employment Act 1980, and applied to all employees by delegated legislation in 1985. The provision for 'pre-hearing review' which would include a deposit of up to £150 is s. 20 of the Employment Act 1989.

25. For detailed discussion, see Leach, S. and Stoker, G. 'The transformation of central-local government relations' in Graham, C. and Prosser, T. (eds) *Waiving the Rules: The Constitution under Thatcherism* (Milton Keynes, Open University Press, 1988) pp. 95–115, and Grant, M. 'Central-local relations: the balance of power' in Jowell, J. and Oliver, D. (eds) *The Changing Constitution* 2nd edn (Oxford, Clarendon Press, 1989) pp. 247–72.

26. A progression that began with 'holdback' and other cuts in the rate support grant took a more radical turn with rate-capping (Rates Act 1985), and continued when, with the abolition of rates and their replacement by the poll tax (Local Government Finance Act 1988), the latter became subject to capping as well when local authorities set charges the government deemed excessive.

27. Transport Act 1983, discussed in Loughlin, M. *Local Government in the Modern State* (London, Sweet & Maxwell, 1986) ch. 3; Housing Act 1988 pt. III, creating Housing Action Trusts; and the Education Reform Act 1988, discussed above.

28. Local Government Act 1985, abolishing the Greater London Council and the six Metropolitan County Councils.

29. Local Government Act 1988 ss. 17, 18.

30. This study was reported in *The Guardian* (28 February 1990). The author is given as Marc Mauer, the project's assistant director.

31. For a discussion of these issues, see NACRO *Black People and the Criminal Justice System*

(London, 1986) and Reiner, R. 'Race and criminal justice' (1989) 16 *New Community* 5.

32. Large organizations of any kind, public or private, profit-seeking or service-providing, engage in monitoring and evaluation as part of the efficient conduct of the enterprise. But only public institutions will use their intelligence capabilities with an eye to considering the redistributive impact of particular policies or activities.

33. The text of the Draft Social Charter may be found at [1989] 3 *CMLR* 642.

34. Under the headline 'Tory loan scheme prompts poor to buy council homes', *The Guardian* of 30 June 1990 reports the progress of the Welsh Flexi-Ownership and the Scottish Rent to Mortgage schemes. Both treat rents as mortgage repayments, and most importantly involve an interest-free loan which requires no repayment so long as the purchaser continues in residence.

35. *Amin v Entry Clearance Officer, Bombay* [1983] 2 AC 818.

36. *Alexander v Home Office* [1988] IRLR 190 does make a limited incursion in relation to work allocation within the prison; the Home Office did not appeal the county court judge's ruling that this fell within s. 20. I doubt very much, however, whether the Act will be held to apply to categorization, transfer and disciplining of prisoners.

37. Lustgarten, L. 'Racial inequality and the limits of law' (1986) 49 *MLR* 68.

38. The Fair Wages Resolution was first adopted in 1891.

39. Note 'Rethinking *Weber*: the business response to affirmative action' (1989) 102 *Harvard Law Review* 658, 659–63.

40. A useful short discussion of the 'culture of affirmative action' in America by a British commentator, is Edwards, J. 'U.S. affirmative action alive and well despite Supreme Court' (forthcoming).

41. Op. cit. (note 37) pp. 77–78.

42. See the essay by Knox and O'Hara in this volume.

43. Fair Employment (Northern Ireland) Act 1989. For a very useful description and review of this legislation see Ellis [1990] PL 161.

44. For example, the anti-racist education policies of some schools such as Manchester's Burnage High School, the subject of the report of a team of enquiry headed by Ian Macdonald QC, delivered to the city council and reported in the press in April 1988.

Index